# Victorian Prose

# Victorian Prose

## An Anthology

Edited by Rosemary J. Mundhenk
and LuAnn McCracken Fletcher

Columbia University Press

NEW YORK

Columbia University Press

Publishers Since 1893

New York    Chichester, West Sussex

Copyright © 1999 Columbia University Press

Library of Congress Cataloging-in-Publication Data

Victorian prose : an anthology / [compiled by] Rosemary J. Mundhenk
and LuAnn McCracken Fletcher.

  p.  cm

  Includes bibliographical references (p. 455).

  ISBN 0–231–11026–X (acid-free paper). — ISBN 0–231–11027–8 (pbk.)

  1. English prose literature — 19th century.  2. Great Britain—
History—Victoria, 1837–1901—Sources. I. Mundhenk, Rosemary J., 1945– .
II. Fletcher, LuAnn McCracken, 1961– .

PR1304.V55  1999

828'.80808—dc21                                98–46151

# CONTENTS

# CHRONOLOGICAL TABLE OF CONTENTS

# THEMATIC TABLE OF CONTENTS ⟫

## III. The Woman Question

## IV. The New Sciences

## V. Victorian Aesthetics

## VI. RELIGION

## VII. THE VICTORIAN SELF: PUBLIC AND PRIVATE

# INTRODUCTION

The "Spirit of the Age" is in some measure a novel expression. I do not believe that it is to be met with in any work exceeding fifty years in antiquity. The idea of comparing one's own age with former ages, or with our notion of those which are yet to come, has occurred to philosophers, but it never before was itself the dominant idea of any age.

It is an idea essentially belonging to an age of change. Before men begin to think much and long on the peculiarities of their own times, they must have begun to think that those times are, or are destined to be, distinguished in a very remarkable manner from the times which preceded them.

—JOHN STUART MILL, "The Spirit of the Age" (1831)

Never since the beginning of Time was there, that we hear of or read of, so intensely self-conscious a Society. Our whole relations to the Universe and to our fellow-man have become an Inquiry, a Doubt; nothing will go on of its own accord, and do its function quietly; but all things must be probed into, the whole working of man's world must be anatomically studied.

—THOMAS CARLYLE, "Characteristics" (1831)

John Stuart Mill and Thomas Carlyle voice what has long been a refrain in historical and literary studies of the nineteenth century: Victorian self-consciousness. The catch-phrases used by Victorians themselves—"the spirit of the age," "the age of transition," "the condition of England"—suggest a preoccupation with their perceived uniqueness in history, an emphasis on *this* issue at *this* moment in time, a belief that no culture ever anywhere faced the same problems and experiences. Given the overwhelming social, economic, religious, and scientific changes introduced during the period, this perception was warranted. Diagnosing his time as an "age of transition," Mill wrote, "Mankind has outgrown old institutions and old doctrines, and has not acquired new ones." Mill's inquiry into the nature of his "age" is but one of many. Victorian men and women from various levels of society and different social backgrounds held and articulated opinions on the important public issues of the day. The volume and variety of that contemplation suggest that latter-day generalizations about the spirit of the age oversimplify the Victorians' complex and many-voiced debates.

The age was prolific. Authors turned out an amount of work that now seems to us humanly impossible. Margaret Oliphant wrote over ninety novels, eight collections of stories, hundreds of articles published in *Blackwood's Edinburgh Magazine* and elsewhere, and twenty-five works of nonfiction, including her *Autobiography*. Anthony Trollope produced not only scores of novels but also biographies, travel accounts, and an autobiography, totaling nearly seventy books. Oliphant and Trollope are admittedly exceptional, but they are representative of an age of productivity. More than fifty thousand Victorian periodicals[1] responded to a perceived need for information and dialogue on the interests and issues faced by the majority of Victorians. Publishers capitalized on the increase in working-class literacy and the growth of leisure by meeting readers' demands for entertainment and education. Although the price of a book was generally beyond the reach of many readers, the price of many periodicals, especially cheap family magazines such as *Chambers's Edinburgh Journal* or *The Penny Magazine*—and the ideas they contained—was not. There were periodicals to suit almost every purpose and audience, from the influential quarterlies—the Whig *Edinburgh Review*, the Tory *Quarterly Review*, the Benthamite *Westminster Review*—to satirical and comic magazines such as *Punch* and *Fun*; from labor periodicals to religious periodicals; from women's magazines, such as the *Englishwoman's Domestic Magazine*, Charlotte Elizabeth Tonna's *Christian Lady's Magazine*, and the feminist *Englishwoman's Review* to art and architectural magazines, such as the *Art Journal* and the *Builder*. Periodicals enabled Victorian prose writers, including Ruskin, Macaulay, Arnold, and Newman, to reach wider audiences, just as they proved to be a successful commercial vehicle for Victorian novelists such as Dickens, Thackeray, Gaskell, and Hardy. The Victorian period also witnessed the development of successful children's magazines, ranging from Samuel Beeton's *Boy's Own Magazine* to the more sensational *Bad Boy's Paper* and, later, the *Girl's Own Paper*, as well as the rise of professional journals, such as the *Lancet*, the *British Medical Journal*, and the *Solicitor's Journal and Reporter*.

Despite growing specialization and fragmentation of knowledge by profession, class, discipline, and avocation, the Victorian reading experience created a more elastic, less narrowly focused perception of the world than our modern experience tends to encourage, a breadth of intellectual exchange as well as varying intellectual depth. As Robin Gilmour notes:

> The prestige and comprehensiveness of the great periodicals (a nineteenth-
> century phenomenon in itself) helped to sustain a common discourse. A
> subscriber to the *Edinburgh Review* or the *Quarterly* was accustomed to move
> from, say, a review of Tennyson's poems to a discussion of the latest work
> in geology, from an article on contemporary astronomy to one on the
> Oxford Movement, without feeling that science, literature, and theology
> belonged in separate intellectual compartments.[2]

A reader of the *Westminster Review* in 1856 would encounter George Eliot's "Silly Novels by Lady Novelists," G. H. Lewes's articles on alchemy, heredity, and lions and lion hunting, and Harriet Martineau's discussion of Christian missions. Juxtaposed with Thomas

1. N. Merrill Distad, "Desiderata and Agenda for the Twenty-first Century," in *Victorian Periodicals: A Guide to Research*, vol. 2, ed. J. Don Vann and Rosemary T. VanArsdel (New York: Modern Language Association, 1989), p. 125.

2. Robin Gilmour, *The Victorian Period: The Intellectual and Cultural Context of English Literature, 1830–1890* (London and New York: Longman, 1993), p. 7.

Carlyle's *Sartor Resartus*, serialized in *Fraser's Magazine* (1833–4), were articles on the character and conduct of household servants, a discussion of Toryism, a description of fishing the Thames, and a satire in the style of Juvenal by "Pierce Pungent." A subscriber to *The Nineteenth Century* in 1889 would discover not only Mary (Mrs. Humphry) Ward's "Appeal Against Female Suffrage" and M. M. Dilke's "Reply" but also political essays by William Gladstone, T. H. Huxley's defense of agnosticism, Oscar Wilde's "Decay of Lying," William Morris's plea for the preservation of Westminster Abbey, a discussion of French theater, and an essay on sport in Nepal.

Not that everyone in 1889 was reading *The Nineteenth Century*, or in 1833, *Fraser's*. With the proliferation of printed material came a proliferation of prose addressing readers from different educational backgrounds, intellectual levels, classes, and interests. This phenomenon, especially in the second half of the century, Richard Altick has called "the democratizing of reading."[3] Educated readers interested in new theories of Political Economy might go directly to the sources and read Jeremy Bentham and James Mill, but others would find Harriet Martineau's popular *Illustrations of Political Economy* (1832–4) a much more accessible introduction to utilitarianism. While some might read Charles Lyell's *Principles of Geology* (1830–3), Mary Somerville's *On the Connexion of the Physical Sciences* (1834), or Charles Darwin's best-selling *On the Origin of Species* (1859), more accessible discussions and summaries of the latest scientific discoveries were available in works such as Gideon Mantell's *The Wonders of Geology* and Robert Chambers's *Vestiges of the Natural History of Creation*, in magazines and series designed for the working classes such as *Chambers's Edinburgh Journal* and Charles Knight's *Penny Cyclopedia*, or in *Household Words*' entertaining distillations of Michael Faraday's lectures. The increased accessibility of new ideas helped to satisfy the Victorian demand for information: as Elizabeth Rigby, Lady Eastlake commented—none too favorably—in her journal, "People see everything nowadays to talk of it; the very wonders of Science made drawing-room tattle."[4]

Victorian prose writers responded to changing social and intellectual conditions of nineteenth-century England, but they also helped to create and shape those conditions. James Phillips Kay (later Kay-Shuttleworth) based *The Moral and Physical Condition of the Working Classes* (1832) on his observations in the poor districts of Manchester; this pamphlet, with its social analysis and graphic depiction of unsanitary living and working conditions, added to the debates preceding the passage of the New Poor Law Amendment in 1834. John Ruskin's defense of the painter J. M. W. Turner in *Modern Painters* (1843–60) helped to create the aesthetic climate out of which Pre-Raphaelitism would grow; his celebration of Gothic architecture in *The Stones of Venice* (1851–3) popularized pinnacles and flying buttresses among the Victorian middle class. Indeed, many writers were aware of the impact that their writing had upon the reading public. Ruskin occasionally betrayed a frustration with his inability to control the direction of his influence on public taste; annoyed that his audience focused on the matter rather than the morality of Gothic, he claimed, in a lecture to the citizens of Bradford, that he was being treated as "a

3. Richard Altick, *The English Common Reader* (Chicago and London: University of Chicago Press, 1957), p. 5.
4. Elizabeth Rigby, Lady Eastlake, in *Journals and Correspondence of Lady Eastlake*, vol. 2, ed. Charles Eastlake Smith (London: John Murray, 1895; rpt. AMS Press, 1975), p. 186.

respectable architectural man-milliner," sent for to give his opinion on "the newest and sweetest thing in pinnacles."[5] But many writers courted the public's response. Encouraged by the editors of *The Nineteenth Century* to champion the cause against suffrage for women, Mrs. Humphry Ward wrote an "Appeal Against Female Suffrage" for the June 1889 issue of the journal. Appended to her appeal was a detachable coupon, with which women readers were invited to record their support of the protest against the vote for women. Some fifteen hundred women responded. Ward's article and the response to it have been credited with hindering the cause of women's suffrage in England for years.[6]

Such active dialogues between writers and culture, writers and readers, preclude any attempt to develop a schematic relationship between the Victorian period and the prose it produced. Nor can we identify one writer as a representative spokesperson for the period. In fact, although we may isolate typical Victorian issues, we can by no means define a standard "Victorian" response to each. Even on the question of British imperialism, although we find notions of European racial superiority common, we discover that the reasons for British colonial expansion and the understanding of England's relationship with other cultures differ from writer to writer. David Livingstone's motive for promoting commerce with Africa stemmed from a desire to stop the slave trade by making it unprofitable. His rationale for British expansion, when placed beside Benjamin Disraeli's celebration of imperialistic expansion as an aspect of Britain's progress and glory, suggests that we should not view imperialist attitudes as one-dimensional. And if our contemporary sensibilities are offended by the racism of Richard Burton's anthropological descriptions of the African societies that he encountered on his travels, we ought to acknowledge the relative open-mindedness of Mary Kingsley toward the West African cultures she studied. Placing the many nineteenth-century documents on other cultures vis-à-vis England next to one another, we discover a richer, more complex texture of opinion. No issue may be understood within a single context or dismissed with a single proffered solution.

The crisis of religious faith, for example, is a subject central to our latter-day understanding of the Victorian period, but this "characteristic" topic of the age also is complicated by a variety of responses, positions, and solutions. Scientific discovery and theories of evolution, the Benthamite emphasis on utility and reason, and the "scientific" study of the Bible as history rather than the inspired word of God threatened to undermine the foundations of belief in the nineteenth century. Some, like Herbert Spencer and T. H. Huxley, questioned religious dogma and replaced religious faith with skepticism. Others, like John Henry Newman, Charles Kingsley, and Charlotte Elizabeth Tonna, remained believers within established religious institutions. Still others forged idiosyncratic belief systems, as Carlyle did in espousing "Natural Supernaturalism." And Matthew Arnold, criticizing narrow religious sectarianism, sought a replacement for religious orthodoxy in culture and conduct. Many, including Charles Kingsley, Frances Power Cobbe, and William Morris, turned to social reform as an outlet for religious and moral fervor. For

---

5. John Ruskin, "Traffic" (1864). Ruskin's lecture was subsequently included in *The Crown of Wild Olive*, published in 1866.

6. John Sutherland, *Mrs Humphry Ward* (Oxford: Clarendon, 1990), p. 199.

some Victorian intellectuals—George Henry Lewes, George Eliot, and Harriet Martineau among them—traditional faith metamorphosed into a "religion of humanity," a secular substitute for traditional religion.

One further example will serve to illustrate the frequently unpredictable combinations that may be found when we juxtapose texts on a single issue. In recent decades students of the Victorian period have made us increasingly aware of how central the question of gender—especially "the woman question"—was to all aspects of Victorian culture, social, economic, and moral. And we have seen that this question spawned a multivoiced debate about women, men, and English life. The divergence in positions on the question of gender cannot be categorized on the basis of sex: John Stuart Mill advocated women's rights, while Mrs. Humphry Ward and Sarah Ellis desired to preserve the status quo. Ellis, who discouraged women from attempting to exercise influence outside of the domestic realm, had—surprisingly—something in common with Frances Power Cobbe, who advocated women's suffrage and participation in public affairs but who also required mothers to raise their children at home. Both Dinah Mulock Craik and W. R. Greg criticized the middle-class norm of women's ornamental status, but Craik blamed lack of education for women's uselessness and restlessness, while Greg blamed women's laziness and love of luxury.

This collection attempts to juxtapose writers and texts in order to suggest the diversity of the prose and the dialogues on many of the central issues of the age. By including texts not previously anthologized, we hope to restore for the modern reader a sense of the depth and breadth of Victorian intellectual exchange, as well as to help the modern reader to rediscover the merits of writers sacrificed in the process of shaping literary history. Furthermore, by setting better-known texts in the context of lesser-known writings, we hope that the known will be seen anew and perhaps be appreciated differently. We provide thematic and chronological tables of contents in addition to an authorial table. Cross-references to other writers included in this volume are indicated by uppercase last names. Even as we have sought to expand the range of voices represented, however, we acknowledge our need to be selective, to leave much out. We hope that the absences of this collection encourage the reader to seek out other voices.

# ACKNOWLEDGMENTS ⤳

We could not have completed this project without the expert advice and generous assistance of many others. Our thanks go to the library staffs at the British Library; at Lehigh University, especially Philip Metzger, Christine Roysden, Margaret Misinco, Marie Boltz, Kathleen Morrow, Roseann Bowerman, Patricia Ward, and the magicians of Interlibrary Loan; and at Cedar Crest College, especially Susan Phillips, Carolyn Nippert, Christopher Raab, and Dana Bart-Bell. We are grateful to Jennifer Bailey, Albert Sears, Anne Dickson, and Stephanie Scordia for their excellent work as editorial assistants; to Stephanie Kramer, Molly O'Brien, Leanne Kittle, Marion Doherty, and Margie Stauffer for their more than able typing. We thank also numerous friends and colleagues: Robert Mundhenk, Robert Fletcher, Jan S. Fergus, James R. Frakes, Scott Gordon, Patricia Ingham, Michael Peterson, Carol Pulham, Carolyn Segal, Elizabeth Meade, and Ryland Greene for their daily support and knowledgeable advice on just about everything; Barbara Pavlock and Robert Phillips for help with Greek and Latin; Mary Anne Kucserik, Marie-Sophie Armstrong, and Carrie Prettiman with French and Italian; and Albert Hartung, Vera Stegmann, and James J. Ward with German; James A. Jones, West Chester University, for assistance with the Livingstone and Burton selections; Carol Laub, Kim Silvestri, and Sandy Edmiston for everything else. Lehigh University and Cedar Crest College supplied travel funds and support for editorial assistants and typists. Jennifer Crewe, Anne McCoy, Susan Heath, and the readers at Columbia University Press offered valuable assistance and insight. To Robert Mundhenk, Robert Fletcher, Christopher Mundhenk, the McCracken, Herbert, Burrell, Karmelich, and Mundhenk families we offer both thanks and apologies for time given and taken. To her father, Leslie G. McCracken, LuAnn McCracken Fletcher dedicates her work on this book in loving remembrance.

The following institutions, publishers, and individuals have graciously granted us permission to print selections from the following works:

Charlotte Brontë, letters to George Henry Lewes of November 6, 1847, November 22, 1847, January 12, 1848, January 18, 1848, January 1850, and January 19, 1850. British Library MS. Add 39763. Reproduced by permission of The British Library Board and Blackwell Publishers.

Jane Welsh Carlyle, letter of 23 September 1845 and letter of 29 September 1845, in Clyde de L. Ryals, Kenneth J. Fielding et al., eds., *The Collected Letters of Thomas and Jane Welsh Carlyle*, vol. 19 (January–September 1845). Copyright 1993, Duke University Press. Reprinted with permission.

Edmund William Gosse, *Father and Son: A Study of Two Temperaments*. Copyright 1907, William Heinemann. Reprinted by permission of Jennifer Gosse.

Florence Nightingale, "Cassandra," in *Suggestions for Thought to the Searchers After Truth Among the Artizans of England*, privately printed by George E. Eyre and William Spottiswoode, 1860. Reprinted by kind permission of the Trustees of the Henry Bonham-Carter Will Trust and The British Library Board.

Arthur William Symons, "The Decadent Movement in Literature," *Harper's New Monthly Magazine*, November 1893. Reproduced by permission of Mr. Brian Read M.A. (Oxon) for the Estate of Arthur Symons.

Queen Victoria, letter of 15 June 1858, letter of 17 November 1858, and letter of 5 June 1872. Acknowledgment is made to the gracious permission of Her Majesty Queen Elizabeth II for the use of this previously published material.

# A NOTE ON THE TEXTS

The sources of our selections are usually the first printed editions. When we have chosen a later edition, that fact is noted in the preface to the selection. Nineteenth-century spelling and punctuation have been preserved, except for the most obvious typographical errors.

The sources of the selections are:

Acton, William. *Prostitution, Considered in Its Moral, Social, and Sanitary Aspects*. 2d. ed. London: John Churchill and Sons, 1870.

Albert, Prince Consort. Speech at the Mansion House, March 21, 1850. In *Prince Albert's Speeches*. People's Edition. London: Bell and Daldy, 1857. Pp. 109–14.

Arnold, Matthew. *Culture and Anarchy: An Essay in Political and Social Criticism*. 2d. ed. London: Smith, Elder, 1875.

—— ——. "Literature and Science." In *Discourses in America*. London: Macmillan, 1885. Pp. 72–137.

Bodichon, Barbara Leigh Smith. *Reasons for the Enfranchisement of Women*. London: London National Society for Women's Suffrage, 1866.

Brontë, Charlotte. Letter to George Henry Lewes, November 6, 1847. British Library MS. Add 39763. In *The Letters of Charlotte Brontë*. Vol. 1. Ed. Margaret Smith. Oxford: Clarendon Press, 1995. Pp. 559–60.

——. Letter to George Henry Lewes, November 22, 1847. British Library MS. Add 39763. In *The Letters of Charlotte Brontë*. P. 566.

——. Letter to George Henry Lewes, January 12, 1848. British Library MS. Add 39763. In *The Brontës: Their Lives, Friendships and Correspondence*. Ed. Thomas J. Wise and J A. Symington. Oxford: Shakespeare Head Press, 1933. No. 340.

——. Letter to George Henry Lewes, January 18, 1848. British Library MS. Add 39763. In *The Brontës: Their Lives, Friendships and Correspondence*. No. 341.

——. Letter to George Henry Lewes, January 1850. British Library MS. Add 39763. In *The Brontës: Their Lives, Friendships and Correspondence*. No. 516.

——. Letter to George Henry Lewes, January 19, 1850. British Library MS. Add 39763. In *The Brontës: Their Lives, Friendships and Correspondence*. No. 518.

Burton, Richard. "A Day Amongst the Fans." *Anthropological Review* 1, no. 1 (1863): 43–54.

Carlyle, Jane Welsh. Letter to Thomas Carlyle, September 23, 1845. In *The Collected Letters of Thomas and Jane Welsh Carlyle*. Vol. 19. Ed. Clyde De L. Ryals, Kenneth J. Fielding, Ian Campbell, Aileen Christianson, Hilary J. Smith. Durham and London: Duke University Press, 1993. Pp. 209–13.

——. Letter to Jeannie Welsh, September 29, 1845. In *The Collected Letters of Thomas and Jane Welsh Carlyle*. Vol. 19. Pp. 227–9.

Carlyle, Thomas. *Sartor Resartus. Fraser's Magazine* 8, no. 47 (November 1833): 581–92; 8, no. 48 (December 1833): 669–84; 9, no. 50 (February 1834): 177–95; 9, no. 51 (March 1834): 301–13; 9, no. 52 (April 1834): 443–55; 9, no. 54 (June 1834): 664–74; 10, no. 55 (July 1834): 77–87; 10, no. 56 (August 1834): 182–95.

———. *Past and Present*. London: Chapman and Hall, 1843.

Chambers, Robert. *Vestiges of the Natural History of Creation*. London: John Churchill, 1844.

Cobbe, Frances Power. "Woman as a Citizen of the State." In *The Duties of Women: A Course of Lectures*. London: Williams and Norgate, 1881.

———. *Life of Frances Power Cobbe*. 2 vols. London: R. Bentley & Son, 1894.

Craik, Dinah Maria Mulock. *A Woman's Thoughts About Women*. London: Hurst and Blackett, 1858.

Darwin, Charles. *On the Origin of Species by Means of Natural Selection, or, The Preservation of Favoured Races in the Struggle for Life*. London: John Murray, 1859.

Disraeli, Benjamin. Speech at the Banquet of the National Union of Conservative and Constitutional Associations at the Crystal Palace. *Publications of the National Union* 16. London: R. J. Mitchell and Sons, 1872.

Duff Gordon, Lucie. *Letters from the Cape*. In *Vacation Tourists and Notes of Travel in 1862–3*. Ed. Francis Galton. London and Cambridge: Macmillan, 1864. Pp. 119–222.

———. *Letters from Egypt, 1863–65*. London: Macmillan, 1865.

Eliot, George. "Silly Novels by Lady Novelists." *Westminster Review* n.s. 10, no. 130 (October 1856): 442–61.

Ellis, Sarah Stickney. *The Women of England, Their Social Duties, and Domestic Habits*. London: Fisher, Son, & Co., 1839.

Gladstone, William Ewart. "England's Mission." *The Nineteenth Century* 19 (September 1878): 560–84.

Gosse, Edmund William. *Father and Son: A Study of Two Temperaments*. London: William Heinemann, 1907.

Greg, William Rathbone. "Why Are Women Redundant?" *National Review* 14, no. 28 (April 1862): 434–60.

Huxley, Thomas Henry. "Science and Culture." In *Science and Culture and Other Essays*. London: Macmillan, 1881. Pp. 1–23.

———. "Agnosticism and Christianity." *The Nineteenth Century* 25, no. 148 (June 1889): 937–64.

Kay[-Shuttleworth], James Phillips. *The Moral and Physical Condition of the Working Classes Employed in the Cotton Manufacture in Manchester*. 2d ed. London: James Ridgway, 1832.

Kingsley, Charles. "The Massacre of the Innocents!" London: Ladies' Sanitary Association, 1859.

Kingsley, Mary H. *Travels in West Africa: Congo Français, Corsico and Cameroons*. London: Macmillan, 1897.

Leigh, Percival. "The Chemistry of a Candle." *Household Words* 5 (1850): 439–44.

Lewes, George Henry. Review of Currer Bell's *Shirley*. *Edinburgh Review* 91, no. 133 (January 1850): 153–73.

———. *Comte's Philosophy of the Sciences*. London: H. G. Bohn, 1853.

Livingstone, David. *Missionary Travels and Researches in South Africa*. London: John Murray, 1857.

Macaulay, Thomas Babington. Review of Robert Southey's *St. Thomas More; or Colloquies on the Progress and Prospects of Society*. *Edinburgh Review* 50, no. 100 (January 1830): 528–65.

Martineau, Harriet. *Eastern Life, Present and Past*. 3 vols. London: Edward Moxon, 1848.

Mayhew, Henry. "Labour and the Poor, Letter II." *The Morning Chronicle*, October 23, 1849. P. 5.

Mill, John Stuart. *The Subjection of Women*. London: Longmans, Green, Reader, and Dyer, 1869.

———. *Autobiography*. London: Longmans, Green, Reader, and Dyer, 1873.

Morris, William. "How We Live and How We Might Live." *Signs of Change: Seven Lectures*. London: Reeves and Turner, 1888. Pp. 1–36.

Newman, John Henry. *Apologia Pro Vita Sua*. 7 pts. London: Longman, Green, Longman, Roberts, and Green, April–June 1864.

Nightingale, Florence. *Suggestions for Thought to the Searchers After Truth among the Artizans of England*. London: George E. Eyre and William Spottiswoode, 1860.

Norton, Caroline. *A Letter to the Queen on Lord Chancellor Cranworth's Marriage and Divorce Bill*. London: Longman, Brown, Green, and Longmans, 1855.

Oastler, Richard. "Slavery in Yorkshire. To the Editors of the Leeds Mercury" *Leeds Mercury*, October 16, 1830. P. 4.

Oliphant, Margaret. *The Autobiography and Letters of Mrs M[argaret] O.W. Oliphant*. Ed. Mrs Harry Coghill. Edinburgh and London: William Blackwood, 1899.

Pater, Walter Horatio. *Studies in the History of the Renaissance*. London: Macmillan, 1873.

Prince, Mary. *The History of Mary Prince, A West Indian Slave. Related by Herself*. London: F. Westley and A. H. Davis; Edinburgh: Waugh and Innes, 1831.

"Punch's Own Report of the Opening of the Great Exhibition." *Punch* 20 (May 1851): 190–1.

Rigby, Elizabeth [Lady Eastlake]. Review of *Vanity Fair*, *Jane Eyre*, and the Governesses' Benevolent Institution Report for 1847. *Quarterly Review* 84, no. 167 (December 1848): 153–85.

Ruskin, John. "Traffic." In *The Crown of Wild Olive: Three Lectures on Work, Traffic, and War*. London: Smith, Elder, 1866. Pp. 79–138.

———. "Of Queens' Gardens." In *Sesame and Lilies: Two Lectures*. London: Smith, Elder, 1865.

Smiles, Samuel. *Self-Help with Illustrations of Character and Conduct*. London: John Murray, 1859.

Spencer, Herbert. "Progress: Its Law and Cause." *Westminster Review* n.s. 11, no. 132 (April 1857): 244–67.

Symons, Arthur. "The Decadent Movement in Literature." *Harper's New Monthly*

*Magazine* 87, no. 522 (November 1893): 858–67.

[Tonna,] Charlotte Elizabeth. *The Wrongs of Woman*. London: W. H. Dalton, 1843–4.

Victoria, Queen. Journal entry, May 1, 1851. In Martin, Theodore. *The Life of His Royal Highness the Prince Consort*. Vol. 2. London: Smith, Elder, 1876. Pp. 364–8.

————. Letter to her daughter Victoria, June 15, 1858. In *Dearest Child: Letters between Queen Victoria and the Princess Royal, 1858–1861*. Ed. Roger Fulford. London: Evans Brothers, 1964.

————. Letter to her daughter Victoria, November 17, 1858. In *Dearest Child: Letters between Queen Victoria and the Princess Royal, 1858–1861*.

————. Letter to her daughter Victoria, June 5, 1872. In *Darling Child: Private Correspondence of Queen Victoria and the Crown Princess of Prussia, 1871–1878*. Ed. Roger Fulford. London: Evans Brothers, 1976.

Ward, Mary Arnold [Mrs. Humphry]. "An Appeal Against Female Suffrage." *The Nineteenth Century* 25, no. 148 (June 1889): 781–8.

Wilde, Oscar. "The Soul of Man Under Socialism." *Fortnightly Review* 49 (February 1, 1891): 292–319.

# Mary Prince

## THE HISTORY OF MARY PRINCE, A WEST INDIAN SLAVE, RELATED BY HERSELF.

*Mary Prince's autobiography chronicles her experience as a West Indian slave and her eventual escape from slavery. The victim of a series of cruel masters and mistresses, Prince managed to leave her final owners, the Woods of Antigua, who had brought her with them when they visited London in 1828. She found shelter and support from members of the Anti-Slavery Society. She told her story to Thomas Pringle, secretary at the London antislavery headquarters, who had Susanna Strickland (later Moodie) transcribe the story. In the transformation from oral to written narrative, Mary Prince's story may have been edited to resemble the accounts of abused slaves published by the* Anti-Slavery Reporter, *as well as earlier male slave narratives such as* The Interesting Narrative of the Life of Olaudah Equiano (1789). The History *nevertheless introduced Prince's own voice and perspective as a resistant female slave to an English audience.*

*A popular publication—three editions in its first year—Prince's* History *was used as antislavery propaganda, in particular as propaganda against flogging. Prince herself allowed the evidence of her body to be used to support the case of the Ladies Anti-Slavery*

*Associations against the practice. Her narrative, championed by abolitionists and viciously attacked by antiabolitionists such as James Macqueen of the* Glasgow Courier, *contributed to the controversies and debates leading to the abolition of slavery in the British colonies in 1834.*                                                                              LMF

I WAS BORN AT BRACKISH-POND, in Bermuda, on a farm belonging to Mr. Charles Myners. My mother was a household slave; and my father, whose name was Prince, was a sawyer belonging to Mr. Trimmingham, a ship-builder at Crow-Lane. When I was an infant, old Mr. Myners died, and there was a division of the slaves and other property among the family. I was bought along with my mother by old Captain Darrel, and given to his grand-child, little Miss Betsey Williams. Captain Williams, Mr. Darrel's son-in-law, was master of a vessel which traded to several places in America and the West Indies, and he was seldom at home long together.

Mrs. Williams was a kind-hearted good woman, and she treated all her slaves well. She had only one daughter, Miss Betsey, for whom I was purchased, and who was about my own age. I was made quite a pet of by Miss Betsey, and loved her very much. She used to lead me about by the hand, and call me her little nigger. This was the happiest period of my life; for I was too young to understand rightly my condition as a slave, and too thoughtless and full of spirits to look forward to the days of toil and sorrow.

My mother was a household slave in the same family. I was under her own care, and my little brothers and sisters were my play-fellows and companions. My mother had several fine children after she came to Mrs. Williams,—three girls and two boys. The tasks given out to us children were light, and we used to play together with Miss Betsey, with as much freedom almost as if she had been our sister.

My master, however, was a very harsh, selfish man; and we always dreaded his return from sea. His wife was herself much afraid of him; and, during his stay at home, seldom dared to shew her usual kindness to the slaves. He often left her, in the most distressed circumstances, to reside in other female society, at some place in the West Indies of which I have forgot the name. My poor mistress bore his ill-treatment with great patience, and all her slaves loved and pitied her. I was truly attached to her, and, next to my own mother, loved her better than any creature in the world. My obedience to her commands was cheerfully given: it sprung solely from the affection I felt for her, and not from fear of the power which the white people's law had given her over me.

I had scarcely reached my twelfth year when my mistress became too poor to keep so many of us at home; and she hired me out to Mrs. Pruden, a lady who lived about five miles off, in the adjoining parish, in a large house near the sea. I cried bitterly at parting with my dear mistress and Miss Betsey, and when I kissed my mother and brothers and sisters, I thought my young heart would break, it pained me so. But there was no help; I was forced to go. Good Mrs. Williams comforted me by saying that I should still be near the home I was about to quit, and might come over and see her and my kindred whenever I could obtain leave of absence from Mrs. Pruden. A few hours after this I was taken to a strange house, and found myself among strange people. This separation seemed a sore trial to me then; but oh! 'twas light, light to the trials I have since endured!—'twas nothing—nothing to be mentioned with them; but I was a child then, and it was according to my strength.

I knew that Mrs. Williams could no longer maintain me; that she was fain to part with me for my food and clothing; and I tried to submit myself to the change. My new mistress was a passionate woman; but yet she did not treat me very unkindly. I do not remember her striking me but once, and that was for going to see Mrs. Williams when I heard she was sick, and staying longer than she had given me leave to do. All my employment at this time was nursing a sweet baby, little Master Daniel; and I grew so fond of my nursling that it was my greatest delight to walk out with him by the sea-shore, accompanied by his brother and sister, Miss Fanny and Master James.—Dear Miss Fanny! She was a sweet, kind young lady, and so fond of me that she wished me to learn all that she knew herself; and her method of teaching me was as follows:—Directly she had said her lessons to her grandmamma, she used to come running to me, and make me repeat them one by one after her; and in a few months I was able not only to say my letters but to spell many small words. But this happy state was not to last long. Those days were too pleasant to last. My heart always softens when I think of them.

At this time Mrs. Williams died. I was told suddenly of her death, and my grief was so great that, forgetting I had the baby in my arms, I ran away directly to my poor mistress's house; but reached it only in time to see the corpse carried out. Oh, that was a day of sorrow,—a heavy day! All the slaves cried. My mother cried and lamented her sore; and I (foolish creature!) vainly entreated them to bring my dear mistress back to life. I knew nothing rightly about death then, and it seemed a hard thing to bear. When I thought about my mistress I felt as if the world was all gone wrong; and for many days and weeks I could think of nothing else. I returned to Mrs. Pruden's; but my sorrow was too great to be comforted, for my own dear mistress was always in my mind. Whether in the house or abroad, my thoughts were always talking to me about her.

I staid at Mrs. Pruden's about three months after this; I was then sent back to Mr. Williams to be sold. Oh, that was a sad sad time! I recollect the day well. Mrs. Pruden came to me and said, "Mary, you will have to go home directly; your master is going to be married, and he means to sell you and two of your sisters to raise money for the wedding." Hearing this I burst out a crying,—though I was then far from being sensible of the full weight of my misfortune, or of the misery that waited for me. Besides, I did not like to leave Mrs. Pruden, and the dear baby, who had grown very fond of me. For some time I could scarcely believe that Mrs. Pruden was in earnest, till I received orders for my immediate return.—Dear Miss Fanny! how she cried at parting with me, whilst I kissed and hugged the baby, thinking I should never see him again. I left Mrs. Pruden's, and walked home with a heart full of sorrow. The idea of being sold away from my mother and Miss Betsey was so frightful, that I dared not trust myself to think about it. We had been bought of Mr. Myners, as I have mentioned, by Miss Betsey's grandfather, and given to her, so that we were by right her property, and I never thought we should be separated or sold away from her.

When I reached the house, I went in directly to Miss Betsey. I found her in great distress; and she cried out as soon as she saw me, "Oh, Mary! my father is going to sell you all to raise money to marry that wicked woman. You are *my* slaves, and he has no right to sell you; but it is all to please her." She then told me that my mother was living with her father's sister at a house close by, and I went there to see her. It was a sorrowful meeting; and we lamented with a great and sore crying our unfortunate situation. "Here comes one of my poor picaninnies!" she said, the moment I came in, "one of the poor slave-brood who are to be sold to-morrow."

Oh dear! I cannot bear to think of that day,—it is too much.—It recalls the great grief that filled my heart, and the woeful thoughts that passed to and fro through my mind, whilst listening to the pitiful words of my poor mother, weeping for the loss of her children. I wish I could find words to tell you all I then felt and suffered. The great God above alone knows the thoughts of the poor slave's heart, and the bitter pains which follow such separations as these. All that we love taken away from us—Oh, it is sad, sad! and sore to be borne!—I got no sleep that night for thinking of the morrow; and dear Miss Betsey was scarcely less distressed. She could not bear to part with her old playmates, and she cried sore and would not be pacified.

The black morning at length came; it came too soon for my poor mother and us. Whilst she was putting on us the new osnaburgs[1] in which we were to be sold, she said, in a sorrowful voice, (I shall never forget it!) "See, I am *shrouding* my poor children; what a task for a mother!" —She then called Miss Betsey to take leave of us. "I am going to carry my little chickens to market," (these were her very words,) "take your last look of them; may be you will see them no more." "Oh, my poor slaves! my own slaves!" said dear Miss Betsey, "you belong to me; and it grieves my heart to part with you."—Miss Betsey kissed us all, and, when she left us, my mother called the rest of the slaves to bid us good bye. One of them, a woman named Moll, came with her infant in her arms. "Ay!" said my mother, seeing her turn away and look at her child with the tears in her eyes, "your turn will come next." The slaves could say nothing to comfort us; they could only weep and lament with us. When I left my dear little brothers and the house in which I had been brought up, I thought my heart would burst.

Our mother, weeping as she went, called me away with the children Hannah and Dinah, and we took the road that led to Hamble Town, which we reached about four o'clock in the afternoon. We followed my mother to the market-place, where she placed us in a row against a large house, with our backs to the wall and our arms folded across our breasts. I, as the eldest, stood first, Hannah next to me, then Dinah; and our mother stood beside, crying over us. My heart throbbed with grief and terror so violently, that I pressed my hands quite tightly across my breast, but I could not keep it still, and it continued to leap as though it would burst out of my body. But who cared for that? Did one of the many by-standers, who were looking at us so carelessly, think of the pain that wrung the hearts of the negro woman and her young ones? No, no! They were not all bad, I dare say, but slavery hardens white people's hearts towards the blacks; and many of them were not slow to make their remarks upon us aloud, without regard to our grief—though their light words fell like cayenne on the fresh wounds of our hearts. Oh those white people have small hearts who can only feel for themselves.

1. Coarse linen dresses.

At length the vendue master,[2] who was to offer us for sale like sheep or cattle, arrived, and asked my mother which was the eldest. She said nothing, but pointed to me. He took me by the hand, and led me out into the middle of the street, and, turning me slowly round, exposed me to the view of those who attended the vendue. I was soon surrounded by strange men, who examined and handled me in the same manner that a butcher would a calf or a lamb he was about to purchase, and who talked about my shape and size in like words—as if I could no more understand their meaning than the dumb beasts. I was then put up to sale. The bidding commenced at a few pounds, and gradually rose to fifty-seven,[3] when I was knocked down to the highest bidder; and the people who stood by said that I had fetched a great sum for so young a slave.

I then saw my sisters led forth, and sold to different owners; so that we had not the sad satisfaction of being partners in bondage. When the sale was over, my mother hugged and kissed us, and mourned over us, begging of us to keep up a good heart, and do our duty to our new masters. It was a sad parting; one went one way, one another, and our poor mammy went home with nothing.[4]

My new master was a Captain I—, who lived at Spanish Point. After parting with my mother and sisters, I followed him to his store, and he gave me into the charge of his son, a lad about my own age, Master Benjy, who took me to my new home. I did not know where I was going, or what my new master would do with me. My heart was quite broken with grief, and my thoughts went back continually to those from whom I had been so suddenly parted. "Oh, my mother! my mother!" I kept saying to myself, "Oh, my mammy and my sisters and my brothers, shall I never see you again!". . .

The next morning my mistress set about instructing me in my tasks. She taught me to do all sorts of household work; to wash and bake, pick cotton and wool, and wash floors, and cook. And she taught me (how can I ever forget it!) more things than these; she caused me to know the exact difference between the smart of the rope, the cart-whip, and the cow-skin, when applied to my naked body by her own cruel hand. And there was scarcely any punishment more dreadful than the blows I received on my face and head from her hard heavy fist. She was a fearful woman, and a savage mistress to her slaves.

There were two little slave boys in the house, on whom she vented her bad temper in a special manner. One of these children was a mulatto, called Cyrus, who had been bought while an infant in his mother's arms; the other, Jack, was an African from the coast of Guinea, whom a sailor had given or sold to my master. Seldom a day passed without these boys receiving the most severe treatment, and often for no fault at all. Both my master and mistress seemed to think that they had a right to ill-use them at their pleasure; and very often accompanied their commands with blows, whether the children were behaving well or ill. I have seen their flesh ragged and raw with licks.—Lick—lick—they were never secure one moment from a blow, and their lives were passed in continual fear. My mistress was not contented with using the whip, but often pinched their cheeks and

2. Auctioneer at a public slave sale.
3. Bermuda currency; about £38 sterling. [Pringle's note]
4. At this point in the text, Pringle includes in a footnote a lengthy excerpt from one of his earlier publications describing the sale of three children before their mother at the Cape of Good Hope. He remarks on the similarity of the accounts.

arms in the most cruel manner. My pity for these poor boys was soon transferred to myself; for I was licked, and flogged, and pinched by her pitiless fingers in the neck and arms, exactly as they were. To strip me naked—to hang me up by the wrists and lay my flesh open with the cow-skin, was an ordinary punishment for even a slight offence. My mistress often robbed me too of the hours that belong to sleep. She used to sit up very late, frequently even until morning; and I had then to stand at a bench and wash during the greater part of the night, or pick wool and cotton; and often I have dropped down overcome by sleep and fatigue, till roused from a state of stupor by the whip, and forced to start up to my tasks.

Poor Hetty, my fellow slave, was very kind to me, and I used to call her my Aunt; but she led a most miserable life, and her death was hastened (at least the slaves all believed and said so,) by the dreadful chastisement she received from my master during her pregnancy. It happened as follows. One of the cows had dragged the rope away from the stake to which Hetty had fastened it, and got loose. My master flew into a terrible passion, and ordered the poor creature to be stripped quite naked, notwithstanding her pregnancy, and to be tied up to a tree in the yard. He then flogged her as hard as he could lick, both with the whip and cow-skin, till she was all over streaming with blood. He rested, and then beat her again and again. Her shrieks were terrible. The consequence was that poor Hetty was brought to bed before her time, and was delivered after severe labour of a dead child. She appeared to recover after her confinement, so far that she was repeatedly flogged by both master and mistress afterwards; but her former strength never returned to her. Ere long her body and limbs swelled to a great size; and she lay on a mat in the kitchen, till the water burst out of her body and she died. All the slaves said that death was a good thing for poor Hetty; but I cried very much for her death. The manner of it filled me with horror. I could not bear to think about it; yet it was always present to my mind for many a day.

After Hetty died all her labours fell upon me, in addition to my own. I had now to milk eleven cows every morning before sunrise, sitting among the damp weeds; to take care of the cattle as well as the children; and to do the work of the house. There was no end to my toils—no end to my blows. I lay down at night and rose up in the morning in fear and sorrow; and often wished that like poor Hetty I could escape from this cruel bondage and be at rest in the grave. But the hand of that God whom then I knew not, was stretched over me; and I was mercifully preserved for better things. It was then, however, my heavy lot to weep, weep, weep, and that for years; to pass from one misery to another, and from one cruel master to a worse. But I must go on with the thread of my story. . . .

For five years after this I remained in his [Captain I—'s] house, and almost daily received the same harsh treatment. At length he put me on board a sloop, and to my great joy sent me away to Turk's Island. I was not permitted to see my mother or father, or poor sisters and brothers, to say good bye, though going away to a strange land, and might never see them again. Oh the Buckra people[5] who keep slaves think that black people are like cattle, without natural affection. But my heart tells me it is far otherwise.

5. White people.

We were nearly four weeks on the voyage, which was unusually long. Sometimes we had a light breeze, sometimes a great calm, and the ship made no way; so that our provisions and water ran very low, and we were put upon short allowance. I should almost have been starved had it not been for the kindness of a black man called Anthony, and his wife, who had brought their own victuals, and shared them with me.

When we went ashore at the Grand Quay, the captain sent me to the house of my new master, Mr. D—-, to whom Captain I— had sold me. Grand Quay is a small town upon a sandbank; the houses low and built of wood. Such was my new master's. The first person I saw, on my arrival, was Mr. D—-, a stout sulky looking man, who carried me through the hall to show me to his wife and children. Next day I was put up by the vendue master to know how much I was worth, and I was valued at one hundred pounds currency.

My new master was one of the owners or holders of the salt ponds, and he received a certain sum for every slave that worked upon his premises, whether they were young or old. This sum was allowed him out of the profits arising from the salt works. I was immediately sent to work in the salt water with the rest of the slaves. This work was perfectly new to me. I was given a half barrel and a shovel, and had to stand up to my knees in the water, from four o'clock in the morning till nine, when we were given some Indian corn boiled in water, which we were obliged to swallow as fast as we could for fear the rain should come on and melt the salt. We were then called again to our tasks, and worked through the heat of the day; the sun flaming upon our heads like fire, and raising salt blisters in those parts which were not completely covered. Our feet and legs, from standing in the salt water for so many hours, soon became full of dreadful boils, which eat down in some cases to the very bone, afflicting the sufferers with great torment. We came home at twelve; ate our corn soup, called *blawly,* as fast as we could, and went back to our employment till dark at night. We then shovelled up the salt in large heaps, and went down to the sea, where we washed the pickle from our limbs, and cleaned the barrows and shovels from the salt. When we returned to the house, our master gave us each our allowance of raw Indian corn, which we pounded in a mortar and boiled in water for our suppers.

We slept in a long shed, divided into narrow slips, like the stalls used for cattle. Boards fixed upon stakes driven into the ground, without mat or covering, were our only beds. On Sundays, after we had washed the salt bags, and done other work required of us, we went into the bush and cut the long soft grass, of which we made trusses for our legs and feet to rest upon, for they were so full of the salt boils that we could get no rest lying upon the bare boards.

Though we worked from morning till night, there was no satisfying Mr. D—. I hoped, when I left Capt. I—, that I should have been better off, but I found it was but going from one butcher to another. There was this difference between them: my former master used to beat me while raging and foaming with passion; Mr. D— was usually quite calm. He would stand by and give orders for a slave to be cruelly whipped, and assist in the punishment, without moving a muscle of his face; walking about and taking snuff with the greatest composure. Nothing could touch his hard heart—neither sighs, nor tears, nor prayers, nor streaming blood; he was deaf to our cries, and careless of our sufferings.—

Mr. D— has often stripped me naked, hung me up by the wrists, and beat me with the cow-skin, with his own hand, till my body was raw with gashes. Yet there was nothing very remarkable in this; for it might serve as a sample of the common usage of the slaves on that horrible island. . . .

I am often much vexed, and I feel great sorrow when I hear some people in this country say, that the slaves do not need better usage, and do not want to be free.[6] They believe the foreign people,[7] who deceive them, and say slaves are happy. I say, Not so. How can slaves be happy when they have the halter round their neck and the whip upon their back? and are disgraced and thought no more of than beasts?—and are separated from their mothers, and husbands, and children, and sisters, just as cattle are sold and separated? Is it happiness for a driver in the field to take down his wife or sister or child, and strip them, and whip them in such a disgraceful manner?—women that have had children exposed in the open field to shame! There is no modesty or decency shown by the owner to his slaves; men, women, and children are exposed alike. Since I have been here I have often wondered how English people can go out into the West Indies and act in such a beastly manner. But when they go to the West Indies, they forget God and all feeling of shame, I think, since they can see and do such things. They tie up slaves like hogs—moor[8] them up like cattle, and they lick them, so as hogs, or cattle, or horses never were flogged;—and yet they come home and say, and make some good people believe, that slaves don't want to get out of slavery. But they put a cloak about the truth. It is not so. All slaves want to be free—to be free is very sweet. I will say the truth to English people who may read this history that my good friend, Miss S—, is now writing down for me. I have been a slave myself—I know what slaves feel—I can tell by myself what other slaves feel, and by what they have told me. The man that says slaves be quite happy in slavery— that they don't want to be free—that man is either ignorant or a lying person. I never heard a slave say so. I never heard a Buckra man say so, till I heard tell of it in England. Such people ought to be ashamed of themselves. They can't do without slaves, they say. What's the reason they can't do without slaves as well as in England? No slaves here—no whips—no stocks—no punishment, except for wicked people. They hire servants in England; and if they don't like them, they send them away: they can't lick them. Let them work ever so hard in England, they are far better off than slaves. If they get a bad master, they give warning and go hire to another. They have their liberty. That's just what *we* want. We don't mind hard work, if we had proper treatment, and proper wages like English servants, and proper time given in the week to keep us from breaking the Sabbath. But they won't give it: they will have work—work—work, night and day, sick or well, till we are quite done up; and we must not speak up nor look amiss, however much we be abused. And then when we are quite done up, who cares for us, more than for a lame horse? This is slavery. I tell it, to let English people know the truth; and I hope they will never leave off to pray God, and call loud to the great King of England, till all the poor blacks be given free, and slavery done up for evermore.

6. The whole of this paragraph especially, is given as nearly as was possible in Mary's precise words. [Pringle's note]
7. She means West Indians. [Pringle's note]
8. A West Indian phrase: to fasten or tie up. [Pringle's note]

# Richard Oastler

1789: Born 20 December at Leeds
1830: "Slavery in Yorkshire" published in *Leeds Mercury*
1841–4: *The Fleet Papers*
1861: Died 22 August at Harrogate

## SLAVERY IN YORKSHIRE

*On October 16, 1830, the* Leeds Mercury *published a morally indignant letter, entitled "Slavery in Yorkshire," protesting the long work day and unsafe, abusive conditions of workers—particularly child laborers—in the Bradford textile mills and comparing their situations to those of slaves in the West Indies. The letter's author, Richard Oastler, a Yorkshire estate steward and opponent of slavery, almost immediately became the outspoken leader of the Factory Movement in Yorkshire, agitating for a ten-hour work day, and later an influential opponent of the implementation of the 1834 Poor Law Amendment. Oastler's inflammatory rhetoric and organizing skills helped to call national attention to the plight of the mill worker. Despite intense opposition, the Factory Movement of the 1830s and 1840s achieved qualified success with the passage of protective legislation for female and child factory operatives, most notably the Factory Acts of 1833, 1847, and 1850.* RM

To The Editors Of The Leeds Mercury

"It is the pride of Britain that a Slave cannot exist on her soil; and if I read the genius of her constitution aright, I find that Slavery is most abhorrent to It—that the air which Britons breathe is free—the ground on which they tread is sacred to liberty."—*Rev.* R. W. Hamilton's *Speech at the Meeting held in the Cloth-hall Yard, Sept. 22d, 1830*

Gentlemen,—No heart responded with truer accents to the sounds of liberty which were heard in the Leeds Cloth-hall yard, on the 22d inst. than did mine, and from none could more sincere and earnest prayers arise to the throne of Heaven, that hereafter Slavery might only be known to Britain in the pages of her history. One shade alone obscured my pleasure, arising not from any difference in principle, but from the want of application of the general principle *to the whole Empire*. The pious and able champions of *Negro* liberty and *Colonial* rights should, if I mistake not, have gone farther than they did; or perhaps, to speak more correctly, before they had travelled so far as the West Indies, should, at least for a few moments, have sojourned in our own immediate neighbourhood, and have directed the attention of the meeting to scenes of misery, acts of oppression and victims of Slavery, even on the threshold of our homes!

Let truth speak out, appalling as the statements may appear. The fact is true. Thousands of our fellow-creatures and fellow-subjects, both male and female, the miserable inhabitants of a *Yorkshire town*, (Yorkshire now represented in Parliament by the giant of anti-slavery principles,[1]) are this very moment existing in a state of Slavery *more horrid* than are the victims of that hellish system—"*Colonial Slavery*." These innocent creatures drawl out unpitied their short but miserable existence, in a place famed for its profession of religious zeal, whose inhabitants are ever foremost in *professing* "Temperance" and "Reformation," and are striving to outrun their neighbours in Missionary exertions, and would fain send the Bible to the farthest corner of the globe—aye in the very place where the anti-slavery fever rages most furiously, her *apparent charity*, is not more admired on earth, than her *real cruelty* is abhorred in heaven. The very streets which receive the droppings of an "Anti-Slavery Society" are every morning wet by the tears of innocent victims at the accursed shrine of avarice, who are *compelled* (not by the cart-whip of the negro slave-driver) but by the dread of the equally appalling thong or strap of the overlooker, to hasten, half-dressed, *but not half-fed*, to those magazines of British Infantile Slavery— *the Worsted Mills in the town and neighbourhood of Bradford!!!*

Would that I had Brougham's eloquence, that I might rouse the hearts of the nation, and make every Briton swear "These innocents shall be free!"

Thousands of little children, both male and female, *but principally female*, from SEVEN to fourteen years of age, are daily *compelled to labour* from six o'clock in the morning to seven in the evening, with only—Britons blush whilst you read it!— *with only thirty minutes allowed for eating and recreation!*—Poor infants! ye are indeed sacrificed at the shrine of avarice, *without even the solace of the negro slave;*— ye are no more than he is, *free agents*— ye are compelled to work as long as the *necessity* of your needy parents may require, or the cold-blooded avarice of your worse than barbarian masters *may demand!* Ye live in the boasted land of freedom, and *feel* and mourn that *ye are Slaves*, and slaves without the only comfort which the Negro has. He knows it is his sordid mercenary master's INTEREST that he should *live*, be *strong* and *healthy*. Not so with you. Ye are doomed to labour from morn till night for one who cares not how soon your weak and tender frames are stretched to breaking! You are not mercifully valued at so much per head; this would assure you at least (even with the worst and most cruel masters), of the mercy shown to their own labouring beasts. No, no! your soft and delicate limbs are tired, and fagged, and jaded at only *so much per week*; and when your joints can act no longer, your emaciated frames are cast aside, the boards on which you lately toiled and wasted life away, are instantly supplied with other victims, who in this boasted land of liberty are HIRED—not sold—as Slaves,

1. Henry Brougham (1778–1868), elected Member of Parliament for Yorkshire in 1830.

and daily forced to *hear* that they are free. Oh! Duncombe! Thou hatest Slavery—I know thou dost resolve that "Yorkshire children shall no more be slaves." And Morpeth! who justly gloriest in the Christian faith—Oh Morpeth listen to the cries and count the tears of these poor babes, and let St. Stephen's hear thee swear—"they shall no longer groan in Slavery!" And Bethell, too! who swears eternal hatred to the name of Slave, whene'er thy manly voice is heard in Britain's senate, assert the rights and liberty of Yorkshire Youths. And Brougham! Thou who art the chosen champion of liberty in every clime! Oh bend thy giant's mind, and listen to the sorrowing accents of these poor Yorkshire little ones, and note their tears; then let thy voice rehearse their woes, and touch the chord thou only holdest—the chord that sounds above the silvery notes in praise of heavenly liberty, and down descending at thy will, groans in the horrid caverns of the deep in muttering sounds of misery accursed to hellish bondage; and as thou soundst these notes, let Yorkshire hear thee swear "Her *children* shall be free!" Yes, all ye four protectors[2] of our rights, chosen by freemen to destroy oppression's rod,

> "Vow one by one, vow altogether, vow
> With heart and voice, eternal enmity
> Against oppression by your brethren's hands;
> Till man nor woman under Britain's laws,
> Nor son nor daughter born within her empire,
> Shall buy, or sell, or HIRE, or BE a Slave!"[3]

The nation is now most resolutely determined that Negroes shall be free. Let them, however, not forget that Briton's have common rights with Afric's sons.

The blacks may be fairly compared to beasts of burden, *kept for their master's use*. The whites to those *which others keep and let for hire*! If I have succeeded in calling the attention of your readers to the horrid and abominable system on which the worsted mills in and near Bradford are conducted, I have done some good. Why should not children working in them be protected by legislative enactments, as well as those who work in cotton mills?[4] Christians should feel and act for those whom Christ so eminently loved and declared that "of such is the kingdom of heaven."

Your insertion of the above in the *Leeds Mercury*, at your earliest convenience, will oblige, Gentlemen,

Your most obedient servant,
RICHARD OASTLER
*Fixby Hall, near Huddersfield, Sept. 29th, 1830.*

2. William Duncombe (1798–1867), George W. F. Howard, Lord Morpeth (1802–64), Richard Bethell (1772–1864), and Henry Brougham represented Yorkshire in Parliament in 1830.
3. James Montgomery, "Inscription under the Picture of an Aged Negro-Woman" (1826).
4. A reference to earlier regulation of child labor in the cotton mills of Lancashire.

# Charlotte Elizabeth Tonna

## THE WRONGS OF WOMAN

*As a novelist, journalist, writer of religious tracts, and editor of religious magazines, Charlotte Elizabeth Tonna sought to awaken her readers' consciences to the plight of the laboring poor.* The Christian Lady's Magazine, *which she wrote for and edited, combined Evangelical piety, practical advice for women, and some fanatical anti-Catholicism with social commentary, informing its women readers of grim factory conditions and insufficient wages and advocating regulation of child labor. Tonna's popular industrial novel,* Helen Fleetwood: A Tale of the Factories, *exposed the exploitation of workers in Manchester cotton mills.* The Wrongs of Woman, *published under the pen-name of "Charlotte Elizabeth" and aimed at a primarily female audience, focused on female and child employment in dress-making, pin-heading, lace-running, and screw-making. By employing women and children at wages substantially below those of men, Tonna argues, manufacturers and merchants increased their profits while simultaneously causing men's unemployment and demoralization, women's neglect of their children and their sacred domestic duties, and consequently the disintegration of the family. By purchasing luxuries such as lace, Tonna charges, women consumers participated in the exploitation of their sisters. Unregulated laissez-faire, in short, was un-Christian; it wrenched women from their divinely ordained domestic mission and it destroyed the family. To make its argument,* The Wrongs of Woman *mixes documentary evidence, drawn from governmental inquiries and reports such as the* Second Report of the Commissioners on the Employment of Children

*(1843), with the fictional accounts of the young women of three families—the Kings, the Smiths, and the Clarkes—who have been driven by circumstances into the labor force and descend rapidly in a spiral of physical, psychological, and moral disintegration to death and prostitution. In the selection below, Kate Clarke, innocently assuming she has been employed as a housemaid, is introduced to the trade of lace-running or embroidery.* RM

## LACE MANUFACTURE

WHO SHALL PLEAD THE CAUSE of the poor? The question forces itself upon us as though it were unanswerable, when we look round and behold the multifarious forms in which oppression causes the land to mourn. The whole land, we repeat, mourns: covetousness smites the poor with a direct stroke, but the recoil upon itself is scarcely less grievous. Those who place their happiness in this world's good, and who, to increase their portion, readily avail themselves of such means as the ways and the maxims of this world sanction, are self-doomed to the greatest curse that can befal an accountable being. . . .

. . .There is an article of female attire, not, like the pin, necessary and of universal adoption, but elegant, tasteful, becoming, and very generally sought after. Of this, some kinds are so costly as to be only within the reach of the most affluent; and, until of late years, our home manufacture could not produce a fabric to compete with the foreign produce, neither can we now equal it. However, this being so promising a speculation, great efforts have been made by men who possessed capital for present outlay; and the lace trade employs an immense number of female hands in constant occupation to supply a market that numbers among its customers, in one branch or another, every grade of society, from the Queen upon the throne to the village barmaid, who cannot serve beer out to her master's customers without a bit of edging to her simple cap.

So far, all is very fair; that any produce of honest industry should find so ready a sale, and that our own poor should enjoy the profit rather than foreigners, is a matter of thankfulness. They, the labourers in this craft, might thereby obtain "food and raiment" with which they would be content, and glad. Their employers might make a fair, though moderate profit, and enjoy through it the greater comforts and advantages to which they have been accustomed; while the tradesman who retails the article would secure his reasonable profits also; and the purchaser of what is, under all circumstances, an addition to her necessaries—in other words, a luxury, must be content by giving a good price to remunerate all these agents for its supply. We find, accordingly, that the shopkeeper never fails to secure his portion; he charges as high a price as, in the midst of competition, he can venture to do; but that competition being extensive and brisk, he cannot grasp so much as he would do if the market were less amply supplied. Still he will not lose; he gives such a price for it as will compensate him, and the manufacturer must take what the tradesman will give.

The manufacturer has then to balance what he gets from the retailer with what he has paid, or must pay, for the raw material, and the wages of those who have wrought it into its present form; and the cost of machinery employed, so far as machinery can be made to go towards doing work for which otherwise the poor must be paid. He buys an immense supply of the article, to answer any sudden demand, and lest any brother in the business should profit by it instead of himself. Accordingly he has many hands at work, among a class who do literally depend for their daily share of the coarsest food, the scantiest raiment, the most miserable shelter, on the daily toil of their own hands; and these being wholly at his mercy, he throws the whole burden upon them. They have no other resource; they can turn to no other quarter for help; they have learnt the business, and however willing, however able to undertake any other branch of industry, they have not a friend in the world to put them in the way of so doing. Moreover, the number of applicants for employment is so large, and the destitution of such as cannot procure any is so fearful, that they dare not, even for a day, relinquish their posts, which hundreds would rush forward to secure, closing the way against their return, if, for the pursuit of another object, or for a little season of rest, they left them unoccupied. They are fettered by their helpless condition not less strongly than is the galley-slave by his iron chain; and they *must* toil on.

In sketching out a supposed village community, to which the Kings and the Smiths originally belonged, we named a widower, Tom Clarke, as being on the look-out for employment for his four daughters, of whom he designed the eldest for service, and the rest for such work as he could find. We will take Kate Clarke to a place recommended by somebody who stopped at the old inn where Tom still loitered; and who, having ascertained that there were more hands than occupations in his family, drew a very flattering picture of the lace-making districts, and of one in particular. One or two suspicious people, indeed, cautioned Clarke; telling him that it was a lure—that the traveller had been asking questions which showed some ulterior object, and that there were agents known to be on the look-out to tempt into these districts such persons as, when once there, were not likely to be able to return, and who must therefore work for such pay as they could get, being even more destitute and helpless than those belonging to the parishes in which they resided. To all this, Tom turned a deaf ear: he had a great dislike to factories, and other places of imprisonment, as he called it; his own outdoor life, and the habits of his family, tended to strengthen the feeling; and as the traveller assured him that the persons of whom he spoke all worked independently at their own cottages, and that he might easily get his daughter received into one of these families, as a domestic helper, filling up her spare time with the beautiful work of lace-making, it seemed both to him and the girls such a splendid opening, that he was prevailed on to promise them all a share in the advantages, as soon as Kate had settled herself there.

Before accompanying this new adventurer in her promising career, it may be well to bring our readers somewhat acquainted with the various branches and peculiarities of the lace-making trade. The manufacture of the main fabric is carried on by machinery, varying in some points. The machines that are worked by hand are sometimes used singly, in separate houses, but more frequently a small number are worked together in a house; while, in a few cases, they are placed together in factories, to the number even of fifty. The main work is laborious, increasing in difficulty when the machine is wider than the common carriage, and requiring the strength of a man to keep it in action. In some very wide machines, there is occasion for two, or even three men, unless a wheel is used, and then children, generally young boys, are employed to attend to the wheels. The work is carried on, very frequently, twenty out of the twenty-four hours; and the labourers of all ages are consequently liable to be called for at all times of the day and night. It is usual, towards the end of the week, to keep it on during the whole night, to make up for time lost in the early part by idleness and debauchery. Of course, whenever the workmen choose to be at the business, all the junior hands must be there also.

The machines propelled by steam-power cannot be thus worked at will, but must be attended to incessantly, while the engines are going. But this usually commences at four in the morning, and continues till twelve at night, making twenty hours of regular work. The work stops at eight on the Saturday, but in many instances they keep it up through the whole of Friday night, to make good the four hours so lost. It is not uncommon in some factories to go on throughout the whole twenty-four hours, allowing one hour for cleansing the engine and machinery. Two sets of men or lads are employed in such cases, each party taking five or six hours at once, called a "shift;" and thus every one has ten or twelve hours' work *per diem*.

The machines are very perfect, making the lace by their own action, but requiring such incessant, watchful care, such a sharp eye kept constantly upon the whole surface of the web to detect and to rectify any blemish or irregularity, that it is beyond any similar employment trying and injurious to the sight; so that at forty, very few indeed can carry it on without the aid of spectacles. This particular mischief belongs to the process in all its branches, the winding, threading, mending, running, drawing, &c. as will be seen by a little further description.

*Winding* consists in winding into the brass bobbins the necessary quantity of thread to make a piece of lace: it is done by young women, requires great care, and, from the delicacy of the material used, and the continued fixing of the eyes on the metal to which it must be adjusted, the sight is strained, weakened, and permanently injured; though by no means to such an extent as in the next department.

*Threading* consists in passing the end of the thread, wound as above, through an aperture often no larger than the eye of a needle, in order that it may be properly spread and woven on the machine. This is the sole occupation of the threaders during the day and night, and the fatigue both of limb and eye is overpowering. There never are relays, or sets, or "shifts" of threaders: the poor children must work as long as they are wanted; they must, even during the intervals, remain at hand to be ready for the next summons; and no provision is ever made, by mattress, blanket, or any accommodation of any kind whatever, for their obtaining rest during the hours of the night, when they may be spared to snatch a little sleep. . . .

*Drawing* consists in pulling out with a needle the threads that join the widths of lace in one broad piece when they come from the manufactory. How, and by whom this is accomplished, we shall see by and by. *Running, hemming, pearling,* as well as *mending,* are done by the needle, and may be said to employ nearly the whole female population of the places where the business is carried on. The enormous price of machines, often becoming useless when fitted up at an expense of some hundreds of pounds, by a sudden change in the fashion which renders that particular pattern of no value, entails a frequent loss on the proprietor; and this forms the general excuse for all hardships imposed on the dependent poor, applying themselves and their children—shall we not rather say, applying themselves and sacrificing their children?—without intermission to a most destructive employment during the livelong day and not a small part of the night, for a pittance that will scarcely purchase for them a sufficiency of bread.

When Kate Clarke arrives at her destination, she finds it is a cottage consisting of two rooms: that on the ground floor extending the whole length and width of the building, but very low in proportion, while the chamber, or rather loft above it, following the form of the roof, slants off, so that it is only in the middle a person of common stature may comfortably stand upright. Here she sees a couple of coarse palliasses, laid on the ground, with a little bedding to each, and all the remaining space cumbered with old boxes, and different tools belonging to the trade at which the master of the house works as a journeyman; whilst in the apartment below, a turn-up bedstead leans against the wall, to make room for a deal table; and a number of small frames are wedged close together, the exact purpose of which she does not yet comprehend. The waggon by which her father brought her hither completed its slow progress on the Sunday afternoon, and no work is done. The man and his wife, both quiet, dull sort of people, and their five or six children, excite no particular interest in the mind of their new inmate, which is by no means of an intellectual order; but she takes a fancy to the youngest, a lovely little girl, under three years old, pale and delicate, yet with more vivacity in her looks than any other of the family, in whom Kate hopes to find a merry companion, when running out on messages, and doing the household work. The child seems no less taken with Kate's round rosy face, her staring blue eyes, and rather unmeaning, but very good-natured grin, and her evident inclination to be on the move. Mrs. Collins gives herself little concern as to the appearance or temper of her new domestic, nor does she seem to require her help in household matters, to which she attends, mechanically enough, herself. . . .

The principal object of Mrs. Collins' attention seemed to be a rather large but light package, loosely done up, from which she occasionally drew forth a corner of what appeared to Kate the most costly article she had ever seen, being fine as a cobweb; and which she rightly conjectured to be lace received from the factory. The children, on the contrary, eye it askance and with unfriendly looks; except the boy, seemingly about nine years old, who is absorbed in a game of dibs, near the door-way, while the little one, whom they call Sally, picks up the bones as they roll down, and jumping and laughing restores them to him. A piece of pork, brought by the villagers as a gift, having been boiled for supper, they all sit down to it, with appetites that seem to have been sharpened by previous abstinence; and Tom Clarke, highly satisfied with his daughter's prospects, takes a cordial leave of her and her employers, pausing at the door, to observe, with a triumphant snap of the fingers, "They sha'n't have it to say of me as they do of John Smith, that he made slaves of his children. I know better than to put mine in a factory prison. No, no; 'Home, sweet home' for me;" and he departs, whistling the tune of that favourite strain.

But in whatever visions of freedom an Englishman who has been taught from the cradle that his house is his castle, and that no tyranny can violate the sacred barrier of his humble threshold, may indulge in connexion with that hallowed domicile, there is a tyranny which enters unresisted to lay the most galling of fetters upon his household group, and to grind them into the dust. What is the precise nature of that tyranny it may be hard to decide: that it is an invited chain, voluntarily assumed, yea, contended for by the inmates of many an Englishman's castle, is undeniable; yet no man can look at the victims, and surmise that the circumstances under which they sought the oppressive yoke were other than sternly compulsory.

The only explanation that can be given of this system of inflicted and invited wrong, is the fact that, in the desperate spirit of speculation, commercial men will set no limits to the production of what they may possibly sell, to the farther increase of their growing capital; and that in the struggle for means to live by the very scanty portion of this accumulated wealth which is allowed to circulate among them, the really destitute class are as little disposed to reject the most inadequate remuneration for their heavy toil; thus at once glutting the market with labourers, and keeping down the price of work, so that those who are not yet quite destitute must submit to the same scale of wages, the same pressure of immoderate task-work, in order to secure a resource, however miserable, when what little they may have shall melt away. To this also we must attribute the pernicious plan of still tempting more adventurers into the manufacturing from the agricultural districts; because the greater the competition among the wretched, who *must* find employment or starve, the more free are those who employ them to impose hard terms; and upon the noble principle that "a penny saved is a penny got," to swell their deposits, and enlarge their outlay with the gain thus "saved" from the pining, famished stomachs of the poor.

## THE FINALE

. . . Ladies of England! under such circumstances as we have laid before you, are the materials of your daily attire prepared by manufacture and embroidery, the articles made up by dress-makers and milliners, and the very pins with which you secure them, formed to answer the purpose. At such a price you make your toilet—we have gone no further than that one branch of the almost numberless productions of British industry, and we will not wrong you by any appeal—if such FACTS do not speak, all language is utterly vain.

The untold horrors, any allusion to which would afford the pretext for an outcry against this book, as injurious to female delicacy, are all, every one, with all their causes and effects, fully open to the eye of Him, who said, in reference to the most beloved of all people, when they sinned to an extent not to be compared with England's sin, "Shall I not visit for these things? Shall not my soul be avenged on such a nation as this?"[1] and the extensive publication of what has so long been concealed from the general eye, is a token that He is about to vindicate His own holiness, justice, and mercy by some fearful act of vengeance against the transgressors. Let us therefore fear.

It has been asked, Why is this little book called "The Wrongs of Woman," seeing it is only to one class of female sufferers that its sad details apply? We answer, that the wrong against woman, against woman in every rank and every class, perpetrated by the means

1. Jeremiah 5: 9, 29.

which have been very briefly sketched in these pages, is alike fearful and universal. Have we not a woman on the throne? and is she not wronged, the Queen of England, while rebellion is cradled, fostered, matured in the ancient nurseries of pure old English loyalty throughout the land? There ever has been, and ever will be, a spirit of restless discontent seeking to unsettle the minds of the lower orders; but so long as the humblest of England's wives and mothers had homes where the frugal meal that fair industry could secure to them might be eaten in peace—so long as those women were left to make such lowly homes pleasant to the labouring men, who, with "a fair day's wages for a fair day's work" filled their proper station in the scale of society, and claimed the poor Englishman's share of that domestic comfort which is, or was, their country's dearest boast—so long a great but most effective opposing force was found in continual operation against the pernicious effects of political incendiarism; and however the man might bluster over imaginary wrongs in a crowd of noisy spouters, the quiet home, the clean-swept hearth, the industrious wife, and rosy prattling children that hailed his return, were better than fifty treatises on loyalty and contentment to reconcile him to his lot. Besides, while God's laws were not outraged, nor His Poor ground down by oppression that actually FORBIDS the woman of a Christian land to be "a keeper at home," to "rule the house," to adorn herself with "shamefacedness and sobriety," or to fulfil even the most sacred duties of a mother to her own baby offspring, yea, compels her to become an infanticide,—so long the blessing was not withdrawn— the curse was not poured out upon the land. But now, through the atrocious system of which a very small, and that too the least revolting part, has been set forth, our women are changed into men, and our men into devils; and the fair inheritance of England's Queen is becoming but as a throne whose pillars rest on an awakening volcano.

Once bursting forth, in the fierce and fiery tumult of universal insurrection, who in that scene of turbulence and violence, of blood and desolation, will not in the wild plainings of those daughters of the land who now dwell quiet and secure, averting their eyes from the sin and the sorrow, the consequences of which they never can avert from their devoted heads—who will not in that unpitied plaint, recognize a dreadful attestation that the cruelties now heaped upon the poorest of our sex, are in the broadest, most inclusive sense, THE WRONGS OF WOMAN?

# Thomas Carlyle

## SARTOR RESARTUS

Sartor Resartus *first appeared serially in* Fraser's Magazine, *from which the following selection is taken. Although many early readers were puzzled and angered by its idiosyncratic, mystifying form and style, George Eliot later would attest that the reading of* Sartor *became "an epoch in the history" of many minds.*[1] *Part fictional biography, part sermon, part philosophical tract,* Sartor Resartus *("The Tailor Re-tailored") is at once comic and deadly serious, allusive and elusive, ironic and didactic, satiric and prophetic.*

*At the narrative's center are two characters. First is the mysterious Diogenes Teufelsdröckh ("God-born Devil's-dung"), Professor of Things in General at Weissnichtwo (Know-not-where). Second is the fictional English editor who introduces English readers to Teufelsdröckh's life and his philosophy of Clothes, expounded in his massive treatise "Die Kleider, ihr Werden und Wirken" ("Clothes, Their Origin and Influence"). Sifting through fragments contained in six paper bags, the editor pieces together the biography of*

---

1. "Thomas Carlyle," *Essays of George Eliot*, ed. Thomas Pinney (London: Routledge and Kegan Paul, 1963), pp. 213–14.

*Teufelsdröckh, from his mysterious origin and childhood, through despair and doubt, to self-renunciation and spiritual rebirth. Beset by skepticism and jilted by his beloved Blumine, Teufelsdröckh has wandered through a world he thinks dead and purposeless. Gradually he experiences a religious and psychological conversion, as he passes through "The Everlasting No" and "The Centre of Indifference" to the "Everlasting Yea." "The Universe is not dead and demoniacal," he affirms, "but godlike, and my Father's." That affirmation of the divinity and mystery of a living universe is the cornerstone of Teufelsdröckh's and Carlyle's philosophy, presented most cogently in the chapter "Natural Supernaturalism," where the fictional editor quotes from and interprets the obscure "Die Kleider." As clothing covers the body and the body cloaks the soul, the visible, finite world both disguises and reveals the invisible and infinite. As clothes (beliefs, institutions, customs, time, and space) become outworn, they must be stripped away to reveal the divine in man and nature. Innovative and often baffling in style and form,* Sartor Resartus *calls for spiritual revolution or rebirth in both the individual and society.*                                                                    RM

## NATURAL SUPERNATURALISM

IT IS IN HIS STUPENDOUS Section, headed *Natural Supernaturalism*, that the Professor first becomes a Seer; and, after long effort, such as we have witnessed, finally subdues under his feet this refractory Clothes-Philosophy, and takes victorious possession thereof. Phantasms enough he has had to struggle with; "Cloth-webs and Cob-webs," of Imperial Mantles, Superannuated Symbols, and what not: yet still did he courageously pierce through. Nay, worst of all, two quite mysterious, world-embracing Phantasms, TIME and SPACE, have ever hovered round him, perplexing and bewildering: but with these also he now resolutely grapples, these also he victoriously rends asunder. In a word, he has looked fixedly on Existence, till one after the other, its earthly hulls and garnitures, have all melted away; and now to his rapt vision the interior, celestial Holy of Holies, lies disclosed.

Here therefore properly it is that the Philosophy of Clothes attains to Transcendentalism; this last leap, can we but clear it, takes us safe into the promised land, where *Palingenesia*,[2] in all senses, may be considered as beginning. "Courage, then!" may our Diogenes exclaim, with better right than Diogenes the First[3] once did. This stupendous Section we, after long, painful meditation, have found not to be unintelligible; but on the contrary to grow clear, nay radiant, and all-illuminating. Let the reader, turning on it what utmost force of speculative intellect is in him, do his part; as we, by judicious selection and adjustment, shall study to do ours:

"Deep has been, and is, the significance of Miracles," thus quietly begins the Professor; "far deeper perhaps than we imagine. Meanwhile, the question of questions were: What specially is a Miracle? To that Dutch King of Siam, an icicle had been a miracle; whoso had carried with him an air-pump, and phial of vitriolic ether, might have worked a mir-

2. Rebirth or new birth.
3. Greek philosopher of Cynic school, who supposedly said, near the end of a long, tedious lecture, "Courage, friends! I see land!"

acle. To my Horse again, who unhappily is still more unscientific, do not I work a miracle, and magical '*open sesame!*' every time I please to pay twopence, and open for him an
impassable *Schlagbaum*, or shut Turnpike?

" 'But is not a real Miracle simply a violation of the Laws of Nature?' ask several.
Whom I answer by this new question: What are the Laws of Nature? To me perhaps the
rising of one from the dead were no violation of these Laws, but a confirmation; were
some far deeper Law, now first penetrated into, and by Spiritual Force, even as the rest
have all been, brought to bear on us with its Material Force.

"Here too may some inquire, not without astonishment: On what ground shall one,
that can make Iron swim,[4] come and declare that therefore he can teach Religion? To us,
truly, of the Nineteenth Century, such declaration were inept enough; which nevertheless to our fathers, of the First Century, was full of meaning.

" 'But is it not the deepest Law of Nature that she be constant?' cries an illuminated
class: 'Is not the Machine of the Universe fixed to move by unalterable rules?' Probable
enough, good friends: nay, I too must believe that the God, whom ancient, inspired men
assert to be 'without variableness or shadow of turning,'[5] does indeed never change; that
Nature, that the Universe, which no one whom it so pleases can be prevented from calling a Machine, does move by the most unalterable rules. And now of you too I make the
old inquiry: What those same unalterable rules, forming the complete Statute-Book of
Nature, may possibly be?

"They stand written in our Works of Science, say you; in the accumulated records of
man's Experience?—Was man with his Experience present at the Creation, then, to see
how it all went on? Have any deepest scientific individuals yet dived down to the foundations of the Universe, and gauged every thing there? Did the Maker take them into His
counsel; that they read His ground-plan of the incomprehensible All; and can say, This
stands marked therein, and no more than this? Alas, not in anywise! These scientific individuals have been nowhere but where we also are; have seen some handbreadths deeper
than we see into the Deep that is infinite, without bottom as without shore.

"Laplace's Book on the Stars,[6] wherein he exhibits that certain Planets, with their
Satellites, gyrate round our worthy Sun, at a rate and in a course, which, by greatest good
fortune, he and the like of him have succeeded in detecting,—is to me as precious as to
another. But is this what thou namest 'Mechanism of the Heavens,' and 'System of the
World;' this, wherein Sirius and the Pleiades, and all Herschel's Fifteen thousand Suns
per minute,[7] being left out, some paltry handful of Moons, and inert Balls, had been—
looked at, nicknamed, and marked in the Zodiacal Waybill; so that we can now prate of
their Whereabout; their How, their Why, their What, being hid from us as in the signless
Inane?

"System of Nature! To the wisest man, wide as is his vision, Nature remains of quite
*infinite* depth, of quite infinite expansion; and all Experience thereof limits itself to some

4. Elisha miraculously makes an ax head float, in 2 Kings 6:4–7.
5. James 1:17.
6. Pierre Laplace, *Celestial Mechanics* (1829–39), trans. Nathaniel Bowditch.
7. Sir William Herschel (1738–1822), astronomer who discovered Uranus, catalogued hundreds of double-stars,
and described the form of the galaxy.

few computed centuries, and measured square-miles. The course of Nature's phases, on this our little fraction of a Planet, is partially known to us; but who knows what deeper courses these depend on; what infinitely larger Cycle (of causes) our little Epicycle revolves on? To the Minnow every cranny and pebble, and quality and accident, of its little native Creek may have become familiar: but does the Minnow understand the Ocean Tides and periodic Currents, the Trade-winds, and Monsoons, and Moon's Eclipses; by all which the condition of its little Creek is regulated, and may, from time to time (*un*miraculously enough), be quite overset and reversed? Such a minnow is man; his Creek this Planet Earth; his Ocean the immeasurable All; his Monsoons and periodic Currents the mysterious Course of Providence through Æons of Æons.

"We speak of the Volume of Nature: and truly a Volume it is,—whose Author and Writer is God. To read it! Dost thou, does man, so much as well know the Alphabet thereof? With its Words, Sentences, and grand descriptive Pages, poetical and philosophical, spread out through Solar Systems, and Thousands of Years, we shall not try thee. It is a Volume written in celestial hieroglyphs, in the true Sacred-writing; of which even Prophets are happy that they can read here a line and there a line. As for your Institutes, and Academies of Science, they strive bravely; and, from amid the thick-crowded, inextricably intertwisted hieroglyphic writing, pick out, by dextrous combination, some Letters in the vulgar Character, and therefrom put together this and the other economic Recipe, of high avail in Practice. That Nature is more than some boundless Volume of such Recipes, or huge, well-nigh inexhaustible Domestic-Cookery Book, of which the whole secret will, in this wise, one day, evolve itself, the fewest dream.

"Custom," continues the Professor, "doth make dotards of us all. Consider well, thou wilt find that Custom is the greatest of Weavers; and weaves air-raiment for all the Spirits of the Universe; whereby indeed these dwell with us visibly, as ministering servants, in our houses and workshops; but their spiritual nature becomes, to the most, for ever hidden. Philosophy complains that Custom has hoodwinked us, from the first; that we do every thing by Custom, even Believe by it; that our very Axioms, let us boast of Free-thinking as we may, are oftenest simply such Beliefs as we have never heard questioned. Nay, what is Philosophy throughout but a continual battle against Custom; an ever-renewed effort to *transcend* the sphere of blind Custom, and so become Transcendental?

"Innumerable are the illusions and legerdemain tricks of Custom: but of all these perhaps the cleverest is her knack of persuading us that the Miraculous, by simple repetition, ceases to be Miraculous. True, it is by this means we live; for man must work as well as wonder: and herein is Custom so far a kind nurse, guiding him to his true benefit. But she is a fond foolish nurse, or rather we are false foolish nurselings, when, in our resting and reflecting hours, we prolong the same deception. Am I to view the Stupendous with stupid indifference, because I have seen it twice, or two hundred, or two million times? There is no reason in Nature or in Art why I should: unless, indeed, I am a mere Work-Machine, for whom the divine gift of Thought were no other than the terrestrial gift of Steam is to the Steam-engine; a power whereby Cotton might be spun, and money and money's worth realised.

"Notable enough too, here as elsewhere, wilt thou find the potency of Names; which indeed are but one kind of such Custom-woven, wonder-hiding garments. Witchcraft, and all manner of Spectre-work, and Demonology, we have now named Madness, and Diseases of the Nerves. Seldom reflecting that still the new question comes upon us: What is Madness, what are Nerves? Ever, as before, does Madness remain a mysterious-terrific, altogether *infernal* boiling up of the Nether Chaotic Deep, through this fair-painted Vision of Creation, which swims thereon, which we name the Real. Was Luther's Picture of the Devil less a Reality,[8] whether it were formed within the bodily eye, or without it? In every the wisest Soul, lies a whole world of internal Madness, an authentic Demon-Empire; out of which, indeed, his world of Wisdom has been creatively built together, and now rests there, as on its dark foundations does a habitable flowery Earth-rind.

"But deepest of all illusory Appearances, for hiding Wonder, as for many other ends, are your two grand fundamental world-enveloping Appearances, SPACE and TIME. These, as spun and woven for us from before Birth itself, to clothe our celestial ME for dwelling here, and yet to blind it,—lie all-embracing, as the universal canvass, or warp and woof, whereby all minor Illusions, in this Phantasm Existence, weave and paint themselves. In vain, while here on Earth, shall you endeavour to strip them off; you can, at best, but rend them asunder for moments, and look through.

"Fortunatus had a wishing Hat, which when he put on, and wished himself Anywhere, behold he was There. By this means had Fortunatus triumphed over Space, he had annihilated Space; for him there was no Where, but all was Here. Were a Hatter to establish himself, in the Wahngasse of Weissnichtwo, and make felts of this sort for all mankind, what a world we should have of it! Still stranger, should, on the opposite side of the street, another Hatter establish himself; and, as his fellow-craftsman made Space-annihilating Hats, make Time-annihilating! Of both would I purchase, were it with my last groschen; but chiefly of this latter. To clap on your felt, and, simply by wishing that you were Any*where*, straightway to be *There!* Next to clap on your other felt, and, simply by wishing that you were Any*when*, straightway to be *Then!* This were indeed the grander: shooting at will from the Fire-Creation of the World to its Fire-Consummation; here historically present in the First Century, conversing face to face with Paul and Seneca;[9] there prophetically in the Thirty-first, conversing also face to face with other Pauls and Senecas, who as yet stand hidden in the depth of that late Time!

"Or thinkest thou, it were impossible, unimaginable? Is the Past annihilated, then, or only past; is the Future non-extant, or only future? Those mystic faculties of thine, Memory and Hope, already answer: already through those mystic avenues, thou the Earth-blinded summonest both Past and Future, and communest with them, though as yet darkly, and with mute beckonings. The curtains of Yesterday drop down, the curtains of To-morrow roll up; but Yesterday and To-morrow both *are*. Pierce through the Time-Element, glance into the Eternal. Believe what thou findest written in the sanctuaries of Man's Soul, even as all Thinkers, in all ages, have devoutly read it there: that Time and

---

8. The devil is said to have appeared before Luther as he translated the Psalms.

9. According to legend, St. Paul and Lucius Annaeus Seneca—first-century Roman philosopher, essayist, and dramatist—once conversed.

Space are not God, but creations of God; that with God as it is a universal HERE, so is it an Everlasting Now.

"And seest thou therein any glimpse of IMMORTALITY?—O Heaven! Is the white Tomb of our Loved One, who died from our arms, and must be left behind us there, which rises in the distance, like a pale, mournfully receding Milestone, to tell how many toilsome uncheered miles we have journeyed on alone,—but a pale spectral Illusion! Is the lost Friend still mysteriously Here, even as we are Here mysteriously, with God!—Know of a truth that only the Time-shadows have perished, or are perishable; that the real Being of whatever was, and whatever is, and whatever will be, *is* even now and for ever. This, should it unhappily seem new, thou mayest ponder, at thy leisure; for the next twenty years, or the next twenty centuries: believe it thou must; understand it thou canst not.

"That the Thought-forms, Space and Time, wherein, once for all, we are sent into this Earth to live, should condition and determine our whole Practical reasonings, conceptions, and imagings (not imaginings),—seems altogether fit, just, and unavoidable. But that they should, farthermore, usurp such sway over pure spiritual Meditation, and blind us to the wonder everywhere lying close on us, seems nowise so. Admit Space and Time to their due rank as Forms of Thought; nay, even, if thou wilt, to their quite undue rank of Realities: and consider, then, with thyself how their thin disguises hide from us the brightest God-effulgences! Thus, were it not miraculous, could I stretch forth my hand, and clutch the Sun? Yet thou seest me daily stretch forth my hand, and therewith clutch many a thing, and swing it hither and thither. Art thou a grown Baby, then, to fancy that the Miracle lies in miles of distance, or in pounds avoirdupois of weight; and not to see that the true inexplicable God-revealing Miracle lies in this, that I can stretch forth my hand at all; that I have free Force to clutch aught therewith? Innumerable other of this sort are the deceptions, and wonder-hiding stupefactions, which Space practises on us.

"Still worse is it with regard to Time. Your grand anti-magician, and universal wonder-hider, is this same lying Time. Had we but the Time-annihilating Hat, to put on for once only, we should see ourselves in a World of Miracles, wherein all fabled or authentic Thaumaturgy, and feats of Magic, were outdone. But unhappily we have not such a Hat; and man, poor fool that he is, can seldom and scantily help himself without one.

"Were it not wonderful, for instance, had Orpheus built the walls of Thebes by the mere sound of his Lyre? Yet tell me, who built these walls of Weissnichtwo; summoning out all the sandstone rocks, to dance along from the *Steinbruch*[10] (now a huge Troglodyte Chasm, with frightful green-mantled pools); and shape themselves into Doric and Ionic pillars, squared ashlar houses and noble streets? Was it not the still higher Orpheus, or Orpheuses, who, in past centuries, by the divine Music of Wisdom, succeeded in civilising Man? Our highest Orpheus walked in Judea, eighteen hundred years ago: his sphere-melody, flowing in wild native tones, took captive the ravished souls of men; and, being of a truth sphere-melody, still flows and sounds, though now with thousandfold Accompaniments, and rich symphonies, through all our hearts; and modulates, and divinely leads them. Is that a wonder, which happens in two hours; and does it cease to be wonderful if happening in two million? Not only was Thebes built by the Music of an

10. A stone quarry.

Orpheus; but without the music of some inspired Orpheus was no city ever built, no work that man glories in ever done.

"Sweep away the Illusion of Time: glance, if thou have eyes, from the near moving-cause to its far distant Mover: The stroke that came transmitted through a whole galaxy of elastic balls, was it less a stroke than if the last ball only had been struck, and sent flying? Oh, could I (with the Time-annihilating Hat) transport thee direct from the Beginnings to the Endings, how were thy eyesight unsealed, and thy heart set flaming in the Light-sea of celestial wonder! Then sawest thou that this fair Universe, were it in the meanest province thereof, is in very deed the star-domed City of God; that through every star, through every grass-blade, and most through every Living Soul, the glory of a present God still beams. But Nature, which is the Time-vesture of God, and reveals Him to the wise, hides Him from the foolish.

"Again, could any thing be more miraculous than an actual authentic Ghost? The English Johnson longed, all his life, to see one; but could not, though he went to Cock Lane, and thence to the church-vaults, and tapped on coffins. Foolish Doctor! Did he never, with the mind's eye as well as with the body's, look round him into that full tide of human Life he so loved; did he never so much as look into Himself? The good Doctor was a Ghost, as actual and authentic as heart could wish; well nigh a million of Ghosts were travelling the streets by his side. Once more I say, sweep away the illusion of Time; compress the three-score years into three minutes: what else was he, what else are we? Are we not Spirits, shaped into a body, into an Appearance; and that fade away again into air, and Invisibility? This is no metaphor, it is a simple scientific *fact*: we start out of Nothingness, take figure, and are Apparitions; round us, as round the veriest spectre, is Eternity; and to Eternity minutes are as years and æons. Come there not tones of Love and Faith, as from celestial harp-strings, like the Song of beatified Souls? And again, do we not squeak and gibber (in our discordant, screech-owlish debatings and recriminatings); and glide bodeful, and feeble, and fearful; or uproar (*poltern*), and revel in our mad Dance of the Dead,—till the scent of the morning-air summons us to our still Home; and dreamy Night becomes awake and Day? Where now is Alexander of Macedon: does the steel Host, that yelled in fierce battle-shouts at Issus and Arbela, remain behind him; or have they all vanished utterly, even as perturbed Goblins must? Napoleon too, and his Moscow Retreats and Austerlitz Campaigns! Was it all other than the veriest Spectre-Hunt; which has now, with its howling tumult that made Night hideous, flitted away?— Ghosts! There are nigh a thousand million walking the earth openly at noontide; some half-hundred have vanished from it, some half-hundred have arisen in it, ere thy watch ticks once.

"O Heaven, it is mysterious, it is awful to consider that we not only carry each a future Ghost within him; but are, in very deed, Ghosts! These Limbs, whence had we them; this stormy Force; this life-blood with its burning Passion? They are dust and shadow; a Shadow-system gathered round our ME; wherein, through some moments or years, the Divine Essence is to be revealed in the Flesh. That warrior on his strong war-horse, fire flashes through his eyes; Force dwells in his arm and heart: but warrior and war-horse are a vision; a revealed Force, nothing more. Stately they tread the Earth, as if it were a firm substance: fool! the Earth is but a film; it cracks in twain, and warrior and war-horse sink beyond plummet's sounding. Plummet's? Fantasy herself will not follow them. A little while ago they were not; a little while and they are not, their very ashes are not.

"So has it been from the beginning, so will it be to the end. Generation after generation takes to itself the Form of a Body; and forth-issuing from Cimmerian[11] Night, on Heaven's mission, APPEARS. What Force and Fire is in each he expends: one grinding in the mill of Industry; one hunter-like climbing the giddy Alpine heights of Science; one madly dashed in pieces on the rocks of Strife, in war with his fellow:—and then the Heaven-sent is recalled; his earthly Vesture falls away, and soon even to Sense becomes a vanished Shadow. Thus, like some wild-flaming, wild-thundering train of Heaven's Artillery, does this mysterious MANKIND thunder and flame, in long-drawn, quick-succeeding grandeur, through the unknown Deep. Thus, like a God-created, fire-breathing Spirit-host, we emerge from the Inane; haste stormfully across the astonished Earth; then plunge again into the Inane. Earth's mountains are levelled, and her seas filled up, in our passage: can the Earth, which is but dead and a vision, resist Spirits which have reality and are alive? On the hardest adamant some foot-print of us is stamped in; the last Rear of the host will read traces of the earliest Van. But whence?—O Heaven, whither? Sense knows not; Faith knows not; only that it is through Mystery to Mystery, from God and to God.

> 'We *are such stuff*
> As Dreams are made of, and our little Life
> Is rounded with a sleep!' "[12]

---

## PAST AND PRESENT

---

*In* Past and Present *Carlyle uses the medieval past to indict the Victorian present and to awaken his audience to a particularly Carlylean vision of the future. The present is the turbulent period of the late 1830s and early 1840s, a time of unemployment, low wages for laborers, strikes, factory closings, and riots—all of which suggested to Carlyle and others that England was rushing toward anarchy and self-destruction. Chartists, disappointed with the compromises of the Reform Bill of 1832, organized massive demonstrations and petitioned Parliament for universal male suffrage, secret ballots, annual elections, pay for members of Parliament, equal electoral districts, and the removal of property qualifications for members of Parliament. The Corn Laws, despite repeated agitation for repeal, restricted trade, kept the price of bread high, and enriched the landed aristocracy. The Poor Law Amendment Act of 1834 created workhouses, which Carlyle called "Poor Law Bastilles," for the unworking poor and aimed to do away with "out-door" relief or welfare payments to the poor. More generally, the present is modern, industrialized England, where Mammon (or*

---

11. In the *Odyssey*, the Cimmerii live in darkness.
12. William Shakespeare, *The Tempest* 4.1.156–8.

*money) is worshipped as a god, and the doctrine of* laissez-faire *sanctions unbridled individualism and exploitation of others. Juxtaposed with the godless, chaotic present is Carlyle's idealized vision of twelfth-century England, drawn from his reading of the chronicle of the monastery at Bury St. Edmunds by Jocelin of Brakelond. In this England dissension is quelled and order restored by coherent religious belief and the emergence of a heroic leader: the just, stern, hardworking Abbot Samson.*

*Carlyle's solutions to the crisis of the present may be regarded as both radical and reactionary. Echoing* Sartor Resartus, Past and Present *calls for a spiritual rebirth, both individual and social: an awakening to the mysterious, purposeful order of the universe and to the interdependence of human beings; and a conversion to a new creed centered on the tenets of hero worship and the gospel of work. Carlyle's new order is decidedly antidemocratic. The rebirth of both the individual and the nation depends upon a realization of the universal, hierarchical order of things, a recognition of one's rightful place in that order and of superiors fit to lead and to be obeyed. In* Past and Present *Carlyle adds Abbot Samson to the pantheon of heroes, including Cromwell, Napoleon, Dante, Shakespeare, Luther, and Knox, which he had discussed in* On Heroes, Hero-Worship, and the Heroic in History. *Most important, he exhorts middle-class industrialists and manufacturers to recognize their own potential heroism and, by discarding* laissez faire *and Mammonism, to become "Captains of Industry," heroic workers and leaders guided by a sense of divine order and justice.*                                                                      RM

## BOOK I

PROEM

### Chapter I

MIDAS

The condition of England, on which many pamphlets are now in the course of publication, and many thoughts unpublished are going on in every reflective head, is justly regarded as one of the most ominous, and withal one of the strangest, ever seen in this world. England is full of wealth, of multifarious produce, supply for human want in every kind; yet England is dying of inanition. With unabated bounty the land of England blooms and grows; waving with yellow harvests; thick-studded with workshops, industrial implements, with fifteen millions of workers, understood to be the strongest, the cunningest and the willingest our Earth ever had; these men are here; the work they have done, the fruit they have realised is here, abundant, exuberant on every hand of us: and behold, some baleful fiat as of Enchantment has gone forth, saying, "Touch it not, ye workers, ye master-workers, ye master-idlers; none of you can touch it, no man of you shall be the better for it; this is enchanted fruit!" On the poor workers such fiat falls first, in its rudest shape; but on the rich master-workers too it falls; neither can the rich master-idlers, nor any richest or highest man escape, but all are like to be brought low with it, and made 'poor' enough, in the money-sense or a far fataller one.

Of these successful skilful workers some two millions, it is now counted, sit in Workhouses, Poor-law Prisons; or have 'out-door relief' flung over the wall to them,—the workhouse Bastille being filled to bursting, and the strong Poor-law broken asunder by a stronger.[1] They sit there, these many months now; their hope of deliverance as yet small. In workhouses, pleasantly so named, because work cannot be done in them. Twelve hundred thousand workers in England alone; their cunning right-hand lamed, lying idle in their sorrowful bosom; their hopes, outlooks, share of this fair world, shut in by narrow walls. They sit there, pent up, as in a kind of horrid enchantment; glad to be imprisoned and enchanted, that they may not perish starved. The picturesque Tourist, in a sunny autumn day, through this bounteous realm of England, descries the Union Workhouse on his path. 'Passing by the Workhouse of St. Ives in Huntingdonshire, on a bright day last autumn,' says the picturesque Tourist, 'I saw sitting on wooden benches, in front of their Bastille and within their ring-wall and its railings, some half-hundred or more of these men. Tall robust figures, young mostly or of middle age; of honest countenance, many of them thoughtful and even intelligent-looking men. They sat there, near by one another; but in a kind of torpor, especially in a silence, which was very striking. In silence: for, alas, what word was to be said? An Earth all lying round, crying, Come and till me, come and reap me;—yet we here sit enchanted! In the eyes and brows of these men hung the gloomiest expression, not of anger, but of grief and shame and manifold inarticulate distress and weariness; they returned my glance with a glance that seemed to say, "Do not look at us. We sit enchanted here, we know not why. The Sun shines and the Earth calls; and, by the governing Powers and Impotences of this England, we are forbidden to obey. It is impossible, they tell us!" There was something that reminded me of Dante's Hell in the look of all this; and I rode swiftly away.'

So many hundred thousands sit in workhouses: and other hundred thousands have not yet got even workhouses; and in thrifty Scotland itself, in Glasgow or Edinburgh City, in their dark lanes, hidden from all but the eye of God, and of rare Benevolence the minister of God, there are scenes of woe and destitution and desolation, such as, one may hope, the Sun never saw before in the most barbarous regions where men dwelt. Competent witnesses, the brave and humane Dr. Alison,[2] who speaks what he knows, whose noble Healing Art in his charitable hands becomes once more a truly sacred one, report these things for us: these things are not of this year, or of last year, have no reference to our present state of commercial stagnation, but only to the common state. Not in sharp fever-fits, but in chronic gangrene of this kind is Scotland suffering. A Poor-law, any and every Poor-law, it may be observed, is but a temporary measure; an anodyne, not a remedy: Rich and Poor, when once the naked facts of their condition have come into collision, cannot long subsist together on a mere Poor-law. True enough:—and yet, human beings cannot be left to die! Scotland too, till something better come, must have a Poor-law, if Scotland is not to be a byword among the nations. O, what a waste is there;

---

1. The Return of Paupers for England and Wales, at Ladyday, 1842, is, 'In-door 221,687, Out-door 1,207,402, Total 1,429,089.'—(*Official Report.*) [Carlyle's note]

2. William P. Alison (1790–1859), physician and author of *Observations on the Management of the Poor in Scotland* (1840).

of noble and thrice-noble national virtues; peasant Stoicisms, Heroisms; valiant manful habits, soul of a Nation's worth,—which all the metal of Potosi[3] cannot purchase back; to which the metal of Potosi, and all you can buy with *it*, is dross and dust! . . .

## Chapter VI

HERO-WORSHIP

To the present Editor, not less than to Bobus,[4] a Government of the Wisest, what Bobus calls an Aristocracy of Talent, seems the one healing remedy: but he is not so sanguine as Bobus with respect to the means of realising it. He thinks that we have at once missed realising it, and come to need it so pressingly, by departing far from the inner eternal Laws and taking up with the temporary outer semblances of Laws. He thinks that 'enlightened Egoism,' never so luminous, is not the rule by which man's life can be led. That 'Laissez-faire,' 'Supply-and-demand,' 'Cash-payment for the sole nexus,' and so forth, were not, are not, and will never be, a practicable Law of Union for a Society of Men. That Poor and Rich, that Governed and Governing, cannot long live together on any such Law of Union. Alas, he thinks that man has a soul in him, *different* from the stomach in any sense of this word; that if said soul be asphyxied, and lie quietly forgotten, the man and his affairs are in a bad way. He thinks that said soul will have to be resuscitated from its asphyxia; that if it prove irresuscitable, the man is not long for this world. In brief, that Midas-eared Mammonism, double-barrelled Dilettantism, and their thousand adjuncts and corollaries, are *not* the Law by which God Almighty has appointed this his Universe to go. That, once for all, these are not the Law: and then farther that we shall have to return to what *is* the Law, not by smooth flowery paths, it is like, and with 'tremendous cheers' in our throat; but over steep untrodden places, through stormclad chasms, waste oceans, and the bosom of tornadoes; thank Heaven, if not through very Chaos and the Abyss! The resuscitating of a soul that has gone to asphyxia is no momentary or pleasant process, but a long and terrible one.

To the present Editor, 'Hero-worship,' as he has elsewhere named it, means much more than an elected Parliament, or stated Aristocracy, of the Wisest; for, in his dialect, it is the summary, ultimate essence, and supreme practical perfection of all manner of 'worship,' and true worships and noblenesses whatsoever. Such blessed Parliament and, were it once in perfection, blessed Aristocracy of the Wisest, god-honoured and man-honoured, he does look for, more and more perfected,—as the topmost blessed practical apex of a whole world reformed from sham-worship, informed anew with worship, with truth and blessedness! He thinks that Hero-worship, done differently in every different epoch of the world, is the soul of all social business among men; that the doing of it well, or the doing of it ill, measures accurately what degree of well-being or of ill-being there is in the world's affairs. He thinks that we, on the whole, do our Hero-worship worse than any Nation in this world ever did it before: that the Burns an Exciseman, the Byron a Literary Lion, are intrinsically, all things considered, a baser and falser phenom-

---

3. Bolivian silver-mine district.
4. One of Carlyle's fictional characters, Bobus Higgins is a prosperous sausage-maker.

enon than the Odin a God, the Mahomet a Prophet of God. It is this Editor's clear opinion, accordingly, that we must learn to do our Hero-worship better; that to do it better and better, means the awakening of the Nation's soul from its asphyxia, and the return of blessed life to us,—Heaven's blessed life, not Mammon's galvanic accursed one. To resuscitate the Asphyxied, apparently now moribund, and in the last agony if not resuscitated: such and no other seems the consummation.

'Hero-worship,' if you will,—yes, friends; but, first of all, by being ourselves of heroic mind. A whole world of Heroes; a world not of Flunkeys, where no Hero-King *can* reign: that is what we aim at! We, for our share, will put away all Flunkeyism, Baseness, Unveracity from us; we shall then hope to have Noblenesses and Veracities set over us; never till then. Let Bobus and Company sneer, "That is your Reform!" Yes, Bobus, that is our Reform; and except in that, and what will follow out of that, we have no hope at all. Reform, like Charity, O Bobus, must begin at home. Once well at home, how will it radiate outwards, irrepressible, into all that we touch and handle, speak and work; kindling ever new light, by incalculable contagion, spreading in geometric ratio, far and wide,— doing good only, wheresoever it spreads, and not evil.

By Reform Bills, Anti-Corn-Law Bills, and thousand other bills and methods, we will demand of our Governors, with emphasis, and for the first time not without effect, that they cease to be quacks, or else depart; that they set no quackeries and blockheadisms anywhere to rule over us, that they utter or act no cant to us,—that it will be better if they do not. For we shall now know quacks when we see them; cant, when we hear it, shall be horrible to us! We will say, with the poor Frenchman at the Bar of the Convention, though in wiser style than he, and 'for the space' not 'of an hour' but of a lifetime: "*Je demande l'arrestation des coquins et des lâches.*" 'Arrestment of the knaves and dastards:' ah, we know what a work that is; how long it will be before *they* are all or mostly got 'arrested:'—but here is one; arrest him, in God's name; it is one fewer! We will, in all practicable ways, by word and silence, by act and refusal to act, energetically demand that arrestment,—"*je demande cette arrestation-là!*"—and by degrees infallibly attain it. Infallibly: for light spreads; all human souls, never so bedarkened, love light; light once kindled spreads, till all is luminous;—till the cry, "*Arrest* your knaves and dastards" rises imperative from millions of hearts, and rings and reigns from sea to sea. Nay, how many of them may we not 'arrest' with our own hands, even now; we! Do not countenance them, thou there: turn away from their lackered sumptuosities, their belauded sophistries, their serpent graciosities, their spoken and acted cant, with a sacred horror, with an *Apage Satanas.*[5]—Bobus and Company, and all men will gradually join us. We demand arrestment of the knaves and dastards, and begin by arresting our own poor selves out of that fraternity. There is no other reform conceivable. Thou and I, my friend, can, in the most flunkey world, make, each of us, *one* non-flunkey, one hero, if we like: that will be two heroes to begin with:—Courage! even that is a whole world of heroes to end with, or what we poor Two can do in furtherance thereof!

Yes, friends: Hero-kings and a whole world not unheroic,—there lies the port and

5. "Get thee hence, Satan," Matthew 4:10.

happy haven, towards which, through all these stormtost seas, French Revolutions, Chartisms, Manchester Insurrections, that make the heart sick in these bad days, the Supreme Powers are driving us. On the whole, blessed be the Supreme Powers, stern as they are! Towards that haven will we, O friends; let all true men, with what of faculty is in them, bend valiantly, incessantly, with thousandfold endeavour, thither, thither! There, or else in the Ocean-abysses, it is very clear to me, we shall arrive.

Well; here truly is no answer to the Sphinx-question; not the answer a disconsolate Public, inquiring at the College of Health,[6] was in hopes of! A total change of regimen, change of constitution and existence from the very centre of it; a new body to be got, with resuscitated soul,—not without convulsive travail-throes; as all birth and new-birth presupposes travail! This is sad news to a disconsolate discerning Public, hoping to have got off by some Morrison's Pill, some Saint-John's corrosive mixture[7] and perhaps a little blistery friction on the back!—We were prepared to part with our Corn-Law, with various Laws and Unlaws: but this, what is this?

Nor has the Editor forgotten how it fares with your ill-boding Cassandras[8] in Sieges of Troy. Imminent perdition is not usually driven away by words of warning. Didactic Destiny has other methods in store; or these would fail always. Such words should, nevertheless, be uttered, when they dwell truly in the soul of any man. Words are hard, are importunate; but how much harder the importunate events they foreshadow! Here and there a human soul may listen to the words,—who knows how many human souls? whereby the importunate events, if not diverted and prevented, will be rendered *less* hard. The present Editor's purpose is to himself full of hope.

For though fierce travails, though wide seas and roaring gulfs lie before us, is it not something if a Loadstar, in the eternal sky, do once more disclose itself; an everlasting light, shining through all cloud-tempests and roaring billows, ever as we emerge from the trough of the sea: the blessed beacon, far off on the edge of far horizons, towards which we are to steer incessantly for life? Is it not something; O Heavens, is it not all? There lies the Heroic Promised Land; under that Heaven's-light, my brethren, bloom the Happy Isles,—there, O there! Thither will we;

'There dwells the great Achilles whom we knew.'[9]

There dwell all Heroes, and will dwell: thither, all ye heroic-minded!—The Heaven's Loadstar once clearly in our eye, how will each true man stand truly to *his* work in the ship; how, with undying hope, will all things be fronted, all be conquered. Nay, with the ship's prow once turned in that direction, is not all, as it were, already well? Sick wasting misery has become noble manful effort with a goal in our eye. 'The choking Nightmare chokes us no longer; for we *stir* under it; the Nightmare has already fled.'—

Certainly, could the present Editor instruct men how to know Wisdom, Heroism, when they see it, that they might do reverence to *it* only, and loyally make it ruler over

---

6. The dispensary of James Morison's "vegetable universal medicine," which for Carlyle is an emblem of quackery and false cure-alls.

7. Another supposed cure-all, created by St. John Long.

8. King Priam's daughter, whose prophecy of the fall of Troy was not heeded.

9. Tennyson's Poems (*Ulysses*). [Carlyle's note]

them,—yes, he were the living epitome of all Editors, Teachers, Prophets, that now teach and prophesy; he were an *Apollo*-Morrison, a Trismegistus[10] and *effective* Cassandra! Let no Able Editor hope such things. It is to be expected the present laws of copyright, rate of reward per sheet, and other considerations, will save him from that peril. Let no Editor hope such things: no;—and yet let all Editors aim towards such things, and even towards such alone! One knows not what the meaning of editing and writing is, if even this be not it.

Enough, to the present Editor it has seemed possible some glimmering of light, for here and there a human soul, might lie in these confused Paper-Masses now intrusted to him; wherefore he determines to edit the same. Out of old Books, new Writings, and much Meditation not of yesterday, he will endeavour to select a thing or two; and from the Past, in a circuitous way, illustrate the Present and the Future. The Past is a dim indubitable fact: the Future too is one, only dimmer; nay properly it is the *same* fact in new dress and development. For the Present holds in it both the whole Past and the whole Future;—as the LIFE-TREE IGDRASIL,[11] wide-waving, many-toned, has its roots down deep in the Death-kingdoms, among the oldest dead dust of men, and with its boughs reaches always beyond the stars; and in all times and places is one and the same Life-tree!

## BOOK II

THE ANCIENT MONK

### Chapter I

JOCELIN OF BRAKELOND

We will, in this Second Portion of our Work, strive to penetrate a little, by means of certain confused Papers, printed and other, into a somewhat remote Century; and to look face to face on it, in hope of perhaps illustrating our own poor Century thereby. It seems a circuitous way; but it may prove a way nevertheless. For man has ever been a striving, struggling, and, in spite of wide-spread calumnies to the contrary, a veracious creature: the Centuries too are all lineal children of one another; and often, in the portrait of early grandfathers, this and the other enigmatic feature of the newest grandson shall disclose itself, to mutual elucidation. . . .

A certain Jocelinus de Brakelonda, a natural-born Englishman, has left us an extremely foreign Book,[12] which the labours of the Camden Society have brought to light in these days. Jocelin's Book, the 'Chronicle,' or private Boswellean Notebook, of Jocelin, a certain old St. Edmundsbury Monk and Boswell, now seven centuries old, how remote is it from us; exotic, extraneous; in all ways, coming from far abroad! The language of it is not foreign only but dead: Monk-Latin lies across not the British Channel, but the ninefold Stygian Marshes, Stream of Lethe, and one knows not where! Roman Latin itself, still alive for us in the Elysian Fields of Memory, is domestic in comparison. And then the

---

10. Greek name for Egyptian god Thoth, patron of letters, learning, and wisdom.
11. The great ash tree, symbolizing the universe, in Norse mythology.
12. Chronica *JOCELINI DE BRAKELONDA, de rebus gestis Samsonis Abbatis Monasterii Sancti Edmundi: nunc primum typis mandata, curante JOHANNE GAGE ROKEWOOD.* (Camden Society, London, 1840.) [Carlyle's note]

ideas, life-furniture, whole workings and ways of this worthy Jocelin; covered deeper than Pompeii with the lava-ashes and inarticulate wreck of seven hundred years!

Jocelin of Brakelond cannot be called a conspicuous literary character; indeed few mortals that have left so visible a work, or footmark, behind them can be more obscure. One other of those vanished Existences, whose work has not yet vanished;—almost a pathetic phenomenon, were not the whole world full of such! The builders of Stonehenge, for example:—or alas, what say we, Stonehenge and builders? The writers of the *Universal Review* and *Homer's Iliad*; the paviers of London streets;—sooner or later, the entire Posterity of Adam! It is a pathetic phenomenon; but an irremediable, nay, if well meditated, a consoling one.

By his dialect of Monk-Latin, and indeed by his name, this Jocelin seems to have been a Norman Englishman; the surname *de Brakelonda* indicates a native of St. Edmundsbury itself, *Brakelond* being the known old name of a street or quarter in that venerable Town. Then farther, sure enough, our Jocelin was a Monk of St. Edmundsbury Convent; held some '*obedientia*,' subaltern officiality there, or rather, in succession several; was, for one thing, 'chaplain to my Lord Abbot, living beside him night and day for the space of six years;'—which last, indeed, is the grand fact of Jocelin's existence, and properly the origin of this present Book, and of the chief meaning it has for us now. He was, as we have hinted, a kind of born *Boswell*, though an infinitesimally small one; neither did he altogether want his *Johnson* even there and then. Johnsons are rare; yet, as has been asserted, Boswells perhaps still rarer,—the more is the pity on both sides! This Jocelin, as we can discern well, was an ingenious and ingenuous, a cheery-hearted, innocent, yet withal shrewd, noticing, quick-witted man; and from under his monk's cowl has looked out on that narrow section of the world in a really *human* manner; not in any *simial*, canine, ovine, or otherwise *inhuman* manner,—afflictive to all that have humanity! The man is of patient, peaceable, loving, clear-smiling nature; open for this and that. A wise simplicity is in him; much natural sense; a *veracity* that goes deeper than words. Veracity: it is the basis of all; and, some say, means genius itself; the prime essence of all genius whatsoever. Our Jocelin, for the rest, has read his classical manuscripts, his Virgilius, his Flaccus, Ovidius Naso; of course still more, his Homilies and Breviaries, and if not the Bible, considerable extracts of the Bible. Then also he has a pleasant wit; and loves a timely joke, though in mild subdued manner: very amiable to see. A learned grown man, yet with the heart as of a good child; whose whole life indeed has been that of a child,—St. Edmundsbury Monastery a larger kind of cradle for him, in which his whole prescribed duty was to *sleep* kindly, and love his mother well! This is the Biography of Jocelin; 'a man of excellent religion,' says one of his contemporary Brother Monks, ' *eximiæ religionis, potens sermone et opere.*'[13] . . .

## Chapter IX

ABBOT SAMSON

So then the bells of St. Edmundsbury clang out one and all, and in church and chapel the organs go: Convent and Town, and all the west side of Suffolk, are in gala; knights, vis-

---

13. A man "of exceptional religion, powerful in word and deed."

counts, weavers, spinners, the entire population, male and female, young and old, the very sockmen with their chubby infants,—out to have a holiday, and see the Lord Abbot arrive! And there is 'stripping barefoot' of the Lord Abbot at the Gate, and solemn leading of him in to the High Altar and Shrine; with sudden 'silence of all the bells and organs,' as we kneel in deep prayer there; and again with outburst of all the bells and organs, and loud *Te Deum* from the general human windpipe; and speeches by the leading viscount, and giving of the kiss of brotherhood; the whole wound up with popular games, and dinner within doors of more than a thousand strong, *plus quam mille comedentibus in gaudio magno.*[14]

In such manner is the selfsame Samson once again returning to us, welcomed on *this* occasion. He that went away with his frock-skirts looped over his arm, comes back riding high; suddenly made one of the dignitaries of this world. Reflective readers will admit that here was a trial for a man. Yesterday a poor mendicant, allowed to possess not above two shillings of money, and without authority to bid a dog run for him, this man today finds himself a *Dominus Abbas*, mitred Peer of Parliament, Lord of manorhouses, farms, manors, and wide lands; a man with 'Fifty Knights under him,' and dependent swiftly obedient multitudes of men. It is a change greater than Napoleon's; so sudden withal. As if one of the Chandos daydrudges[15] had, on awakening some morning, found that *he* overnight was become Duke! Let Samson with his clear-beaming eyes see into that, and discern it if he can. We shall now get the measure of him by a new scale of inches, considerably more rigorous than the former was. For if a noble soul is rendered tenfold beautifuller by victory and prosperity, springing now radiant as into his own due element and sunthrone; an ignoble one is rendered tenfold and hundredfold uglier, pitifuller. Whatsoever vices, whatsoever weaknesses were in the man, the parvenu will shew us them enlarged, as in the solar microscope, into frightful distortion. Nay, how many mere seminal principles of vice, hitherto all wholesomely kept latent, may we now see unfolded, as in the solar hothouse, into growth, into huge universally-conspicuous luxuriance and development!

But is not this, at any rate, a singular aspect of what political and social capabilities, nay let us say what depth and opulence of true social vitality, lay in those old barbarous ages, That the fit Governor could be met with under such disguises, could be recognised and laid hold of under such? Here he is discovered with a maximum of two shillings in his pocket, and a leather scrip round his neck; trudging along the highway, his frock-skirts looped over his arm. They think this is he nevertheless, the true Governor; and he proves to be so. Brethren, have we no need of discovering true Governors, but will sham ones forever do for us? These were absurd superstitious blockheads of Monks; and we are enlightened Tenpound Franchisers, without taxes on knowledge![16] Where, I say, are our superior, are our similar or at all comparable discoveries? We also have eyes, or ought to have; we have hustings, telescopes; we have lights, link-lights and rush-lights of an

---

14. "More than a thousand people at dinner in great joy."
15. Richard Chandos Grenville, second Duke of Buckingham and Chandos (1797–1861), a supporter of the Corn Laws, known for underpaying his laborers.
16. Taxes on newspapers and paper.

enlightened free Press, burning and dancing everywhere, as in a universal torch-dance; singeing your whiskers as you traverse the public thoroughfares in town and country. Great souls, true Governors, go about under all manner of disguises now as then. Such telescopes, such enlightenment,—and such discovery! How comes it, I say; how comes it? Is it not lamentable; is it not even, in some sense, amazing?

Alas, the defect, as we must often urge and again urge, is less a defect of telescopes than of some eyesight. Those superstitious blockheads of the Twelfth Century had no telescopes, but they had still an eye: not ballot-boxes; only reverence for Worth, abhorrence of Unworth. It is the way with all barbarians. Thus Mr. Sale informs me, the old Arab Tribes would gather in liveliest *gaudeamus*,[17] and sing, and kindle bonfires, and wreathe crowns of honour, and solemnly thank the gods that, in their Tribe too, a Poet had shewn himself. As indeed they well might; for what usefuller, I say not nobler and heavenlier thing could the gods, doing their very kindest, send to any Tribe or Nation, in any time or circumstances? I declare to thee, my afflicted quack-ridden brother, in spite of thy astonishment, it is very lamentable! We English find a Poet, as brave a man as has been made for a hundred years or so anywhere under the Sun; and do we kindle bonfires, thank the gods? Not at all. We, taking due counsel of it, set the man to gauge ale-barrels in the Burgh of Dumfries; and pique ourselves on our 'patronage of genius.' . . .

Abbot Samson had found a Convent all in dilapidation; rain beating through it, material rain and metaphorical, from all quarters of the compass. Willelmus Sacrista sits drinking nightly, and doing mere *tacenda*. Our larders are reduced to leanness, Jew Harpies and unclean creatures our purveyors; in our basket is no bread. Old women with their distaffs rush out on a distressed Cellarer in shrill Chartism. 'You cannot stir abroad but Jews and Christians pounce upon you with unsettled bonds;' debts boundless seemingly as the National Debt of England. For four years our new Lord Abbot never went abroad but Jew creditors and Christian, and all manner of creditors, were about him; driving him to very despair. Our Prior is remiss; our Cellarers, officials are remiss, our monks are remiss: what man is not remiss? Front this, Samson, thou alone art there to front it; it is thy task to front and fight this, and to die or kill it. May the Lord have mercy on thee!

To our antiquarian interest in poor Jocelin and his Convent, where the whole aspect of existence, the whole dialect, of thought, of speech, of activity, is so obsolete, strange, long-vanished, there now superadds itself a mild glow of human interest for Abbot Samson; a real pleasure, as at sight of man's work, especially of governing, which is man's highest work, done *well*. Abbot Samson had no experience in governing; had served no apprenticeship to the trade of governing, alas, only the hardest apprenticeship to that of obeying. He had never in any court given *vadium* or *plegium*,[18] says Jocelin; hardly ever seen a court, when he was set to preside in one. But it is astonishing, continues Jocelin, how soon he learned the ways of business; and, in all sort of affairs, became expert beyond others. Of the many persons offering him their service 'he retained one Knight skilled in taking *vadia* and *plegia*;' and within the year was himself well skilled. Nay, by

17. George Sale (ca. 1697–1736), translator of the *Koran*. "Gaudeamus": "revelry" or "funmaking."
18. Guarantees of an individual's appearance in court, by property, money, or another person.

and by, the Pope appoints him Justiciary in certain causes; the King one of his new Circuit Judges: official Osbert is heard saying, "That Abbot is one of your shrewd ones, *disputator est*; if he go on as he begins, he will cut out every lawyer of us!"[19]

Why not? What is to hinder this Samson from governing? There is in him what far transcends all apprenticeships; in the man himself there exists a model of governing, something to govern by! There exists in him a heart-abhorrence of whatever is incoherent, pusillanimous, unveracious,—that is to say, chaotic, *ungoverned*; of the Devil, not of God. A man of this kind cannot help governing! He has the living ideal of a governor in him; and the incessant necessity of struggling to unfold the same out of him. Not the Devil or Chaos, for any wages, will he serve; no, this man is the born servant of Another than them. Alas, how little avail all apprenticeships, when there is in your governor himself what we may well call *nothing* to govern by: nothing;—a general grey twilight, looming with shapes of expediencies, parliamentary traditions, division-lists, election-funds, leading-articles; this, with what of vulpine alertness and adroitness soever, is not much!

But indeed what say we, apprenticeship? Had not this Samson served, in his way, a right good apprenticeship to governing; namely, the harshest slave-apprenticeship to obeying! Walk this world with no friend in it but God and St. Edmund, you will either fall into the ditch, or learn a good many things. To learn obeying is the fundamental art of governing. How much would many a Serene Highness have learned, had he travelled through the world with water-jug and empty wallet, *sine omni expensa*; and, at his victorious return, sat down not to newspaper-paragraphs and city-illuminations, but at the foot of St. Edmund's Shrine to shackles and bread and water! He that cannot be servant of many, will never be master, true guide and deliverer of many;—that is the meaning of true mastership. Had not the Monk-life extraordinary 'political capabilities' in it; if not imitable by us, yet enviable? Heavens, had a Duke of Logwood, now rolling sumptuously to his place in the Collective Wisdom, but himself happened to plough daily, at one time, on seven-and-sixpence a week, with no out-door relief,—what a light, unquenchable by logic and statistic and arithmetic, would it have thrown on several things for him!

In all cases, therefore, we will agree with the judicious Mrs. Glass: 'First catch your hare!'[20] First get your man; all is got: he can learn to do all things, from making boots, to decreeing judgments, governing communities; and will do them like a man. Catch your no-man,—alas, have you not caught the terriblest Tartar in the world! Perhaps all the terribler, the quieter and gentler he looks. For the mischief that one blockhead, that every blockhead does, in a world so feracious, teeming with endless results as ours, no ciphering will sum up. The quack bootmaker is considerable; as corn-cutters can testify, and desperate men reduced to buckskin and list-shoes. But the quack priest, quack highpriest, the quack king! Why do not all just citizens rush, half-frantic, to stop him, as they would a conflagration? Surely a just citizen *is* admonished by God and his own Soul, by all silent and articulate voices of this Universe, to do what in *him* lies towards relief of this poor blockhead-quack, and of a world that groans under him. Run swiftly; relieve him,—

---

19. Jocelini Chronica, p. 25. [Carlyle's note]
20. Proverbial phrase, erroneously thought to appear at beginning of recipe in Hannah Glasse, *The Art of Cookery Made Plain and Easy* (1747).

were it even by extinguishing him! For all things have grown so old, tinder-dry, com-
bustible; and he is more ruinous than conflagration. Sweep him *down*, at least; keep him
strictly within the hearth: he will then cease to be conflagration; he will then become useful, more or less, as culinary fire. Fire is the best of servants; but what a master! This poor
blockhead too is born for uses: why, elevating him to mastership, will you make a conflagration, a parish-curse or world-curse of him?

## BOOK III

THE MODERN WORKER

## Chapter II

GOSPEL OF MAMMONISM

. . . O sumptuous Merchant-Prince, illustrious game-preserving Duke, is there no way of
'killing' thy brother but Cain's rude way! 'A good man by the very look of him, by his
very presence with us as a fellow wayfarer in this Life-pilgrimage, *promises* so much:'
wo[e] to him if he forget all such promises, if he never know that they were given! To a
deadened soul, seared with the brute Idolatry of Sense, to whom going to Hell is equivalent to not making money, all 'promises,' and moral duties, that cannot be pleaded for
in Courts of Requests, address themselves in vain. Money he can be ordered to pay, but
nothing more. I have not heard in all Past History, and expect not to hear in all Future
History, of any Society anywhere under God's Heaven supporting itself on such
Philosophy. The Universe is not made so; it is made otherwise than so. The man or nation
of men that thinks it is made so, marches forward nothing doubting, step after step; but
marches—whither we know! In these last two centuries of Atheistic Government (near
two centuries now, since the blessed restoration of his Sacred Majesty, and Defender of
the Faith,[21] Charles Second), I reckon that we have pretty well exhausted what of 'firm
earth' there was for us to march on;—and are now, very ominously, shuddering, reeling,
and let us hope trying to recoil, on the cliff's edge!—

For out of this that we call Atheism come so many other *isms* and falsities, each falsity
with its misery at its heels!—A SOUL is not like wind (*spiritus*, or breath) contained within a capsule; the ALMIGHTY MAKER is not like a Clockmaker that once, in old immemo-
rial ages, having *made* his Horologe of a Universe, sits ever since and sees it go! Not at all.
Hence comes Atheism; come, as we say, many other *isms*; and as the sum of all, comes
Valetism, the *reverse* of Heroism; sad root of all woes whatsoever. For indeed, as no man
ever saw the above-said wind-element enclosed within its capsule, and finds it at bottom
more deniable than conceivable; so too he finds, in spite of Bridgewater Bequests,[22] your
Clockmaker Almighty an entirely questionable affair, a deniable affair;—and accordingly
denies it, and along with it so much else. Alas, one knows not what and how much else!

---

21. Title first conferred by Pope Leo X on Henry VIII for his defense of the Church against Luther.
22. Bequest, left by Francis Henry Egerton, 8th Earl of Bridgewater (1756–1829) and shared by the authors of
Bridgewater Treatises on natural theology for the best work on the "Power, Wisdom, and Goodness of God, as
manifested in the Creation."

For the faith in an Invisible, Unnameable, Godlike, present everywhere in all that we see and work and suffer, is the essence of all faith whatsoever; and that once denied, or still worse, asserted with lips only, and out of bound prayerbooks only, what other thing remains believable? That Cant well-ordered is marketable Cant; that Heroism means gas-lighted Histrionism; that seen with 'clear eyes' (as they call Valet-eyes), no man is a Hero, or ever was a Hero, but all men are Valets and Varlets. The accursed practical quintessence of all sorts of Unbelief! For if there be now no Hero, and the Histrio himself begin to be seen into, what hope is there for the seed of Adam here below? We are the doomed ever-lasting prey of the Quack; who, now in this guise, now in that, is to filch us, to pluck and eat us, by such modes as are convenient for him. For the modes and guises I care little. The Quack once inevitable, let him come swiftly, let him pluck and eat me;—swiftly, that I may at least have done with him; for in his Quack-world I can have no wish to linger. Though he slay me, yet will I despise him.[23] Though he conquer nations, and have all the Flunkeys of the Universe shouting at his heels, yet will I know well that *he* is an Inanity; that for him and his there is no continuance appointed, save only in Gehenna and the Pool.[24] Alas, the Atheist world, from its utmost summits of Heaven and Westminster Hall, downwards through poor seven-feet Hats and 'Unveracities fallen hungry,' down to the lowest cellars and neglected hunger-dens of it, is very wretched.

One of Dr. Alison's Scotch facts struck us much.[25] A poor Irish Widow, her husband having died in one of the Lanes of Edinburgh, went forth with her three children, bare of all resource, to solicit help from the Charitable Establishments of that City. At this Charitable Establishment and then at that she was refused; referred from one to the other, helped by none;—till she had exhausted them all; till her strength and heart failed her: she sank down in typhus-fever; died, and infected her Lane with fever, so that 'seventeen other persons' died of fever there in consequence. The humane Physician asks thereupon, as with a heart too full for speaking, Would it not have been *economy* to help this poor Widow? She took typhus-fever, and killed seventeen of you!—Very curious. The forlorn Irish Widow applies to her fellow-creatures, as if saying, "Behold I am sinking, bare of help: ye must help me! I am your sister, bone of your bone; one God made us: ye must help me!" They answer, "No; impossible: thou art no sister of ours." But she proves her sisterhood; her typhus-fever kills *them*: they actually were her brothers, though denying it! Had man ever to go lower for a proof?

For, as indeed was very natural in such case, all government of the Poor by the Rich has long ago been given over to Supply-and-demand, Laissez-faire and such like, and uni-versally declared to be 'impossible.' "You are no sister of ours; what shadow of proof is there? Here are our parchments, our padlocks, proving indisputably our money-safes to be *ours*, and you to have no business with them. Depart! It is impossible!"—Nay, what wouldst thou thyself have us do? cry indignant readers. Nothing, my friends,—till you have got a soul for yourselves again. Till then all things are 'impossible.' Till then I cannot

23. A reference to Job 13:15: "Though he slay me, yet will I trust in him."
24. Hell.
25. Observations on the Management of the Poor in Scotland: By William Pulteney Alison, M.D. (Edinburgh, 1840.) [Carlyle's note]

even bid you buy, as the old Spartans would have done, two-pence worth of powder and lead, and compendiously shoot to death this poor Irish Widow: even that is 'impossible' for you. Nothing is left but that she prove her sisterhood by dying, and infecting you with typhus. Seventeen of you lying dead will not deny such proof that she *was* flesh of your flesh; and perhaps some of the living may lay it to heart.

'Impossible:' of a certain two-legged animal with feathers, it is said if you draw a distinct chalk-circle round him, he sits imprisoned, as if girt with the iron ring of Fate; and will die there, though within sight of victuals,—or sit in sick misery there, and be fatted to death. The name of this poor two-legged animal is—Goose; and they make of him, when well fattened, *Pâté de foie gras*, much prized by some!

## Chapter IV

### HAPPY

All work, even cotton-spinning, is noble; work is alone noble: be that here said and asserted once more. And in like manner too all dignity is painful; a life of ease is not for any man, nor for any god. The life of all gods figures itself to us as a Sublime Sadness— earnestness of Infinite Battle against Infinite Labour. Our highest religion is named the 'Worship of Sorrow.' For the son of man there is no noble crown, well worn, or even ill worn, but is a crown of thorns!—These things, in spoken words, or still better, in felt instincts alive in every heart, were once well known.

Does not the whole wretchedness, the whole *Atheism* as I call it, of man's ways, in these generations, shadow itself for us in that unspeakable Life-philosophy of his: The pretension to be what he calls 'happy?' Every pitifulest whipster that walks within a skin has his head filled with the notion that he is, shall be, or by all human and divine laws ought to be, 'happy.' His wishes, the pitifulest whipster's, are to be fulfilled for him; his days, the pitifulest whipster's, are to flow on in ever-gentle current of enjoyment, impossible even for the gods. The prophets preach to us, Thou shalt be happy; thou shalt love pleasant things, and find them. The people clamour, Why have we not found pleasant things?

We construct our theory of Human Duties, not on any Greatest-Nobleness Principle, never so mistaken; no, but on a Greatest-Happiness Principle. 'The word *Soul* with us, as in some Slavonic dialects, seems to be synonymous with *Stomach*.' We plead and speak, in our Parliaments and elsewhere, not as from the Soul, but from the Stomach;—wherefore, indeed, our pleadings are so slow to profit. We plead not for God's Justice; we are not ashamed to stand clamouring and pleading for our own 'interests,' our own rents and trade-profits; we say, They are the 'interests' of so many; there is such an intense desire for them in us! We demand Free-Trade, with much just vociferation and benevolence, That the poorer classes, who are terribly ill off at present, may have cheaper New-Orleans bacon. Men ask on Free-trade platforms, How can the indomitable spirit of Englishmen be kept up without plenty of bacon? We shall become a ruined Nation!— Surely, my friends, plenty of bacon is good and indispensable: but, I doubt, you will never get even bacon by aiming only at that. You are men, not animals of prey, well-used or ill-used! Your Greatest-Happiness Principle seems to me fast becoming a rather unhappy one.——What if we should cease babbling about 'happiness,' and leave *it* resting on its own basis, as it used to do! . . .

Truly, I think the man who goes about pothering and uproaring for his 'happiness,'—pothering, and were it ballot-boxing, poem-making, or in what way soever fussing and exerting himself,—he is not the man that will help us to 'get our knaves and dastards arrested!' No; he rather is on the way to increase the number,—by at least one unit and *his* tail! Observe, too, that this is all a modern affair; belongs not to the old heroic times, but to these dastard new times. 'Happiness our being's end and aim'[26] is at bottom, if we will count well, not yet two centuries old in the world.

The only happiness a brave man ever troubled himself with asking much about was, happiness enough to get his work done. Not "I can't eat!" but "I can't work!" that was the burden of all wise complaining among men. It is, after all, the one unhappiness of a man. That he cannot work; that he cannot get his destiny as a man fulfilled. Behold, the day is passing swiftly over, our life is passing swiftly over; and the night cometh, wherein no man can work.[27] The night once come, our happiness, our unhappiness,—it is all abolished; vanished, clean gone; a thing that has been: 'not of the slightest consequence' whether we were happy as eupeptic Curtis,[28] as the fattest pig of Epicurus, or unhappy as Job with potsherds, as musical Byron with Giaours and sensibilities of the heart; as the unmusical Meat-jack with hard labour and rust! But our work,—behold that is not abolished, that has not vanished: our work, behold, it remains, or the want of it remains;—for endless Times and Eternities, remains; and that is now the sole question with us forevermore! Brief brawling Day, with its noisy phantasms, its poor paper-crowns tinsel-gilt, is gone; and divine everlasting Night, with her star-diadems, with her silences and her veracities, is come! What hast thou done, and how? Happiness, unhappiness: all that was but the *wages* thou hadst; thou hast spent all that, in sustaining thyself hitherward; not a coin of it remains with thee, it is all spent, eaten: and now thy work, where is thy work? Swift, out with it, let us see thy work!

Of a truth, if man were not a poor hungry dastard, and even much of a blockhead withal, he would cease criticising his victuals to such extent; and criticise himself rather, what he does with his victuals!

## Chapter XIII

### DEMOCRACY

If the Serene Highnesses and Majesties do not take note of that,[29] then, as I perceive, *that* will take note of itself! The time for levity, insincerity, and idle babble and play-acting, in all kinds, is gone by; it is a serious, grave time. Old long-vexed questions, not yet solved

---

26. Alexander Pope, *Essay on Man*, 4.1.
27. John 9:4.
28. Sir William Curtis (1752–1829), Tory Member of Parliament, merchant, and infamous epicure.
29. In the preceding chapter Carlyle has argued that the epic of the current age is not "Arms and the Man," but "Tools and the Man" and admonished legislators to help the manufacturers do their work, by abolishing legislation that hinders industry, namely the Corn Laws.

in logical words or parliamentary laws, are fast solving themselves in facts, somewhat unblessed to behold! This largest of questions, this question of Work and Wages, which ought, had we heeded Heaven's voice, to have begun two generations ago or more, cannot be delayed longer without hearing Earth's voice. 'Labour' will verily need to be somewhat 'organised,' as they say,—God knows with what difficulty. Man will actually need to have his debts and earnings a little better paid by man; which, let Parliaments speak of them or be silent of them, are eternally his due from man, and cannot, without penalty and at length not without death-penalty, be withheld. How much ought to cease among us straightway; how much ought to begin straightway, while the hours yet are!

Truly they are strange results to which this of leaving all to 'Cash;' of quietly shutting up the God's Temple, and gradually opening wide-open the Mammon's Temple, with 'Laissez-faire, and Every man for himself,'—have led us in these days! We have Upper, speaking Classes, who indeed do 'speak' as never man spake before; the withered flimsiness, the godless baseness and barrenness of whose Speech might of itself indicate what kind of Doing and practical Governing went on under it! For Speech is the gaseous element out of which most kinds of Practice and Performance, especially all kinds of moral Performance, condense themselves, and take shape; as the one is, so will the other be. Descending, accordingly, into the Dumb Class in its Stockport Cellars[30] and Poor-Law Bastilles, have we not to announce that they also are hitherto unexampled in the History of Adam's Posterity?

Life was never a May-game for men: in all times the lot of the dumb millions born to toil was defaced with manifold sufferings, injustices, heavy burdens, avoidable and unavoidable; not play at all, but hard work that made the sinews sore, and the heart sore. As bond-slaves, *villani, bordarii, sochemanni,* nay indeed as dukes, earls and kings, men were oftentimes made weary of their life; and had to say, in the sweat of their brow and of their soul, Behold it is not sport, it is grim earnest, and our back can bear no more! Who knows not what massacrings and harryings there have been; grinding, long-continuing, unbearable injustices,—till the heart had to rise in madness, and some "*Eu Sachsen, nimith euer sachses,*You Saxons, out with your gully-knives then!" You Saxons, some 'arrestment,' partial 'arrestment of the Knaves and Dastards' has become indispensable!—The page of Dryasdust[31] is heavy with such details.

And yet I will venture to believe that in no time, since the beginnings of Society, was the lot of those same dumb millions of toilers so entirely unbearable as it is even in the days now passing over us. It is not to die, or even to die of hunger, that makes a man wretched; many men have died; all men must die,—the last exit of us all is in a Fire-Chariot of Pain. But it is to live miserable we know not why; to work sore and yet gain nothing; to be heart-worn, weary, yet isolated, unrelated, girt in with a cold universal Laissez-faire: it is to die slowly all our life long, imprisoned in a deaf, dead, Infinite Injustice, as in the accursed iron belly of a Phalaris' Bull![32] This is and remains forever

---

30. Earlier in the text Carlyle refers to the 1841 trial of a poverty-stricken couple in Stockport, who were charged with poisoning their children in order to receive burial insurance.
31. Carlyle's name for a pedantic historian.
32. Phalaris, sixth-century B.C. tyrant, who roasted his victims in a hollow brazen bull.

intolerable to all men whom God has made. Do we wonder at French Revolutions, Chartisms, Revolts of Three Days?[33] The times, if we will consider them, are really unexampled.

Never before did I hear of an Irish Widow reduced to 'prove her sisterhood by dying of typhus-fever and infecting seventeen persons,'—saying in such undeniable way, "You *see*, I was your sister!" Sisterhood, brotherhood was often forgotten; but not till the rise of these ultimate Mammon and Shotbelt Gospels, did I ever see it so expressly denied. If no pious Lord or *Law-ward* would remember it, always some pious Lady ('*Hlaf-dig*,' Benefactress, '*Loaf-giveress*,' they say she is,—blessings on her beautiful heart!) was there, with mild mother-voice and hand, to remember it; some pious thoughtful *Elder*, what we now call 'Prester,' *Presbyter* or 'Priest,' was there to put all men in mind of it, in the name of the God who had made all.

Not even in Black Dahomey was it ever, I think, forgotten to the typhus-fever length. Mungo Park,[34] resourceless, had sunk down to die under the Negro Village-Tree, a horrible White object in the eyes of all. But in the poor Black Woman, and her daughter who stood aghast at him, whose earthly wealth and funded capital consisted of one small calabash of rice, there lived a heart richer than '*Laissez-faire:*' they, with a royal munificence, boiled their rice for him; they sang all night to him, spinning assiduous on their cotton distaffs, as he lay to sleep: "Let us pity the poor white man; no mother has he to fetch him milk, no sister to grind him corn!" Thou poor black Noble One,—thou *Lady* too: did not a God make thee too; was there not in thee too something of a God!—

Gurth[35] born thrall of Cedric the Saxon has been greatly pitied by Dryasdust and others. Gurth with the brass collar round his neck, tending Cedric's pigs in the glades of the wood, is not what I call an exemplar of human felicity: but Gurth, with the sky above him, with the free air and tinted boscage and umbrage round him, and in him at least the certainty of supper and social lodging when he came home; Gurth to me seems happy, in comparison with many a Lancashire and Buckinghamshire man, of these days, not born thrall of anybody! Gurth's brass collar did not gall him: Cedric *deserved* to be his Master. The pigs were Cedric's, but Gurth too would get his parings of them. Gurth had the inexpressible satisfaction of feeling himself related indissolubly, though in a rude brass-collar way, to his fellow-mortals in this Earth. He had superiors, inferiors, equals.—Gurth is now 'emancipated' long since; has what we call 'Liberty.' Liberty, I am told, is a Divine thing. Liberty when it becomes the 'Liberty to die by starvation' is not so divine!

Liberty? The true liberty of a man, you would say, consisted in his finding out, or being forced to find out the right path, and to walk thereon. To learn, or to be taught, what work he actually was able for; and then, by permission, persuasion, and even compulsion, to set about doing of the same! That is his true blessedness, honour, 'liberty' and maximum of wellbeing: if liberty be not that, I for one have small care about liberty. You do not allow a palpable madman to leap over precipices; you violate his liberty, you that are wise; and keep him, were it in strait-waistcoats, away from the precipices! Every stupid,

---

33. A reference to the three-day revolution in Paris in 1830.
34. Mungo Park (1771–1806), Scottish explorer of the Niger River.
35. A swineherd in Walter Scott's *Ivanhoe* (1819).

every cowardly and foolish man is but a less palpable madman: his true liberty were that a wiser man, that any and every wiser man, could, by brass collars, or in whatever milder or sharper way, lay hold of him when he was going wrong, and order and compel him to go a little righter. O if thou really art my *Senior*, Seigneur, my *Elder*, Presbyter or Priest,—if thou art in very deed my *Wiser*, may a beneficent instinct lead and impel thee to 'conquer' me, to command me! If thou do know better than I what is good and right, I conjure thee in the name of God, force me to do it; were it by never such brass collars, whips and handcuffs, leave me not to walk over precipices! That I have been called, by all the Newspapers, a 'free man' will avail me little, if my pilgrimage have ended in death and wreck. O that the Newspapers had called me slave, coward, fool, or what it pleased their sweet voices to name me, and I had attained not death, but life!—Liberty requires new definitions.

A conscious abhorrence and intolerance of Folly, of Baseness, Stupidity, Poltroonery and all that brood of things, dwells deep in some men: still deeper in others an *uncon-scious* abhorrence and intolerance, clothed moreover by the beneficent Supreme Powers in what stout appetites, energies, egoisms so-called, are suitable to it;—these latter are your Conquerors, Romans, Normans, Russians, Indo-English; Founders of what we call Aristocracies. Which indeed have they not the most 'divine right' to found;—being them-selves very truly "Αριστοι, BRAVEST, BEST; and conquering generally a confused rabble of WORST, or at lowest, clearly enough, of WORSE? I think their divine right, tried, with affirmatory verdict, in the greatest Law-Court known to me, was good! A class of men who are dreadfully exclaimed against by Dryasdust; of whom nevertheless beneficent Nature has oftentimes had need; and may, alas, again have need.

When, across the hundredfold poor scepticisms, trivialisms, and constitutional cob-webberies of Dryasdust, you catch any glimpse of a William the Conqueror, a Tancred of Hauteville[36] or such like,—do you not discern veritably some rude outline of a true God-made King; whom not the Champion of England cased in tin, but all Nature and the Universe were calling to the throne? It is absolutely necessary that he get thither. Nature does not mean her poor Saxon children to perish, of obesity, stupor or other malady, as yet: a stern Ruler and Line of Rulers therefore is called in,—a stern but most beneficent *Perpetual House-Surgeon* is called in, by Nature, and even the appropriate *fees* are provided for him! Dryasdust talks lamentably about Hereward and the Fen Counties; fate of Earl Waltheof; Yorkshire and the North reduced to ashes;[37] all which is undoubtedly lamenta-ble. But even Dryasdust apprises me of one fact: 'A child, in this William's reign, might have carried a purse of gold from end to end of England.' My erudite friend, it is a fact which outweighs a thousand! Sweep away thy constitutional, sentimental and other cob-webberies; look eye to eye, if thou still have any eye, in the face of this big burly William Bastard: thou wilt see a fellow of most flashing discernment, of most strong lion-heart; — in whom, as it were, within a frame of oak and iron, the gods have planted the soul of 'a man of genius!' Dost thou call that nothing? I call it an immense thing!—Rage enough

---

36. William I, King of England, who reigned from 1066 to 1087; Carlyle later refers to his illegitimate birth. Tancred, Norman hero of the First Crusade.
37. Hereward the Wake, the legendary outlaw, led a rising of the Fen counties against William the Conqueror in 1070. Waltheof, Earl of Northumbria, was executed in 1076 for conspiring against William.

was in this Willelmus Conquestor, rage enough for his occasions;—and yet the essential element of him, as of all such men, is not scorching *fire*, but shining illuminative *light*. Fire and light are strangely interchangeable; nay, at bottom, I have found them different forms of the same most godlike 'elementary substance' in our world: a thing worth stating in these days. The essential element of this Conquestor is, first of all, the most sun-eyed perception of what *is* really what on this God's-Earth;—which, thou wilt find, does mean at bottom 'Justice,' and 'Virtues' not a few: *Conformity* to what the Maker has seen good to make; that, I suppose, will mean Justice and a Virtue or two?—

Dost thou think Willelmus Conquestor would have tolerated ten years' jargon, one hour's jargon, on the propriety of killing Cotton-manufactures by partridge Corn-Laws? I fancy, this was not the man to knock out of his night's-rest with nothing but a noisy bedlamism in your mouth! "Assist us still better to bush the partridges; strangle Plugson who spins the shirts?"—"*Par la Splendeur de Dieu!*"— — Dost thou think Willelmus Conquestor, in this new time, with Steamengine Captains of Industry on one hand of him, and Joe-Manton Captains of Idleness[38] on the other, would have doubted which *was* really the BEST; which did deserve strangling, and which not?

I have a certain indestructible regard for Willelmus Conquestor. A resident House-Surgeon, provided by Nature for her beloved English People, and even furnished with the requisite 'fees,' as I said; for he by no means felt himself doing Nature's work, this Willelmus, but his own work exclusively! And his own work withal it was; informed '*par la Splendeur de Dieu.*'—I say, it is necessary to get the work out of such a man, however harsh that be! When a world, not yet doomed for death, is rushing down to ever-deeper Baseness and Confusion, it is a dire necessity of Nature's to bring in her ARISTOCRACIES, her BEST, even by forcible methods. When their descendants or representatives cease entirely to *be* the Best, Nature's poor world will very soon rush down again to Baseness; and it becomes a dire necessity of Nature's to cast them out. Hence French Revolutions, Five-point Charters, Democracies, and a mournful list of *Etceteras*, in these our afflicted times. . . .

Democracy, the chase of Liberty in that direction, shall go its full course; unrestrainable by him of Pferdefuss-Quacksalber,[39] or any of *his* household. The Toiling Millions of Mankind, in most vital need and passionate instinctive desire of Guidance, shall cast away False-Guidance; and hope, for an hour, that No-Guidance will suffice them: but it can be for an hour only. The smallest item of human Slavery is the oppression of man by his Mock-Superiors; the palpablest, but I say at bottom the smallest. Let him shake off such oppression, trample it indignantly under his feet; I blame him not, I pity and commend him. But oppression by your Mock-Superiors well shaken off, the grand problem yet remains to solve: That of finding government by your Real-Superiors! Alas, how shall we ever learn the solution of that, benighted, bewildered, sniffing, sneering, godforgetting unfortunates as we are? It is a work for centuries; to be taught us by tribulations, confusions, insurrections, obstructions; who knows if not by conflagration and despair! It is a lesson inclusive of all other lessons; the hardest of all lessons to learn. . . .

---

38. Joseph Manton, London gunsmith, supplied the "idle" aristocracy with guns for hunting.
39. Horsefoot-Quackdoctor, a reference to Prime Minister Robert Peel.

# BOOK IV

HOROSCOPE

## Chapter IV

CAPTAINS OF INDUSTRY

If I believed that Mammonism with its adjuncts was to continue henceforth the one serious principle of our existence, I should reckon it idle to solicit remedial measures from any Government, the disease being insusceptible of remedy. Government can do much, but it can in no wise do all. Government, as the most conspicuous object in Society, is called upon to give signal of what shall be done; and, in many ways, to preside over, further, and command the doing of it. But the Government cannot do, by all its signalling and commanding, what the Society is radically indisposed to do. In the long-run every Government is the exact symbol of its People, with their wisdom and unwisdom; we have to say, Like People like Government.—The main substance of this immense Problem of Organising Labour, and first of all of Managing the Working Classes, will, it is very clear, have to be solved by those who stand practically in the middle of it; by those who themselves work and preside over work. Of all that can be enacted by any Parliament in regard to it, the germs must already lie potentially extant in those two Classes, who are to obey such enactment. A Human Chaos in which there is no light, you vainly attempt to irradiate by light shed on it: order never can arise there.

But it is my firm conviction that the 'Hell of England' will *cease* to be that of 'not making money;' that we shall get a nobler Hell and a nobler Heaven! I anticipate light *in* the Human Chaos, glimmering, shining more and more; under manifold true signals from without That light shall shine. Our deity no longer being Mammon,—O Heavens, each man will then say to himself: "Why such deadly haste to make money? I shall not go to Hell, even if I do not make money! There is another Hell, I am told!" Competition, at railway-speed, in all branches of commerce and work will then abate:—good felt-hats for the head, in every sense, instead of seven-feet lath-and-plaster hats on wheels,[40] will then be discoverable! Bubble-periods,[41] with their panics and commercial crises, will again become infrequent; steady modest industry will take the place of gambling speculation. To be a noble Master, among noble Workers, will again be the first ambition with some few; to be a rich Master only the second. How the Inventive Genius of England, with the whirr of its bobbins and billy-rollers shoved somewhat into the backgrounds of the brain, will contrive and devise, not cheaper produce exclusively, but fairer distribution of the produce at its present cheapness! By degrees, we shall again have a Society with something of Heroism in it, something of Heaven's Blessing on it; we shall again have, as my German friend asserts, 'instead of Mammon-Feudalism with unsold cotton-shirts and Preservation of the Game, noble just Industrialism and Government by the Wisest!'

It is with the hope of awakening here and there a British man to know himself for a man and divine soul, that a few words of parting admonition, to all persons to whom the Heavenly Powers have lent power of any kind in this land, may now be addressed. And

40. A reference to advertisements for a London hatter.
41. Periods of "Bubbles" or dangerous financial speculation, such as the notorious South Sea Bubble of 1720.

first to those same Master-Workers, Leaders of Industry; who stand nearest, and in fact powerfulest, though not most prominent, being as yet in too many senses a Virtuality rather than an Actuality.

The Leaders of Industry, if Industry is ever to be led, are virtually the Captains of the World; if there be no nobleness in them, there will never be an Aristocracy more. But let the Captains of Industry consider: once again, are they born of other clay than the old Captains of Slaughter; doomed forever to be no Chivalry, but a mere gold-plated *Doggery*,—what the French well name *Canaille*, 'Doggery' with more or less gold carrion at its disposal? Captains of Industry are the true Fighters, henceforth recognisable as the only true ones: Fighters against Chaos, Necessity and the Devils and Jötuns[42]; and lead on Mankind in that great, and alone true, and universal warfare; the stars in their courses fighting for them, and all Heaven and all Earth saying audibly, Well-done! Let the Captains of Industry retire into their own hearts, and ask solemnly, If there is nothing but vulturous hunger, for fine wines, valet reputation and gilt carriages, discoverable there? Of hearts made by the Almighty God I will not believe such a thing. Deep-hidden under wretchedest godforgetting Cants, Epicurisms, Dead-Sea Apisms[43]; forgotten as under foulest fat Lethe mud and weeds, there is yet, in all hearts born into this God's-World, a spark of the Godlike slumbering. Awake, O nightmare sleepers; awake, arise, or be forever fallen! This is not playhouse poetry; it is sober fact. Our England, our world cannot live as it is. It will connect itself with a God again, or go down with nameless throes and fire-consummation to the Devils. Thou who feelest aught of such a Godlike stirring in thee, any faintest intimation of it as through heavy-laden dreams, follow *it*, I conjure thee. Arise, save thyself, be one of those that save thy country.

Bucaniers, Chactaw Indians, whose supreme aim in fighting is that they may get the scalps, the money, that they may amass scalps and money: out of such came no Chivalry, and never will! Out of such came only gore and wreck, infernal rage and misery; desperation quenched in annihilation. Behold it, I bid thee, behold there, and consider! What is it that thou have a hundred thousand-pound bills laid up in thy strong-room, a hundred scalps hung up in thy wigwam? I value not them or thee. Thy scalps and thy thousand-pound bills are as yet nothing, if no nobleness from within irradiate them; if no Chivalry, in action, or in embryo ever struggling towards birth and action, be there.

Love of men cannot be bought by cash-payment; and without love, men cannot endure to be together. You cannot lead a Fighting World without having it regimented, chivalried: the thing, in a day, becomes impossible; all men in it, the highest at first, the very lowest at last, discern consciously, or by a noble instinct, this necessity. And can you any more continue to lead a Working World unregimented, anarchic? I answer, and the Heavens and Earth are now answering, No! The thing becomes not 'in a day' impossible; but in some two generations it does. Yes, when fathers and mothers, in Stockport hunger-cellars, begin to eat their children, and Irish widows have to prove their relationship by dying of typhus-fever; and amid Governing 'Corporations of the Best and Bravest,' busy to preserve their game by 'bushing,' dark millions of God's human creatures start up in mad

---

42. Giants in Scandinavian mythology.
43. Earlier in the text, Carlyle tells of a fabled Dead Sea tribe that ignored Moses's warnings and turned into apes.

Chartisms, impracticable Sacred-Months, and Manchester Insurrections;—and there is a virtual Industrial Aristocracy as yet only half-alive, spellbound amid money-bags and ledgers; and an actual Idle Aristocracy seemingly near dead in somnolent delusions, in trespasses and double-barrels; 'sliding,' as on inclined-planes, which every new year they *soap* with new Hansard's-jargon[44] under God's sky, and so are 'sliding' ever faster, towards a 'scale' and balance-scale whereon is written *Thou art foundWanting:*—in such days, after a generation or two, I say, it does become, even to the low and simple, very palpably impossible! No Working World, any more than a Fighting World, can be led on without a noble Chivalry of Work, and laws and fixed rules which follow out of that,—far nobler than any Chivalry of Fighting was. As an anarchic multitude on mere Supply-and-demand, it is becoming inevitable that we dwindle in horrid suicidal convulsion, and self-abrasion, frightful to the imagination, into *Chactaw* Workers. With wigwam and scalps,—with palaces and thousand-pound bills; with savagery, depopulation, chaotic desolation! Good Heavens, will not one French Revolution and Reign of Terror suffice us, but must there be two? There will be two if needed; there will be twenty if needed; there will be precisely as many as are needed. The Laws of Nature will have themselves fulfilled. That is a thing certain to me.

Your gallant battle-hosts and work-hosts, as the others did, will need to be made loyally yours; they must and will be regulated, methodically secured in their just share of conquest under you;—joined with you in veritable brotherhood, sonhood, by quite other and deeper ties than those of temporary day's wages! How would mere redcoated regiments, to say nothing of chivalries, fight for you, if you could discharge them on the evening of the battle, on payment of the stipulated shillings,—and they discharge you on the morning of it! Chelsea Hospitals,[45] pensions, promotions, rigorous lasting covenant on the one side and on the other, are indispensable even for a hired fighter. The Feudal Baron, much more,—how could he subsist with mere temporary mercenaries round him, at sixpence a day; ready to go over to the other side, if sevenpence were offered? He could not have subsisted;—and his noble instinct saved him from the necessity of even trying! The Feudal Baron had a Man's Soul in him; to which anarchy, mutiny, and the other fruits of temporary mercenaries, were intolerable: he had never been a Baron otherwise, but had continued a Chactaw and Bucanier. He felt it precious, and at last it became habitual, and his fruitful enlarged existence included it as a necessity, to have men round him who in heart loved him; whose life he watched over with rigour yet with love; who were prepared to give their life for him, if need came. It was beautiful; it was human! Man lives not otherwise, nor can live contented, anywhere or anywhen. Isolation is the sum-total of wretchedness to man. To be cut off, to be left solitary: to have a world alien, not your world; all a hostile camp for you; not a home at all, of hearts and faces who are yours, whose you are! It is the frightfulest enchantment; too truly a work of the Evil One. To have neither superior, nor inferior, nor equal, united manlike to you. Without father, without child, without brother. Man knows no sadder destiny. 'How is each of us,' exclaims Jean Paul, 'so lonely, in the wide bosom of the All!'[46] Encased each as in his

44. A reference to parliamentary debates, printed by Hansard.
45. Hospital for disabled and infirm soldiers.
46. Jean Paul [F. Richter], *Siebenkäs* (1796–97).

transparent 'ice-palace;' our brother visible in his, making signals and gesticulations to us;—visible, but forever unattainable: on his bosom we shall never rest, nor he on ours. It was not a God that did this; no!

Awake, ye noble Workers, warriors in the one true war: all this must be remedied. It is you who are already half-alive, whom I will welcome into life; whom I will conjure in God's name to shake off your enchanted sleep, and live wholly! Cease to count scalps, gold-purses; not in these lies your or our salvation. Even these, if you count only these, will not long be left. Let bucaniering be put far from you; alter, speedily abrogate all laws of the bucaniers, if you would gain any victory that shall endure. Let God's justice, let pity, nobleness and manly valour, with more gold-purses or with fewer, testify themselves in this your brief Life-transit to all the Eternities, the Gods and Silences. It is to you I call; for ye are not dead, ye are already half-alive: there is in you a sleepless dauntless energy, the prime-matter of all nobleness in man. Honour to you in your kind. It is to you I call: ye know at least this, That the mandate of God to His creature man is: Work! The future Epic of the World rests not with those that are near dead, but with those that are alive, and those that are coming into life.

Look around you. Your world-hosts are all in mutiny, in confusion, destitution; on the eve of fiery wreck and madness! They will not march farther for you, on the sixpence a day and supply-and-demand principle: they will not; nor ought they, nor can they. Ye shall reduce them to order, begin reducing them. To order, to just subordination; noble loyalty in return for noble guidance. Their souls are driven nigh mad; let yours be sane and ever saner. Not as a bewildered bewildering mob; but as a firm regimented mass, with real captains over them, will these men march any more. All human interests, combined human endeavours, and social growths in this world, have, at a certain stage of their development, required organising: and Work, the grandest of human interests, does now require it.

God knows, the task will be hard: but no noble task was ever easy. This task will wear away your lives, and the lives of your sons and grandsons: but for what purpose, if not for tasks like this, were lives given to men? Ye shall cease to count your thousand-pound scalps, the noble of you shall cease! Nay the very scalps, as I say, will not long be left if you count only these. Ye shall cease wholly to be barbarous vulturous Chactaws, and become noble European Nineteenth-Century Men. Ye shall know that Mammon, in never such gigs and flunkey 'respectabilities,' is not the alone God; that of himself he is but a Devil, and even a Brute-god.

Difficult? Yes, it will be difficult. The short-fibre cotton; that too was difficult. The waste cotton-shrub, long useless, disobedient, as the thistle by the wayside,—have ye not conquered it; made it into beautiful bandana webs; white woven shirts for men; bright-tinted air-garments wherein flit goddesses? Ye have shivered mountains asunder, made the hard iron pliant to you as soft putty: the Forest-giants, Marsh-jötuns bear sheaves of golden grain; Ægir the Sea-demon himself stretches his back for a sleek highway to you, and on Firehorses and Windhorses ye career. Ye are most strong. Thor red-bearded, with his blue sun-eyes, with his cheery heart and strong thunder-hammer, he and you have prevailed. Ye are most strong, ye Sons of the icy North, of the far East,—far marching from your rugged Eastern Wildernesses, hitherward from the grey Dawn of Time! Ye are Sons of the *Jötun*-land; the land of Difficulties Conquered. Difficult? You must try this thing. Once try it with the understanding that it will and shall have to be done. Try it as ye try the paltrier thing, making of money! I will bet on you once more, against all Jötuns, Tailor-gods, Double-barrelled Law-wards, and Denizens of Chaos whatsoever!

# Sarah Stickney Ellis

## THE WOMEN OF ENGLAND, THEIR SOCIAL DUTIES, AND DOMESTIC HABITS

*Sarah Stickney Ellis wrote poetry and didactic fiction, and established a school for young women in Hertfordshire. Her highly popular conduct manuals, aimed toward middle-class women living in a capitalist society, suggested that women had a duty to civilize men who had become brutish under the stress of economic competition. Despite her own success as a professional writer, Ellis insisted that women had to learn to repress their own desires and ambitions in order to serve others, creating homes that would refresh the spirits of weary husbands, sons, and brothers. Ellis has been credited with helping to formulate what has come to be known as the "doctrine of separate spheres"—that is, separate areas of influence, public and private, for men and women, respectively. Her belief in the superiority of the domestic Englishwoman influenced mainstream English thought for decades: thirty years after* The Women of England *first appeared, John RUSKIN celebrated Ellis's ideal of womanly morality in his lecture "Of Queens' Gardens" (1864), and Eliza Lynn Linton invoked Ellis's ideal of woman's selflessness to criticize the modern, middle-class young woman in her essay "The Girl of the Period," published in the* Saturday Review *(1868).*     LMF

. . . THE IMMEDIATE OBJECT OF THE present work is to show how intimate is the connexion which exists between the *women* of England, and the *moral* character maintained by their country in the scale of nations. For a woman to undertake such a task, may at first sight appear like an act of presumption; yet when it is considered that the appropriate business of men is to direct, and expatiate upon, those expansive and important measures for which their capabilities are more peculiarly adapted, and that to women belongs the minute and particular observance of all those trifles which fill up the sum of human happiness or misery, it may surely be deemed pardonable for a woman to solicit the serious attention of her own sex, while she endeavours to prove that it is the minor morals of domestic life which give the tone to English character, and that over this sphere of duty it is her peculiar province to preside. . . .

No one could be farther than the writer of these pages from wishing to point out as objects of laudable emulation those domestic drudges, who, because of some affinity between culinary operations, and the natural tone and character of their own minds, prefer the kitchen to the drawing-room,—of their own free choice, employ their whole lives in the constant bustle of providing for mere animal appetite, and waste their ingenuity in the creation of new wants and wishes, which all their faculties again are taxed to supply. This class of individuals have, by a sad mistake in our nomenclature, been called *useful*, and hence, in some degree, may arise the unpopular reception which this valuable word is apt to meet with in female society.

It does not require much consideration to perceive that these are not the women to give a high moral tone to the national character of England; yet so entirely do human actions derive their dignity or their meanness from the *motives* by which they are prompted, that it is no violation of truth to say, the most servile drudgery may be ennobled by the self-sacrifice, the patience, the cheerful submission to duty, with which it is performed. Thus a high-minded and intellectual woman is never more truly great than when willingly and judiciously performing kind offices for the sick; and much as may be said, and said justly, in praise of the public virtues of women, the voice of nature is so powerful in every human heart, that, could the question of superiority on these two points be universally proposed, a response would be heard throughout the world, in favour of woman in her private and domestic character.

Nor would the higher and more expansive powers of usefulness with which women are endowed, suffer from want of exercise, did they devote themselves assiduously to their domestic duties. I am rather inclined to think they would receive additional vigour from the healthy tone of their own minds, and the leisure and liberty afforded by the systematic regularity of their household affairs. Time would never hang heavily on their hands, but each moment being husbanded with care, and every agent acting under their influence being properly chosen and instructed, they would find ample opportunity to go forth on errands of mercy, secure that in their absence the machinery they had set in motion would still continue to work, and to work well.

But if, on the other hand, all was confusion and neglect at home—filial appeals unanswered—domestic comforts uncalculated—husbands, sons, and brothers referred to servants for all the little offices of social kindness, in order that the ladies of the family might hurry away at the appointed time to some committee-room, scientific lecture, or public assembly; however laudable the object for which they met, there would be sufficient cause why their cheeks should be mantled with the blush of burning shame, when they heard the women of England and their virtues spoken of in that high tone of approbation and applause, which those who aspire only to be about their Master's business will feel little pleasure in listening to, and which those whose charity has not begun at home, ought never to appropriate to themselves.

It is a widely mistaken notion to suppose that the sphere of usefulness recommended here, is a humiliating and degraded one. As if the earth that fosters and nourishes in its lovely bosom the roots of all the plants and trees which ornament the garden of the world, feeding them from her secret storehouse with supplies that never fail, were less important, in the economy of vegetation, than the sun that brings to light their verdure and their flowers, or the genial atmosphere that perfects their growth, and diffuses their perfume abroad upon the earth. To carry out the simile still farther, it is but just to give the preference to that element which, in the absence of all other favouring circumstances, withholds not its support; but when the sun is shrouded, and the showers forget to fall, and blighting winds go forth, and the hand of culture is withdrawn, still opens out its hidden fountains, and yields up its resources, to invigorate, to cherish, and sustain.

It would be an easy and a grateful task, thus, by metaphor and illustration, to prove the various excellencies and amiable peculiarities of woman, did not the utility of the present work demand a more minute and homely detail of that which constitutes her practical and individual duty. It is too much the custom with writers, to speak in these general terms of the *loveliness* of the female character; as if woman were some fragrant flower, created only to bloom, and exhale in sweets; when perhaps these very writers are themselves most strict in requiring that the domestic drudgery of their own households should each day be faithfully filled up. How much more generous, just, and noble would it be to deal fairly by woman in these matters, and to tell her that to be *individually*, what she is praised for being *in general*, it is necessary for her to lay aside all her natural caprice, her love of self-indulgence, her vanity, her indolence—in short, her very *self*—and assuming a new nature, which nothing less than watchfulness and prayer can enable her constantly to maintain, to spend her mental and moral capabilities in devising means for promoting the happiness of others, while her own derives a remote and secondary existence from theirs.

If an admiration almost unbounded for the perfection of female character, with a sisterly participation in all the errors and weaknesses to which she is liable, and a profound sympathy with all that she is necessarily compelled to feel and suffer, are qualifications for the task I have undertaken, these certainly are points on which I yield to none; but at the same time that I do my feeble best, I must deeply regret that so few are the voices lifted up in her defence against the dangerous influence of popular applause, and the still more dangerous tendency of modern habits, and modern education. Perhaps it is not to be expected that those who write most powerfully, should most clearly perceive the influence of the one, or the tendency of the other; because the very strength and consistency of their own minds must in some measure exempt them from participation in either. While, therefore, in the art of reasoning, a writer like myself must be painfully sensible of her own deficiency, in sympathy of feeling, she is perhaps the better qualified to address the weakest of her sex.

With such, it is a favourite plea, brought forward in extenuation of their own uselessness, that they have no influence—that they are not leading women—that society takes no note of them;—forgetting, while they shelter themselves beneath these indolent excuses, that the very feather on the stream may serve to warn the doubtful mariner of the rapid and fatal current by which his bark might be hurried to destruction. It is, moreover, from amongst this class that wives are more frequently chosen; for there is a peculiarity in men—I would fain call it *benevolence*—which inclines them to offer the benefit of their protection to the most helpless and dependent of the female sex; and therefore it is upon this class that the duty of training up the young most frequently devolves. . . .

It is therefore not only false in reasoning, but wrong in principle, for women to assert, as they not unfrequently do with a degree of puerile satisfaction, that they have no influence. An influence fraught either with good or evil, they must have; and though the one may be above their ambition, and the other beyond their fears, by neglecting to obtain an influence which shall be beneficial to society, they necessarily assume a bad one: just in the same proportion as their selfishness, indolence, or vacuity of mind, render them in youth an easy prey to every species of unamiable temper, in middle age the melancholy victims of mental disease, and, long before the curtain of death conceals their follies from the world, a burden and a bane to society at large.

A superficial observer might rank with this class many of those exemplary women, who pass to and fro upon the earth with noiseless step, whose names are never heard, and who, even in society, if they attempt to speak, have scarcely the ability to command an attentive audience. Yet amongst this unpretending class are found striking and noble instances of women, who, apparently feeble and insignificant, when called into action by pressing and peculiar circumstances, can accomplish great and glorious purposes, supported and carried forward by that most valuable of all faculties—*moral power*. And just in proportion as women cultivate this faculty (under the blessing of heaven) independently of all personal attractions, and unaccompanied by any high attainments in learning or art, is their influence over their fellow-creatures, and consequently their power of doing good.

It is not to be presumed that women *possess* more moral power than men; but happily for them, such are their early impressions, associations, and general position in the world, that their moral feelings are less liable to be impaired by the pecuniary objects which too often constitute the chief end of man, and which, even under the limitations of better principle, necessarily engage a large portion of his thoughts. There are many humble-minded women, not remarkable for any particular intellectual endowments, who yet possess so clear a sense of the right and wrong of individual actions, as to be of essential service in aiding the judgments of their husbands, brothers, or sons, in those intricate affairs in which it is sometimes difficult to dissever worldly wisdom from religious duty.

To men belongs the potent—(I had almost said the *omnipotent*) consideration of worldly aggrandisement; and it is constantly misleading their steps, closing their ears against the voice of conscience, and beguiling them with the promise of peace, where peace was never found. Long before the boy has learned to exult in the dignity of the man, his mind has become familiarized to the habit of investing with supreme importance, all considerations relating to the acquisition of wealth. He hears on the Sabbath, and on stated occasions, when men meet for that especial purpose, of a God to be worshipped, a Saviour to be trusted in, and a holy law to be observed; but he sees before him, every day and every hour, a strife, which is nothing less than deadly to the highest impulses of the soul, after another god—the Mammon of unrighteousness—the Moloch[1] of this world; and believing rather what men do, than what they preach, he learns too soon to mingle with the living mass, and to unite his labours with theirs. To unite? Alas! there is no union in the great field of action in which he is engaged; but envy, and hatred, and opposition, to the close of the day,—every man's hand against his brother, and each struggling to exalt himself, not merely by trampling upon his fallen foe, but by usurping the place of his weaker brother, who faints by his side, from not having brought an equal portion of strength unto the conflict, and who is consequently borne down by numbers, hurried over, and forgotten.

This may be an extreme, but it is scarcely an exaggerated picture of the engagements of men of business in the present day. And surely they now need more than ever all the assistance which Providence has kindly provided, to win them away from this warfare, to remind them that they are hastening on towards a world into which none of the treasures they are amassing can be admitted; and, next to those holier influences which operate through the medium of revelation, or through the mysterious instrumentality of Divine love, I have little hesitation in saying, that the society of woman, in her highest moral capacity, is best calculated to effect this purpose.

How often has man returned to his home with a mind confused by the many voices, which in the mart, the exchange, or the public assembly, have addressed themselves to his inborn selfishness, or his worldly pride; and while his integrity was shaken, and his resolution gave way beneath the pressure of apparent necessity, or the insidious pretences of expediency, he has stood corrected before the clear eye of woman, as it looked directly to the naked truth, and detected the lurking evil of the specious act he was about to commit. Nay, so potent may have become this secret influence, that he may have borne it about with him like a kind of second conscience, for mental reference, and spiritual counsel, in moments of trial; and when the snares of the world were around him, and temptations from within and without have bribed over the witness in his own bosom, he has thought of the humble monitress who sat alone, guarding the fireside comforts of his distant home; and the remembrance of her character, clothed in moral beauty, has scattered the clouds before his mental vision, and sent him back to that beloved home, a wiser and a better man.

The women of England, possessing the grand privilege of being better instructed than those of any other country in the minutiæ of domestic comfort, have obtained a degree of importance in society far beyond what their unobtrusive virtues would appear to claim. The long-established customs of their country have placed in their hands the high and holy duty of cherishing and protecting the minor morals of life, from whence springs all that is elevated in purpose, and glorious in action. The sphere of their direct personal influence is central, and consequently small; but its extreme operations are as widely extended as the range of human feeling. . . .

1. Mammon: the personification of riches, avarice, and worldly gain. Moloch: Old Testament god to whom parents sacrificed their children; also a personification of the power to exact merciless sacrifices.

# Thomas Babington Macaulay

1800: BORN 25 OCTOBER IN LEICESTERSHIRE

1825: BECAME A REGULAR CONTRIBUTOR TO THE *EDINBURGH REVIEW* UNTIL 1844

1830: ENTERED THE HOUSE OF COMMONS

1834: ACCEPTED A SEAT ON THE SUPREME COUNCIL OF INDIA

1842: *LAYS OF ANCIENT ROME*

1848–61: *HISTORY OF ENGLAND*, VOLUMES 1–5

1859: DIED 28 DECEMBER IN KENSINGTON

## SOUTHEY'S "COLLOQUIES"

*In both his prose and his politics, Thomas Babington Macaulay exuded early Victorian con-
fidence. A member of Parliament, a government official, and one of the foremost nineteenth-
century historians, Macaulay subscribed to the Whig philosophy of* laissez-faire *government
and placed much faith in progress, education, and the middle classes. His 1830 review of
Robert Southey's* Sir Thomas More; or Colloquies on the Progress and Prospects of
Society *(1829) appeared in the Whig* Edinburgh Review. *Macaulay attacks Southey's
Tory traditionalism by claiming that Southey's ideal rural, paternalistic English past was
imagined, not real. Southey's* Colloquies *as well as Macaulay's review are products of the
worries that arose as England's development into a modern industrial state touched off a
series of social, economic, and political crises in the early part of the century. While some
writers responded to the changes accompanying industrialization with alarm, skepticism,
and distaste, Macaulay, particularly in this review, responded with optimism. He dismissed
the evils of industrialism that Southey foresaw by calling attention to technological, medical, and economic advances. Ultimately, Macaulay faulted Southey for attempting to evalu
ate the quality of human life by aesthetic standards, rather than measuring progress by
comparing past and present standards of living. Macaulay's faith in the ability of the growing middle class to govern wisely led him to champion the First Reform Bill of 1832.
Macaulay's optimism should be weighed against the sobering observations of Richard
*OASTLER *and James Phillips* KAY-SHUTTLEWORTH. LMF

. . . WE NOW COME TO THE conversations which pass between Mr Southey and Sir Thomas More, or rather between two Southeys, equally eloquent, equally angry, equally unreasonable, and equally given to talking about what they do not understand.[1] . . .

It is in the same manner that Mr Southey appears to have formed his opinion of the manufacturing system. There is nothing which he hates so bitterly. It is, according to him, a system more tyrannical than that of the feudal ages,—a system of actual servitude,—a system which destroys the bodies and degrades the minds of those who are engaged in it. He expresses a hope that the competition of other nations may drive us out of the field; that our foreign trade may decline, and that we may thus enjoy a restoration of national sanity and strength. But he seems to think that the extermination of the whole manufacturing population would be a blessing, if the evil could be removed in no other way.

Mr Southey does not bring forward a single fact in support of these views, and, as it seems to us, there are facts which lead to a very different conclusion. In the first place, the poor-rate is very decidedly lower in the manufacturing than in the agricultural districts.[2] If Mr Southey will look over the Parliamentary returns on this subject, he will find that the amount of parish relief required by the labourers in the different counties of England, is almost exactly in inverse proportion to the degree in which the manufacturing system has been introduced into those counties. The returns for the years ending in March 1825, and in March 1828, are now before us. In the former year, we find the poor-rate highest in Sussex,—about 20s. to every inhabitant. Then come Buckinghamshire, Essex, Suffolk, Bedfordshire, Huntingdonshire, Kent, and Norfolk. In all these the rate is above 15s. a-head. We will not go through the whole. Even in Westmoreland, and the North Riding of Yorkshire, the rate is at more than 8s. In Cumberland and Monmouthshire, the most fortunate of all the agricultural districts, it is at 6s. But in the West Riding of Yorkshire, it is as low as 5s.; and when we come to Lancashire, we find it at 4s.,—one-fifth of what it is in Sussex. The returns of the year ending in March 1828, are a little, and but a little, more unfavourable to the manufacturing districts. Lancashire, even in that season of distress, required a smaller poor-rate than any other district, and little more than one-fourth of the poor-rate raised in Sussex. Cumberland alone, of the agricultural districts, was as well off as the West Riding of Yorkshire. These facts seem to indicate that the manufacturer is both in a more comfortable and in a less dependent situation than the agricultural labourer.

As to the effect of the manufacturing system on the bodily health, we must beg leave to estimate it by a standard far too low and vulgar for a mind so imaginative as that of Mr Southey—the proportion of births and deaths. We know that, during the growth of this atrocious system—this new misery,—(we use the phrases of Mr Southey,)—this new enormity—this birth of a portentous age—this pest, which no man can approve whose heart is not seared, or whose understanding has not been darkened—there has been a great diminution of mortality—and that this diminution has been greater in the manufacturing towns than anywhere else. The mortality still is, as it always was, greater in

1. In his *Colloquies*, Southey imagines a dialogue between Sir Thomas More and Montesinos, Southey's persona.
2. Taxes on property to provide food and shelter for the unemployed and the unemployable were assessed by district according to the number of unemployed persons in that district.

towns than in the country. But the difference has diminished in an extraordinary degree. There is the best reason to believe, that the annual mortality of Manchester, about the middle of the last century, was one in twenty-eight. It is now reckoned at one in forty-five. In Glasgow and Leeds a similar improvement has taken place. Nay, the rate of mortality in those three great capitals of the manufacturing districts, is now considerably less than it was fifty years ago over England and Wales taken together—open country and all. We might with some plausibility maintain, that the people live longer because they are better fed, better lodged, better clothed, and better attended in sickness; and that these improvements are owing to that increase of national wealth which the manufacturing system has produced.

Much more might be said on this subject. But to what end? It is not from bills of mortality and statistical tables that Mr Southey has learned his political creed. He cannot stoop to study the history of the system which he abuses—to strike the balance between the good and evil which it has produced—to compare district with district, or generation with generation. We will give his own reason for his opinion—the only reason which he gives for it—in his own words:

'We remained awhile in silence, looking upon the assemblage of dwellings below. Here, and in the adjoining hamlet of Millbeck, the effects of manufactures and of agriculture may be seen and compared. The old cottages are such as the poet and the painter equally delight in beholding. Substantially built of the native stone without mortar, dirtied with no white lime, and their long, low roofs covered with slate, if they had been raised by the magic of some indigenous Amphion's music,[3] the materials could not have adjusted themselves more beautifully in accord with the surrounding scene; and time has still further harmonized them with weather-stains, lichens, and moss, short grasses, and short fern, and stone-plants of various kinds. The ornamented chimneys, round or square, less adorned than those which, like little turrets, crest the houses of the Portuguese peasantry; and yet not less happily suited to their place, the hedge of clipt box beneath the windows, the rose-bushes beside the door, the little patch of flower-ground, with its tall hollyocks in front; the garden beside, the bee-hives, and the orchard with its bank of daffodils and snow-drops, the earliest and the profusest in these parts, indicate in the owners some portion of ease and leisure, some regard to neatness and comfort, some sense of natural, and innocent, and healthful enjoyment. The new cottages of the manufacturers are upon the manufacturing pattern—naked, and in a row.

'How is it,' said I, 'that every thing which is connected with manufactures presents such features of unqualified deformity? From the largest of

3. In Greek mythology, Amphion was a son of Zeus and Antiope who, with his twin brother Zethus, built the walls of Thebes by the music of a magical lyre.

Mammon's temples down to the poorest hovel in which his helotry are
stalled, these edifices have all one character. Time will not mellow them;
nature will neither clothe nor conceal them; and they will remain always as
offensive to the eye as to the mind.'

Here is wisdom. Here are the principles on which nations are to be governed. Rose-
bushes and poor-rates, rather than steam-engines and independence. Mortality and cottages with weather-stains, rather than health and long life with edifices which time cannot mellow. We are told, that our age has invented atrocities beyond the imagination of
our fathers; that society has been brought into a state, compared with which extermination would be a blessing;—and all because the dwellings of cotton-spinners are naked and
rectangular. Mr Southey has found out a way, he tells us, in which the effects of manufactures and agriculture may be compared. And what is this way? To stand on a hill, to
look at a cottage and a manufactory, and to see which is the prettier. Does Mr Southey
think that the body of the English peasantry live, or ever lived, in substantial and ornamented cottages, with box-hedges, flower-gardens, bee-hives, and orchards? . . .

Mr Southey entertains as exaggerated a notion of the wisdom of governments as of
their power. He speaks with the greatest disgust of the respect now paid to public opinion. That opinion is, according to him, to be distrusted and dreaded; its usurpation ought
to be vigorously resisted; and the practice of yielding to it is likely to ruin the country. To
maintain police is, according to him, only one of the ends of government. Its duties are
patriarchal and paternal. It ought to consider the moral discipline of the people as its first
object, to establish a religion, to train the whole community in that religion, and to consider all dissenters as its own enemies.

> 'Nothing,' says Sir Thomas, 'is more certain, than that religion is the
> basis upon which civil government rests; that from religion power derives
> its authority, laws their efficacy, and both their zeal and sanction; and it is
> necessary that this religion be established as for the security of the state,
> and for the welfare of the people, who would otherwise be moved to and
> fro with every wind of doctrine. A state is secure in proportion as the peo-
> ple are attached to its institutions; it is, therefore, the first and plainest
> rule of sound policy, that the people be trained up in the way they should
> go. The state that neglects this prepares its own destruction; and they who
> train them in any other way are undermining it. Nothing in abstract sci-
> ence can be more certain than these positions are.'
>
> 'All of which,' answers Montesinos, 'are nevertheless denied by our
> professors of the arts Babblative and Scribblative; some in the audacity of
> evil designs, and others in the glorious assurance of impenetrable igno-
> rance.'

The greater part of the two volumes before us is merely an amplification of these
absurd paragraphs. What does Mr Southey mean by saying, that religion is demonstrably

the basis of civil government? He cannot surely mean that men have no motives except those derived from religion for establishing and supporting civil government, that no temporal advantage is derived from civil government, that man would experience no temporal inconvenience from living in a state of anarchy? If he allows, as we think he must allow, that it is for the good of mankind in this world to have civil government, and that the great majority of mankind have always thought it for their good in this world to have civil government, we then have a basis for government quite distinct from religion. It is true, that the Christian religion sanctions government, as it sanctions every thing which promotes the happiness and virtue of our species. But we are at a loss to conceive in what sense religion can be said to be the basis of government, in which it is not also the basis of the practices of eating, drinking, and lighting fires in cold weather. Nothing in history is more certain than that government has existed, has received some obedience and given some protection, in times in which it derived no support from religion,—in times in which there was no religion that influenced the hearts and lives of men. It was not from dread of Tartarus, or belief in the Elysian fields, that an Athenian wished to have some institutions which might keep Orestes from filching his cloak, or Midias from breaking his head.[4] 'It is from religion,' says Mr Southey, 'that power derives its authority, and laws their efficacy.' From what religion does our power over the Hindoos derive its authority, or the law in virtue of which we hang Brahmins its efficacy? For thousands of years civil government has existed in almost every corner of the world,—in ages of priestcraft,—in ages of fanaticism,—in ages of Epicurean indifference,—in ages of enlightened piety. However pure or impure the faith of the people might be, whether they adored a benef icent or a malignant power, whether they thought the soul mortal or immortal, they have, as soon as they ceased to be absolute savages, found out their need of civil government, and instituted it accordingly. It is as universal as the practice of cookery. Yet, it is as certain, says Mr Southey, as any thing in abstract science, that government is founded on religion. We should like to know what notion Mr Southey has of the demonstrations of abstract science. But a vague one, we suspect.

The proof proceeds. As religion is the basis of government, and as the state is secure in proportion as the people are attached to its institutions, it is therefore, says Mr Southey, the first rule of policy, that the government should train the people in the way in which they should go; and it is plain, that those who train them in any other way, are undermining the state.

Now it does not appear to us to be the first object that people should always believe in the established religion, and be attached to the established government. A religion may be false. A government may be oppressive. And whatever support government gives to false religions, or religion to oppressive governments, we consider as a clear evil.

The maxim, that governments ought to train the people in the way in which they should go, sounds well. But is there any reason for believing that a government is more likely to lead the people in the right way, than the people to fall into the right way of

---

4. In Greek mythology, Tartarus was the abyss below Hades; the Elysian Fields, the land of the blessed dead. Orestes, son of Agamemnon and Clytemnestra, avenged his father's murder by killing his mother and her lover Aegisthus. Athenian Midias was accused of bribery and physical assault by Demosthenes.

themselves? Have there not been governments which were blind leaders of the blind? Are there not still such governments? Can it be laid down as a general rule that the movement of political and religious truth is rather downwards from the government to the people, than upwards from the people to the government? These are questions which it is of importance to have clearly resolved. Mr Southey declaims against public opinion, which is now, he tells us, usurping supreme power. Formerly, according to him, the laws governed; now public opinion governs. What are laws but expressions of the opinion of some class which has power over the rest of the community? By what was the world ever governed, but by the opinion of some person or persons? By what else can it ever be governed? What are all systems, religious, political, or scientific, but opinions resting on evidence more or less satisfactory? The question is not between human opinion, and some higher and more certain mode of arriving at truth, but between opinion and opinion,— between the opinion of one man and another, or of one class and another, or of one generation and another. Public opinion is not infallible; but can Mr Southey construct any institutions which shall secure to us the guidance of an infallible opinion? Can Mr Southey select any family,—any profession—any class, in short, distinguished by any plain badge from the rest of the community, whose opinion is more likely to be just than this much-abused public opinion? Would he choose the peers, for example? Or the two hundred tallest men in the country? Or the poor Knights of Windsor? Or children who are born with cawls, seventh sons of seventh sons? We cannot suppose that he would recommend popular election; for that is merely an appeal to public opinion. And to say that society ought to be governed by the opinion of the wisest and best, though true, is useless. Whose opinion is to decide, who are the wisest and best?

Mr Southey and many other respectable people seem to think that when they have once proved the moral and religious training of the people to be a most important object, it follows, of course, that it is an object which the government ought to pursue. They forget that we have to consider, not merely the goodness of the end, but also the fitness of the means. Neither in the natural nor in the political body have all members the same office. There is surely no contradiction in saying that a certain section of the community may be quite competent to protect the persons and property of the rest, yet quite unfit to direct our opinions, or to superintend our private habits.

So strong is the interest of a ruler, to protect his subjects against all depredations and outrages except his own,—so clear and simple are the means by which this end is to be effected, that men are probably better off under the worst governments in the world, than they would be in a state of anarchy. Even when the appointment of magistrates has been left to chance, as in the Italian Republics, things have gone on better than they would have done, if there had been no magistrates at all, and every man had done what seemed right in his own eyes. But we see no reason for thinking that the opinions of the magistrate are more likely to be right than those of any other man. None of the modes by which rulers are appointed,—popular election, the accident of the lot, or the accident of birth,—afford, as far as we can perceive, much security for their being wiser than any of their neighbours. The chance of their being wiser than all their neighbours together is still smaller. Now we cannot conceive how it can be laid down, that it is the duty and the right of one class to direct the opinions of another, unless it can be proved that the former class is more likely to form just opinions than the latter.

The duties of government would be, as Mr Southey says that they are, paternal, if a government were necessarily as much superior in wisdom to a people, as the most foolish father, for a time, is to the most intelligent child, and if a government loved a people as fathers generally love their children. But there is no reason to believe, that a government will either have the paternal warmth of affection or the paternal superiority of intellect. Mr Southey might as well say, that the duties of the shoemaker are paternal, and that it is an usurpation in any man not of the craft to say that his shoes are bad, and to insist on having better. The division of labour would be no blessing, if those by whom a thing is done were to pay no attention to the opinion of those for whom it is done. The shoemaker, in the Relapse, tells Lord Foppington, that his lordship is mistaken in supposing that his shoe pinches. 'It does not pinch—it cannot pinch—I know my business— and I never made a better shoe.' This is the way in which Mr Southey would have a government treat a people who usurp the privilege of thinking. Nay, the shoemaker of Vanbrugh has the advantage in the comparison. He contented himself with regulating his customer's shoes, about which he knew something, and did not presume to dictate about the coat and hat. But Mr Southey would have the rulers of a country prescribe opinions to the people, not only about politics, but about matters concerning which a government has no peculiar sources of information,—concerning which any man in the streets may know as much, and think as justly, as a king,—religion and morals.

Men are never so likely to settle a question rightly, as when they discuss it freely. A government can interfere in discussion, only by making it less free than it would otherwise be. Men are most likely to form just opinions, when they have no other wish than to know the truth, and are exempt from all influence, either of hope or fear. . . .

The labouring classes . . . were, according to Mr Southey, better fed three hundred years ago than at present. We believe that he is completely in error on this point. The condition of servants in noble and wealthy families, and of scholars at the Universities, must surely have been better in those times than that of common day-labourers; and we are sure that it was not better than that of our workhouse paupers. From the household book of the Northumberland family, we find that in one of the greatest establishments of the kingdom the servants lived almost entirely on salt meat, without any bread at all. A more unwholesome diet can scarcely be conceived. In the reign of Edward the Sixth, the state of the students at Cambridge is described to us, on the very best authority, as most wretched. Many of them dined on pottage made of a farthing's worth of beef with a little salt and oatmeal, and literally nothing else. This account we have from a contemporary master of St Johns. Our parish poor now eat wheaten bread. In the sixteenth century the labourer was glad to get barley, and was often forced to content himself with poorer fare. In Harrison's introduction to Holinshed[5] we have an account of the state of our working population in the 'golden days,' as Mr Southey calls them, of good Queen Bess. 'The gentilitie,' says he, 'commonly provide themselves sufficiently of wheat for their

5. William Harrison (1534–93) published a "Description of England" with Raphael Holinshed's *Chronicles* (1577).

own tables, whylest their household and poore neighbours in some shires are inforced to content themselves with rice or barleie; yea, and in time of dearth, many with bread made eyther of beanes, peason, or otes, or of altogether, and some acornes among. I will not say that this extremity is oft so well to be seen in time of plentie as of dearth; but if I should I could easily bring my trial: for albeit there be much more grounde eared nowe almost in everye place then hath beene of late yeares, yet such a price of corne continueth in eache towne and markete, without any just cause, that the artificer and poore labouring man is not able to reach unto it, but is driven to content himself with horse-corne; I mean beanes, peason, otes, tares, and lintelles.' We should like to see what the effect would be of putting any parish in England now on allowance of 'horse-corne.' The helotry of Mammon are not, in our day, so easily enforced to content themselves as the peasantry of that happy period, as Mr Southey considers it, which elapsed between the fall of the feudal and the rise of the commercial tyranny.

'The people,' says Mr Southey, 'are worse fed than when they were fishers.' And yet in another place he complains that they will not eat fish. 'They have contracted,' says he, 'I know not how, some obstinate prejudice against a kind of food at once wholesome and delicate, and everywhere to be obtained cheaply and in abundance, were the demand for it as general as it ought to be.' It is true that the lower orders have an obstinate prejudice against fish. But hunger has no such obstinate prejudices. If what was formerly a common diet is now eaten only in times of severe pressure, the inference is plain. The people must be fed with what they at least think better food than that of their ancestors.

The advice and medicine which the poorest labourer can now obtain, in disease or after an accident, is far superior to what Henry the Eighth could have commanded. Scarcely any part of the country is out of the reach of practioners, who are probably not so far inferior to Sir Henry Halford as they are superior to Sir Anthony Denny.[6] That there has been a great improvement in this respect Mr Southey allows. Indeed he could not well have denied it. 'But,' says he, 'the evils for which these sciences are the palliative, have increased since the time of the Druids, in a proportion that heavily overweighs the benefit of improved therapeutics.' We know nothing either of the diseases or the remedies of the Druids. But we are quite sure that the improvement of medicine has far more than kept pace with the increase of disease during the last three centuries. This is proved by the best possible evidence. The term of human life is decidedly longer in England than in any former age, respecting which we possess any information on which we can rely. All the rants in the world about picturesque cottages and temples of Mammon will not shake this argument. No test of the state of society can be named so decisive as that which is furnished by bills of mortality. That the lives of the people of this country have been gradually lengthening during the course of several generations, is as certain as any fact in statistics, and that the lives of men should become longer and longer, while their physical condition, during life, is becoming worse and worse, is utterly incredible.

Let our readers think over these circumstances. Let them take into the account the sweating sickness and the plague. Let them take into the account that fearful disease

---

6. Henry Halford (1766–1844), English physician who attended George IV, William IV, and Victoria. Anthony Denny (1501–49), counsellor to Henry VIII.

which first made its appearance in the generation to which Mr Southey assigns the palm of felicity, and raged through Europe with a fury at which the physician stood aghast, and before which the people were swept away by thousands. Let them consider the state of the northern counties, constantly the scene of robberies, rapes, massacres, and conflagrations. Let them add to all this the fact that seventy-two thousand persons suffered death by the hands of the executioner during the reign of Henry the Eighth, and judge between the nineteenth and the sixteenth century.

We do not say that the lower orders in England do not suffer severe hardships. But, in spite of Mr Southey's assertions, and in spite of the assertions of a class of politicians, who, differing from Mr Southey in every other point, agree with him in this, we are inclined to doubt whether they really suffer greater physical distress than the labouring classes of the most flourishing countries of the Continent. . . .

It is not strange that, differing so widely from Mr Southey as to the past progress of society, we should differ from him also as to its probable destiny. He thinks, that to all outward appearance, the country is hastening to destruction; but he relies firmly on the goodness of God. We do not see either the piety, or the rationality, of thus confidently expecting that the Supreme Being will interfere to disturb the common succession of causes and effects. We, too, rely on his goodness,—on his goodness as manifested, not in extraordinary interpositions, but in those general laws which it has pleased him to establish in the physical and in the moral world. We rely on the natural tendency of the human intellect to truth, and on the natural tendency of society to improvement. We know no well authenticated instance of a people which has decidedly retrograded in civilisation and prosperity, except from the influence of violent and terrible calamities,—such as those which laid the Roman Empire in ruins, or those which, about the beginning of the sixteenth century, desolated Italy. We know of no country which, at the end of fifty years of peace and tolerably good government, has been less prosperous than at the beginning of that period. The political importance of a state may decline, as the balance of power is disturbed by the introduction of new forces. Thus the influence of Holland and of Spain is much diminished. But are Holland and Spain poorer than formerly? We doubt it. Other countries have outrun them. But we suspect that they have been positively, though not relatively, advancing. We suspect that Holland is richer than when she sent her navies up the Thames,—that Spain is richer than when a French king was brought captive to the footstool of Charles the Fifth.[7]

History is full of the signs of this natural progress of society. We see in almost every part of the annals of mankind how the industry of individuals, struggling up against wars, taxes, famines, conflagrations, mischievous prohibitions, and more mischievous protections, creates faster than governments can squander, and repairs whatever invaders can destroy. We see the capital of nations increasing, and all the arts of life approaching nearer and nearer to perfection, in spite of the grossest corruption and the wildest profusion on the part of rulers.

The present moment is one of great distress. But how small will that distress appear

---

7. A display of Dutch power in 1667. In 1525, Charles V of Spain captured Francis I of France.

when we think over the history of the last forty years;—a war,[8] compared with which, all other wars sink into insignificance;—taxation, such as the most heavily taxed people of former times could not have conceived;—a debt larger than all the public debts that ever existed in the world added together;—the food of the people studiously rendered dear;—the currency imprudently debased, and imprudently restored. Yet is the country poorer than in 1790? We fully believe that, in spite of all the misgovernment of her rulers, she has been almost constantly becoming richer and richer. Now and then there has been a stoppage, now and then a short retrogression; but as to the general tendency there can be no doubt. A single breaker may recede, but the tide is evidently coming in.

If we were to prophesy that in the year 1930, a population of fifty millions, better fed, clad, and lodged than the English of our time, will cover these islands,—that Sussex and Huntingdonshire will be wealthier than the wealthiest parts of the West-Riding of Yorkshire now are,—that cultivation, rich as that of a flower-garden, will be carried up to the very tops of Ben Nevis and Helvellyn,[9]—that machines, constructed on principles yet undiscovered, will be in every house,—that there will be no highways but rail-roads, no travelling but by steam,—that our debt, vast as it seems to us, will appear to our great-grandchildren a trifling encumbrance, which might easily be paid off in a year or two,—many people would think us insane. We prophesy nothing; but this we say—If any person had told the Parliament which met in perplexity and terror after the crash in 1720, that in 1830 the wealth of England would surpass all their wildest dreams—that the annual revenue would equal the principal of that debt which they considered as an intolerable burden—that for one man of £10,000 then living, there would be five men of £50,000; that London would be twice as large and twice as populous, and that neverthe-less the mortality would have diminished to one-half what it then was,—that the post-office would bring more into the exchequer than the excise and customs had brought in together under Charles II,—that stagecoaches would run from London to York in twen-ty-four hours—that men would sail without wind, and would be beginning to ride with-out horses—our ancestors would have given as much credit to the prediction as they gave to Gulliver's Travels. Yet the prediction would have been true; and they would have per-ceived that it was not altogether absurd, if they had considered that the country was then raising every year a sum which would have purchased the fee-simple of the revenue of the Plantagenets—ten times what supported the government of Elizabeth—three times what, in the time of Oliver Cromwell, had been thought intolerably oppressive. To almost all men the state of things under which they have been used to live seems to be the nec-essary state of things. We have heard it said, that five per cent is the natural interest of money, that twelve is the natural number of a jury, that forty shillings is the natural qual-ification of a county voter. Hence it is, that though, in every age, every body knows that up to his own time progressive improvement has been taking place, nobody seems to reckon on any improvement during the next generation. We cannot absolutely prove that those are in error who tell us that society has reached a turning point—that we have seen

---

8. England was at war with France from 1792–1815, barring some periods of peace.
9. Mountains in Scotland and the Lake District of England.

our best days. But so said all who came before us, and with just as much apparent reason. 'A million a-year will beggar us,' said the patriots of 1640. 'Two millions a-year will grind the country to powder,' was the cry in 1660. 'Six millions a-year, and a debt of fifty millions!' exclaimed Swift—'the high allies have been the ruin of us.' 'A hundred and forty millions of debt!' said Junius[10]—'well may we say that we owe Lord Chatham more than we shall ever pay, if we owe him such a load as this.' 'Two hundred and forty millions of debt!' cried all the statesmen of 1783 in chorus—'what abilities, or what economy on the part of a minister, can save a country so burdened?' We know that if, since 1783, no fresh debt had been incurred, the increased resources of the country would have enabled us to defray that burden, at which Pitt, Fox, and Burke stood aghast[11]—to defray it over and over again, and that with much lighter taxation than what we have actually borne. On what principle is it, that when we see nothing but improvement behind us, we are to expect nothing but deterioration before us?

It is not by the intermeddling of Mr Southey's idol, the omniscient and omnipotent State—but by the prudence and energy of the people, that England has hitherto been carried forward in civilisation; and it is to the same prudence and the same energy that we now look with comfort and good hope. Our rulers will best promote the improvement of the people by strictly confining themselves to their own legitimate duties—by leaving capital to find its most lucrative course, commodities their fair price, industry and intelligence their natural reward, idleness and folly their natural punishment—by maintaining peace, by defending property, by diminishing the price of law, and by observing strict economy in every department of the state. Let the Government do this—the People will assuredly do the rest.

---

10. Pseudonym of Whig writer whose letters to the *Public Advertiser* from 1769 to 1771 attacked the ministry of the Duke of Crafton in favor of William Pitt, Earl of Chatham.
11. William Pitt (1759–1806), English statesman and Prime Minister under George III; Charles James Fox (1749–1806) and Edmund Burke (1729–97), statesmen and orators.

# John Henry Newman

## APOLOGIA PRO VITA SUA

Newman's Apologia *is both a spiritual autobiography and a defense of his life. For decades before its 1864 publication, Newman had been embroiled in controversy. First, his leadership of the Oxford or Tractarian Movement—an attempt to revive the Anglican Church from within, by showing the continuity between the Church of England and the early Christian Church, by combatting Liberal and rationalistic threats to faith and the Church, and by rediscovering sacraments and ritual—placed him at the center of religious debates of the 1830s and 1840s. Second, his conversion to Roman Catholicism in 1845, an event predicted by his detractors, and his subsequent entry into the Catholic priesthood lost him many of his Oxford friends and raised the ire of English anti-Papists. Newman had contemplated publishing an explanation of his spiritual journey for some time. But Charles* KINGSLEY's *questioning of Newman's honesty (and implicitly Newman's choice of celibacy) in the January 1864 issue of* Macmillan's *provided both the immediate provocation and the opportunity. Kingsley charged:"Truth, for its own sake, had never been a virtue with the Roman clergy. Father Newman informs us that it need not, and on the whole ought not to*

*be; that cunning is the weapon which Heaven has given to the Saints wherewith to with-*
*stand the brute male force of the wicked world which marries and is given in marriage."*
*Following a series of ferocious attacks and counterattacks, including Kingsley's "What, Then,*
*Does Dr. Newman Mean?," Newman quickly wrote and published his* Apologia, *first as a*
*series of pamphlets (April–June 1864), from which the selection below is taken, and later*
*in revised editions in book form.*

*Newman's rhetorical strategy, as apologist and spiritual autobiographer, reflects his*
*belief that Providence led him gradually and inevitably to the theology and authority of*
*the Roman Church. He traces his beliefs and doubts from Evangelicalism and his encounter*
*with Calvinism in youth, through his studies and the influences of teachers and friends at*
*Oxford, to his leadership in the Oxford Movement and his contributions to the* Tracts *for*
*the* Times, *and ultimately to his reluctant leaving of Oxford and Anglicanism and his con-*
*version to Roman Catholicism. Ever the scholar, Newman examines his earlier writings to*
*reveal the continuities and transitions in his beliefs. If Newman's theological struggles seem*
*to float in a somewhat rarefied air, we should attempt to see them in the context of the*
*intense religious controversies of the mid-nineteenth century—a context partially created*
*by John Henry Newman himself.*                                                        RM

## PART 3

### History of My Religious Opinions

IT MAY EASILY BE CONCEIVED how great a trial it is to me to write the following history of myself; but I must not shrink from the task. The words, "Secretum meum mihi,"[1] keep ringing in my ears; but as men draw towards their end, they care less for disclosures. Nor is it the least part of my trial, to anticipate that my friends may, upon first reading what I have written, consider much in it irrelevant to my purpose; yet I cannot help thinking that, viewed as a whole, it will effect what I wish it to do.

I was brought up from a child to take great delight in reading the Bible; but I had no formed religious convictions till I was fifteen. Of course I had perfect knowledge of my Catechism.

After I was grown up, I put on paper such recollections as I had of my thoughts and feelings on religious subjects, at the time that I was a child and a boy. Out of these I select two, which are at once the most definite among them, and also have a bearing on my later convictions.

In the paper to which I have referred, written either in the Long Vacation of 1820, or in October, 1823, the following notices of my school days were sufficiently prominent in my memory for me to consider them worth recording:—"I used to wish the Arabian Tales were true: my imagination ran on unknown influences, on magical powers, and talismans. . . . . I thought life might be a dream, or I an Angel, and all this world a deception, my fellow-angels by a playful device concealing themselves from me, and deceiving me with the semblance of a material world."

---

1. "My secret unto me" or "My secret is my own."

Again, "Reading in the Spring of 1816 a sentence from [Dr. Watts's] 'Remnants of Time,' entitled 'the Saints unknown to the world,' to the effect, that 'there is nothing in their figure or countenance to distinguish them,' &c. &c.,[2] I supposed he spoke of Angels who lived in the world, as it were disguised."

The other remark is this: "I was very superstitious, and for some time previous to my conversion" [when I was fifteen] "used constantly to cross myself on going into the dark."

Of course I must have got this practice from some external source or other; but I can make no sort of conjecture whence; and certainly no one had ever spoken to me on the subject of the Catholic religion, which I only knew by name. The French master was an émigré Priest, but he was simply made a butt, as French masters too commonly were in that day, and spoke English very imperfectly. There was a Catholic family in the village, old maiden ladies we used to think; but I knew nothing but their name. I have of late years heard that there were one or two Catholic boys in the school; but either we were carefully kept from knowing this, or the knowledge of it made simply no impression on our minds. My brother will bear witness how free the school was from Catholic ideas.

I had once been into Warwick Street Chapel, with my father, who, I believe, wanted to hear some piece of music; all that I bore away from it was the recollection of a pulpit and a preacher and a boy swinging a censer.

When I was at Littlemore,[3] I was looking over old copy-books of my school days, and I found among them my first Latin verse-book; and in the first page of it, there was a device which almost took my breath away with surprise. I have the book before me now, and have just been showing it to others. I have written in the first page, in my school-boy hand, "John H. Newman, February 11th, 1811, Verse Book;" then follow my first Verses. Between "Verse" and "Book" I have drawn the figure of a solid cross upright, and next to it is, what may indeed be meant for a necklace, but what I cannot make out to be any thing else than a set of beads suspended, with a little cross attached. At this time I was not quite ten years old. I suppose I got the idea from some romance, Mrs. Radcliffe's or Miss Porter's;[4] or from some religious picture; but the strange thing is, how, among the thousand objects which meet a boy's eyes, these in particular should so have fixed themselves in my mind, that I made them thus practically my own. I am certain there was nothing in the churches I attended, or the prayer books I read, to suggest them. It must be recollected that churches and prayer books were not decorated in those days as I believe they are now.

When I was fourteen, I read Paine's Tracts against the Old Testament, and found pleasure in thinking of the objections which were contained in them. Also, I read some of Hume's Essays; and perhaps that on Miracles. So at least I gave my father to understand; but perhaps it was a brag. Also, I recollect copying out some French verses, perhaps Voltaire's, against the immortality of the soul, and saying to myself something like "How dreadful, but how plausible!"[5]

2. Isaac Watts (1674–1748), *The Improvement of the Mind* (1741).
3. Littlemore, village near Oxford, where Newman became vicar in 1828 and retired after leaving Oxford in 1842.
4. Ann Radcliffe (1764–1823), author of *The Italian* and *The Mysteries of Udolpho*; Jane Porter (1776–1850), author of *The Scottish Chiefs*.
5. Thomas Paine (1737–1809), deist; David Hume (1711–76), Scottish philosopher/historian; Voltaire (1694–1778), French writer and philosopher.

When I was fifteen, (in the autumn of 1816,) a great change of thought took place in me. I fell under the influences of a definite Creed, and received into my intellect impressions of dogma, which, through God's mercy, have never been effaced or obscured. Above and beyond the conversations and sermons of the excellent man, long dead, who was the human means of this beginning of divine faith in me, was the effect of the books which he put into my hands, all of the school of Calvin. . . .

The two persons who knew me best at that time[6] are still alive, beneficed clergymen, no longer my friends. They could tell better than any one else what I was in those years. From this time my tongue was, as it were, loosened, and I spoke spontaneously and without effort. A shrewd man, who knew me at this time, said, "Here is a man who, when he is silent, will never begin to speak; and when he once begins to speak, will never stop." It was at this time that I began to have influence, which steadily increased for a course of years. I gained upon my pupils, and was in particular intimate and affectionate with two of our probationer Fellows, Robert I. Wilberforce (afterwards Archdeacon) and Richard Hurrell Froude.[7] Whately[8] then, an acute man, perhaps saw around me the signs of an incipient party of which I was not conscious myself. And thus we discern the first elements of that movement afterwards called Tractarian.

The true and primary author of it, however, as is usual with great motive-powers, was out of sight. Having carried off as a mere boy the highest honours of the University, he had turned from the admiration which haunted his steps, and sought for a better and holier satisfaction in pastoral work in the country. Need I say that I am speaking of John Keble? The first time that I was in a room with him was on occasion of my election to a fellowship at Oriel, when I was sent for into the Tower, to shake hands with the Provost and Fellows. How is that hour fixed in my memory after the changes of forty-two years, forty-two this very day on which I write! I have lately had a letter in my hands, which I sent at the time to my great friend, John Bowden,[9] with whom I passed almost exclusively my Undergraduate years. "I had to hasten to the Tower," I say to him, "to receive the congratulations of all the Fellows. I bore it till Keble took my hand, and then felt so abashed and unworthy of the honour done me, that I seemed desirous of quite sinking into the ground." His had been the first name which I had heard spoken of, with reverence rather than admiration, when I came up to Oxford. When one day I was walking in High Street with my dear earliest friend just mentioned, with what eagerness did he cry out, "There's Keble!" and with what awe did I look at him! Then at another time I heard a Master of Arts of my college give an account how he had just then had occasion to introduce himself on some business to Keble, and how gentle, courteous, and unaffected Keble had been, so as almost to put him out of countenance. Then too it was reported, truly or falsely, how a rising man of brilliant reputation, the present Dean of St. Paul's, Dr. Milman, admired and loved him, adding, that somehow he was unlike any one else.

6. At Oxford during the 1820s when Newman was a fellow and tutor.
7. Robert Isaac Wilberforce (1802–57), son of Evangelical reformer William Wilberforce. Richard Hurrell Froude (1803–36), author of *Remains* (1837–9), participated with Newman, Edward Pusey (1800–82), and John Keble (1792–1866) in the Tractarian Movement.
8. Despite their later estrangement, Richard Whately (1787–1863) exercised a profound influence on Newman. Whately became Principal of Alban Hall in 1825 and made Newman his vice-principal and tutor.
9. John William Bowden (1798–1844).

However, at the time when I was elected Fellow of Oriel he was not in residence, and he was shy of me for years in consequence of the marks which I bore upon me of the evangelical and liberal schools. At least so I have ever thought. Hurrell Froude brought us together about 1828: it is one of the sayings preserved in his "Remains,"—"Do you know the story of the murderer who had done one good thing in his life? Well; if I was ever asked what good deed I had ever done, I should say that I had brought Keble and Newman to understand each other."

The Christian Year made its appearance in 1827. It is not necessary, and scarcely becoming, to praise a book which has already become one of the classics of the language. When the general tone of religious literature was so nerveless and impotent, as it was at that time, Keble struck an original note and woke up in the hearts of thousands a new music, the music of a school, long unknown in England. Nor can I pretend to analyze, in my own instance, the effect of religious teaching so deep, so pure, so beautiful. I have never till now tried to do so; yet I think I am not wrong in saying, that the two main intellectual truths which it brought home to me, were the same two, which I had learned from Butler,[10] though recast in the creative mind of my new master. The first of these was what may be called, in a large sense of the word, the Sacramental system; that is, the doctrine that material phenomena are both the types and the instruments of real things unseen,— a doctrine, which embraces, not only what Anglicans, as well as Catholics, believe about Sacraments properly so called; but also the article of "the Communion of Saints" in its fulness; and likewise the Mysteries of the faith. The connexion of this philosophy of religion with what is sometimes called "Berkeleyism" has been mentioned above; I knew little of Berkeley[11] at this time except by name; nor have I ever studied him.

On the second intellectual principle which I gained from Mr. Keble, I could say a great deal; if this were the place for it. It runs through very much that I have written, and has gained for me many hard names. Butler teaches us that probability is the guide of life. The danger of this doctrine, in the case of many minds, is, its tendency to destroy in them absolute certainty, leading them to consider every conclusion as doubtful, and resolving truth into an opinion, which it is safe to obey or to profess, but not possible to embrace with full internal assent. If this were to be allowed, then the celebrated saying, "O God, if there be a God, save my soul, if I have a soul!" would be the highest measure of devotion:—but who can really pray to a Being, about whose existence he is seriously in doubt?

I considered that Mr. Keble met this difficulty by ascribing the firmness of assent which we give to religious doctrine, not to the probabilities which introduced it, but to the living power of faith and love which accepted it. In matters of religion, he seemed to say, it is not merely probability which makes us intellectually certain, but probability as it is put to account by faith and love. It is faith and love which give to probability a force which it has not in itself. Faith and love are directed towards an Object; in the vision of that Object they live; it is that Object, received in faith and love, which renders it rea-

10. Bishop Joseph Butler (1692–1752), whose defense of religion against deism, *Analogy of Religion, Natural and Revealed, to the Constitution and Course of Nature* (1736), Newman had read earlier.
11. George Berkeley (1685–1753), Bishop of Cloyne, author of *Treatise Concerning the Principles of Human Knowledge* (1710).

sonable to take probability as sufficient for internal conviction. Thus the argument about Probability, in the matter of religion, became an argument from Personality, which in fact is one form of the argument from Authority.

In illustration, Mr. Keble used to quote the words of the Psalm: "I will guide thee with mine *eye*. Be ye not like to horse and mule, which have no understanding; whose mouths must be held with bit and bridle, lest they fall upon thee." This is the very difference, he used to say, between slaves, and friends or children. Friends do not ask for literal commands; but, from their knowledge of the speaker, they understand his half-words, and from love of him they anticipate his wishes. Hence it is, that in his Poem for St. Bartholomew's Day, he speaks of the "Eye of God's word;" and in the note quotes Mr. Miller, of Worcester College, who remarks, in his Bampton Lectures, on the special power of Scripture, as having "this Eye, like that of a portrait, uniformly fixed upon us, turn where we will." The view thus suggested by Mr. Keble, is brought forward in one of the earliest of the "Tracts for the Times." In No. 8 I say, "The Gospel is a Law of Liberty. We are treated as sons, not as servants; not subjected to a code of formal commandments, but addressed as those who love God, and wish to please Him."

I did not at all dispute this view of the matter, for I made use of it myself; but I was dissatisfied, because it did not go to the root of the difficulty. It was beautiful and religious, but it did not even profess to be logical; and accordingly I tried to complete it by considerations of my own, which are implied in my University Sermons, Essay on Ecclesiastical Miracles, and Essay on Development of Doctrine. My argument is in outline as follows: that that absolute certitude which we were able to possess, whether as to the truths of natural theology, or as to the fact of a revelation, was the result of an *assemblage* of concurring and converging probabilities, and that, both according to the constitution of the human mind and the will of its Maker; that certitude was a habit of mind, that certainty was a quality of propositions; that probabilities which did not reach to logical certainty, might create a mental certitude; that the certitude thus created might equal in measure and strength the certitude which was created by the strictest scientific demonstration; and that to have such certitude might in given cases and to given individuals be a plain duty, though not to others in other circumstances:—

Moreover, that as there were probabilities which sufficed to create certitude, so there were other probabilities which were legitimately adapted to create opinion; that it might be quite as much a matter of duty in given cases and to given persons to have about a fact an opinion of a definite strength and consistency, as in the case of greater or of more numerous probabilities it was a duty to have a certitude; that accordingly we were bound to be more or less sure, on a sort of (as it were) graduated scale of assent, viz. according as the probabilities attaching to a professed fact were brought home to us, and, as the case might be, to entertain about it a pious belief, or a pious opinion, or a religious conjecture, or at least, a tolerance of such belief, or opinion, or conjecture in others; that on the other hand, as it was a duty to have a belief, of more or less strong texture, in given cases, so in other cases it was a duty not to believe, not to opine, not to conjecture, not even to tolerate the notion that a professed fact was true, inasmuch as it would be credulity or superstition, or some other moral fault, to do so. This was the region of Private

Judgment in religion; that is, of a Private Judgment, not formed arbitrarily and according to one's fancy or liking, but conscientiously, and under a sense of duty. . . .

## PART 4

HISTORY OF MY RELIGIOUS OPINIONS

. . . I have spoken of my firm confidence in my position;[12] and now let me state more definitely what the position was which I took up, and the propositions about which I was so confident. These were three:—

1. First was the principle of dogma: my battle was with liberalism; by liberalism I meant the anti-dogmatic principle and its developments. This was the first point on which I was certain. Here I make a remark: persistence in a given belief is no sufficient test of its truth; but departure from it is at least a slur upon the man who has felt so certain about it. In proportion then as I had in 1832 a strong persuasion in beliefs which I have since given up, so far a sort of guilt attaches to me, not only for that vain confidence, but for my multiform conduct in consequence of it. But here I have the satisfaction of feeling that I have nothing to retract, and nothing to repent of. The main principle of the Movement is as dear to me now, as it ever was. I have changed in many things: in this I have not. From the age of fifteen, dogma has been the fundamental principle of my religion: I know no other religion; I cannot enter into the idea of any other sort of religion; religion, as a mere sentiment, is to me a dream and a mockery. As well can there be filial love without the fact of a father, as devotion without the fact of a Supreme Being. What I held in 1816, I held in 1833, and I hold in 1864. Please God, I shall hold it to the end. Even when I was under Dr. Whately's influence, I had no temptation to be less zealous for the great dogmas of the faith, and at various times I used to resist such trains of thought on his part, as seemed to me (rightly or wrongly) to obscure them. Such was the fundamental principle of the Movement of 1833.

2. Secondly, I was confident in the truth of a certain definite religious teaching, based upon this foundation of dogma; viz. that there was a visible Church with sacraments and rites which are the channels of invisible grace. I thought that this was the doctrine of Scripture, of the early Church, and of the Anglican Church. Here again, I have not changed in opinion; I am as certain now on this point as I was in 1833, and have never ceased to be certain. In 1834 and the following years I put this ecclesiastical doctrine on a broader basis, after reading Laud, Bramhall, and Stillingfleet[13] and other Anglican divines on the one hand, and after prosecuting the study of the Fathers on the other; but the doctrine of 1833 was strengthened in me, not changed. When I began the Tracts for the Times I rested the main doctrine, of which I am speaking, upon Scripture, on St. Ignatius's Epistles,[14] and on the Anglican Prayer Book. As to the existence of a visible

12. On July 14, 1833, John Keble delivered his sermon on "National Apostasy," criticizing governmental interference in Church matters and condemning specifically a bill to reduce the number of bishoprics in Ireland. Newman regarded this sermon as the beginning of the Oxford Movement, whose main principles he now summarizes.
13. Seventeenth-century Anglicans: William Laud (1573–1645), John Bramhall (1594–1663), and Edward Stillingfleet (1635–99).
14. St. Ignatius (d. c. 110 A.D.), early Church father and Bishop of Antioch.

Church, I especially argued out the point from Scripture, in Tract 11, viz. from the Acts of the Apostles and the Epistles. As to the Sacraments and Sacramental rites, I stood on the Prayer Book. I appealed to the Ordination Service, in which the Bishop says, "Receive the Holy Ghost;" to the Visitation Service, which teaches confession and absolution; to the Baptismal Service, in which the Priest speaks of the child after baptism as regenerate; to the Catechism, in which Sacramental Communion is receiving "verily the Body and Blood of Christ;" to the Commination Service, in which we are told to do "works of penance;" to the Collects, Epistles, and Gospels, to the calendar and rubricks, wherein we find the festivals of the Apostles, notice of certain other Saints, and days of fasting and abstinence.

And further, as to the Episcopal system, I founded it upon the Epistles of St. Ignatius, which inculcated it in various ways. One passage especially impressed itself upon me: speaking of cases of disobedience to ecclesiastical authority, he says, "A man does not deceive that Bishop whom he sees, but he practises rather with the Bishop Invisible, and so the question is not with flesh, but with God, who knows the secret heart." I wished to act on this principle to the letter, and I may say with confidence that I never consciously transgressed it. I loved to act in the sight of my Bishop, as if I was, as it were, in the sight of God. It was one of my special safeguards against myself and of my supports; I could not go very wrong while I had reason to believe that I was in no respect displeasing him. It was not a mere formal obedience to rule that I put before me, but I desired to please him personally, as I considered him set over me by the Divine Hand. I was strict in observing my clerical engagements, not only because they *were* engagements, but because I considered myself simply as the servant and instrument of my Bishop. I did not care much for the Bench of Bishops, except as they might be the voice of my Church: nor should I have cared much for a Provincial Council; nor for a Diocesan Synod presided over by my Bishop; all these matters seemed to me to be *jure ecclesiastico*, but what to me was *jure divino* was the voice of my Bishop in his own person. My own Bishop was my Pope; I knew no other; the successor of the Apostles, the Vicar of Christ. This was but a practical exhibition of the Anglican theory of Church Government, as I had already drawn it out myself. This continued all through my course; when at length in 1845 I wrote to Bishop Wiseman, in whose Vicariate I found myself, to announce my conversion, I could find nothing better to say to him, than that I would obey the Pope as I had obeyed my own Bishop in the Anglican Church. My duty to him was my point of honour; his disapprobation was the one thing which I could not bear. I believe it to have been a generous and honest feeling; and in consequence I was rewarded by having all my time for ecclesiastical superior a man, whom had I had a choice, I should have preferred, out and out, to any other Bishop on the Bench, and for whose memory I have a special affection, Dr. Bagot[15]—a man of noble mind, and as kind-hearted and as considerate as he was noble. He ever sympathized with me in my trials which followed; it was my own fault, that I was not brought into more familiar personal relations with him than it was my happiness to be. May his name be ever blessed!

15. Richard Bagot (1782–1854), Bishop of Oxford (1829–45).

And now in concluding my remarks on the second point on which my confidence rested, I observe that here again I have no retractation to announce as to its main outline. While I am now as clear in my acceptance of the principle of dogma, as I was in 1833 and 1816, so again I am now as firm in my belief of a visible Church, of the authority of Bishops, of the grace of the sacraments, of the religious worth of works of penance, as I was in 1833. I have added Articles to my Creed; but the old ones, which I then held with a divine faith, remain.

3. But now, as to the third point on which I stood in 1833, and which I have utterly renounced and trampled upon since,—my then view of the Church of Rome;—I will speak about it as exactly as I can. When I was young, as I have said already, and after I was grown up, I thought the Pope to be Antichrist. At Christmas 1824–5 I preached a Sermon to that effect. In 1827 I accepted eagerly the stanza in the Christian Year, which many people thought too charitable, "Speak *gently* of thy sister's fall." From the time that I knew Froude I got less and less bitter on the subject. I spoke (successively, but I cannot tell in what order or at what dates) of the Roman Church as being bound up with "the *cause* of Antichrist," as being *one* of the "*many* antichrists" foretold by St. John, as being influenced by "the *spirit* of Antichrist," and as having something "very Antichristian" or "unchristian" about her. From my boyhood and in 1824 I considered, after Protestant authorities, that St. Gregory I. about A.D. 600 was the first Pope that was Antichrist, and again that he was also a great and holy man; in 1832–3 I thought the Church of Rome was bound up with the cause of Antichrist by the Council of Trent.[16] When it was that in my deliberate judgment I gave up the notion altogether in any shape, that some special reproach was attached to her name, I cannot tell; but I had a shrinking from renouncing it, even when my reason so ordered me, from a sort of conscience or prejudice, I think up to 1843. Moreover, at least during the Tract Movement, I thought the essence of her offence to consist in the honours which she paid to the Blessed Virgin and the Saints; and the more I grew in devotion, both to the Saints and to Our Lady, the more impatient was I at the Roman practices, as if those glorified creations of God must be gravely shocked, if pain could be theirs, at the undue veneration of which they were the objects.

On the other hand, Hurrell Froude in his familiar conversations was always tending to rub the idea out of my mind. In a passage of one of his letters from abroad, alluding, I suppose, to what I used to say in opposition to him, he observes: "I think people are injudicious who talk against the Roman Catholics for worshipping Saints, and honouring the Virgin and images, &c. These things may perhaps be idolatrous; I cannot make up my mind about it; but to my mind it is the Carnival that is real practical idolatry, as it is written, 'the people sat down to eat and drink, and rose up to play.' " The Carnival, I observe in passing, is, in fact, one of those very excesses, to which, for at least three centuries, religious Catholics have ever opposed themselves, as we see in the life of St. Philip,[17] to say nothing of the present day; but this he did not know. Moreover, from Froude I learned to admire the great medieval Pontiffs; and, of course, when I had come to consider the Council of Trent to be the turning-point of the history of Christian Rome, I found myself

16. Ecumenical council (1545–63), beginning of Roman Catholic Counter-Reformation.
17. St. Philip Neri (1515–95), founder of the Oratorians.

as free, as I was rejoiced, to speak in their praise. Then, when I was abroad, the sight of so many great places, venerable shrines, and noble churches, much impressed my imagination. And my heart was touched also. Making an expedition on foot across some wild country in Sicily, at six in the morning I came upon a small church; I heard voices, and I looked in. It was crowded, and the congregation was singing. Of course it was the Mass, though I did not know it at the time. And, in my weary days at Palermo, I was not ungrateful for the comfort which I had received in frequenting the Churches, nor did I ever forget it. Then, again, her zealous maintenance of the doctrine and the rule of celibacy, which I recognized as Apostolic, and her faithful agreement with Antiquity in so many points besides, which were dear to me, was an argument as well as a plea in favour of the great Church of Rome. Thus I learned to have tender feelings towards her; but still my reason was not affected at all. My judgment was against her, when viewed as an institution, as truly as it ever had been.

This conflict between reason and affection I expressed in one of the early Tracts, published July, 1834. "Considering the high gifts and the strong claims of the Church of Rome and its dependencies on our admiration, reverence, love, and gratitude; how could we withstand it, as we do, how could we refrain from being melted into tenderness, and rushing into communion with it, but for the words of Truth itself, which bid us prefer It to the whole world? 'He that loveth father or mother more than Me, is not worthy of me.' How could 'we learn to be severe, and execute judgment,' but for the warning of Moses against even a divinely-gifted teacher, who should preach new gods; and the anathema of St. Paul even against Angels and Apostles, who should bring in a new doctrine?"—*Records*, No. 24. My feeling was something like that of a man, who is obliged in a court of justice to bear witness against a friend; or like my own now, when I have said, and shall say, so many things on which I had rather be silent. . . .

And now I come to the very point, for which I have introduced the subject of my feelings about Rome. I felt such confidence in the substantial justice of the charges which I advanced against her, that I considered them to be a safeguard and an assurance that no harm could ever arise from the freest exposition of what I used to call Anglican principles. All the world was astounded at what Froude and I were saying: men said that it was sheer Popery. I answered, "True, we seem to be making straight for it; but go on awhile, and you will come to a deep chasm across the path, which makes real approximation impossible." And I urged in addition, that many Anglican divines had been accused of Popery, yet had died in their Anglicanism;—now, the ecclesiastical principles which I professed, they had professed also; and the judgment against Rome which they had formed, I had formed also. Whatever faults then the Anglican system might have, and however boldly I might point them out, any how that system was not vulnerable on the side of Rome, and might be mended in spite of her. In that very agreement of the two forms of faith, close as it might seem, would really be found, on examination, the elements and principles of an essential discordance.

It was with this supreme persuasion on my mind that I fancied that there could be no rashness in giving to the world in fullest measure the teaching and the writings of the Fathers. I thought that the Church of England was substantially founded upon them. I did not know all that the Fathers had said, but I felt that, even when their tenets happened to differ from the Anglican, no harm could come of reporting them. I said out what I was clear they had said; I spoke vaguely and imperfectly, of what I thought they said, or what some of them had said. Any how, no harm could come of bending the crooked stick the other way, in the process of straightening it; it was impossible to break it. If there was any thing in the Fathers of a startling character, it would be only for a time; it would admit of explanation; it could not lead to Rome. I express this view of the matter in a passage of the Preface to the first volume, which I edited, of the Library of the Fathers.[18] Speaking of the strangeness at first sight, presented to the Anglican mind, of some of their principles and opinions, I bid the reader go forward hopefully, and not indulge his criticism till he knows more about them, than he will learn at the outset. "Since the evil," I say, "is in the nature of the case itself, we can do no more than have patience, and recommend patience to others, and, with the racer in the Tragedy, look forward steadily and hopefully to the *event*, τῷ τέλει πίστιν φέρων,[19] when, as we trust, all that is inharmonious and anomalous in the details, will at length be practically smoothed."

Such was the position, such the defences, such the tactics, by which I thought it was both incumbent on us, and possible to us, to meet that onset of Liberal principles, of which we were all in immediate anticipation, whether in the Church or in the University.

. . .

There was another motive for my publishing, of a personal nature, which I think I should mention. I felt then, and all along felt, that there was an intellectual cowardice in not having a basis in reason for my belief, and a moral cowardice in not avowing that basis. I should have felt myself less than a man, if I did not bring it out, whatever it was. This is one principal reason why I wrote and published the "Prophetical Office."[20] It was on the same feeling, that in the spring of 1836, at a meeting of residents on the subject of the struggle then proceeding, some one wanted us all merely to act on college and conservative grounds (as I understood him), with as few published statements as possible: I answered, that the person whom we were resisting had committed himself in writing, and that we ought to commit ourselves too. This again was a main reason for the publication of Tract 90.[21] Alas! it was my portion for whole years to remain without any satisfactory basis for my religious profession, in a state of moral sickness, neither able to acquiesce in Anglicanism, nor able to go to Rome. But I bore it, till in course of time my way was made clear to me. If here it be objected to me, that as time went on, I often in my writings hinted at things which I did not fully bring out, I submit for consideration whether this occurred except when I was in great difficulties, how to speak, or how to be silent, with due regard for the position of mind or the feelings of others. However, I may

18. "The Library of the Fathers of the Holy Catholic Church," a series of translations begun by the Tractarians. The first volume was E. B. Pusey's translation of Augustine's *Confessions* (1838).
19. Sophocles, *Electra*, 735. Translation in context: "Orestes had been driving last and holding / his horses back, putting his trust in the finish."
20. "The Prophetical Office of the Church viewed relatively to Romanism and Popular Protestantism."
21. Newman's controversial Tract 90, arguing that the Church of England's Thirty-nine Articles were not incompatible with Catholicism and essentially giving the articles a Catholic interpretation, was widely condemned and led to a cessation of the tracts.

have an opportunity to say more on this subject. But to return to the "Prophetical Office."

I thus speak in the Introduction to my Volume:—

"It is proposed," I say, "to offer helps towards the formation of a recognized Anglican theology in one of its departments. The present state of our divinity is as follows: the most vigorous, the clearest, the most fertile minds, have through God's mercy been employed in the service of our Church: minds too as reverential and holy, and as fully imbued with Ancient Truth, and as well versed in the writings of the Fathers, as they were intellectually gifted. This is God's great mercy indeed, for which we must ever be thankful. Primitive doctrine has been explored for us in every direction, and the original principles of the Gospel and the Church patiently brought to light. But one thing is still wanting: our champions and teachers have lived in stormy times: political and other influences have acted upon them variously in their day, and have since obstructed a careful consolidation of their judgments. We have a vast inheritance, but no inventory of our treasures. All is given us in profusion; it remains for us to catalogue, sort, distribute, select, harmonize, and complete. We have more than we know how to use; stores of learning, but little that is precise and serviceable; Catholic truth and individual opinion, first principles and the guesses of genius, all mingled in the same works, and requiring to be discriminated. We meet with truths overstated or misdirected, matters of detail variously taken, facts incompletely proved or applied, and rules inconsistently urged or discordantly interpreted. Such indeed is the state of every deep philosophy in its first stages, and therefore of theological knowledge. What we need at present for our Church's well-being, is not invention, nor originality, nor sagacity, nor even learning in our divines, at least in the first place, though all gifts of God are in a measure needed, and never can be unseasonable when used religiously, but we need peculiarly a sound judgment, patient thought, discrimination, a comprehensive mind, an abstinence from all private fancies and caprices and personal tastes,—in a word, Divine Wisdom."

The subject of the Volume is the doctrine of the *Via Media*, a name which had already been applied to the Anglican system by writers of name. It is an expressive title, but not altogether satisfactory, because it is at first sight negative. This had been the reason of my dislike to the word "Protestant;" in the idea which it conveyed, it was not the profession of any religion at all, and was compatible with infidelity. A *Via Media* was but a receding from extremes, therefore I had to draw it out into a shape, and a character; before it had claims on our respect, it must first be shown to be one, intelligible, and consistent. This was the first condition of any reasonable treatise on the *Via Media*. The second condition, and necessary too, was not in my power. I could only hope that it would one day be fulfilled. Even if the *Via Media* were ever so positive a religious system, it was not as yet objective and real; it had no original any where of which it was the representative. It was at present a paper religion. This I confess in my Introduction; I say, "Protestantism and Popery are real religions . . . but the *Via Media*, viewed as an integral system, has scarcely had existence except on paper." I grant the objection and proceed to lessen it. There I say, "It still remains to be tried, whether what is called Anglo-Catholicism, the religion of Andrewes, Laud, Hammond, Butler, and Wilson,[22] is capable of being professed, acted

22. High-Church divines of the previous three centuries.

on, and maintained on a large sphere of action, or whether it be a mere modification or transition-state of either Romanism or popular Protestantism." I trusted that some day it would prove to be a substantive religion.

Lest I should be misunderstood, let me observe that this hesitation about the validity of the theory of the *Via Media* implied no doubt of the three fundamental points on which it was based, as I have described above, dogma, the sacramental system, and opposition to the Church of Rome. . . .

## PART 5

### HISTORY OF MY RELIGIOUS OPINIONS

And now that I am about to trace, as far as I can, the course of that great revolution of mind, which led me to leave my own home, to which I was bound by so many strong and tender ties, I feel overcome with the difficulty of satisfying myself in my account of it, and have recoiled from doing so, till the near approach of the day, on which these lines must be given to the world, forces me to set about the task. For who can know himself, and the multitude of subtle influences which act upon him? and who can recollect, at the distance of twenty-five years, all that he once knew about his thoughts and his deeds, and that, during a portion of his life, when even at the time his observation, whether of himself or of the external world, was less than before or after, by very reason of the perplexity and dismay which weighed upon him,—when, though it would be most unthankful to seem to imply that he had not all-sufficient light amid his darkness, yet a darkness it emphatically was? And who can gird himself suddenly to a new and anxious undertaking, which he might be able indeed to perform well, had he full and calm leisure to look through every thing that he has written, whether in published works or private letters? but, on the other hand, as to that calm contemplation of the past, in itself so desirable, who can afford to be leisurely and deliberate, while he practises on himself a cruel operation, the ripping up of old griefs, and the venturing again upon the "infandum dolorem"[23] of years, in which the stars of this lower heaven were one by one going out? I could not in cool blood, nor except upon the imperious call of duty, attempt what I have set myself to do. It is both to head and heart an extreme trial, thus to analyze what has so long gone by, and to bring out the results of that examination. I have done various bold things in my life: this is the boldest: and, were I not sure I should after all succeed in my object, it would be madness to set about it.

In the spring of 1839 my position in the Anglican Church was at its height. I had supreme confidence in my controversial *status*, and I had a great and still growing success, in recommending it to others. I had in the foregoing autumn been somewhat sore at the Bishop's Charge,[24] but I have a letter which shows that all annoyance had passed from my mind. In January, if I recollect aright, in order to meet the popular clamour against myself and others, and to satisfy the Bishop, I had collected into one all the strong things which they, and especially I, had said against the Church of Rome, in order to their insertion

---

23. "Grief beyond words" or "Unspeakable sorrow." Virgil, *Aeneid*, 2.
24. Criticism of the tracts by Richard Bagot, Bishop of Oxford.

among the advertisements appended to our publications. Conscious as I was that my opinions in religion were not gained, as the world said, from Roman sources, but were, on the contrary, the birth of my own mind and of the circumstances in which I had been placed, I had a scorn of the imputations which were heaped upon me. It was true that I held a large bold system of religion, very unlike the Protestantism of the day, but it was the concentration and adjustment of the statements of great Anglican authorities, and I had as much right to do so, as the Evangelical party had, and more right than the Liberal, to hold their own respective doctrines. As I spoke on occasion of Tract 90, I claimed, in behalf of who would, that he might hold in the Anglican Church a comprecation with the Saints with Bramhall, and the Mass all but Transubstantiation with Andrewes, or with Hooker that Transubstantiation itself is not a point for Churches to part communion upon, or with Hammond that a General Council, truly such, never did, never shall err in a matter of faith, or with Bull that man lost inward grace by the fall, or with Thorndike that penance is a propitiation for post-baptismal sin, or with Pearson that the all-powerful name of Jesus is no otherwise given than in the Catholic Church.[25] "Two can play at that," was often in my mouth, when men of Protestant sentiments appealed to the Articles, Homilies, or Reformers; in the sense that, if they had a right to speak loud, I had both the liberty and the means of giving them tit for tat. I thought that the Anglican Church had been tyrannized over by a party, and I aimed at bringing into effect the promise contained in the motto to the Lyra, "They shall know the difference now." I only asked to be allowed to show them the difference.

What will best describe my state of mind at the early part of 1839, is an Article in the British Critic for that April. I have looked over it now, for the first time since it was published; and have been struck by it for this reason:—it contains the last words which I ever spoke as an Anglican to Anglicans. It may now be read as my parting address and valediction, made to my friends. I little knew it at the time. It reviews the actual state of things, and it ends by looking towards the future. It is not altogether mine; for my memory goes to this,—that I had asked a friend to do the work; that then, the thought came on me, that I would do it myself: and that he was good enough to put into my hands what he had with great appositeness written, and I embodied it into my Article. Every one, I think, will recognize the greater part of it as mine. It was published two years before the affair of Tract 90, and was entitled "The State of Religious Parties."

In this Article, I begin by bringing together testimonies from our enemies to the remarkable success of our exertions. One writer said: "Opinions and views of a theology of a very marked and peculiar kind have been extensively adopted and strenuously upheld, and are daily gaining ground among a considerable and influential portion of the members, as well as ministers of the Established Church." Another: the Movement has manifested itself "with the most rapid growth of the hot-bed of these evil days.". . . And, lastly, a bishop in a Charge:—It "is daily assuming a more serious and alarming aspect. Under the specious pretence of deference to Antiquity and respect for primitive models, the foundations of the Protestant Church are undermined by men, who dwell within her walls, and those who sit in the Reformers' seat are traducing the Reformation."

25. Anglican clergy of sixteenth and seventeenth centuries.

After thus stating the phenomenon of the time, as it presented itself to those who did not sympathize in it, the Article proceeds to account for it; and this it does by considering it as a re-action from the dry and superficial character of the religious teaching and the literature of the last generation, or century, and as a result of the need which was felt both by the hearts and the intellects of the nation for a deeper philosophy, and as the evidence and as the partial fulfilment of that need, to which even the chief authors of the then generation had borne witness. First, I mentioned the literary influence of Walter Scott, who turned men's minds to the direction of the middle ages. "The general need," I said, "of something deeper and more attractive, than what had offered itself elsewhere, may be considered to have led to his popularity; and by means of his popularity he reacted on his readers, stimulating their mental thirst, feeding their hopes, setting before them visions, which, when once seen, are not easily forgotten, and silently indoctrinating them with nobler ideas, which might afterwards be appealed to as first principles."

Then I spoke of Coleridge, thus: "While history in prose and verse was thus made the instrument of Church feelings and opinions, a philosophical basis for the same was laid in England by a very original thinker, who, while he indulged a liberty of speculation which no Christian can tolerate, and advocated conclusions which were often heathen rather than Christian, yet after all instilled a higher philosophy into inquiring minds, than they had hitherto been accustomed to accept. In this way he made trial of his age, and succeeded in interesting its genius in the cause of the Catholic truth." . . .

Lastly, I proceeded to the question of that future of the Anglican Church, which was to be a new birth of the Ancient Religion. And I did not venture to pronounce upon it. "About the future, we have no prospect before our minds whatever, good or bad. Ever since that great luminary, Augustine, proved to be the last bishop of Hippo, Christians have had a lesson against attempting to foretell, *how* Providence will prosper and" [or?] "bring to an end, what it begins." Perhaps the lately-revived principles would prevail in the Anglican Church; perhaps they would be lost in "some miserable schism, or some more miserable compromise"; but there was nothing rash in venturing to predict that "neither Puritanism nor Liberalism had any permanent inheritance within her." I suppose I meant to say that in the present age, without the aid of the Apostolical principles, the Anglican Church would, in the event, cease to exist.

"As to Liberalism, we think the formularies of the Church will ever, with the aid of a good Providence, keep it from making any serious inroads upon the Clergy. Besides, it is too cold a principle to prevail with the multitude." But as regarded what was called Evangelical Religion or Puritanism, there was more to cause alarm. I observed upon its organization; but on the other hand it had no intellectual basis; no internal idea, no principle of unity, no theology. "Its adherents," I said, "are already separating from each other; they will melt away like a snow drift. It has no straightforward view on any one point, on which it professes to teach, and to hide its poverty, it has dressed itself out in a maze of words. We have no dread of it at all; we only fear what it may lead to. It does not stand on intrenched ground, or make any pretence to a position; it does but occupy the space between contending powers, Catholic Truth and Rationalism. Then indeed will be the stern encounter, when two real and living principles, simple, entire, and consistent, one in the Church, the other out of it, at length rush upon each other, contending not for names and words, or half-views, but for elementary notions and distinctive moral characters."

Whether the ideas of the coming age upon religion were true or false, they would be real. "In the present day," I said, "mistiness is the mother of wisdom. A man who can set down half-a-dozen general propositions, which escape from destroying one another only by being diluted into truisms, who can hold the balance between opposites so skilfully as to do without fulcrum or beam, who never enunciates a truth without guarding himself against being supposed to exclude the contradictory,—who holds that Scripture is the only authority, yet that the Church is to be deferred to, that faith only justifies, yet that it does not justify without works, that grace does not depend on the sacraments, yet is not given without them, that bishops are a divine ordinance, yet those who have them not are in the same religious condition as those who have,—this is your safe man and the hope of the Church; this is what the Church is said to want, not party men, but sensible, temperate, sober, well-judging persons, to guide it through the channel of no-meaning, between the Scylla and Charybdis of Aye and No."

This state of things, however, I said, could not last, if men were to read and think. They "will not keep standing in that very attitude which you call sound Church-of-Englandism or orthodox Protestantism. They cannot go on for ever standing on one leg, or sitting without a chair, or walking with their feet tied, or grazing like Tityrus's stags in the air. They will take one view or another, but it will be a consistent view. It may be Liberalism, or Erastianism, or Popery, or Catholicity; but it will be real."

I concluded the Article by saying, that all who did not wish to be "democratic, or pantheistic, or popish," must "look out for *some* Via Media which will preserve us from what threatens, though it cannot restore the dead. The spirit of Luther is dead; but Hildebrand and Loyola are alive.[26] Is it sensible, sober, judicious, to be so very angry with those writers of the day, who point to the fact, that our divines of the seventeenth century have occupied a ground which is the true and intelligible mean between extremes? Is it wise to quarrel with this ground, because it is not exactly what we should choose, had we the power of choice? Is it true moderation, instead of trying to fortify a middle doctrine, to fling stones at those who do? . . . Would you rather have your sons and daughters members of the Church of England or of the Church of Rome?"

And thus I left the matter. But, while I was thus speaking of the future of the Movement, I was in truth winding up my accounts with it, little dreaming that it was so to be;—while I was still, in some way or other, feeling about for an available *Via Media*, I was soon to receive a shock which was to cast out of my imagination all middle courses and compromises for ever. . . .[27]

---

26. Hildebrand, Pope Gregory VII; St. Ignatius Loyola, founder of the Jesuit Order.
27. Further study led Newman to the discovery that the Anglican position, specifically his *via media* or middle way between Roman Catholicism and Protestantism, resembled the tenets of fourth- to sixth-century heresies. After this realization in the summer of 1839, Newman nevertheless struggled during the next few years to find "new ground" for his Anglicanism.

# Jane Welsh Carlyle

1801: Born 14 July at Haddington, Scotland

1826: Married Thomas Carlyle

1834: Carlyles settled in Chelsea, London

1866: Died 21 April in London

1883: *Letters and Memorials of Jane Welsh Carlyle*

## LETTERS

*Although Jane Welsh had produced poetry and a tragedy by the age of fourteen, it was as a writer of letters that she excelled. She was the intellectual partner of her husband, the great "sage" Thomas Carlyle, as well as his protector from the noise and bother of everyday living. Together they became the center of an illustrious circle that included at various times Charles Dickens, John Stuart Mill, Harriet Taylor, William Makepeace Thackeray, Alfred Tennyson, John Ruskin, Robert Browning, and Geraldine Jewsbury. The "most caustic, the most concrete, the most clear-sighted of women," according to Virginia Woolf,[1] Jane Carlyle was a witty, often cynical observer of social manners and mores. In the two letters included below—one to her husband and one to her cousin Jeannie Welsh, or "Babbie"—she describes, with both irreverence and self-mockery, her overhauling of her home while Thomas Carlyle is away and her attendance, accompanied by her brother-in-law John Carlyle, at Charles Dickens's amateur production of Ben Jonson's* Every Man in His Humour. RM*

*Tuesday [23 September 1845]*

To Thomas Carlyle

'*Nothink*' for you today in the shape of enclosure; unless I enclose a letter from Mrs Paulet to myself which you will find as "*entertaining*," to the full, as any of mine. And *nothink* to be *told* either, except all about *the Play*, and, upon *my* honour, I do not feel as if I had penny-a-liner-genius enough this cold morning to make much entertainment out of

1. "Geraldine and Jane," *The Common Reader, Second Series,* 1932.

*that*— Enough to clasp one's hands, and exclaim like Helen[2] before *The Virgin and Child* "*Oh! how EXPENSIVE*"! —But "how did the Creatures get thro' it"? *Too well* and *not well enough!* The Public Theatre, scenes painted by Stanfield, costumes "rather exquisite" together with the *certain* amount of *proficiency* in the Amateurs overlaid all idea of *Private Theatricals* and considering it as *Public* Theatricals the acting was "most insipid," not one performer among them that could be called *good*, and none that could be called absolutely *bad*. Douglas Gerold seemed to me the best, the oddity of his appearance greatly helping him—he played *Stephen the Gull*—Forster as Kitely and Dickens Captain Bobadil were much on a par—but Forster preserved his identity even thro his loftiest flights of *Macreadyism*, while poor little Dickens all painted in black and red, and affecting the voice of a man of six feet, would have been unrecognisable for the Mother that bore him![3] On the whole, to *get up* the smallest interest in the thing one needed to be always reminding oneself "all these actors were once *men*!" and will be men again tomorrow morning! The greatest wonder for me was how they had contrived to get together some six or seven hundred *Ladies and gentlemen* (judging from the clothes) at this season of the year! and all utterly unknown to me except some half dozen! So long as I kept my own seat in the Dress Circle I recognised only Mrs Macready—(in one of the four private boxes) and in my nearer neighbourhood Sir Alexander and Lady Gordon.[4] But in the interval betwixt the Play and the Farce, I took a notion to make my way to Mrs Macready—John of course declared the thing "clearly impossible—no use trying it"—but a servant of the Theatre over hearing our debate politely offered to escort me where I wished, and then John having no longer any difficulties to surmount followed to have his share in what advantages might accrue from the change. Passing thro a long dim passage I came on a tall man leant to the wall with his head touching the ceiling like a *Caryatide*—to all appearance *asleep*, or resolutely *trying* it under most unfavourable circumstances! "*Alfred* Tennyson" I exclaimed in joyful surprise— "*Well!*" said he taking the hand I held out to him and *forgetting* to let it go again. "I did not know you were in town" said I— "I should like to know—who you are"! said he— "I *know* that I *know* you but cannot tell your name"!— and I had actually to name myself to him— Then he *woke up* in good earnest, and said he had been meaning and was still meaning to come to Chelsea "But Carlyle is in Scotland" I told him with due humility. "So I heard from Spedding[5] already, but I asked Spedding would he go with me to see Mrs Carlyle and he said he would." I told him if he really meant to come he had better not wait for *backing* under the *present* circumstances. And then pursued my way to the Macready's box where I was received by *William* (whom I had not divined) with a "Gracious Heavens!" and spontaneous dramatic start, which made *me* all but answer "Gracious Heavens"! and start dramatically in my turn. And then I was

2. Helen Mitchell, the Carlyles' maid.
3. Dramatist and journalist Douglas Jerrold; novelist Charles Dickens; and Dickens's friend and future biographer, John Forster. "Macreadyism" is a reference to the acting style of prominent actor and theater manager William C. Macready, who attended the performance.
4. Alexander Cornewall Duff Gordon (1811–72) and his wife Lucie DUFF GORDON (1821–69), translator and travel writer.
5. James Spedding (1808–81), writer and Alfred Tennyson's friend from Cambridge.

kissed all round by his women—and poor Nell Gwyn—Mrs Millner Gibson,[6] seemed almost pushed by the general enthusiasm on the distracted idea of *kissing* me also! They would not let me return to my stupid place but put in a third chair for me in front of their box—and "the latter end of that *woman* was better than the beginning." Macready was in perfect ecstasies over *The Life of Schiller*[7] —spoke of it *with tears in his eyes.*

As "a sign of the Times," I may mention that in the box opposite sat the Duke of Devonshire with Payne Collier! next to us were D'Orsay and "mi Laddy"![8] — Between eleven and twelve it was *all over*—and the practical result? eight and sixpence for a fly and a headach for twentyfour hours! I went to bed as wearied as a little woman could be, and dreamt that I was plunging thro a quagmire seeking some herbs which were to save the life of—Mrs Maurice! and that Maurice was waiting at home for them in an agony of impatience while I could not get out of the mud-water![9]

Craik[10] arrived next evening (Sunday) to make his compliments of "*Kerrag*" [carriage]—all he had to be thankful for, as *his* ticket was for another part of the House than Johns and mine— Decidedly a man who cannot get in a finger without thrusting in a whole hand! Helen had gone to visit *Numbers*—John was smoking in the Kitchen—I was lying on the sofa *headachy* leaving Craik to put himself to the chief expenditure of wind, when a cab drove up—Mr Strachey?— No! Alfred Tennyson—*alone!!!* Actually; by a superhuman effort of volition he had *put himself* into a cab—nay *brought himself* away from a dinnerparty, and was there to smoke and talk with me! by myself *me*! But no such blessedness was in store for him—Craik prosed and John babbled for his entertainment, and I whom he had come to see got scarcely any speech with him.—The exertion however of having to provide him with tea thro' my own unassisted Ingenuity (Helen being gone for the evening) drove away my headach; also perhaps a little feminine vanity at having inspired such a man with the *energy* to take a cab on his own responsibility, and to throw himself on Providence for getting away again!

He staid till eleven; Craik *sitting him out* as he sat out Lady Harriet[11] —and would sit out the Virgin Mary and *Monsieur son Fils* should he find them here—

What with these unfortunate mattrasses (a work of necessity) and other processes *almost* equally indispensable; I have my hands full—and feel "*worried*" which is worse   I fancy my earthquake begins to "come it rather strong" for Johns comfort and ease—but I cannot help *that*—if I do not get on with my work—such as it is—what am I here for?. . .

*Monday Night [29 September 1845]*

TO JEANNIE WELSH

. . . I have been and am busy, as "little ant or honey bee that speedily away doth flee"— turning up my whole house from top to bottom *painting*, sweeping chimneys, beating car-

---

6. Susanna Arethusa Milner-Gibson (1814–85), whom Jane Carlyle calls "Nell Gwyn" after the seventeenth-century actress and mistress of Charles II.

7. Thomas Carlyle's biography of Johann Schiller, published in 1823–4.

8. Marguerite, Countess of Blessington (1789–1849).

9. Anna Maurice, wife of theological writer and Christian Socialist F. D. Maurice, had died in March 1845.

10. George Lillie Craik, nicknamed "Creek" (1798–1866), historian, scholar, and friend of the Carlyles.

11. Harriet Baring, Lady Ashburton (1805–57), whose close relationship with Thomas Carlyle did not please Jane Carlyle.

pets, making the house into "Hell and Tommy" (I "*Tommy*") and when it will be all subsided into its normal state lies beyond my immediate sphere of contemplation—To complicate my household difficulties, I found on my return two wool-mattrasses perfectly swarming with *moths*! had all the wool to *boil* and *dry*—and the heavens constantly pouring down rain! did you ever see the wool of a large mattrass all afloat? If not; pray the superior powers that you never may! it is a sight before which the female human mind is struck stupid with a sense of *the Impossible*! moreover I have had an immense letter-debt, at first almost as hopeless looking as the National Debt, to discharge—in addition to the letter *every second day*, required of me by Carlyle. Happily I am not much taken up with visitors— "nobody in town"— At least nobody *ought* to be *in town* at this season: still stray human beings do occasionally drop in upon me—enough to keep me in mind that I am still in an inhabited world—a still more forcible reminiscence of the same was our recent "Amateur Play"—the "realized Ideal" of Forster and Dickens— It was—what shall I say?—best perhaps characterized by Helens favorite Phrase of admiration "*Oh how expensive*"! The "fulecreturs" must have spent a mint of money on it—a public Theatre engaged for the occasion—scenes painted by Stanfield—costumes according to the strictly historical style of Macready—*cost* "no object"— In fact Macready himself could not have *got up* the material of the thing any more sumptuously—and all this for *one* night— "To think of the *loaves* Babbie" that their frolic might have supplied to "the poor people"! "the working classes eating boiled dog"! For the *acting*; it is much praised in the newspapers—much praised by the majority but there is a small *minority* of *one* at least that thinks it was nothing "to speak of"— There were six or seven hundred people invited and these present by heaven knows what amount of locomotion *at this season of the year!* from hundreds of miles they came—among them were many of the leading Aristocracy; *I was told*—but to my matter of fact eye that looked rather *a rum set*— To be sure the Duke of Devonshire *did* sit opposite to me, with his nose "looking towards Damascus," and old Lady Holland graced *it* (not the nose but the Play) with her hideous presence— I must confess "as one solitary Individual" that it needed me to be always reminding myself "all these *Actors* were once *Men*"! to keep myself from being shamefully bored—With John Carlyle for my only companion, it would have needed a rather unexampled excellence of acting to have awakened me into anything like enthusiasm. I saw Alfred Tennyson in the lobby—and *that* was the best of it! And better still he came to take tea, and talk, and *smoke* with me—me by myself me—the following evening—such at least was his *intention*, not a little flattering to my vanity considering his normal state of indolence—but the result was, that he found *Creek* and *John* and they made a *mess* of it—"the Devil fly away with" them both! In fact the Devil *has* flown away with one of them (John) within the last few days. I fairly *painted him out!* blessings on my powers of invention! There he was; waiting to "see his way clearly" and never so much as wiping his spectacles—babbling and boring, and holding oyster-like to the external accommodations of one's house, without a thought beyond!—an element of confusion hindering all my efforts at order!— But never let a living woman despair— I wielded the Earthquake in my small right hand, and one morning he awoke and found himself "in his old Lodging"—where there was no vestige of a reason why he should not have been all this while! Carlyle has not fixed a time for his return but says in every letter "it will not be long"— Lady Harriet is unexpectedly in town for two days—"too ill to go out" she sent me a note to that effect and the carriage to take me to see her—more than *gracious! incomprehensible* upon *my* honour!— She insisted that I had promised to "give her *my whole winter* at Alverstoke"!— and yet I have an unconquerable persuasion that she does not and never can like me! Well by and by I shall (like John) "See my way clearly" a bushel of kisses to my own Uncle—with so many daughters all taught the art of writing—pity that I can hear of him so seldom— Ever your affectionate

JC

# Harriet Martineau

## EASTERN LIFE, PRESENT AND PAST

*Travel books by well-known novelists and journalists provided many nineteenth-century readers with their images of other lands and cultures. Charles Dickens wrote about his impressions of America; Anthony Trollope, about his visits to the West Indies, North America, and South Africa; and Harriet Martineau, about America and the Middle East. By 1846, when Martineau left Liverpool for an eight-month tour of Egypt, Palestine, Syria, and Lebanon, she had established a reputation as a novelist, a writer of children's narratives, and the popularizer of the theories of Jeremy Bentham, James Mill, David Ricardo, and Thomas Malthus in her* Illustrations of Political Economy. *Her account of her trip,* Eastern Life, Present and Past, *is both a story of spiritual pilgrimage and a travel narrative. Already skeptical about traditional Christianity, Martineau found in her meditative visits to sites of ancient religions a confirmation of her antitheological convictions and evidence of her evolutionary theory of religious history. Christianity, Martineau argued, was a transitional stage in the progression, faith by faith, to enlightenment. At the same time, though, Martineau could not rid herself of her Western convictions and prejudices. A middle-class English Radical, an outspoken abolitionist, and a proponent of women's education and increased opportunities for female employment, she was appalled by polygamy, by*

*slavery, and by the women she met in her visits to "hareems." Her delineation of Eastern*
*women's oppression implicitly reinforced the notion of Western culture's enlightenment*
*and superiority.*                                                                        RM

I SAW TWO HAREEMS IN the East; and it would be wrong to pass them over in an account
of my travels; though the subject is as little agreeable as any I can have to treat. I cannot
now think of the two mornings thus employed without a heaviness of heart greater than
I have ever brought away from Deaf and Dumb Schools, Lunatic Asylums, or even
Prisons. As such are my impressions of hareems, of course I shall not say whose they were
that I visited. Suffice it that one was at Cairo and the other at Damascus. . . .

Before I went abroad, more than one sensible friend had warned me to leave behind
as many prejudices as possible; and especially on this subject, on which the prejudices of
Europeans are the strongest. I was reminded of the wide extent, both of time and space,
in which Polygamy had existed; and that openness of mind was as necessary to the accurate observation of this institution as of every other. I had really taken this advice to heart:
I had been struck by the view taken by Mr. Milnes in his beautiful poem of "the Hareem;"[1]
and I am sure I did meet this subject with every desire to investigate the ideas and general feelings involved in it. I learned a very great deal about the working of the institution; and I believe I apprehend the thoughts and feelings of the persons concerned in it:
and I declare that if we are to look for a hell upon earth, it is where polygamy exists: and
that, as polygamy runs riot in Egypt, Egypt is the lowest depth of this hell. I always before
believed that every arrangement and prevalent practice had some one fair side,—some
one redeeming quality: and diligently did I look for this fair side in regard to polygamy:
but there is none. The longer one studies the subject, and the deeper one penetrates into
it,—the more is one's mind confounded with the intricacy of its iniquity, and the more
does one's heart feel as if it would break.

I shall say but little of what I know. If there were the slightest chance of doing any
good, I would speak out at all hazards;—I would meet all the danger, and endure all the
disgust. But there is no reaching the minds of any who live under the accursed system. It
is a system which belongs to a totally different region of ideas from ours: and there is
nothing to appeal to in the minds of those who, knowing the facts of the institution, can
endure it: and at home, no one needs appealing to and convincing. Any plea for liberality that we meet at home proceeds from some poetical fancy, or some laudable desire for
impartiality in the absence of knowledge of the facts. Such pleas are not operative enough
to render it worth while to shock and sadden many hearts by statements which no one
should be required needlessly to endure. I will tell only something of what I saw; and but
little of what I thought and know.

At ten o'clock one morning, Mrs. Y.[2] and I were home from our early ride, and
dressed for a visit to a hareem of a high order. The lady to whose kindness we mainly
owed this opportunity, accompanied us, with her daughter. We had a disagreeable drive
in the carriage belonging to the hotel, knocking against asses, horses and people all the

1. Richard Monckton Milnes (1809–85), "The Hareem."
2. Mr. and Mrs. Richard Yates were Martineau's travel companions.

way. We alighted at the entrance of a paved passage leading to a court which we crossed: and then, in a second court, we were before the entrance of the hareem.

A party of eunuchs stood before a faded curtain, which they held aside when the gentlemen of our party and the dragoman had gone forward. Retired some way behind the curtain stood, in a half circle, eight or ten slave girls, in an attitude of deep obeisance. Two of them then took charge of each of us, holding us by the arms above the elbows, to help us upstairs.—After crossing a lobby at the top of the stairs, we entered a handsome apartment, where lay the chief wife,—at that time an invalid.—The ceiling was gaily painted; and so were the walls,—the latter with curiously bad attempts at domestic perspective. There were four handsome mirrors; and the curtains in the doorway were of a beautiful shawl fabric, fringed and tasselled. A Turkey carpet not only covered the whole floor, but was turned up at the corners. Deewáns extended round nearly the whole room,—a lower one for ordinary use, and a high one for the seat of honour. The windows, which had a sufficient fence of blinds, looked upon a pretty garden, where I saw orange trees and many others, and the fences were hung with rich creepers.

On cushions on the floor lay the chief lady, ill and miserable-looking. She rose as we entered; but we made her lie down again: and she was then covered with a silk counterpane. Her dress was, as we saw when she rose, loose trowsers of blue striped cotton under her black silk jacket: and the same blue cotton appeared at the wrists, under her black sleeves. Her headdress was of black net, bunched out curiously behind. Her hair was braided down the sides of this headdress behind, and the ends were pinned over her forehead. Some of the black net was brought round her face, and under the chin, showing the outline of a face which had no beauty in it, nor traces of former beauty, but which was interesting to-day from her manifest illness and unhappiness. There was a strong expression of waywardness and peevishness about the mouth, however. She wore two handsome diamond rings; and she and one other lady had watches and gold chains. She complained of her head; and her left hand was bound up: she made signs, by pressing her bosom, and imitating the dandling of a baby, which, with her occasional tears, persuaded my companions that she had met with some accident and had lost her infant. On leaving the hareem, we found that it was not a child of her own that she was mourning, but that of a white girl in the hareem: and that the wife's illness was wholly from grief for the loss of this baby;—a curious illustration of the feelings and manners of the place! The children born in large hareems are extremely few: and they are usually idolised, and sometimes murdered. It is known that in the houses at home which morally most resemble these hareems (though little enough externally) when the rare event of the birth of a child happens, a passionate joy extends over the wretched household:—jars are quieted, drunkenness is moderated, and there is no self-denial which the poor creatures will not undergo during this gratification of their feminine instincts. They will nurse the child all night in illness, and pamper it all day with sweetmeats and toys; they will fight for the possession of it, and be almost heartbroken at its loss: and lose it they must; for the child always dies,—killed with kindness, even if born healthy. This natural outbreak of feminine instinct takes place in the too populous hareem, when a child is given to any one of the many who are longing for the gift: and if it dies naturally, it is mourned as we saw

through a wonderful conquest of personal jealousy by this general instinct. But when the
jealousy is uppermost,—what happens then?—why, the strangling the innocent in its
sleep,—or the letting it slip from the window into the river below,—or the mixing poison with its food;—the mother and the murderess, always rivals and now fiends, being
shut up together for life. If the child lives, what then? If a girl, she sees before her from
the beginning the nothingness of external life, and the chaos of interior existence, in
which she is to dwell for life. If a boy, he remains among the women till ten years old,
seeing things when the eunuchs come in to romp, and hearing things among the chatter
of the ignorant women, which brutalise him for life before the age of rationality comes.
But I will not dwell on these hopeless miseries.

A sensible looking old lady, who had lost an eye, sat at the head of the invalid: and a
nun-like elderly woman, whose head and throat were wrapped in unstarched muslin, sat
behind for a time, and then went away, after an affectionate salutation to the invalid.—
Towards the end of the visit, the husband's mother came in,—looking like a little old man
in her coat trimmed with fur. Her countenance was cheerful and pleasant. We saw, I
think, about twenty more women,—some slaves,—most or all young,—some good-
looking, but none handsome. Some few were black; and the rest very light:—Nubians or
Abyssinians and Circassians, no doubt. One of the best figures, as a picture, in the
hareem, was a Nubian girl, in an amber-coloured watered silk, embroidered with black,
looped up in festoons, and finished with a black boddice. The richness of the gay printed
cotton skirts and sleeves surprised us: the finest shawls could hardly have looked better.
One graceful girl had her pretty figure well shown by a tight-fitting black dress. Their
heads were dressed much like the chief lady's. Two, who must have been sisters, if not
twins, had patches between the eyes. One handmaid was barefoot, and several were without shoes. Though there were none of the whole large number who could be called particularly pretty individually, the scene was, on the whole, exceedingly striking, as the
realisation of what one knew before, but as in a dream. The girls went and came in, but,
for the most part, stood in a half circle. Two sat on their heels for a time: and some went
to play in the neighbouring apartments. . . .

The mourning worn by the lady who went with us was the subject of much speculation: and many questions were asked about her home and family. To appease the curiosity about her home, she gave her card. As I anticipated, this did not answer. It was the great
puzzle of the whole interview. At first the poor lady thought it was to do her head good:
then, she fidgetted about it, in the evident fear of omitting some observance: but at last,
she understood that she was to keep it. When we had taken our departure, however, a
eunuch was sent after us to inquire of the dragoman what "the letter" was which our companion had given to the lady.

The difficulty is to get away, when one is visiting a hareem. The poor ladies cannot
conceive of one's having anything to do; and the only reason they can understand for the
interview coming to an end is the arrival of sunset, after which it would, they think, be
improper for any woman to be abroad. And the amusement to them of such a visit is so
great that they protract it to the utmost, even in such a case as ours to-day, when all intercourse was conducted by dumb show. It is certainly very tiresome; and the only wonder

is that the hostesses can like it. To sit hour after hour on the deewán, without any exchange of ideas, having our clothes examined, and being plied with successive cups of coffee and sherbet, and pipes, and being gazed at by a half-circle of girls in brocade and shawls, and made to sit down again as soon as one attempts to rise, is as wearisome an experience as one meets with in foreign lands.——The weariness of heart is, however, the worst part of it. I noted all the faces well during our constrained stay; and I saw no trace of mind in any one except in the homely one-eyed old lady. All the younger ones were dull, soulless, brutish, or peevish. How should it be otherwise, when the only idea of their whole lives is that which, with all our interests and engagements, we consider too prominent with us? There cannot be a woman of them all who is not dwarfed and with-ered in mind and soul by being kept wholly engrossed with that one interest,——detained at that stage in existence which, though most important in its place, is so as a means to ulterior ends. The ignorance is fearful enough: but the grossness is revolting.

At the third move, and when it was by some means understood that we were waited for, we were permitted to go,——after a visit of above two hours. The sick lady rose from her cushions, notwithstanding our opposition, and we were conducted forth with much observance. On each side of the curtain which overhung the outer entrance stood a girl with a bottle of rose water, some of which was splashed in our faces as we passed out.

We had reached the carriage when we were called back:——his Excellency was waiting for us. So we visited him in a pretty apartment, paved with variegated marbles, and with a fountain in the centre. His Excellency was a sensible-looking man, with gay, easy and graceful manners. He lamented the mistake about the interpreter, and said we must go again, when we might have conversation. He insisted upon attending us to the carriage, actually passing between the files of beggars which lined the outer passage. The dragoman was so excessively shocked by this degree of condescension that we felt obliged to be so too, and remonstrated; but in vain. He stood till the door was shut and, the whip was cracked. He is a liberal-minded man; and his hareem is nearly as favourable a specimen as could be selected for a visit; but what is this best specimen? I find these words written down on the same day, in my journal: written, as I well remember, in heaviness of heart. "I am glad of the opportunity of seeing a hareem: but it leaves an impression of discon tent and uneasiness which I shall be glad to sleep off. And I am not conscious that there is prejudice in this. I feel that a visit to the worst room in the Rookery in St. Giles's would have affected me less painfully. There are there at least the elements of a rational life, however perverted; while here humanity is wholly and hopelessly baulked. It will never do to look on this as a case for cosmopolitan philosophy to regard complacently, and require a good construction for. It is not a phase of natural early manners. It is as pure a conventionalism as our representative monarchy, or German heraldry, or Hindoo caste; and the most atrocious in the world."

And of this atrocious system, Egypt is the most atrocious example. It has unequalled facilities for the importation of black and white slaves; and these facilities are used to the utmost; yet the population is incessantly on the decline. But for the importation of slaves, the upper classes, where polygamy runs riot, must soon die out,——so few are the chil-dren born, and so fatal to health are the arrangements of society. The finest children are those born of Circassian or Georgian mothers; and but for these, we should soon hear lit-tle more of an upper class in Egypt.—Large numbers are brought from the south,—the girls to be made attendants or concubines in the hareem, and the boys to be made, in a vast proportion, those guards to the female part of the establishment whose mere pres-ence is a perpetual insult and shame to humanity. The business of keeping up the supply of these miserable wretches,—of whom the Pasha's eldest daughter has fifty for her exclusive service,—is in the hands of the Christians of Asyoot. It is these Christians who provide a sufficient supply, and cause a sufficient mortality to keep the number of the sexes pretty equal: in consideration of which we cannot much wonder that Christianity does not appear very venerable in the eyes of Mohammedans.

These eunuchs are indulged in regard to dress, personal liberty, and often the posses-sion of office, domestic, military, or political. When retained as guards of the hareem, they are in their master's confidence,—acting as his spies, and indispensable to the ladies as a medium of communication with the world, and as furnishing their amusements,—being at once playmates and servants. It is no unusual thing for the eunuchs to whip the ladies away from a window, whence they had hoped for amusement; or to call them opprobrious names; or to inform against them to their owner; and it is also no unusual thing for them to romp with the ladies, to obtain their confidence, and to try their dis-positions. Cases have been known of one of them becoming the friend of some poor girl of higher nature and tendencies than her companions; and even of a closer attachment, which is not objected to by the proprietor of both. It is a case too high for his jealousy, so long as he knows that the cage is secure. It has become rather the fashion to extenuate the lot of the captive of either sex: to point out how the Nubian girl, who would have ground corn, and woven garments, and nursed her infants in comparative poverty all her days, is now surrounded by luxury, and provided for for life: and how the Circassian girl may become a wife of the son of her proprietor, and hold a high rank in the hareem: and how the wretched brothers of these slaves may rise to posts of military command or political confidence; but it is enough to see them to be disabused of all impressions of their good fortune. It is enough to see the dull and gross face of the handmaid of the hareem, and to remember at the moment the cheerful, modest countenance of the Nubian girl, busy about her household tasks, or of the Nubian mother, with her infants hanging about her as she looks, with face open to the sky, for her husband's return from the field, or meets him on the river bank. It is enough to observe the wretched health, and abject, or worn, or insolent look of the guard of the hareem, and to remember that he ought to have been the head of a household of his own, however humble: and in this contrast of what is with what ought to have been, slavery is seen to be fully as detestable here as anywhere else. These two hellish practices, slavery and polygamy, which, as prac-tices, can clearly never be separated, are here avowedly connected; and, in that connex-ion, are exalted into a double institution, whose working is such as to make one almost wish that the Nile would rise to cover the tops of the hills, and sweep away the whole abomination. Till this happens, there is, in the condition of Egypt, a fearful warning before the eyes of all men. The Egyptians laugh at the marriage arrangements of Europe, declaring that virtual polygamy exists everywhere, and is not improved by hypocritical concealment. The European may see, when startled by the state of Egypt, that virtual slavery is indispensably required by the practice of polygamy; virtual proprietorship of the women involved, without the obligations imposed by actual proprietorship; and cruel oppression of the men who should have been the husbands of these women. And again, the Carolina planter, who knows as well as any Egyptian that polygamy is a natural concomitant of slavery, may see in the state of Egypt and the Egyptians what his country and his children must come to, if either of those vile arrangements is permitted which necessitates the other.

It is scarcely needful to say that those benevolent persons are mistaken who believe that Slavery in Egypt has been abolished by the Pasha, and the importation of slaves effectually prohibited. Neither the Pasha nor any other human power can abolish slavery while Polygamy is an institution of the country, the proportion of the sexes remaining in Egypt what it is, there and everywhere else. . . .

# Robert Chambers

## VESTIGES OF THE NATURAL HISTORY OF CREATION

*Published anonymously in 1844,* Vestiges *created an immediate sensation. Its author, Scottish publisher and amateur geologist Robert Chambers, constructed a sweeping narrative of the origin of the earth and the evolution of life. Accepting the controversial nebular hypothesis of the formation of the universe from a "fiery mist" (a position he would later modify), Chambers plotted a step-by-step history of the composition of the cosmos, the geological transformations of the earth, and the ascending development of organic forms from marine life to land vegetation and animals and ultimately human beings. He insisted that his version of the origin and development of life was consistent with the descriptions of creation in* Genesis *and that progressive creation was determined by natural laws emanating from a divine will. Critics denounced* Vestiges *on religious as well as scientific grounds. To many readers its account of evolution by divine law suggested that God was but a "Divine Author," withdrawn from his creation, and seemed to deny individual moral responsibility. Professional scientists attacked its amateurism, its blunders in details, and its speculations about spontaneous generation and embryology. Despite the criticism, or perhaps because of it, the book was immensely popular and influential, reaching four editions in six months and selling well over twenty thousand copies by 1860. Charles* Darwin *regarded it as a pioneering text in the field of evolution: "In my opinion, it has done excellent service in this country in calling attention to the subject, in removing prejudice, in thus preparing the ground for the reception of analogous views."[1]* RM

1. "Historical Introduction," *On the Origin of Species,* 3rd edition (1861).

## GENERAL CONSIDERATIONS RESPECTING THE ORIGIN OF THE ANIMATED TRIBES

. . . IF THERE IS ANY THING more than another impressed on our minds by the course of the geological history, it is, that the same laws and conditions of nature now apparent to us have existed throughout the whole time, though the operation of some of these laws may now be less conspicuous than in the early ages, from some of the conditions having come to a settlement and a close. That seas have flowed and ebbed, and winds disturbed their surfaces, in the time of the secondary rocks, we have proof on the yet preserved surfaces of the sands which constituted margins of the seas in those days. Even the fall of wind-slanted rain is evidenced on the same tablets. The washing down of detached matter from elevated grounds, which we see rivers constantly engaged in at the present time, and which is daily shallowing the seas adjacent to their mouths, only appears to have proceeded on a greater scale in earlier epochs. The volcanic subterranean force, which we see belching forth lavas on the sides of mountains, and throwing up new elevations by land and sea, was only more powerfully operative in distant ages. To turn to organic nature, vegetation seems to have proceeded then exactly as now. The very alternations of the seasons have been read in unmistakable characters in sections of the trees of those days, precisely as it might be read in a section of a tree cut down yesterday. The system of prey amongst animals flourished throughout the whole of the pre-human period; and the adaptation of all plants and animals to their respective spheres of existence was as perfect in those early ages as it is still.

But, as has been observed, the operation of the laws may be modified by conditions. At one early age, if there was any dry land at all, it was perhaps enveloped in an atmosphere unfit for the existence of terrestrial animals, and which had to go through some changes before that condition was altered. In the carbonigenous era, dry land seems to have consisted only of clusters of islands, and the temperature was much above what now obtains at the same places. Volcanic forces, and perhaps also the disintegrating power, seem to have been on the decrease since the first, or we have at least long enjoyed an exemption from such paroxysms of the former, as appear to have prevailed at the close of the coal formation in England and throughout the tertiary era. The surface has also undergone a gradual progress by which it has become always more and more variegated, and thereby fitted for the residence of a higher class of animals.

In pursuing the progress of the development of both plants and animals upon the globe, we have seen an advance in both cases, along the line leading to the higher forms of organization. Amongst plants, we have first sea-weeds, afterwards land plants; and amongst these the simpler (cellular and cryptogamic) before the more complex. In the department of zoology, we see zoophytes, radiata, mollusca, articulata, existing for ages before there were any higher forms. The first step forward gives fishes, the humblest class of the vertebrata; and, moreover, the earliest fishes partake of the character of the next lowest sub-kingdom, the articulata. Afterwards come land animals, of which the first are reptiles, universally allowed to be the type next in advance from fishes, and to be connected with these by the links of an insensible gradation. From reptiles we advance to birds, and thence to mammalia, which are commenced by marsupialia, acknowledgedly low forms in their class. That there is thus a progress of some kind, the most superficial glance at the geological history is sufficient to convince us. Indeed the doctrine of the gradation of animal forms has received a remarkable support from the discoveries of this science, as several types formerly wanting to a completion of the series have been found in a fossil state.[2]

It is scarcely less evident, from the geological record, that the progress of organic life has observed some correspondence with the progress of physical conditions on the surface. We do not know for certain that the sea, at the time when it supported radiated, molluscous, and articulated families, was incapable of supporting fishes; but causes for such a limitation are far from inconceivable. The huge saurians appear to have been precisely adapted to the low muddy coasts and sea margins of the time when they flourished. Marsupials appear at the time when the surface was generally in that flat, imperfectly variegated state in which we find Australia, the region where they now live in the greatest abundance, and one which has no higher native mammalian type. Finally, it was not till the land and sea had come into their present relations, and the former, in its principal continents, had acquired the irregularity of surface necessary for man, that man appeared. We have likewise seen reason for supposing that land animals could not have lived before the carbonigenous era, owing to the great charge of carbonic acid gas presumed to have been contained in the atmosphere down to that time. The surplus of this having gone, as M. Brogniart[3] suggests, to form the vegetation, whose ruins became coal, and the air being thus brought to its present state, land animals immediately appeared. So also, sea-plants were at first the only specimens of vegetation, because there appears to have been no place where other plants could be produced or supported. Land vegetation followed, at first simple, afterwards complex, probably in conformity with an advance of the conditions required by the higher class of plants. In short, we see everywhere throughout the geological history, strong traces of a parallel advance of the physical conditions and the organic forms. . . .

A candid consideration of all these circumstances can scarcely fail to introduce into our minds a somewhat different idea of organic creation from what has hitherto been generally entertained. That God created animated beings, as well as the terraqueous theatre of their being, is a fact so powerfully evidenced, and so universally received, that I at once take it for granted. But in the particulars of this so highly supported idea, we surely here see cause for some re-consideration. It may now be inquired,—In what way was the creation of animated beings effected? The ordinary notion may, I think, be not unjustly described as this,—that the Almighty author produced the progenitors of all existing species by some sort of personal or immediate exertion. But how does this notion comport with what we have seen of the gradual advance of species, from the humblest to the highest? How can we suppose an immediate exertion of this creative power at one time to produce zoophytes, another time to add a few marine mollusks, another to bring in one or two conchifers, again to produce crustaceous fishes, again perfect fishes, and so on

2. Intervals in the series were numerous in the department of the pachydermata; many of these gaps are now filled up from the extinct genera found in the tertiary formation. [Chambers's note]
3. Alexandre Brongniart (1770–1847), French geologist.

to the end? This would surely be to take a very mean view of the Creative Power—to, in short, anthropomorphize it, or reduce it to some such character as that borne by the ordinary proceedings of mankind. And yet this would be unavoidable; for that the organic creation was thus progressive through a long space of time, rests on evidence which nothing can overturn or gainsay. Some other idea must then be come to with regard to *the mode* in which the Divine Author proceeded in the organic creation. Let us seek in the history of the earth's formation for a new suggestion on this point. We have seen powerful evidence, that the construction of this globe and its associates, and inferentially that of all the other globes of space, was the result, not of any immediate or personal exertion on the part of the Deity, but of natural laws which are expressions of his will. What is to hinder our supposing that the organic creation is also a result of natural laws, which are in like manner an expression of his will? More than this, the fact of the cosmical arrangements being an effect of natural law, is a powerful argument for the organic arrangements being so likewise, for how can we suppose that the august Being who brought all these countless worlds into form by the simple establishment of a natural principle flowing from his mind, was to interfere personally and specially on every occasion when a new shell-fish or reptile was to be ushered into existence on *one* of these worlds? Surely this idea is too ridiculous to be for a moment entertained.

It will be objected that the ordinary conceptions of Christian nations on this subject are directly derived from Scripture, or, at least, are in conformity with it. If they were clearly and unequivocally supported by Scripture, it may readily be allowed that there would be a strong objection to the reception of any opposite hypothesis. But the fact is, however startling the present announcement of it may be, that the first chapter of the Mosaic record is not only not in harmony with the ordinary ideas of mankind respecting cosmical and organic creation, but is opposed to them, and only in accordance with the views here taken. When we carefully peruse it with awakened minds, we find that all the procedure is represented primarily and pre-eminently as flowing *from commands and expressions of will, not from direct acts.* Let there be light—let there be a firmament—let the dry land appear—let the earth bring forth grass, the herb, the tree—let the waters bring forth the moving creature that hath life—let the earth bring forth the living creature after his kind—these are the terms in which the principal acts are described. The additional expressions,—God made the firmament—God made the beast of the earth, &c., occur subordinately, and only in a few instances; they do not necessarily convey a different idea of the mode of creation, and indeed only appear as alternative phrases, in the usual duplicative manner of Eastern narrative. Keeping this in view, the words used in a subsequent place, "God *formed* man in his own image," cannot well be understood as implying any more than what was implied before,—namely, that man was produced in consequence of an expression of the Divine will to that effect. Thus, the scriptural objection quickly vanishes, and the prevalent ideas about the organic creation appear only as a mistaken inference from the text, formed at a time when man's ignorance prevented him from drawing therefrom a just conclusion. At the same time, I freely own that I do not think it right to adduce the Mosaic record, either in objection to, or support of any natural hypothesis, and this for many reasons, but particularly for this, that there is not the least appearance of an intention in that book to give philosophically exact views of nature.

To a reasonable mind the Divine attributes must appear, not diminished or reduced in any way, by supposing a creation by law, but infinitely exalted. It is the narrowest of all views of the Deity, and characteristic of a humble class of intellects, to suppose him acting constantly in particular ways for particular occasions. It, for one thing, greatly detracts from his foresight, the most undeniable of all the attributes of Omnipotence. It lowers him towards the level of our own humble intellects. Much more worthy of him it surely is, to suppose that all things have been commissioned by him from the first, though neither is he absent from a particle of the current of natural affairs in one sense, seeing that the whole system is continually supported by his providence. Even in human affairs, if I may be allowed to adopt a familiar illustration, there is a constant progress from specific action for particular occasions, to arrangements which, once established, shall continue to answer for a great multitude of occasions. Such plans the enlightened readily form for themselves, and conceive as being adopted by all who have to attend to a multitude of affairs, while the ignorant suppose every act of the greatest public functionary to be the result of some special consideration and care on his part alone. Are we to suppose the Deity adopting plans which harmonize only with the modes of procedure of the less enlightened of our race? Those who would object to the hypothesis of a creation by the intervention of law, do not perhaps consider how powerful an argument in favour of the existence of God is lost by rejecting this doctrine. When all is seen to be the result of law, the idea of an Almighty Author becomes irresistible, for the creation of a law for an endless series of phenomena—an act of intelligence above all else that we can conceive—could have no other imaginable source, and tells, moreover, as powerfully for a sustaining as for an originating power. . . .

# James Phillips Kay-Shuttleworth

1804: Born 20 July at Rochdale, Lancashire

1824–7: Studied medicine at Edinburgh University

1832: *The Moral and Physical Condition of the Working Classes*

1835: Appointed Assistant Poor Law Commissioner, under the 1834 Poor Law Amendment

1862: *Four Periods of Public Education*

1877: Died 26 May in London

---

## THE MORAL AND PHYSICAL CONDITION OF THE WORKING CLASSES EMPLOYED IN THE COTTON MANUFACTURE IN MANCHESTER

---

*James Phillips Kay, who became Kay-Shuttleworth after his marriage in 1842, published his pamphlet on the working classes in 1832, and, later that same year, an enlarged second edition, from which the following excerpt is taken. A physician in the growing manufacturing city of Manchester, Kay served as a dispensary medical officer and secretary of the Manchester Board of Health. He visited the streets of depressed and overcrowded neighborhoods, inspected the homes of the working poor, and tabulated information about physical environments and habits. His 1832 pamphlet, intended to expose poverty and its sources, focused as much on the "demoralization" or moral "degradation" of the mill worker as on the physical conditions of home and workplace. To combat the "evils" that Kay identified as the sources of urban poverty—restricted trade, low wages, the current Poor Law, Irish immigration, ignorance, and lack of "domestic economy"—he proposed medical, municipal, and legislative "intervention." Later he would concentrate his efforts on the education of pauper children and the establishment of a national system of public education.* RM

SELF-KNOWLEDGE, INCULCATED BY THE maxim of the ancient philosopher, is a precept not less appropriate to societies than to individuals. The physical and moral evils by which we are personally surrounded, may be more easily avoided when we are distinctly conscious

of their existence; and the virtue and health of society may be preserved, with less difficulty, when we are acquainted with the sources of its errors and diseases.

The sensorium of the animal structure, to which converge the sensibilities of each
organ, is endowed with a consciousness of every change in the sensations to which each
member is liable; and few diseases are so subtle as to escape its delicate perceptive power.
Pain thus reveals to us the existence of evils, which, unless arrested in their progress,
might insidiously invade the sources of vital action.

Society were well preserved, did a similar faculty preside, with an equal sensibility,
over its constitution; making every order immediately conscious of the evils affecting any
portion of the general mass, and thus rendering their removal equally necessary for the
immediate ease, as it is for the ultimate welfare of the whole social system. The mutual
dependance of the individual members of society and of its various orders, for the supply of their necessities and the gratification of their desires, is acknowledged, and it
imperfectly compensates for the want of a faculty, resembling that pervading consciousness which presides over the animal economy. But a knowledge of the moral and physical evils oppressing one order of the community, is by these means slowly communicated to those which are remote; and general efforts are seldom made for the relief of partial ills, until they threaten to convulse the whole social constitution. . . .

The introduction into this country of a singularly malignant contagious malady,[1]
which, though it selects its victims from every order of society, is chiefly propagated
amongst those whose health is depressed by disease, mental anxiety, or want of the comforts and conveniences of life, has directed public attention to an investigation of the state
of the poor. In Manchester, Boards of Health were established, in each of the fourteen districts of Police, for the purpose of minutely inspecting the state of the houses and streets.
These districts were divided into minute sections, to each of which two or more inspec-
tors were appointed from among the most respectable inhabitants of the vicinity, and they
were provided with tabular queries, applying to each particular house and street.
Individual exceptions only exist, in which minute returns were not furnished to the
Special Board: and as the investigation was prompted equally by the demands of benevolence, of personal security, and of the general welfare, the results may be esteemed as
accurate as the nature of the investigation would permit. The other facts contained in this
pamphlet have been obtained from the public offices of the town, or are the results of the
author's personal observation.

The township of Manchester chiefly consists of dense masses of houses, inhabited by
the population engaged in the great manufactories of the cotton trade. Some of the central divisions are occupied by warehouses and shops, and a few streets by the dwellings of
some of the more wealthy inhabitants; but the opulent merchants chiefly reside in the
country, and even the superior servants of their establishments inhabit the suburban
townships. Manchester, properly so called, is chiefly inhabited by shopkeepers and the
labouring classes.[2] Those districts where the poor dwell are of very recent origin. The

1. Cholera.
2. To the stranger, it is also necessary to observe, that the investigations on whose results the conclusions of this
pamphlet are founded, were of necessity conducted *in the township of Manchester only*; and that the inhabitants of a

rapid growth of the cotton manufacture has attracted hither operatives from every part of the kingdom, and Ireland has poured forth the most destitute of her hordes to supply the constantly increasing demand for labour. This immigration has been, in one important respect, a serious evil. The Irish have taught the labouring classes of this country a pernicious lesson. The system of cottier farming,[3] the demoralization and barbarism of the people, and the general use of the potato as the chief article of food, have encouraged the population in Ireland more rapidly than the *available* means of subsistence have been increased. Debased alike by ignorance and pauperism, they have discovered, with the savage, what is the minimum of the means of life, upon which existence may be prolonged. The paucity of the amount of means and comforts *necessary for the mere support of life*, is not known by a more civilized population, and this secret has been taught the labourers of this country by the Irish. As competition and the restrictions and burdens of trade diminished the profits of capital, and consequently reduced the price of labour, the contagious example of ignorance and a barbarous disregard of forethought and economy, exhibited by the Irish, spread. The colonization of savage tribes has ever been attended with effects on civilization as fatal as those which have marked the progress of the sand flood over the fertile plains of Egypt. Instructed in the fatal secret of subsisting on what is barely necessary to life—yielding partly to necessity, and partly to example,—the labouring classes have ceased to entertain a laudable pride in furnishing their houses, and in multiplying the decent comforts which minister to happiness. What is superfluous to the mere exigencies of nature, is too often expended at the tavern; and for the provision of old age and infirmity, they too frequently trust either to charity, to the support of their children, or to the protection of the poor laws.

When this example is considered in connexion with the unremitted labour of the whole population engaged in the various branches of the cotton manufacture, our wonder will be less excited by their fatal demoralization. Prolonged and exhausting labour, continued from day to day, and from year to year, is not calculated to develop the intellectual or moral faculties of man. The dull routine of a ceaseless drudgery, in which the same mechanical process is incessantly repeated, resembles the torment of Sisyphus—the toil, like the rock, recoils perpetually on the wearied operative. The mind gathers neither stores nor strength from the constant extension and retraction of the same muscles. The intellect slumbers in supine inertness; but the grosser parts of our nature attain a rank development. To condemn man to such severity of toil is, in some measure, to cultivate in him the habits of an animal. He becomes reckless. He disregards the distinguishing appetites and habits of his species. He neglects the comforts and delicacies of life. He lives in squalid wretchedness, on meager food, and expends his superfluous gains in debauchery.

The population employed in the cotton factories rises at five o'clock in the morning, works in the mills from six till eight o'clock, and returns home for half an hour or forty minutes to breakfast. This meal generally consists of tea or coffee, with a little bread.

---

great part of the adjacent townships are in a condition superior to that described in these pages. The most respectable portion of the operative population has, we think, a tendency to avoid the central districts of Manchester, and to congregate in the suburban townships. [Kay's note]

3. Tenant farming.

Oatmeal porridge is sometimes, but of late rarely used, and chiefly by the men; but the stimulus of tea is preferred, and especially by the women. The tea is almost always of a bad, and sometimes of a deleterious quality; the infusion is weak, and little or no milk is added. The operatives return to the mills and workshops until twelve o'clock, when an hour is allowed for dinner. Amongst those who obtain the lower rates of wages this meal generally consists of boiled potatoes. The mess of potatoes is put into one large dish; melted lard and butter are poured upon them, and a few pieces of fried fat bacon are sometimes mingled with them, and but seldom a little meat. Those who obtain better wages, or families whose aggregate income is larger, add a greater proportion of animal food to this meal, at least three times in the week; but the quantity consumed by the labouring population is not great. The family sits round the table, and each rapidly appropriates his portion on a plate, or they all plunge their spoons into the dish, and with an animal eagerness satisfy the cravings of their appetite. At the expiration of the hour, they are all again employed in the workshops or mills, where they continue until seven o'clock or a later hour, when they generally again indulge in the use of tea, often mingled with spirits accompanied by a little bread. Oatmeal or potatoes are however taken by some a second time in the evening.

The comparatively innutritious qualities of these articles of diet are most evident. We are, however, by no means prepared to say that an individual living in a healthy atmosphere, and engaged in active employment in the open air, would not be able to continue protracted and severe labour, without any suffering, whilst nourished by this food. We should rather be disposed on the contrary to affirm, that any ill effects must necessarily be so much diminished, that, from the influence of habit, and the benefits derived from the constant inhalation of an uncontaminated atmosphere, during healthy exercise in agricultural pursuits, few if any evil results would ensue. But the population nourished on this aliment is crowded into one dense mass, in cottages separated by narrow, unpaved, and almost pestilential streets, in an atmosphere loaded with the smoke and exhalations of a large manufacturing city. The operatives are congregated in rooms and workshops during twelve hours in the day, in an enervating, heated atmosphere, which is frequently loaded with dust or filaments of cotton, or impure from constant respiration, or from other causes. They are engaged in an employment which absorbs their attention, and unremittingly employs their physical energies.[4] They are drudges who watch the movements, and assist the operations, of a mighty material force, which toils with an energy ever unconscious of fatigue. The persevering labour of the operative must rival the mathematical precision, the incessant motion, and the exhaustless power of the machine.

Hence, besides the negative results—the abstraction of moral and intellectual stimuli—the absence of variety—banishment from the grateful air and the cheering influences of light, the physical energies are impaired by toil, and imperfect nutrition. The artisan too seldom possesses sufficient moral dignity or intellectual or organic strength to resist the seductions of appetite. His wife and children, subjected to the same process,

4. A gentleman, whose opinions on these subjects command universal respect, suggests to me, that the intensity of this application is exceedingly increased by the system of paying, not for time, but according to the result of labour. [Kay's note]

have little power to cheer his remaining moments of leisure. Domestic economy is neglected, domestic comforts are too frequently unknown. A meal of coarse food is hastily prepared, and devoured with precipitation. Home has little other relation to him than that of shelter—few pleasures are there—it chiefly presents to him a scene of physical exhaustion, from which he is glad to escape. His house is ill furnished, uncleanly, often ill ventilated—perhaps damp; his food, from want of forethought and domestic economy, is meagre and innutritious; he generally becomes debilitated and hypochondriacal, and unless supported by principle, falls the victim of dissipation. In all these respects, it is grateful to add, that those among the operatives of the mills, who are employed *in the process of spinning*, and especially of fine spinning, (who receive a high rate of wages and who are elevated on account of their skill) are more attentive to their domestic arrangements, have better furnished houses, are consequently more regular in their habits, and more observant of their duties than those engaged in other branches of the manufacture. . . .

Visiting Manchester, the metropolis of the commercial system, a stranger regards with wonder the ingenuity and comprehensive capacity, which, in the short space of half a century, have here established the staple manufacture of this kingdom. He beholds with astonishment the establishments of its merchants—monuments of fertile genius and successful design:—the masses of capital which have been accumulated by those who crowd upon its mart, and the restless but sagacious spirit which has made every part of the known world the scene of their enterprise. The sudden creation of the mighty system of commercial organization which covers this county, and stretches its arms to the most distant seas, attests the power and the dignity of man. Commerce, it appears to such a spectator, here gathers in her storehouses the productions of every clime, that she may minister to the happiness of a favoured race.

When he turns from the great capitalists, he contemplates the fearful strength only of that multitude of the labouring population, which lies like a slumbering giant at their feet. He has heard of the turbulent riots of the people—of machine breaking—of the secret and sullen organization which has suddenly lit the torch of incendiarism, or well nigh uplifted the arm of rebellion in the land. He remembers that political desperadoes have ever loved to tempt this population to the hazards of the swindling game of revolution, and have scarcely failed. In the midst of so much opulence, however, he has disbelieved the cry of need.

Believing that the natural tendency of unrestricted commerce, (unchecked by the prevailing want of education, and the incentives afforded by imperfect laws to improvidence and vice,) is to develop the energies of society, to increase the comforts and luxuries of life, and to *elevate the physical condition* of every member of the social body, we have exposed, with a faithful, though a friendly hand, the condition of the lower orders connected with the manufactures of this town, because we conceive that the evils affecting them result *from foreign and accidental causes*. A system, which promotes the advance of civilization, and diffuses it over the world—which promises to maintain the peace of nations, by establishing a permanent international law, founded on the benefits of commercial association, cannot be inconsistent with the happiness of the *great mass of the peo-*

*ple.* There are men who believe that the labouring classes are condemned for ever, by an inexorable fate, to the unmitigated curse of toil, scarcely rewarded by the bare necessaries of existence, and often visited by the horrors of hunger and disease—that the heritage of ignorance, labour, and misery, is entailed upon them as an eternal doom. Such an opinion might appear to receive a gloomy confirmation, were we content with the evidence of fact, derived only from the history of uncivilized races, and of feudal institutions. No modern Rousseau[5] now rhapsodises on the happiness of the state of nature. Moral and physical degradation are inseparable from barbarism. The unsheltered, naked savage, starving on food common to the denizens of the wilderness, never knew the comforts contained in the most wretched cabin of our poor.

Civilization, to which feudality is inimical, but which is most powerfully promoted by commerce, surrounds man with innumerable inventions. It has thus a constant tendency to multiply, without limit, the comforts of existence, and that by an amount of labour, at all times undergoing an indefinite diminution. It continually expands the sphere of his relations, from a dependance on his own limited resources, until it has combined into one mighty league, alike the members of communities, and the powers of the most distant regions. The cultivation of the faculties, the extension of knowledge, the improvement of the arts, enable man to extend his dominion over matter, and to minister, not merely to all the exigencies, but to the capricious tastes and the imaginary appetites of his nature. When, therefore, every zone has contributed its most precious stores—science has revealed her secret laws—genius has applied the mightiest powers of nature to familiar use, making matter the patient and silent slave of the will of man—if want prey upon the heart of the people, we may strongly presume that, besides the effects of existing manners, some accidental barrier exists, arresting their natural and rightful supply.

The evils affecting the working classes, *so far from being the necessary results of the commercial system, furnish evidence of a disease which impairs its energies, if it does not threaten its vitality.*

The increase of the manufacturing establishments, and the consequent colonization of the district, have been exceedingly more rapid than the growth of its civic institutions. The eager antagonization of commercial enterprise, has absorbed the attention, and concentrated the energies of every member of the community. In this strife, the remote influence of arrangements has sometimes been neglected, not from the want of humanity, but from the pressure of occupation, and the deficiency of time. Thus, some years ago, the internal arrangements of mills (now so much improved) as regarded temperature, ventilation, cleanliness, and the proper separation of the sexes, &c., were such as to be extremely objectionable. The same cause has, we think, chiefly occasioned the want of police regulations, to prevent the gross neglect of the streets and houses of the poor.

The great and sudden fluctuations to which trade is liable, are often the sources of severe embarrassment. Sometimes the demand for labour diminishes, and its price consequently falls in a corresponding ratio. On the other hand, the existing population has often been totally inadequate to the required production; and capitalists have eagerly

5. Jean-Jacques Rousseau (1712–78), French philosopher, whose condemnation of civilization and society as corrupting influences on nature is rejected by Kay.

invited a supply of labour from distant counties, and the sister kingdom. The colonization of the Irish was thus first encouraged; and has proved one chief source of the demoralization, and consequent physical depression of the people.

The effects of this immigration, even when regarded as a simple economical question, do not merely include an equation of the comparative cheapness of labour; its influence on civilization and morals, as *they tend to affect the production of wealth*, cannot be neglected. . . .

Morality is therefore worthy of the attention of the economist, even when considered as simply ministering to the production of wealth. Civilization creates artificial wants, introduces economy, and cultivates the moral and physical capabilities of society. Hence the introduction of an uncivilized race does not tend even primarily to increase the power of producing wealth, in a ratio by any means commensurate with the cheapness of its labour, and may ultimately retard the increase of the fund for the maintenance of that labour. Such a race is useful only as a mass of animal organization, which consumes the smallest amount of wages. The low price of the labour of such people depends, however, on the paucity of their wants, and their savage habits. When they assist the production of wealth, therefore, their barbarous habits and consequent moral depression must form a part of the equation. They are only necessary to a state of commerce *inconsistent* with such a reward for labour as is calculated to maintain the standard of civilization. A few years pass, and they become burdens to a community whose morals and physical power they have depressed; and dissipate wealth which they did not accumulate.

# Benjamin Disraeli

1804: Born 21 December in London

1826–7: *Vivian Grey*

1837: Elected to House of Commons

1844: *Coningsby; or, The New Generation*

1845: *Sybil; or, The Two Nations*

1847: *Tancred; or, The New Crusade*

1868: Served as Prime Minister

1870: *Lothair*

1874–80: Prime Minister

1881: Died 19 April, London

## CONSERVATIVE AND LIBERAL PRINCIPLES

### Speech at the Crystal Palace, June 24, 1872

*Before members of the National Union of Conservative and Constitutional Associations, gathered at the Crystal Palace, Benjamin Disraeli delivered a speech that came to be regarded as a major statement of British nationalistic and imperialistic sentiment. It was a political speech, designed to gain wider support for the Conservative party and to reassert the ex-Prime Minister's leadership of that party. Applying a Tory reinterpretation of recent history, Disraeli attacks the Liberals, who had dominated English politics for decades, for undermining traditional institutions under the guise of reform and progress, and assails Prime Minister William GLADSTONE for his foreign and colonial policies. The Tory Party, Disraeli asserts, has three great objects: to maintain the nation's institutions    its monarchy, House of Lords, and Church; to elevate the condition of the people; and to uphold the Empire. Assuming the superiority of the nation and its institutions, he advocates "a great policy of Imperial consolidation," in order to insure England's international power and reputation. Later, during Disraeli's second administration, the government both enacted important social reforms related to public health, housing, factory conditions, and trade unions*

*and pursued an aggressive foreign policy, marked by the purchase of the Suez Canal, the*
*checking of Russian expansion, and in 1876 the proclaiming of Victoria as "Empress of*
*India."*

                                                                                    RM

My Lord Duke and Gentlemen,—I am very sensible of the honour which you have done me in requesting that I should be your guest to-day, and still more for your having associated my name with the important toast which has been proposed by the Lord Mayor. In the few observations that I shall presume to make on this occasion I will confine myself to some suggestions as to the present state of the Constitutional cause and the prospects which you, as a great Constitutional party, have before you. Gentlemen, some years ago—now, indeed, not an inconsiderable period, but within the memory of many who are present—the Tory party experienced a great overthrow. I am here to admit that in my opinion it was deserved. A long course of power and prosperity had induced it to sink into a state of apathy and indifference, and it had deviated from the great principles of that political association which had so long regulated the affairs and been identified with the glory of England. Instead of the principles professed by Mr. Pitt and Lord Grenville,[1] and which those great men inherited from Tory statesmen who had preceded them not less illustrious, the Tory system had degenerated into a policy which found an adequate basis on the principles of exclusiveness and restriction. Gentlemen, the Tory party, unless it is a national party, is nothing. It is not a confederacy of nobles, it is not a democratic multitude; it is a party formed from all the numerous classes in the realm— classes alike and equal before the law, but whose different conditions and different aims give vigour and variety to our national life.

Gentlemen, a body of public men distinguished by their capacity took advantage of these circumstances. They seized the helm of affairs in a manner the honour of which I do not for a moment question, but they introduced a new system into our political life. Influenced in a great degree by the philosophy and the politics of the Continent, they endeavoured to substitute cosmopolitan for national principles; and they baptized the new scheme of politics with the plausible name of "Liberalism." Far be it from me for a moment to intimate that a country like England should not profit by the political experience of Continental nations of not inferior civilisation; far be it from me for a moment to maintain that the party which then obtained power and which has since generally possessed it did not make many suggestions for our public life that were of great value, and bring forward many measures which, though changes, were nevertheless improvements. But the tone and tendency of Liberalism cannot be long concealed. It is to attack the institutions of the country under the name of Reform, and to make war on the manners and customs of the people of this country under the pretext of Progress. During the forty years that have elapsed since the commencement of this new system—although the superficial have seen upon its surface only the contentions of political parties—the real state of affairs has been this: the attempt of one party to establish in this country cos-

---

1. William Pitt (1759–1806), prime minister 1783–1801 and 1804–6; William Wyndham Grenville (1759–1834), foreign secretary under Pitt.

mopolitan ideas, and the efforts of another—unconscious efforts, sometimes, but always continued—to recur to and resume those national principles to which they attribute the greatness and glory of the country. . . . Now, I have always been of opinion that the Tory party has three great objects. The first is to maintain the institutions of the country—not from any sentiment of political superstition, but because we believe that it embodies the principles upon which a community like England can alone safely rest. The principles of liberty, of order, of law, and of religion ought not to be entrusted to individual opinion or to the caprice and passion of multitudes, but should be embodied in a form of permanence and power. We associate with the Monarchy the ideas which it represents—the majesty of law, the administration of justice, the fountain of mercy and of honour. We know that in the Estates of the Realm and the privileges they enjoy, is the best security for public liberty and good government. We believe that a national profession of faith can only be maintained by an Established Church, and that no society is safe unless there is a public recognition of the Providential government of the world, and of the future responsibility of man. . . .

. . . Gentlemen, I have referred to what I look upon as the first object of the Tory party—namely, to maintain the institutions of the country, and reviewing what has occurred, and referring to the present temper of the times upon these subjects, I think that the Tory party, or, as I will venture to call it, the National party, has everything to encourage it. I think that the nation, tested by many and severe trials, has arrived at the conclusion which we have always maintained, that it is the first duty of England to maintain its institutions, because to them we principally ascribe the power and prosperity of the country.

Gentlemen, there is another and second great object of the Tory party. If the first is to maintain the institutions of the country, the second is, in my opinion, to uphold the Empire of England. If you look to the history of this country since the advent of Liberalism—40 years ago—you will find that there has been no effort so continuous, so subtle, supported by so much energy, and carried on with so much ability and acumen, as the attempts of Liberalism to effect the disintegration of the Empire of England. And, gentlemen, of all its efforts, this is the one which has been the nearest to success. Statesmen of the highest character, writers of the most distinguished ability, the most organised and efficient means have been employed in this endeavour. It has been proved to all of us that we have lost money by our Colonies. It has been shewn with precise, with mathematical demonstration, that there never was a jewel in the Crown of England that was so truly costly as the possession of India. How often has it been suggested that we should at once emancipate ourselves from this incubus. Well, that result was nearly accomplished. When those subtle views were adopted by the country under the plausible plea of granting self-government to the Colonies, I confess that I myself thought that the tie was broken. Not that I for one object to self-government. I cannot conceive how our distant Colonies can have their affairs administered except by self-government. But self-government, in my opinion, when it was conceded, ought to have been conceded as part of a great policy of Imperial consolidation. It ought to have been accompanied by an Imperial tariff, by securities for the people of England for the enjoyment of the unappropriated lands which belonged to the Sovereign as their trustee, and by a military code which should have precisely defined the means and the responsibilities by which the Colonies should be defended, and by which, if necessary, this country should call for aid from the Colonies themselves. It ought, further, to have been accompanied by the institution of some representative council in the metropolis, which would have brought the Colonies into constant and continuous relations with the Home Government. All this, however, was omitted because those who advised that policy—and I believe their convictions were sincere—looked upon the Colonies of England, looked even upon our connection with India, as a burden upon this country, viewing everything in a financial aspect, and totally passing by those moral and political considerations which make nations great, and by the influence of which alone men are distinguished from animals. Well, what has been the result of this attempt during the reign of Liberalism for the disintegration of the Empire? It has entirely failed. But how has it failed? Through the sympathy of the Colonies with the Mother Country. They have decided that the Empire shall not be destroyed, and in my opinion no Minister in this country will do his duty who neglects any opportunity of reconstructing as much as possible our Colonial Empire, and of responding to those distant sympathies which may become the source of incalculable strength and happiness to this land. Therefore, gentlemen, with respect to the second great object of the Tory party also—the maintenance of the Empire—public opinion appears to be in favour of our principles—that public opinion which, I am bound to say, thirty years ago, was not favourable to our principles, and which, during a long interval of controversy, in the interval had been doubtful.

Gentlemen, another great object of the Tory party, and one not inferior to the maintenance of the Empire, or the upholding of our institutions, is the elevation of the condition of the people. Let us see in this great struggle between Toryism and Liberalism that has prevailed in this country during the last forty years what are the salient features. It must be obvious to all who consider the condition of the multitude with a desire to improve and elevate it, that no important step can be gained unless you can effect some reduction of their hours of labour and humanise their toil. The great problem is to be able to achieve such results without violating those principles of economic truth upon which the prosperity of all States depends. . . . And I can tell you this, gentlemen, from personal conversation with some of the most intelligent of the labouring class—and I think there are many of them in this room who can bear witness to what I say—that the policy of the Tory party—the hereditary, the traditionary policy of the Tory party, that would improve the condition of the people—is more appreciated by the people than the ineffable mysteries and all the pains and penalties of the Ballot Bill. Gentlemen, is that wonderful? Consider the condition of the great body of the working classes of this country. They are in possession of personal privileges—of personal rights and liberties—which are not enjoyed by the aristocracies of other countries. Recently they have obtained—and wisely obtained—a great extension of political rights; and when the people of England see that under the constitution of this country, by means of the constitutional cause which my right hon. friend the Lord Mayor has proposed, they possess every personal right of freedom, and, according to the conviction of the whole country, also an adequate concession of political rights, is it at all wonderful that they should wish to elevate and improve their condition, and is it unreasonable that they should ask the Legislature to assist them in that behest as far as it is consistent with the general welfare of the realm?. . .

Before sitting down, I would make one remark particularly applicable to those whom I am now addressing. This is a numerous assembly; this is an assembly individually influential; but it is not on account of its numbers, it is not on account of its individual influence, that I find it to me deeply interesting. It is because I know that I am addressing a representative assembly. It is because I know that there are men here who come from all districts and all quarters of England, who represent classes and powerful societies, and who meet here not merely for the pleasure of a festival, but because they believe that our assembling together may lead to national advantage. Yes, I tell all who are here present that there is a responsibility which you have incurred to-day, and which you must meet like men. When you return to your homes, when you return to your counties and to your cities, you must tell to all those whom you can influence that the time is at hand, that, at least, it cannot be far distant when England will have to decide between national and cosmopolitan principles. The issue is not a mean one. It is whether you will be content to be a comfortable England, modelled and moulded upon Continental principles and meeting in due course an inevitable fate, or whether you will be a great country,—an Imperial country—a country where your sons, when they rise, rise to paramount positions, and obtain not merely the esteem of their countrymen, but command the respect of the world. . . .

# John Stuart Mill

## THE SUBJECTION OF WOMEN

*Liberal philosopher and social reformer, John Stuart Mill earned the respect of his readers with his philosophical treatises on political economy, logic, government, and individual liberty. Mill's commitment to women's rights was lifelong, beginning publicly in 1824 with an essay he published in the Utilitarian* Westminster Review. *His belief in women's abilities and the need for women's legal and political emancipation was fostered by his training in philosophy as well as his encounters with intellectual, politically astute women, including Harriet MARTINEAU, Sarah Austin, Harriet Grote, and especially Harriet Taylor, who eventually became his wife, and Helen Taylor, her daughter. In 1867, during the Parliamentary debates on the proposed extension of the franchise, Mill moved that the word "man" in the bill be replaced by the word "person." The motion did not carry, but it generated some interest. Mill continued to raise the issue by helping to form the National Society for Women's Suffrage and by publishing* The Subjection of Women *in 1869, which was written, according to Mill himself, with Harriet Taylor Mill's help in 1861.*

*Subjection generated the most controversy of all Mill's works. James Fitzjames Stephens and Herbert SPENCER disliked it. Anne Mozley in* Blackwood's Magazine *and Margaret*

*OLIPHANT in the* Edinburgh Review *attacked it. But other women, including Elizabeth Cady Stanton and Barbara BODICHON, were delighted by Mill's insight into women's oppression. In* The Subjection of Women, *Mill challenged his readers' assumptions about the supposed "nature" of women, but he avoided taking what would have been considered extreme political positions—on divorce, for example. Although a bill for women's suffrage was not enacted until 1918, Mill's influence on the issue led indirectly to support for other significant reforms, including the Married Women's Property Act, and the promotion of women's education. The selection below is from chapter 1.*                                LMF

THE OBJECT OF THIS ESSAY is to explain as clearly as I am able, the grounds of an opinion which I have held from the very earliest period when I had formed any opinions at all on social or political matters, and which, instead of being weakened or modified, has been constantly growing stronger by the progress of reflection and the experience of life: That the principle which regulates the existing social relations between the two sexes—the legal subordination of one sex to the other—is wrong in itself, and now one of the chief hindrances to human improvement; and that it ought to be replaced by a principle of perfect equality, admitting no power or privilege on the one side, nor disability on the other.

The very words necessary to express the task I have undertaken, show how arduous it is. But it would be a mistake to suppose that the difficulty of the case must lie in the insufficiency or obscurity of the grounds of reason on which my conviction rests. The difficulty is that which exists in all cases in which there is a mass of feeling to be contended against. So long as an opinion is strongly rooted in the feelings, it gains rather than loses in stability by having a preponderating weight of argument against it. For if it were accepted as a result of argument, the refutation of the argument might shake the solidity of the conviction; but when it rests solely on feeling, the worse it fares in argumentative contest, the more persuaded its adherents are that their feeling must have some deeper ground, which the arguments do not reach; and while the feeling remains, it is always throwing up fresh intrenchments of argument to repair any breach made in the old. And there are so many causes tending to make the feelings connected with this subject the most intense and most deeply-rooted of all those which gather round and protect old institutions and customs, that we need not wonder to find them as yet less undermined and loosened than any of the rest by the progress of the great modern spiritual and social transition; nor suppose that the barbarisms to which men cling longest must be less barbarisms than those which they earlier shake off. . . .

The generality of a practice is in some cases a strong presumption that it is, or at all events once was, conducive to laudable ends. This is the case, when the practice was first adopted, or afterwards kept up, as a means to such ends, and was grounded on experience of the mode in which they could be most effectually attained. If the authority of men over women, when first established, had been the result of a conscientious comparison between different modes of constituting the government of society; if, after trying various other modes of social organization—the government of women over men, equality between the two, and such mixed and divided modes of government as might be invented—it had been decided, on the testimony of experience, that the mode in which women are wholly under the rule of men, having no share at all in public concerns, and each in private being under the legal obligation of obedience to the man with whom she has associated her destiny, was the arrangement most conducive to the happiness and well being of both; its general adoption might then be fairly thought to be some evidence that, at the time when it was adopted, it was the best: though even then the considerations which recommended it may, like so many other primeval social facts of the greatest importance, have subsequently, in the course of ages, ceased to exist. But the state of the case is in every respect the reverse of this. In the first place, the opinion in favour of the present system, which entirely subordinates the weaker sex to the stronger, rests upon theory only; for there never has been trial made of any other: so that experience, in the sense in which it is vulgarly opposed to theory, cannot be pretended to have pronounced any verdict. And in the second place, the adoption of this system of inequality never was the result of deliberation, or forethought, or any social ideas, or any notion whatever of what conduced to the benefit of humanity or the good order of society. It arose simply from the fact that from the very earliest twilight of human society, every woman (owing to the value attached to her by men, combined with her inferiority in muscular strength) was found in a state of bondage to some man. Laws and systems of polity always begin by recognising the relations they find already existing between individuals. They convert what was a mere physical fact into a legal right, give it the sanction of society, and principally aim at the substitution of public and organized means of asserting and protecting these rights, instead of the irregular and lawless conflict of physical strength. Those who had already been compelled to obedience became in this manner legally bound to it. Slavery, from being a mere affair of force between the master and the slave, became regularized and a matter of compact among the masters, who, binding themselves to one another for common protection, guaranteed by their collective strength the private possessions of each, including his slaves. In early times, the great majority of the male sex were slaves, as well as the whole of the female. And many ages elapsed, some of them ages of high cultivation, before any thinker was bold enough to question the rightfulness, and the absolute social necessity, either of the one slavery or of the other. By degrees such thinkers did arise: and (the general progress of society assisting) the slavery of the male sex has, in all the countries of Christian Europe at least (though, in one of them, only within the last few years[1]) been at length abolished, and that of the female sex has been gradually changed into a milder form of dependence. But this dependence, as it exists at present, is not an original institution, taking a fresh start from considerations of justice and social expediency—it is the primitive state of slavery lasting on, through successive mitigations and modifications occasioned by the same causes which have softened the general manners, and brought all human relations more under the control of justice and the influence of humanity. It has not lost the taint of its brutal origin. No presumption in its favour, therefore, can be drawn from the fact of its existence. The only such presumption which it could be supposed to have, must be grounded on its having lasted till now, when so many other things which came down from the same odious source have been

1. Mill probably alludes to the emancipation of the serfs in Russia in 1861.

done away with. And this, indeed, is what makes it strange to ordinary ears, to hear it asserted that the inequality of rights between men and women has no other source than the law of the strongest. . . .

If people are mostly so little aware how completely, during the greater part of the duration of our species, the law of force was the avowed rule of general conduct, any other being only a special and exceptional consequence of peculiar ties—and from how very recent a date it is that the affairs of society in general have been even pretended to be regulated according to any moral law; as little do people remember or consider, how institutions and customs which never had any ground but the law of force, last on into ages and states of general opinion which never would have permitted their first establishment. Less than forty years ago, Englishmen might still by law hold human beings in bondage as saleable property: within the present century they might kidnap them and carry them off, and work them literally to death. This absolutely extreme case of the law of force, condemned by those who can tolerate almost every other form of arbitrary power, and which, of all others, presents features the most revolting to the feelings of all who look at it from an impartial position, was the law of civilized and Christian England within the memory of persons now living: and in one half of Anglo-Saxon America three or four years ago, not only did slavery exist, but the slave trade, and the breeding of slaves expressly for it, was a general practice between slave states. Yet not only was there a greater strength of sentiment against it, but, in England at least, a less amount either of feeling or of interest in favour of it, than of any other of the customary abuses of force: for its motive was the love of gain, unmixed and undisguised; and those who profited by it were a very small numerical fraction of the country, while the natural feeling of all who were not personally interested in it, was unmitigated abhorrence. So extreme an instance makes it almost superfluous to refer to any other: but consider the long duration of absolute monarchy. In England at present it is the almost universal conviction that military despotism is a case of the law of force, having no other origin or justification. Yet in all the great nations of Europe except England it either still exists, or has only just ceased to exist, and has even now a strong party favourable to it in all ranks of the people, especially among persons of station and consequence. Such is the power of an established system, even when far from universal; when not only in almost every period of history there have been great and well-known examples of the contrary system, but these have almost invariably been afforded by the most illustrious and most prosperous communities. In this case, too, the possessor of the undue power, the person directly interested in it, is only one person, while those who are subject to it and suffer from it are literally all the rest. The yoke is naturally and necessarily humiliating to all persons, except the one who is on the throne, together with, at most, the one who expects to succeed to it. How different are these cases from that of the power of men over women! I am not now prejudging the question of its justifiableness. I am showing how vastly more permanent it could not but be, even if not justifiable, than these other dominations which have nevertheless lasted down to our own time. Whatever gratification of pride there is in the possession of power, and whatever personal interest in its exercise, is in this case not confined to a limited class, but common to the whole male sex. Instead of being, to most of its supporters, a thing desirable chiefly in the abstract, or, like the political ends usually contended for by factions, of little private importance to any but the leaders; it comes home to the person and hearth of every male head of a family, and of every one who looks forward to being so. The clodhopper exercises, or is to exercise, his share of the power equally with the highest nobleman. And the case is that in which the desire of power is the strongest: for every one who desires power, desires it most over those who are nearest to him, with whom his life is passed, with whom he has most concerns in common, and in whom any independence of his authority is oftenest likely to interfere with his individual preferences. If, in the other cases specified, powers manifestly grounded only on force, and having so much less to support them, are so slowly and with so much difficulty got rid of, much more must it be so with this, even if it rests on no better foundation than those. We must consider, too, that the possessors of the power have facilities in this case, greater than in any other, to prevent any uprising against it. Every one of the subjects lives under the very eye, and almost, it may be said, in the hands, of one of the masters—in closer intimacy with him than with any of her fellow-subjects; with no means of combining against him, no power of even locally overmastering him, and, on the other hand, with the strongest motives for seeking his favour and avoiding to give him offence. In struggles for political emancipation, everybody knows how often its champions are bought off by bribes, or daunted by terrors. In the case of women, each individual of the subject-class is in a chronic state of bribery and intimidation combined. In setting up the standard of resistance, a large number of the leaders, and still more of the followers, must make an almost complete sacrifice of the pleasures or the alleviations of their own individual lot. If ever any system of privilege and enforced subjection had its yoke tightly riveted on the necks of those who are kept down by it, this has. I have not yet shown that it is a wrong system: but every one who is capable of thinking on the subject must see that even if it is, it was certain to outlast all other forms of unjust authority. And when some of the grossest of the other forms still exist in many civilized countries, and have only recently been got rid of in others, it would be strange if that which is so much the deepest-rooted had yet been perceptibly shaken anywhere. There is more reason to wonder that the protests and testimonies against it should have been so numerous and so weighty as they are. . . .

. . . The subjection of women to men being a universal custom, any departure from it quite naturally appears unnatural. But how entirely, even in this case, the feeling is dependent on custom, appears by ample experience. Nothing so much astonishes the people of distant parts of the world, when they first learn anything about England, as to be told that it is under a queen: the thing seems to them so unnatural as to be almost incredible. To Englishmen this does not seem in the least degree unnatural, because they are used to it; but they do feel it unnatural that women should be soldiers or members of parliament. In the feudal ages, on the contrary, war and politics were not thought unnatural to women, because not unusual; it seemed natural that women of the privileged classes should be of manly character, inferior in nothing but bodily strength to their husbands and fathers. The independence of women seemed rather less unnatural to the Greeks than to other ancients, on account of the fabulous Amazons (whom they believed to be historical), and the partial example afforded by the Spartan women; who, though no less subordinate by law than in other Greek states, were more free in fact, and being trained to bodily exercises in the same manner with men, gave ample proof that they were not naturally disqualified for them. There can be little doubt that Spartan experience suggested to Plato, among many other of his doctrines, that of the social and political equality of the two sexes.[2]

But, it will be said, the rule of men over women differs from all these others in not being a rule of force: it is accepted voluntarily; women make no complaint, and are consenting parties to it. . . .

All causes, social and natural, combine to make it unlikely that women should be collectively rebellious to the power of men. They are so far in a position different from all other subject classes, that their masters require something more from them than actual service. Men do not want solely the obedience of women, they want their sentiments. All men, except the most brutish, desire to have, in the woman most nearly connected with them, not a forced slave, but a willing one, not a slave merely, but a favourite. They have therefore put everything in practice to enslave their minds. The masters of all other slaves rely, for maintaining obedience, on fear; either fear of themselves, or religious fears. The masters of women wanted more than simple obedience, and they turned the whole force of education to effect their purpose. All women are brought up from the very earliest years in the belief that their ideal of character is the very opposite to that of men; not self-will, and government by self-control, but submission, and yielding to the control of others. All the moralities tell them that it is the duty of women, and all the current sentimentalities that it is their nature, to live for others; to make complete abnegation of themselves, and to have no life but in their affections. And by their affections are meant the only ones they are allowed to have—those to the men with whom they are connected, or to the children who constitute an additional and indefeasible tie between them and a man. When we put together three things—first, the natural attraction between opposite sexes; secondly, the wife's entire dependence on the husband, every privilege or pleasure she has being either his gift, or depending entirely on his will; and lastly, that the principal object of human pursuit, consideration, and all objects of social ambition, can in general be sought or obtained by her only through him, it would be a miracle if the object of being attractive to men had not become the polar star of feminine education and formation of character. And, this great means of influence over the minds of women having been acquired, an instinct of selfishness made men avail themselves of it to the utmost as a means of holding women in subjection, by representing to them meekness, submissiveness, and resignation of all individual will into the hands of a man, as an essential part of sexual attractiveness. Can it be doubted that any of the other yokes which mankind have succeeded in breaking, would have subsisted till now if the same means had existed, and had been as sedulously used, to bow down their minds to it? If it had been made the object of the life of every young plebeian to find personal favour in the eyes of some patrician, of every young serf with some seigneur; if domestication with him, and a share of his personal affections, had been held out as the prize which they all should look out for,

---

2. See Plato, *Republic*, 5.

the most gifted and aspiring being able to reckon on the most desirable prizes; and if, when this prize had been obtained, they had been shut out by a wall of brass from all interests not centering in him, all feelings and desires but those which he shared or inculcated; would not serfs and seigneurs, plebeians and patricians, have been as broadly distinguished at this day as men and women are? and would not all but a thinker here and there, have believed the distinction to be a fundamental and unalterable fact in human nature?

The preceding considerations are amply sufficient to show that custom, however universal it may be, affords in this case no presumption, and ought not to create any prejudice, in favour of the arrangements which place women in social and political subjection to men. But I may go farther, and maintain that the course of history, and the tendencies of progressive human society, afford not only no presumption in favour of this system of inequality of rights, but a strong one against it; and that, so far as the whole course of human improvement up to this time, the whole stream of modern tendencies, warrants any inference on the subject, it is, that this relic of the past is discordant with the future, and must necessarily disappear.

For, what is the peculiar character of the modern world—the difference which chiefly distinguishes modern institutions, modern social ideas, modern life itself, from those of times long past? It is, that human beings are no longer born to their place in life, and chained down by an inexorable bond to the place they are born to, but are free to employ their faculties, and such favourable chances as offer, to achieve the lot which may appear to them most desirable. Human society of old was constituted on a very different principle. All were born to a fixed social position, and were mostly kept in it by law, or interdicted from any means by which they could emerge from it. As some men are born white and others black, so some were born slaves and others freemen and citizens; some were born patricians, other plebeians; some were born feudal nobles, others commoners and roturiers.[3] A slave or serf could never make himself free, nor, except by the will of his master, become so. In most European countries it was not till towards the close of the middle ages, and as a consequence of the growth of regal power, that commoners could be ennobled. Even among nobles, the eldest son was born the exclusive heir to the paternal possessions, and a long time elapsed before it was fully established that the father could disinherit him. Among the industrious classes, only those who were born members of a guild, or were admitted into it by its members, could lawfully practise their calling within its local limits; and nobody could practise any calling deemed important, in any but the legal manner—by processes authoritatively prescribed. Manufacturers have stood in the pillory for presuming to carry on their business by new and improved methods. In modern Europe, and most in those parts of it which have participated most largely in all other modern improvements, diametrically opposite doctrines now prevail. Law and government do not undertake to prescribe by whom any social or industrial operation shall or shall not be conducted, or what modes of conducting them shall be lawful. These things are left to the unfettered choice of individuals. . . .

3. Plebeians.

At present, in the more improved countries, the disabilities of women are the only case, save one, in which laws and institutions take persons at their birth, and ordain that they shall never in all their lives be allowed to compete for certain things. The one exception is that of royalty. Persons still are born to the throne; no one, not of the reigning family, can ever occupy it, and no one even of that family can, by any means but the course of hereditary succession, attain it. All other dignities and social advantages are open to the whole male sex: many indeed are only attainable by wealth, but wealth may be striven for by any one, and is actually obtained by many men of the very humblest origin. The difficulties, to the majority, are indeed insuperable without the aid of fortunate accidents; but no male human being is under any legal ban: neither law nor opinion superadd artificial obstacles to the natural ones. Royalty, as I have said, is excepted: but in this case every one feels it to be an exception—an anomaly in the modern world, in marked opposition to its customs and principles, and to be justified only by extraordinary special expediencies, which, though individuals and nations differ in estimating their weight, unquestionably do in fact exist. But in this exceptional case, in which a high social function is, for important reasons, bestowed on birth instead of being put up to competition, all free nations contrive to adhere in substance to the principle from which they nominally derogate; for they circumscribe this high function by conditions avowedly intended to prevent the person to whom it ostensibly belongs from really performing it; while the person by whom it is performed, the responsible minister, does obtain the post by a competition from which no full-grown citizen of the male sex is legally excluded. The disabilities, therefore, to which women are subject from the mere fact of their birth, are the solitary examples of the kind in modern legislation. In no instance except this, which comprehends half the human race, are the higher social functions closed against any one by a fatality of birth which no exertions, and no change of circumstances, can overcome; for even religious disabilities (besides that in England and in Europe they have practically almost ceased to exist) do not close any career to the disqualified person in case of conversion. . . .

Neither does it avail anything to say that the *nature* of the two sexes adapts them to their present functions and position, and renders these appropriate to them. Standing on the ground of common sense and the constitution of the human mind, I deny that any one knows, or can know, the nature of the two sexes, as long as they have only been seen in their present relation to one another. If men had ever been found in society without women, or women without men, or if there had been a society of men and women in which the women were not under the control of the men, something might have been positively known about the mental and moral differences which may be inherent in the nature of each. What is now called the nature of women is an eminently artificial thing—the result of forced repression in some directions, unnatural stimulation in others. It may be asserted without scruple, that no other class of dependents have had their character so entirely distorted from its natural proportions by their relation with their masters; for, if conquered and slave races have been, in some respects, more forcibly repressed, whatever in them has not been crushed down by an iron heel has generally been let alone, and if left with any liberty of development, it has developed itself according to its own laws;

but in the case of women, a hot-house and stove cultivation has always been carried on of some of the capabilities of their nature, for the benefit and pleasure of their masters. Then, because certain products of the general vital force sprout luxuriantly and reach a great development in this heated atmosphere and under this active nurture and watering, while other shoots from the same root, which are left outside in the wintry air, with ice purposely heaped all round them, have a stunted growth, and some are burnt off with fire and disappear; men, with that inability to recognise their own work which distinguishes the unanalytic mind, indolently believe that the tree grows of itself in the way they have made it grow, and that it would die if one half of it were not kept in a vapour bath and the other half in the snow.

Of all difficulties which impede the progress of thought, and the formation of well-grounded opinions on life and social arrangements, the greatest is now the unspeakable ignorance and inattention of mankind in respect to the influences which form human character. Whatever any portion of the human species now are, or seem to be, such, it is supposed, they have a natural tendency to be: even when the most elementary knowledge of the circumstances in which they have been placed, clearly points out the causes that have made them what they are. Because a cottier deeply in arrears to his landlord is not industrious, there are people who think that the Irish are naturally idle. Because constitutions can be overthrown when the authorities appointed to execute them turn their arms against them, there are people who think the French incapable of free government. Because the Greeks cheated the Turks, and the Turks only plundered the Greeks, there are persons who think that the Turks are naturally more sincere: and because women, as is often said, care nothing about politics except their personalities, it is supposed that the general good is naturally less interesting to women than to men. History, which is now so much better understood than formerly, teaches another lesson. if only by showing the extraordinary susceptibility of human nature to external influences, and the extreme variableness of those of its manifestations which are supposed to be most universal and uniform. But in history, as in travelling, men usually see only what they already had in their own minds; and few learn much from history, who do not bring much with them to its study.

Hence, in regard to that most difficult question, what are the natural differences between the two sexes—a subject on which it is impossible in the present state of society to obtain complete and correct knowledge—while almost everybody dogmatizes upon it, almost all neglect and make light of the only means by which any partial insight can be obtained into it. This is, an analytic study of the most important department of psychology, the laws of the influence of circumstances on character. For, however great and apparently ineradicable the moral and intellectual differences between men and women might be, the evidence of their being natural differences could only be negative. Those only could be inferred to be natural which could not possibly be artificial—the residuum, after deducting every characteristic of either sex which can admit of being explained from education or external circumstances. The profoundest knowledge of the laws of the formation of character is indispensable to entitle any one to affirm even that there is any difference, much more what the difference is, between the two sexes considered as moral and rational beings; and since no one, as yet, has that knowledge, (for there is hardly any subject which, in proportion to its importance, has been so little stud-ied), no one is thus far entitled to any positive opinion on the subject. Conjectures are all that can at present be made; conjectures more or less probable, according as more or less authorized by such knowledge as we yet have of the laws of psychology, as applied to the formation of character.

Even the preliminary knowledge, what the differences between the sexes now are, apart from all question as to how they are made what they are, is still in the crudest and most incomplete state. Medical practitioners and physiologists have ascertained, to some extent, the differences in bodily constitution; and this is an important element to the psy-chologist: but hardly any medical practitioner is a psychologist. Respecting the mental characteristics of women; their observations are of no more worth than those of common men. It is a subject on which nothing final can be known, so long as those who alone can really know it, women themselves, have given but little testimony, and that little, mostly suborned. . . . The most favourable case which a man can generally have for studying the character of a woman, is that of his own wife: for the opportunities are greater, and the cases of complete sympathy not so unspeakably rare. And in fact, this is the source from which any knowledge worth having on the subject has, I believe, generally come. But most men have not had the opportunity of studying in this way more than a single case: accordingly one can, to an almost laughable degree, infer what a man's wife is like, from his opinions about women in general. To make even this one case yield any result, the woman must be worth knowing, and the man not only a competent judge, but of a char-acter so sympathetic in itself, and so well adapted to hers, that he can either read her mind by sympathetic intuition, or has nothing in himself which makes her shy of disclos-ing it. Hardly anything, I believe, can be more rare than this conjunction. It often happens that there is the most complete unity of feeling and community of interests as to all exter-nal things, yet the one has as little admission into the internal life of the other as if they were common acquaintance. Even with true affection, authority on the one side and sub-ordination on the other prevent perfect confidence. Though nothing may be intentional-ly withheld, much is not shown. In the analogous relation of parent and child, the corre-sponding phenomenon must have been in the observation of every one. As between father and son, how many are the cases in which the father, in spite of real affection on both sides, obviously to all the world does not know, nor suspect, parts of the son's character familiar to his companions and equals. The truth is, that the position of looking up to another is extremely unpropitious to complete sincerity and openness with him. The fear of losing ground in his opinion or in his feelings is so strong, that even in an upright char-acter, there is an unconscious tendency to show only the best side, or the side which, though not the best, is that which he most likes to see: and it may be confidently said that thorough knowledge of one another hardly ever exists, but between persons who, besides being intimates, are equals. How much more true, then, must all this be, when the one is not only under the authority of the other, but has it inculcated on her as a duty to reck-on everything else subordinate to his comfort and pleasure, and to let him neither see nor feel anything coming from her, except what is agreeable to him. All these difficulties stand in the way of a man's obtaining any thorough knowledge even of the one woman whom alone, in general, he has sufficient opportunity of studying. When we further consider that to understand one woman is not necessarily to understand any other woman; that even if he could study many women of one rank, or of one country, he would not thereby understand women of other ranks or countries; and even if he did, they are still only the women of a single period of history; we may safely assert that the knowledge which men can acquire of women, even as they have been and are, without reference to what they might be, is wretchedly imperfect and superficial, and always will be so, until women themselves have told all that they have to tell.

And this time has not come; nor will it come otherwise than gradually. It is but of yesterday that women have either been qualified by literary accomplishments, or permitted by society, to tell anything to the general public. As yet very few of them dare tell anything, which men, on whom their literary success depends, are unwilling to hear. Let us remember in what manner, up to a very recent time, the expression, even by a male author, of uncustomary opinions, or what are deemed eccentric feelings, usually was, and in some degree still is, received; and we may form some faint conception under what impediments a woman, who is brought up to think custom and opinion her sovereign rule, attempts to express in books anything drawn from the depths of her own nature. The greatest woman who has left writings behind her sufficient to give her an eminent rank in the literature of her country, thought it necessary to prefix as a motto to her boldest work, "Un homme peut braver l'opinion; une femme doit s'y soumettre."[4] The greater part of what women write about women is mere sycophancy to men. In the case of unmarried women, much of it seems only intended to increase their chance of a husband. Many, both married and unmarried, overstep the mark, and inculcate a servility beyond what is desired or relished by any man, except the very vulgarest. But this is not so often the case as, even at a quite late period, it still was. Literary women are becoming more freespoken, and more willing to express their real sentiments. Unfortunately, in this country especially, they are themselves such artificial products, that their sentiments are compounded of a small element of individual observation and consciousness, and a very large one of acquired associations. This will be less and less the case, but it will remain true to a great extent, as long as social institutions do not admit the same free development of originality in women which is possible to men. When that time comes, and not before, we shall see, and not merely hear, as much as it is necessary to know of the nature of women, and the adaptation of other things to it. . . .

# AUTOBIOGRAPHY

*Mill hoped that his autobiography would serve as an illustration of an unusual education, as an example of continuous intellectual and moral development in an age of transition,*

---

4. Title-page of Mme. de Stael's "Delphine." [Mill's note] Translation: "A man can defy prejudice; a woman must submit to it."

*and as a means by which others could reflect on their own intellectual development. Much of the* Autobiography *describes Mill's "early training" up to the age of fourteen, an education conducted by his father, Utilitarian James Mill, according to theories adapted partly from Jeremy Bentham, the founder of Utilitarianism. J. S. Mill studied Greek at the age of three; Latin at seven or eight; logic, algebra, and calculus at twelve; and political economy at thirteen. In 1826, when Mill was successfully launched upon a professional career as an employee of the East India Company and a political essayist and Radical reformer, he experienced an emotional and intellectual breakdown. The selection included here from chapter 5, "A Crisis in My Mental History," describes this breakdown and its effects on his life and thought. The crisis was attributed by some Victorian readers to overwork and fatigue; it has been seen also as a subtle indictment of James Mill's educational "system" and, recently, as an expression of Mill's suppressed anger at his father's control of his life. However one psychoanalyzes J. S. Mill, he himself saw the episode as a turning point in his emotional and intellectual life, one that led him to recognize the importance of emotion and "internal culture" and to develop the less mechanistic, more humanized Utilitarianism of his later writings.*

*With the assistance of his wife, Harriet Taylor Mill, J. S. Mill completed a draft of his* Autobiography *by 1856. He added to it in 1869–70, and it was published in 1873.* LMF

## CHAPTER 1

### CHILDHOOD AND EARLY EDUCATION

It seems proper that I should prefix to the following biographical sketch, some mention of the reasons which have made me think it desirable that I should leave behind me such a memorial of so uneventful a life as mine. I do not for a moment imagine that any part of what I have to relate, can be interesting to the public as a narrative, or as being connected with myself. But I have thought that in an age in which education, and its improvement, are the subject of more, if not of profounder study than at any former period of English history, it may be useful that there should be some record of an education which was unusual and remarkable, and which, whatever else it may have done, has proved how much more than is commonly supposed may be taught, and well taught, in those early years which, in the common modes of what is called instruction, are little better than wasted. It has also seemed to me that in an age of transition in opinions, there may be somewhat both of interest and of benefit in noting the successive phases of any mind which was always pressing forward, equally ready to learn and to unlearn either from its own thoughts or from those of others. But a motive which weighs more with me than either of these, is a desire to make acknowledgment of the debts which my intellectual and moral development owes to other persons; some of them of recognised eminence, others less known than they deserve to be, and the one to whom most of all is due, one whom the world had no opportunity of knowing. . . .[1]

1. Mill refers to his wife, Harriet Taylor Mill.

# CHAPTER 5

A CRISIS IN MY MENTAL HISTORY. ONE STAGE ONWARD

. . . From the winter of 1821, when I first read Bentham,[2] and especially from the commencement of the Westminster Review, I had what might truly be called an object in life; to be a reformer of the world. My conception of my own happiness was entirely identified with this object. The personal sympathies I wished for were those of fellow labourers in this enterprise. I endeavoured to pick up as many flowers as I could by the way; but as a serious and permanent personal satisfaction to rest upon, my whole reliance was placed on this; and I was accustomed to felicitate myself on the certainty of a happy life which I enjoyed, through placing my happiness in something durable and distant, in which some progress might be always making, while it could never be exhausted by complete attainment. This did very well for several years, during which the general improvement going on in the world and the idea of myself as engaged with others in struggling to promote it, seemed enough to fill up an interesting and animated existence. But the time came when I awakened from this as from a dream. It was in the autumn of 1826. I was in a dull state of nerves, such as everybody is occasionally liable to; unsusceptible to enjoyment or pleasurable excitement; one of those moods when what is pleasure at other times, becomes insipid or indifferent; the state, I should think, in which converts to Methodism usually are, when smitten by their first "conviction of sin." In this frame of mind it occurred to me to put the question directly to myself: "Suppose that all your objects in life were realized; that all the changes in institutions and opinions which you are looking forward to, could be completely effected at this very instant: would this be a great joy and happiness to you?" And an irrepressible self consciousness distinctly answered, "No!" At this my heart sank within me: the whole foundation on which my life was constructed fell down. All my happiness was to have been found in the continual pursuit of this end. The end had ceased to charm, and how could there ever again be any interest in the means? I seemed to have nothing left to live for.

At first I hoped that the cloud would pass away of itself; but it did not. A night's sleep, the sovereign remedy for the smaller vexations of life, had no effect on it. I awoke to a renewed consciousness of the woful fact. I carried it with me into all companies, into all occupations. Hardly anything had power to cause me even a few minutes' oblivion of it. For some months the cloud seemed to grow thicker and thicker. The lines in Coleridge's "Dejection"—I was not then acquainted with them—exactly describe my case:

> "A grief without a pang, void, dark and drear,
> A drowsy, stifled, unimpassioned grief,
> Which finds no natural outlet or relief
> In word, or sigh, or tear."

In vain I sought relief from my favourite books; those memorials of past nobleness and greatness from which I had always hitherto drawn strength and animation. I read them

---

2. Jeremy Bentham (1748–1832), founder of Utilitarianism, which is sometimes called Benthamism or Philosophical Radicalism.

now without feeling, or with the accustomed feeling *minus* all its charm; and I became persuaded, that my love of mankind, and of excellence for its own sake, had worn itself out. I sought no comfort by speaking to others of what I felt. If I had loved any one sufficiently to make confiding my griefs a necessity, I should not have been in the condition I was. I felt, too, that mine was not an interesting, or in any way respectable distress. There was nothing in it to attract sympathy. Advice, if I had known where to seek it, would have been most precious. The words of Macbeth to the physician often occurred to my thoughts.[3] But there was no one on whom I could build the faintest hope of such assistance. My father, to whom it would have been natural to me to have recourse in any practical difficulties, was the last person to whom, in such a case as this, I looked for help. Everything convinced me that he had no knowledge of any such mental state as I was suffering from, and that even if he could be made to understand it, he was not the physician who could heal it. My education, which was wholly his work, had been conducted without any regard to the possibility of its ending in this result; and I saw no use in giving him the pain of thinking that his plans had failed, when the failure was probably irremediable, and, at all events, beyond the power of *his* remedies. Of other friends, I had at that time none to whom I had any hope of making my condition intelligible. It was however abundantly intelligible to myself; and the more I dwelt upon it, the more hopeless it appeared.

My course of study had led me to believe, that all mental and moral feelings and qualities, whether of a good or of a bad kind, were the results of association; that we love one thing, and hate another, take pleasure in one sort of action or contemplation, and pain in another sort, through the clinging of pleasurable or painful ideas to those things, from the effect of education or of experience. As a corollary from this, I had always heard it maintained by my father, and was myself convinced, that the object of education should be to form the strongest possible associations of the salutary class; associations of pleasure with all things beneficial to the great whole, and of pain with all things hurtful to it. This doctrine appeared inexpugnable; but it now seemed to me, on retrospect, that my teachers had occupied themselves but superficially with the means of forming and keeping up these salutary associations. They seemed to have trusted altogether to the old familiar instruments, praise and blame, reward and punishment. Now, I did not doubt that by these means, begun early, and applied unremittingly, intense associations of pain and pleasure, especially of pain, might be created, and might produce desires and aversions capable of lasting undiminished to the end of life. But there must always be something artificial and casual in associations thus produced. The pains and pleasures thus forcibly associated with things, are not connected with them by any natural tie; and it is therefore, I thought, essential to the durability of these associations, that they should have become so intense and inveterate as to be practically indissoluble, before the habitual exercise of the power of analysis had commenced. For I now saw, or thought I saw, what I had always before received with incredulity—that the habit of analysis has a tendency to wear away the feelings: as indeed it has, when no other mental habit is cultivated, and the analysing spirit remains without its natural complements and correctives. The very excellence of analysis (I argued) is that it tends to weaken and undermine whatever is the result of prej-

3. "Canst thou not minister to a mind diseas'd?" from William Shakespeare's *Macbeth*, 5.3.

udice; that it enables us mentally to separate ideas which have only casually clung together: and no associations whatever could ultimately resist this dissolving force, were it not
that we owe to analysis our clearest knowledge of the permanent sequences in nature; the
real connexions between Things, not dependent on our will and feelings; natural laws, by
virtue of which, in many cases, one thing is inseparable from another in fact; which laws,
in proportion as they are clearly perceived and imaginatively realized, cause our ideas of
things which are always joined together in Nature, to cohere more and more closely in
our thoughts. Analytic habits may thus even strengthen the associations between causes
and effects, means and ends, but tend altogether to weaken those which are, to speak
familiarly, a *mere* matter of feeling. They are therefore (I thought) favourable to prudence
and clear-sightedness, but a perpetual worm at the root both of the passions and of the
virtues; and, above all, fearfully undermine all desires, and all pleasures, which are the
effects of association, that is, according to the theory I held, all except the purely physical and organic; of the entire insufficiency of which to make life desirable, no one had a
stronger conviction than I had. These were the laws of human nature, by which, as it
seemed to me, I had been brought to my present state. All those to whom I looked up,
were of opinion that the pleasure of sympathy with human beings, and the feelings which
made the good of others, and especially of mankind on a large scale, the object of existence, were the greatest and surest sources of happiness. Of the truth of this I was convinced, but to know that a feeling would make me happy if I had it, did not give me the
feeling. My education, I thought, had failed to create these feelings in sufficient strength
to resist the dissolving influence of analysis, while the whole course of my intellectual
cultivation had made precocious and premature analysis the inveterate habit of my mind.
I was thus, as I said to myself, left stranded at the commencement of my voyage, with a
well-equipped ship and a rudder, but no sail; without any real desire for the ends which
I had been so carefully fitted out to work for: no delight in virtue, or the general good,
but also just as little in anything else. The fountains of vanity and ambition seemed to have
dried up within me, as completely as those of benevolence. I had had (as I reflected) some
gratification of vanity at too early an age: I had obtained some distinction, and felt myself
of some importance, before the desire of distinction and of importance had grown into a
passion: and little as it was which I had attained, yet having been attained too early, like
all pleasures enjoyed too soon, it had made me *blasé* and indifferent to the pursuit. Thus
neither selfish nor unselfish pleasures were pleasures to me. And there seemed no power
in nature sufficient to begin the formation of my character anew, and create in a mind
now irretrievably analytic, fresh associations of pleasure with any of the objects of human
desire.

　　These were the thoughts which mingled with the dry heavy dejection of the melancholy winter of 1826–7. During this time I was not incapable of my usual occupations. I
went on with them mechanically, by the mere force of habit. I had been so drilled in a
certain sort of mental exercise, that I could still carry it on when all the spirit had gone
out of it. I even composed and spoke several speeches at the debating society,[4] how, or
with what degree of success, I know not. Of four years continual speaking at that society,

4. The London Debating Society, which Mill helped to found in 1829.

this is the only year of which I remember next to nothing. Two lines of Coleridge, in whom alone of all writers I have found a true description of what I felt, were often in my thoughts, not at this time (for I had never read them), but in a later period of the same mental malady:

"Work without hope draws nectar in a sieve,
And hope without an object cannot live."[5]

In all probability my case was by no means so peculiar as I fancied it, and I doubt not that many others have passed through a similar state; but the idiosyncrasies of my education had given to the general phenomenon a special character, which made it seem the natural effect of causes that it was hardly possible for time to remove. I frequently asked myself, if I could, or if I was bound to go on living, when life must be passed in this manner. I generally answered to myself, that I did not think I could possibly bear it beyond a year. When, however, not more than half that duration of time had elapsed, a small ray of light broke in upon my gloom. I was reading, accidentally, Marmontel's "Memoires,"[6] and came to the passage which relates his father's death, the distressed position of the family, and the sudden inspiration by which he, then a mere boy, felt and made them feel that he would be everything to them—would supply the place of all that they had lost. A vivid conception of the scene and its feelings came over me, and I was moved to tears. From this moment my burden grew lighter. The oppression of the thought that all feeling was dead within me, was gone. I was no longer hopeless: I was not a stock or a stone. I had still, it seemed, some of the material out of which all worth of character, and all capacity for happiness, are made. Relieved from my ever present sense of irremediable wretchedness, I gradually found that the ordinary incidents of life could again give me some pleasure; that I could again find enjoyment, not intense, but sufficient for cheerfulness, in sunshine and sky, in books, in conversation, in public affairs; and that there was, once more, excitement, though of a moderate kind, in exerting myself for my opinions, and for the public good. Thus the cloud gradually drew off, and I again enjoyed life: and though I had several relapses, some of which lasted many months, I never again was as miserable as I had been.

The experiences of this period had two very marked effects on my opinions and character. In the first place, they led me to adopt a theory of life, very unlike that on which I had before acted, and having much in common with what at that time I certainly had never heard of, the anti-self-consciousness theory of Carlyle.[7] I never, indeed, wavered in the conviction that happiness is the test of all rules of conduct, and the end of life. But I now thought that this end was only to be attained by not making it the direct end. Those only are happy (I thought) who have their minds fixed on some object other than their own happiness; on the happiness of others, on the improvement of mankind, even on some art or pursuit, followed not as a means, but as itself an ideal end. Aiming thus at

---

5. From "Work Without Hope" (1828).
6. Jean François Marmontel (1723–99), French writer and author of *Mémoires d'un père* (1804).
7. See Thomas CARLYLE, *Sartor Resartus* and "Characteristics" (1831).

something else, they find happiness by the way. The enjoyments of life (such was now my theory) are sufficient to make it a pleasant thing, when they are taken *en passant*, without being made a principal object. Once make them so, and they are immediately felt to be insufficient. They will not bear a scrutinizing examination. Ask yourself whether you are happy, and you cease to be so. The only chance is to treat, not happiness, but some end external to it, as the purpose of life. Let your self-consciousness, your scrutiny, your self-interrogation, exhaust themselves on that; and if otherwise fortunately circumstanced you will inhale happiness with the air you breathe, without dwelling on it or thinking about it, without either forestalling it in imagination, or putting it to flight by fatal questioning. This theory now became the basis of my philosophy of life. And I still hold to it as the best theory for all those who have but a moderate degree of sensibility and of capacity for enjoyment, that is, for the great majority of mankind.

The other important change which my opinions at this time underwent, was that I, for the first time, gave its proper place, among the prime necessities of human well-being, to the internal culture of the individual. I ceased to attach almost exclusive importance to the ordering of outward circumstances, and the training of the human being for speculation and for action.

I had now learnt by experience that the passive susceptibilities needed to be cultivated as well as the active capacities, and required to be nourished and enriched as well as guided. I did not, for an instant, lose sight of, or undervalue, that part of the truth which I had seen before; I never turned recreant to intellectual culture, or ceased to consider the power and practice of analysis as an essential condition both of individual and of social improvement. But I thought that it had consequences which required to be corrected, by joining other kinds of cultivation with it. The maintenance of a due balance among the faculties, now seemed to me of primary importance. The cultivation of the feelings became one of the cardinal points in my ethical and philosophical creed. And my thoughts and inclinations turned in an increasing degree towards whatever seemed capable of being instrumental to that object.

I now began to find meaning in the things which I had read or heard about the importance of poetry and art as instruments of human culture. But it was some time longer before I began to know this by personal experience. The only one of the imaginative arts in which I had from childhood taken great pleasure, was music; the best effect of which (and in this it surpasses perhaps every other art) consists in exciting enthusiasm; in winding up to a high pitch those feelings of an elevated kind which are already in the character, but to which this excitement gives a glow and a fervour, which, though transitory at its utmost height, is precious for sustaining them at other times. This effect of music I had often experienced; but like all my pleasurable susceptibilities it was suspended during the gloomy period. I had sought relief again and again from this quarter, but found none. After the tide had turned, and I was in process of recovery, I had been helped forward by music, but in a much less elevated manner. I at this time first became acquainted with Weber's Oberon, and the extreme pleasure which I drew from its delicious melodies did me good, by showing me a source of pleasure to which I was as susceptible as ever. The good, however, was much impaired by the thought, that the pleasure of music (as is quite true of such pleasure as this was, that of mere tune) fades with familiarity, and requires either to be revived by intermittence, or fed by continual novelty. And it is very characteristic both of my then state, and of the general tone of my mind at this period of my life, that I was seriously tormented by the thought of the exhaustibility of musical combinations. The octave consists only of five tones and two semitones, which can be put together in only a limited number of ways, of which but a small proportion are beautiful: most of these, it seemed to me, must have been already discovered, and there could not be room for a long succession of Mozarts and Webers, to strike out, as these had done, entirely new and surpassingly rich veins of musical beauty. This source of anxiety may, perhaps, be thought to resemble that of the philosophers of Laputa, who feared lest the sun should be burnt out.[8] It was, however, connected with the best feature in my character, and the only good point to be found in my very unromantic and in no way honourable distress. For though my dejection, honestly looked at, could not be called other than egotistical, produced by the ruin, as I thought, of my fabric of happiness, yet the destiny of mankind in general was ever in my thoughts, and could not be separated from my own. I felt that the flaw in my life, must be a flaw in life itself; that the question was, whether, if the reformers of society and government could succeed in their objects, and every person in the community were free and in a state of physical comfort, the pleasures of life, being no longer kept up by struggle and privation, would cease to be pleasures. And I felt that unless I could see my way to some better hope than this for human happiness in general, my dejection must continue; but that if I could see such an outlet, I should then look on the world with pleasure; content as far as I was myself concerned, with any fair share of the general lot.

This state of my thoughts and feelings made the fact of my reading Wordsworth for the first time (in the autumn of 1828), an important event in my life. I took up the collection of his poems from curiosity, with no expectation of mental relief from it, though I had before resorted to poetry with that hope. In the worst period of my depression, I had read through the whole of Byron (then new to me), to try whether a poet, whose peculiar department was supposed to be that of the intenser feelings, could rouse any feeling in me. As might be expected, I got no good from this reading, but the reverse. The poet's state of mind was too like my own. His was the lament of a man who had worn out all pleasures, and who seemed to think that life, to all who possess the good things of it, must necessarily be the vapid, uninteresting thing which I found it. His Harold and Manfred had the same burden on them which I had; and I was not in a frame of mind to desire any comfort from the vehement sensual passion of his Giaours, or the sullenness of his Laras. But while Byron was exactly what did not suit my condition, Wordsworth was exactly what did. I had looked into the Excursion two or three years before, and found little in it; and I should probably have found as little, had I read it at this time. But the miscellaneous poems, in the two-volume edition of 1815 (to which little of value was added in the latter part of the author's life), proved to be the precise thing for my mental wants at that particular juncture.

8. An episode in Jonathan Swift's *Gulliver's Travels*.

In the first place, these poems addressed themselves powerfully to one of the strongest of my pleasurable susceptibilities, the love of rural objects and natural scenery; to which I had been indebted not only for much of the pleasure of my life, but quite recently for relief from one of my longest relapses into depression. In this power of rural beauty over me, there was a foundation laid for taking pleasure in Wordsworth's poetry; the more so, as his scenery lies mostly among mountains, which, owing to my early Pyrenean excursion, were my ideal of natural beauty. But Wordsworth would never have had any great effect on me, if he had merely placed before me beautiful pictures of natural scenery. Scott does this still better than Wordsworth, and a very second-rate landscape does it more effectually than any poet. What made Wordsworth's poems a medicine for my state of mind, was that they expressed, not mere outward beauty, but states of feeling, and of thought coloured by feeling, under the excitement of beauty. They seemed to be the very culture of the feelings, which I was in quest of. In them I seemed to draw from a source of inward joy, of sympathetic and imaginative pleasure, which could be shared in by all human beings; which had no connexion with struggle or imperfection, but would be made richer by every improvement in the physical or social condition of mankind. From them I seemed to learn what would be the perennial sources of happiness, when all the greater evils of life shall have been removed. And I felt myself at once better and happier as I came under their influence. There have certainly been, even in our own age, greater poets than Wordsworth; but poetry of deeper and loftier feeling could not have done for me at that time what his did. I needed to be made to feel that there was real, permanent happiness in tranquil contemplation. Wordsworth taught me this, not only without turning away from, but with a greatly increased interest in the common feelings and common destiny of human beings. And the delight which these poems gave me, proved that with culture of this sort, there was nothing to dread from the most confirmed habit of analysis. At the conclusion of the Poems came the famous Ode, falsely called Platonic, "Intimations of Immortality:" in which, along with more than his usual sweetness of melody and rhythm, and along with the two passages of grand imagery but bad philosophy so often quoted, I found that he too had had similar experience to mine; that he also had felt that the first freshness of youthful enjoyment of life was not lasting; but that he had sought for compensation, and found it, in the way in which he was now teaching me to find it. The result was that I gradually, but completely, emerged from my habitual depression, and was never again subject to it. I long continued to value Wordsworth less according to his intrinsic merits, than by the measure of what he had done for me. Compared with the greatest poets, he may be said to be the poet of unpoetical natures, possessed of quiet and contemplative tastes. But unpoetical natures are precisely those which require poetic cultivation. This cultivation Wordsworth is much more fitted to give, than poets who are intrinsically far more poets than he. . . .

In giving an account of this period of my life, I have only specified such of my new impressions as appeared to me, both at the time and since, to be a kind of turning points, marking a definite progress in my mode of thought. But these few selected points give a very insufficient idea of the quantity of thinking which I carried on respecting a host of subjects during these years of transition. Much of this, it is true, consisted in rediscovering things known to all the world, which I had previously disbelieved, or disregarded. But the rediscovery was to me a discovery, giving me plenary possession of the truths, not as traditional platitudes, but fresh from their source: and it seldom failed to place them in some new light, by which they were reconciled with, and seemed to confirm while they modified, the truths less generally known which lay in my early opinions, and in no essential part of which I at any time wavered. All my new thinking only laid the foundation of these more deeply and strongly, while it often removed misapprehension and confusion of ideas which had perverted their effect. For example, during the later returns of my dejection, the doctrine of what is called Philosophical Necessity weighed on my existence like an incubus. I felt as if I was scientifically proved to be the helpless slave of antecedent circumstances; as if my character and that of all others had been formed for us by agencies beyond our control, and was wholly out of our own power. I often said to myself, what a relief it would be if I could disbelieve the doctrine of the formation of character by circumstances; and remembering the wish of Fox[9] respecting the doctrine of resistance to governments, that it might never be forgotten by kings, nor remembered by subjects, I said that it would be a blessing if the doctrine of necessity could be believed by all quoad[10] the characters of others, and disbelieved in regard to their own. I pondered painfully on the subject, till gradually I saw light through it. I perceived, that the word Necessity, as a name for the doctrine of Cause and Effect applied to human action, carried with it a misleading association; and that this association was the operative force in the depressing and paralysing influence which I had experienced: I saw that though our character is formed by circumstances, our own desires can do much to shape those circumstances; and that what is really inspiriting and ennobling in the doctrine of freewill, is the conviction that we have real power over the formation of our own character; that our will, by influencing some of our circumstances, can modify our future habits or capabilities of willing. All this was entirely consistent with the doctrine of circumstances, or rather, was that doctrine itself, properly understood. From that time I drew in my own mind, a clear distinction between the doctrine of circumstances, and Fatalism; discarding altogether the misleading word Necessity. The theory, which I now for the first time rightly apprehended, ceased altogether to be discouraging, and besides the relief to my spirits, I no longer suffered under the burden, so heavy to one who aims at being a reformer in opinions, of thinking one doctrine true, and the contrary doctrine morally beneficial. The train of thought which had extricated me from this dilemma, seemed to me, in after years, fitted to render a similar service to others; and it now forms the chapter on Liberty and Necessity in the concluding Book of my System of Logic.

Again, in politics, though I no longer accepted the doctrine of the Essay on Government[11] as a scientific theory; though I ceased to consider representative democracy as an absolute principle, and regarded it as a question of time, place, and circumstance; though I now looked upon the choice of political institutions as a moral and educational question more than one of material interests, thinking that it ought to be decid-

9. Probably Charles James Fox (1749–1806), Whig statesman and orator.
10. "With respect to."
11. James Mill's article on government for the *Encyclopaedia Britannica* was republished in 1828 and reviewed by Thomas Babington MACAULAY in the *Edinburgh Review* (March 1829).

ed mainly by the consideration, what great improvement in life and culture stands next in order for the people concerned, as the condition of their further progress, and what institutions are most likely to promote that; nevertheless, this change in the premises of my political philosophy did not alter my practical political creed as to the requirements of my own time and country. I was as much as ever a Radical and Democrat for Europe, and especially for England. I thought the predominance of the aristocratic classes, the noble and the rich, in the English constitution, an evil worth any struggle to get rid of; not on account of taxes, or any such comparatively small inconvenience, but as the great demoralizing agency in the country. Demoralizing, first, because it made the conduct of the Government an example of gross public immorality, through the predominance of private over public interests in the State, and the abuse of the powers of legislation for the advantage of classes. Secondly, and in a still greater degree, because the respect of the multitude always attaching itself principally to that which, in the existing state of society, is the chief passport to power; and under English institutions, riches, hereditary or acquired, being the almost exclusive source of political importance; riches, and the signs of riches, were almost the only things really respected, and the life of the people was mainly devoted to the pursuit of them. I thought, that while the higher and richer class- es held the power of government, the instruction and improvement of the mass of the people were contrary to the self interest of those classes, because tending to render the people more powerful for throwing off the yoke: but if the democracy obtained a large, and perhaps the principal share, in the governing power, it would become the interest of the opulent classes to promote their education, in order to ward off really mischievous errors, and especially those which would lead to unjust violations of property. On these grounds I was not only as ardent as ever for democratic institutions, but earnestly hoped that Owenite, St. Simonian,[12] and all other anti-property doctrines might spread widely among the poorer classes; not that I thought those doctrines true, or desired that they should be acted on, but in order that the higher classes might be made to see that they had more to fear from the poor when uneducated, than when educated. . . .

My father's tone of thought and feeling, I now felt myself at a great distance from: greater, indeed, than a full and calm explanation and reconsideration on both sides, might have shown to exist in reality. But my father was not one with whom calm and full expla- nations on fundamental points of doctrine could be expected, at least with one whom he might consider as, in some sort, a deserter from his standard. Fortunately we were almost always in strong agreement on the political questions of the day, which engrossed a large part of his interest and of his conversation. On those matters of opinion on which we differed, we talked little. He knew that the habit of thinking for myself, which his mode of education had fostered, sometimes led me to opinions different from his, and he perceived from time to time that I did not always tell him *how* different. I expected no good, but only pain to both of us, from discussing our differences: and I never expressed them but when he gave utterance to some opinion or feeling repugnant to mine, in a manner which would have made it disingenuousness on my part to remain silent. . . .

12. Robert Owen (1771–1858), British social reformer and founder of experimental communities based upon socialist principles. Claude Saint-Simon (1760–1825), founder of French socialism.

# Caroline Norton

## A LETTER TO THE QUEEN ON LORD CHANCELLOR CRANWORTH'S MARRIAGE AND DIVORCE BILL

In the 1830s the private details of Caroline Norton's unhappy, apparently violent marriage to George Norton became public knowledge in court and through her own writings. The granddaughter of playwright Richard Brinsley Sheridan and a poet and fiction writer in her own right, Caroline Norton battled with her husband for nearly two decades over finances, property, and the custody of their children. Following their separation in 1836, Norton's husband denied her contact with her children, as he was legally able to do, and charged Prime Minister Lord Melbourne with adultery. Melbourne was acquitted, but the notoriety of the scandal would follow Caroline Norton. In 1853 their problems were again aired in court after George Norton refused to pay her allowance and her debts because of her income from an inheritance and her publications.

Norton's personal experiences led her to use her pen and her name to champion legal rights for married women. She published pamphlets that influenced the passage of the 1839 Custody of Infants Bill, granting separated wives the ability to petition for custody of children under seven and access to older children. After the second lawsuit, she wrote "English

*Laws for Women in the Nineteenth Century" and her "Letter to the Queen," intending to*
*influence Parliamentary discussions of modifications to the Marriage Laws. Critical of Lord*
*Chancellor Cranworth's Divorce Bill, introduced in 1854, Norton exposed the anomaly that*
*in a nation "with a Queen on the throne, all other married women are legally NON-EXIS-*
*TENT." The Divorce Bill and Matrimonial Causes Act, with amendments reflecting Norton's*
*arguments, was passed in 1857. Another bill, the Married Women's Property Act—far more*
*ambitious in its attempt to rectify the problem of women's legal "non-existence," and cham-*
*pioned by Barbara BODICHON and Harriet MARTINEAU—was debated in Parliament at the*
*same time as Cranworth's bill. But Parliament, reluctant to appear to undercut the sanctity*
*of marriage by granting wives financial independence, endorsed the more conservative*
*Divorce Bill. The First Married Women's Property Act became law in 1870.*     LMF

MADAM,

ON TUESDAY, JUNE 13TH, OF last session, Lord Chancellor Cranworth[1] brought forward
a measure for the reform of the Marriage laws of England; which measure was afterwards withdrawn. In March, 1855, in this present session, the Solicitor General stated,
that a bill on the same subject was "nearly prepared," and would be brought forward
"immediately after the Easter recess." On May 10th, being pressed to name a time, he
stated that it would be proposed "*as soon as the House had expressed an opinion on the*
*Testamentary Jurisdiction Bill.*" That time has not arrived: and meanwhile,—as one who
has grievously suffered, and is still suffering, under the present imperfect state of the
law,—I address your Majesty on the subject.

I do not do so in the way of appeal. The vague romance of "carrying my wrongs to the
foot of the throne," forms no part of my intention: for I know the throne is powerless to
redress them. I know those pleasant tales of an earlier and simpler time, when oppressed
subjects travelled to the presence of some glorious prince or princess, who instantly set
their affairs to rights without reference to law, are quaint old histories, or fairy fables, fit
only for the amusement of children.

I connect your Majesty's name with these pages from a different motive; for two reasons: of which one, indeed, is a sequence to the other. First, because I desire to point out
the grotesque anomaly which ordains that married women shall be "non-existent" in a
country governed by a female Sovereign; and secondly, because, whatever measure for
the reform of these statutes may be proposed, it cannot become "the law of the land"
without your Majesty's assent and sign manual. In England there is no Salique law.[2] If
there were,—if the principles which guide all legislation for the inferior sex in this country, were carried out in their integrity as far as the throne,—your Majesty would be by
birth a subject, and Hanover and England would be still under one King.[3]

It is not so. Your Majesty is Queen of England; Head of the Church; Head of the Law;
Ruler of millions of men; and the assembled Senate who meet to debate and frame leg-

1. Robert Monsey Rolfe, Lord Cranworth (1790–1868).
2. The Salique or Salic law, derived from a fifth-century Germanic law that specified that only males could inherit
land, excluded females from succession to the throne.
3. After King William's death, the next male in line for the throne was the Duke of Cumberland, King of Hanover.

islative enactments in each succeeding year, *begin* their sessional labours by reverently listening to that clear woman's voice,—rebellion against whose command is treason.

In the year 1845, on the occasion of the opening of the new Hall of Lincoln's Inn, your Majesty honoured that Hall with your presence: when His Royal Highness Prince Albert was invited to become a Barrister: "the keeping of his terms and exercises, and the payment of all fees and expenses, being dispensed with." It was an occasion of great pomp and rejoicing. No reigning sovereign had visited the Inns of Court since Charles II., in 1671. In the magnificent library of Lincoln's Inn, seated on a chair of state (Prince Albert standing), your Majesty held a levee; and received an address from the benchers, barristers, and students-at-law, which was read by the treasurer on his knee: thanking your Majesty for the proof given by your presence of your "gracious regard for the profession of the law,"—offering congratulations "on the great amendments of the law, effected since your Majesty's accession;" and affirming that "the pure glory of those labours must be dear to your Majesty's heart."

To that address your Majesty was graciously pleased to return a suitable answer; adding,—"I gladly testify my respect for the profession of the law; by which I am aided in administering JUSTICE, and in maintaining the prerogative of the Crown and the rights of my people."

A banquet followed. The health of the new barrister, the Prince Consort, was drunk with loud cheers. His Royal Highness put on a student's gown, over his Field Marshal's uniform, and so wore it on returning from the Hall; and then that glittering courtly vision—of a young beloved queen, with ladies in waiting, and attendant officers of state, and dignitaries in rich dresses, melted out of the solemn library; and left the dingy law courts once more to the dull quiet, which had been undisturbed by such a gorgeous sight for nearly two hundred years. Only, on the grand day of the following Trinity term, the new Barrister, His Royal Highness Prince Albert, dined in the Hall as a Bencher, in compliment to those who had elected him.

Now this was not a great mockery; but a great ceremony. It was entered into with the serious loyalty of faithful subjects: with the enthusiasm of attached hearts: and I know not what sight could be more graceful or touching, than the homage of those venerable and learned men to their young female sovereign. The image of Lawful Power, coming in such fragile person, to meet them on that vantage ground of Justice, where students are taught, by sublime theories, how Right can be defended against Might, the poor against the rich, the weak against the strong, in their legal practice; and how entirely the civilised intelligence of the nineteenth century rejects, as barbarous, those bandit rules of old, based on the "simple plan,"

> "That they should take, who have the power,
> And they should keep, who *can*."[4]

It was the very poetry of allegiance, when the Lord Chancellor and the other great law officers did obeisance in that Hall to their Queen; and the Treasurer knelt at a woman's

---

4. William Wordsworth, "Rob Roy's Grave" (1807).

feet, to read of the amendments in that great stern science by which governments themselves are governed; whose thrall all nations submit to; whose value even the savage acknowledges,—and checks by its means the wild liberty he enjoys, with some rude form of polity and order.

Madam,—I will not do your Majesty the injustice of supposing, that the very different aspect the law wears in England for the female sovereign and the female subject, must render you indifferent to what those subjects may suffer; or what reform may be proposed, in the rules more immediately affecting them. I therefore submit a brief and familiar exposition of the laws relating to women,—as taught and practised in those Inns of Court, where your Majesty received homage, and Prince Albert was elected a Bencher.

A married woman in England has *no legal existence*: her being is absorbed in that of her husband. Years of separation or desertion cannot alter this position. Unless divorced by special enactment in the House of Lords, the legal fiction holds her to be "*one*" with her husband, even though she may never see or hear of him.

She has no possessions, unless by special settlement; her property is *his* property. Lord Ellenborough[5] mentions a case in which a sailor bequeathed "all he was worth" to a woman he cohabited with; and afterwards married, in the West Indies, a woman of considerable fortune. At this man's death it was held,—notwithstanding the hardship of the case,—that the will swept away from his widow, in favour of his mistress, every shilling of the property. It is now provided that a will shall be revoked by marriage: but the claim of *the husband* to all that is his wife's exists in full force. An English wife has no legal right even to her clothes or ornaments; her husband may take them and sell them if he pleases, even though they be the gifts of relatives or friends, or bought before marriage.

An English wife cannot make a will. She may have children or kindred whom she may earnestly desire to benefit;—she may be separated from her husband, who may be living with a mistress; no matter: the law gives what she has to him, and no will she could make would be valid.

An English wife cannot legally claim her own earnings. Whether wages for manual labour, or payment for intellectual exertion, whether she weed potatoes, or keep a school, her salary is *the husband's*; and he could compel a second payment, and treat the first as void, if paid to the wife without his sanction.

An English wife may not leave her husband's house. Not only can he sue her for "restitution of conjugal rights," but he has a right to enter the house of any friend or relation with whom she may take refuge, and who may "harbour her,"—as it is termed,—and carry her away by force, with or without the aid of the police.

If the wife sue for separation for cruelty, it must be "cruelty that endangers life or limb," and if she has once forgiven, or, in legal phrase, "*condoned*" his offences, she cannot plead them; though her past forgiveness only proves that she endured as long as endurance was possible.

If her husband take proceedings for a divorce, she is not, in the first instance, allowed to defend herself. She has no means of proving the falsehood of his allegations. She is not represented by attorney, nor permitted to be considered a party to the suit between him

---

5. Probably Edward Law, Baron Ellenborough (1750–1818), Lord Chief Justice.

and her supposed lover, for "damages." Lord Brougham[6] affirmed in the House of Lords: *"in that action the character of the woman was at immediate issue, although she was not prosecuted. The consequence not unfrequently was, that the character of a woman was sworn away; instances were known in which, by collusion between the husband and a pretended paramour, the character of the wife has been destroyed. All this could take place, and yet the wife had no defence; she was excluded from Westminster-hall, and behind her back, by the principles of our jurisprudence, her character was tried between her husband and the man called her paramour."*

If an English wife be guilty of infidelity, her husband can divorce *her* so as to marry again; but she cannot divorce the husband *a vinculo*,[7] however profligate he may be. No law court can divorce in England. A special Act of Parliament annulling the marriage, is passed for each case. The House of Lords grants this almost as a matter of course to the husband, but not to the wife. In only four instances (two of which were cases of incest), has the wife obtained a divorce to marry again.

She cannot prosecute for a libel. Her husband must prosecute; and in cases of enmity and separation, of course she is without a remedy.

She cannot sign a lease, or transact responsible business.

She cannot claim support, as a matter of personal right, from her husband. The general belief and nominal rule is, that her husband is "bound to maintain her." That is not the law. He is not bound to *her*. He is bound to his country; bound to see that she does not cumber the parish in which she resides. If it be proved that means sufficient are at her disposal, from relatives or friends, her husband is quit of his obligation, and need not contribute a farthing: even if he have deserted her; or be in receipt of money which is hers by inheritance.

She cannot bind her husband by any agreement, except through a third party. A contract formally drawn out by a lawyer, –witnessed, and signed by her husband,—is *void in law*; and he can evade payment of an income so assured, by the legal quibble that "a man cannot contract with his own wife."

Separation from her husband by consent, or for his ill usage, does not alter their mutual relation. He retains the right to divorce her *after* separation,—as before,—though he himself be unfaithful.

Her being, on the other hand, of spotless character, and without reproach, gives her no advantage in law. She may have withdrawn from his roof knowing that he lives with "his faithful housekeeper": having suffered personal violence at his hands; having "condoned" much, and being able to prove it by unimpeachable testimony: or he may have shut the doors of her house against her: all this is quite immaterial: the law takes no cognisance of which is to blame. As *her husband*, he has a right to all that is hers: as *his wife*, she has no right to anything that is his. As her husband, he may divorce her (if truth or false swearing can do it): as his wife, the utmost "divorce" she could obtain, is permission to reside alone,—married to his name. The marriage ceremony is a civil bond for him,—and an indissoluble sacrament for her; and the rights of mutual property which that ceremony is ignorantly supposed to confer, are made absolute for him, and null for her.

6. Henry Peter Brougham, first Baron Brougham and Vaux (1778–1868).
7. "From the bonds" (of marriage).

Of course an opposite picture may be drawn. There are bad, wanton, irreclaimable women, as there are vicious, profligate, tyrannical men: but the difference is *this*: that to punish and restrain bad wives, there are laws, and very severe laws (to say nothing of social condemnation); while to punish or restrain bad husbands, there is, in England, no adequate law whatever. Indeed, the English law holds out a sort of premium on infidelity; for there is no doubt that the woman who is divorced for a lover and marries him, suffers less (except in conscience) than the woman who *does not deserve to suffer at all*—the wife of a bad husband, who can inflict what he pleases, whether she remain in her home, or attempt to leave it.

Such, however, is "the law": and if anything could add to the ridicule, confusion, and injustice of its provisions, it would be the fact, that though it is law for the rich, it is not law for the poor; and though it is the law in England, it is not the law in Scotland!

It is not law for the poor.

Since the days of King Henry VIII., for whose passions it was contrived, our method of divorce has remained an indulgence sacred to the aristocracy of England. The poorer classes have no form of divorce amongst them. The rich man makes a new marriage, having divorced his wife in the House of Lords: his new marriage is legal; his children are legitimate; his bride occupies, in all respects, the same social position as if he had never previously been wedded. The poor man makes a new marriage, *not* having divorced his wife in the House of Lords; his new marriage is null; his children are bastards; and he himself is liable to be put on his trial for bigamy: the allotted punishment for which crime, at one time was hanging, and is now imprisonment. Not always offending knowingly,—for nothing can exceed the ignorance of the poor on this subject; they believe a Magistrate can divorce them; that an absence of seven years constitutes a nullity of the marriage tie; or that they can give each other reciprocal permission to divorce: and among some of our rural populations, the grosser belief prevails, that a man may legally *sell* his wife, and so break the bond of union! They believe anything,—rather than what is the fact,—viz., that *they* cannot do legally, that which they know is done legally in the classes above them; that the comfort of the rich man's home, or the indulgence of the rich man's passions, receives a consideration in England which the poor need not expect to obtain.

It is not the law of Scotland. In your Majesty's kingdom, nothing but
> "The rapid running of the silver Tweed"

divides that portion of the realm where women are protected by law,—from that portion where they are *un*protected, though living under the same Sovereign and the same government!

When, in Queen Anne's reign, the legislative union of Scotland was completed, the laws relating to trade, customs, and excise, were assimilated to those of England; but other laws remained untouched; and in nothing is there a larger difference than in all matters relating to marriage, divorce, and legitimation of children.

In Scotland, the wife accused of infidelity defends herself as a matter of course, and as a first process,—instead of suffering by the infamous English action for "damages," where she is not allowed to interfere, though the result may be to ruin her.

In Scotland, the property of the wife is protected; rules are made for her "aliment" or support; and her clothes and "paraphernalia" cannot be seized by her husband.

In Scotland, above all, the law *has* power to divorce *a vinculo*, so as to enable *either* party to marry again; and the right of the wife to apply for such divorce is equal with the right of the husband; that license for inconstancy, taken out under the English law by the English husband,—as one of the masculine gender,—being utterly unknown to the Scottish courts.

This condition of the English law; its anomalies, its injustice, its actions for damages and crim. con.,[8] and its perpetual contradictions, have long marked it out for reform. At various times, and on various occasions, it has been pronounced,—not by wailing, angry, and complaining women, but by *men*,—senators and judges,—to be "barbarous"—"indecent"—"oppressive"—"anomalous and preposterous"—"utterly disgraceful." When the Marriage Reform Bill was brought in, the late Lord Beaumont[9] stigmatised the examinations before the House of Lords in divorce cases, as "*disgusting and demoralising.*" Lord Campbell spoke of passing Bills of Divorce through the two Houses of Parliament as a "*scandalous practice.*" Lord St. Leonards, while he affirmed that no measure would be satisfactory, that did not reconcile the conflict of our jurisdiction with the Scottish law, declared the present English action for "damages" to be a "*disgrace to the country*"—"*a stigma on the law of England*"—"*an action which shocked one's sense of what was right.*" Lord Brougham,—so long as sixteen years ago,—spoke of the law as regards a woman's earnings in this most forcible language,—"*Could anything be more harsh or cruel,*" he said, "*than that the wife's goods and chattels should be at the mercy of the husband, and that she might work and toil for an unkind father to support his family and children, while the husband repaid her with harshness and brutality, he all the time rioting and revelling in extravagance and dissipation, and squandering in the company of guilty paramours the produce of her industry? The law was silent to the complaints of such a woman.*"

In short, the gentlemen of England—members of both Houses—have severally denounced in the most unmeasured terms, the present laws for women; and unanimously agreed that they ought to be reformed. Commissioners were accordingly "ordered to report," and they reported. Lord Cranworth undertook to bring in the measure which was to set all to rights; and after some delay, he presented a bill, with his plan for future alterations. Any one would have imagined, after the decided admissions of evil on the part of all concerned, that this bill would have proposed some sweeping change; the establishment of a judicial tribunal, as in Scotland and France, which should have *complete power* in matrimonial causes; and better laws of protection for women. Not at all. The gist of the new bill, was simply to take away power from the Ecclesiastical Courts, and transfer it to the Court of Chancery. It was full of contradictions. It professed to deprive the House of Lords of the power of granting divorces, and yet made the House of Lords the court of appeal "*en dernier ressort,*"[10] from the proposed new tribunal. It proposed to "leave

---

8. "Criminal conversation," the legal term for adultery.
9. Thomas Wentworth Beaumont (1792–1848). Norton next mentions John Campbell (1779–1861) and Edward Burthenshaw Sugden, Baron St. Leonards (1781–1875).
10. "As the last resort."

the law as it stood," with regard to the right of the wife to apply for divorce; and, in reality, created a new, definite, and anomalous limit; for whereas at present the power of *applying for* (if not of *obtaining*) a Divorce Act, exists for all women who conceive themselves wronged—the Chancellor proposed to classify what were insupportable wrongs, and grant the remedy only to such women as could plead them. Stripped of confusion and technicalities, the object of the bill was simply this; to make it statute law, (instead of Parliamentary practice, as at present,) that marriage should be dissoluble in England; that husbands should divorce their wives, but not wives their husbands; and that the richer class should have the benefit of their riches, by the process remaining comparatively expensive. Only that all this was to be arranged by a different and more decent method. The bill was discussed; opposed; and withdrawn. No lawyer, of whatever eminence, ever yet proposed a measure in either House of Parliament, that all the other lawyers did not rise one by one to tell him that they "objected to the machinery of his bill," and that its provisions were "wholly impracticable." They did so on the present occasion. In one thing only they generally agreed, they congratulated Lord Cranworth upon that portion of his plan which provided that Justice should have her scales ready weighted in favour of the stronger party—viz., that women should by no means be discouraged from forgiving their husbands, by enacting that adultery in the male sex should be considered a ground of divorce—"as in Scotland."

It is with timid reluctance, that I permit myself to allude to the social condition of that unhappy country. To all loyal minds it must be matter for grave and sorrowful reflection, that while your Majesty is surrounded with faithful wives and discreet ladies in London,—Windsor,—and Osborne,—the less cautious portion of the realm in which Balmoral is situated, is plunged in the grossest immorality. England is virtuous; but Scotland is "a hot-bed of vice." It is a land dedicated to Cupid. Statues of Venus are set up in all the principal squares of Edinburgh. The marriage-tie is a mere true lovers' knot. The ladies who present themselves at Holyrood are triumphant Messalinas.[11] And on the decks of the emigrant vessels which crowd the harbour of Leith, groups of melancholy cast-off husbands may be seen, bidding reproachful farewell to that inhospitable country where they only exist to be repudiated! . . .

The natural position of woman is inferiority to man. Amen! That is a thing of God's appointing, not of man's devising. I believe it sincerely, as a part of my religion: and I accept it as a matter proved to my reason. I never pretended to the wild and ridiculous doctrine of equality. I will even hold that (as one coming under the general rule that the wife must be inferior to the husband), *I* occupy that position. *Uxor fulget radiis Mariti*[12]; I am Mr Norton's inferior; I am the clouded moon of that sun. Put me then—(my ambition extends no further)—in the same position as all his other inferiors! In that of his housekeeper, whom he could not libel with impunity, and without possible defence; of an apprentice whom he could not maltreat lawlessly, even if the boy "condoned" original ill-usage; of a scullion, whose wages he could not refuse on the plea that she is legally "non-

11. Valeria Messallina, third wife of the Roman emperor Claudius, forced a young man to divorce his wife and marry her.
12. "The wife shines in the husband's beams."

existent"; of the day-labourer, with whom he would not argue that his signature to a contract is "worthless." Put me under *some* law of protection; and do not leave me to the mercy of one who has never shewn me mercy. For want of such a law of protection, all other protection has been vain! I have had the upholding (and I set it first, because it has been of greater comfort and value to me than any other), of as generous and affectionate a family as ever combined to shield one of its members from undeserved disgrace. Sisters of spotless reputation, who stood by me "through evil report and good report," tenderly and steadily for restless years. Brothers and brothers-in-law, among the best gentlemen of England. Relations and intimate friendships among the noblest and purest of its women.

I have sons whom I love and am proud of, and who (thank God!), love and are proud of *me*, in spite of past misery. I had the verdict of twelve English gentlemen, sworn to a verdict of *truth*; and the solemn word,—living and dying,—of the friend who was accused with me of sin. . . .

. . . In all cases of great injustice among men, there comes a culminating point, after which that injustice *is not borne*: whether that point arrive on the wrong of a peasant or the wrong of a king. Things ripen in health and in disease: ripen alike for bloom and for disgust. There is no standing still, in a world which God set moving.

In our little corner of the earth,—where so much besides is busy and fermenting for change,—the time is ripely come for alteration in the laws for women. And they will be changed.

In vain would the sneerers declare, "This is folly; this is the mere rebellion of a clever woman against the authority of her natural lord and master." It is not so. Real superiority will make itself felt—and my heart bows low and reverentially before it, for I hold that it does not depend on the glitter of human gifts. That man is not my superior who has greater comeliness of appearance, or a quicker human intelligence; but he that is better, stronger-hearted, and a more faithful servant of God. He who stands nearer to glory than I, on that ladder to Heaven which angels tread; and will so stand in its clear light, when human comeliness shall be black mould, and the sparkle of human intelligence—darkness.

Madam,—in families, as in nations, Rebellion is a disease that springs from the *malaria* of bad government. WRONGS make REBELS. Those who would dwell submissive in the wholesome atmosphere of authority, revolt in the jail fever of tyranny.

There is tyranny in these laws which uphold the strong against the weak; which make so monstrous a difference between rich and poor. It ought not to be *possible*, in this realm of England, that poor men should be able to say,—"We are brought up for judgment before these gentlemen, because laws are made against *us*, but not against *them*: we get six months' prison for ill-treating our wives, but gentlemen seem able to do as they please. *We* get twelve months (as Lord Brougham has said) for the embezzlement or theft of a few pence,—but *they* can creep out of a money contract, and no law to check them. *We* go to prison for bigamy, because we aint rich enough to buy a divorce act; but, as for the rich man, who *can* pay for a divorce act, his bigamy sets his son among the gentry, or among the peers of England, and his lady among the other ladies of the land. Our hearts revolt against being judged by men who are, in fact, more guilty than ourselves, though we are prisoners, and some of them are magistrates." By a very recently enacted statute, the law compels the poor man to be responsible to the community at large, for the mal-treatment of his wife. Why should it seem grievous and shocking to make new laws of restraint for gentlemen as well as for poor men? Is the right of ill-usage a luxury belong-ing (like the possibility of divorce) to the superior and wealthy classes? . . .

It is impossible for me, when I reflect on my unjust position as an English subject, not also to reflect on your Majesty's position, as Queen of the country where such laws are in force: and on the peculiar circumstances which,—even had the case occurred to per-sons obscure and unknown, instead of to your Majesty's Prime Minister,—would war-rant the hope, that the present Sovereign of England might take peculiar interest in the reform of the laws which have made such events possible.

Not lone and vainglorious, like the virgin Queen Elizabeth,—nor childless, like the hypochondriac Mary,—nor heirless, like the feeble-minded Anne,[13]—more of "the beau-ty of womanhood" adorns the destiny of Queen Victoria, than has belonged to the barren reigns of former English Queens; and the link to all the interests of woman's life should be greater. More mercy may be expected from her, than from the embittered daughter of wronged Catherine of Spain,—more love, than from the haughty scion of degraded Anne Boleyn,—more justice, than from the weak and capricious niece of Charles II.,—more thankfulness to God, and willingness to help His less fortunate creatures, may be supposed to exist in the heart of that royal wife and mother, who has been permitted by Him to sail so far on the sea of life, without one storm (as yet) to ruffle its changeful sur-face!

In the history of those preceding female reigns, I find no trace of any attempt to bet-ter the condition of laws for women.

In the hard, stern, persecuting reign of her whose mother had been set aside for the sake of the "Gospel light" that shone in Boleyn's eyes,—women were burnt for faith's sake; and that gentle and learned "child-wife," Lady Jane Grey,[14] suffered unreprieved, for the ambition of others. Sending her last patient sigh to heaven, on the same day (chris-tened Black Monday), that fifteen gibbets were erected for other executions. Mary was gloomy and pitiless: forsaken, like her mother, by a king sooner wearied (and more just-ly wearied) than her inconstant father, she left no trace of woman's softness to relieve the fierce and joyless history of her brief rule over England.

Nor Anne; though governed by waiting women and female favourites; though the poor crowned slave of the passionate Duchess of Marlborough, and the wily intrigante Mrs Masham;[15] though as "womanly" as folly could make her, and the incapacity for a great position; feebly declaring, during the quarrels of Harley and Bolingbroke, that "the dis-

---

13. Elizabeth I (1533–1603), daughter of Henry VIII and his second wife, Anne Boleyn (ca. 1507–36); Mary I (1516–1558), daughter of Henry VIII and his first wife, Catherine of Aragon; Anne (1665–1714), daughter of James II and niece of Charles II.
14. Lady Jane Grey (1537–54) was proclaimed queen at the death of Edward VI in order to prevent the Catholic Mary I from taking the throne. Lady Jane reigned nine days and was later executed for treason by Mary.
15. Queen Anne was influenced by her friendships with Sarah Jennings Churchill, Duchess of Marlborough (1660–1744), and, later, Abigail Hill, Mrs. Masham (d. 1734); and troubled by the disputes between Henry St. John, First Viscount Bolingbroke (1678–1751) and Robert Harley, Earl of Oxford (1661–1724).

putes of her ministers would kill her." (A disease which, fortunately for us, is less dangerous in the present reign; considering the height to which the fever of such disputes has risen.) In all the thirteen years of her non-government, we find no further protection of women than for the sake of that which is always made the *one* plea of protection in mercantile England—property: and we are rather startled than satisfied, when we read, that under Queen Anne, one Haagen Swensden was tried and executed "for stealing and marrying Mistress Pleasant Rawlins," because she was an heiress. . . .

And now it is the fashion amongst legists to work very heartily at "*assimilating*" this law and that law,—"assimilating" the law of evidence in England and Scotland; and the law of partnership; and the commercial law for bills of exchange. On this last, the Lord Advocate observes, that "*it is a matter of astonishment that the law of bills of exchange has remained so long in the barbarous state it is at present.*" And Sir Erskine Perry[16] (who has been in India) says, much remains to do, but much has been done since Bentham's time, when the field of English law was "a wild jungle." Does it not occur to these and other authorities, that the law of "*might is right*" savours also rather of the "wild jungle," than of the calm enactments of a civilised Christian country? and that the principle of "assimilation" might be extended with advantage to those laws between husband and wife, which are utterly at variance North and South of the river Tweed? . . .

I hope, during this period of tranquil reflection, the rebellious thought may not occur to the tapestry-working sex, that the obstacle to this legal reform must be, that men fear to curb the license of their own pleasures. It is impossible, seeing how eager, energetic, and enthusiastic, men are in *other* reforms whose necessity is once proved and admitted, not to fancy that the reason why this particular change is "*so surrounded with difficulty*" is because it is extremely unpalatable to the reformers! I think—to use the words of the Solicitor-General—the House "will express an opinion on the Testamentary Jurisdiction Bill" with infinitely more speed, clearness, and decision, than on a Marriage Reform Bill. Every man seems to dread that he is surrendering some portion of his own rights over woman, in allowing these laws to be revised; even while he admits that abuses which are "a disgrace to England," blot the strange barbarous code, which remains intact while other barbarous laws have gradually been repealed or altered.

To all that women can read on the subject, I add this more familiarly easy treatise; and I shall follow this treatise by a published selection of "*Cases, decided according to Law, and contrary to Justice*;" admitted to be so decided even by the judges and counsel engaged in them; the sentences given being often accompanied by courteous and sincere expressions of regret at their manifest oppression; and by a hope that the code might be altered, which made such sentences compulsory on the persons whose duty it was "to administer the law as they found it." My husband has taught me, by subpœnaing my publishers to account for my earnings,—that my gift of writing was not meant for the purposes to which I have hitherto applied it. It was not intended that I should "strive for peace and ensue it" through a life of much occasional bitterness and many unjust trials; that I should prove my literary ability, by publishing melodies and songs for young girls and women to

---

16. Sir Thomas Erskine Perry (1806–82) introduced legislation in 1856 to amend laws relating to women's property.

sing in happier homes than mine,—or poetry and prose for them to read in leisure hours,—or even please myself by better and more serious attempts to advocate the rights of the people, or the education and interests of the poor.

When Mr Norton allowed me, I say, to be publicly subpœnaed in court, to defend himself by a quibble from a just debt, and subpœnaed my publishers to meet me there, he taught me what my gift of writing was worth. Since he would not leave even *that* source tranquil and free in my destiny, let him have the triumph of being able at once to embitter and to turn its former current. He has made me dream that it was meant for a higher and stronger purpose,—that gift which came not from man, but from God. It was meant to enable me to rouse the hearts of others to examine into all the gross injustice of these laws,—to ask the "nation of gallant gentlemen," whose countrywoman I am, for once to hear a woman's pleading on the subject. Not because I deserve more at their hands than other women. Well I know, on the contrary, how many hundreds, infinitely better than I,—more pious, more patient, and less rash under injury,—have watered their bread with tears! My plea to attention is, that in pleading for myself I am able to plead for all these others. Not that my sufferings or my deserts are greater than theirs; but that I combine, with the fact of having suffered wrong, the power to comment on and explain the cause of that wrong; which few women are able to do.

For *this*, I believe, God gave me the power of writing. To this I devote that power. I abjure all other writing, till I see these laws altered. I care not what ridicule or abuse may be the result of that declaration. They who cannot bear ridicule and abuse, are unfit and unable to advance *any* cause: and once more I deny that this is my personal cause; it is the cause of all the women of England. If *I* could be justified and happy to-morrow, I would still strive and labour in it; and if I were to die to-morrow, it would still be a satisfaction to me that I had so striven. Meanwhile, my husband has a legal lien (as he has publicly proved), on the copyright of my works. Let him claim the copyright of THIS: and let the Lord Chancellor, whose office is thus described in Chamberlayne's State of England,— "To judge, not according to the Common Law, as other Civil Courts do, but to moderate the rigour of the Law, and to judge according to Equity, Conscience, and Reason: and his Oath is to do right to all manner of People, poor and rich, after the Laws and Customs of the Realm, and truly counsel the King,"—let the Lord Chancellor, I say,—the "Summa Cancellarius" of Great Britain, cancel, in Mr Norton's favour,—according to the laws and customs of this realm of England,—my right to the labour of my own brain and pen; and docket it, among forgotten Chancery Papers, with a parody of Swift's contemptuous labelling.

"*Only a Woman's Pamphlet.*"[17]

But let the recollection of what I write, remain with those who read; and above all, let the recollection remain with your Majesty, to whom it is addressed; the one woman in England who *cannot* suffer wrong; and whose royal assent will be formally necessary

---

17. Norton alludes to the epigraph placed on the title page of her pamphlet, "Only a woman's hair," taken from William Makepeace Thackeray's lecture on Jonathan Swift, one of his series on "The English Humourists of the Eighteenth Century," given 1851–3. The reference is to a paper on which Swift had written the words of the epigraph and in which he had enclosed a lock of his wife's hair.

to any Marriage Reform Bill which the Lord Chancellor, assembled Peers, and assembled Commons, may think fit to pass, in the Parliament of this free nation; where, with a Queen on the throne, all other married women are legally NON-EXISTENT.

I remain,
With the sincerest loyalty and respect,
Your Majesty's humble and devoted
Subject and Servant,
CAROLINE ELIZABETH SARAH NORTON

# William Rathbone Greg

## WHY ARE WOMEN REDUNDANT?

*Originally a mill manager and owner, W. R. Greg gave up his business in 1850 to devote himself to writing on political, economic, and theological questions. He contributed numerous articles to the leading journals and produced several well-received volumes of essays on political and social philosophy. While interested in philanthropy, Greg did not favor major social or political reform. He believed that the problems of an industrial society would be corrected by time and by trust in the legislative system and social structures already in place. "Why Are Women Redundant?," published in* The National Review *(1862), illustrates Greg's reliance on "natural" laws, in this case supply and demand, to solve social problems. When the census of 1851 made it clear that a large number of women between the ages of twenty and forty were unmarried, social commentators became alarmed. If the duty of the middle-class woman was to marry and raise a family, as Sarah Stickney ELLIS suggested, then here was evidence that the middle-class ideal was in danger. Ignoring the consideration that the ideal itself and the issue of employment for women needed to be addressed, Greg worked out an elaborate scheme for female emigration to reduce the excess population of single women. His scheme resembled an earlier emigration plan that had been proposed to relieve distressed needlewomen, one of several groups of "surplus women" who were victims of economic pressures and restrictive social conventions. Such calls for female emigration were perhaps not quite as absurd as they seem to us now: they were a response, albeit transposed to women, to the problems raised by male emigration during the period. Nevertheless, soon after Greg's essay was published, Francis Power COBBE attacked Greg's*

*solution in her essay "What Shall We Do with Our Old Maids?" (Fraser's Magazine,*
*November 1862) and called for a reconsideration of the "profession" of marriage and for the*
*provision of greater occupational opportunities for women.*                    LMF

. . . THE BRITISH WORLD—PHILANTHROPIC AS well as political—takes up only one thing
at a time; or, rather and usually, only a fragment of a thing. It discovers an island, and proceeds to reason on it and deal with it as such; and it is long before it learns that it is only
the promontory of a vast continent. WOMAN is the subject which for some time back our
benevolence has been disposed to take in hand, fitfully and piecemeal. We have been
grieved, startled, shocked, perplexed, baffled: still, with our usual activity, we have been
long at work; beating about the bush; flying at this symptom; attacking that fragment;
relieving this distress; denouncing that abomination. First it was the factory girls; then the
distressed needlewomen; then aged and decayed governesses; latterly, Magdalens, *in esse*
or *in futurum.*[1] The cry of "Woman's Rights" reached us chiefly from America, and created only a faint echo here. *We* have occupied ourselves more with "Woman's Mission," and
"Woman's Employment;" and, as usual, have been both more practical and more superficial than our neighbours across the Channel and across the Atlantic: but the "condition of
women," in one form or another—their wants, their woes, their difficulties—have taken
possession of our thoughts, and seem likely to occupy us busily and painfully enough for
some time to come. And well they may; for not only do the mischiefs, anomalies, and falsities in that condition unveil themselves more and more as we study the subject, but are,
we believe, every day actually on the increase.

The problem, which is so generally though so dimly perceived, and which so many are
spasmodically and ambitiously bent on solving, when looked at with a certain degree of
completeness,—with an endeavour, that is, to bring together all the scattered phenomena which are usually only seen separately and in detail,—appears to resolve itself into
this: that there is an enormous and increasing number of single women in the nation, a
number quite disproportionate and quite abnormal; a number which, positively and relatively, is indicative of an unwholesome social state, and is both productive and prognos-
tic of much wretchedness and wrong. There are hundreds of thousands of women—not
to speak more largely still—scattered through all ranks, but proportionally most numerous in the middle and upper classes,—who have to earn their own living, instead of
spending and husbanding the earnings of men; who, not having the natural duties and
labours of wives and mothers, have to carve out artificial and painfully-sought occupations for themselves; who, in place of completing, sweetening, and embellishing the existence of others, are compelled to lead an independent and incomplete existence of their
own. In the manufacturing districts thousands of girls are working in mills and earning
ample wages, instead of performing, or preparing and learning to perform, the functions
and labours of domestic life. In great cities, thousands, again, are toiling in the ill-paid
*métier* of sempstresses and needlewomen, wasting life and soul, gathering the scantiest
subsistence, and surrounded by the most overpowering and insidious temptations. As we

1. In actuality or in the future.

go a few steps higher in the social scale, we find two classes of similar abnormal existences: women, more or less well educated, spending youth and middle life as governesses, living laboriously, yet perhaps not uncomfortably, but laying by nothing, and
retiring to a lonely and destitute old age; and old maids, with just enough income to live
upon, but wretched and deteriorating, their minds narrowing, and their hearts withering, because they have nothing to do, and none to love, cherish, and obey. A little further
upwards, how many do we daily see, how many have we all known, who are raised by fortune above the necessity of caring for their own subsistence, but to whom employment
is a necessity as imperious as to the milliner or the husbandman, because only employment can fill the dreary void of an unshared existence;—beautiful lay nuns, involuntary
takers of the veil,—who pine for work, who beg for occupation, who pant for interest in
life, as the hart panteth after the water-brooks, and dig for it more earnestly than for hid
treasures. With most women, probably, this phase comes at some epoch in their course;
with numbers, alas, it never passes into any other. Some rush to charity, and do much
good or much mischief; some find solace in literary interests and work, and these, though
the fewest, are perhaps the most fortunate of all; some seek in the exclusive development
of the religious affections a pale ideal substitute for the denied human ones,—a substitute of which God forbid that we should speak slightingly, but which is seldom wholly
satisfactory or wholly safe. Lastly, as we ascend into the highest ranks of all, we come
upon crowds of the same unfulfilled destinies—the same *existences manquées*[2]—women
who have gay society, but no sacred or sufficing home, whose dreary round of pleasure is
yet sadder, less remunerative, and less satisfying, than the dreary round of toil trodden by
their humbler sisters The very being of all these various classes is a standing proof of, and
protest against, that "something wrong," on which we have a few words to say,—that
besetting problem which, like the sphinx's, society must solve or die. . . .

    . . . Hundreds of women remain single in our distorted civilisation because they have
never been asked at all. Thousands remain single because the offers they have received
threatened to expose them to privations and sacrifices which they shrank from even more
than from celibacy. Thousands more, because one abortive love in the past has closed their
hearts to every other sentiment; or because they have waited long years in persistent faith
and silent hope for that one special love which never came; or because ambition deluded
them into setting their claims higher than fate or fortune was prepared to realise. But we
are satisfied that no one whose experience of life has been large, whose insight into life
has been deep, and whose questionings of life have been honest, will demur to our assertion that the women who adopt a single life from positive (not *relative*) choice—we do
not say from preference, but from love—who deliberately resolve upon celibacy as that
which they like for itself, and not as a mere escape from the *lottery* of marriage—will not
in their combined numbers exceed, if they even reach, that three or four per cent, for
whom, as statistics show us, Nature has provided no exclusive partners. The residue—the
large excess over this proportion—*who remain unmarried constitute the problem to be solved,
the evil and anomaly to be cured.* . . .

2. Wasted lives.

. . . There were in *England and Wales*, in 1851, 1,248,000 women in the prime of life, *i.e.* between the ages of twenty and forty years, who were unmarried, out of a total number of rather less than 3,000,000. According to our assumption there ought only to have been 150,000 (or five per cent) in that condition, which would leave 1,100,000 women in the best and most attractive period of life, who must be classed as unnaturally, if not all unintentionally, single. There is no need, however, to place either figures or inferences in too strong a light; and as unquestionably many women do marry between the ages of twenty and thirty years, we may perhaps reduce the number of those who are spinsters, in consequence of social disorders, or anomalies of some sort, and not from choice, to about 750,000, or three-quarters of a million,—a figure large enough in all conscience.

We have now to consider to what causes this startling anomaly is to be traced, and by what means it may be cured; for, as we premised at the outset, we must search for remedies before we can safely begin to think of applying anodynes. The chief causes we shall find to be three in number: the first we shall notice is EMIGRATION.

I. In the last forty-five years, upwards of 5,000,000 persons have definitively left our shores to find new homes either in our various colonies or in the United States. Of this number we know that the vast majority were men, though the proportions of the sexes has, we believe, been nowhere published. A considerable amount of that excess of women, which we have recorded as prevailing in the mother country, is thus at once accounted for, and is shown to be artificial and not natural, apparent rather than real. Nature makes no mistakes; Nature has no redundancies; and, as we shall see, the excess here is counterbalanced by a corresponding deficiency elsewhere. . . .

In 1840 (we still depend on the Registrar-General) the *total* excess of males over females in the United States was 309,000; the excess, after the age of twenty, was 198,000. This disproportion has assuredly been largely aggravated since, and we shall be within the mark if we assume that at least 250,000 adult women are needed in America to redress the balance among the free white population of that country. The deficiency of female life there is, as nearly as possible, the same as the redundancy in England, *viz. five per cent.* . . .

These figures, then, clearly indicate, and even loudly proclaim, the first remedy to be applied. We must redress the balance. We must restore by an emigration of women that natural proportion between the sexes in the old country and in the new ones, which was disturbed by an emigration of men, and the disturbance of which has wrought so much mischief in both lands. There are, however, two serious difficulties in the way; but difficulties are only obstacles to be overcome;—as soon as we see with sufficient clearness and feel with sufficient conviction the course that *ought to be* pursued, we cannot doubt that some practicable mode will be devised in which it *can* be pursued.

The first difficulty is chiefly mechanical. It is not easy to convey a multitude of women across the Atlantic, or to the antipodes, by any ordinary means of transit. To transport the half million from where they are redundant to where they are wanted, at an average rate of fifty passengers in each ship, would require 10,000 vessels, or at least 10,000 voyages. Still, as 350,000 emigrants *have* left our shores in a single year before now, and as we do not need and do not wish to expatriate the whole number at once, or with any great rapidity, the undertaking, though difficult, would seem to be quite possible. But far the greater portion of the 350,000 emigrants were bound for the shorter voyage to America, and of the 440,000 women who should emigrate, the larger number are wanted for the longer voyage to Australia. Still it would be feasible enough to find passenger ships to take out 10,000, 20,000, or 40,000 every year, if they were men. But to contrive some plan of taking out such a number of women, especially on a three months' voyage, in comfort, in safety, and in honour, is a problem yet to be solved. . . .

II. In female emigration, then, must be sought the rectification of that disturbance in the normal proportions between men and women which the excess of male emigration has created. But when this remedy has been applied as extensively as shall be found feasible, there will still remain a large "residual phenomenon" to be dealt with. We have seen that the extensive annual exodus from Great Britain, which has now grown almost into a national habit, has only raised the excess of adult women to about *six* per cent, whereas the proportion of adult women who are unmarried is *thirty* per cent. The second cause for this vast amount of super-normal celibacy is undoubtably to be found in the growing and morbid LUXURY of the age. The number of women who remain unmarried, because marriage—such marriage, that is, as is within their reach, or may be offered them—would entail a sacrifice of that "position," which they value more than the attractions of domestic life, is considerable in the middle ranks, and is enormous in the higher ranks. This word "position" we use as one which includes all the various forms and disguises which the motive in question puts on. Sometimes it is luxury proper which is thus inordinately valued,—dainty living, splendid dressing, large houses, carriages *ad libitum*,[3] gay society, and exoneration from all useful exertion. Sometimes it is the more shadowy sentiment which values these things, not for themselves,—for to many they are wearisome even to nausea,—but for their appearance. Hundreds of women would be really *happier* in a simpler and a less lazy life, and know that they would; but to accept that life would be, or would be deemed to be, a derogation from their social status; a virtual ejection, to a greater or less degree, from that society, that mode of existence, which they do not enjoy, but cannot make up their minds to surrender. Hundreds again—probably thousands—forego the joys of married life, not because they really cling to unrelished luxuries or empty show, but because they shrink from the loss of those actual *comforts* which refined taste or delicate organisations render almost indispensable, and which it is supposed (often most erroneously) that a small income could not sufficiently procure. . . .

. . . *Female servants do not constitute any part* (or at least only a very small part) *of the problem we are endeavouring to solve.* They are in no sense redundant; we have not to cudgel our brains to find a niche or an occupation for *them*; they are fully and usefully employed; they discharge a most important and indispensable function in social life; they do not follow an obligatorily independent, and therefore for their sex an unnatural, career:—on the contrary, they are attached to others and are connected with other existences, which they embellish, facilitate, and serve. In a word, they fulfil both essentials of woman's being; *they are supported by, and they minister to, men.* We could not possibly do without them.

3. At pleasure.

Nature has not provided one too many. If society were in a perfectly healthy state, we should no doubt have to manage with fewer female servants than at present; they would earn higher wages; they would meet with more uniform consideration; and they would, as a rule, remain in service only for a few years, and not for life:—but they must always be a numerous class, and no portion of their sex is more useful or more worthy.

III. We have now to treat of the third and last chief cause of the abnormal extent of female celibacy in our country,—a cause respecting which a speech is difficult, but respecting which silence would be undutiful and cowardly. We will be plain, because we wish both to be brief and to be true. So many women are single because so many men are profligate. Probably, among all the sources of the social anomaly in question, this, if fully analysed, would be found to be the most fertile, and to lie the deepest. The case lies in a nutshell. Few men—incalculably few—are truly celibate by nature or by choice. There are few who would not purchase love, or the indulgences which are its coarse equivalents, by the surrender or the curtailment of nearly all other luxuries and shadows, if they could obtain them on no cheaper terms. In a word, few—comparatively very few—would not marry as soon as they could maintain a wife in any thing like decency or comfort, if only through marriage they could satisfy their cravings and gratify their passions. If their sole choice lay between entire chastity,—a celibacy as strict and absolute as that of women,—or obedience to the natural dictates of the senses and the heart in the only legitimate mode, the decision of nine out of ten of those who now remain bachelors during the whole or a great portion of their lives would, there can be no doubt, be in favour of marriage. If therefore, every man among the middle and higher ranks were compelled to lead a life of stainless abstinence till he married, and unless he married, we may be perfectly sure that every woman in those ranks would have so many offers, such earnest and such rationally eligible ones, that no one would remain single except those to whom nature dictated celibacy as a vocation, or those whose cold hearts, independent tempers, or indulgent selfishness, made them select it as a preferable and more luxurious career. Unhappily, as matters are managed now, thousands of men find it perfectly feasible to combine all the freedom, luxury, and self-indulgence of a bachelor's career with the pleasures of female society and the enjoyments they seek for there. As long as this is so, so long, we fear, a vast proportion of the best women in the educated classes—women especially who have no dowry beyond their goodness and their beauty—will be doomed to remain involuntarily single. . . .

To sum up the whole matter. Nature makes no mistakes and creates no redundancies. Nature, honestly and courageously interrogated, gives no erroneous or ambiguous replies. In the case before us, Nature cries out against the malady, and plainly indicates the remedy. The first point to fix firmly in our minds is, that in the excess of single women in Great Britain we have a curable evil to be mended, not an irreparable evil to be borne. The mischief is to be eradicated, not to be counterbalanced, mitigated, or accepted. To speak in round numbers, we have one million and a half adult unmarried women in Great Britain. Of these half a million are wanted in the colonies; half a million more are usefully, happily, and indispensably occupied in domestic service;—the evil, thus viewed, assumes manageable dimensions, and only half a million remain to be practically dealt

with. As an immediate result of the removal of 500,000 women from the mother-coun-
try, where they are redundant, to the colonies, where they are sorely needed, all who
remain at home will rise in value, will be more sought, will be better rewarded. The number who compete for the few functions and the limited work at the disposal of women
being so much reduced, the competition will be less cruelly severe, and the pay less
ruinously beaten down. As the redundancy at home diminishes, and the value is thereby
increased, men will not be able to obtain women's society and women's care so cheaply
on illicit terms. . . . We are satisfied that IF the gulf could be practically bridged over, so
that women went where they are clamoured for; and IF we were contented with the *actu-
alities* instead of the empty and unreal and unrewarding shadows of luxury and refinement; and IF men were necessitated either to marry or be chaste,—*all of which things it is
a discreditable incapacity in us not to be able to accomplish*,—so far from there being too many
women for the work that must be done and that only women can do well, there would
be too few. The work would be seeking for the women, instead of, as now, the women
seeking for the work. We are disordered, we are suffering, we are astray, because we have
*gone wrong*; and our philanthropists are labouring, not to make us go backward and go
right, but to make it easier and smoother to persist in wrong.

# Charles Darwin

## ON THE ORIGIN OF SPECIES

*Although the terms "Darwinism" and "Evolution" are sometimes used synonymously, Charles Darwin was not the first to speak of evolutionary theory. By midcentury, scientists and the educated reading public were already familiar with Charles Lyell's discussion of uniformitarianism or gradual change in* Principles of Geology *(1830–3), with Robert* Chambers's *popular* Vestiges of the Natural History of Creation *(1844), and perhaps with the earlier theories of Georges Buffon, Jean Baptiste de Lamarck, Erasmus Darwin, and Georges Cuvier. But Darwin's idea of natural selection provided a mechanism, a method, an explanation of how evolution could occur. What was convincing to some and unsettling to many was the stunning authority of Darwin's evidence, drawn from almost two decades of observation and collection of specimen and fossils.*

*In July 1858 two papers on natural selection were read before the Linnean Society in London: one by Darwin and the other by Alfred Russel Wallace, who independently had developed an almost identical theory of common descent by natural selection. The following year Darwin published* On the Origin of Species by Means of Natural Selection, or, The Preservation of Favoured Races in the Struggle for Life. *Its publication sparked immediate interest (selling 1,250 copies on the first day), shock, and controversy. "No work of our time," said G. H. Lewes, "has been so general in its influence."*[1] *Some, most notably T. H. Huxley, who became Darwin's advocate or "bulldog," welcomed Darwin's conclusions enthusiastically. Others, including scientists and religious leaders, deplored the implications of evolution and natural selection in challenging literal readings of Genesis and belief in individual creation by a Creator. Adam Sedgwick, Professor of Geology at Cambridge and a believer in natural theology, condemned Darwin's work for not being sufficiently inductive and expressed his "detestation" of "its unflinching materialism."*[2] *Although Darwin had studiously avoided the subject of human evolution in* Origin, *the implications of natural selection, with its slow process of modification producing new variations and new species, were evident to many, including Samuel Wilberforce, Bishop of Oxford, who wrote: "Man's derived supremacy over the earth; man's power of articulate speech; man's gift of reason; man's free-will and responsibility; man's fall and redemption; the incarnation of the Eternal Son; the indwelling of the Eternal Spirit,—all are equally and utterly irreconcilable with the degrading notion of the brute origin of him who was created in the image of God."*[3]

RM

## RECAPITULATION AND CONCLUSION

. . . That many and grave objections may be advanced against the theory of descent with modification through natural selection, I do not deny. I have endeavoured to give to them their full force. Nothing at first can appear more difficult to believe than that the more complex organs and instincts should have been perfected, not by means superior to, though analogous with, human reason, but by the accumulation of innumerable slight variations, each good for the individual possessor. Nevertheless, this difficulty, though appearing to our imagination insuperably great, cannot be considered real if we admit the following propositions, namely,—that gradations in the perfection of any organ or instinct, which we may consider, either do now exist or could have existed, each good of its kind,—that all organs and instincts are, in ever so slight a degree, variable,—and, lastly, that there is a struggle for existence leading to the preservation of each profitable deviation of structure or instinct. The truth of these propositions cannot, I think, be disputed. . . .

As natural selection acts solely by accumulating slight, successive, favourable variations, it can produce no great or sudden modification; it can act only by very short and slow steps. Hence the canon of "Natura non facit saltum,"[4] which every fresh addition to our knowledge tends to make more strictly correct, is on this theory simply intelligible. We can plainly see why nature is prodigal in variety, though niggard in innovation. But why this should be a law of nature if each species has been independently created, no man can explain.

1. "Mr. Darwin's Hypotheses," *The Fortnightly Review* 16 (April 1868): 353.
2. "Objections to Mr. Darwin's Theory of the Origin of Species," *The Spectator* 33 (March 24, 1860): 286.
3. Review of *On the Origin, Quarterly Review* 108 (July 1860): 258.
4. Nature does not make a leap.

Many other facts are, as it seems to me, explicable on this theory. How strange it is that a bird, under the form of woodpecker, should have been created to prey on insects on the ground; that upland geese, which never or rarely swim, should have been created with webbed feet; that a thrush should have been created to dive and feed on sub-aquatic insects; and that a petrel should have been created with habits and structure fitting it for the life of an auk or grebe! and so on in endless other cases. But on the view of each species constantly trying to increase in number, with natural selection always ready to adapt the slowly varying descendants of each to any unoccupied or ill-occupied place in nature, these facts cease to be strange, or perhaps might even have been anticipated.

As natural selection acts by competition, it adapts the inhabitants of each country only in relation to the degree of perfection of their associates; so that we need feel no surprise at the inhabitants of any one country, although on the ordinary view supposed to have been specially created and adapted for that country, being beaten and supplanted by the naturalised productions from another land. Nor ought we to marvel if all the contrivances in nature be not, as far as we can judge, absolutely perfect; and if some of them be abhorrent to our ideas of fitness. We need not marvel at the sting of the bee causing the bee's own death; at drones being produced in such vast numbers for one single act, and being then slaughtered by their sterile sisters; at the astonishing waste of pollen by our fir-trees; at the instinctive hatred of the queen bee for her own fertile daughters; at ichneumonidæ[5] feeding within the live bodies of caterpillars; and at other such cases. The wonder indeed is, on the theory of natural selection, that more cases of the want of absolute perfection have not been observed.

The complex and little known laws governing variation are the same, as far as we can see, with the laws which have governed the production of so-called specific forms. In both cases physical conditions seem to have produced but little direct effect; yet when varieties enter any zone, they occasionally assume some of the characters of the species proper to that zone. In both varieties and species, use and disuse seem to have produced some effect; for it is difficult to resist this conclusion when we look, for instance, at the logger-headed duck, which has wings incapable of flight, in nearly the same condition as in the domestic duck; or when we look at the burrowing tucutucu,[6] which is occasionally blind, and then at certain moles, which are habitually blind and have their eyes covered with skin; or when we look at the blind animals inhabiting the dark caves of America and Europe. In both varieties and species correlation of growth seems to have played a most important part, so that when one part has been modified other parts are necessarily modified. In both varieties and species reversions to long-lost characters occur. How inexplicable on the theory of creation is the occasional appearance of stripes on the shoulder and legs of the several species of the horse-genus and in their hybrids! How simply is this fact explained if we believe that these species have descended from a striped progenitor, in the same manner as the several domestic breeds of pigeon have descended from the blue and barred rock-pigeon!

5. A wasplike insect, having larvae that are parasitic on the larvae of other insects.
6. Nocturnal rodent.

On the ordinary view of each species having been independently created, why should the specific characters, or those by which the species of the same genus differ from each other, be more variable than the generic characters in which they all agree? Why, for instance, should the colour of a flower be more likely to vary in any one species of a genus, if the other species, supposed to have been created independently, have different-ly coloured flowers, than if all the species of the genus have the same coloured flowers? If species are only well-marked varieties, of which the characters have become in a high degree permanent, we can understand this fact; for they have already varied since they branched off from a common progenitor in certain characters, by which they have come to be specifically distinct from each other; and therefore these same characters would be more likely still to be variable than the generic characters which have been inherited without change for an enormous period. It is inexplicable on the theory of creation why a part developed in a very unusual manner in any one species of a genus, and therefore, as we may naturally infer, of great importance to the species, should be eminently liable to variation; but, on my view, this part has undergone, since the several species branched off from a common progenitor, an unusual amount of variability and modification, and therefore we might expect this part generally to be still variable. But a part may be devel-oped in the most unusual manner, like the wing of a bat, and yet not be more variable than any other structure, if the part be common to many subordinate forms, that is, if it has been inherited for a very long period; for in this case it will have been rendered con-stant by long-continued natural selection.

Glancing at instincts, marvellous as some are, they offer no greater difficulty than does corporeal structure on the theory of the natural selection of successive, slight, but prof-itable modifications. We can thus understand why nature moves by graduated steps in endowing different animals of the same class with their several instincts. I have attempt-ed to show how much light the principle of gradation throws on the admirable architec-tural powers of the hive-bee. Habit no doubt sometimes comes into play in modifying instincts; but it certainly is not indispensable, as we see, in the case of neuter insects, which leave no progeny to inherit the effects of long-continued habit. On the view of all the species of the same genus having descended from a common parent, and having inher-ited much in common, we can understand how it is that allied species, when placed under considerably different conditions of life, yet should follow nearly the same instincts; why the thrush of South America, for instance, lines her nest with mud like our British species. On the view of instincts having been slowly acquired through natural selection we need not marvel at some instincts being apparently not perfect and liable to mistakes, and at many instincts causing other animals to suffer.

If species be only well-marked and permanent varieties, we can at once see why their crossed offspring should follow the same complex laws in their degrees and kinds of resemblance to their parents,—in being absorbed into each other by successive crosses, and in other such points,—as do the crossed offspring of acknowledged varieties. On the other hand, these would be strange facts if species have been independently created, and varieties have been produced by secondary laws. . . .

The fact, as we have seen, that all past and present organic beings constitute one grand natural system, with group subordinate to group, and with extinct groups often falling in between recent groups, is intelligible on the theory of natural selection with its contingencies of extinction and divergence of character. On these same principles we see how it is, that the mutual affinities of the species and genera within each class are so complex and circuitous. We see why certain characters are far more serviceable than others for classification;—why adaptive characters, though of paramount importance to the being, are of hardly any importance in classification; why characters derived from rudimentary parts, though of no service to the being, are often of high classificatory value; and why embryological characters are the most valuable of all. The real affinities of all organic beings are due to inheritance or community of descent. The natural system is a genealogical arrangement, in which we have to discover the lines of descent by the most permanent characters, however slight their vital importance may be.

The framework of bones being the same in the hand of a man, wing of a bat, fin of the porpoise, and leg of the horse,—the same number of vertebræ forming the neck of the giraffe and of the elephant,—and innumerable other such facts, at once explain themselves on the theory of descent with slow and slight successive modifications. The similarity of pattern in the wing and leg of a bat, though used for such different purpose,—in the jaws and legs of a crab,—in the petals, stamens, and pistils of a flower, is likewise intelligible on the view of the gradual modification of parts or organs, which were alike in the early progenitor of each class. On the principle of successive variations not always supervening at an early age, and being inherited at a corresponding not early period of life, we can clearly see why the embryos of mammals, birds, reptiles, and fishes should be so closely alike, and should be so unlike the adult forms. We may cease marvelling at the embryo of an air breathing mammal or bird having branchial slits and arteries running in loops, like those in a fish which has to breathe the air dissolved in water, by the aid of well-developed branchiæ.

Disuse, aided sometimes by natural selection, will often tend to reduce an organ, when it has become useless by changed habits or under changed conditions of life; and we can clearly understand on this view the meaning of rudimentary organs. But disuse and selection will generally act on each creature, when it has come to maturity and has to play its full part in the struggle for existence, and will thus have little power of acting on an organ during early life; hence the organ will not be much reduced or rendered rudimentary at this early age. The calf, for instance, has inherited teeth, which never cut through the gums of the upper jaw, from an early progenitor having well-developed teeth; and we may believe, that the teeth in the mature animal were reduced, during successive generations, by disuse or by the tongue and palate having been fitted by natural selection to browse without their aid; whereas in the calf, the teeth have been left untouched by selection or disuse, and on the principle of inheritance at corresponding ages have been inherited from a remote period to the present day. On the view of each organic being and each separate organ having been specially created, how utterly inexplicable it is that parts, like the teeth in the embryonic calf or like the shrivelled wings under the soldered wing-covers of some beetles, should thus so frequently bear the plain stamp of inutility! Nature may be said to have taken pains to reveal, by rudimentary organs and by homologous structures, her scheme of modification, which it seems that we wilfully will not understand.

I have now recapitulated the chief facts and considerations which have thoroughly convinced me that species have changed, and are still slowly changing by the preservation and accumulation of successive slight favourable variations. Why, it may be asked, have all the most eminent living naturalists and geologists rejected this view of the mutability of species? It cannot be asserted that organic beings in a state of nature are subject to no variation; it cannot be proved that the amount of variation in the course of long ages is a limited quantity; no clear distinction has been, or can be, drawn between species and well-marked varieties. It cannot be maintained that species when intercrossed are invariably sterile, and varieties invariably fertile; or that sterility is a special endowment and sign of creation. The belief that species were immutable productions was almost unavoidable as long as the history of the world was thought to be short of duration; and now that we have acquired some idea of the lapse of time, we are too apt to assume, without proof, that the geological record is so perfect that it would have afforded us plain evidence of the mutation of species, if they had undergone mutation.

But the chief cause of our natural unwillingness to admit that one species has given birth to other and distinct species, is that we are always slow in admitting any great change of which we do not see the intermediate steps. The difficulty is the same as that felt by so many geologists, when Lyell[7] first insisted that long lines of inland cliffs had been formed, and great valleys excavated, by the slow action of the coast-waves. The mind cannot possibly grasp the full meaning of the term of a hundred million years; it cannot add up and perceive the full effects of many slight variations, accumulated during an almost infinite number of generations.

Although I am fully convinced of the truth of the views given in this volume under the form of an abstract, I by no means expect to convince experienced naturalists whose minds are stocked with a multitude of facts all viewed, during a long course of years, from a point of view directly opposite to mine. It is so easy to hide our ignorance under such expressions as the "plan of creation," "unity of design," &c., and to think that we give an explanation when we only restate a fact. Any one whose disposition leads him to attach more weight to unexplained difficulties than to the explanation of a certain number of facts will certainly reject my theory. A few naturalists, endowed with much flexibility of mind, and who have already begun to doubt on the immutability of species, may be influenced by this volume; but I look with confidence to the future, to young and rising naturalists, who will be able to view both sides of the question with impartiality. Whoever is led to believe that species are mutable will do good service by conscientiously expressing his conviction; for only thus can the load of prejudice by which this subject is overwhelmed be removed.

Several eminent naturalists have of late published their belief that a multitude of reputed species in each genus are not real species; but that other species are real, that is, have been independently created. This seems to me a strange conclusion to arrive at. They

7. Sir Charles Lyell (1797–1875), author of *Principles of Geology* (1830–3).

admit that a multitude of forms, which till lately they themselves thought were special creations, and which are still thus looked at by the majority of naturalists, and which consequently have every external characteristic feature of true species,—they admit that these have been produced by variation, but they refuse to extend the same view to other and very slightly different forms. Nevertheless they do not pretend that they can define, or even conjecture, which are the created forms of life, and which are those produced by secondary laws. They admit variation as a *vera causa*[8] in one case, they arbitrarily reject it in another, without assigning any distinction in the two cases. The day will come when this will be given as a curious illustration of the blindness of preconceived opinion. These authors seem no more startled at a miraculous act of creation than at an ordinary birth. But do they really believe that at innumerable periods in the earth's history certain elemental atoms have been commanded suddenly to flash into living tissues? Do they believe that at each supposed act of creation one individual or many were produced? Were all the infinitely numerous kinds of animals and plants created as eggs or seed, or as full grown? and in the case of mammals, were they created bearing the false marks of nourishment from the mother's womb? Although naturalists very properly demand a full explanation of every difficulty from those who believe in the mutability of species, on their own side they ignore the whole subject of the first appearance of species in what they consider reverent silence.

It may be asked how far I extend the doctrine of the modification of species. The question is difficult to answer, because the more distinct the forms are which we may consider, by so much the arguments fall away in force. But some arguments of the greatest weight extend very far. All the members of whole classes can be connected together by chains of affinities, and all can be classified on the same principle, in groups subordinate to groups. Fossil remains sometimes tend to fill up very wide intervals between existing orders. Organs in a rudimentary condition plainly show that an early progenitor had the organ in a fully developed state; and this in some instances necessarily implies an enormous amount of modification in the descendants. Throughout whole classes various structures are formed on the same pattern, and at an embryonic age the species closely resemble each other. Therefore I cannot doubt that the theory of descent with modification embraces all the members of the same class. I believe that animals have descended from at most only four or five progenitors, and plants from an equal or lesser number.

Analogy would lead me one step further, namely, to the belief that all animals and plants have descended from some one prototype. But analogy may be a deceitful guide. Nevertheless all living things have much in common, in their chemical composition, their germinal vesicles, their cellular structure, and their laws of growth and reproduction. We see this even in so trifling a circumstance as that the same poison often similarly affects plants and animals; or that the poison secreted by the gall-fly produces monstrous growths on the wild rose or oak-tree. Therefore I should infer from analogy that probably all the organic beings which have ever lived on this earth have descended from some one primordial form, into which life was first breathed.

8. True or real cause.

When the views entertained in this volume on the origin of species, or when analogous views are generally admitted, we can dimly foresee that there will be a considerable revolution in natural history. . . . In short, we shall have to treat species in the same manner as those naturalists treat genera, who admit that genera are merely artificial combinations made for convenience. This may not be a cheering prospect; but we shall at least be freed from the vain search for the undiscovered and undiscoverable essence of the term species.

The other and more general departments of natural history will rise greatly in interest. The terms used by naturalists of affinity, relationship, community of type, paternity, morphology, adaptive characters, rudimentary and aborted organs, &c., will cease to be metaphorical, and will have a plain signification. When we no longer look at an organic being as a savage looks at a ship, as at something wholly beyond his comprehension; when we regard every production of nature as one which has had a history; when we contemplate every complex structure and instinct as the summing up of many contrivances, each useful to the possessor, nearly in the same way as when we look at any great mechanical invention as the summing up of the labour, the experience, the reason, and even the blunders of numerous workmen; when we thus view each organic being, how far more interesting, I speak from experience, will the study of natural history become! . . .

In the distant future I see open fields for far more important researches. Psychology will be based on a new foundation, that of the necessary acquirement of each mental power and capacity by gradation. Light will be thrown on the origin of man and his history.

Authors of the highest eminence seem to be fully satisfied with the view that each species has been independently created. To my mind it accords better with what we know of the laws impressed on matter by the Creator, that the production and extinction of the past and present inhabitants of the world should have been due to secondary causes, like those determining the birth and death of the individual. When I view all beings not as special creations, but as the lineal descendants of some few beings which lived long before the first bed of the Silurian system was deposited, they seem to me to become ennobled. Judging from the past, we may safely infer that not one living species will transmit its unaltered likeness to a distant futurity. And of the species now living very few will transmit progeny of any kind to a far distant futurity; for the manner in which all organic beings are grouped, shows that the greater number of species of each genus, and all the species of many genera, have left no descendants, but have become utterly extinct. We can so far take a prophetic glance into futurity as to foretel that it will be the common and widely-spread species, belonging to the larger and dominant groups, which will ultimately prevail and procreate new and dominant species. As all the living forms of life are the lineal descendants of those which lived long before the Silurian epoch, we may feel certain that the ordinary succession by generation has never once been broken, and that no cataclysm has desolated the whole world. Hence we may look with some confidence to a secure future of equally inappreciable length. And as natural selection works solely by and for the good of each being, all corporeal and mental endowments will tend to progress towards perfection.

It is interesting to contemplate an entangled bank, clothed with many plants of many kinds, with birds singing on the bushes, with various insects flitting about, and with worms crawling through the damp earth, and to reflect that these elaborately constructed forms, so different from each other, and dependent on each other in so complex a manner, have all been produced by laws acting around us. These laws, taken in the largest sense, being Growth with Reproduction; Inheritance which is almost implied by reproduction; Variability from the indirect and direct action of the external conditions of life, and from use and disuse; a Ratio of Increase so high as to lead to a Struggle for Life, and as a consequence to Natural Selection, entailing Divergence of Character and the Extinction of less-improved forms. Thus, from the war of nature, from famine and death, the most exalted object which we are capable of conceiving, namely, the production of the higher animals, directly follows. There is grandeur in this view of life, with its several powers, having been originally breathed into a few forms or into one; and that, whilst this planet has gone cycling on according to the fixed law of gravity, from so simple a beginning endless forms most beautiful and most wonderful have been, and are being, evolved.

# Elizabeth Rigby, Lady Eastlake

1809: Born 17 November at Norwich

1841: *A Residence on the Shores of the Baltic*, a collection of letters about Russian life

1846: *Livonian Tales*

1848: Review of *Vanity Fair*, *Jane Eyre*, and the 1847 Report of the Governesses' Benevolent Institution

1856: Review of Ruskin's *Modern Painters* in the *Quarterly Review*

1893: Died 2 October in London

---

## REVIEW OF *VANITY FAIR*, *JANE EYRE*, AND THE 1847 REPORT OF THE GOVERNESSES' BENEVOLENT INSTITUTION

*Elizabeth Rigby Eastlake was a well-informed art historian, practicing artist, fluent trans-lator, reviewer, social commentator, and author of several short works of fiction. But she is perhaps best known to modern readers for her 1848 attack on the author of* Jane Eyre *in the* Quarterly Review *and her erroneous belief—resting on what she saw as "Currer Bell's" ignorance of feminine social custom—that the novelist was a man. Eastlake's review of Charlotte* Brontë's *novel is part of a larger review, which includes her commentary on Thackeray's* Vanity Fair *and the 1847 Report of the Governesses' Benevolent Institution and examines the use—and exploitation—of governesses by upper-middle-class households. Astutely analyzing the circumstances by which "ladies," often as a result of their fathers' eco-nomic failures, are forced to become "servants of ladies" in order to support parents, siblings, and themselves, Eastlake calls her readers' attention to the hypocrisy of employers who desire an employee of their own class but refuse to offer a salary reflecting the governess's social and educational background. Rigby's analysis of the governess class is one of many discussions of the governesses' plight appearing throughout the 1840's; these essays reflect middle-class anxieties about the fluidity of class identities, a concern exacerbated by the economic and social uncertainties that characterized the first half of the century.[1]* LMF

---

1. See Mary Poovey, "The Anathematized Race: The Governess and *Jane Eyre*," *Uneven Developments* (Chicago: University of Chicago Press, 1988), pp. 126–63.

. . . Jane Eyre is throughout the personification of an unregenerate and undisciplined spirit, the more dangerous to exhibit from that prestige of principle and self-control which is liable to dazzle the eye too much for it to observe the inefficient and unsound foundation on which it rests. It is true Jane does right, and exerts great moral strength, but it is the strength of a mere heathen mind which is a law unto itself. No Christian grace is perceptible upon her. She has inherited in fullest measure the worst sin of our fallen nature—the sin of pride. Jane Eyre is proud, and therefore she is ungrateful too. It pleased God to make her an orphan, friendless, and penniless—yet she thanks nobody, and least of all Him, for the food and raiment, the friends, companions, and instructors of her helpless youth—for the care and education vouchsafed to her till she was capable in mind as fitted in years to provide for herself. On the contrary, she looks upon all that has been done for her not only as her undoubted right, but as falling far short of it. The doctrine of humility is not more foreign to her mind that it is repudiated by her heart. It is by her own talents, virtues, and courage that she is made to attain the summit of human happiness, and, as far as Jane Eyre's own statement is concerned, no one would think that she owed anything either to God above or to man below. She flees from Mr. Rochester, and has not a being to turn to. Why was this? The excellence of the present institution at Casterton, which succeeded that of Cowan Bridge near Kirkby Lonsdale—these being distinctly, as we hear, the original and the reformed Lowoods of the book—is pretty generally known. Jane had lived there for eight years with 110 girls and fifteen teachers. Why had she formed no friendships among them? Other orphans have left the same and similar institutions, furnished with friends for life, and puzzled with homes to choose from. How comes it that Jane had acquired neither? Among that number of associates there were surely some exceptions to what she so presumptuously stigmatises as 'the society of inferior minds.' Of course it suited the author's end to represent the heroine as utterly destitute of the common means of assistance, in order to exhibit both her trials and her powers of self-support—the whole book rests on this assumption—but it is one which, under the circumstances, is very unnatural and very unjust.

Altogether the auto-biography of Jane Eyre is pre-eminently an anti-Christian composition. There is throughout it a murmuring against the comforts of the rich and against the privations of the poor, which, as far as each individual is concerned, is a murmuring against God's appointment—there is a proud and perpetual assertion of the rights of man, for which we find no authority either in God's word or in God's providence—there is that pervading tone of ungodly discontent which is at once the most prominent and the most subtle evil which the law and the pulpit, which all civilized society in fact has at the present day to contend with. We do not hesitate to say that the tone of mind and thought which has overthrown authority and violated every code human and divine abroad, and fostered Chartism[2] and rebellion at home, is the same which has also written Jane Eyre.

Still we say again this is a very remarkable book. We are painfully alive to the moral, religious, and literary deficiencies of the picture, and . . . passages of beauty and power . . . cannot redeem it, but it is impossible not to be spell-bound with the freedom of the

2. The 1830s–1840s movement for political reform. Chartists formulated their demands in a six-point petition, or People's Charter, presented unsuccessfully to Parliament in 1839, 1842, and 1848.

touch. It would be mere hackneyed courtesy to call it 'fine writing.' It bears no impress of being written at all, but is poured out rather in the heat and hurry of an instinct, which flows ungovernably on to its object, indifferent by what means it reaches it, and unconscious too. As regards the author's chief object, however, it is a failure—that, namely, of making a plain, odd woman, destitute of all the conventional features of feminine attraction, interesting in our sight. We deny that he has succeeded in this. Jane Eyre, in spite of some grand things about her, is a being totally uncongenial to our feelings from beginning to end. We acknowledge her firmness—we respect her determination—we feel for her struggles; but, for all that, and setting aside higher considerations, the impression she leaves on our mind is that of a decidedly vulgar-minded woman—one whom we should not care for as an acquaintance, whom we should not seek as a friend, whom we should not desire for a relation, and whom we should scrupulously avoid for a governess.

There seem to have arisen in the novel-reading world some doubts as to who really wrote this book; and various rumours, more or less romantic, have been current in Mayfair, the metropolis of gossip, as to the authorship. For example, Jane Eyre is sentimentally assumed to have proceeded from the pen of Mr. Thackeray's governess, whom he had himself chosen as his model of Becky, and who, in mingled love and revenge, personified him in return as Mr. Rochester. In this case, it is evident that the author of 'Vanity Fair,' whose own pencil makes him grey-haired, has had the best of it, though his children may have had the worst, having, at all events, succeeded in hitting that vulnerable point in the Becky bosom, which it is our firm belief no man born of woman, from her Soho to her Ostend days, had ever so much as grazed. To this ingenious rumour the coincidence of the second edition of Jane Eyre being dedicated to Mr. Thackeray has probably given rise. For our parts, we see no great interest in the question at all. The first edition of Jane Eyre purports to be edited by Currer Bell, one of a trio of brothers, or sisters, or cousins, by names Currer, Acton, and Ellis Bell, already known as the joint-authors of a volume of poems. The second edition the same—dedicated, however, 'by the author,' to Mr. Thackeray; and the dedication (itself an indubitable chip of Jane Eyre) signed Currer Bell. Author and editor therefore are one, and we are as much satisfied to accept this double individual under the name of 'Currer Bell,' as under any other, more or less euphonious. Whoever it be, it is a person who, with great mental powers, combines a total ignorance of the habits of society, a great coarseness of taste, and a heathenish doctrine of religion. And as these characteristics appear more or less in the writings of all three, Currer, Acton, and Ellis alike, for their poems differ less in degree of power than in kind, we are ready to accept the fact of their identity or of their relationship with equal satisfaction. At all events there can be no interest attached to the writer of 'Wuthering Heights'—a novel succeeding 'Jane Eyre,' and purporting to be written by Ellis Bell—unless it were for the sake of more individual reprobation. For though there is a decided family likeness between the two, yet the aspect of the Jane and Rochester animals in their native state, as Catherine and Heathfield,[3] is too odiously and abominably pagan to be palatable even to the most vitiated class of English readers. With all the unscrupulousness of the French school of novels it combines that repulsive vulgarity in the choice of its vice which sup-

3. Obviously, she means Heathcliff.

plies its own antidote. The question of authorship, therefore, can deserve a moment's curiosity only as far as 'Jane Eyre' is concerned, and though we cannot pronounce that it appertains to a real Mr. Currer Bell and to no other, yet that it appertains to a man, and not, as many assert, to a woman, we are strongly inclined to affirm. Without entering into the question whether the power of the writing be above her, or the vulgarity below her, there are, we believe, minutiæ of circumstantial evidence which at once acquit the feminine hand. No woman—a lady friend, whom we are always happy to consult, assures us—makes mistakes in her own *métier*—no woman *trusses game* and garnishes dessert-dishes with the same hands, or talks of so doing in the same breath. Above all, no woman attires another in such fancy dresses as Jane's ladies assume—Miss Ingram coming down, irresistible, 'in a *morning* robe of sky-blue crape, a gauze azure scarf twisted in her hair!!' No lady, we understand, when suddenly roused in the night, would think of hurrying on '*a frock.*' They have garments more convenient for such occasions, and more becoming too. This evidence seems incontrovertible. Even granting that these incongruities were purposely assumed, for the sake of disguising the female pen, there is nothing gained; for if we ascribe the book to a woman at all, we have no alternative but to ascribe it to one who has, for some sufficient reason, long forfeited the society of her own sex.

And if by no woman, it is certainly also by no artist. The Thackeray eye has had no part there. There is not more disparity between the art of drawing Jane assumes and her evident total ignorance of its first principles, than between the report she gives of her own character and the conclusions we form for ourselves. Not but what, in another sense, the author may be classed as an artist of very high grade. Let him describe the simplest things in nature—a rainy landscape, a cloudy sky, or a bare moorside, and he shows the hand of a master; but the moment he talks of the art itself, it is obvious that he is a complete ignoramus.

We cannot help feeling that this work must be far from beneficial to that class of ladies whose cause it affects to advocate. Jane Eyre is not precisely the mouthpiece one would select to plead the cause of governesses, and it is therefore the greater pity that she has chosen it: for there is none we are convinced which, at the present time, more deserves and demands an earnest and judicious befriending. If these times puzzle us how to meet the claims and wants of the lower classes of our dependants, they puzzle and shame us too in the case of that highest dependant of all, the governess—who is not only entitled to our gratitude and respect by her position, but, in nine cases out of ten, by the circumstances which reduced her to it. For the case of the governess is so much the harder than that of any other class of the community, in that they are not only quite as liable to all the vicissitudes of life, but are absolutely supplied by them. There may be, and are, exceptions to this rule, but the real definition of a governess, in the English sense, is a being who is our equal in birth, manners, and education, but our inferior in wordly wealth. Take a lady, in every meaning of the word, born and bred, and let her father pass through the gazette,[4] and she wants nothing more to suit our highest *beau idéal* of a guide and instructress to our children. We need the imprudencies, extravagancies, mistakes, or crimes of a certain number of fathers, to sow that seed from which we reap the harvest

4. The *London Gazette* published the names of persons declaring bankruptcy.

of governesses. There is no other class of labourers for hire who are thus systematically supplied by the misfortunes of our fellow-creatures. There is no other class which so cruelly requires its members to be, in birth, mind, and manners, above their station, in order to fit them for their station. From this peculiarity in their very qualifications for office result all the peculiar and most painful anomalies of their professional existence. The line which severs the governess from her employers is not one which will take care of itself, as in the case of a servant. If she sits at table she does not shock you—if she opens her mouth she does not distress you—her appearance and manners are likely to be as good as your own—her education rather better; there is nothing upon the face of the thing to stamp her as having been called to a different state of life from that in which it has pleased God to place you; and therefore the distinction has to be kept up by a fictitious barrier which presses with cruel weight upon the mental strength or constitutional vanity of a woman. People talk of the prevailing vanity of governesses, and we grant it in one sense fully—but how should it not be so? If a governess have a grain of vanity in her composition, it is sought and probed for by every species of slight and mortification, intentional or not, till it starts into unnatural life beneath the irritation. She must be a saint, or no woman at all, who can rise above those perpetual little dropping-water trials to which the self-love of an averagely-placed governess is exposed. That fearful fact that the lunatic asylums of this country are supplied with a larger proportion of their inmates from the ranks of young governesses than from any other class of life, is a sufficient proof how seldom she can. But it is not her vanity which sends her there, but her *wounded* vanity—the distinction is great—and wounded vanity, as all medical men will tell us, is the rock on which most minds go to pieces.

Man cannot live by the head alone, far less woman. A governess has no equals, and therefore can have no sympathy. She is a burden and restraint in society, as all must be who are placed ostensibly at the same table and yet are forbidden to help themselves or to be helped to the same viands. She is a bore to almost any gentleman, as a tabooed woman, to whom he is interdicted from granting the usual privileges of the sex, and yet who is perpetually crossing his path. She is a bore to most ladies by the same rule, and a reproach too—for her dull, fagging, bread-and-water life is perpetually putting their pampered listlessness to shame. The servants invariably detest her, for she is a dependant like themselves, and yet, for all that, as much their superior in other respects as the family they both serve. Her pupils may love her, and she may take the deepest interest in them, but they cannot be her friends. She must, to all intents and purposes, live alone, or she transgresses that invisible but rigid line which alone establishes the distance between herself and her employers.

We do not deny that there are exceptions to this statement—that there are many governesses who are treated with an almost undue equality and kindness—that there are many who suffer from slights which they entirely make for themselves, and affect a humility which is never needed—and also that there is no class in which there are women so encroaching, so *exigeantes*,[5] and so disagreeable. But still these are exceptions, let them be ever so numerous. The broad and real characteristics of the governess's qualifications,

5. Demanding.

position, and trials are such as we have described, and must be such. Nor have we brought them forward with any view, or hope, or even with any wish to see them remedied, for in the inherent constitution of English habits, feelings, and prejudices, there is no possibility that they should be. We say English, for foreign life is far more favourable to a governess's happiness. In its less stringent domestic habits, the company of a *teacher*, for she is nothing more abroad, is no interruption—often an acquisition; she herself, again, is pleased with that mere surface of politeness and attention which would not satisfy an Englishwoman's heart or pride; the difference of birth, too, is more obvious, from the nonexistence in any other country of an untitled aristocracy like our own. But all this cannot be altered with us. We shall ever prefer to place those immediately about our children who have been born and bred with somewhat of the same refinement as ourselves. We must ever keep them in a sort of isolation, for it is the only means for maintaining that distance which the reserve of English manners and the decorum of English families exact. That true justice and delicacy in the employer which would make a sunshine even in a barren schoolroom must ever be too rare to be depended upon. That familiarity which should level all distinction a right-thinking governess would scorn to accept;—all this must be continued as it is. But there *is* one thing, the absence of which need not be added to the other drawbacks of her lot; which would go far to compensate to her for the misfortunes which reduced her to this mode of life, and for the trials attendant upon it— for the years of chilly solitude through which the heart is kept shivering upon a diet that can never sufficiently warm it, and that in the longing season of youth—for the nothing less than maternal cares and solicitudes for which she reaps no maternal reward—for a life spent in harness from morning till night, and from one year's end to another—for the old age and incapacity creeping on and threatening to deprive her even of that mode of existence which habit has made endurable—there is something that would compensate for all this, and that is *better pay*. We quite agree with Mr. Rochester, in answer to one of Jane's sententious speeches, that 'most freeborn things will submit to anything for a salary;' in other words, that most men and women of average sense will put up with much that is fatiguing to do, or irksome to bear, if you make it worth their while; and we know of no process of reasoning by which it can be proved that governesses, as is too often required from them, can dispense with this potent stimulus.

There is something positively usurious in the manner with which the misfortunes of the individual or the general difficulty of the times is now-a-days constantly taken advantage of to cut the stipend of the governess down to the lowest ratio that she will accept. The Jew raises his rate of interest because the heedless spendthrift will pay anything to get that loan he needs; and by the same rule the Christian parent lowers the salary because the friendless orphan will take anything rather than be without a situation. Each traffics with the necessities, and not with the merits of the case; but the one proceeding is so much the harder than the other, because it presses not upon a selfish, thoughtless, extravagant man, but upon a poor, patient, and industrious woman. 'And they are very glad to get that, I can tell you,' is the cold-hearted rejoinder, if you expostulate on the injustice of throwing all the labour of the teacher and many of the chief duties of a parent upon the shoulders of a young woman, for the remuneration of thirty or even twenty pounds a-year. It may be quite true that she is glad to get even this; and if so, it is very deplorable: but this has no relation to the services exacted and the assistance given; and these should be more especially the standard where the plaintiff, as in the case of the governess, possesses no means of resistance. Workmen may rebel, and tradesmen may combine, not to let you have their labour or their wares under a certain rate; but the governess has no refuge—no escape; she is a needy *lady*, whose services are of far too precious a kind to have any stated market value, and is therefore left to the mercy, or what they call the *means*, of the family that engages her.

But is not this an all-sufficient plea? it may be urged. If parents have not the means to give higher salaries, what can they do? We admit the argument, though it might be easily proved how often the cheap governess and the expensive servant are to be found in the same establishment; but the question is in truth whether they have the means or the excuse to keep a governess at all? Whether it be conscientiously honest to engage the best years of a hard-working, penniless woman, without the power of making her an adequate return? The fine-ladyism of the day has, we regret to observe, crept into a lower class than that one was wont to associate it with, and where, from its greater sacrifice of the com forts and rights of others, it is still more objectionable. Women, whose husbands leave them in peace from morning till night, for counting-houses or lawyers' offices—certainly leave them with nothing better to do than to educate and attend to their children—must now, forsooth, be keeping ill-paid governesses for those duties which one would hope a peeress only unwillingly relinquishes. Women, from whom society requires nothing but that they should quietly and unremittingly do that for which their station offers them the happy leisure, must now treat themselves to one of those *pro-mammas* who, owing to various causes, more or less distressing, have become so plentiful that they may be had *cheap*! If more governesses find a penurious maintenance by these means, more mothers are encouraged to neglect those duties, which, one would have thought, they would have been as jealous of as of that first duty of all that infancy requires from them. It is evident, too, that by this unfair demand the supply has been suddenly increased. Farmers and tradespeople are now educating their daughters for governesses as a mode of advancing them a step in life, and thus a number of underbred young women have crept into the profession who have brought down the value of salaries and interfered with the rights of those whose birth and misfortunes leave them no other refuge. . . .

While we therefore applaud heartily the efforts for their comfort and relief which have been made within the last few years, in the establishment of the Governesses' Benevolent Institution, we look with sorrow, and almost with horror, at the disclosures which those efforts have brought to light. There is no document which more painfully exposes the peculiar tyranny of our present state of civilization than those pages in the Report of this Society containing the list of candidates for the few and small annuities which the Institution is as yet in the condition to give. We know of nothing, in truth or fiction, more affecting than the sad and simple annals of these afflicted and destitute ladies, many of them with their aristocratic names, who, having passed through that course of servitude which, as we have shown, is peculiarly and inevitably deprived of most of those endearing sympathies which gladden this life, are now left in their old age or sickness without even the absolute necessaries for existence. With minds also which, from their original refinement and constant cultivation, have the keener sense of the misery and injustice of their lot; for the delicate and well-bred lady we at first congratulated ourselves on having engaged in our family is equally the same when we cast her off to shift for herself. What a mockery must all this thankless acquisition of knowledge, which has been the object of her study and the puff in her credentials, appear to her now! Conversant with several languages—skilled in many accomplishments—crammed with every possible fact in history, geography, and the use of the globes—and scarcely the daily bread to put into her mouth! . . .

# William Ewart Gladstone

1809: Born 29 December, Liverpool

1832: Entered House of Commons as Tory

1838: *The State in its Relations with the Church*

1868–74: First term as Liberal Prime Minister

1880–5: Second ministry

1886: Third ministry

1892–4: Fourth ministry

1898: Died 19 May, at Hawarden, Wales

## ENGLAND'S MISSION

*England's expansionist colonial politics and sentiments in the last three decades of the century did not go uncontested. One of the most outspoken critics of aggressive imperialism, Liberal William Gladstone characterized the foreign policies and activities of his Conservative rival Benjamin Disraeli's government as unprincipled, jingoistic, and excessive. In 1878 Prime Minister Disraeli (Lord Beaconsfield) and his foreign secretary Lord Salisbury returned from the Congress of Berlin, where, under the guise of settling the Russo-Turkish War and achieving "peace with honour," the major European powers had helped themselves to the spoils, with England appropriating Cyprus as a Mediterranean base. The morally indignant Gladstone responded in "England's Mission," published in the September 1878 issue of* The Nineteenth Century. *He charged that Disraeli and his foreign minister had allied England with the Turkish oppressors of Balkan Christians and, by annexing Cyprus, pursued a policy of territorial acquisitiveness that would drain the economy and reduce England's international reputation.*

*Not that Gladstone was anti-Empire: "The sentiment of empire," he admitted, "may be called innate in every Briton." But his notion of empire was less militaristic and expansionist than Disraeli's. Advocating free trade and the "equal rights of nations," Gladstone envisioned, somewhat paternally, a community or family of colonies, bound together not by force*

*but by mutual interests and trust. Ironically, during Gladstone's second administration,*
*England would display its military power and occupy Egypt.*          RM

'GENTLEMEN, WE BRING YOU PEACE; and peace with honour.' Such are the reputed words, with which Lord Beaconsfield and Lord Salisbury, the two British Plenipotentiaries at Berlin, rewarded the admiring crowds who, on their return to London in July, formed part of the well-organised machinery of an obsequious reception, unexampled, I suppose, in the history of our civilians; and meant, perhaps, to recall the pomp of the triumphs which Rome awarded to her most successful generals.

> Deliis
> Ornatum foliis ducem,
> Quod regum tumidas contuderit minas,
> Ostendet Capitolio.[1]

To whatever criticism it may be open, it was certainly a bold challenge to Fortune thus to blazon deeds which at best were no more than inchoate. Peace and honour are most musical, most attractive words. But as to the first of this 'blest pair of Sirens,' two questions at once occur: what was it that they brought, and in what sense were they the bringers? . . .

. . . Territorial aggrandisement, backed by military display, is the *cheval de bataille*[2] of the administration. Empire is greatness; leagues of land are empire; your safety is measured by the fear you strike into other nations; trade follows the flag: he that doubts is an enemy to his country. This creed of aggrandisement, made real to the public imagination by the acquisition of a Mediterranean and virtually European island,[3] has operated a relative success: it has covered the miscarriages of the Government, and it enables them to say that they have not been condemned to capital punishment by the country.

It is very disagreeable for an Englishman to hint to Englishmen that the self-love and pride, which all condemn in individuals, have often lured nations to their ruin or their loss; that they are apt to entail a great deal of meanness, as well as a great deal of violence; that they begin with a forfeiture of respect abroad, and end even in the loss of self-respect; that their effect is to destroy all sobriety in the estimation of human affairs, and to generate a temperament of excitability which errs alternately on the side of arrogance, and of womanish and unworthy fears. For the performance of this disagreeable duty, we are entitled to look in the first place to the Queen's Government; which ought in foreign affairs invariably to play, and which in other times usually has played, the part of moderator; and which thus has supplied much of that correction, which in domestic matters we supply to one another by the free contact, and even conflict, of opinion. It is their duty

---

1. Hor. *Od*. IV. iii. 6. [Gladstone's note] Gladstone quotes a fragment of the following passage, literally translated: "Isthmian labor will not make him famous as a boxer, whom you have once looked at with kindly eye when he was born, Melpomene, nor will an unsluggish horse lead him as a victor in an Achaean chariot, nor will military affairs show him to the Capitoline as a leader adorned with the Delian leaves, because he has crushed the proud threats of kings."
2. Fad, obsession, or hobbyhorse.
3. Cyprus.

to act as counsel for the absent. It is bad enough when men without the responsibilities of office condescend to appeal to selfishness and prejudice. When, on the occasion of Mr. Pitt's treaty with France, Mr. Fox made himself the organ of an old antipathy, and described France as our natural enemy,[4] he greatly erred; but had the parts been reversed, and had Mr. Pitt given utterance to such a sentiment, the offence committed, and the mischief done, would each have been multiplied an hundredfold. Substantially it is just that inversion of parts, which has taken place in our controversy on the Eastern Question. The doctrines of national self-restraint, of the equal obligations of States to public law, and of their equal rights to fair construction as to words and deeds, have been left to unofficial persons. The Government, not uniformly nor consistently, but in the main and on the whole, have opened up and relied on an illegitimate source of power, which never wholly fails: they have appealed, under the prostituted name of patriotism, to exaggerated fears, to imaginary interests, and to the acquisitiveness of a race which has surpassed every other known to history in the faculty of appropriating to itself vast spaces of the earth, and establishing its supremacy over men of every race and language. Now I hold that to stimulate these tendencies, to overlook the proportion between our resources and our obligations, and above all to claim anything more than equality of rights in the moral and political intercourse of the world, is not the way to make England great, but to make it both morally and materially little.

The sentiment of empire may be called innate in every Briton. If there are exceptions, they are like those of men born blind or lame among us. It is part of our patrimony: born with our birth, dying only with our death; incorporating itself in the first elements of our knowledge, and interwoven with all our habits of mental action upon public affairs. It is a portion of our national stock, which has never been deficient, but which has more than once run to rank excess, and brought us to mischief accordingly, mischief that for a time we have weakly thought was ruin. In its normal action, it made for us the American colonies, the grandest monument ever erected by a people of modern times, and second only to the Greek colonisation in the whole history of the world. In its domineering excess, always under the name of British interests and British honour, it lost them by obstinacy and pride. Lord Chatham who forbade us to tax, Mr. Burke who forbade us to legislate for them, would have saved them.[5] But they had to argue for a limitation of English power; and to meet the reproach of the political wiseacres, who first blustered on our greatness, and then, when they reaped as they had sown, whined over our calamities. Undoubtedly the peace of 1782–3, with its adjuncts in exasperated feeling, was a terrible dismemberment. But England was England still: and one of the damning signs of the politics of the school is their total blindness to the fact, that the central strength of England lies in England. Their eye travels with satisfaction over the wide space upon the map covered by the huge ice-bound deserts of North America or the unpenetrated wastes of Australasia, but rests with mortification on the narrow bounds of latitude and longitude marked by nature for the United Kingdom. They are the materialists of politics: their

4. In 1787 Charles James Fox (1749–1806) opposed the commercial treaty with France negotiated by Prime Minister William Pitt the Younger (1759–1806).
5. The Earl of Chatham, William Pitt the Elder (1708–78); Edmund Burke (1729–1797).

faith is in acres and in leagues, in sounding titles and long lists of territories. They forget that the entire fabric of the British Empire was reared and consolidated by the energies of a people, which was (though it is not now) insignificant in numbers, when compared with the leading States of the Continent; and that if by some vast convulsion our transmarine possessions could be all submerged, the very same energies of that very same people would either discover other inhabited or inhabitable spaces of the globe on which to repeat its work, or would without them in other modes assert its undiminished greatness. Of all the opinions disparaging to England, there is not one which can lower her like that which teaches that the source of strength for this almost measureless body lies in its extremities, and not in the heart which has so long propelled the blood through all its regions, and in the brain which has bound and binds them into one.

In the sphere of personal life, most men are misled through the medium of the dominant faculty of their nature. It is round that dominant faculty that folly and flattery are wont to buzz. They play upon vainglory by exaggerating and commending what it does, and by piquing it on what it sees cause to forbear from doing. It is so with nations. For all of them the supreme want really is, to be warned against the indulgence of the dominant passion. The dominant passion of France was military glory. Twice, in this century, it has towered beyond what is allowed to man; and twice has paid the tremendous forfeit of opening to the foe the proudest capital in the world. The dominant passion of England is extended empire. It has heretofore been kept in check by the integrity and sagacity of her statesmen, who have not shrunk from teaching her the lessons of self-denial and self-restraint. But a new race has arisen; and the most essential or the noblest among all the duties of government, the exercise of moral control over ambition and cupidity, have been left to the intermittent and feeble handling of those who do not govern.

Between the two parties in this controversy there is a perfect agreement that England has a mighty mission in the world; but there is a discord as fundamental upon the question what that mission is.

I. With the one party, her first care is held to be the care of her own children within her own shores, the redress of wrongs, the supply of needs, the improvement of laws and institutions. Against this homespun doctrine, the present Government appears to set up territorial aggrandisement, large establishments, and the accumulation of a multitude of fictitious interests abroad, as if our real interests were not enough; and since the available store of national time and attention is a fixed quantity, there ensues that comparative remissness in domestic affairs, which is too conclusively shown by the beggarly returns of our legislation, the aggravation of our burdens, and the fast-growing arrears of business.

II. With the one party, the great duty and honour and charge of our transmarine Colonial Empire is, to rear up free congenital communities. They receive a minority of our emigrants, of whom the larger number go to the United States of America; but, in receiving this minority, they enlarge for our outgoing population the field of choice, and by keeping them within the Empire diminish the shock and severance of change. Commercially our colonies unhappily embrace to a great extent, like the United States, the principles of Protectionism, and they are quietly suffered to carry them even into caricature by enforcing them against the parent country; but they have not within themselves the same scope and variety of production which allow those principles to receive in the United States such large effect; and from many causes, none of them involving coercion or command, the capitative addition made by their population to our commerce is larger than in the case of any foreign country. It is felt at the same time that Great Britain has, against the merely material advantages of these possessions, greatly enlarged her military responsibilities in time of war. Energetic efforts, indeed, have been necessary to relieve the mother country from military charge for the colonies in ordinary years of peace; and these have been largely, but not as yet uniformly, successful. Still, whatever be in these respects the just balance of the account, it is felt that the colonial relation involves far higher elements of consideration; that the founding of these free, growing, and vigorous communities has been a specific part of the work providentially assigned to Britain. The day has gone by, when she would dream of compelling them by force to remain in political connection with her. But, on the other hand, she would never suffer them to be torn away from her; and would no more grudge the cost of defending them against such a consummation, than the father of a family grudges the expense of the food necessary to maintain his children. . . .

Of all the Empires whose rise and fall have been recorded in history, there is not one that has owed its ruin or decay to checking the lust of unmeasured territorial acquisition. The wisest of the Roman Emperors was also the one, who even recalled the boundaries of his dominions from beyond the Danube. Every one can discern and denounce the private folly of the farmer who covets more and more land, when he has neither capital nor skill to turn to account what he has already got; though he does not commonly proceed by covenants taken in the dark lest his landlord should come to know what sort of deed he is signing. But it requires a steady eye and a firm resolution to maintain the good tradition of all our bygone statesmen at a juncture when all tradition is discarded for newfangled, or, as Mr. Roebuck[6] calls them, 'original' devices, and the mind of folly finds utterance through the voice of authority. England, which has grown so great, may easily become little; through the effeminate selfishness of luxurious living; through neglecting realities at home to amuse herself everywhere else in stalking phantoms; through putting again on her resources a strain like that of the great French war, which brought her people to misery, and her Throne to peril; through that denial of equal rights to others, which taught us so severe a lesson at the epoch of the Armed Neutrality. But she will never lose by the modesty in thought and language, which most of all beseems the greatest of mankind; never by forwardness to allow, and to assert, the equal rights of all states and nations; never by refusing to be made the tool of foreign cunning, for ends alien to her principles and feelings; never by keeping her engagements in due relation to her means, or by husbanding those means for the day of need, and for the noble duty of defending, as occasion offers, the cause of public right, and of rational freedom, over the broad expanse of Christendom.

---

6. John Arthur Roebuck (1801–79), radical politician and reformer.

# Henry Mayhew

1812: Born 25 November in London

1835: Became editor of *Figaro in London*, a comic weekly

1841: Helped to found *Punch*; became coeditor with Mark Lemon

1847: *The Greatest Plague of Life: Or The Adventures of a Lady in Search of a Good Servant*, with his brother Augustus

1849–50: Metropolitan Correspondent for *Morning Chronicle* investigation of "Labour and the Poor"

1851–2: *London Labour and the London Poor*

1862: *The Criminal Prisons of London*

1887: Died 25 July in London

## LABOUR AND THE POOR

Henry Mayhew's reputation rests on his series of investigations into the lives of London's poor, which he considered "under three separate phases, according as they will work, they can't work, and they won't work." He began with a study of London's manufacturing trades for the Morning Chronicle's series on "Labour and the Poor," from which we take our selection. A response to middle-class interest in the poor—stimulated by an attempt to understand the recent Chartist movement and the 1848–9 cholera epidemic—the series was an ambitious project. At first "Labour and the Poor" comprised three sections: each week a reader would see articles or "letters" by Mayhew as "Special Correspondent for the Metropolis" and other letters from a provincial correspondent who covered the manufacturing and mining districts and a correspondent who covered the rural districts. In October 1850 Mayhew left the Morning Chronicle and began publishing London Labour and the London Poor in parts, binding the parts into volumes in 1851 and 1852, with later volumes appearing in 1861 and 1862. London Labour and the London Poor expanded upon Mayhew's Morning Chronicle articles, incorporating more detailed interviews, a widened range of street folk interviewed, and more fully developed discussions of political economy. Nevertheless, the four-volume study reveals some redundancy as well as Mayhew's *indebtedness to materials he collected for his original investigations.*

*The* Morning Chronicle *series followed two decades of investigation into the living and working conditions of the poor: governmental commissions had looked into industrial working conditions and the functioning of the Poor Laws and issued "blue books" reporting their observations; James KAY-SHUTTLEWORTH and Edwin Chadwick had studied sanitary conditions; philanthropists had gathered information about working-class morality. Mayhew, however, was as interested in the opinions of the working poor as in questions of morality and statistics about living conditions. A journalist and amateur sociologist, he conducted detailed interviews with a number of people from each group he studied. Some readers criticized his technique, his accuracy (with some justification), and the series as a whole for exploiting the sordidness and pathos of poverty in order to boost readership. Manufacturers were angered. But many were sobered by Mayhew's findings, including Charles KINGSLEY, who drew upon Mayhew's series when writing his novel* Alton Locke.

LMF

## LETTER 2 (*THE MORNING CHRONICLE*, OCTOBER 23, 1849)

IN MY FIRST LETTER I STATED that I purposed considering the whole of the metropolitan poor under three distinct phases—according as they will work, as they *can't* work, and as they *won't* work. The causes of poverty among such as are willing to work, appeared to me to be two: 1. The workman might receive for his labour less than sufficient to satisfy his wants. 2. He might receive a sufficiency, and yet be in want, either from having to pay an exorbitant price for the commodities he requires in exchange for his wages, or else from a deficiency of economy and prudence in the regulation of his desires by his means and chances of subsistence. Or, to say the same thing in a more concise manner, the privations of the industrious classes admit of being referred either to (1) low wages, (2) high prices, or (3) improvident habits.

In opening the subject which has been entrusted to me, and setting forth the plan I purpose pursuing, so as to methodize and consequently simplify the investigation of it, I stated it to be my intention to devote myself primarily to the consideration of that class of poor whose privations seemed to be due to the insufficiency of their wages. In accordance with this object, I directed my steps first towards Bethnal-green, with the view of inquiring into the rate of wages received by the Spitalfields weavers. My motive for making this selection was, principally, because the manufacture of silk is one of the few arts that continue localized—that is, restricted to a particular quarter—in London. The tanners of Bermondsey—the watchmakers of Clerkenwell—the coachmakers of Long-acre—the marine-store dealers of Saffron-hill—the old clothesmen of Holywell-street and Rosemary-lane—the potters of Lambeth—the hatters of the Borough, are among the few handicrafts and trades that, as in the bazaars of the East, are confined to particular parts of the town. Moreover, the weavers of Spitalfields have always been notorious for their privations, and being all grouped together within a comparatively small space, they could be more easily visited, and a greater mass of information obtained in a less space of time, than in the case of any other ill-paid metropolitan handicraft with which I am acquainted. In my inquiry I have sought to obtain information from the artizans of Spitalfields upon two points in particular. I was desirous to ascertain from the workmen themselves, not only the average rate of wages received by them, but also to hear their opinions as to the cause of the depreciation in the value of their labour. The result of my inquiries on these two points I purpose setting forth in my present communication; but, before entering upon the subject, I wish the reader distinctly to understand that the sentiments here recorded are those wholly and solely of the weavers themselves. My vocation is to collect facts, and to register opinions. I have undertaken the subject with a rigid determination neither to be biased nor prejudiced by my own individual notions, whatever they may be, upon the matter. I know that as in science the love of theorising warps the mind, and causes it to see only those natural phenomena that it wishes to see—so in politics, party-feeling is the coloured spectacles through which too many invariably look at the social events of this and other countries. The truth will be given in its stark nakedness. Indeed, hardly a line will be written but what a note of the matter recorded has been taken upon the spot, so that, no matter how startling or incredible the circumstances may seem, the reader may rest assured that it is his experience rather than the reporter's veracity that is at fault.

With this preamble let me now seek to set before the reader the peculiar characteristics, first, of the district to which the Spitalfields weaver is indigenous, and, secondly, of the art he follows. "Owing to the vastness of London," says Mr. Martin, in one of his Sanitary Reports—"owing to the moral gulf which there separates the various classes of its inhabitants, its several quarters may be designated as assemblages of towns rather than as one city; and so it is, in a social sense and on a smaller scale, in other towns: the rich know nothing of the poor— the mass of misery that festers beneath the affluence of London and of the great towns is not known to their wealthy occupants." . . .

. . . The history of weaving in Spitalfields is interesting, and tends to elucidate several of the habits existing to this day among the class. Upon the revocation of the edict of Nantes[1] in 1685, numerous French artizans left their native country, and took refuge in the neighbouring states. King James II. encouraged these settlers, and William III. published a proclamation, dated April 25, 1689, for the encouraging the French Protestants to transport themselves into this kingdom, promising them his royal protection, and to render their living here comfortable and easy to them. For a considerable time the population of Spitalfields might be considered as exclusively French; that language was universally spoken, and even within the memory of persons now living their religious rites were performed in French in chapels erected for that purpose. The weavers were, formerly, almost the only botanists in the metropolis, and their love of flowers to this day is a strongly marked characteristic of the class. Some years back, we are told, they passed their leisure hours, and generally the whole family dined on Sundays, at the little gardens in the environs of London, now mostly built upon. Not very long ago there was an Entomological Society, and they were among the most diligent entomologists in the

---

1. The Edict of Nantes (1598) allowed limited religious freedom to French Huguenots. Its revocation in 1685 by Louis XIV led many Protestants to emigrate from France.

kingdom. This taste, though far less general than formerly, still continues to be a type of the class. There was at one time a Floricultural Society, an Historical Society, and a Mathematical Society, all maintained by the operative silk-weavers; and the celebrated Dollond, the inventor of the achromatic telescope, was a weaver; so too were Simpson and Edwards, the mathematicians, before they were taken from the loom into the employ of Government, to teach mathematics to the cadets at Woolwich and Chatham.[2] Such *were* the Spitalfields weavers at the beginning of the present century; possessing tastes and following pursuits the refinement and intelligence of which would be an honour and a grace to the artisan even of the present day, but which shone out with a double lustre at a time when the amusements of society were almost all of a gross and brutalizing kind. The weaver of our own time, however, though still far above the ordinary artisan, both in refinement and intellect, falls far short of the weaver of former years.

Of the importance of the silk trade, as a branch of manufacture, to the country, we may obtain some idea from the estimate of the total value of the produce, drawn up by Mr. M'Culloch, with great care, as he tells us, from the statements of intelligent, practical men in all parts of the country, conversant with the trade, and well able to form an opinion upon it. The total amount of wages paid in the year 1836 (since when, he says, the circumstances have changed but little) was upwards of £370,000; the total number of hands employed, 200,000; the interest on capital, wear, tear, profit, &c., £2,600,000; and the estimated total value of the silk manufacture of Great Britain, £10,480,000. Now, according to the census of the weavers of the Spitalfields district, taken at the time of the Government inquiry in 1838, and which appears to be considered by the weavers themselves of a generally accurate character, the number of looms at work was 9,302, and those unemployed, 894. But every two of the looms employed would occupy five hands; so that the total number of hands engaged in the silk manufacture in Spitalfields, in 1838, must have been more than double that number—say 20,000. This would show about one-tenth of the silk goods that were produced in Great Britain in that year to have been manufactured in Spitalfields, and hence the total value of the produce of that district must have been upwards of one million of money, and the amount paid in wages about £370,000. Now, from inquiries made among the operatives, I find that there has been a depreciation in the value of their labour of from 15 to 20 per cent. since the year 1839; so that, according to the above calculation, the total amount of wages now paid to the weavers is £60,000 less than what it was ten years back. By the preceding estimate it will be seen that the average amount of wages in the trade would have been in 1839 about 7s. a week per hand, and that now the wages would be about 5s. 6d. for each of the parties employed. This appears to agree with a printed statement put forward by the men themselves, wherein it is affirmed that "the average weekly earnings of the operative silk weaver in 1824, under the act then repealed, taking the whole body of operatives employed, partially employed, and unemployed, was 14s. 6d. Deprived of legislative protection," they say, "there is now no means of readily ascertaining the average weekly earnings of the whole body of the employed and unemployed operative silk weavers; but,

2. John Dollond (1706–61). Thomas Simpson (1710–61).

according to the best approximation to an average which can be made in Spitalfields, the average of the weekly earnings of the operative silk weaver is now, taking the unemployed and the partially employed, with the employed of those remaining attached to the occupation of weaver, only 4s. 9d. But this weekly average would be much less if it included those who have gone to other trades, or who have become perpetual paupers." Hence it would appear that the estimate before given of 5s. 6d. for the weekly average wages of the employed is not very far from the truth. It may therefore be safely asserted that the operative silk weavers, as a body, obtain £50,000 worth less of food, clothing, and comfort per annum now than in the year 1839.

Now let us see what was the state of the weaver in that year, as detailed by the Government report, so that we may be the better able to comprehend what his state must be at present: "Mr. Thomas Heath, of No. 8, Pedley-street," says the Blue Book of 1839, "has been represented by many persons as one of the most skilful workmen in Spitalfields. He handed in about 40 samples of figured silk done by him, and they appear exceedingly beautiful. This weaver also gave a minute and detailed account of all his earnings for 430 weeks, being upwards of eight years, with the names of the manufacture and the fabrics at which he worked. The sum of the gross earnings for 430 weeks is £322 3s. 4d., being about 14s. 11 3/4 d.—say 15s. a week. He estimates his expenses (for quill-winding, picking, &c.) at 4s., which would leave 11s. net wages; but take the expenses at 3s. 6d., it is still only 11s. 6d. He states his wife's earnings at about 3s. a week. He gives the following remarkable evidence:—Have you any children? No; I had two, but they are both dead, thanks be to God! Do you express satisfaction at the death of your children? I do! I thank God for it. I am relieved from the burden of maintaining them, and they, poor dear creatures, are relieved from the troubles of this mortal life." If this, then, was the condition and feeling of one of the most skilful workmen ten years ago, earning 11s. 6d. a week, and when it was proved in evidence by Mr. Cole that 8s. 6d. per week was the average net earnings of twenty plain weavers—what must be the condition and feeling of the weaver now that wages have fallen from 15 to 20 per cent. since that period?

I will now proceed to give the result of my inquiries into the subject; though, before doing so, it will be as well to make the reader acquainted with the precautions adopted to arrive at a fair and unbiassed estimate as to the feelings and condition of the workmen in the trade. In the first place, having put myself in communication with the surgeon of the district, and one of the principal and most intelligent of the operatives, it was agreed among us that we should go into a particular street, and visit the first six weavers' houses that we came to. Accordingly we made the best of our way to the nearest street. The houses were far above the average abodes of the weavers, the street being wide and airy, and the houses open at the back, with gardens filled with many-coloured dahlias. The "long lights" at top, as the attic window stretching the whole length of the house is technically called, showed that almost the whole line of houses were occupied by weavers. As we entered the street, a coal cart, with a chime of bells above the horse's collar, went jingling past us. Another circumstance peculiar to the place was the absence of children. In such a street, had the labour of the young been less valuable, the gutters and door-steps would have swarmed with juveniles. We knocked at the door of the first house, and, requesting permission to speak with the workman on the subject of his trade, were all three ushered up a steep staircase, and through a trap in the floor into the "shop." This was a long, narrow apartment, with a window back and front, extending the entire length of the house—running from one end of the room to the other. The man was the ideal of his class—a short, spare figure, with a thin face and sunken cheeks. In the room were three looms and some spinning wheels, at one of which sat a boy winding "quills." Working at a loom was a plump, pleasant-looking girl, busy making "plain goods." Along the windows, on each side, were ranged small pots of fuchsias, with their long scarlet drops swinging gently backwards and forwards, as the room shook with the clatter of the looms. The man was a velvet weaver. He was making a drab velvet for coat collars. We sat down on a wooden chair beside him, and talked as he worked. He told us he was to have 3s. 6d. per yard for the fabric he was engaged upon, and that he could make about half a yard a day. They were six in family, he said, and he had three looms at work. He got from 20s. to 25s. for the labour of five of them, and that only when they all are employed. But one loom is generally out of work waiting for fresh "cane." Up to 1824, the price for the same work as he is now doing was 6s. The reduction, he was convinced, arose from the competition in the trade, and one master cutting under the other. "The workmen are obliged to take the low prices, because they have not the means to hold out, and they know that if they don't take the work others will. There are always plenty of weavers unemployed, and the cause of that is owing to the lowness of prices, and the people being compelled to do double the quantity of work that they used to do, in order to live. I have made a stand against the lowness of prices, and have lost my work through refusing to take the price. Circumstances compel us to take it at last. The cupboard gets low, and the landlord comes for his weekly rent. The masters are all trying to undersell one another. They never will advance wages. Go get my neighbour to do it, each says, and then *I'll* advance. It's been a continuation of reduction for the last six-and-twenty years, and a continuation of suffering for just as long. Never a month passes but what you hear of something being lowered. Manufacturers may be divided into two classes—those who care for their men's comforts and welfare, and those who care for none but themselves. In the work of reduction certain houses take the lead, taking advantage of the least depression to offer the workmen less wages. It's useless talking about French goods. Why, we've driven the French out of the market in umbrellas and parasols—but the people are a-starving while they're a-driving of 'em out. A little time back he'd had only one loom at work for eight persons, and lived by making away with his clothes. Labour is so low he can't afford to send his children to school. He only sends them of a Sunday—can't afford it of a work-a-day."

At the next house the man took rather a more gloomy view of his calling. He was at work at brown silk for umbrellas. "His wife worked when she was able, but she was nursing a sick child. He had made the same work he was then engaged upon at 1s. a yard not six months ago. He was to have 10d. for it, and he didn't know that there might not be another penny taken off next time. Weavers were all a-getting poorer, and masters all a-getting country houses. His master had been a-losing terrible, he said, and yet he'd just taken a country mansion. They only give you work just to oblige you, as an act of charity, and not to do themselves any good—oh, no! Works fifteen hours, and often more. When he knocks off at ten at night, leaves lights up all round him—many go on till eleven. All he knows is, he can't! They are possessed of greater strength than he is, he imagines. In the dead of night he can always see one light somewhere—some man "on the finish." Wakes at five, and then he can hear the looms going. Low prices arise entirely from competition among the masters. The umbrella silk he was making would most likely be charged a guinea; what would sixpence extra on that be to the purchaser, and yet that extra sixpence would be three or four shillings per week to him, and go a long way towards the rent? Isn't able to tell exactly what is the cause of the depression— "I only know I suffers from it—aye, that I do! I do! and have severely for some time," said the man, striking the silk before him with his clenched fist. "The man that used to make this here is dead and buried; he died of the cholera. I went to see him buried. He had 11d. for what I get 10d. What it will be next God only knows, and I'm sure I don't care—it can't be much worse." "Mary," said he, to his wife, as she sat blowing the fire, with the dying infant on her lap, "how much leg of beef do we use?—4lb., ain't it, in the week, and 3lb. of flank on Sunday—lucky to get that, too, eh?—and that's among half a dozen of us. Now, I should like a piece of roast beef, with the potatoes done under it, but I shall never taste that again. And yet," said he, with a savage chuckle, "that there sixpence on this umbrella would just do it. But what's that to people? What's it to them if we starve?—and there is many at that game just now, I can tell you. If we could depend upon a constancy of work, and get a good price, why we should be happy men; but I'm sure I don't know whether I shall get any more work when my 'cane's' out. My children I'm quite disheartened about. They must turn out in the world somewhere, but where Heaven only knows. I often bother myself over that—more than my father bothered him self over me. What's to become of us all? What's to become of us all—nine thousand of us here—besides wives and children—I can't say."

These two specimens will give the reader a conception of the feelings and state of the rest of the weavers in the same street. In all there was the same want of hope—the same doggedness and half-indifference as to their fate. All agreed in referring their misery to the spirit of competition on the part of the masters, the same desire to "cut under." They all spoke most bitterly of one manufacturer in particular, and attributed to him the ruin of the trade. One weaver said he was anxious to get to America, and not stop "in this infernal country," for he could see the object of the Government was the starvation of the labouring classes. "If you was to come round here of a Sunday," said he, addressing himself to us, "you'd hear the looms going all about; they're obligated to do it or starve." . . .

It was now growing late, and as I was anxious to see some case of destitution in the trade, which might be taken as a fair average of the state of the second or third rate workman, I requested my guide, before I quitted the district, to conduct me to some such individual if it were not too late. He took me towards Shoreditch, and on reaching a narrow back street he stood opposite a three-storied house to see whether there was still a light shining through the long window in the attic. By the flickering shadows the lamp seemed to be dying out. He thought, however, that we might venture to knock. We did so, and in the silent street the noise echoed from house to house. But no one came. We knocked again still louder. A third time, and louder still, we clattered at the door. A voice from the cellar demanded to know whom we wanted. He told us to lift the latch of the street door. We did so—and it opened. The passage looked almost solid in the darkness. My guide groped his way by the wall to the staircase, bidding me follow him. I did so, and reached the stairs. "Keep away from the banisters," said my companion, "as they are rather rotten and might give way." I clung close to the wall, and we groped our way to the second floor, where a light shone through the closed door in a long luminous line. At last we gained the top room, and knocking, were told to enter. "Oh, Billy, is that you," said an old man sitting up, and looking out from between the curtains of a turn-up bedstead. "Here, Tilly," he continued to a girl who was still dressed, "get another lamp, and hang it up again the loom, and give the gentleman a chair." A backless seat was placed at the foot of the old weaver's bedstead; and when the fresh lamp was lighted, I never beheld so strange scene. In the room were three large looms. From the head of the old weaver's bed a clothes line ran to a loom opposite, and on it were a few old ragged shirts and petticoats hanging to dry. Under the "porry" of another loom was stretched a second clothes line, and more linen drying. Behind me on the floor was spread a bed, on which lay four boys, two with their heads in one direction and two in another, for the more convenient stowage of the number. They were covered with old sacks and coats. Beside the bed of the old man was a mattress on the ground without any covering, and the tick positively chocolate-coloured with dirt. "Oh, Billy, I am so glad to see you," said the old weaver to my companion; "I've been dreadful bad, nearly dead with the cholera. I was took dreadful about one o'clock in the morning; just the time the good 'ooman down below were taken. What agony I suffered to be sure! I hope to God you may never have it. I've known four hundred die about here in fourteen days. I couldn't work! Oh, no! It took all the use of my strength from me, as if I'd been on a sick bed for months. And how I lived I can't tell. To tell you the real truth, I wanted, such as I never ought to want—why, I wanted for common necessaries. I got round as well as I could; but how I did it I don't know—God knows; I don't, that's true enough. I hadn't got any money to buy anything. Why, there's seven on us here—yes, seven on us—all dependent on the weaving here—nothing else. What was four shilling a yard is paid one and nine now, so I leaves you to judge, sir—an't it Billy? My work stopped for seven days, and I was larning my boy, so his stopped too, and we had nothing to live upon. God knows how we lived. I pawned my things—and shall never get 'em again—to buy some bread, tea, and sugar, for my young ones there. Oh! it's like a famine in these parts just now among the people, now they're getting well. It's no use talking about the parish; you might as well talk to a wall. There was hardly anybody well just round about here, from the back of Shoreditch Church, you may say to Swan-street. The prices of weaving is so low, that we're ashamed to say what it is, because it's the means of pulling down other poor men's wages and other trades. Why, to tell you the truth, you must need suppose that 1s. 9d. a yard ain't much, and some of the masters is so cruel, that they gives no more than 1s. 3d.—that's it. But it's the competitive system; that's what the Government ought to put a stop to. I knows persons who makes the same work as mine—scores on 'em—at 1s. 3d. a yard. Wretched is their condition! The people is a being brought to that state of destitution, that many say it's a blessing from the

Almighty that takes 'em from the world. They lose all love of country—yes, and all hopes; and they prays to be tortured no longer. Why want is common to a hundred of families close here to-morrow morning; and this it is to have cheap silks. I should like to ask a question here, as I sees you a-writing, sir. When is the people of England to see that there big loaf they was promised—that's it—the people wants to know when they're to have it. I am sure if the ladies who wears what we makes, or the Queen of England was to see our state, she'd never let her subjects suffer such privations in a land of plenty. Yes, I was comfortable in '24. I kept a good little house, and I thought as my young ones growed up—why I thought as I should be comfortable in my old age, and 'stead of that, I've got no wages. I could live by my labour then, but now, why it's wretched in the extreme. Then I'd a nice little garden, and some nice tulips for my hobby, when my work was done. There they lay, up in my old hat now. As for animal food, why it's a stranger to us. Once a week, may be, we gets a taste of it, but that's a hard struggle, and many a family don't have it once a month—a jint we never sees. Oh, it's too bad! There's seven on us here in this room—but it's a very large room to some weavers'—their's a'n't above half the size of this here. The weavers is in general five or six all living and working in the same room. There's four on us here in this bed. One head to foot—one at our back along the bolster; and me and my wife side by side. And there's four on 'em over there. My brother Tom makes up the other one. There's a nice state in a Christian land! How many do you think lives in this house? Why 23 living souls. Oh! a'n't it too bad? But the people is frightened to say how bad they're off, for fear of their masters and losing their work, so they keeps it to themselves—poor creatures. But oh, there's many wuss than me. Many's gone to the docks, and some turned costermongers. But none goes a stealing nor a sojering, that I hears on. They goes out to get a loaf of bread—oh, its a shocking scene! I can't say what I thinks about the young uns. Why you loses your nat'ral affection for 'em. The people in general is ashamed to say how they thinks on their children. It's wretched in the extreme to see one's children, and not be able to do to 'em as a parent ought, and I'll say this here after all you've heerd me state—that the Government of my native land ought to interpose their powerful arm to put a stop to such things. Unless they do, civil society with us is all at an end. Everybody is becoming brutal—unnatural. Billy, just turn up that shell now, and let the gentlemen see what beautiful fabrics we're in the habit of producing—and then he shall say whether we ought to be in the filthy state we are. Just show the light, Tilly! That's for ladies to wear and adorn them, and make them handsome." [It was an exquisite piece of moroon coloured velvet, that, amidst all the squalor of the place, seemed marvellously beautiful, and it was a wonder to see it unsoiled amid all the filth that surrounded it]. "I say, just turn it up Billy, and show the gentleman the back. That's cotton partly, you see, sir, just for the manufacturers to cheat the public, and get a cheap article, and have all the gold out of the poor working creatures they can, and don't care nothing about them. But death, Billy—death gets all the gold out of them. They're playing a deep game, but Death wins after all. Oh, when this here's made known, won't the manufacturers be in a way to find the public aware on their tricks. They've lowered the wages so low, that one would hardly believe the people would take the work. But what's one to do?—the children can't *quite* starve. Oh no!—oh no!"

# Samuel Smiles

1812: Born 23 December at Haddington, Scotland

1829–32: Studied medicine at Edinburgh University

1838: Became editor of *Leeds Times*

1845: Employed by Leeds and Thirsk Railroad

1854: Became secretary to South Eastern Railway

1859: *Self-Help*

1861–2: *Lives of the Engineers*

1875: *Thrift*

1904: Died 16 April at Kensington

## SELF-HELP WITH ILLUSTRATIONS OF CHARACTER AND CONDUCT

*Edinburgh-educated surgeon, journalist, railway official, and insurance officer, Samuel Smiles became the popular spokesman for mid-century individualism, self-discipline, and optimism with the publication of his best-selling* Self-Help. *Smiles's book joined an existing body of self-help literature and a self-improvement culture of Mechanics Institutes and evening adult schools. Yet* Self-Help's *particular blend of aphoristic plain-speaking, common-sense wisdom, widely chosen illustrative biographies, and rousing exhortations to self-improvement seems to have guaranteed its immediate and long-lived popularity. Its biographical sketches celebrate those ideals we associate with the mid-century middle-class: hard work, diligence, perseverance, honesty, self discipline, self reliance, thrift, duty. Success, for Smiles, has less to do with luck or genius than with industry, energy, and will. Although his heroes rise from all backgrounds and ranks and include some who did not achieve financial success, Smiles's prototypical biography charts the individual's rise from humble background, through adverse circumstances, to a position of distinction, influence, and social usefulness. Criticized by some for encouraging raw ambition, pursuit of financial gain, and social climbing,* Self-Help *in fact warns against the temptations of wealth and superficial respectability, and argues that the rewards of, as well as the means to, self-help are character formation, moral reform, and service to others and to country. The progress of the indi-*

*vidual serves the progress of England. Yet, despite its advocacy of service and duty, Smiles's bestseller does appeal to desires for social mobility and material success. Finally, although female as well as male readers surely are invited to practice its virtues,* Self-Help *is gendered masculine: women are conspicuously absent from its pantheon of heroes, and its final chapter celebrates the ideal of "the true gentleman," albeit redefined in terms of morality, not class, as the "man of character."*　　　RM

## SELF-HELP—NATIONAL AND INDIVIDUAL

"The worth of a State, in the long run, is the worth of the individuals composing it." –J. S. MILL.

"We put too much faith in systems, and look too little to men." –B. DISRAELI.

"HEAVEN HELPS THOSE WHO HELP THEMSELVES" is a well-worn maxim, embodying in a small compass the results of vast human experience. The spirit of self-help is the root of all genuine growth in the individual; and, exhibited in the lives of many, it constitutes the true source of national vigour and strength. Help from without is often enfeebling in its effects, but help from within invariably invigorates. Whatever is done *for* men or classes, to a certain extent takes away the stimulus and necessity of doing for themselves; and where men are subjected to over-guidance and over-government, the inevitable tendency is to render them comparatively helpless.

Even the best institutions can give a man no active aid. Perhaps the utmost they can do is, to leave him *free* to develop himself and improve his individual condition. But in all times men have been prone to believe that their happiness and well-being were to be secured by means of institutions rather than by their own conduct. Hence the value of legislation as an agent in human advancement has always been greatly over-estimated. To constitute the millionth part of a Legislature, by voting for one or two men once in three or five years, however conscientiously this duty may be performed, can exercise but little active influence upon any man's life and character. Moreover, it is every day becoming more clearly understood, that the function of Government is negative and restrictive, rather than positive and active; being resolvable principally into protection—protection of life, liberty, and property. Hence the chief "reforms" of the last fifty years have consisted mainly in abolitions and disenactments. But there is no power of law that can make the idle man industrious, the thriftless provident, or the drunken sober; though every individual can be each and all of these if he will, by the exercise of his own free powers of action and self-denial. Indeed all experience serves to prove that the worth and strength of a State depend far less on the form of its institutions than upon the character of its men. For the nation is only the aggregate of individual conditions, and civilization itself is but a question of personal improvement.

National progress is the sum of individual industry, energy, and uprightness, as national decay is of individual idleness, selfishness, and vice. What we are accustomed to decry as great social evils, will, for the most part, be found to be only the outgrowth of our own perverted life; and though we may endeavor to cut them down and extirpate them by means of Law, they will only spring up again with fresh luxuriance in some other form, unless the individual conditions of human life and character are radically improved. If this view be correct, then it follows that the highest patriotism and philanthropy consist, not so much in altering laws and modifying institutions, as in helping and stimulating men to elevate and improve themselves by their own free and independent action as individuals.

The Government of a nation itself is usually found to be but the reflex of the individuals composing it. The Government that is ahead of the people will be inevitably dragged down to their level, as the Government that is behind them will in the long run be dragged up. In the order of nature, the collective character of a nation will as surely find its befitting results in its law and its government, as water finds its own level. The noble people will be nobly ruled, and the ignorant and corrupt ignobly. Indeed, liberty is quite as much a moral as a political growth—the result of free individual action, energy, and independence. It may be of comparatively little consequence how a man is governed from without, whilst everything depends upon how he governs himself from within. The greatest slave is not he who is ruled by a despot, great though that evil be, but he who is the thrall of his own moral ignorance, selfishness, and vice. There have been, and perhaps there still are, so-called patriots abroad, who hold it to be the greatest stroke for liberty to kill a tyrant, forgetting that the tyrant usually represents only too faithfully the millions of people over whom he reigns. But nations who are enslaved at heart cannot be freed by any mere changes of masters or of institutions; and so long as the fatal delusion prevails, that liberty solely depends upon and consists in government, so long will such changes, no matter at what cost they be effected, have as little practical and lasting result as the shifting of the figures in a phantasmagoria. The solid foundations of liberty must rest upon individual character, which is also the only sure guarantee for social security and national progress. In this consists the real strength of English liberty. Englishmen feel that they are free, not merely because they live under those free institutions which they have so laboriously built up, but because each member of society has to a greater or less extent got the root of the matter within himself; and they continue to hold fast and enjoy their liberty, not by freedom of speech merely, but by their steadfast life and energetic action as free individual men.

Such as England is, she has been made by the thinking and working of many generations: the action of even the least significant person having contributed towards the production of the general result. Laborious and patient men of all ranks—cultivators of the soil and explorers of the mine—inventors and discoverers—tradesmen, mechanics, and labourers —poets, thinkers, and politicians—all have worked together, one generation carrying forward the labours of another, building up the character of the country, and establishing its prosperity on solid foundations. This succession of noble workers—the artisans of civilization—has created order out of chaos, in industry, science, and art: and as our forefathers laboured for us, and we have succeeded to the inheritance which they have bequeathed to us, so is it our duty to hand it down, not only unimpaired, but improved, to our successors.

This spirit of self-help, as exhibited in the energetic action of individuals, has in all times been a marked feature in the English character, and furnishes the true measure of our power as a nation. Rising above the heads of the mass, there have always been a series of individuals distinguished beyond others, who have commanded the public homage. But our progress has been owing also to multitudes of smaller and unknown men. Though only the generals' names may be remembered in the history of any great campaign, it has been mainly through the individual valour and heroism of the privates that victories have been won. And life, too, is "a soldiers' battle," the greatest workers in all times having been men in the ranks. Many are the lives of men unwritten, which have nevertheless as powerfully influenced civilization and progress as the more fortunate Great whose names are recorded in biography. Even the humblest person, who sets before his fellows an example of industry, sobriety, and upright honesty of purpose in life, has a present as well as a future influence upon the well-being of his country; for his life and character pass unconsciously into the lives of others, and propagate good example for all time to come.

Biographies of great, but especially of good men, are, nevertheless, most instructive and useful, as helps, guides, and incentives to others. Some of the best are almost equivalent to Gospels—teaching high living, high thinking, and energetic action for their own and the world's good. British biography is studded over, as "with patines of bright gold," with illustrious examples of the power of self-help, of patient purpose, resolute working, and steadfast integrity, issuing in the formation of truly noble and manly character; exhibiting in language not to be misunderstood, what it is in the power of each to accomplish for himself; and illustrating the efficacy of self-respect and self-reliance in enabling men of even the humblest rank to work out for themselves an honorable competency and a solid reputation.

Foreign observers have been keen to note, as one of the most marked characteristics of the Englishman, his strong individuality and distinctive personal energy,—refusing to merge himself in institutions, but retaining throughout his perfect freedom of thought, and speech, and action. "Que j'aime la hardiesse Anglaise! que j'aime les gens qui disent ce qu'ils pensent!" was the expressive exclamation of Voltaire.[1] It is this strong individualism which makes and keeps the Englishman really free, and brings out fully the action of the social body. The energies of the strong form so many living centres of action, round which other individual energies group and cluster themselves; thus the life of all is quickened, and, on great occasions, a powerful energetic action of the nation is secured. . . .

. . . One of our most distinguished writers has, it is true, lamented the decay of that strength of individual character which has been the glory of the English nation; yet, if we mistake not, no age in our history so little justifies such a lament as the present. Never did sudden calamity more severely test the individual pluck, endurance, and energy of a people, than did the recent outbreak of the rebellion in India[2]; but it only served to bring out the unflinching self-reliance and dormant heroism of the English race. In that terrible trial all proved almost equally great—women, civilians, and soldiers—from the gen-

1. "How I love English audacity! How I love people who say what they think!" Smiles attributes the line to Voltaire (1694–1778), French philosopher, man of letters, and visitor to England in the 1720s. See his *Letters Concerning the English Nation* (1733) and *Lettres philosophiques* (1734).
2. The Sepoy Mutiny or Rebellion (1857–8), beginning in May of 1857 with the mutiny of aggrieved Sepoys or Indian soldiers and eventually becoming a major rebellion against British rule, was marked by brutality on both sides. It occasioned the sort of imperialist pride voiced by Smiles here and led to a transfer of authority in India from the East India Company to the Crown.

eral down through all grades to the private and bugleman. The men were not picked—they belonged to the same every-day people whom we daily meet at home—in the streets, in workshops, in the fields, at clubs; yet when sudden disaster fell upon them, each and all displayed a wealth of personal resources and energy, and became as it were individually heroic. . . .

Equally brilliant instances of individual force of character are also to be found in more peaceful and scientific walks. Is there not Livingstone, with a heroism greater than that of Xavier, penetrating the wilds of South Africa on his mission of Christian civilization; Layard, labouring for years to disinter the remains of the buried city of Babylon; Rawlinson, the decipherer of their cuneiform inscriptions; Brooke, establishing a nucleus of European enterprise and colonization amongst the piratical tribes of the Indian Ocean; Franklin, Maclure, Collinson, and others, cleaving their way through storms, and ice, and darkness, to solve the problem of the north-west passage;— enterprises which, for individual daring, self-denial, energy, and heroism, are unsurpassed by those of any age or country.[3]

## LEADERS OF INDUSTRY—INVENTORS AND PRODUCERS

"Rich are the diligent, who can command
  Time, nature's stock! and could his hour-glass fall,
Would, as for seed of stars, stoop for the sand,
  And, by incessant labour, gather all." –D'AVENANT

One of the most strongly marked features of the English people is their indomitable spirit of industry, standing out prominent and distinct in all their past history, and as strikingly characteristic of them now as at any former period. It is this spirit, displayed by the commons of England, which has laid the foundations and built up the industrial greatness of the empire, at home and in the colonies. This vigorous growth of the nation has been mainly the result of the free industrial energy of individuals; and it has been contingent upon the number of hands and minds from time to time actively employed within it, whether as cultivators of the soil, producers of articles of utility, contrivers of tools and machines, writers of books, or creators of works of art. And while this spirit of active industry has been the vital principle of the nation, it has also been its saving and remedial one, counter-acting from time to time the effects of errors in our laws and imperfections in our constitution.

The career of industry which the nation has pursued, has also proved its best education. As steady application to work is the healthiest training for every individual, so it is the best discipline of a state. Honourable industry always travels the same road with enjoyment and duty; and progress is altogether impossible without it. The idle pass through life leaving as little trace of their existence as foam upon the water or smoke upon the air; whereas the industrious stamp their character upon their age, and influence not only their own but all succeeding generations. Labour is the best test of the energies

---

3. David LIVINGSTONE (1813–73). Austen Layard (1817–94). Henry Rawlinson (1810–95). James Brooke (1803–68). John Franklin (1786–1847). Robert McClure (1807–73). Richard Collinson (1811–83).

of men, and furnishes an admirable training for practical wisdom. A life of manual employment is not incompatible with even the highest culture. Hugh Miller,[4] than whom none knew better the strength and the weakness belonging to the lot of labour, stated the result of his experience to be, that Work, even the hardest, is full of pleasure and materials for self-improvement. He held honest labour to be the best of teachers, and that the school of toil is the noblest of schools—save only the Christian one,—that it is a school in which the ability of being useful is imparted, the spirit of independence is learnt, and the habit of persevering effort is acquired. He was even of opinion that the training of the mechanic, by the exercise which it gives to his observant faculties, from his daily dealing with things actual and practical, and the close experience of life which he acquires, better fits him for picking his way through the journey of life, and is more favourable to his growth as a Man, emphatically speaking, than the training afforded by any other condition of life.

The array of great names which we have already cursorily cited, of men springing from the ranks of the industrial classes, who have achieved distinction in various walks of life—in science, commerce, literature, and art—shows that at all events the difficulties interposed by poverty and labour are not insurmountable. . . .

. . . The steam-engine was nothing . . . until it emerged from the state of theory, and was taken in hand by practical mechanics; and what a noble story of patient, laborious investigation, of difficulties encountered and overcome by heroic industry, does not that marvellous machine tell of! It is, indeed, in itself, a monument of the power of self-help in man. Grouped around it we find Savary, the Cornish miner; Newcomen, the Dartmouth blacksmith; Cawley, the glazier; Potter, the engine-boy; Smeaton, the engineer; and, towering above all, the laborious, patient, never-tiring James Watt, the mathematical instrument maker.[5]

Watt was one of the most industrious of men. Whatever subject came under his notice in the course of his business, immediately became to him an object of study; and the story of his life proves, what all experience confirms, that it is not the man of the greatest natural vigour and capacity who achieves the highest results, but he who employs his powers with the greatest industry and the most carefully disciplined skill—the skill that comes by labour, application, and experience. Many men in his time knew far more than Watt, but none laboured so assiduously as he did to turn all that he did know to useful practical purposes. He was, above all things, most persevering in his pursuit of facts. He cultivated carefully that habit of active attention on which all the higher working qualities of the mind mainly depend. Indeed, Mr. Edgworth entertained the opinion, that many of the great differences of intellect which are found in men depend more upon the early cultivation of this *habit of attention*, than upon any great disparity between the powers of one individual and another.[6]

4. Hugh Miller (1802–56), self-educated popularizer of geology.
5. Inventors and pioneers in the development of the steam engine: Thomas Savery (1650–1715); Thomas Newcomen (1663–1729); John Cawley or Calley (?–1717); John Smeaton (1724–92); James Watt (1736–1819). According to legend, a boy named Humphrey Potter, attending a steam engine in 1713, improved its operation by his ingenious use of a piece of string.
6. Richard Lovell Edgeworth (1744–1817), author of *Practical Education* (1798).

Even when a boy, Watt found science in his toys. The quadrants lying about his father's carpenter's shop led him to the study of optics and astronomy; his ill health induced him to pry into the secrets of physiology; and his solitary walks through the country attracted him to the study of botany, history, and antiquarianism. While carrying on the business of a mathematical instrument maker, he received an order to build an organ; and, though without any ear for music, he undertook the study of harmonics, and successfully constructed the instrument. And, in like manner, when the little model of Newcomen's steam-engine, belonging to the University of Glasgow, was placed in his hands for repair, he forthwith set himself to learn all that was then known about heat, evaporation, and condensation,—at the same time plodding his way in mechanics and the science of construction,—the results of which he at length embodied in the condensing steam-engine.

For ten years he went on contriving and inventing—with little hope to cheer him— with few friends to encourage him—struggling with difficulties, and earning but a slender living at his trade. Even when he had brought his engine into a practicable working condition, his difficulties seemed to be as far from an end as ever; and he could find no capitalist to join him in his great undertaking, and bring the invention to a successful practical issue. He went on, meanwhile, earning bread for his family by making and selling quadrants, making and mending fiddles, flutes, and other musical instruments; measuring mason work, surveying roads, superintending the construction of canals, or doing anything that turned up, and offered a prospect of honest gain. At length, Watt found a fit partner in another eminent leader of industry—Mathew Boulton, of Birmingham; a skilful, energetic, and far-seeing man, who vigourously undertook the enterprise of introducing the condensing engine into general use as a working power[7]; and his success is now a matter of history.

A succession of eminent workmen have, from time to time, added new power to the steam-engine; and, by numerous modifications, rendered it capable of being applied to nearly all the purposes of manufacture—driving machinery, impelling ships, grinding corn, printing books, stamping money, hammering, planing, and turning iron; in short, of performing any description of mechanical labour where power is required. One of the most useful modifications in the engine was that devised by Trevithick, another Cornish miner, and eventually perfected by George Stephenson,[8] the colliery engine-man, in the invention of the railway locomotive, by which social changes of immense importance have been brought about, of even greater consequence, considered in their results on human progress and civilization, than the condensing-engine of Watt. These successive advances, however, have not been the result of the genius of any one inventor; but of the continuous and successive industry and inventiveness of many generations. What Mr. Robert Stephenson[9] recently said of the locomotive, at a meeting of engineers at Newcastle, is true of nearly every other capital invention: "It is due," he said, "not to one man, but to the efforts of a nation of mechanical engineers."

7. Matthew Boulton (1728–1809).
8. Richard Trevithick (1771–1833); George Stephenson (1781–1848), railway engineer, inventor of the locomotive, and founder of railways, whose biography by Smiles appeared in 1857.
9. Robert Stephenson (1803–59), railway engineer, son of George Stephenson.

# David Livingstone

## MISSIONARY TRAVELS AND RESEARCHES IN SOUTH AFRICA

*Lionized by the English people as a heroic explorer upon his death, Livingstone first went to Africa as a missionary, and, although his own evangelizing efforts were nearly futile, he never relinquished his hope of bringing Christianity to the native peoples he encountered. Published in 1857 after his return to England,* Missionary Travels *describes Livingstone's transcontinental expedition across Africa. The first European to complete such a journey, he named Victoria Falls for the Queen of England. Livingstone's popular book sold seventy thousand copies and influenced British attitudes about Africa for years. Many of the English participants in his second African expedition, as well as young missionaries during his lifetime and afterward, were inspired to come to Africa by Livingstone's excessively optimistic projections for the colonization and Christianization of the African interior. Unlike Richard Burton, whom Livingstone disliked partly for what he saw as Burton's assumption that Africans were unfit for progress, but sharing Burton's views of European racial superiority, Livingstone believed that by introducing capitalist commerce and values into the interior of Africa, the slave trade might be stopped and the people improved morally, economically, and socially. One of the main reasons for his last expedition was his hope of proving that the interior of Africa might easily be colonized by the English and, thus, that the slave trade might be suppressed by the civilizing influence of agricultural and commercial ven-*

*tures. Livingstone's desire for increased British influence in Africa became a reality after his death, when Britain expanded its empire into central and eastern Africa.*                    LMF

## CHAPTER 1

IN ADDITION TO OTHER ADVERSE influences, the general uncertainty, though not absolute want of food, and the necessity of frequent absence for the purpose of either hunting game or collecting roots and fruits, proved a serious barrier to the progress of the people in knowledge. Our own education in England is carried on at the comfortable breakfast and dinner table and by the cosy fire, as well as in the church and school. Few English people with stomachs painfully empty would be decorous at church any more than they are when these organs are overcharged. Ragged schools[1] would have been a failure had not the teachers wisely provided food for the body as well as food for the mind; and not only must we show a friendly interest in the bodily comfort of the objects of our sympathy as a Christian duty, but we can no more hope for healthy feelings among the poor, either at home or abroad, without feeding them into them, than we can hope to see an ordinary working-bee reared into a queen-mother by the ordinary food of the hive.

Sending the Gospel to the heathen must, if this view be correct, include much more than is implied in the usual picture of a missionary, namely, a man going about with a Bible under his arm. The promotion of commerce ought to be specially attended to, as this, more speedily than any thing else, demolishes that sense of isolation which heathenism engenders, and makes the tribes feel themselves mutually dependent on, and mutually beneficial to, each other. With a view to this, the missionaries at Kuruman[2] got permission from the Government for a trader to reside at the station, and a considerable trade has been the result; the trader himself has become rich enough to retire with a competence. Those laws which still prevent free commercial intercourse among the civilized nations seem to be nothing else but the remains of our own heathenism. My observations on this subject make me extremely desirous to promote the preparation of the raw materials of European manufactures in Africa, for by that means we may not only put a stop to the slave-trade, but introduce the negro family into the body corporate of nations, no one member of which can suffer without the others suffering with it. Success in this, in both Eastern and Western Africa, would lead, in the course of time, to a much larger diffusion of the blessings of civilization than efforts exclusively spiritual and educational confined to any one small tribe. These, however, it would of course be extremely desirable to carry on at the same time at large central and healthy stations, for neither civilization nor Christianity can be promoted alone. In fact, they are inseparable.

## CHAPTER 8

The Bakalahari,[3] who live at Motlatsa wells, have always been very friendly to us, and listen attentively to instruction conveyed to them in their own tongue. It is, however, difficult to give an idea to a European of the little effect teaching produces, because no one

1. Schools originally established by evangelical organizations for the education of the poor.
2. London Missionary Society station in Botswana. At the time of Livingstone's arrival, Kuruman was the most remote mission station in southern Africa.
3. "Ba-Kalahari" is literally "people of the Kalahari" desert.

can realize the degradation to which their minds have been sunk by centuries of barbarism and hard struggling for the necessaries of life: like most others, they listen with
respect and attention, but, when we kneel down and address an unseen Being, the position and the act often appear to them so ridiculous that they can not refrain from bursting into uncontrollable laughter. After a few services they get over this tendency. I was
once present when a missionary attempted to sing among a wild heathen tribe of
Bechuanas,[4] who had no music in their composition; the effect on the risible faculties of
the audience was such that the tears actually ran down their cheeks. Nearly all their
thoughts are directed to the supply of their bodily wants, and this has been the case with
the race for ages. If asked, then, what effect the preaching of the Gospel has at the commencement on such individuals, I am unable to tell, except that some have confessed long
afterward that they then first began to pray in secret. Of the effects of a long-continued
course of instruction there can be no reasonable doubt, as mere nominal belief has never
been considered sufficient proof of conversion by any body of missionaries; and, after the
change which has been brought about by this agency, we have good reason to hope well
for the future: those I have myself witnessed behaving in the manner described, when
kindly treated in sickness often utter imploring words to Jesus, and I believe sometimes
really do pray to him in their afflictions. As that great Redeemer of the guilty seeks to save
all he can, we may hope that they find mercy through His blood, though little able to
appreciate the sacrifice He made. The indirect and scarcely appreciable blessings of
Christian missionaries going about doing good are thus probably not so despicable as
some might imagine; there is no necessity for beginning to tell even the most degraded
of these people of the existence of a God, or of a future state, the facts being universally
admitted. Every thing that cannot be accounted for by common causes is ascribed to the
Deity, as creation, sudden death, &c. "How curiously God made these things!" is a common expression; as is also, "He was not killed by disease, he was killed by God." And,
when speaking of the departed—though there is naught in the physical appearance of the
dead to justify the expression—they say, "He has gone to the gods," the phrase being identical with "*abiit ad plures*."

On questioning intelligent men among the Bakwains[5] as to their former knowledge of
good and evil, of God and the future state, they have scouted the idea of any of them ever
having been without a tolerably clear conception on all these subjects. Respecting their
sense of right and wrong, they profess that nothing we indicate as sin ever appeared to
them as otherwise, except the statement that it was wrong to have more wives than one;
and they declare that they spoke in the same way of the direct influence exercised by God
in giving rain in answer to prayers of the rain-makers, and in granting deliverances in
times of danger, as they do now, before they ever heard of white men. The want, however, of any form of public worship, or of idols, or of formal prayers or sacrifice, make both
Caffres[6] and Bechuanas appear as among the most godless races of mortals known any-

4. The Ba-tswana, variously spelled "Botswana" or "Bechuana," are the Tswana-speaking peoples north of the
Orange River, one of the many groups in that region.
5. Probably a subgroup of the Bechuana; it is likely that Bakwain corresponds to the modern ethnic group San.
6. An alternate spelling for the derogatory Afrikaans word "kaffir." Livingstone appears to use the word to represent
black Africans resident south of the Orange River.

where. But, though they all possess a distinct knowledge of a deity and of a future state, they show so little reverence, and feel so little connection with either, that it is not surprising that some have supposed them entirely ignorant on the subject. At Lotlakani we met an old Bushman[7] who at first seemed to have no conception of morality whatever; when his heart was warmed by our presents of meat, he sat by the fire relating his early adventures: among these was killing five other Bushmen. "Two," said he, counting on his fingers, "were females, one a male, and the other two calves."—"What a villain you are, to boast of killing women and children of your own nation! what will God say when you appear before him?"—"He will say," replied he, "that I was a very clever fellow." This man now appeared to me as without any conscience, and, of course, responsibility, but, on trying to enlighten him by further conversation, I discovered that, though he was employing the word which is used among the Bakwains when speaking of the Deity, he had only the idea of a chief, and was all the while referring to Sekomi, while his victims were a party of rebel Bushmen against whom he had been sent. If I had known the name of God in the Bushman tongue the mistake could scarcely have occurred. It must, however, be recollected, while reflecting on the degradation of the natives of South Africa, that the farther north, the more distinct do the native ideas on religious subjects become, and I have not had any intercourse with either Caffres or Bushmen in their own tongues. . . .

## CHAPTER 32

. . . As far as I am myself concerned, the opening of the new central country is a matter for congratulation only in so far as it opens up a prospect for the elevation of the inhabitants. As I have elsewhere remarked, I view the end of the geographical feat as the beginning of the missionary enterprise. I take the latter term in its most extended signification, and include every effort made for the amelioration of our race; the promotion of all those means by which God in His providence is working, and bringing all His dealings with man to a glorious consummation. Each man in his sphere, either knowingly or unwittingly, is performing the will of our Father in heaven. Men of science, searching after hidden truths, which when discovered, will, like the electric telegraph, bind men more closely together—soldiers battling for the right against tyranny—sailors rescuing the victims of oppression from the grasp of heartless men-stealers—merchants teaching the nations lessons of mutual dependence—and many others, as well as missionaries, all work in the same direction, and all efforts are overruled for one glorious end.

If the reader has accompanied me thus far, he may perhaps be disposed to take an interest in the objects I propose to myself, should God mercifully grant me the honor of doing something more for Africa. As the highlands on the borders of the central basin are comparatively healthy, the first object seems to be to secure a permanent path thither, in order that Europeans may pass as quickly as possible through the unhealthy region near the coast. The river has not been surveyed, but at the time I came down there was abundance of water for a large vessel, and this continues to be the case during four or five months of each year. . . .

---

7. "Bushman" is the English colonial word for the San hunter-gatherers who inhabit the dry regions of southern Africa. The term is considered pejorative in modern usage.

. . . Let it not, however, be thought that a vessel by going thither would return laden with ivory and gold-dust. The Portuguese of Tete[8] pick up all the merchandise of the tribes in their vicinity, and, though I came out by traversing the people with whom the Portuguese have been at war, it does not follow that it will be perfectly safe for others to go in whose goods may be a stronger temptation to cupidity than any thing I possessed. When we get beyond the hostile population mentioned, we reach a very different race. On the latter my chief hopes at present rest. All of them, however, are willing and anxious to engage in trade, and, while eager for this, none have ever been encouraged to cultivate the raw materials of commerce. Their country is well adapted for cotton; and I venture to entertain the hope that by distributing seeds of better kinds than that which is found indigenous, and stimulating the natives to cultivate it by affording them the certainty of a market for all they may produce, we may engender a feeling of mutual dependence between them and ourselves. I have a two-fold object in view, and believe that, by guiding our missionary labors so as to benefit our own country, we shall thereby more effectually and permanently benefit the heathen. Seven years were spent at Kolobeng in instructing my friends there; but the country being incapable of raising materials for exportation, when the Boers[9] made their murderous attack and scattered the tribe for a season, none sympathized except a few Christian friends. Had the people of Kolobeng been in the habit of raising the raw materials of English commerce, the outrage would have been felt in England; or, what is more likely to have been the case, the people would have raised themselves in the scale by barter, and have become, like the Basutos of Moshesh[10] and people of Kuruman, possessed of fire-arms, and the Boers would never have made the attack at all. We ought to encourage the Africans to cultivate for our markets, as the most effectual means, next to the Gospel, of their elevation.

It is in the hope of working out this idea that I propose the formation of stations on the Zambesi beyond the Portuguese territory, but having communication through them with the coast. A chain of stations admitting of easy and speedy intercourse, such as might be formed along the flank of the eastern ridge, would be in a favorable position for carrying out the objects in view. The London Missionary Society has resolved to have a station among the Makololo on the north bank, and another on the south among the Matebele. The Church—Wesleyan, Baptist, and that most energetic body, the Free Church—could each find desirable locations among the Batoka and adjacent tribes. The country is so extensive there is no fear of clashing. All classes of Christians find that sectarian rancor soon dies out when they are working together among and for the real heathen. Only let the healthy locality be searched for, and fixed upon, and then there will be free scope to work in the same cause in various directions, without that loss of men which the system of missions on the unhealthy coasts entails. While respectfully submitting the plan to these influential societies, I can positively state that, when fairly in the interior,

8. Portuguese settlement on the lower Zambesi River.
9. South African Dutch farmers who migrated to the east of the Cape Colony and settled in the Transvaal and the Orange Free State.
10. The Basuto were predominantly Sotho-speaking people who lived in the area around modern Lesotho. Moshoeshoe ("Moshesh") was a leader who organized the Sotho-speaking refugees from the Zulu wars between 1821 and 1823.

there is perfect security for life and property among a people who will at least listen and reason. . . .

If the reader remembers the way in which I was led, while teaching the Bakwains, to commence exploration, he will, I think, recognize the hand of Providence. Anterior to that, when Mr. Moffat began to give the Bible—the Magna Charta of all the rights and privileges of modern civilization—to the Bechuanas, Sebituane[11] went north, and spread the language into which he was translating the sacred oracles in a new region larger than France. Sebituane, at the same time, rooted out hordes of bloody savages among whom no white man could have gone, without leaving his skull to ornament some village. He opened up the way for me—let us hope also for the Bible. Then, again, while I was laboring at Kolobeng, seeing only a small arc of the cycle of Providence, I could not understand it, and felt inclined to ascribe our successive and prolonged droughts to the wicked one. But when forced by these, and the Boers, to become explorer, and open a new country in the north rather than set my face southward, where missionaries are not needed; the gracious Spirit of God influenced the minds of the heathen to regard me with favor; the Divine hand is again perceived. Then I turned away westward, rather than in the opposite direction, chiefly from observing that some native Portuguese, though influenced by the hope of a reward from their government to cross the continent, had been obliged to return from the east without accomplishing their object. Had I gone at first in the eastern direction, which the course of the great Leeambye seemed to invite, I should have come among the belligerents near Tete, when the war was raging at its height, instead of, as it happened, when all was over. And again, when enabled to reach Loanda, the resolution to do my duty by going back to Linyanti probably saved me from the fate of my papers in the "Forerunner."[12] And then, last of all, this new country is partially opened to the sympathies of Christendom, and I find that Sechele[13] himself has, though unbidden by man, been teaching his own people. In fact, he has been doing all that I was prevented from doing, and I have been employed in exploring–a work I had no previous intention of performing. I think that I see the operation of the unseen hand in all this, and I humbly hope, that it will still guide me to do good in my day and generation in Africa.

Viewing the success awarded to opening up the new country as a development of Divine Providence in relation to the African family, the mind naturally turns to the probable influence it may have on negro slavery; and more especially on the practice of it by a large portion of our own race. We now demand increased supplies of cotton and sugar, and then reprobate the means our American brethren adopt to supply our wants. We claim a right to speak about this evil, and also to act in reference to its removal, the more especially because we are of one blood. It is on the Anglo-American race that the hopes of the world for liberty and progress rest. Now it is very grievous to find one portion of

11. Robert Moffat: missionary at Kuruman and Livingstone's father-in-law. Sebituane: chief of the Makololo before Sekeletu. Sebituane, also spelled Sebetwane, was a migrant warrior who created a conquest state in western Zambia. His interest in Livingstone was chiefly a matter of pragmatic diplomacy.

12. Loanda or Luanda: port city located in Portuguese Angola, where Livingstone began his return journey across the African continent. His letters to England from Luanda were lost in a shipwreck. Linyanti: the Makololo town on the river Chobe, in modern Botswana.

13. Chief of the Kwena tribe and Livingstone's only convert to Christianity.

this race practicing the gigantic evil, and the other aiding, by increased demands for the produce of slave-labor, in perpetuating the enormous wrong. The Mauritius,[14] a mere speck on the ocean, yields sugar, by means of guano, improved machinery, and free labor, equal in amount to one-fourth part of the entire consumption of Great Britain. On that island, land is excessively dear, and far from rich: no crop can be raised except by means of guano, and labor has to be brought all the way from India. But in Africa the land is cheap, the soil good, and free labor is to be found on the spot. Our chief hopes rest with the natives themselves; and if the point to which I have given prominence, of healthy inland commercial stations, be realized, where all the produce raised may be collected, there is little doubt but that slavery among our kinsmen across the Atlantic will, in the course of some years, cease to assume the form of a necessity to even the slaveholders themselves. Natives alone can collect produce from the more distant hamlets, and bring it to the stations contemplated. This is the system pursued so successfully in Angola. If England had possessed that strip of land, by civilly declining to enrich her "Frontier colonists" by "Caffre wars," the inborn energy of English colonists would have developed its resources, and the exports would not have been £100,000 as now, but one million at least. The establishment of the necessary agency must be a work of time, and greater difficulty will be experienced on the eastern than on the western side of the continent, because in the one region we have a people who know none but slave-traders, while in the other we have tribes who have felt the influence of the coast missionaries, and of the great Niger expedition; one invaluable benefit it conferred was the dissemination of the knowledge of English love of commerce and English hatred of slavery, and it therefore was no failure. But on the east, there is a river which may become a good pathway to a central population who are friendly to the English; and if we can conciliate the less amicable people on the river, and introduce commerce, an effectual blow will be struck at the slave-trade in that quarter. By linking the Africans there to ourselves in the manner proposed, it is hoped that their elevation will eventually be the result. In this hope and proposed effort I am joined by my brother Charles, who has come from America, after seventeen years' separation, for the purpose. We expect success through the influence of that Spirit who already aided the efforts to open the country, and who has since turned the public mind toward it. A failure may be experienced by sudden rash speculation overstocking the markets there, and raising the prices against ourselves. But I propose to spend some more years of labor, and shall be thankful if I see the system fairly begun in an open pathway which will eventually benefit both Africa and England. . . .

14. Island located in the Indian Ocean east of Madagascar and a French possession in the mid-nineteenth century.

# Percival Leigh

1813: Born 3 November in Haddington
1835: Became member of Royal College of Surgeons
1840: *The Comic Latin Grammar*
1841: Joined the staff of *Punch*
1859: *Paul Prendergast: or, The Comic Schoolmaster*
1889: Died 24 October at Hammersmith

## THE CHEMISTRY OF A CANDLE

*During its short existence (1850–9), the popular weekly journal* Household Words *provided a wide audience with "instruction and entertainment." Conceived and edited by Charles Dickens, the periodical combined fiction (including Elizabeth Gaskell's* North and South *and Dickens's* Hard Times*) with articles on art, politics, travel, London local color, and science. In the following piece, one of a series on scientific principles and applied science, humorist Percival Leigh adopts a fictional frame to dramatize a lecture that chemist and pioneer in electromagnetism Michael Faraday delivered for children at the Royal Institution. Faraday's popular lectures, and other lectures for lay audiences at the Royal Institution, were themselves vehicles for introducing nonscientific audiences to scientific principles and discoveries. When Dickens suggested to Faraday that the publication in* Household Words *of versions of some of his juvenile lectures would reach an even larger audience, Faraday provided his lecture notes, and Leigh distilled them into "The Laboratory in the Chest" (September 7, 1850), "The Mysteries of a Teapot" (November 16, 1850), and "The Chemistry of a Candle" (August 3, 1850).*       RM

The Wilkinsons were having a small party,—it consisted of themselves and Uncle Bagges—at which the younger members of the family, home for the holidays, had been just admitted to assist after dinner. Uncle Bagges was a gentleman from whom his affectionate relatives cherished expectations of a testamentary nature. Hence the greatest attention was paid by them to the wishes of Mr. Bagges, as well as to every observation which he might be pleased to make.

"Eh! what? you sir," said Mr. Bagges, facetiously addressing himself to his eldest nephew, Harry,—"Eh! what? I am glad to hear, sir, that you are doing well at school. Now—eh? now, are you clever enough to tell me where was Moses when he put the candle out?"

"That depends, uncle," answered the young gentleman, "on whether he had lighted the candle to see with at night, or by daylight, to seal a letter."

"Eh! Very good, now! 'Pon my word, very good," exclaimed Uncle Bagges. "You must be Lord Chancellor, sir—Lord Chancellor, one of these days."

"And now, uncle," asked Harry, who was a favourite with the old gentleman, "can you tell me what you do when you put a candle out?"

"Clap an extinguisher on it, you young rogue, to be sure."

"Oh! but I mean, you cut off its supply of oxygen," said Master Harry.

"Cut off its ox's—eh? what? I shall cut off your nose, you young dog, one of these fine days."

"He means something he heard at the Royal Institution," observed Mrs. Wilkinson. "He reads a great deal about chemistry, and he attended Professor Faraday's lectures there on the chemical history of a candle, and has been full of it ever since."

"Now, you sir," said Uncle Bagges, "come you here to me, and tell me what you have to say about this chemical, eh?—or comical; which?—this comical chemical history of a candle."

"He'll bore you, Bagges," said Mr. Wilkinson. "Harry, don't be troublesome to your uncle."

"Troublesome! Oh, not at all. He amuses me. I like to hear him. So let him teach his old uncle the comicality and chemicality of a farthing rushlight."

"A wax candle will be nicer and cleaner, uncle, and answer the same purpose. There's one on the mantel-shelf. Let me light it."

"Take care you don't burn your fingers, or set anything on fire," said Mrs. Wilkinson.

"Now, uncle," commenced Harry, having drawn his chair to the side of Mr. Bagges, "we have got our candle burning. What do you see?"

"Let me put on my spectacles," answered the uncle.

"Look down on the top of the candle around the wick. See, it is a little cup full of melted wax. The heat of the flame has melted the wax just round the wick. The cold air keeps the outside of it hard, so as to make the rim of it. The melted wax in the little cup goes up through the wick to be burnt, just as oil does in the wick of a lamp. What do you think makes it go up, uncle?"

"Why—why, the flame draws it up, doesn't it?"

"Not exactly, uncle. It goes up through little tiny passages in the cotton wick, because very, very small channels, or pipes, or pores, have the power in themselves of sucking up liquids. What they do it by is called cap—something."

"Capillary attraction, Harry," suggested Mr. Wilkinson.

"Yes, that's it; just as a sponge sucks up water, or a bit of lump-sugar the little drop of tea or coffee left in the bottom of a cup. But I mustn't say much more about this, or else you will tell me I am doing something very much like teaching my grandmother to—you know what."

"Your grandmother, eh, young sharpshins?"

"No—I mean my uncle. Now, I'll blow the candle out, like Moses; not to be in the dark, though, but to see into what it is. Look at the smoke rising from the wick. I'll hold a bit of lighted paper in the smoke, so as not to touch the wick. But see, for all that, the candle lights again. So this shows that the melted wax sucked up through the wick is turned into vapour; and the vapour burns. The heat of the burning vapour keeps on melting more wax, and that is sucked up too within the flame, and turned into vapour, and burnt, and so on till the wax is all used up, and the candle is gone. So the flame, uncle, you see, is the last of the candle, and the candle seems to go through the flame into nothing—although it doesn't, but goes into several things, and isn't it curious, as Professor Faraday said, that the candle should look so splendid and glorious in going away?"

"How well he remembers, doesn't he?" observed Mrs. Wilkinson.

"I dare say," proceeded Harry, "that the flame of the candle looks flat to you; but if we were to put a lamp glass over it, so as to shelter it from the draught, you would see it is round,—round sideways, and running up to a peak. It is drawn up by the hot air; you know that hot air always rises, and that is the way smoke is taken up the chimney. What should you think was in the middle of the flame?"

"I should say, fire," replied Uncle Bagges.

"Oh, no! The flame is hollow. The bright flame we see is something no thicker than a thin peel, or skin; and it doesn't touch the wick. Inside of it is the vapour I told you of just now. If you put one end of a bent pipe into the middle of the flame, and let the other end of the pipe dip into a bottle, the vapour or gas from the candle will mix with the air there; and if you set fire to the mixture of gas from the candle and air in the bottle, it would go off with a bang."

"I wish you'd do that, Harry," said Master Tom, the younger brother of the juvenile lecturer.

"I want the proper things," answered Harry. "Well, uncle, the flame of the candle is a little shining case, with gas in the inside of it, and air on the outside, so that the case of flame is between the air and the gas. The gas keeps going into the flame to burn, and when the candle burns properly, none of it ever passes out through the flame; and none of the air ever gets in through the flame to the gas. The greatest heat of the candle is in this skin, or peel, or case of flame."

"Case of flame!" repeated Mr. Bagges. "Live and learn. I should have thought a candle-flame was as thick as my poor old noddle."

"I can show you the contrary," said Harry. "I take this piece of white paper, look, and hold it a second or two down upon the candle-flame, keeping the flame very steady. Now I'll rub off the black of the smoke, and—there—you find that the paper is scorched in the shape of a ring; but inside the ring it is only dirtied, and not singed at all."

"Seeing is believing," remarked the uncle.

"But," proceeded Harry, "there is more in the candle-flame than the gas that comes out of the candle. You know a candle won't burn without air. There must be always air around the gas, and touching it like, to make it burn. If a candle hasn't got enough air, it goes out, or burns badly, so that some of the vapour inside of the flame comes out through it in the form of smoke, and this is the reason of a candle smoking. So now you know why a great clumsy dip smokes more than a neat wax candle; it is because the thick wick of the dip makes too much fuel in proportion to the air that can get to it."

"Dear me! Well, I suppose there is a reason for everything," exclaimed the young philosopher's mamma.

"What should you say, now," continued Harry, "if I told you that the smoke that comes out of a candle is the very thing that makes a candle light? Yes; a candle shines by consuming its own smoke. The smoke of a candle is a cloud of small dust, and the little grains of the dust are bits of charcoal, or carbon, as chemists call it. They are made in the flame, and burnt in the flame, and, while burning, make the flame bright. They are burnt the moment they are made; but the flame goes on making more of them as fast as it burns them; and that is how it keeps bright. The place they are made in, is in the case of flame itself, where the strongest heat is. The great heat separates them from the gas which comes from the melted wax, and, as soon as they touch the air on the outside of the thin case of flame, they burn."

"Can you tell how it is that the little bits of carbon cause the brightness of the flame?" asked Mr. Wilkinson.

"Because they are pieces of solid matter," answered Harry. "To make a flame shine, there must always be some solid—or at least liquid—matter in it."

"Very good," said Mr. Bagges,—"solid stuff necessary to brightness."

"Some gases and other things," resumed Harry, "that burn with a flame you can hardly see, burn splendidly when something solid is put into them. Oxygen and hydrogen—tell me if I use too hard words, uncle—oxygen and hydrogen gases, if mixed together and blown through a pipe, burn with plenty of heat but with very little light. But if their flame is blown upon a piece of quicklime, it gets so bright as to be quite dazzling. Make the smoke of oil of turpentine pass through the same flame, and it gives the flame a beautiful brightness directly."

"I wonder," observed Uncle Bagges, "what has made you such a bright youth."

"Taking after uncle, perhaps," retorted his nephew. "Don't put my candle and me out. Well, carbon or charcoal is what causes the brightness of all lamps, and candles, and other common lights; so, of course, there is carbon in what they are all made of."

"So carbon is smoke, eh? and light is owing to your carbon. Giving light out of smoke, eh? as they say in the classics," observed Mr. Bagges. . . .

"I said that there was carbon or charcoal in all common lights,—so there is in every common kind of fuel. If you heat coal or wood away from the air, some gas comes away, and leaves behind coke from coal, and charcoal from wood; both carbon, though not pure. Heat carbon as much as you will in a close vessel, and it does not change in the least; but let the air get to it, and then it burns and flies off in carbonic acid gas. This makes carbon so convenient for fuel. But it is ornamental as well as useful, uncle. The diamond is nothing else than carbon."

"The diamond, eh? You mean the black diamond."

"No; the diamond, really and truly. The diamond is only carbon in the shape of a crystal."

"Eh? and can't some of your clever chemists crystallise a little bit of carbon, and make a Koh-i-noor?"[1]

"Ah, uncle, perhaps we shall, some day. In the meantime I suppose we must be content with making carbon so brilliant as it is in the flame of a candle. Well; now you see that a candle-flame is vapour burning, and the vapour, in burning, turns into water and carbonic acid gas. The oxygen of both the carbonic acid gas and the water comes from the air, and the hydrogen and carbon together are the vapour. They are distilled out of the melted wax by the heat. But, you know, carbon alone can't be distilled by any heat. It can be distilled, though, when it is joined with hydrogen, as it is in the wax, and then the mixed hydrogen and carbon rise in gas of the same kind as the gas in the streets, and that also is distilled by heat from coal. So a candle is a little gas manufactory in itself, that burns the gas as fast as it makes it."

"Haven't you pretty nearly come to your candle's end?" said Mr. Wilkinson.

"Nearly. I only want to tell uncle, that the burning of a candle is almost exactly like our breathing. Breathing is consuming oxygen, only not so fast as burning. In breathing we throw out water in vapour and carbonic acid from our lungs, and take oxygen in. Oxygen is as necessary to support the life of the body, as it is to keep up the flame of a candle."

"So," said Mr. Bagges, "man is a candle, eh? and Shakespeare knew that, I suppose, (as he did most things,) when he wrote—

'Out, out, brief candle!'

Well, well; we old ones are moulds, and you young squires are dips and rushlights, eh? Any more to tell us about the candle?"

"I could tell you a great deal more about oxygen, and hydrogen, and carbon, and water, and breathing, that Professor Faraday said, if I had time; but you should go and hear him yourself, uncle."

"Eh? well! I think I will. Some of us seniors may learn something from a juvenile lecture, at any rate, if given by a Faraday. And now, my boy, I will tell you what," added Mr. Bagges, "I am very glad to find you so fond of study and science; and you deserve to be encouraged: and so I'll give you a what-d'ye-call-it?—a Galvanic Battery on your next birth-day; and so much for your teaching your old uncle the chemistry of a candle."

1. An enormous diamond, the Kohinor or "Mountain of Light" was acquired by the British Crown with the annexation of the Punjab in 1849.

# William Acton

1814: BORN IN SHILLINGSTONE, DORSET

1840: BECAME A MEMBER OF THE ROYAL COLLEGE OF SURGEONS

1841: *A COMPLETE PRACTICAL TREATISE ON VENEREAL DISEASES*

1857: *THE FUNCTIONS AND DISORDERS OF THE REPRODUCTIVE ORGANS, IN YOUTH, IN ADULT AGE, AND IN ADVANCED LIFE, CONSIDERED IN THEIR PHYSIOLOGICAL, SOCIAL, AND PSYCHOLOGICAL RELATIONS; PROSTITUTION, CONSIDERED IN ITS MORAL, SOCIAL, AND SANITARY ASPECTS, IN LONDON AND OTHER LARGE CITIES: WITH PROPOSALS FOR THE MITIGATION AND PREVENTION OF ITS ATTENDANT EVILS* (EXPANDED AND REVISED EDITION PUBLISHED IN 1870)

1875: DIED 7 DECEMBER IN LONDON

## PROSTITUTION, CONSIDERED IN ITS MORAL, SOCIAL, AND SANITARY ASPECTS

*A physician who studied venereology and urology in Paris, William Acton wrote chiefly about sexuality, venereal disease, and related social problems. In his study of prostitution, he participated in the mid-Victorian discussion of what was termed "the great social evil." Fiction and official studies represented the prostitute as a sinner, an embodiment of the poverty and social upheaval brought about by the Industrial Revolution, or a lower-class victim of aristocratic oppression. The prostitute was also the subject of the sociological research conducted by Acton, Henry MAYHEW, and W. R. GREG. Acton's writings, which were often derivative and directed toward the general reader rather than the medical profession, illustrate the tendency in popular mid-century social research to rely on anecdotal evidence and religious and social assumptions. Prostitution, originally published in 1857, was edited, expanded, and reprinted in 1870. This selection is taken from the 1870 edition, in which Acton enlarged the scope of the earlier discussion and reduced his reliance on others' words.*

*Acton has been referred to as a pioneer in publicly acknowledging the male sexual drive as a natural impulse; however, many of his readers already believed that male sexual desire was biologically based. In fact, the Victorian acceptance of male desire paved the way for*

*Acton's argument that the regulation of prostitutes would promote the social good.*
*Claiming that many prostitutes eventually left the profession for "respectable" work and*
*marriage, he concluded that regulation would protect their own and the general health. His*
*discussion of prostitution and his call for regulation influenced the passage of the*
*Contagious Diseases Acts of the 1860s. This controversial legislation ordered women sus-*
*pected of prostitution to undergo medical examinations. Florence* NIGHTINGALE, *Harriet*
MARTINEAU, *Josephine Butler, and other Victorian feminists opposed the acts on the grounds*
*that women were being singled out and their rights denied, while men's failure to regulate*
*their desire went unaddressed.*                                              LMF

## CAUSES OF PROSTITUTION

. . . THE DEMAND FOR PROSTITUTION ARISES . . . from ill-regulated and uncontrolled
desire, and may be referred to the following heads:—

The natural instinct of man.

His sinful nature.

The artificial state of society rendering early marriages difficult if not impossible.

The unwillingness of many, who can afford marriage, to submit to its restraint, and
incur its obligations.

To a man's calling preventing him from marrying, or debarring him when married
from conjugal intercourse.

The unrestrained want and lawless demand, call for the infamous supply; but want and
demand are insufficient of themselves to create supply; they are strong provoking causes,
but not creative. We must go a step further to discover the sources of supply. It is derived
from the vice of women, which is occasioned by

Natural desire.

Natural sinfulness.

The preferment of indolent ease to labour.

Vicious inclinations strengthened and ingrained by early neglect, or evil training, bad
associates, and an indecent mode of life.

Necessity, imbued by

The inability to obtain a living by honest means consequent on a fall from
virtue.

Extreme poverty.

To this black list may be added love of drink, love of dress, love of amusement, while the
fall from virtue may result either from a woman's love being bestowed on an unworthy
object, who fulfils his professions of attachment by deliberately accomplishing her ruin,
or from the woman's calling peculiarly exposing her to temptation.

I have now called attention to the principal causes of the impure desire and the supply attendant on it.

I shall presently examine them more in detail, but will first of all notice one or two other points connected with this subject that seem not unworthy of consideration. And first I may remark that this demand and supply may either be left to themselves or artificially stimulated—that is, men may be left to find the means of gratifying their impure desires; women to find for themselves the market for their persons, or there may be third parties directly interested in stimulating the demand and increasing the supply. I allude, of course, to procurers and brothel-keepers, who, though it is hardly accurate to include them among the causes of prostitution, as they are themselves rather results of it, undoubtedly cause its continuance and increase.

I may further observe that prostitution is at once a result produced by and a cause producing immorality. Every unchaste woman is not a prostitute. By unchastity a woman becomes liable to lose character, position, and the means of living; and when these are lost is too often reduced to prostitution for support, which, therefore, may be described as the trade adopted by all women who have abandoned or are precluded from an honest course of life, or who lack the power or the inclination to obtain a livelihood from other sources. What is a prostitute? She is a woman who gives for money that which she ought to give only for love; who ministers to passion and lust alone, to the exclusion and extinction of all the higher qualities, and nobler sources of enjoyment which combine with desire, to produce the happiness derived from the intercourse of the sexes. She is a woman with half the woman gone, and that half containing all that elevates her nature, leaving her a mere instrument of impurity; degraded and fallen she extracts from the sin of others the means of living, corrupt and dependent on corruption, and therefore interested directly in the increase of immorality—a social pest, carrying contamination and foulness to every quarter to which she has access, who—

> "like a disease,
> Creeps, no precaution used, among the crowd,
> Makes wicked lightnings of her eyes,"
> ———— —- "and stirs the pulse,
> With devil's leaps, and poisons half the young."[1]

Such women, ministers of evil passions, not only gratify desire, but also arouse it. Compelled by necessity to seek for customers, they throng our streets and public places, and suggest evil thoughts and desires which might otherwise remain undeveloped. Confirmed profligates will seek out the means of gratifying their desires; the young from a craving to discover unknown mysteries may approach the haunts of sin, but thousands would remain uncontaminated if temptation did not seek them out. Prostitutes have the power of soliciting and tempting. Gunpowder remains harmless till the spark falls upon it; the match, until struck, retains the hidden fire, so lust remains dormant till called into being by an exciting cause.

The sexual passion is strong in every man, but it is strong in proportion as it is encouraged or restrained; and every act of indulgence only makes future abstinence more hard, and in time almost impossible. Some consider that prostitution is the safety valve of soci-

---

1. Quoted inexactly from Alfred Tennyson's "Guinevere," in *Idylls of the King* (1859).

ety, and that any serious diminution of the number of prostitutes would be attended with an increase of clandestine immodesty. Such a consequence is not one that I think need be apprehended; the insinuation that virtuous women, to be made to yield, require only to be assaulted, is a base and unworthy calumny; nor is it to be supposed that the man who will use a harlot is prepared to insult or injure a modest woman. But intercourse with depraved women debases the mind, and gradually hardens the heart, and each act of gratification stimulates desire and necessitates fresh indulgence; and when grown into a habit, not only breeds distaste for virtuous society, but causes the mind to form a degraded estimate of the sex, until all women seem mere objects of desire and vehicles of indulgence. The prostitute is a sad burlesque of woman, presenting herself as an object of lust instead of an object of honourable love—a source of base gratification, instead of a reason for self-restraint; familiarising man with this aspect of women till he can see no other, and his indulged body and debased mind lead him to seek in them only sensual gratification, and to make, if possible, of every woman the thing that he desires—a toy; a plaything, an animated doll; a thing to wear like a glove, and fling away; to use like a horse, and send to the knackers[2] when worn out; the mere object of his fancy and servant of his appetite, instead of an immortal being, composed, like himself, of body, soul and spirit—his associate and consort, endowed with memory and hope and strong affections, with a heart to love, to feel, to suffer; man's highest prize and surest safeguard; the inspirer of honest love and manly exertion, powerful

> "Not only to keep down the base in man,
> But teach high thought and amiable words,
> And courtliness, and the desire of fame,
> And love of truth, and all that makes a man."[3]

It thus appears that prostitution depends not only on demand and supply, and external causes, but is itself a cause of its own existence, because the possibility of indulgence weakens the force of self-restraint, by creating the idea in the mind of unlawfully and basely gratifying the natural instinct, to which indulgence adds force and intensity, and thus in a measure creates the want, producing from a desire capable of restraint a habit impossible to shake off; while the supply being active, and itself desiring exercise, does not wait for the demand, but goes about to seek it, suggesting, arousing, stimulating evil thoughts and unhallowed passions. . . .

. . . [P]rostitution abounds not only in places where large numbers of unmarried men are collected together, but also where in the course of their daily work the sexes are brought into close and intimate relations. Factory towns, therefore, must be included in the list of places peculiarly liable to the presence of prostitution, though perhaps in this case the prevailing mischief may be more accurately termed general immorality, or depravity, than prostitution proper; the difference, however, is not very great, and, for the purposes of this work, immaterial. I must not forget to include among local causes

2. Those who buy and slaughter old and disabled horses for their hides and meat.
3. Tennyson, "Guinevere."

the serious mischief incidental to the gang system[4] in various agricultural districts. Public attention has on several recent occasions been prominently called to the evils thus arising, and it is not unreasonable to hope that adequate steps will be taken for improving the moral condition of the agricultural poor. Where women and men, and girls and boys are working together indiscriminately in the fields, with, in many cases, long distances to traverse in going to and returning from the scenes of their labours, it is obvious that opportunity cannot be wanting, and that temptations must not unfrequently be yielded to, and that the morals and habits of the people will be of a very low order. We may, however, expect to find large cities contribute in a greater degree than other places to the manufacture and employment of prostitutes. Here always abound idle and wealthy men, with vicious tastes, which they spare neither pains nor expense to gratify. Here also are the needy, the improvident, and the ill-instructed, from whose ranks the victims of sensuality may be readily recruited. The close proximity of luxury and indigence cannot fail to produce a demoralizing effect upon the latter. Garrison, seaport, and factory towns, and large cities, are all places peculiarly liable to the presence of prostitution, containing, as they do, within themselves in an eminent degree the seeds and causes of vice. Some places, such as London, combine within themselves all these qualities, and are therefore notably and exceptionally exposed to this evil. It is impossible to suppose that in such localities prostitution can ever become extinct. Wherever men are peculiarly exposed to temptation by the state, it seems only just that the state should take care that the evil condition that it imposes should be rendered as little injurious as possible.[5] This position has of late years, as we have seen, received a tardy recognition; it is reasonable, I think, to extend this principle a little further, and to adopt a similar course in all cases where we know that the existence of vice is inevitable; it is useless to shut our eyes to a fact; it is better to recognise it—to regulate the system, and ameliorate, if possible, the condition of its victims. . . .

We have seen that many women stray from the paths of virtue, and ultimately swell the ranks of prostitution through being by their position peculiarly exposed to temptation. The women to whom this remark applies are chiefly actresses, milliners, shop girls, domestic servants, and women employed in factories or working in agricultural gangs. Of these many, no doubt, fall through vanity and idleness, love of dress, love of excitement, love of drink, but by far the larger proportion are driven to evil courses by cruel biting poverty. It is a shameful fact, but no less true, that the lowness of the wages paid to workwomen in various trades is a fruitful source of prostitution; unable to obtain by their labour the means of procuring the bare necessaries of life, they gain, by surrendering their bodies to evil uses, food to sustain and clothes to cover them. Many thousand young women in the metropolis are unable by drudgery that lasts from early morning till late into the night to earn more than from 3s. to 5s. weekly. Many have to eke out their living as best they may on a miserable pittance for less than the least of the sums above-

4. Groups of farm laborers were generally hired seasonally as needed and often had to travel from location to location to plant and harvest crops as these jobs became available.

5. Acton alludes here to the Contagious Diseases Acts, which were a response to the high incidence of venereal disease among soldiers and sailors in garrison towns.

mentioned. What wonder if, urged on by want and toil, encouraged by evil advisers, and exposed to selfish tempters, a large proportion of these poor girls fall from the path of virtue? Is it not a greater wonder that any of them are found abiding in it? Instances innumerable might be adduced in support of this statement. I have said enough to acquaint the reader with the miserable condition of these children of want; it is not my purpose to pain and horrify or to distract the attention from the main purpose of my book; those who desire a narrative of facts fully supporting this statement, I would refer to Mr. Mayhew's work on London Labour and London Poor. Misplaced love, then, inordinate vanity, and sheer destitution are the causes that lead to woman's fall and that help to fill the ranks of prostitution. But love should not lead to the forfeiture of self-respect. Vanity may be restrained; want may be relieved from other sources. A still more frightful cause remains behind—more frightful because here the sinner has had no choice, so far as man can see, except to sin. Neither love nor vanity nor want have induced the surrender of virtue, for in this case virtue never existed, not even the negative form of virtue, the not-sinning state, the children of the very poor or very vile, what is their lot? It is a picture from which one recoils with horror, and the reality of which in this Christian country it is hard to believe. The cause to which I now allude is found in the promiscuous herding of the sexes (no other word is applicable) through the want of sufficient house accommodation. . . .

Bad as are these pauper dens, nurseries of vice more fearful still abound in our Christian capital. In the former some effort after decency may be made, but in the latter, not only is there no such effort, but the smallest remnant of modesty is scouted and trampled down as an insult and reproach. I allude to the low lodging-houses which afford to the homeless poor a refuge still more cruel than the pitiless streets from which they fly. In these detestable haunts of vice men, women, and children are received indiscriminately, and pass the night huddled together, without distinction of age or sex, not merely in one common room, but often one common bed; even if privacy is desired, it is impossible of attainment; no accommodation is made for decency, and the practices of the inmates are on a par with the accommodation. It is fearful to contemplate human beings so utterly abandoned, reduced below the level of the brute creation. By constant practice, vice has become a second nature; with such associates, children of tender years soon become old in vice. This is no fancy sketch, or highly-coloured picture. In this manner thousands pass from childhood to youth, from youth to age, with every good feeling trampled out and every evil instinct cherished and matured; trained to no useful art, and yet dependent for a living on their own exertions, what wonder if all the males are thieves and all the females prostitutes. . . .

The extreme youth of the junior portion of the "street-walkers" is a remarkable feature of London prostitution, and has been the subject of much comment by foreign travellers who have published their impressions of social London. Certain quarters of the town are positively infested by juvenile offenders, whose effrontery is more intolerably disgusting than that of their elder sisters. It is true, these young things spring from the lowest dregs of the population; and, from what I can learn of their habits, their seduction—if seduction it can be called—has been effected, with their own consent, by boys no older than themselves, and is an all but natural consequence of promiscuous herding, that mainspring of corruption among our lower orders. That such as these are generally the victims of panders and old *débauchées* is as untrue as many of the wretched fallacies set about by some who write fictions about social matters in the guise of facts; but whatever the prime cause of their appearance in the streets as prostitutes, it is none the less strange and sad—none the less worth amending, that the London poor should furnish, and London immorality should maintain, so many of these half-fledged nurselings, who take to prostitution, as do their brothers of the same age to thieving and other evil courses, for a bare subsistence.

Although a large number of women fall victims as above, it cannot be denied that others early evince a natural indisposition to do work when they might obtain it, and may thus be said to court admission into the ranks of prostitution. That idleness and vanity are almost inevitable bequests from parent to child, is proved by the fact that the children of the numerous diseased prostitutes, consigned by the police to the St. Lazare Hospital in Paris, notwithstanding all the religious teachings of the Sisters of Charity, and the excellent secular education given them within the walls of that institution, where they are received as old as seven or eight years, almost invariably become prostitutes. The foundlings, or deserted children, oftentimes illegitimate, who crowd our workhouses, are in like manner a very fruitful source for the recruitment of the metropolitan pavé.[6]

With the absolute neglect of children by parents, and the interminable scheming of lustful men, I may end the roll of causes which have operated in this direction since the dawn of civilization, and, singly or combined, will so continue, I presume, to operate for all time.

6. Streetwalkers.

# Charlotte Brontë

## LETTERS TO GEORGE HENRY LEWES

*Charlotte Brontë's correspondence with George Henry* Lewes *began in 1847, when Lewes wrote to Currer Bell to announce that he was writing a review of* Jane Eyre *for* Fraser's Magazine. *An advocate of realistic fiction, Lewes advised the newly published author to avoid melodrama, to focus on the real, and to draw upon experience. Charlotte Brontë's responses to Lewes offer readers an insight into her ideas about writing fiction, especially her claims for the place of imagination and "poetry" in novels. Lewes's favorable review (December, 1847) of* Jane Eyre *pleased Brontë; she found his praise "generous." But his negative review of* Shirley *in 1850, with its discussion of female authorship, clearly did not, as her letters of 1850 indicate. Brontë and Lewes met briefly in 1850 during one of her visits to London.* RM

*November 6, 1847*

Dear Sir

Your LETTER REACHED ME YESTERDAY; I beg to assure you that I appreciate fully the intention with which it was written, and I thank you sincerely both for its cheering commendation and valuable advice.

You warn me to beware of Melodram[a] and you exhort me to adhere to the real. When I first began to write, so impressed was I with the truth of the principles you advocate that I determined to take Nature and Truth as my sole guides and to follow in their very footprints; I restrained imagination, eschewed romance, repressed excitement: over-bright colouring too I avoided, and sought to produce something which should be soft, grave and true.

My work (a tale in 1 vol.)[1] being completed, I offered it to a publisher. He said it was original, faithful to Nature, but he did not feel warranted in accepting it, such a work would not sell. I tried six publishers in succession; they all told me it was deficient in "startling incident" and "thrilling excitement," that it would never suit the circulating libraries, and as it was on those libraries the success of works of fiction mainly depended they could not undertake to publish what would be overlooked there—"Jane Eyre" was rather objected to at first [on] the same grounds—but finally found acceptance.

I mention this to you, not with a view of pleading exemption from censure, but in order to direct your attention to the root of certain literary evils—if in your forthcoming article in "Frazer"[2] you would bestow a few words of enlightenment on the public who support the circulating libraries, you might, with your powers, do some good.

You advise me too, not to stray far from the ground of experience as I become weak when I enter the region of fiction; and you say "real experience is perennially interesting and to all men. ."

I feel that this also is true, but, dear Sir, is not the real experience of each individual very limited? and if a writer dwells upon that solely or principally is he not in danger of repeating himself, and also of becoming an egotist?

Then too, Imagination is a strong, restless faculty which claims to be heard and exercised, are we to be quite deaf to her cry and insensate to her struggles? When she shews us bright pictures are we never to look at them and try to reproduce them? And when she is eloquent and speaks rapidly and urgently in our ear are we not to write to her dictation[?]

I shall anxiously search the next number of "Frazer" for your opinions on these points.

Believe me, dear Sir,

Yours gratefully

C Bell

*November 22, 1847*

DEAR SIR

I have now read "Ranthorpe";[3] I could not get it till a day or two ago, but I have got it and read it at last; And in reading "Ranthorpe," I have read a new book; not a reprint, not a reflection of any other book, but a *new book*. I did not know such books were written now. It is very different to any of the popular works of fiction. It fills the mind with fresh knowledge. Your experience and your convictions are made the reader's, and to an author at least they have a value and an interest quite unusual.

1. *The Professor*, Brontë's first completed novel, which was not published until after her death.
2. *Fraser's Magazine*, December 1847.
3. Lewes's first novel, published anonymously in 1847.

I await your criticism on "Jane Eyre" now with other sentiments than I entertained before the perusal of "Ranthorpe." You were a stranger to me—I did not particularly respect you—I did not feel that your praise or blame would have any special weight—I knew little of your right to condemn or approve—*now* I am informed on these points.

You will be severe—your last letter taught me so much—. Well—I shall try to extract good out of your severity; and besides, though I am now sure you are a just, discriminating man, yet, being mortal, you must be fallible, and if any part of your censure galls me too keenly to the quick, gives me deadly pain, I shall for the present disbelieve it and put it quite aside till such time as I feel able to receive it without torture.

I am, dear Sir

Yours very respectfully

C Bell

*January 12, 1848*

Dear Sir

Mr. Williams[4] did well on the whole to tell you I regretted not having sent the note of thanks I wrote, as I am thus afforded the opportunity of repairing that omission.

I thank you then sincerely for your generous review, and it is with a sense of double content I express my gratitude, because I am now sure the tribute is not superfluous or obtrusive. You were not severe on "Jane Eyre" you were very lenient: I am glad you told me my faults plainly in private, for in your public notice you touch on them so lightly, I should perhaps have passed them over thus indicated, with too little reflection.

I mean to observe your warning about being careful how I undertake new works: my stock of materials is not abundant but very slender, and besides neither my experience, my acquirements, nor my powers are sufficiently varied to justify my ever becoming a frequent writer.

I tell you this because your article in "Frazer" left on me an uneasy impression that you were disposed to think better of the author of "Jane Eyre" than that individual deserved, and I would rather you had a correct than a flattering opinion of me, even though I should never see you.

If I ever *do* write another book, I think I will have nothing of what you call "melodram[a]"; I *think* so, but I am not sure. I *think* too I will endeavour to follow the counsel which shines out of Miss Austen's "mild eyes"; "to finish more, and be more subdued"; but neither am I sure of that. When authors write best, or at least, when they write most fluently, an influence seems to waken in them which becomes their master, which will have its own way, putting out of view all behests but its own, dictating certain words, and insisting on their being used, whether vehement or measured in their nature; new moulding characters, giving unthought-of turns to incidents, rejecting carefully elaborated old ideas, and suddenly creating and adopting new ones. Is it not so? And should we try to

---

4. William Smith Williams, reader for Smith, Elder & Company, who recommended *Jane Eyre* for publication and became a frequent correspondent of the author.

counteract this influence? Can we indeed counteract it?

I am glad that another work of yours will soon appear;[5] most curious shall I be to see whether you will write up to your own principles, and work out your own theories. You did not do it altogether in "Ranthorpe," at least not in the latter part; but the first portion was, I think, nearly without fault; then it had a pith, truth, significance in it which gave the book sterling value: but to write so one must have seen and known a great deal, and I have seen and known very little.

Why do you like Miss Austen so very much? I am puzzled on that point.

What induced you to say that you would rather have written "Pride and Prejudice" or "Tom Jones" than any of the Waverly Novels?

I had not seen "Pride and Prejudice" till I read that sentence of yours, and then I got the book and studied it. And what did I find? An accurate daguerreotyped portrait of a common-place face; a carefully-fenced, highly cultivated garden with neat borders and delicate flowers—but no glance of a bright vivid physiognomy—no open country—no fresh air—no blue hill—no bonny beck. I should hardly like to live with her ladies and gentlemen in their elegant but confined houses. These observations will probably irritate you, but I shall run the risk.

Now I can understand admiration of George Sand[6]—for though I never saw any of her works which I admired throughout (even "Consuelo" which is the best, or the best I have read, appears to me to me [sic] to couple strange extravagance with wondrous excellence) yet she has a grasp of mind which if I cannot fully comprehend, I can very deeply respect; she is sagacious and profound; Miss Austen is only shrewd and observant. Am I wrong—or were you hasty in what you said?

If you have time, I should be glad to hear you further on this subject—if not—or if you think the questions frivolous do not trouble yourself to reply.

I am yours respectfully
C Bell

*January 18, 1848*

DEAR SIR

I must write to you one more note, though I had not intended to trouble you again so soon. I have to agree with you, and to differ from you.

You correct my crude remarks on the subject of the "influence" well: I accept your definition of what the effects of that influence should be; I recognize the wisdom of your rules for its regulation.

About "Ranthorpe" I am right. By the last part of that work I understand only from page 271 to the end; the first portion, in which I include the episode of the Hawbuckes,[7] is the best. You yourself admit it. You say "the great merit of the book lies in its views of literature and literary life, and in the reflections." So I think, and it is in the first part these

---

5. Probably Lewes's second novel, *Rose, Blanche, and Violet* (1848).
6. French novelist (1804–76). Her *Consuelo* was published in 1842.
7. The unhappy marriage of Florence and Sir Frederick Hawbucke forms one of the subplots of Lewes's novel.

views are disclosed, and these reflections made. I like them. The views are just, the reflec
tions profound; both are instructive.

What a strange sentence comes next in your letter! You say I must familiarize my mind
with the fact that "Miss Austen is not a poetess, has no 'sentiment' (you scornfully enclose
the word in inverted commas) no eloquence, none of the ravishing enthusiasm of poetry"—and then you add, I *must* "learn to acknowledge her as *one of the greatest artists, of the
greatest painters of human character*, and one of the writers with the nicest sense of means
to an end that ever lived."

The last point only will I ever acknowledge. Can there be a great artist without poetry? What I call—what I will bend to as a great artist, there cannot be destitute of the
divine gift. But by *poetry* I am sure you understand something different to what I do—as
you do by "sentiment." It is *poetry*, as I comprehend the word which elevates that masculine George Sand, and makes out of something coarse, something godlike. It is "sentiment," in my sense of the term, sentiment jealously hidden, but genuine, which extracts
the venom from that formidable Thackeray, and converts what might be only corrosive
poison into purifying elixir. If Thackeray did not cherish in his large heart deep feeling
for his kind, he would delight to exterminate; as it is, I believe he wishes only to reform.

Miss Austen, being as you say without "sentiment," without *poetry*, may be—*is* sensible, *real* (more *real* than *true*) but she cannot be great.

I submit to your anger which I have now excited (for have I not questioned the perfection of your darling?) the storm may pass over me. Nevertheless I will, when I can (I
do not know when that will be as I have no access to a circulating library) diligently
peruse all Miss Austen's works, as you recommend.

I have something else to say. You mention the authoress of "Azeth the Egyptian":[8] you
say you think I should sympathize "with her daring imagination and pictorial fancy."
Permit me to undeceive you: with infinitely more relish can I sympathize with Miss
Austen's clear common sense and subtle shrewdness. If you find no inspiration in Miss
Austen's page, neither do you find there windy wordiness: to use your words once again,
she exquisitely adapts her means to her end: both are very subdued, a little contracted,
but never absurd. I have not read "Azeth"; but I did read or begin to read a tale in the
"New Monthly" from the same pen, and harsh as the opinion may sound to you, I must
candidly avow that I thought it both turgid and feeble: it reminded me of some of the
most inflated and emptiest parts of Bulwer's[9] novels: I found in it neither strength, sense,
nor originality.

You must forgive me for not always being able to think as you do, and still believe me

Yours gratefully
C Bell

*[January 1850]*

I can be on my guard against my enemies, but God deliver me from my friends!

Currer Bell

8. Eliza Lynn Linton (1822–98).
9. Edward Bulwer-Lytton (1803–73), author of *Eugene Aram* (1832), *The Last Days of Pompeii* (1834), *Paul Clifford*
(1830), and *Pelham* (1828).

*January 19, 1850*

My dear Sir

I will tell you why I was so hurt by that review in the Edinburgh; not because its criticism was keen or its blame sometimes severe; not because its praise was stinted (for indeed I think you give me quite as much praise as I deserve) but because, after I had said earnestly that I wished critics would judge me as an *author* not as a woman, you so roughly—I even thought—so cruelly handled the question of sex. I daresay you meant no harm, and perhaps you will not now be able to understand why I was so grieved at, what you will probably deem, such a trifle; but grieved I was, and indignant too.

There was a passage or two which you did quite wrong to write.

However I will not bear malice against you for it: I know what your nature is; it is not a bad or an unkind one, though you would often jar terribly on some feelings with whose recoil and quiver you could not possibly sympathize. I imagine you are both enthusiastic and implacable, as you are at once sagacious and careless. You know much and discover much, but you are in such a hurry to tell it all, you never give yourself time to think how your reckless eloquence may affect others, and, what is more, if you knew how it did affect them you would not much care.

However I shake hands with you: you have excellent points; you can be generous: I still feel angry and think I do well to be angry, but it is the anger one experiences for rough play rather than for foul play.

I am yours with a certain respect and some chagrin

Currer Bell

# George Henry Lewes

## REVIEW OF *SHIRLEY*

*In 1847 journalist and critic George Henry Lewes, having read an advance copy of* Jane Eyre *by Currer Bell, offered to review the novel for* Fraser's Magazine *and began corresponding with the novelist (later revealed to be Charlotte* Brontë*). The review, appearing in December 1847, praised* Jane Eyre *for its evocation of "deep, significant reality," its passion and power, and its "truth in the delineation of life and character." But Lewes's reaction to Currer Bell's second published novel,* Shirley, *prompted Brontë to respond, "I can be on my guard against my enemies, but God deliver me from my friends!" Published in the January 1850* Edinburgh Review, *his review reveals not only his disappointment in Brontë's latest novel but also his developing theories of realism in fiction. Lewes, who preferred the novels of Jane Austen and, later, George Eliot for their psychological "truthfulness" and representation of the "actual experience of life," argues that* Shirley's *characters, particularly its male ones, are untrue and improbable, their characterization unrealistic. While admiring some passages of powerful feeling, he says the novel fails because it lacks a unified, organically evolving plot. As troubling to Charlotte Brontë as Lewes's criticism of her own work were his introductory comments about the limitations of female writers in general. Here the usually unconventional Lewes falls into conventional, essentialist assumptions about "organic" differences between men and women.* RM

The gallant suggestion of our great Peasant Poet, that Nature 'tried her 'prentice hand' on Man, before venturing on the finer task of fashioning Woman,[1] has not yet found acceptance otherwise than as a sportive caprice of fancy—the sort of playful resignation of superiority which threw Samson at the feet of Dalilah, and made Hercules put aside his strength,—

'Spinning with Omphale,—and all for Love!'[2]

Men in general, when serious and *not* gallant, are slow to admit woman even to an equality with themselves; and the prevalent opinion certainly is that women are inferior in respect of intellect. This opinion may be correct. The question is a delicate one. We very much doubt, however, whether sufficient *data* exist for any safe or confident decision. For the position of women in society has never yet been—perhaps never can be—such as to give fair play to their capabilities. It is true, no doubt, that none of them have yet attained to the highest eminence in the highest departments of intellect. They have had no Shakspeare, no Bacon, no Newton, no Milton, no Raphael, no Mozart, no Watt, no Burke. But while this is admitted, it is surely not to be forgotten that these are the *few* who have carried off the high prizes to which millions of *Men* were equally qualified by their training and education to aspire, and for which, by their actual pursuits, they may be held to have been contending; while the number of *Women* who have had either the benefit of such training, or the incitement of such pursuits, has been comparatively insignificant. When the bearded competitors were numbered by thousands, and the smooth-chinned by scores, what was the chance of the latter? Or with what reason could their failure be ascribed to their inferiority as a class?

Nevertheless, with this consideration distinctly borne in mind, we must confess our doubts whether women will ever rival men in *some* departments of intellectual exertion; and especially in those which demand either a long preparation, or a protracted effort of pure thought. But we do not, by this, prejudge the question of superiority. We assume no general organic inferiority; we simply assert an organic *difference*. Women, we are entirely disposed to admit, are substantially *equal* in the aggregate worth of their endowments: But equality does not imply identity. They may be equal, but not exactly alike. Many of their endowments are specifically different. Mentally as well as bodily there seem to be organic diversities; and these must make themselves felt, whenever the two sexes come into competition.

The grand function of woman, it must always be recollected, is, and ever must be, *Maternity*: and this we regard not only as her distinctive characteristic, and most endearing charm, but as a high and holy office—the prolific source, not only of the best affections and virtues of which our nature is capable, but also of the wisest thoughtfulness, and most useful habits of observation, by which that nature can be elevated and adorned. But with all this, we think it impossible to deny, that it must essentially interfere both with that steady and unbroken application, without which no proud eminence in science can

1. Robert Burns, "Green Grow the Rashes, O" (1787).
2. As slave to Omphale of Lydia, Hercules or Heracles was forced to dress in women's clothing and perform women's work, including spinning.

be gained—and with the discharge of all official or professional functions that do not admit of long or frequent postponement. All women are intended by Nature to be mothers; and by far the greater number—not less, we suppose, than nine tenths—are called upon to act in that sacred character; and, consequently, for twenty of the best years of their lives—those very years in which men either rear the grand fabric or lay the solid foundations of their fame and fortune—women are mainly occupied by the cares, the duties, the enjoyments and the sufferings of maternity. During large parts of these years, too, their bodily health is generally so broken and precarious as to incapacitate them for any strenuous exertion; and, health apart, the greater portion of their time, thoughts, interests, and anxieties ought to be, and generally are, centered in the care and the training of their children. But how could such occupations consort with the intense and unremitting studies which seared the eyeballs of Milton, and for a time unsettled even the powerful brain of Newton? High art and science always require the whole man; and never yield their great prizes but to the devotion of a life. But the life of a woman, from her cradle upwards, is otherwise devoted: and those whose lot it is to expend their best energies, from the age of twenty to the age of forty, in the cares and duties of maternity, have but slender chances of carrying off these great prizes. It is the same with the high functions of statesmanship, legislation, generalship, judgeship, and other elevated stations and pursuits, to which some women, we believe, have recently asserted the equal pretensions of their sex. Their still higher and *indispensable* functions of maternity afford the answer to all such claims. What should we do with a leader of opposition in the seventh month of her pregnancy? or a general in chief who at the opening of a campaign was 'doing as well as could be expected'? or a chief justice with twins?[3] . . .

It is in literature, however, that women have most distinguished themselves; and probably because hundreds have cultivated literature, for one that has cultivated science or art. Their list of names in this department is a list that would rank high even among literary males. Madame de Stael was certainly as powerful a writer as any man of her age or country; and whatever may be the errors of George Sand's opinions, she is almost without a rival in eloquence, power, and invention. Mrs. Hemans, Miss Edgeworth, Miss Baillie, Miss Austen, Mrs. Norton, Miss Mitford, Miss Landon, are second only to the first-rate men of their day; and would probably have ranked even higher, had they not been too solicitous about male excellence,—had they not often written from the man's point of view, instead of from the woman's. That which irretrievably condemns the whole literature of Rome to the second rank,—viz. imitation,—has also kept down the literature of women. The Roman only thought of rivalling a Greek,—not of mirroring life in his own nationality; and so women have too often thought but of rivalling men. It is their boast to be mistaken for men,—instead of speaking sincerely and energetically as women. So true is this, that in the department where they have least followed men, and spoken more as women,—we mean in Fiction,—their success has been greatest. Not to mention other

3. Plato, indeed, argues that women should be trained to exercises of war, since the female dogs guard sheep as well as the male! But this is one of the many 'exquisite reasons' of the Divine Philosopher, which look very like puerility. Duncan's strange account of the King of Dahomey's Amazonian corps, several thousands strong, is the only real experiment of the sort we ever heard of. [Lewes's note]

names, surely no man has surpassed Miss Austen as a delineator of common life? Her range, to be sure, is limited; but her art is perfect. She does not touch those profounder and more impassioned chords which vibrate to the heart's core—never ascends to its grand or heroic movements, nor descends to its deeper throes and agonies; but in all she attempts she is uniformly and completely successful.

It is curious too, and worthy of a passing remark, that women have achieved success in every department of fiction but that of *humour*. They deal, no doubt, in sly humorous touches often enough; but the broad provinces of that great domain are almost uninvaded by them; beyond the outskirts, and open borders, they have never ventured to pass. Compare Miss Austen, Miss Ferriar, and Miss Edgeworth, with the lusty mirth and riotous humour of Shakspeare, Rabelais, Butler, Swift, Fielding, Smollett, or Dickens and Thackeray. It is like comparing a quiet smile with the 'inextinguishable laughter' of the Homeric gods! So also on the stage,—there have been comic actresses of incomparable merit, lively, pleasant, humorous women, gladdening the scene with their airy brightness and gladsome presence; but they have no comic energy. There has been no female Munden, Liston, Matthews, or Keeley. To be sure, our drama has no female parts, the representation of which after such a fashion would not have been a caricature.

But we must pursue this topic no further; and fear our readers may have been wondering how we have wandered away to it, from the theme which seemed to be suggested by the title of the work now before us. The explanation and apology is, that we take Currer Bell to be one of the most remarkable of *female* writers; and believe it is now scarcely a secret that Currer Bell is the pseudonyme of a woman. An eminent contemporary,[4] indeed, has employed the sharp vivacity of a female pen to prove 'upon irresistible evidence' that 'Jane Eyre' *must be* the work of a man! But all that 'irresistible evidence' is set aside by the simple fact that Currer Bell *is* a woman. We never, for our own parts, had a moment's doubt on the subject. That Jane herself was drawn by a woman's delicate hand, and that Rochester equally betrayed the sex of the artist, was to our minds so obvious, as absolutely to shut our ears to all the evidence which could be adduced by the erudition even of a *marchande des modes*;[5] and that simply because we knew that there were women profoundly ignorant of the mysteries of the toilette, and the terminology of fashion (independent of the obvious solution, that such ignorance might be counterfeited, to mislead), and felt that there was no man who *could so* have delineated a woman— or *would so* have delineated a man. The fair and ingenious critic was misled by her own acuteness in the perception of details; and misled also in some other way, and more uncharitably, in concluding that the *author* of 'Jane Eyre' was a heathen educated among heathens,—the *fact* being, that the *authoress* is the daughter of a clergyman!

This question of authorship, which was somewhat hotly debated a little while ago, helped to keep up the excitement about 'Jane Eyre'; but, independently of that title to notoriety, it is certain that, for many years, there had been no work of such power, piquancy, and originality. Its very faults were faults on the side of vigour; and its beauties

---

4. Elizabeth RIGBY (Lady Eastlake), whose very negative, unsigned review of *Jane Eyre* appeared in the December 1848 *Quarterly Review*.

5. "Merchant of fashions."

were all original. The grand secret of its success, however,—as of all genuine and lasting success,—was its *reality*. From out the depths of a sorrowing experience, here was a voice speaking to the experience of thousands. The aspects of external nature, too, were painted with equal fidelity,—the long cheerless winter days, chilled with rolling mists occasionally gathering into the strength of rains,—the bright spring mornings,—the clear solemn nights,—were all painted to your *soul* as well as to your eye by a pencil dipped into a soul's experience for its colours. Faults enough the book has undoubtedly: faults of conception, faults of taste, faults of ignorance, but in spite of all, it remains a book of singular fascination. A more masculine book, in the sense of vigour, was never written. Indeed that vigour often amounts to coarseness,—and is certainly the very antipode to 'lady like.'

This same over-masculine vigour is even more prominent in 'Shirley,' and does not increase the pleasantness of the book. A pleasant book, indeed, we are not sure that we can style it. Power it has unquestionably, and interest too, of a peculiar sort; but not the agreeableness of a work of art. Through its pages we are carried as over a wild and desolate heath, with a sharp east wind blowing the hair into our eyes, and making the blood tingle in our veins: There is health perhaps in the drive; but not much pleasantness. Nature speaks to us distinctly enough, but she does not speak sweetly. She is in her stern and sombre mood, and we see only her dreary aspects.

'Shirley' is inferior to 'Jane Eyre' in several important points. It is not quite so true; and it is not so fascinating. It does not so rivet the reader's attention, nor hurry him through all obstacles of improbability, with so keen a sympathy in its reality. It is even coarser in texture, too, and not unfrequently flippant; while the characters are almost all disagreeable, and exhibit intolerable rudeness of manner. In 'Jane Eyre' life was viewed from the standing point of individual experience; in 'Shirley' that standing point is frequently abandoned, and the artist paints only a panorama of which she, as well as you, are but spectators. Hence the unity of 'Jane Eyre' in spite of its clumsy and improbable contrivances, was great and effective: the fire of one passion fused the discordant materials into one mould. But in 'Shirley' all unity, in consequence of defective art, is wanting. There is no passionate link; nor is there any artistic fusion, or intergrowth, by which one part evolves itself from another. Hence its falling-off in interest, coherent movement, and life. The book may be laid down at any chapter, and almost any chapter might be omitted. The various scenes are gathered up into three volumes,—they have not grown into a work. The characters often need a justification for their introduction; as in the case of the three Curates, who are offensive, uninstructive, and unamusing.[6] That they are not *inventions*, however, we feel persuaded. For nothing but a strong sense of their reality could have seduced the authoress into such a mistake as admitting them at all. We are confident she has seen them, known them, despised them; and *therefore* she paints them! although they have no relation with the story, have no interest in themselves, and cannot be accepted as types of a class,—for they are not *Curates* but *boors*: and although not inventions, we must be permitted to say that they are *not true*. Some such objection the

---

6. The curates are introduced in Brontë's controversial first chapter.

authoress seems indeed to have anticipated; and thus towards the close of her work defends herself against it. 'Note well! wherever you present *the actual simple truth, it is somehow always denounced as a lie*: they disown it, cast it off, throw it on the parish; whereas the product of your imagination, the mere figment, the sheer fiction, is adopted, petted, termed pretty, proper, sweetly natural.' Now Currer Bell, we fear, has here fallen into a vulgar error. It is one, indeed, into which even Miss Edgeworth has also fallen: who conceived that she justified the introduction of an improbable anecdote in her text, by averring in a note that it was a 'fact.' But, the intrusion is not less an error for all that. Truth is never rejected, unless it be truth so exceptional as to stagger our belief; and in that case the artist is wrong to employ it, without so *preparing* our minds that we might receive it unquestioned. The coinage of imagination, on the other hand, is not accepted *because* it departs from the actual truth, but only because it presents the recognised attributes of our nature in new and striking combinations. If it falsify these attributes, or the known laws of their associations, the fiction is at once pronounced to be *monstrous*, and is rejected. Art, in short, deals with the broad principles of human nature, not with idiosyncracies: and, although it requires an experience of life both comprehensive and profound, to enable us to say with confidence, that '*this* motive is unnatural,' or '*that* passion is untrue,' it requires no great experience to say 'this character has not the air of reality; it may be copied from nature, but it does not *look* so.' Were Currer Bell's defence allowable, all criticism must be silenced at once. An author has only to say that his characters *are copied from nature*, and the discussion is closed. But though the portraits may be like the oddities from whom they are copied, they are faulty as works of art, if they strike all who never met with these oddities, as unnatural. The curious anomalies of life, which find their proper niches in Southey's 'Omniana, or Common-place Book,'[7] are not suitable to a novel. It is the same with incidents.

Again we say that 'Shirley' cannot be received as a work of art. It is not a picture; but a portfolio of random sketches for one or more pictures. The authoress never seems distinctly to have made up her mind as to what she was to do; whether to describe the habits and manners of Yorkshire and its social aspects in the days of King Lud,[8] or to paint character, or to tell a love story. All are by turns attempted and abandoned; and the book consequently moves slowly, and by starts—leaving behind it no distinct or satisfactory impression. Power is stamped on various parts of it; power unmistakeable, but often misapplied. Currer Bell has much yet to learn,—and, especially, the discipline of her own tumultuous energies. She must learn also to sacrifice a little of her Yorkshire roughness to the demands of good taste, neither saturating her writings with such rudeness and offensive harshness, nor suffering her style to wander into such vulgarities as would be inexcusable—even in a man. No good critic will object to the homeliness of natural diction, or to the racy flavour of conversational idiom; but every one must object to such phrases as 'Miss Mary, *getting up the steam* in her turn, now asked,' &c., or as 'making hard-handed worsted spinners *cash up to the tune of* four or five hundred per cent.,' or as 'Malone

7. Robert Southey's *Omniana* (1812), a pastiche of miscellaneous curiosities.
8. *Shirley* is set in Yorkshire during the 1811–12 outbreak of Luddism or machine-breaking. The names "King Lud" or "Ned Ludd" apply to Luddism's mythical leader.

much chagrined at hearing him *pipe up in most superior style;*' all which phrases occur with-in the space of about a dozen pages, and that not in dialogue, but in the authoress's own narrative. And while touching on this minor, yet not trivial point, we may also venture a word of quiet remonstrance against a most inappropriate obtrusion of French phrases. When Gerard Moore and his sister talk in French, *which the authoress translates*, it surely is not allowable to leave scraps of French in the translation. A French word or two may be introduced now and then on account of some peculiar fitness, but Currer Bell's use of the language is little better than that of the 'fashionable' novelists. To speak of a grandmoth-er as *une grand'mère*, and of treacle as *mélasse*, or of a young lady being angry as *courroucée*, gives an air of affectation to the style strangely at variance with the frankness of its gen-eral tone. . . .

Our closing word shall be one of exhortation. Schiller, writing to Goethe about Madame de Stael's 'Corinne,' says, 'This person wants every thing that is graceful in a woman; and, nevertheless, the faults of her book are altogether womanly faults. She steps out of her sex—without elevating herself above it.' This brief and pregnant criticism is quite as applicable to Currer Bell: For she, too, has genius enough to create a great name for herself; and if we seem to have insisted too gravely on her faults, it is only because we are ourselves sufficiently her admirers to be most desirous to see her remove these blem-ishes from her writings, and take the rank within her reach. She has extraordinary power—but let her remember that '*on tombe du côté où l'on penche!*'[9]

# COMTE'S PHILOSOPHY OF THE SCIENCES

*Largely self-taught, Lewes was an intellectual and social nonconformist. He quickly accept-ed Charles DARWIN's theory of natural selection, praised the novels of George Sand, and explained for the common reader the major Western systems of philosophy in his important Biographical History of Philosophy. In this history Lewes expressed his interest in the positivist theory of Auguste Comte (1798–1857). Lewes and other mid-Victorians, includ-ing John Stuart MILL, George ELIOT, and Harriet MARTINEAU, found Comte's Cours de philosophie positive (1830–42) appealing because, in an increasingly scientific age, Comte's "sociology" (Comte's term) and his belief in human progress seemed to fulfill the needs of those who could no longer hold traditional religious beliefs but who still desired a foundation for morality. In 1852 Lewes wrote a series of essays about Comte's positivist sys-tem and philosophy for the Leader. He published this series in 1853 as a volume in "Bohn's Scientific Library," from which this selection is taken. As in the case of J. S. Mill, who first introduced him to Comte's ideas, Lewes's initial enthusiasm for Comte's empiricism and optimism was replaced by skepticism, when he became disillusioned by Comte's development of a kind of authoritarian pseudoreligion. Throughout his life, Lewes continued his attempt to wed philosophy and science: his final work,* Problems of Life and Mind, *tried to explain psychology in terms of physiology.*                    LMF

9. "One falls in the direction that one leans."

## GENERAL CONSIDERATIONS ON THE AIM AND SCOPE OF POSITIVISM

THERE is one very injurious, though very intelligible mistake current on the subject of the Positive Philosophy. It is supposed to be a thing of dry, severe science, only interesting to scientific men—presenting only the scientific aspect of things, and leaving untouched the great questions of Emotion, of Art, of Morality, of Religion; a philosophy which may amuse the intellect of the speculative few, but can never claim the submission of the mass. The mistake is injurious, because the thinking world happens, unfortunately, to be divided into two classes—men of science destitute of a philosophy, because incompetent for the most part to the thorough grasp of those generalities which form a philosophy; and metaphysicians, whose tendency towards generalities causes them to disdain the creeping specialities of physical science. Thus, between Science which ignores Philosophy, and Philosophy which ignores Science, Comte is in danger of being set aside altogether. These pages will probably convince the reader, that the Positive Philosophy must necessarily reconcile these discrepancies, and that, while rendering due recognition to the specialities of experimentalists, it gives full scope to the generalizing tendency of philosophers. Meanwhile, the moralist, the metaphysician, and the man of letters, may be assured, that if Comte's system has one capital distinction more remarkable than another, it is the absolute predominance of the moral point of view—the rigorous subordination of the intellect to the heart. Speculation, as a mere display of intellectual energy, it denounces; science, as commonly understood, it looks upon with something of the feeling which may move the moralist contemplating the routine of pin-makers. The half-repugnant feeling about science, in the minds of literary men, artists, and moralists, is a natural and proper insurgence of the emotions against the domineering tendency of the intellect: men know that the moral life is larger and more intense than the intellectual life—they know that this moral life has its needs, which no science can pretend to regulate, and they reject a philosophy which speaks to them only of the Laboratory. But in Comte, Science has no such position. It is the basis upon which the social superstructure may be raised. It gives Philosophy materials and a Method; that is all.

If the Positive Philosophy be anything, it is a doctrine capable of embracing all that can regulate Humanity; not a treatise on physical science, not a treatise on social science, but a system which absorbs all intellectual activity. "Positivism," he says, in his recent work, "is essentially composed of a Philosophy and a Polity, which are necessarily inseparable because they constitute the basis and aim of a system wherein intellect and sociability are intimately connected." And farther on, "This then is the mission of Positivism: to generalize science, and to systematize sociality." In other words, it aims at creating a Philosophy of the Sciences as a basis for a new social faith. A social doctrine is the *aim* of Positivism, a scientific doctrine the *means*; just as in man, intelligence is the minister and interpreter of life. "En effet, si le cœur doit toujours poser les questions, c'est toujours à l'esprit qu'il appartient de les résoudre."[1]

So much for the aim. Let me now call attention to Comte's initial conceptions; and first, to the luminous conception of *all the sciences—physical and social—as branches of one Science, to be investigated on one and the same Method.*

1. "In effect, if the heart must always ask questions, it is the mind which is always concerned with resolving them."

To say that Science is one, and that the Method should be one, may, to the hasty reader, seem more like a truism than a discovery; but on inquiry he will find, that before Comte, although a general idea of the connection of the physical sciences was prevalent, yet, to judge from Mrs. Somerville's work, or Herschel's *Discourse*,[2] it was neither very precise nor very profound; no one had thought of a Social Science issuing from the Physical Sciences, and *investigated on the same method*. In fact, to talk of moral questions being reduced to a positive science will even now be generally regarded as absurd. Men use the phrase "Social Science," "Ethical Science," but they never mean thereby that Ethics forms one branch of the great tree, rising higher than the physical sciences, but rising from the *same* root. On the contrary, they interpret ethical phenomena by metaphysical or theological methods, and believe History to be under the governance not of Laws, but of caprice.

The second initial conception which the reader should familiarize his mind with, is that of the fundamental Law of human development:—*There are but three phases of intellectual evolution—for the individual as well as for the mass—the Theological (Supernatural), the Metaphysical, and the Positive.*

Hereafter this law will be illustrated in detail, and a very brief indication will be sufficient now. In the *Supernatural* phase the mind seeks *causes*; it aspires to know the *essences* of things, and the How and Why of their operation. It regards all effects as the productions of supernatural agents. Unusual phenomena are interpreted as the signs of the pleasure or displeasure of some god. In the *Metaphysical* phase, a modification takes place; the supernatural agents are set aside for abstract forces or Entities supposed to inhere in various substances, and capable of engendering phenomena. In the *Positive* phase the mind, convinced of the futility of all inquiry into *causes* and *essences*, restricts itself to the observation and classification of phenomena, and to the discovery of the invariable *relations* of succession and similitude which things bear to each other: in a word, to the discovery of the *laws* of phenomena.

The third initial conception is that beautiful classification of the sciences co-ordinated by the luminous principle of *commencing with the study of the simplest (most general) phenomena, and proceeding successively to the most complex and particular*; thus arranging the sciences according to their *dependence* on each other.

The three great conceptions just stated no one can be expected to appreciate until he has applied them. But how would he appreciate any general conception—say the law of gravitation—if it were simply presented to him as a formula which he had not verified? Let an honest verification of the three formulas be made, and I have the deepest conviction that no competent mind will fail to recognise them as the grandest contributions to philosophy since Descartes and Bacon inaugurated the positive method.[3]

And now a word on the part Positivism is to play in the coming years of struggle. That a new epoch is dawning, that a new form of social life is growing up out of the ruins of

2. Mary Somerville (1780–1872), *On the Connexion of the Physical Sciences* (1834). John Herschel (1792–1871), *Preliminary Discourse on the Study of Natural Philosophy* (1830).
3. René Descartes (1596–1650); Sir Francis Bacon (1561–1626).

feudalism, the most superficial observer cannot fail to see; and as signs of the deep unrest now agitating society, no less than as evidence of the indestructible aspiration after an Ideal which has always moved mankind, the systems of Communism so confidently promulgated attract the attention of most thinkers. But can any system of Communism yet devised be accepted as an efficient solution of the social problem? Positivism says No; and for this reason: Communism is simply a *political* solution of a problem which embraces far deeper and higher questions than politics. Communism is the *goal* towards which society tends, not a *path* by which the goal may be reached. Neither cooperation, nor watchwords of fraternity, however sincerely translated into action, can pretend to compass the whole problem. For let us suppose the political questions settled; let us imagine a parallelogram of harmonious success—a human bee-hive of cooperative activity,—will *all* be settled then? Will not the deep and urgent questions of Religion and Philosophy still demand an answer? Just where man most obviously rises above the bee, Communism leaves him to the care of Priests and Teachers, who cannot agree among themselves! and as all polity is founded on a system of ideas believed in common, as we cannot in social problems isolate the political from the moral, the moral from the religious system, Communism leaves society to its anarchy.

The present anarchy of politics arises from the anarchy of ideas. The ancient faiths are shaken where they are not shattered. The new faith which must replace them is still to come. What Europe wants is a Doctrine which will embrace the whole system of our conceptions, which will satisfactorily answer the questions of Science, Life, and Religion; teaching us our relations to the World, to Duty, and to God. A mere glance at the present state of Europe will detect the want of *unity*, caused by the absence of any one Doctrine *general* enough to embrace the variety of questions, and *positive* enough to carry with it irresistible conviction. This last reservation is made because Catholicism has the requisite *generality*, but fails in convincing Protestants. The existence of *sects* is enough to prove, if proof were needed, that none of the Religions are competent to their mission of *binding together* all men under one faith. As with religion, so with philosophy: no one doctrine is universal; there are almost as many philosophies as philosophers. The dogmas of Germany are laughed at in England and Scotland; the psychology of Scotland is scorned in Germany, and neglected in England. Besides these sectarian divisions, we see Religion and Philosophy more or less avowedly opposed to each other.

This, then, is the fact with respect to general doctrines:—Religions are opposed to religions, philosophies are opposed to philosophies; while religion and philosophy are essentially opposed to each other.

In positive Science there is less dissidence, but there is a similar absence of any general Doctrine. Each science rests on a broad firm basis of ascertained truth, and rapidly improves; but a Philosophy of the Sciences is nowhere to be found, except in the pages of Auguste Comte. The *speciality* of most scientific men, and their seeming incapacity of either producing or apprehending general ideas, has long been a matter of just complaint; they are Hodmen,[4] and fancy themselves Architects. This incapacity is one of the reasons

---

4. Suppliers of bricks or mortar to builders.

why nebulous metaphysics still waste the fine activity of noble minds; men see clearly enough that, however exact each separate science may be, these sciences do not of themselves constitute philosophy: bricks are not a house. In the early days of science, general views were easily attained. As the materials became more complex, various divisions took place; one man devoted himself to one science, another to another. Even then, general ideas were not absent. But, as the tide swept on, discovery succeeding discovery, like advancing waves, new tracks of inquiry opening vast wildernesses of undiscovered truth, it became absolutely necessary for one man to devote the labour of a life to some small fraction of a science, leaving to others the task of ranging his discoveries under their general head. The result has been, that most men of science regard only their speciality, and leave to metaphysicians the task of constructing a general doctrine. Hence we find at present abundance of ideas powerless, because they are not positive; and the positive sciences powerless, because they are not general. The aim of Comte is to present a doctrine *positive*, because elaborated from positive science, and yet possessing all the desired *generality* of metaphysical schemes, without their vagueness, baselessness, and inapplicability. . . .

# John Ruskin

## TRAFFIC

*Ruskin delivered his lecture "Traffic" on April 21, 1864, to the citizens of Bradford, who had requested his advice about the proper architectural style for their new stock exchange. With* Modern Painters *and* The Stones of Venice, *Ruskin had become an important art critic, teaching the Victorian public to see and appreciate art, and helping to create a national interest in Gothic architecture. Beginning in the 1850s, Ruskin increasingly used the lecture platform to educate the public in matters of taste, which for him were inseparable from matters of social justice. He had discovered, however, that his audience was more interested in being fashionable than in seeing art as an expression of a culture's ethical principles. As he expressed his frustration in* The Seven Lamps of Architecture, *"how is it that the tradesmen cannot understand that custom is to be had only by selling good tea and cheese and cloth, and that people come to them for their honesty, and their right wares, and not because they have Greek cornices over their windows?"[1]* "Traffic" *voices Ruskin's concern that*

---

1. Ruskin, *The Seven Lamps of Architecture* (New York: Farrar, 1986), p. 115.

*his social message was being ignored; it follows his outspoken* Unto This Last, *in which he turned from his role as an art critic to a commentator on the dangers of laissez-faire economics, in the vein of Thomas* CARLYLE. *Probably Ruskin hoped to unsettle his complacent middle-class audience with "Traffic," but he did not make the desired impression: by the time "Traffic" was published in* The Crown of Wild Olive, *the Bradford design committee had decided to build their exchange in the Venetian Gothic style.*                    LMF

MY GOOD YORKSHIRE FRIENDS, YOU asked me down here among your hills that I might talk to you about this Exchange you are going to build: but earnestly and seriously asking you to pardon me, I am going to do nothing of the kind. I cannot talk, or at least can say very little, about this same Exchange. I must talk of quite other things, though not willingly;—I could not deserve your pardon, if, when you invited me to speak on one subject, I wilfully spoke on another. But I cannot speak, to purpose, of anything about which I do not care; and most simply and sorrowfully I have to tell you, in the outset, that I do *not* care about this Exchange of yours.

If, however, when you sent me your invitation, I had answered, 'I won't come, I don't care about the Exchange of Bradford,' you would have been justly offended with me, not knowing the reasons of so blunt a carelessness. So I have come down, hoping that you will patiently let me tell you why, on this, and many other such occasions, I now remain silent, when formerly I should have caught at the opportunity of speaking to a gracious audience.

In a word, then, I do not care about this Exchange,—because *you* don't; and because you know perfectly well I cannot make you. Look at the essential circumstances of the case, which you, as business men, know perfectly well, though perhaps you think I forget them. You are going to spend 30,000*l.*, which to you, collectively, is nothing; the buying a new coat is, as to the cost of it, a much more important matter of consideration to me than building a new Exchange is to you. But you think you may as well have the right thing for your money. You know there are a great many odd styles of architecture about; you don't want to do anything ridiculous; you hear of me, among others, as a respectable architectural man-milliner: and you send for me, that I may tell you the leading fashion; and what is, in our shops, for the moment, the newest and sweetest thing in pinnacles.

Now, pardon me for telling you frankly, you cannot have good architecture merely by asking people's advice on occasion. All good architecture is the expression of national life and character; and it is produced by a prevalent and eager national taste, or desire for beauty. And I want you to think a little of the deep significance of this word 'taste;' for no statement of mine has been more earnestly or oftener controverted than that good taste is essentially a moral quality. 'No,' say many of my antagonists, 'taste is one thing, morality is another. Tell us what is pretty; we shall be glad to know that: but preach no sermons to us.'

Permit me, therefore, to fortify this old dogma of mine somewhat. Taste is not only a part and an index of morality;—it is the ONLY morality. . . .

And so completely and unexceptionally is this so, that, if I had time to-night, I could show you that a nation cannot be affected by any vice, or weakness, without expressing it, legibly, and for ever, either in bad art, or by want of art; and that there is no national virtue, small or great, which is not manifestly expressed in all the art which circumstances enable the people possessing that virtue to produce. Take, for instance, your great English virtue of enduring and patient courage. You have at present in England only one art of any consequence—that is, iron-working. You know thoroughly well how to cast and hammer iron. Now, do you think in those masses of lava which you build volcanic cones to melt, and which you forge at the mouths of the Infernos you have created; do you think, on those iron plates, your courage and endurance are not written for ever—not merely with an iron pen, but on iron parchment? And take also your great English vice—European vice—vice of all the world—vice of all other worlds that roll or shine in heaven, bearing with them yet the atmosphere of hell—the vice of jealousy, which brings competition into your commerce, treachery into your councils, and dishonour into your wars—that vice which has rendered for you, and for your next neighbouring nation, the daily occupations of existence no longer possible, but with the mail upon your breasts and the sword loose in its sheath; so that, at last, you have realised for all the multitudes of the two great peoples[2] who lead the so-called civilisation of the earth,—you have realised for them all, I say, in person and in policy, what was once true only of the rough Border riders of your Cheviot hills—

> They carved at the meal
> With gloves of steel,
> And they drank the red wine through the helmet barr'd;—[3]

do you think that this national shame and dastardliness of heart are not written as legibly on every rivet of your iron armour as the strength of the right hands that forged it? Friends, I know not whether this thing be the more ludicrous or the more melancholy. It is quite unspeakably both. Suppose, instead of being now sent for by you, I had been sent for by some private gentleman, living in a suburban house, with his garden separated only by a fruit-wall from his next door neighbour's; and he had called me to consult with him on the furnishing of his drawing-room. I begin looking about me, and find the walls rather bare; I think such and such a paper might be desirable—perhaps a little fresco here and there on the ceiling—a damask curtain or so at the windows. 'Ah,' says my employer, 'damask curtains, indeed! That's all very fine, but you know I can't afford that kind of thing just now!' 'Yet the world credits you with a splendid income!' 'Ah, yes,' says my friend, 'but do you know, at present, I am obliged to spend it nearly all in steel-traps?' 'Steel-traps! for whom?' 'Why, for that fellow on the other side the wall, you know: we're very good friends, capital friends; but we are obliged to keep our traps set on both sides of the wall; we could not possibly keep on friendly terms without them, and our spring guns. The worst of it is, we are both clever fellows enough; and there's never a day passes that we don't find out a new trap, or a new gun-barrel, or something; we spend about fifteen millions a year each in our traps, take it all together; and I don't see how we're to do with less.' A highly comic state of life for two private gentlemen! but for two

2. Britain and France.
3. Sir Walter Scott, *The Lay of the Last Minstrel* (1805).

nations, it seems to me, not wholly comic? Bedlam would be comic, perhaps, if there were only one madman in it; and your Christmas pantomime is comic, when there is only one clown in it; but when the whole world turns clown, and paints itself red with its own heart's blood instead of vermilion, it is something else than comic, I think.

Mind, I know a great deal of this is play, and willingly allow for that. You don't know what to do with yourselves for a sensation: fox-hunting and cricketing will not carry you through the whole of this unendurably long mortal life: you liked pop-guns when you were schoolboys, and rifles and Armstrongs[4] are only the same things better made: but then the worst of it is, that what was play to you when boys, was not play to the sparrows; and what is play to you now, is not play to the small birds of State neither; and for the black eagles, you are somewhat shy of taking shots at them, if I mistake not.[5]

I must get back to the matter in hand, however. Believe me, without farther instance, I could show you, in all time, that every nation's vice, or virtue, was written in its art: the soldiership of early Greece; the sensuality of late Italy; the visionary religion of Tuscany; the splendid human energy and beauty of Venice. I have no time to do this to-night, (I have done it elsewhere before now); but I proceed to apply the principle to ourselves in a more searching manner.

I notice that among all the new buildings which cover your once wild hills, churches and schools are mixed in due, that is to say, in large proportion, with your mills and mansions; and I notice also that the churches and schools are almost always Gothic, and the mansions and mills are never Gothic. Will you allow me to ask precisely the meaning of this? For, remember, it is peculiarly a modern phenomenon. When Gothic was invented, houses were Gothic as well as churches; and when the Italian style superseded the Gothic, churches were Italian as well as houses. If there is a Gothic spire to the cathedral of Antwerp, there is a Gothic belfry to the Hôtel de Ville at Brussels; if Inigo Jones builds an Italian Whitehall, Sir Christopher Wren builds an Italian St. Paul's. But now you live under one school of architecture, and worship under another. What do you mean by doing this? Am I to understand that you are thinking of changing your architecture back to Gothic; and that you treat your churches experimentally, because it does not matter what mistakes you make in a church? Or am I to understand that you consider Gothic a pre-eminently sacred and beautiful mode of building, which you think, like the fine frankincense, should be mixed for the tabernacle only, and reserved for your religious services? For if this be the feeling, though it may seem at first as if it were graceful and reverent, you will find that, at the root of the matter, it signifies neither more nor less than that you have separated your religion from your life. . . .

Now, you feel, as I say this to you—I know you feel—as if I were trying to take away the honour of your churches. Not so; I am trying to prove to you the honour of your houses and your hills; I am trying to show you—not that the Church is not sacred—but that the whole Earth IS. I would have you feel, what careless, what constant, what infectious sin there is in all modes of thought, whereby, in calling your churches only 'holy,'

---

4. Heavy guns made by Armstrong and used in the Crimean War.
5. Both Prussia and Austria had black eagles on their flags. Ruskin alludes to Britain's reluctance to aid Denmark in the Schleswig-Holstein conflict because of Prussian influence.

you call your hearths and homes profane; and have separated yourselves from the heathen by casting all your household gods to the ground, instead of recognising, in the places of their many and feeble Lares, the presence of your One and Mighty Lord and Lar.

'But what has all this to do with our Exchange?' you ask me, impatiently. My dear friends, it has just everything to do with it; on these inner and great questions depend all the outer and little ones; and if you have asked me down here to speak to you, because you had before been interested in anything I have written, you must know that all I have yet said about architecture was to show this. The book I called 'The Seven Lamps' was to show that certain right states of temper and moral feeling were the magic powers by which all good architecture, without exception, had been produced. 'The Stones of Venice' had, from beginning to end, no other aim than to show that the Gothic architecture of Venice had arisen out of, and indicated in all its features, a state of pure national faith, and of domestic virtue; and that its Renaissance architecture had arisen out of, and in all its features indicated, a state of concealed national infidelity, and of domestic corruption. And now, you ask me what style is best to build in; and how can I answer, knowing the meaning of the two styles, but by another question—do you mean to build as Christians or as Infidels? And still more—do you mean to build as honest Christians or as honest Infidels? as thoroughly and confessedly either one or the other? You don't like to be asked such rude questions. I cannot help it; they are of much more importance than this Exchange business; and if they can be at once answered, the Exchange business settles itself in a moment. But, before I press them farther, I must ask leave to explain one point clearly. In all my past work, my endeavour has been to show that good architecture is essentially religious—the production of a faithful and virtuous, not of an infidel and corrupted people. But in the course of doing this, I have had also to show that good architecture is not *ecclesiastical*. People are so apt to look upon religion as the business of the clergy, not their own, that the moment they hear of anything depending on 'religion,' they think it must also have depended on the priesthood; and I have had to take what place was to be occupied between these two errors, and fight both, often with seeming contradiction. Good architecture is the work of good and believing men; therefore, you say, at least some people say, 'Good architecture must essentially have been the work of the clergy, not of the laity.' No—a thousand times no; good architecture has always been the work of the commonalty, *not* of the clergy. What, you say, those glorious cathedrals—the pride of Europe—did their builders not form Gothic architecture? No; they corrupted Gothic architecture. Gothic was formed in the baron's castle, and the burgher's street. It was formed by the thoughts, and hands, and powers of free citizens and soldier kings. By the monk it was used as an instrument for the aid of his superstition: when that superstition became a beautiful madness, and the best hearts of Europe vainly dreamed and pined in the cloister, and vainly raged and perished in the crusade,—through that fury of perverted faith and wasted war, the Gothic rose also to its loveliest, most fantastic, and finally, most foolish dreams; and, in those dreams, was lost.

I hope, now, that there is no risk of your misunderstanding me when I come to the gist of what I want to say to-night;—when I repeat, that every great national architecture has been the result and exponent of a great national religion. You can't have bits of it here,

bits there—you must have it everywhere, or nowhere. It is not the monopoly of a clerical company—it is not the exponent of a theological dogma—it is not the hieroglyphic
writing of an initiated priesthood; it is the manly language of a people inspired by resolute and common purpose, and rendering resolute and common fidelity to the legible
laws of an undoubted God.

Now there have as yet been three distinct schools of European architecture. I say,
European, because Asiatic and African architectures belong so entirely to other races and
climates, that there is no question of them here; only, in passing, I will simply assure you
that whatever is good or great in Egypt, and Syria, and India, is just good or great for the
same reasons as the buildings on our side of the Bosphorus. We Europeans, then, have had
three great religions: the Greek, which was the worship of the God of Wisdom and
Power; the Mediæval, which was the worship of the God of Judgment and Consolation;
the Renaissance, which was the worship of the God of Pride and Beauty: these three we
have had—they are past,—and now, at last, we English have got a fourth religion, and a God
of our own, about which I want to ask you. But I must explain these three old ones first.

I repeat, first, the Greeks essentially worshipped the God of Wisdom; so that whatever contended against their religion,—to the Jews a stumbling block,—was, to the
Greeks—*Foolishness*.

The first Greek idea of deity was that expressed in the word, of which we keep the
remnant in our words '*Di*-urnal' and '*Di*-vine'—the god of *Day*, Jupiter the revealer.
Athena is his daughter, but especially daughter of the Intellect, springing armed from the
head. We are only with the help of recent investigation beginning to penetrate the depth
of meaning couched under the Athenaic symbols: but I may note rapidly, that her ægis,
the mantle with the serpent fringes, in which she often, in the best statues, is represented as folding up her left hand for better guard, and the Gorgon on her shield, are both
representative mainly of the chilling horror and sadness, (turning men to stone, as it
were,) of the outmost and superficial spheres of knowledge—that knowledge which separates, in bitterness, hardness, and sorrow, the heart of the full-grown man from the
heart of the child. For out of imperfect knowledge spring terror, dissension, danger, and
disdain; but from perfect knowledge, given by the full-revealed Athena, strength and
peace, in sign of which she is crowned with the olive spray, and bears the resistless spear.

This, then, was the Greek conception of purest Deity, and every habit of life, and
every form of his art developed themselves from the seeking this bright, serene, resistless wisdom; and setting himself, as a man, to do things evermore rightly and strongly;[6]
not with any ardent affection or ultimate hope; but with a resolute and continent energy
of will, as knowing that for failure there was no consolation, and for sin there was no
remission. And the Greek architecture rose unerring, bright, clearly defined, and self-
contained.

---

6. It is an error to suppose that the Greek worship, or seeking, was chiefly of Beauty. It was essentially of Rightness
and Strength, founded on Forethought: the principal character of Greek art is not beauty, but Design: and the
Dorian Apollo-worship and Athenian Virgin-worship are both expressions of adoration of divine Wisdom and
Purity. Next to these great deities rank, in power over the national mind, Dionysus and Ceres, the givers of human
strength and life: then, for heroic example, Hercules. There is no Venus-worship among the Greeks in the great
times: and the Muses are essentially teachers of Truth, and of its harmonies. [Ruskin's note]

Next followed in Europe the great Christian faith, which was essentially the religion of Comfort. Its great doctrine is the remission of sins; for which cause it happens, too often, in certain phases of Christianity, that sin and sickness themselves are partly glorified, as if, the more you had to be healed of, the more divine was the healing. The practical result of this doctrine, in art, is a continual contemplation of sin and disease, and of imaginary states of purification from them; thus we have an architecture conceived in a mingled sentiment of melancholy and aspiration, partly severe, partly luxuriant, which will bend itself to every one of our needs, and every one of our fancies, and be strong or weak with us, as we are strong or weak ourselves. It is, of all architecture, the basest, when base people build it—of all, the noblest, when built by the noble.

And now note that both these religions—Greek and Mediæval—perished by falsehood in their own main purpose. The Greek religion of Wisdom perished in a false philosophy—'Oppositions of science, falsely so called.' The Mediæval religion of Consolation perished in false comfort; in remission of sins given lyingly. It was the selling of absolution that ended the Mediæval faith; and I can tell you more, it is the selling of absolution which, to the end of time, will mark false Christianity. Pure Christianity gives her remission of sins only by *ending* them; but false Christianity gets her remission of sins by *compounding for* them. And there are many ways of compounding for them. We English have beautiful little quiet ways of buying absolution, whether in low Church or high, far more cunning than any of Tetzel's trading.[7]

Then, thirdly, there followed the religion of Pleasure, in which all Europe gave itself to luxury, ending in death. First, *bals masqués* in every saloon, and then guillotines in every square. And all these three worships issue in vast temple building. Your Greek worshipped Wisdom, and built you the Parthenon—the Virgin's temple. The Mediæval worshipped Consolation, and built you Virgin temples also—but to our Lady of Salvation. Then the Revivalist worshipped beauty, of a sort, and built you Versailles, and the Vatican. Now, lastly, will you tell me what *we* worship, and what *we* build?

You know we are speaking always of the real, active, continual, national worship; that by which men act while they live; not that which they talk of when they die. Now, we have, indeed, a nominal religion, to which we pay tithes of property and sevenths of time; but we have also a practical and earnest religion, to which we devote nine-tenths of our property and six-sevenths of our time. And we dispute a great deal about the nominal religion; but we are all unanimous about this practical one, of which I think you will admit that the ruling goddess may be best generally described as the 'Goddess of Getting-on,' or 'Britannia of the Market.' The Athenians had an 'Athena Agoraia,' or Minerva of the Market; but she was a subordinate type of their goddess, while our Britannia Agoraia is the principal type of ours. And all your great architectural works are, of course, built to her. It is long since you built a great cathedral; and how you would laugh at me, if I proposed building a cathedral on the top of one of these hills of yours, taking it for an Acropolis! But your railroad mounds, prolonged masses of Acropolis; your railroad stations, vaster than the Parthenon, and innumerable; your chimneys, how much more mighty and costly than cathedral spires! your harbour-piers; your warehouses; your

7. Johann Tetzel (c. 1460–1519), preacher and seller of papal indulgences.

exchanges!—all these are built to your great Goddess of 'Getting-on;' and she has formed, and will continue to form, your architecture, as long as you worship her; and it is quite vain to ask me to tell you how to build to *her*; you know far better than I.

There might indeed, on some theories, be a conceivably good architecture for Exchanges—that is to say if there were any heroism in the fact or deed of exchange, which might be typically carved on the outside of your building. For, you know, all beautiful architecture must be adorned with sculpture or painting; and for sculpture or painting, you must have a subject. And hitherto it has been a received opinion among the nations of the world that the only right subjects for either, were *heroisms* of some sort. Even on his pots and his flagons, the Greek put a Hercules slaying lions, or an Apollo slaying serpents, or Bacchus slaying melancholy giants, and earth-born despondencies. On his temples, the Greek put contests of great warriors in founding states, or of gods with evil spirits. On his houses and temples alike, the Christian put carvings of angels conquering devils; or of hero-martyrs exchanging this world for another; subject inappropriate, I think, to our manner of exchange here. And the Master of Christians not only left his followers without any orders as to the sculpture of affairs of exchange on the outside of buildings, but gave some strong evidence of his dislike of affairs of exchange within them. And yet there might surely be a heroism in such affairs; and all commerce become a kind of selling of doves, not impious. The wonder has always been great to me, that heroism has never been supposed to be in anywise consistent with the practice of supplying people with food, or clothes; but rather with that of quartering oneself upon them for food, and stripping them of their clothes. Spoiling of armour is an heroic deed in all ages; but the selling of clothes, old, or new, has never taken any colour of magnanimity. Yet one does not see why feeding the hungry and clothing the naked should ever become base businesses, even when engaged in on a large scale. If one could contrive to attach the notion of conquest to them anyhow? so that, supposing there were anywhere an obstinate race, who refused to be comforted, one might take some pride in giving them compulsory comfort; and as it were, 'occupying a country' with one's gifts, instead of one's armies? If one could only consider it as much a victory to get a barren field sown, as to get an eared field stripped; and contend who should build villages, instead of who should 'carry' them. Are not all forms of heroism, conceivable in doing these serviceable deeds? You doubt who is strongest? It might be ascertained by push of spade, as well as push of sword. Who is wisest? There are witty things to be thought of in planning other business than campaigns. Who is bravest? There are always the elements to fight with, stronger than men; and nearly as merciless. The only absolutely and unapproachably heroic element in the soldier's work seems to be—that he is paid little for it—and regularly: while you traffickers, and exchangers, and others occupied in presumably benevolent business, like to be paid much for it—and by chance. I never can make out how it is that a knight-errant does not expect to be paid for his trouble, but a pedlar-errant always does;— that people are willing to take hard knocks for nothing, but never to sell ribands cheap;—that they are ready to go on fervent crusades to recover the tomb of a buried God, never on any travels to fulfil the orders of a living God;—that they will go anywhere barefoot to preach their faith, but must be well bribed to practise it, and are perfectly ready to give the Gospel gratis, but never the loaves and fishes. If you chose to take the matter up on any such soldierly principle, to do your commerce, and your feeding of nations, for fixed salaries; and to be as particular about giving people the best food, and the best cloth, as soldiers are about giving them the best gunpowder, I could carve something for you on your exchange worth looking at. But I can only at present suggest decorating its frieze with pendant purses; and making its pillars broad at the base, for the sticking of bills. And in the innermost chambers of it there might be a statue of Britannia of the Market, who may have, perhaps advisably, a partridge for her crest, typical at once of her courage in fighting for noble ideas; and of her interest in game; and round its neck the inscription in golden letters, 'Perdix fovit quæ non peperit,'[8] Then, for her spear, she might have a weaver's beam; and on her shield, instead of her Cross, the Milanese boar, semi-fleeced, with the town of Gennesaret proper, in the field and the legend 'In the best market,' and her corslet, of leather, folded over her heart in the shape of a purse, with thirty slits in it for a piece of money to go in at, on each day of the month. And I doubt not but that people would come to see your exchange, and its goddess, with applause.

Nevertheless, I want to point out to you certain strange characters in this goddess of yours. She differs from the great Greek and Mediæval deities essentially in two things— first, as to the continuance of her presumed power; secondly, as to the extent of it.

1st, as to the Continuance.

The Greek Goddess of Wisdom gave continual increase of wisdom, as the Christian Spirit of Comfort (or Comforter) continual increase of comfort. There was no question, with these, of any limit or cessation of function. But with your Agora Goddess, that is just the most important question. Getting on—but where to? Gathering together—but how much? Do you mean to gather always—never to spend? If so, I wish you joy of your goddess, for I am just as well-off as you, without the trouble of worshipping her at all. But if you do not spend, somebody else will—somebody else must. And it is because of this (among many other such errors) that I have fearlessly declared your so-called science of Political Economy to be no science; because, namely, it has omitted the study of exactly the most important branch of the business— the study of *spending*. For spend you must, and as much as you make, ultimately. You gather corn:—will you bury England under a heap of grain; or will you, when you have gathered, finally eat? You gather gold:—will you make your house-roofs of it, or pave your streets with it? That is still one way of spending it. But if you keep it, that you may get more, I'll give you more; I'll give you all the gold you want—all you can imagine—if you can tell me what you'll do with it. You shall have thousands of gold pieces;—thousands of thousands—millions—mountains, of gold: where will you keep them? Will you put an Olympus of silver upon a golden Pelion—make Ossa like a wart?[9] Do you think the rain and dew would then come down to you, in the streams from such mountains, more blessedly than they will down the

---

8. Jerem. xvii. II (best in Septuagint and Vulgate). 'As the partridge, fostering what she brought not forth, so he that getteth riches, not by right, shall leave them in the midst of his days, and at his end shall be a fool.' [Ruskin's note]
9. Allusion to William Shakespeare's *Hamlet* 5.1. Olympus, Pelion, and Ossa—mountains in Thessaly—figure in the Greek story of the giants' attempt to overthrow Zeus by piling Ossa on Pelion to reach heaven.

mountains which God has made for you, of moss and whinstone? But it is not gold that you want to gather! What is it? greenbacks? No; not those neither. What is it then—is it ciphers after a capital I? Cannot you practise writing ciphers, and write as many as you want? Write ciphers for an hour every morning, in a big book, and say every evening, I am worth all those noughts more than I was yesterday. Won't that do? Well, what in the name of Plutus[10] is it you want? Not gold, not greenbacks, not ciphers after a capital I? You will have to answer, after all, 'No; we want, somehow or other, money's *worth*.' Well, what is that? Let your Goddess of Getting-on discover it, and let her learn to stay therein.

II. But there is yet another question to be asked respecting this Goddess of Getting on. The first was of the continuance of her power; the second is of its extent.

Pallas and the Madonna were supposed to be all the world's Pallas, and all the world's Madonna. They could teach all men, and they could comfort all men. But, look strictly into the nature of the power of your Goddess of Getting-on; and you will find she is the Goddess—not of everybody's getting on—but only of somebody's getting on. This is a vital, or rather deathful, distinction. Examine it in your own ideal of the state of national life which this Goddess is to evoke and maintain. I asked you what it was, when I was last here;[11]—you have never told me. Now, shall I try to tell you?

Your ideal of human life then is, I think, that it should be passed in a pleasant undulating world, with iron and coal everywhere underneath it. On each pleasant bank of this world is to be a beautiful mansion, with two wings; and stables, and coachhouses; a moderately sized park; a large garden and hot-houses; and pleasant carriage drives through the shrubberies. In this mansion are to live the favoured votaries of the Goddess; the English gentleman, with his gracious wife, and his beautiful family; always able to have the boudoir and the jewels for the wife, and the beautiful ball dresses for the daughters, and hunters for the sons, and a shooting in the Highlands for himself. At the bottom of the bank, is to be the mill; not less than a quarter of a mile long, with a steam engine at each end, and two in the middle, and a chimney three hundred feet high. In this mill are to be in constant employment from eight hundred to a thousand workers, who never drink, never strike, always go to church on Sunday, and always express themselves in respectful language.

Is not that, broadly, and in the main features, the kind of thing you propose to yourselves? It is very pretty indeed, seen from above; not at all so pretty, seen from below. For, observe, while to one family this deity is indeed the Goddess of Getting on, to a thousand families she is the Goddess of *not* Getting on. 'Nay,' you say, 'they have all their chance.' Yes, so has every one in a lottery, but there must always be the same number of blanks. 'Ah! but in a lottery it is not skill and intelligence which take the lead, but blind chance.' What then! do you think the old practice, that 'they should take who have the power, and they should keep who can,'[12] is less iniquitous, when the power has become

---

10. The god of wealth.
11. Two Paths, p. 117. [Ruskin's note] Ruskin spoke on "Modern Manufacture and Design" at Bradford, a lecture he subsequently published in *The Two Paths* (1859).
12. William Wordsworth, "Rob Roy's Grave" (1807).

power of brains instead of fist? and that, though we may not take advantage of a child's or a woman's weakness, we may of a man's foolishness? 'Nay, but finally, work must be done, and some one must be at the top, some one at the bottom.' Granted, my friends. Work must always be, and captains of work must always be; and if you in the least remember the tone of any of my writings, you must know that they are thought unfit for this age, because they are always insisting on need of government, and speaking with scorn of liberty. But I beg you to observe that there is a wide difference between being captains or governors of work, and taking the profits of it. It does not follow, because you are general of an army, that you are to take all the treasure, or land, it wins (if it fight for treasure or land); neither, because you are king of a nation, that you are to consume all the profits of the nation's work. Real kings, on the contrary, are known invariably by their doing quite the reverse of this,—by their taking the least possible quantity of the nation's work for themselves. There is no test of real kinghood so infallible as that. Does the crowned creature live simply, bravely, unostentatiously? probably he *is* a King. Does he cover his body with jewels, and his table with delicates? in all probability he is *not* a King. It is possible he may be, as Solomon was; but that is when the nation shares his splendour with him. Solomon made gold, not only to be in his own palace as stones, but to be in Jerusalem as stones. But, even so, for the most part, these splendid kinghoods expire in ruin, and only the true kinghoods live, which are of royal labourers governing loyal labourers; who, both leading rough lives, establish the true dynasties. Conclusively you will find that because you are king of a nation, it does not follow that you are to gather for yourself all the wealth of that nation; neither, because you are king of a small part of the nation, and lord over the means of its maintenance—over field, or mill, or mine, are you to take all the produce of that piece of the foundation of national existence for yourself.

You will tell me I need not preach against these things, for I cannot mend them. No, good friends, I cannot; but you can, and you will; or something else can and will. Do you think these phenomena are to stay always in their present power or aspect? All history shows, on the contrary, that to be the exact thing they never can do. Change *must* come; but it is ours to determine whether change of growth, or change of death. Shall the Parthenon be in ruins on its rock, and Bolton priory in its meadow, but these mills of yours be the consummation of the buildings of the earth, and their wheels be as the wheels of eternity? Think you that 'men may come, and men may go,'[13] but—mills—go on for ever? Not so; out of these, better or worse shall come; and it is for you to choose which.

I know that none of this wrong is done with deliberate purpose. I know, on the contrary, that you wish your workmen well; that you do much for them, and that you desire to do more for them, if you saw your way to it, safely. I know that many of you have done, and are every day doing, whatever you feel to be in your power; and that even all this wrong and misery are brought about by a warped sense of duty, each of you striving to do his best, without noticing that this best is essentially and centrally the best for himself,

13. Alfred Tennyson, "The Brook" (1855).

not for others. And all this has come of the spreading of that thrice accursed, thrice impious doctrine of the modern economist, that 'To do the best for yourself, is finally to do the best for others.' Friends, our great Master said not so; and most absolutely we shall find this world is not made so. Indeed, to do the best for others, is finally to do the best for ourselves; but it will not do to have our eyes fixed on that issue. The Pagans had got beyond that. Hear what a Pagan says of this matter; hear what were, perhaps, the last written words of Plato,—if not the last actually written, (for this we cannot know), yet assuredly in fact and power his parting words—in which, endeavouring to give full crowning and harmonious close to all his thoughts, and to speak the sum of them by the imagined sentence of the Great Spirit, his strength and his heart fail him, and the words cease, broken off for ever. It is the close of the dialogue called 'Critias,' in which he describes, partly from real tradition, partly in ideal dream, the early state of Athens; and the genesis, and order, and religion, of the fabled isle of Atlantis; in which genesis he conceives the same first perfection and final degeneracy of man, which in our own Scriptural tradition is expressed by saying that the Sons of God intermarried with the daughters of men, for he supposes the earliest race to have been indeed the children of God; and to have corrupted themselves, until 'their spot was not the spot of his children.'[14] And this, he says, was the end; that indeed

> 'through many generations, so long as the God's nature in them yet was
> full, they were submissive to the sacred laws, and carried themselves lov-
> ingly to all that had kindred with them in divineness; for their uttermost
> spirit was faithful and true, and in every wise great; so that, in all meek-
> ness of wisdom, they dealt with each other, and took all the chances of life;
> and despising all things except virtue, they cared little what happened day
> by day, and *bore lightly the burden* of gold and of possessions; for they saw
> that, if only their common love and virtue increased, all these things would
> be increased together with them; but to set their esteem and ardent pur-
> suit upon material possession, would be to lose that first, and their virtue
> and affection together with it. And by such reasoning, and what of the
> divine nature remained in them, they gained all this greatness of which we
> have already told; but when the God's part of them faded and became
> extinct, being mixed again and again, and effaced by the prevalent mortali-
> ty; and the human nature at last exceeded, they then became unable to
> endure the courses of fortune; and fell into shapelessness of life, and base-
> ness in the sight of him who could see, having lost everything that was
> fairest of their honour; while to the blind hearts which could not discern
> the true life, tending to happiness, it seemed that they were then chiefly
> noble and happy, being filled with all iniquity of inordinate possession and
> power. Whereupon, the God of Gods, whose Kinghood is in laws, behold-

14. Deuteronomy 32:5.

ing a once just nation thus cast into misery, and desiring to lay such punishment upon them as might make them repent into restraining, gathered
together all the gods into his dwelling place, which from heaven's centre
overlooks whatever has part in creation; and having assembled them, he
said'—

The rest is silence. So ended are the last words of the chief wisdom of the heathen,
spoken of this idol of riches; this idol of yours; this golden image, high by measureless
cubits, set up where your green fields of England are furnace-burnt into the likeness of
the plain of Dura[15]: this idol, forbidden to us, first of all idols, by our own Master and
faith; forbidden to us also by every human lip that has ever, in any age or people, been
accounted of as able to speak according to the purposes of God. Continue to make that
forbidden deity your principal one, and soon no more art, no more science, no more
pleasure will be possible. Catastrophe will come; or, worse than catastrophe, slow moul-
dering and withering into Hades. But if you can fix some conception of a true human
state of life to be striven for—life for all men as for yourselves—if you can determine
some honest and simple order of existence; following those trodden ways of wisdom,
which are pleasantness, and seeking her quiet and withdrawn paths, which are peace;—
then, and so sanctifying wealth into 'commonwealth,' all your art, your literature, your
daily labours, your domestic affection, and citizen's duty, will join and increase into one
magnificent harmony. You will know then how to build, well enough; you will build with
stone well, but with flesh better; temples not made with hands, but riveted of hearts; and
that kind of marble, crimson-veined, is indeed eternal.

## OF QUEENS' GARDENS

*Ruskin's lecture "Of Queens' Gardens" was delivered in December 1864 at Manchester and
was subsequently published, along with "Of Kings' Treasuries," in Sesame and Lilies, the
most popular of Ruskin's works in his day: 160,000 copies were printed during his lifetime. Its popularity suggests that it expressed and reinforced widely-held assumptions about
women's moral influence. Ruskin's discussion of separate spheres of activity for men and
women is, to our modern sensibility, uncomfortably conservative. But such an evaluation
ignores the lecture's more radical elements, in particular Ruskin's emphasis on the education of women. Ruskin actively promoted women's education. He contributed funds, collections of art, and time to women's colleges and girls' schools. He financially supported a
number of women artists, including Kate Greenaway, Lizzie Siddal, and Anna Blunden, and
encouraged their professional careers. While Ruskin's view of women's "proper" duties is
smugly patriarchal, he does concede that there is value in men's learning things "in a womanly sort of way"—that is, intuitively, with the goal of sympathy rather than mastery—
and so anticipates recent essentialist feminist arguments.*                                    LMF

15. Babylonian plain where Nebuchadnezzar constructed a huge golden image. See Daniel 3:1.

. . . I AM NOW GOING TO ask you to consider with me farther, what special portion or kind of this royal authority, arising out of noble education, may rightly be possessed by women; and how far they also are called to a true queenly power. Not in their households merely, but over all within their sphere. And in what sense, if they rightly understood and exercised this royal or gracious influence, the order and beauty induced by such benignant power would justify us in speaking of the territories over which each of them reigned, as "Queens' Gardens."

And here, in the very outset, we are met by a far deeper question, which—strange though this may seem—remains among many of us yet quite undecided, in spite of its infinite importance.

We cannot determine what the queenly power of women should be, until we are agreed what their ordinary power should be. We cannot consider how education may fit them for any widely extending duty, until we are agreed what is their true constant duty. And there never was a time when wilder words were spoken, or more vain imagination permitted, respecting this question—quite vital to all social happiness. The relations of the womanly to the manly nature, their different capacities of intellect or of virtue, seem never to have been yet estimated with entire consent. We hear of the mission and of the rights of Woman, as if these could ever be separate from the mission and the rights of Man;—as if she and her lord were creatures of independent kind, and of irreconcileable claim. This, at least, is wrong. And not less wrong—perhaps even more foolishly wrong (for I will anticipate thus far what I hope to prove)—is the idea that woman is only the shadow and attendant image of her lord, owing him a thoughtless and servile obedience, and supported altogether in her weakness by the pre-eminence of his fortitude.

This, I say, is the most foolish of all errors respecting her who was made to be the helpmate of man. As if he could be helped effectively by a shadow, or worthily by a slave!

Let us try, then, whether we cannot get at some clear and harmonious idea (it must be harmonious if it is true) of what womanly mind and virtue are in power and office, with respect to man's; and how their relations, rightly accepted, aid, and increase, the vigour, and honour, and authority of both. . . .

We are foolish, and without excuse foolish, in speaking of the "superiority" of one sex to the other, as if they could be compared in similar things. Each has what the other has not: each completes the other, and is completed by the other: they are in nothing alike, and the happiness and perfection of both depends on each asking and receiving from the other what the other only can give.

Now their separate characters are briefly these. The man's power is active, progressive, defensive. He is eminently the doer, the creator, the discoverer, the defender. His intellect is for speculation and invention; his energy for adventure, for war, and for conquest, wherever war is just, wherever conquest necessary. But the woman's power is for rule, not for battle,—and her intellect is not for invention or creation, but for sweet ordering, arrangement, and decision. She sees the qualities of things, their claims, and their places. Her great function is Praise: she enters into no contest, but infallibly adjudges the crown of contest. By her office, and place, she is protected from all danger and temptation. The man, in his rough work in the open world, must encounter all peril and trial:——to him, therefore, the failure, the offence, the inevitable error: often he must be wounded, or subdued, often misled, and *always* hardened. But he guards the woman from all this; within his house, as ruled by her, unless she herself has sought it, need enter no danger, no temptation, no cause of error or offence. This is the true nature of home— it is the place of Peace; the shelter, not only from all injury, but from all terror, doubt, and division. In so far as it is not this, it is not home; so far as the anxieties of the outer life penetrate into it, and the inconsistently-minded, unknown, unloved, or hostile society of the outer world is allowed by either husband or wife to cross the threshold, it ceases to be home; it is then only a part of that outer world which you have roofed over and lighted fire in. But so far as it is a sacred place, a vestal temple, a temple of the hearth watched over by Household Gods, before whose faces none may come but those whom they can receive with love,——so far as it is this, and roof and fire are types only of a nobler shade and light,——shade as of the rock in a weary land, and light as of the Pharos in the stormy sea;——so far it vindicates the name, and fulfils the praise, of Home.

And wherever a true wife comes, this home is always round her. The stars only may be over her head; the glowworm in the night-cold grass may be the only fire at her foot: but home is yet wherever she is; and for a noble woman it stretches far round her, better than ceiled with cedar, or painted with vermilion, shedding its quiet light far, for those who else were homeless.

This, then, I believe to be,——will you not admit it to be,——the woman's true place and power? But do not you see that, to fulfil this, she must—as far as one can use such terms of a human creature—be incapable of error? So far as she rules, all must be right, or nothing is. She must be enduringly, incorruptibly good, instinctively, infallibly wise—wise, not for self-development, but for self-renunciation: wise, not that she may set herself above her husband, but that she may never fail from his side: wise, not with the narrowness of insolent and loveless pride, but with the passionate gentleness of an infinitely variable, because infinitely applicable, modesty of service—the true changefulness of woman. In that great sense—"La donna e mobile," not "Qual piùm' al vento;"[1] no, nor yet "Variable as the shade, by the light quivering aspen made;"[2] but variable as the *light*, manifold in fair and serene division, that it may take the colour of all that it falls upon, and exalt it.

I have been trying, thus far, to show you what should be the place, and what the power of woman. Now, secondly, we ask, What kind of education is to fit her for these?

And if you indeed think this a true conception of her office and dignity, it will not be difficult to trace the course of education which would fit her for the one, and raise her to the other.

The first of our duties to her—no thoughtful persons now doubt this—is to secure for her such physical training and exercise as may confirm her health and perfect her beauty; the highest refinement of that beauty being unattainable without splendor of activity and of delicate strength. . . .

1. "Woman is changeful," not "like a feather in the wind." Phrases from an aria in Verdi's *Rigoletto* (1851).
2. Sir Walter Scott, *Marmion* (1808), Canto 6.

. . . Do not think you can make a girl lovely, if you do not make her happy. There is not one restraint you put on a good girl's nature—there is not one check you give to her instincts of affection or of effort—which will not be indelibly written on her features, with a hardness which is all the more painful because it takes away the brightness from the eyes of innocence, and the charm from the brow of virtue. . . .

The perfect loveliness of a woman's countenance can only consist in that majestic peace, which is founded in the memory of happy and useful years,—full of sweet records; and from the joining of this with that yet more majestic childishness, which is still full of change and promise;—opening always—modest at once, and bright, with hope of better things to be won, and to be bestowed. There is no old age where there is still that promise—it is eternal youth.

Thus, then, you have first to mould her physical frame, and then, as the strength she gains will permit you, to fill and temper her mind with all knowledge and thoughts which tend to confirm its natural instincts of justice, and refine its natural tact of love.

All such knowledge should be given her as may enable her to understand, and even to aid, the work of men: and yet it should be given, not as knowledge,—not as if it were, or could be, for her an object to know; but only to feel, and to judge. It is of no moment, as a matter of pride or perfectness in herself, whether she knows many languages or one; but it is of the utmost that she should be able to show kindness to a stranger, and to understand the sweetness of a stranger's tongue. It is of no moment to her own worth or dignity that she should be acquainted with this science or that; but it is of the highest that she should be trained in habits of accurate thought; that she should understand the mean-ing, the inevitableness, and the loveliness of natural laws, and follow at least some one path of scientific attainment, as far as to the threshold of that bitter Valley of Humiliation, into which only the wisest and bravest of men can descend, owning themselves for ever children, gathering pebbles on a boundless shore. It is of little consequence how many positions of cities she knows, or how many dates of events, or how many names of cele-brated persons—it is not the object of education to turn a woman into a dictionary; but it is deeply necessary that she should be taught to enter with her whole personality into the history she reads; to picture the passages of it vitally in her own bright imagination; to apprehend, with her fine instincts, the pathetic circumstances and dramatic relations, which the historian too often only eclipses by his reasoning, and disconnects by his arrangement: it is for her to trace the hidden equities of divine reward, and catch sight, through the darkness, of the fateful threads of woven fire that connect error with its ret-ribution. But chiefly of all, she is to be taught to extend the limits of her sympathy with respect to that history which is being for ever determined, as the moments pass in which she draws her peaceful breath; and to the contemporary calamity which, were it but rightly mourned by her, would recur no more hereafter. She is to exercise herself in imagining what would be the effects upon her mind and conduct, if she were daily brought into the presence of the suffering which is not the less real because shut from her sight. She is to be taught somewhat to understand the nothingness of the proportion which that little world in which she lives and loves, bears to the world in which God lives and loves;—and solemnly she is to be taught to strive that her thoughts of piety may not be feeble in proportion to the number they embrace, nor her prayer more languid than it is for the momentary relief from pain of her husband or her child, when it is uttered for the multitudes of those who have none to love them,—and is "for all who are desolate and oppressed." . . .

I believe, then, . . . that a girl's education should be nearly, in its course and material of study, the same as a boy's; but quite differently directed. A woman in any rank of life, ought to know whatever her husband is likely to know, but to know it in a different way. His command of it should be foundational and progressive, hers, general and accomplished for daily and helpful use. Not but that it would often be wiser in men to learn things in a womanly sort of way, for present use, and to seek for the discipline and training of their mental powers in such branches of study as will be afterwards fitted for social service; but, speaking broadly, a man ought to know any language or science he learns, thoroughly while a woman ought to know the same language, or science, only so far as may enable her to sympathise in her husband's pleasures, and in those of his best friends.

Yet, observe, with exquisite accuracy as far as she reaches. There is a wide difference between elementary knowledge and superficial knowledge between a firm beginning, and a feeble smattering. A woman may always help her husband by what she knows, however little; by what she half-knows, or mis-knows, she will only teaze him.

And indeed, if there were to be any difference between a girl's education and a boy's, I should say that of the two the girl should be earlier led, as her intellect ripens faster, into deep and serious subjects; and that her range of literature should be, not more, but less frivolous, calculated to add the qualities of patience and seriousness to her natural poignancy of thought and quickness of wit; and also to keep her in a lofty and pure element of thought. I enter not now into any question of choice of books; only be sure that her books are not heaped up in her lap as they fall out of the package of the circulating library, wet with the last and lightest spray of the fountain of folly. . . .

Without, however, venturing here on any attempt at decision how much novel reading should be allowed, let me at least clearly assert this, that whether novels, or poetry, or history be read, they should be chosen, not for what is *out* of them, but for what is *in* them. The chance and scattered evil that may here and there haunt, or hide itself in, a powerful book, never does any harm to a noble girl; but the emptiness of an author oppresses her, and his amiable folly degrades her. And if she can have access to a good library of old and classical books, there need be no choosing at all. Keep the modern magazine and novel out of your girl's way: turn her loose into the old library every wet day, and let her alone. She will find what is good for her; you cannot; for there is just this difference between the making of a girl's character and a boy's—you may chisel a boy into shape, as you would a rock, or hammer him into it, if he be of a better kind, as you would a piece of bronze. But you cannot hammer a girl into anything. She grows as a flower does,—she will wither without sun; she will decay in her sheath, as the narcissus does, if you do not give her air enough; she may fall, and defile her head in dust, if you leave her without help at some moments of her life; but you cannot fetter her; she must take her own fair form and way, if she take any, and in mind as in body, must have always—

"Her household motions light and free,
    And steps of virgin liberty."[3]

Let her loose in the library, I say, as you do a fawn in a field. It knows the bad weeds twenty times better than you; and the good ones too, and will eat some bitter and prickly ones, good for it, which you had not the slightest thought were good. . . .

And not only in the material and in the course, but yet more earnestly in the spirit of it, let a girl's education be as serious as a boy's. You bring up your girls as if they were meant for sideboard ornaments, and then complain of their frivolity. Give them the same advantages that you give their brothers—appeal to the same grand instincts of virtue in them; teach *them* also that courage and truth are the pillars of their being: do you think that they would not answer that appeal, brave and true as they are even now, when you know that there is hardly a girls' school in this Christian kingdom where the children's courage or sincerity would be thought of half so much importance as their way of coming in at a door; and when the whole system of society, as respects the mode of establishing them in life, is one rotten plague of cowardice and imposture—cowardice, in not daring to let them live, or love, except as their neighbours choose; and imposture, in bringing, for the purposes of our own pride, the full glow of the world's worst vanity upon a girl's eyes, at the very period when the whole happiness of her future existence depends upon her remaining undazzled? . . .

Thus far, then, of the nature, thus far of the teaching, of woman, and thus of her household office, and queenliness. We come now to our last, our widest question,—What is her queenly office with respect to the state?

Generally, we are under an impression that a man's duties are public, and a woman's private. But this is not altogether so. A man has a personal work or duty, relating to his own home, and a public work or duty, which is the expansion of the other, relating to the state. So a woman has a personal work or duty, relating to her own home, and a public work and duty, which is also the expansion of that.

Now, the man's work for his own home is, as has been said, to secure its maintenance, progress, and defence; the woman's to secure its order, comfort, and loveliness.

Expand both these functions. The man's duty, as a member of a commonwealth, is to assist in the maintenance, in the advance, in the defence of the state. The woman's duty, as a member of the commonwealth, is to assist in the ordering, in the comforting, and in the beautiful adornment of the state.

What the man is at his own gate, defending it, if need be, against insult and spoil, that also, not in a less, but in a more devoted measure, he is to be at the gate of his country, leaving his home, if need be, even to the spoiler, to do his more incumbent work there.

And, in like manner, what the woman is to be within her gates, as the centre of order, the balm of distress, and the mirror of beauty; that she is also to be without her gates, where order is more difficult, distress more imminent, loveliness more rare. . . .

. . . There is no putting by that crown; queens you must always be; queens to your lovers; queens to your husbands and your sons; queens of higher mystery to the world

3. William Wordsworth, "She Was a Phantom of Delight" (1807).

beyond, which bows itself, and will for ever bow, before the myrtle crown, and the stainless sceptre, of womanhood. But, alas! you are too often idle and careless queens, grasping at majesty in the least things, while you abdicate it in the greatest; and leaving misrule and violence to work their will among men, in defiance of the power, which, holding straight in gift from the Prince of all Peace, the wicked among you betray, and the good forget.

"Prince of Peace." Note that name. When kings rule in that name, and nobles, and the judges of the earth, they also, in their narrow place, and mortal measure, receive the power of it. There are no other rulers than they: other rule than theirs is but *mis*rule; they who govern verily "*Dei Gratiâ*" are all princes, yes, or princesses, of peace. There is not a war in the world, no, nor an injustice, but you women are answerable for it; not in that you have provoked, but in that you have not hindered. Men, by their nature, are prone to fight; they will fight for any cause, or for none. It is for you to choose their cause for them, and to forbid them when there is no cause. There is no suffering, no injustice, no misery in the earth, but the guilt of it lies lastly with you. Men can bear the sight of it, but you should not be able to bear it. Men may tread it down without sympathy in their own struggle; but men are feeble in sympathy, and contracted in hope; it is you only who can feel the depths of pain; and conceive the way of its healing. Instead of trying to do this, you turn away from it; you shut yourselves within your park walls and garden gates; and you are content to know that there is beyond them a whole world in wilderness—a world of secrets which you dare not penetrate, and of suffering which you dare not conceive. . . .

# Queen Victoria

1819: BORN 24 MAY AT KENSINGTON PALACE

1837: BECAME QUEEN AFTER WILLIAM IV's DEATH

1840: MARRIED PRINCE ALBERT OF SAXE-COBURG AND GOTHA

1861: PRINCE ALBERT's DEATH AND BEGINNING OF QUEEN's LONG PERIOD OF MOURNING

1876: PROCLAIMED EMPRESS OF INDIA

1901: DIED 22 JANUARY AT OSBORNE

## JOURNAL ENTRY ON THE GREAT EXHIBITION, 1851

The Great Exhibition of the Works of Industry of All Nations opened May 1, 1851, at Hyde Park. Its massive "crystal palace" of glass and metal, designed by Joseph Paxton, housed over one hundred thousand exhibits by nearly fourteen thousand exhibitors from England, its Empire, and other nations. A tribute to international commerce and a celebration of the wedding of technology and art, the festival also proclaimed England's world leadership, mid-century prosperity, and professed superiority in industry, design, and trade.

Queen Victoria's journal entry of May 1 offers a unique eyewitness account of the opening day's ceremonies. As monarch, she observed an extravagant display of her country's international prominence in manufacturing and commerce, and, as wife, she applauded PRINCE ALBERT's success as a driving force behind the "Peace-Festival." In its planning stages, the Great Exhibition was not without detractors, as Victoria's account reveals: the Times assailed it; some objected to the "desecration" of Hyde Park; others feared an invasion of foreigners, revolutionaries, and persons of questionable honesty. Its opening-day ceremony silenced or converted most of its critics. To the relieved and thankful Queen, who described the ceremony in quasireligious terms, May 1 represented Albert's vindication and a confirmation of her realm's order and peace.

Victoria's journals, including this entry, were not necessarily the private documents they seem. Her Leaves from the Journal of Our Life in the Highlands appeared publicly in

*1868, for example. The following description of the exhibition's opening day was published
in 1876 in Theodore Martin's* The Life of His Royal Highness the Prince Consort.[1]

RM

MAY 1.—THE GREAT EVENT has taken place—a complete and beautiful triumph—a glorious and touching sight, one which I shall ever be proud of for my beloved Albert and my country. . . . Yes! it is a day which makes my heart swell with pride and glory and thankfulness!

We began it with tenderest greetings for the birthday of our dear little Arthur.[2] At breakfast there was nothing but congratulations. . . . Mama and Victor[3] were there and all the children and our guests. Our humble gifts of toys were added to by a beautiful little bronze *replica* of the Amazon (Kiss's[4]) from the Prince (of Prussia), a beautiful paper-knife from the Princess (of Prussia), and a nice little clock from Mama.

The Park presented a wonderful spectacle, crowds streaming through it, carriages and troops passing, quite like the Coronation day, and for me the same anxiety,—no, much greater anxiety on account of my beloved Albert. The day was bright and all bustle and excitement. . . . . At half-past eleven the whole procession in state carriages was in motion. . . . . The Green Park and Hyde Park were one densely crowded mass of human beings, in the highest good humour and most enthusiastic. I never saw Hyde Park look as it did,—as far as the eye could reach. A little rain fell just as we started; but before we came near the Crystal Palace the sun shone and gleamed upon the gigantic edifice, upon which the flags of all the Nations were floating. We drove up Rotten Row and got out at the entrance on that side.

The glimpse of the transept through the iron gates, the waving palms, flowers, statues, myriads of people filling the galleries and seats around, with the flourish of trumpets as we entered, gave us a sensation which I can never forget, and I felt much moved. We went for a moment to a little side room, where we left our shawls, and where we found Mama and Mary (now Princess of Teck), and outside which were standing the other Princes. In a few seconds we proceeded, Albert leading me, having Vicky at his hand, and Bertie holding mine.[5] The sight, as we came to the middle, where the steps and chair (which I did *not* sit on) were placed, with the beautiful Crystal fountain just in front of it,—was magical,—so vast, so glorious, so touching. One felt,—as so many did whom I have since spoken to—filled with devotion,—more so than by any service I have ever heard. The tremendous cheers, the joy expressed in every face, the immensity of the building, the mixture of palms, flowers, trees, statues, fountains,—the organ (with 200 instruments and 600 voices, which sounded like nothing), and my beloved husband the author of this "Peace-Festival," which united the industry of all nations of the earth,—all this was moving indeed, and it was and is a day to live for ever. God bless my dearest Albert, God bless my dearest country, which has shown itself so great to-day! One felt so grateful to the

1. Another version of this entry is the edited transcript made by Princess Beatrice after the Queen's death. The version in Martin is reprinted here because it was published during Victoria's reign.
2. Prince Arthur, born May 1, 1850.
3. Duchess of Kent and Prince Victor of Hohenlohe-Langenbourg.
4. August Karl Eduard Kiss (1802–65), German sculptor.
5. Victoria, the Princess Royal (1840–1901); Albert Edward, Prince of Wales (1841–1910).

great God, who seemed to pervade all and to bless all! The only event it in the slightest degree reminded me of was the Coronation, but this day's festival was a thousand times superior. In fact, it is unique, and can bear no comparison, from its peculiarity, beauty, and combination of such different and striking objects. I mean the slight resemblance only as to its solemnity: the enthusiasm and cheering, too, were much more touching, for in a church naturally all is silent.

Albert left my side after "God Save the Queen" had been sung, and at the head of the Commissioners—a curious assemblage of political and distinguished men—read me the Report, which is a long one, and to which I read a short answer. After which the Archbishop of Canterbury offered up a short and appropriate prayer, followed by the "Hallelujah Chorus," during which the Chinese Mandarin came forward and made his obeisance. This concluded, the procession began. It was beautifully arranged, and of great length,—the prescribed order being exactly adhered to. The Nave was full, which had not been intended; but still there was no difficulty, and the whole long walk from one end to the other was made in the midst of continued and deafening cheers and waving of hand-kerchiefs. Every one's face was bright and smiling, many with tears in their eyes. Many Frenchmen called out "Vive la Reine!" One could, of course, see nothing but what was near in the Nave, and nothing in the Courts. The organs were but little heard, but the Military Band, at one end, had a very fine effect as we passed along. They played the March from *Athalie*. The beautiful Amazon, in bronze, by Kiss, looked very magnificent. The old Duke and Lord Anglesey[6] walked arm in arm, which was a touching sight. I saw many acquaintances amongst those present.

We returned to our own place, and Albert told Lord Breadalbane to declare that the Exhibition was opened, which he did in a loud voice—"Her Majesty commands me to declare this Exhibition open,"—which was followed by a flourish of trumpets and immense cheering. All the Commissioners, the Executive Committee, &c., who worked so hard and to whom such immense praise is due, seemed truly happy, and no one more so than Paxton, who may be justly proud; he rose from being a common gardener's boy. Everybody was astonished and delighted, Sir George Grey in tears.

The return was equally satisfactory,—the crowd most enthusiastic, the order perfect. We reached the Palace at twenty minutes past one, and went out on the balcony, and were loudly cheered. The Prince and Princess quite delighted and impressed. That *we* felt happy—thankful—I need not say; proud of all that had passed, of my darling husband's success, and of the behaviour of my good people. I was more impressed than I can say by the scene. It was one that can never be effaced from my memory, and never will be from that of any one who witnessed it. Albert's name is immortalised, and the wicked and absurd reports of dangers of every kind, which a set of people, viz. the *soi-disant* fashion-ables and the most violent Protectionists, spread, are silenced. It is therefore doubly sat-isfactory, that all should have gone off so well, and without the slightest accident or mishap . . . . Albert's emphatic words last year, when he said that the feeling would be, *"that of deep thankfulness to the Almighty for the blessings which he has bestowed upon us already here below,"* this day realized. . . .

6. Arthur Wellesley, Duke of Wellington (1769–1852), national hero, victor at Waterloo, and former prime minis-ter; Henry Paget, Marquess of Anglesey (1768–1854).

# LETTERS TO HER DAUGHTER, THE PRINCESS ROYAL

*A prolific letter writer, Victoria corresponded regularly with her prime ministers and with members of her family. She began exchanging letters with her daughter Victoria, the Princess Royal and later Empress of Germany, in 1858 when the Princess married Prince Frederick of Prussia. In the context of Victoria's contradictory public image as both monarch and bourgeois, domestic woman (an image she fostered), her letters reveal the tensions between and the intersection of her public and private roles.*                    RM

*Stoneleigh Abbey, Kenilworth*
*June 15, 1858*

. . . So far I got before dinner, and can hardly hold my pen for the awful steaming heat this morning after a heavy thunderstorm and violent rain during the night which was too fearfully hot! Still I think it will get better as soon as the steaming is over—so many people ask kindly after you and say I must so feel the separation which God knows I do. It is so nice to see all these married daughters of Lady Westminster's here together, such charming people—all so happily and so richly married and all together. It is what I hope often to see. These are Lord and Lady Macclesfield (the second daughter) Lord and Lady Wenlock (the third) Lord and Lady Leigh themselves (she the fourth daughter) Sir M. and Lady Octavia Shaw Stewart; and Lady Agnes (the sixth) and her bridegroom Sir Archibald Campbell (also a rich Scotch Baronet) are also here. Lady Leigh has charming children. There are two married and one unmarried not here. The old entrance was illuminated both nights as well as the front door—and we took a walk to refresh ourselves, the band playing. I send you a Birmingham newspaper. Tuesday at one we go to Warwick Castle where we lunch and we ordered our train at five in order not to travel at the very hottest time.

What you say of the pride of giving life to an immortal soul is very fine, dear, but I own I cannot enter into that; I think much more of our being like a cow or a dog at such moments; when our poor nature becomes so very animal and unecstatic—but for you, dear, if you are sensible and reasonable not in ecstasy nor spending your day with nurses and wet nurses, which is the ruin of many a refined and intellectual young lady, without adding to her real maternal duties, a child will be a great resource. Above all, dear, do remember never to lose the modesty of a young girl towards others (without being prude); though you are married don't become a matron at once to whom everything can be said, and who minds saying nothing herself—I remained particular to a degree (indeed feel so now) and often feel shocked at the confidences of other married ladies. I fear abroad they are very indelicate about these things. Think of me who at that first time, very unreasonable, and perfectly furious as I was to be caught, having to have drawing rooms and levées and made to sit down—and be stared at and take every sort of precaution.

Don't give way to melancholy, dear. I found the best way when Papa was away—and a feeling of loneliness and sorrow came over me to say to myself—it must not be, it must be conquered and I must control it from a sense of duty and unselfishness, and I always did—particularly by occupying myself and trying to do and see as much as I could. . . .

*Windsor Castle*
*November 17, 1858*

. . . Miss Bennett is coming here next week. Let me advise you dear, not to complain any more of poor Anne G.—she is going and the less said about it the better for you and for her. She is not the first maid who has failed: I could give a long list of my failures, and it does no-one any good to complain of all her "forgets," which moreover are no worse than many I could tell of others, as it will soon be over. So pray let this subject be dropped.

I know that the little being will be a great reward for all your trouble and suffering— but I know you will not forget, dear, your promise not to indulge in "baby worship", or to neglect your other greater duties in becoming a nurse. You know how manifold your duties are, and as my dear child is a little disorderly in regulating her time, I fear you might lose a great deal of it, if you overdid the passion for the nursery. No lady, and still less a Princess, is fit for her husband or her position, if she does that. I know, dear, that you will feel and guard against this, but I only just wish to remind you and warn you, as with your great passion for little children (which are mere little plants for the first six months) it would be very natural for you to be carried away by your pleasure at having a child.

I can not bear to think Bertie is going to you and I can't—and when I look at the baby things, and feel I shall not be, where every other mother is—and I ought to be and can't  it makes me sick and almost frantic. Why in the world did you manage to choose a time when we could not be with you? In Nov: Dec: or the beginning of January we could have done it so easily.

Well, it is no use complaining. Let us hope on another similar occasion to be more fortunate. . . .

*Balmoral*
*June 5, 1872*

It gave me much pleasure to receive your dear letter, dated 2nd, as it showed me that you can understand what I meant about the relations of children and parents. The higher the position the more difficult it is.—And for a woman alone to be head of so large a family and at the same time reigning Sovereign is I can assure you almost more than human strength can bear. I assure you I feel so done by the amount of work and interruption all day long that it affects my health and also my spirits very much at times. I feel so disheartened. I should like to retire quietly to a cottage in the hills and rest and see almost no one. As long as my health and strength will bear it—I will go on—but I often fear I shall not be able for many years (if I live). If only our dear Bertie was fit to replace me! Alas! Alas! I feel very anxious for the future, as I see by your observations in your letter of the 30th—for which many thanks also—that you also are. And so is every one.

# Charles Kingsley

1819: Born 12 June at Holne, Devonshire

1842: Became curate at Eversley, Hampshire; rector in 1844

1848: *Yeast* in *Fraser's Magazine*

1850: *Cheap Clothes and Nasty*; *Alton Locke*

1855: *Westward Ho!*

1856: *The Heroes; or Greek Fairy Tales for My Children*

1858: *Andromeda and Other Poems*

1860: Appointed Regius Professor of Modern History at Cambridge

1863: *The Water-Babies*

1875: Died 23 January at Eversley

## THE MASSACRE OF THE INNOCENTS!

*A man of many interests, occupations, and avocations, Charles Kingsley served as curate and rector of Eversley Church, Canon of Chester and Westminster, chaplain to the Queen, and Professor of Modern History at Cambridge, while also becoming a successful novelist, poet, popularizer of science, defender of Protestantism, and political pamphleteer. Sparked by his sympathy with—though not approval of—Chartist agitators, Kingsley was drawn to Christian Socialism in 1848, under the influence of F. D. Maurice and John Ludlow. Wishing to promote the movement's vision of social regeneration, to be achieved by moral reform and communal responsibility, Kingsley and his friends created a penny weekly addressed to the working classes,* Politics for the People, *to which Kingsley contributed a number of essays and poems. His* Cheap Clothes and Nasty, *which exposed the appalling working conditions of tailors, appeared in the series "Tracts by Christian Socialists." It was quickly followed by his novel about Chartism,* Alton Locke, *which caused many reviewers to bristle, but was widely read.*

*Concern for the living conditions of the poor led to Kingsley's interest in sanitary reform. He shared this interest with others who, responding to studies such as Edwin Chadwick's* Report on the Sanitary Condition of the Labouring Population *(1842),*

*began a public campaign for change in sanitary practices and laws. After seeing the*
*unhealthy conditions of the cholera-ridden Bermondsey district of London, Kingsley helped*
*to bring fresh water to the inhabitants and proposed the formation of a Sanitary League.*
*He delivered "The Massacre of the Innocents!" at St. James Hall, London in 1859, at the*
*first public meeting of the Ladies' Sanitary Association. Kingsley's lecture exemplifies his*
*progressive interest in the living conditions of the poor and in physical health, but also his*
*imperialist tendencies.*                                                        LMF

AFTER THE ADMIRABLE SPEECH AND *resumé* of the whole intent of this meeting that you
have just heard from the Chairman,[1] there seems at first sight very little to be said. But
let me say one thing to the ladies who are interested in this matter. Have they really seriously considered what they are about to do in carrying out their own plans? Are they
aware that if their Society really succeeds, they will produce a very serious, some would
think a very dangerous, change in the state of this nation? Are they aware that they would
probably save the lives of some thirty or forty per cent. of the children who are born in
England, and that therefore they would cause the subjects of Queen Victoria to increase
at a very far more rapid rate than they do now? And are they aware that some very wise
men inform us that England is already over-peopled, and that it is an exceedingly puz-
zling question where we shall soon be able to find work or food for our masses, so rapidly do they increase already, in spite of the thirty or forty per cent. kind Nature carries off
yearly before they are five years old? Have they considered what they are to do with all
those children whom they are going to save alive? That has to be thought of; and if they
really do believe, with political economists now, that over-population is a possibility to a
country which has the greatest colonial empire that the world has ever seen, then I think
they had better stop in their course, and let the children die, as they have been dying.

But if, on the other hand, it seems to them, as I confess it does to me, that the most
precious thing in the world is a human being: that the lowest, and poorest, and the most
degraded of human beings is better than all the dumb animals in the world; that there is
an infinite, priceless capability in that creature, degraded as it may be—a capability of
virtue, and of social and industrial use, which, if it is taken in time, may be developed up
to a pitch, of which at first sight the child gives no hint whatsoever: if they believe again,
that of all races upon earth now, the English race is the finest, and that it gives not the
slightest sign whatever of exhaustion; that it seems to be on the whole a young race, and
to have very great capabilities in it which have not yet been developed, and above all, the
most marvellous capability of adapting itself to every sort of climate, and every form of
life that any nation, except the old Roman, ever had in the world: if they consider with
me that it is worth the while of political economists and social philosophers to look at the
map, and see that about four-fifths of the globe cannot be said as yet to be in anywise
inhabited or cultivated, or in the state in which men could make it by any fair supply of
population and industry and human intellect:—then, perhaps, they may think with me
that it is a duty, one of the noblest of duties, to help the increase of the English race as

1. Anthony Ashley Cooper, Lord Shaftesbury (1801–85).

much as possible, and to see that every child that is born into this great nation of England be developed to the highest pitch to which we can develop him, in physical strength and in beauty, as well as in intellect and in virtue. And then, in that light, it does seem to me, that this Association—small now, but I do hope some day to become great, and to become the mother Association of many and valuable children—is one of the noblest, most right-minded, straightforward, and practical conceptions that I have come across for some years.

We all know the difficulties of Sanitary Legislation. One looks at them at times almost with despair. I have my own reasons, with which I will not trouble this meeting, for look-ing on them with more despair than ever; not on account of the government of the time, or any possible government that could come to England, but on account of the peculiar class of persons in whom the ownership of the small houses has become more and more vested, and who are becoming more and more, I had almost said, the arbiters of the pop-ular opinion, and of every election of parliament. However, that is no business of mine here; that must be settled somewhere else; and a fearfully long time, it seems to me, it will be before it is settled. But, in the mean time, what legislation cannot do, I believe private help, and, above all, woman's help, can do even better. It can do this; it can not only improve the condition of the working man; I am not speaking of working men just at this time, I am speaking of the middle classes, of the man who owns the house in which the working-man lives. I am speaking, too, of the wealthy tradesman; I am speaking, it is a sad thing to have to say, of our own class as well as of others. Sanitary Reform, as it is called, or, in plain English, the art of health, is so very recent a discovery, as all true phys-ical science is, that we ourselves and our own class know very little about it, and practise it very ill. And this Society, I do hope, will bear in mind that it is not simply to affect the working-man, not only to go into the foul alley; but it is to go to the door of the farmer, to the door of the shopkeeper, aye, to the door of ladies and gentlemen of the same rank as ourselves. Women can do in that work what men cannot do. Private correspondence, private conversation, private example, may do what no legislation can do. I am struck more and more with the amount of disease and death I see around me in all classes, which no sanitary legislation whatsoever could touch, unless you had a complete house-to-house visitation by a government officer, with powers to enter every house, to drain and ventilate it, and not only that, but to regulate the clothes and the diet of every inhabitant, and that among all ranks. I can conceive of nothing short of that, which would be absurd and impossible and most harmful, which would stop the present amount of disease and death which I see around me, without some such private exertion on the part of women, above all of mothers, as I do hope will spring from this Institution more and more. . . .

Now, I do believe that if those tracts which you are publishing, which I have read, and of which I cannot speak too highly, are spread over the length and breadth of the land, and if women, clergymen's wives, the wives of manufacturers and of great employers, district visitors and school mistresses, have these books put into their hands, and are per-suaded to spread them, and to enforce them, by their own example and by their own counsel, then in the course of a few years, this system being thoroughly carried out, you would see a sensible and large increase in the rate of population. When you have saved your children alive, then you must settle what to do with them. But a living dog is better than a dead lion; I would rather have the living child, and let it take its chance, than let it return to God—wasted. Oh! it is a distressing thing to see children die. God gives the most beautiful and precious thing that earth can have, and we just take it and cast it away; we toss our pearls upon the dunghill, and leave them. A dying child is to me one of the most dreadful sights in the world. A dying man, a man dying on the field of battle, that is a small sight: he has taken his chance; he has had his excitement; he has had his glory, if that will be any consolation to him; if he is a wise man, he has the feeling that he is doing his duty by his country, or by his king, or by his queen. I am not horrified or shocked at the sight of the man who dies on the field of battle: let him die so. It does not horrify or shock me to see a man dying in a good old age, even though it be painful at the last as it too often is. But it does shock me, it does make me feel that the world is indeed out of joint, to see a child die. I believe it to be a priceless boon to the child to have lived for a week, or a day; but oh, what has God given to this thankless earth, and what has the earth thrown away, in nine cases out of ten, from its own neglect and carelessness! What that boy might have been, what he might have done as an Englishman, if he could have lived and grown up healthy and strong! And I entreat you to bear this in mind, that it is not as if our lower or our middle classes were not worth saving; bear in mind that the physical beauty and strength and intellectual power of the middle classes,—the shopkeeping class, the farming class, the working class—whenever you give them a fair chance, whenever you give them fair food and air, and physical education of any kind, prove them to be the finest race in Europe. Not merely the aristocracy, splendid race as they are: but down and down and down to the lowest labouring man, to the navigator;—why, there is not such a body of men in Europe as our navigators, and no body of men perhaps have had a worse chance of growing to be what they are; and yet see what they have done. See the magnificent men they become in spite of all that is against them, all that is dragging them back, all that is tending to give them rickets and consumption, and all the miserable diseases which children contract; see what men they are, and then conceive what they might be!

It has been said, again, that there are no more beautiful races of women in Europe than the wives and daughters of our London shopkeepers, and yet there are few races of people who lead a life more in opposition to all rules of hygiene. But, in spite of all that, so wonderful is the vitality of the English race, they are what they are; and therefore we have the finest material to work upon that people ever had. And therefore, again, we have the less excuse if we do allow English people to grow up puny, stunted, and diseased. . . .

It is in the power, I believe, of any woman in this room to save three or four lives, human lives, during the next six months. It is in your power, ladies, and it is *so* easy. You might save several lives a-piece, if you choose, without, I believe, interfering with your daily business, or with your daily pleasure, or, if you choose, with your daily frivolities, in any way whatsoever. Let me ask, then, those who are here, and who have not yet laid these things to heart: Will you let this meeting to-day be a mere passing matter of two or three hours interest, which you may go away and forget for the next book or the next amusement? Or will you be in earnest? Will you learn—I say it openly—from the noble chairman, how easy it is to be in earnest in life; how every one of you, amid all the artificial complications of English society in the nineteenth century, can find a work to do, and a noble work to do, and a chivalrous work to do—just as chivalrous as if you lived in any old fairy land, such as Spenser talked of in his 'Faery Queen;' how you can be as true a knight-errant, or lady-errant in the present century, as if you had lived far away in the dark ages of violence and rapine? Will you, I ask, learn this? Will you learn to be in earnest, and to use the position, and the station, and the talent that God has given you, to save alive those who should live? And will you remember that it is not the will of your Father that is in Heaven that one little one that plays in the kennel outside should perish, either in body or in soul?

# Prince Albert

1819: Born 26 August near Coburg, Germany

1840: Married Victoria, Queen of England

1845: Became President of the Society of Arts

1857: Received title of Prince Consort

1861: Died 14 December at Windsor

## SPEECH AT THE MANSION HOUSE, MARCH 21, 1850

*An ardent sponsor and major planner of the Great Exhibition of 1851, Prince Albert served as chairman of the Royal Commission for the international festival, officially titled "The Great Exhibition of Works of Industry of All Nations." The Prince's March 1850 address, before Her Majesty's ministers, foreign ambassadors, and one hundred and eighty British mayors, reveals his idealism about the project: the massive collection of exhibits at the Crystal Palace was to form a "living picture" of the progress of civilization, of the union of science and art, and of world cooperation and free trade.*

*As a foreigner in a country wary of foreigners and foreign influence, Prince Albert peri-odically found himself the subject of controversy and suspicion, given his position as the Queen's clearly adored husband and confidential adviser. But the success of the Great Exhibition—its celebration of the British Empire's prominence as well as of world peace and commerce—marked the popular triumph of his short career.*                RM

I AM SINCERELY GRATEFUL FOR the kindness with which you have proposed my health, and to you, Gentlemen, for the cordiality with which you have received this proposal.

It must indeed be most gratifying to me to find that a suggestion which I had thrown out, as appearing to me of importance at this time, should have met with such universal concurrence and approbation; for this has proved to me that the view I took of the peculiar character and claims of the time we live in was in accordance with the feelings and opinions of the country.

Gentlemen—I conceive it to be the duty of every educated person closely to watch and study the time in which he lives, and, as far as in him lies, to add his humble mite of individual exertion to further the accomplishment of what he believes Providence to have ordained.

Nobody, however, who has paid any attention to the peculiar features of our present era, will doubt for a moment that we are living at a period of most wonderful transition, which tends rapidly to accomplish that great end to which, indeed, all history points— *the realization of the unity of mankind*. Not a unity which breaks down the limits and levels the peculiar characteristics of the different nations of the earth, but rather a unity, the *result and product* of those very national varieties and antagonistic qualities.

The distances which separated the different nations and parts of the globe are rapidly vanishing before the achievements of modern invention, and we can traverse them with incredible ease; the languages of all nations are known, and their acquirement placed within the reach of everybody; thought is communicated with the rapidity, and even by the power, of lightning. On the other hand, the *great principle of division of labour*, which may be called the moving power of civilization, is being extended to all branches of science, industry, and art.

Whilst formerly the greatest mental energies strove at universal knowledge, and that knowledge was confined to the few, now they are directed on specialities, and in these, again, even to the minutest points; but the knowledge acquired becomes at once the property of the community at large; for, whilst formerly discovery was wrapped in secrecy, the publicity of the present day causes that no sooner is a discovery or invention made than it is already improved upon and surpassed by competing efforts. The products of all quarters of the globe are placed at our disposal, and we have only to choose which is the best and the cheapest for our purposes, and the powers of production are entrusted to the stimulus of *competition and capital*.

So man is approaching a more complete fulfilment of that great and sacred mission which he has to perform in this world. His reason being created after the image of God, he has to use it to discover the laws by which the Almighty governs His creation, and, by making these laws his standard of action, to conquer nature to his use; himself a divine instrument.

Science discovers these laws of power, motion, and transformation; industry applies them to the raw matter, which the earth yields us in abundance, but which becomes valuable only by knowledge. Art teaches us the immutable laws of beauty and symmetry, and gives to our productions forms in accordance to them.

Gentlemen—the Exhibition of 1851 is to give us a true test and a living picture of the point of development at which the whole of mankind has arrived in this great task, and a new starting-point from which all nations will be able to direct their further exertions.

I confidently hope that the first impression which the view of this vast collection will produce upon the spectator will be that of deep thankfulness to the Almighty for the blessings which He has bestowed upon us already here below; and the second, the conviction that they can only be realized in proportion to the help which we are prepared to render each other; therefore, only by peace, love, and ready assistance, not only between individuals, but between the nations of the earth.

This being my conviction, I must be highly gratified to see here assembled the magistrates of all the important towns of this realm, sinking all their local and possibly political differences, the representatives of the different political opinions of the country, and the representatives of the different Foreign Nations—to-day representing only *one interest!*

Gentlemen—my original plan had been to carry out this undertaking with the help of the Society of Arts of London, which had long and usefully laboured in this direction, and by the means of private capital and enterprise. You have wished it otherwise, and declared that it was a work which the British people as a whole ought to undertake. I at once yielded to your wishes, feeling that it proceeded from a patriotic, noble, and generous spirit. On *your* courage, perseverance, and liberality, the undertaking now entirely depends. I feel the strongest confidence in these qualities of the British people, and I am sure that they will repose confidence in themselves—confidence that they will honourably sustain the contest of emulation, and that they will nobly carry out their proffered hospitality to their foreign competitors.

We, Her Majesty's Commissioners, are quite alive to the innumerable difficulties which we shall have to overcome in carrying out the scheme; but, having confidence in you and in our own zeal and perseverance, at least, we require only *your confidence in us* to make us contemplate the result without any apprehension.

# Punch

## PUNCH'S OWN REPORT OF THE OPENING OF THE GREAT EXHIBITION

*Founded in 1841, Punch—the popular journal of social, political, and cultural satire—*
*amused its readers with articles by William Makepeace Thackeray, Mark Lemon, and*
*Douglas Jerrold, and the cartoons of John Tenniel, John Leech, Charles Keene, and George*
*du Maurier. Especially in its early decades, Punch attacked the pretensions of aristocrats,*
*royalty, and political parties A favorite target of Punch's lampoons was PRINCE ALBERT. But*
*Punch, although initially skeptical, quickly became a convert to the Prince's grand plans*
*for the Great Exhibition of 1851 a nineteenth-century version of a world's fair, display-*
*ing the art and manufactures of England, her Empire, and the world. It was Punch in fact*
*that dubbed architect John Paxton's massive building the "Crystal Palace." The gentle irony*
*in its coverage of the May 1, 1851 opening of the Great Exhibition suggests that Mr. Punch,*
*like many early skeptics, was carried away by nationalistic euphoria surrounding the event.*

RM

MAY HAS OFTEN BELIED ITS character for merriment by occasional fits of gloom, and by appearing in the woolly paletôt or over-coat of fleecy clouds; but the first of May in the present year has sufficed to retrieve all former faults of that frequently fickle month, and render it for ever famous in the annals of glorious sunshine and cheerfulness. We had intended to get up with the lark, but there being no local lark to regulate our movements, we accepted as a substitute for the early bird, those well known London black-birds, the sweeps, whose cry was the signal for our rising.

Everything seemed auspicious. Even our razor was in excellent temper, which was fortunate, for had it been obstinate, we should have had a terribly close shave to join in sufficient time the line of equipages, which already, before eight o'clock, extended in one rank—a rank in which no aristocratic distinctions were observed—from the doors of the Crystal Palace to the very centre of the Metropolis. The proudest equipage of the peer was obliged to fall in behind the humblest fly or the ugliest Hansom; there being no privileged order, but the order of arrival. The student in armorial bearings would have had a miscellaneous feast in examining the panels of the various vehicles, which combined all the brilliant blazonry of BURKE, with all the mysterious heraldry of the cab-stand.

During the time of waiting for the opening of the doors, good-humour kept up the spirits of all, except some of those who, being driven impatiently by the side of the line, found themselves obliged to retrace their steps on arriving at the park gates, and take their places at the back of the whole string, which had lengthened a mile or so since they had foolishly quitted it. The contents—or rather the non-contents—of the vehicles in this dilemma afforded amusement to those who had fallen in at once with the regulations, and, as the former were seen returning a good deal farther back than the place they came from, it was clear that the occupants of each carriage were throwing, sometimes upon each other, but more often on the unfortunate driver, the blame of their failure. Nevertheless, the arrangements were so excellent, and every foot of ground was so well apportioned, that scarcely any one had room for complaint, except, perhaps, when a passing coal-waggon made every one wish the Wall's-end at the World's End, or when the carts of a suburban milk company, returning from the morning supply of their customers, intruded with their "pure milk" among many who thought themselves for the moment the cream of elegance, and turned somewhat sour at the contact.

The doors were at length reached, and the crowd waiting the arrival of HER MAJESTY, furnished an exhibition of various kinds of industry not represented within the doors of the Crystal Palace. Every available place for catching a sight of the procession had been taken possession of in every available manner. Our friends, the Bedouins, who, according to the Astleian views of their habits, run about piled on each others' shoulders in pyramids, four or five human stories high, were equalled, if not surpassed, by our native acrobats. Looking at the doubtful security of those forming the capitals of these strangely constructed pillars, we could not help philosophising inwardly on the danger of a high position, even when resting on the shoulders of the people. The trees opposite the principal door seemed to have burst out suddenly into a crop of eager boys, who, in spite of the warnings of the police against the forbidden fruits of juvenile industry, seemed to think every tree a legitimate tree of knowledge, if anything could be learned or seen by climbing it. . . .

With our usual good fortune, we secured a front place; and, indeed, where should *Punch* be, but in the foremost ranks of those desirous of showing loyalty and affection to the Sovereign? Having taken up our quarters, we had leisure, for the first time, to admire the wondrous magnificence—the grandeur enhanced by the simplicity—of MR. PAXTON's building. We will not enlarge upon its merits; for *Punch* disdains to echo the general voice; which, in this instance, is, in fact, the echo of the approval *Punch* himself was pleased to bestow on the first design of the architect. Where were the croakers and detractors who knew the building was unsafe, though it was strong enough to bear the weight of their stupidity and malignity combined?—and where, oh where, were the formidable sparrows which we had been told had got irremediably into the building; but which, if they inhabit any nest at all, must occupy some mare's nest or other, of which, happily, no trace is visible?

At length a cheer without, and a flourish of trumpets within, announce the arrival of the QUEEN—and the PRINCE, who, by the idea of this Exhibition, has given to Royal Consortship a new glory, or, rather, has rendered for ever illustrious, in his own case, a position too often vibrating between the mischievous and the insignificant. PRINCE ALBERT has done a grand service to humanity, and earned imperishable fame for himself by an idea, the greatness of which, instead of becoming less, will appear still greater as it recedes from us. We are as yet too completely face to face with the object to see at once all its grandeur; but it will be more perceptible as we advance, just as the height and extent of the mountain are but partially developed to the traveller who has not yet quitted it.

During the ceremonial, which was of a solemn and imposing nature—and for which we refer to our merely matter-of-fact contemporaries,—it was not surprising that several eyes, including the Royal one, were slightly crystallised in graceful harmony with the Crystal Palace. While the proceedings were going on, the attempt to keep the ladies off the seats was given up as hopeless, and it was a pardonable instance of the weakness of human nature, even in that stern piece of stuff, a metropolitan policeman, that the constable, gradually growing absorbed in the overwhelming interest of the scene, appeared to think that the country would excuse him for attending more to the throbbings of his heart than his ordinary beat, and that England would not be too rigorous in expecting every man—that is to say, every policeman—at such a moment to do his duty. Nevertheless, so admirable were the arrangements, that there was at the time specified really no duty to do.

At the conclusion of the ceremonial, a Chinese, carried away, or rather pushed forward, by his enthusiasm, performed suddenly, before HER MAJESTY, an elaborate salaam, consisting of a sudden act of prostration on his face, and when the individual rose up, the custom at once occurred to us as the cause of the general flatness of feature and particular squareness of nose of that flowery people, who, from their countenance, appear to have been sown broad-cast over a large tract of country.

Beyond comparison, the most gratifying incident of the day was the promenade of the QUEEN and PRINCE, holding by the hand their two eldest children, through the whole of the lower range of the building. It was a magnificent lesson for foreigners—and especially for the Prussian princes, who cannot stir abroad without an armed escort—to see how securely and confidently a young female Sovereign and her family could walk in the closest possible contact, near enough to be touched by almost everyone, with five-and-twenty thousand people, selected from no class, and requiring only the sum of forty-two shillings as a qualification for the nearest proximity with royalty. Here was a splendid example of that real freedom on the one hand, and perfect security on the other, which are the result of our constitutional monarchy, and which all the despotism and republicanism of the world cannot obtain elsewhere, let them go on as long as they may, executing each other in the name of order, or cutting each other's throats in the name of liberty. It was delightful to see the smiling confidence of the QUEEN, as—leaning on her husband's arm, the father and the mother each holding by the hand one of the royal children—she acknowledged the heartfelt cheerings of the enthusiastic but perfectly orderly multitude.

The only blot, as we thought, upon the whole proceedings, were the unnatural and crab-like movements of one of our wealthiest peers, the MARQUESS OF WESTMINSTER, and his fellow-official, the LORD CHAMBERLAIN, whose part in the pageant consisted of the difficult, but not very dignified, feat of walking backwards, during the progress of the procession. We hope the time is not far distant when, among the other sensible arrangements of the present reign, a wealthy nobleman may be released from the humiliation of having to perform before the Sovereign and the public a series of awkward evolutions, which not all the skill of the posture-master can redeem from the absurdity attaching to the contortions of the mountebank.

Not the least interesting incident of the day was a little bit of byplay between the DUKE OF WELLINGTON and the MARQUESS OF ANGLESEY,[1] who, when preparing to form the procession, engaged in a slight contest, or rather passage, of arms, one attempting to pass the arm of the other through his own as the privilege due to seniority. The Duke eventually succeeded in causing the Marquess to surrender his arm, which the latter never did before; and the two veterans, who had been often side by side on the field of battle, proceeded side by side among the triumphs of the peaceful contest of Industry.

We have left ourselves no space, had our emotions left us inclination, to notice all, or any, of the wonders of the Great Exhibition, to which we hope often to go, for the profit, not of ourselves alone, but of the public, whom we mean to make our constant companions in our numerous anticipated visits. We could not help, however, being struck by the glaring contrast between large pretension and little performance, as exemplified in the dreary and empty aspect of the large space claimed by and allotted to America. An enormous banner betokened the whole of the east end as devoted to the United States; but what was our astonishment, on arriving there, to find that their contribution to the world's industry consists as yet of a few wine-glasses, a square or two of soap, and a pair of salt-cellars! For a calculating people, our friends the Americans are thus far terribly out in their calculations.

.

1. Arthur Wellesley, Duke of Wellington (1769–1852), national hero, victor at Waterloo, and former prime minister; Henry Paget, Marquess of Anglesey (1768–1854).

# George Eliot

## SILLY NOVELS BY LADY NOVELISTS

*George Eliot is best known for her psychologically astute, socially complex, realist novels. But she began her writing career as, first, a translator of German philosophical critiques of traditional Christianity and, second, a contributor to and behind-the-scenes editor of the* Westminster Review. *Her wide reading and intellectual rigor served her well in her career as both journalist and novelist, while shaping her critical responses to some of the popular fiction of her day.* "Silly Novels by Lady Novelists," *written less than two weeks before Eliot began the first in a series of tales she titled* Scenes of Clerical Life, *objects to the improbabilities that characterize didactic novels or "romances," written for circulating libraries such as Mudie's. Eliot's endorsement of realism as a characteristic of serious fiction has been compared to the aesthetic theories of G. H. Lewes, whose relationship with Eliot began in the early 1850s. But, while Lewes certainly influenced Eliot's ideas about fiction, she had formed her own opinions as early as 1839, when she complained to a friend that* "Religious novels . . . are a sort of Centaur or Mermaid and like other monsters that we do not know how to class should be destroyed for the public good as soon as born."[1]

---

1. Letter to Maria Lewis, March 16, 1839, in *The George Eliot Letters*, vol. 1, ed. Gordon S. Haight (New Haven: Yale University Press, 1954), p. 23.

*Eliot's essay in the* Westminster Review *appeared at the end of a series of articles in which she examined over one hundred and fifty books. Clearly, Eliot's remarks in "Silly Novels" were grounded in a familiarity with a range of contemporary fiction. She does not condemn women for writing novels, but she assumes that the work of both sexes should be judged by the same aesthetic criteria, an expectation not generally held by writers or reviewers.*

LMF

SILLY NOVELS BY LADY NOVELISTS are a genus with many species, determined by the particular quality of silliness that predominates in them—the frothy, the prosy, the pious, or the pedantic. But it is a mixture of all these—a composite order of feminine fatuity, that produces the largest class of such novels, which we shall distinguish as the *mind-and-millinery* species. The heroine is usually an heiress, probably a peeress in her own right, with perhaps a vicious baronet, an amiable duke, and an irresistible younger son of a marquis as lovers in the foreground, a clergyman and a poet sighing for her in the middle distance, and a crowd of undefined adorers dimly indicated beyond. Her eyes and her wit are both dazzling; her nose and her morals are alike free from any tendency to irregularity; she has a superb *contralto* and a superb intellect; she is perfectly well-dressed and perfectly religious; she dances like a sylph, and reads the Bible in the original tongues. Or it may be that the heroine is not an heiress—that rank and wealth are the only things in which she is deficient; but she infallibly gets into high society, she has the triumph of refusing many matches and securing the best, and she wears some family jewels or other as a sort of crown of righteousness at the end. Rakish men either bite their lips in impotent confusion at her repartees, or are touched to penitence by her reproofs, which, on appropriate occasions, rise to a lofty strain of rhetoric; indeed, there is a general propensity in her to make speeches, and to rhapsodize at some length when she retires to her bedroom. In her recorded conversations she is amazingly eloquent, and in her unrecorded conversations, amazingly witty. She is understood to have a depth of insight that looks through and through the shallow theories of philosophers, and her superior instincts are a sort of dial by which men have only to set their clocks and watches, and all will go well. The men play a very subordinate part by her side. You are consoled now and then by a hint that they have affairs, which keeps you in mind that the working-day business of the world is somehow being carried on, but ostensibly the final cause of their existence is that they may accompany the heroine on her "starring" expedition through life. They see her at a ball, and are dazzled; at a flower-show, and they are fascinated; on a riding excursion, and they are witched by her noble horsemanship; at church, and they are awed by the sweet solemnity of her demeanour. She is the ideal woman in feelings, faculties, and flounces. For all this, she as often as not marries the wrong person to begin with, and she suffers terribly from the plots and intrigues of the vicious baronet; but even death has a soft place in his heart for such a paragon, and remedies all mistakes for her just at the right moment. The vicious baronet is sure to be killed in a duel, and the tedious husband dies in his bed requesting his wife, as a particular favour to him, to marry the man she loves best, and having already dispatched a note to the lover informing him of the comfortable arrangement. Before matters arrive at this desirable issue our feelings are tried by seeing the noble, lovely, and gifted heroine pass through many *mauvais moments*,[2] but we have the satisfaction of knowing that her sorrows are wept into embroidered pocket-handkerchiefs, that her fainting form reclines on the very best upholstery, and that whatever vicissitudes she may undergo, from being dashed out of her carriage to having her head shaved in a fever, she comes out of them all with a complexion more blooming and locks more redundant than ever.

We may remark, by the way, that we have been relieved from a serious scruple by discovering that silly novels by lady novelists rarely introduce us into any other than very lofty and fashionable society. We had imagined that destitute women turned novelists, as they turned governesses, because they had no other "lady-like" means of getting their bread. On this supposition, vacillating syntax and improbable incident had a certain pathos for us, like the extremely supererogatory pincushions and ill-devised nightcaps that are offered for sale by a blind man. We felt the commodity to be a nuisance, but we were glad to think that the money went to relieve the necessitous, and we pictured to ourselves lonely women struggling for a maintenance, or wives and daughters devoting themselves to the production of "copy" out of pure heroism,—perhaps to pay their husband's debts, or to purchase luxuries for a sick father. Under these impressions we shrank from criticising a lady's novel: her English might be faulty, but, we said to ourselves, her motives are irreproachable; her imagination may be uninventive, but her patience is untiring. Empty writing was excused by an empty stomach, and twaddle was consecrated by tears. But no! This theory of ours, like many other pretty theories, has had to give way before observation. Women's silly novels, we are now convinced, are written under totally different circumstances. The fair writers have evidently never talked to a tradesman except from a carriage window; they have no notion of the working-classes except as "dependents;" they think five hundred a-year a miserable pittance; Belgravia and "baronial halls" are their primary truths; and they have no idea of feeling interest in any man who is not at least a great landed proprietor, if not a prime minister. It is clear that they write in elegant boudoirs, with violet-coloured ink and a ruby pen; that they must be entirely indifferent to publishers' accounts, and inexperienced in every form of poverty except poverty of brains. It is true that we are constantly struck with the want of verisimilitude in their representations of the high society in which they seem to live; but then they betray no closer acquaintance with any other form of life. If their peers and peeresses are improbable, their literary men, tradespeople, and cottagers are impossible; and their intellect seems to have the peculiar impartiality of reproducing both what they *have* seen and heard, and what they have *not* seen and heard, with equal unfaithfulness. . . .

Writers of the mind-and-millinery school are remarkably unanimous in their choice of diction. In their novels, there is usually a lady or gentleman who is more or less of a upas tree[3]: the lover has a manly breast; minds are redolent of various things; hearts are hollow; events are utilized; friends are consigned to the tomb; infancy is an engaging period; the sun is a luminary that goes to his western couch, or gathers the rain-drops into his refulgent bosom; life is a melancholy boon; Albion and Scotia are conversational

2. Bad moments.
3. A tall tree with a poisonous sap.

epithets. There is a striking resemblance, too, in the character of their moral comments, such, for instance, as that "It is a fact, no less true than melancholy, that all people, more or less, richer or poorer, are swayed by bad example;" that "Books, however trivial, contain some subjects from which useful information may be drawn;" that "Vice can too often borrow the language of virtue;" that "Merit and nobility of nature must exist, to be accepted, for clamour and pretension cannot impose upon those too well read in human nature to be easily deceived;" and that, "In order to forgive, we must have been injured." There is, doubtless, a class of readers to whom these remarks appear peculiarly pointed and pungent; for we often find them doubly and trebly scored with the pencil, and delicate hands giving in their determined adhesion to these hardy novelties by a distinct *très vrai*,[4] emphasized by many notes of exclamation. The colloquial style of these novels is often marked by much ingenious inversion, and a careful avoidance of such cheap phraseology as can be heard every day. Angry young gentlemen exclaim—" 'Tis ever thus, methinks;" and in the half-hour before dinner a young lady informs her next neighbour that the first day she read Shakspeare she "stole away into the park, and beneath the shadow of the greenwood tree, devoured with rapture the inspired page of the great magician." But the most remarkable efforts of the mind-and-millinery writers lie in their philosophic reflections. The authoress of "Laura Gay,"[5] for example, having married her hero and heroine, improves the event by observing that "if those sceptics, whose eyes have so long gazed on matter that they can no longer see aught else in man, could once enter with heart and soul into such bliss as this, they would come to say that the soul of man and the polypus are not of common origin, or of the same texture." Lady novelists, it appears, can see something else besides matter; they are not limited to phenomena, but can relieve their eyesight by occasional glimpses of the *noumenon*, and are, therefore, naturally better able than any one else to confound sceptics, even of that remarkable, but to us unknown school, which maintains that the soul of man is of the same texture as the polypus.

The most pitiable of all silly novels by lady novelists are what we may call the *oracular* species—novels intended to expound the writer's religious, philosophical, or moral theories. There seems to be a notion abroad among women, rather akin to the superstition that the speech and actions of idiots are inspired, and that the human being most entirely exhausted of common sense is the fittest vehicle of revelation. To judge from their writings, there are certain ladies who think that an amazing ignorance, both of science and of life, is the best possible qualification for forming an opinion on the knottiest moral and speculative questions. Apparently, their recipe for solving all such difficulties is something like this:—Take a woman's head, stuff it with a smattering of philosophy and literature chopped small, and with false notions of society baked hard, let it hang over a desk a few hours every day, and serve up hot in feeble English, when not required. You will rarely meet with a lady novelist of the oracular class who is diffident of her ability to decide on theological questions,—who has any suspicion that she is not capable of discriminating with the nicest accuracy between the good and evil in all church parties,—who does not see precisely how it is that men have gone wrong hitherto,—and pity philosophers in general that they have not had the opportunity of consulting her. Great writers, who have modestly contented themselves with putting their experience into fiction, and have thought it quite a sufficient task to exhibit men and things as they are, she sighs over as deplorably deficient in the application of their powers. "They have solved no great questions"—and she is ready to remedy their omission by setting before you a complete theory of life and manual of divinity, in a love story, where ladies and gentlemen of good family go through genteel vicissitudes, to the utter confusion of Deists, Puseyites, and ultra-Protestants,[6] and to the perfect establishment of that particular view of Christianity which either condenses itself into a sentence of small caps, or explodes into a cluster of stars on the three hundred and thirtieth page. It is true, the ladies and gentlemen will probably seem to you remarkably little like any you have had the fortune or misfortune to meet with, for, as a general rule, the ability of a lady novelist to describe actual life and her fellow-men, is in inverse proportion to her confident eloquence about God and the other world, and the means by which she usually chooses to conduct you to true ideas of the invisible is a totally false picture of the visible. . . .

The epithet "silly" may seem impertinent, applied to a novel which indicates so much reading and intellectual activity as "The Enigma;"[7] but we use this epithet advisedly. If, as the world has long agreed, a very great amount of instruction will not make a wise man, still less will a very mediocre amount of instruction make a wise woman. And the most mischievous form of feminine silliness is the literary form, because it tends to confirm the popular prejudice against the more solid education of women. When men see girls wasting their time in consultations about bonnets and ball dresses, and in giggling or sentimental love-confidences, or middle-aged women mismanaging their children, and solacing themselves with acrid gossip, they can hardly help saying, "For Heaven's sake, let girls be better educated; let them have some better objects of thought—some more solid occupations." But after a few hours' conversation with an oracular literary woman, or a few hours' reading of her books, they are likely enough to say, "After all, when a woman gets some knowledge, see what use she makes of it! Her knowledge remains acquisition, instead of passing into culture; instead of being subdued into modesty and simplicity by a larger acquaintance with thought and fact, she has a feverish consciousness of her attainments; she keeps a sort of mental pocket-mirror, and is continually looking in it at her own 'intellectuality;' she spoils the taste of one's muffin by questions of metaphysics; 'puts down' men at a dinner table with her superior information; and seizes the opportunity of a *soirée* to catechise us on the vital question of the relation between mind and matter. And then, look at her writings! She mistakes vagueness for depth, bombast for eloquence, and affectation for originality; she struts on one page, rolls her eyes on another, grimaces in a third, and is hysterical in a fourth. She may have read many writings of great men, and a few writings of great women; but she is as unable to discern the difference between

6. Deists were freethinkers who sought to maintain a belief in God while making it compatible with the rationalism of the Enlightenment. Puseyites were followers of Dr. Edward Pusey, English theologian and one of the leaders of the Oxford Movement.
7. *The Enigma: A Leaf from the Archives of the Wolchorley House*, by "an old chronicler" (1856).

her own style and theirs as a Yorkshireman is to discern the difference between his own English and a Londoner's: rodomontade is the native accent of her intellect. No—the average nature of women is too shallow and feeble a soil to bear much tillage; it is only fit for the very lightest crops."

It is true that the men who come to such a decision on such very superficial and imperfect observation may not be among the wisest in the world; but we have not now to contest their opinion—we are only pointing out how it is unconsciously encouraged by many women who have volunteered themselves as representatives of the feminine intellect. We do not believe that a man was ever strengthened in such an opinion by associating with a woman of true culture, whose mind had absorbed her knowledge instead of being absorbed by it. A really cultured woman, like a really cultured man, is all the simpler and the less obtrusive for her knowledge; it has made her see herself and her opinions in something like just proportions; she does not make it a pedestal from which she flatters herself that she commands a complete view of men and things, but makes it a point of observation from which to form a right estimate of herself. She neither spouts poetry nor quotes Cicero on slight provocation; not because she thinks that a sacrifice must be made to the prejudices of men, but because that mode of exhibiting her memory and Latinity does not present itself to her as edifying or graceful. She does not write books to confound philosophers, perhaps because she is able to write books that delight them. In conversation she is the least formidable of women, because she understands you, without wanting to make you aware that you *can't* understand her. She does not give you information, which is the raw material of culture,—she gives you sympathy, which is its subtlest essence. . . .

"Be not a baker if your head be made of butter," says a homely proverb, which, being interpreted, may mean, let no woman rush into print who is not prepared for the consequences. We are aware that our remarks are in a very different tone from that of the reviewers who, with a perennial recurrence of precisely similar emotions, only paralleled, we imagine, in the experience of monthly nurses, tell one lady novelist after another that they "hail" her productions "with delight." We are aware that the ladies at whom our criticism is pointed are accustomed to be told, in the choicest phraseology of puffery, that their pictures of life are brilliant, their characters well drawn, their style fascinating, and their sentiments lofty. But if they are inclined to resent our plainness of speech, we ask them to reflect for a moment on the chary praise, and often captious blame, which their panegyrists give to writers whose works are on the way to become classics. No sooner does a woman show that she has genius or effective talent, than she receives the tribute of being moderately praised and severely criticised. By a peculiar thermometric adjustment, when a woman's talent is at zero, journalistic approbation is at the boiling pitch; when she attains mediocrity, it is already at no more than summer heat; and if ever she reaches excellence, critical enthusiasm drops to the freezing point. Harriet Martineau, Currer Bell, and Mrs. Gaskell have been treated as cavalierly as if they had been men. And every critic who forms a high estimate of the share women may ultimately take in literature, will, on principle, abstain from any exceptional indulgence towards the productions of literary women. For it must be plain to every one who looks impartially and extensively into feminine literature, that its greatest deficiencies are due hardly more to the want of intellectual power than to the want of those moral qualities that contribute to literary excellence—patient diligence, a sense of the responsibility involved in publication, and an appreciation of the sacredness of the writer's art. In the majority of women's books you see that kind of facility which springs from the absence of any high standard; that fertility in imbecile combination or feeble imitation which a little self-criticism would check and reduce to barrenness; just as with a total want of musical ear people will sing out of tune, while a degree more melodic sensibility would suffice to render them silent. The foolish vanity of wishing to appear in print, instead of being counterbalanced by any consciousness of the intellectual or moral derogation implied in futile authorship, seems to be encouraged by the extremely false impression that to write *at all* is a proof of superiority in a woman. On this ground, we believe that the average intellect of women is unfairly represented by the mass of feminine literature, and that while the few women who write well are very far above the ordinary intellectual level of their sex, the many women who write ill are very far below it. So that, after all, the severer critics are fulfilling a chivalrous duty in depriving the mere fact of feminine authorship of any false prestige which may give it a delusive attraction, and in recommending women of mediocre faculties—as at least a negative service they can render their sex—to abstain from writing.

The standing apology for women who become writers without any special qualification is, that society shuts them out from other spheres of occupation. Society is a very culpable entity, and has to answer for the manufacture of many unwholesome commodities, from bad pickles to bad poetry. But society, like "matter," and Her Majesty's Government, and other lofty abstractions, has its share of excessive blame as well as excessive praise. Where there is one woman who writes from necessity, we believe there are three women who write from vanity; and, besides, there is something so antiseptic in the mere healthy fact of working for one's bread, that the most trashy and rotten kind of feminine literature is not likely to have been produced under such circumstances. "In all labour there is profit;" but ladies' silly novels, we imagine, are less the result of labour than of busy idleness.

Happily, we are not dependent on argument to prove that Fiction is a department of literature in which women can, after their kind, fully equal men. A cluster of great names, both living and dead, rush to our memories in evidence that women can produce novels not only fine, but among the very finest;—novels, too, that have a precious speciality, lying quite apart from masculine aptitudes and experience. No educational restrictions can shut women out from the materials of fiction, and there is no species of art which is so free from rigid requirements. Like crystalline masses, it may take any form, and yet be beautiful; we have only to pour in the right elements—genuine observation, humour, and passion. But it is precisely this absence of rigid requirement which constitutes the fatal seduction of novel-writing to incompetent women. Ladies are not wont to be very grossly deceived as to their power of playing on the piano; here certain positive difficulties of execution have to be conquered, and incompetence inevitably breaks down. Every art which has its absolute *technique* is, to a certain extent, guarded from the intru-

sions of mere left-handed imbecility. But in novel-writing there are no barriers for incapacity to stumble against, no external criteria to prevent a writer from mistaking foolish
facility for mastery. And so we have again and again the old story of La Fontaine's ass, who
puts his nose to the flute, and, finding that he elicits some sound, exclaims, "Moi, aussi,
je joue de la flute;"[8]—a fable which we commend, at parting, to the consideration of any
feminine reader who is in danger of adding to the number of "silly novels by lady novelists."

8. "Me, too, I play the flute."

# Herbert Spencer

## PROGRESS: ITS LAW AND CAUSE

In a time of increasing disciplinary specialization, Herbert Spencer was a generalist, a philosopher-scientist of encyclopedic interests. He attempted to unify the physical sciences and the nascent social sciences under the mantle of developmental theory. He extended the hypothesis of progressive evolution from geology and biology to sociology. Spencer's early essay "Progress: Its Law and Cause," published in the Westminster Review in April 1857, makes the argument that was to inform his later work: organic progress consists in the change, through continuous differentiation, from simple to complex forms, from homogeneity to heterogeneity, and, further, "the law of organic progress is the law of all progress." His all-encompassing hypothesis provided a rationalization for a hierarchical division of labor, laissez-faire economics, eugenics, and a racial theory that differentiated the lower "savage" from the civilized European. It was Spencer, not Charles Darwin, who coined the phrase "survival of the fittest." If his science, his social analysis, and his grand theory have been largely discredited, his attempt to synthesize knowledge—aided by his lucid prose—helped to popularize science and contributed to its growing authority in the second half of the century. RM

THE CURRENT CONCEPTION OF PROGRESS is somewhat shifting and indefinite. Sometimes it comprehends little more than simple growth—as of a nation in the number of its members and the extent of territory over which it has spread. Sometimes it has reference to quantity of material products—as when the advance of agriculture and manufactures is the topic. Sometimes the superior quality of these products is contemplated; and sometimes the new or improved appliances by which they are produced. When, again, we speak of moral or intellectual progress, we refer to the state of the individual or people exhibiting it; whilst, when the progress of Knowledge, of Science, of Art, is commented upon, we have in view certain abstract results of human thought and action. Not only, however, is the current conception of Progress more or less vague, but it is in great measure erroneous. It takes in not so much the reality of Progress as its accompaniments—not so much the substance as the shadow. That progress in intelligence which takes place during the evolution of the child into the man, or the savage into the philosopher, is commonly regarded as consisting in the greater number of facts known and laws understood: whereas the actual progress consists in those internal modifications of which this increased knowledge is the expression. Social progress is supposed to consist in the produce of a greater quantity and variety of the articles required for the satisfaction of men's wants; in the increasing security of person and property; in the widening freedom of action enjoyed: whereas, rightly understood, social progress consists in those changes of structure in the social organism which have entailed these consequences. The current conception is a teleological one. The phenomena are contemplated solely as bearing on human happiness. Only those changes are held to constitute progress which directly or indirectly tend to heighten human happiness. And they are thought to constitute progress simply *because* they tend to heighten human happiness. But rightly to understand Progress, we must inquire what is the nature of these changes, considered apart from our interests. Ceasing, for example, to regard the successive geological modifications that have taken place in the Earth, as modifications that have gradually fitted it for the habitation of Man, and as *therefore* a geological progress, we must seek to determine the character common to these modifications—the law to which they all conform. And similarly in every other case. Leaving out of sight concomitants and beneficial consequences, let us ask what Progress is in itself.

In respect to that progress which individual organisms display in the course of their evolution, this question has been answered by the Germans. The investigations of Wolff, Goethe, and Von Baer,[1] have established the truth that the series of changes gone through during the development of a seed into a tree, or an ovum into an animal, constitute an advance from homogeneity of structure to heterogeneity of structure. In its primary stage, every germ consists of a substance that is uniform throughout, both in texture and chemical composition. The first step in its development is the appearance of a difference between two parts of this substance; or, as the phenomenon is described in physiological language—a differentiation. Each of these differentiated divisions presently begins itself to exhibit some contrast of parts; and by and bye these secondary differentiations become

---

1. Kaspar Friederich Wolff (1734–94), physiologist; Johann Wolfgang von Goethe (1749–1832), poet and scientist; Karl Ernst von Baer (1792–1876), embryologist.

as definite as the original one. This process is continuously repeated—is simultaneously going on in all parts of the growing embryo; and by endless multiplication of these differentiations there is ultimately produced that complex combination of tissues and organs constituting the adult animal or plant. This is the course of evolution followed by all organisms whatever. It is settled beyond dispute that organic progress consists in a change from the homogeneous to the heterogeneous.

Now, we propose in the first place to show, that this law of organic progress is the law of all progress. Whether it be in the development of the Earth, in the development of Life upon its surface, in the development of Society, of Government, of Manufactures, of Commerce, of Language, Literature, Science, Art, this same evolution of the simple into the complex, through a process of continuous differentiation, holds throughout. From the earliest traceable cosmical changes down to the latest results of civilization, we shall find that the transformation of the homogeneous into the heterogeneous, is that in which Progress essentially consists. . . .

Whether an advance from the homogeneous to the heterogeneous is or is not displayed in the biological history of the globe, it is clearly enough displayed in the progress of the latest and most heterogeneous creature—Man. It is alike true that, during the period in which the Earth has been peopled, the human organism has become more heterogeneous among the civilized divisions of the species; and that the species, as a whole, has been growing more heterogeneous in virtue of the multiplication of races and the differentiation of these races from each other. In proof of the first of these positions, we may cite the fact that, in the relative development of the limbs, the civilized man departs more widely from the general type of the placental mammalia than do the lower human races. Whilst often possessing well-developed body and arms, the Papuan has extremely small legs: reminding us in this respect of the quadrumana, in which there is no great contrast in size between the hind and fore limbs. But in the European, the greater length and massiveness of the legs has become very marked—the fore and hind limbs are relatively more heterogeneous. Again, in the greater ratio which the cranial bones bear to the facial bones, we may see the same truth. Among the vertebrata in general, progress is marked by an increasing heterogeneity in the vertebral column, and more especially in the vertebræ constituting the skull: the higher forms being distinguished by the relatively larger size of the bones which cover the brain, and the relatively smaller size of those which form the jaws, &c. Now, this characteristic, which is more marked in Man than in any other creature, is more marked in the European than in the savage. Judging from the greater extent and variety of faculty he exhibits, we may infer that the civilized man has also a more complex or heterogeneous nervous system than the uncivilized man: and indeed the fact is in part visible in the increased ratio which his cerebrum bears to the subjacent ganglia. If further elucidation be needed, we may find it in every nursery. The infant European has sundry marked points of resemblance to the lower human races; as in the flatness of the alæ of the nose, the depression of its bridge, the divergence and forward opening of the nostrils, the form of the lips, the absence of a frontal sinus, the width between the eyes, the smallness of the legs. Now, as the developmental process by which these characteristics are changed into those of the adult European, in a continuation of that change from the homogeneous to the heterogeneous exhibited during the previous evolution of the embryo, which every physiologist will admit; it follows that the parallel developmental process by which the like characteristics of the barbarous races have been changed into those of the civilized races, has also been a continuation of the change from the homogeneous to the heterogeneous. The truth of the second position—that Mankind, as a whole, have become more heterogeneous—is so obvious as scarcely to need illustration. Every work on Ethnology, by its divisions and subdivisions of races, bears testimony to it. Even were we to admit the hypothesis that Mankind originated from several separate stocks, it would still remain true, that as, from each of these stocks, there have sprung many now widely different tribes, which are proved by philological evidence to have had a common origin, the race as a whole is far less homogeneous than it was at first. Add to which, that we have, in the Anglo-Americans, an example of a new variety arising within these few generations; and that, if we may trust to the descriptions of observers, we are likely soon to have another such example in Australia.

On passing from Humanity under its individual form, to Humanity as socially embodied, we find the general law still more variously exemplified. The change from the homogeneous to the heterogeneous is displayed equally in the evolution of civilization as a whole, and in the progress of every tribe or nation; and is still going on with increasing rapidity. As we see in still existing barbarous tribes, society in its first and lowest form is a homogeneous aggregation of individuals having like powers and performing like functions: the only differentiation of function being that which accompanies difference of sex. Every man is warrior, hunter, fisherman, tool-maker, builder; every woman performs the same drudgeries; every family is self-sufficing, and, save for purposes of aggression and defence, might as well live apart from the rest. Very early, however, in the process of social evolution, we find an incipient differentiation between the governing and the governed. Some kind of chieftainship seems almost co-ordinate with the first advance from the state of separate wandering families to that of a nomadic tribe. The authority of the strongest makes itself felt among a body of savages as in a herd of animals, or a posse of schoolboys. At first, however, it is indefinite, uncertain,—is shared by others of scarcely inferior power, and is unaccompanied by any difference in occupation or style of living: the first ruler kills his own game, makes his own weapons, builds his own hut, and, economically considered, does not differ from others of his tribe. Gradually, as the tribe progresses, the contrast between the governing and the governed grows more marked. Supreme power becomes hereditary in one family; the head of that family ceasing to provide for his own wants, is served by others, and he begins to assume the sole office of ruling. . . .

. . . In the course of ages, there arises, as among ourselves, a highly complex political organization of monarch, ministers, lords and commons, with their subordinate administrative departments, courts of justice, revenue offices, &c., supplemented in the provinces by municipal governments, county governments, parish or union governments—all of them more or less elaborated. By its side there grows up a highly complex religious organization, with its various grades of officials, from archbishops down to sextons, its colleges, convocations, ecclesiastical courts, &c.; to all which must be added the ever-multiplying independent sects, each with its general and local authorities. And at the same time there is developed a highly complex aggregation of customs, manners, and temporary fashions, enforced by society at large, and serving to control those minor transactions between man and man which are not regulated by civil and religious law. Moreover it is to be observed that this ever-increasing heterogeneity in the governmental appliances of each nation, has been accompanied by an increasing heterogeneity in the governmental appliances of different nations; all of which are more or less unlike in their political systems and legislation, in their creeds and religious institutions, in their customs and ceremonial usages.

Simultaneously there has been going on a second differentiation of a still more familiar kind; that, namely, by which the mass of the community has become segregated into distinct classes and orders of workers. While the governing part has been undergoing the complex development above described, the governed part has been undergoing an equally complex development, which has resulted in that minute division of labour characterizing advanced nations. It is needless to trace out this progress from its first stages, up through the caste divisions of the East and the incorporated guilds of Europe, to the elaborate producing and distributing organization existing among ourselves. Political economists have made familiar to all, the evolution which, beginning with a tribe whose members severally perform the same actions each for himself, ends with a civilized community whose members severally perform different actions for each other; and they have further explained the evolution through which the solitary producer of any one commodity, is transformed into a combination of producers, who, united under a master, take separate parts in the manufacture of such commodity. But there are yet other and higher phases of this advance from the homogeneous to the heterogeneous in the industrial structure of the social organism. Long after considerable progress had been made in the division of labour among different classes of workers, there is still little or no division of labour among the widely separated parts of the community: the nation continues comparatively homogeneous in the respect that in each district the same occupations are pursued. But when roads and other means of transit become numerous and good, the different districts begin to assume different functions, and to become mutually dependent. The calico manufacture locates itself in this county, the woollen-cloth manufacture in that; silks are produced here, lace there; stockings in one place, shoes in another; pottery, hardware, cutlery, come to have their special towns: and ultimately every locality becomes more or less distinguished from the rest by the leading occupation carried on in it. Nay, more, this subdivision of functions shows itself not only among the different parts of the same nation, but among different nations. That exchange of commodities which free-trade promises so greatly to increase will ultimately have the effect of specializing, in a greater or less degree, the industry of each people. So that beginning with a barbarous tribe, almost if not quite homogeneous in the functions of its members, the progress has been, and still is, towards an economic aggregation of the whole human race, growing ever more heterogeneous in respect to the separate functions assumed by separate nations, the separate functions assumed by the local sections of each nation, the separate functions assumed by the many kinds of makers and traders in each town, and the separate functions assumed by the workers united in producing each commodity. . . .

And now, from this uniformity of procedure, may we not infer some fundamental necessity whence it results? May we not rationally seek for some all-pervading principle which determines this all-pervading process of things? Does not the universality of the *law* imply a universal *cause*?

That we can fathom such cause, noumenally considered, is not to be supposed. To do this would be to solve that ultimate mystery which must ever transcend human intelligence. But it still may be possible for us to reduce the law of all Progress, above established, from the condition of an empirical generalization, to the condition of a rational generalization. Just as it was possible to interpret Kepler's laws[2] as necessary consequences of the law of gravitation; so it may be possible to interpret this law of Progress, in its multiform manifestations, as the necessary consequence of some similarly universal principle. As gravitation was assignable as the *cause* of each of the groups of phenomena which Kepler formulated; so may some equally simple attribute of things be assignable as the cause of each of the groups of phenomena formulated in the foregoing pages. We may be able to affiliate all these varied and complex evolutions of the homogeneous into the heterogeneous, upon certain simple facts of immediate experience, which, in virtue of endless repetition, we regard as necessary.

The probability of a common cause, and the possibility of formulating it, being granted, it will be well, before going further, to consider what must be the general characteristics of such cause, and in what direction we ought to look for it. We can with certainty predict that it has a high degree of generality; seeing that it is common to such infinitely varied phenomena: just in proportion to the universality of its application must be the abstractness of its character. We need not expect to see in it an obvious solution of this or that form of Progress; because it equally refers to forms of Progress bearing little apparent resemblance to them: its association with multiform orders of facts, involves its dissociation from any particular order of facts. Being that which determines Progress of every kind—astronomic, geologic, organic, ethnologic, social, economic, artistic, &c.— it must be concerned with some fundamental attribute possessed in common by all these; and must be expressible in terms of this fundamental attribute. The only obvious respect in which all kinds of Progress are alike, is, that they are modes of *change*; and hence, in some characteristic of changes in general, the desired solution will probably be found. We may suspect *à priori* that in some law of change lies the explanation of this universal transformation of the homogeneous into the heterogeneous.

Thus much premised, we pass at once to the statement of the law, which is this:— *Every active force produces more than one change—every cause produces more than one effect* . . . .

Our limits will not allow us to trace out this process in its higher complications; else might we show how the localization of special industries in special parts of a kingdom, as well as the minute subdivision of labour in the production of each commodity, are similarly determined. Or, turning to a somewhat different order of illustrations, we might dwell on the multitudinous changes—material, intellectual, moral,—caused by printing; or the further extensive series of changes wrought by gunpowder. But leaving the inter-

---

2. Johannes Kepler (1571–1630), astronomer, theorist on planetary motion.

mediate phases of social development, let us take a few illustrations from its most recent and its passing phases. To trace out the effects of steam-power in its manifold applications to mining, navigation, and manufactures of all kinds, would carry us into unmanageable detail. Let us confine ourselves to the latest embodiment of steam-power—the locomotive engine. This, as the proximate cause of our railway system, has changed the face of the country, the course of trade, and the habits of the people. Consider, first, the complicated sets of changes that precede the making of every railway—the provisional arrangements, the meetings, the registration, the trial section, the parliamentary survey, the lithographed plans, the books of reference, the local deposits and notices, the application to Parliament, the passing Standing-Orders Committee, the first, second, and third readings: each of which brief heads indicates a multiplicity of transactions, and the development of sundry occupations—as those of engineers, surveyors, lithographers, parliamentary agents, share-brokers; and the creation of sundry others—as those of traffic-takers, reference-takers. Consider, next, the yet more marked changes implied in railway construction—the cuttings, embankings, tunnellings, diversions of roads; the building of bridges and stations; the laying down of ballast, sleepers, and rails; the making of engines, tenders, carriages, and wagons: which processes, acting upon numerous trades, increase the importation of timber, the quarrying of stone, the manufacture of iron, the mining of coal, the burning of bricks; institute a variety of special manufactures weekly advertised in the *Railway Times*; and, finally, open the way to sundry new occupations, as those of drivers, stokers, cleaners, plate-layers, &c., &c. And then consider the changes, more numerous and involved still, which railways in action produce upon the community at large. The organization of every business is more or less modified; facility of communication makes it better to do directly what was before done by proxy; agencies are established where previously they would not have paid; goods are obtained from distant wholesale houses instead of near retail ones; and commodities are used which distance previously rendered inaccessible. Again, the rapidity and small cost of carriage tend to specialize more than ever the industries of different districts—to confine each manufacture to the parts in which, from local advantages, it can be best carried on. Further, the diminished cost of carriage facilitating distribution, equalizes prices, and also, on the average, lowers prices: thus bringing sundry articles within the means of those before unable to buy them, and so increasing their comforts and improving their habits. At the same time the practice of travelling is immensely extended. Classes who never before thought of it, take annual trips to the sea; visit their distant relations; make tours; and so we are benefited in body, feelings, and intellect. Moreover, the more prompt transmission of letters and of news produces further changes—makes the pulse of the nation faster. Yet more, there arises an extensive dissemination of cheap literature through railway book-stalls, and of advertisements in railway carriages: both of them aiding ulterior progress. And all the innumerable changes here briefly indicated are consequent on the invention of the locomotive engine. The social organism has been rendered more heterogeneous in virtue of the various new occupations introduced, and the many old ones further specialized; prices in every place have been altered; each trader has, more or less, modified his way of doing business; and almost every member of the community has been affected in his actions, thoughts, emotions. . . .

A few words must be added on the ontological bearings of our argument. Probably not a few will conclude that here is an attempted solution of the great questions with which Philosophy in all ages has perplexed itself. Let none thus deceive themselves. Only such as know not the scope and the limits of Science can fall into so grave an error. After all that has been said, the ultimate mystery of things remains just as it was. The explanation of that which is explicable, does but bring out into greater clearness the inexplicableness of that which remains behind. However we may succeed in reducing the equation to its lowest terms, we are not thereby enabled to determine the unknown quantity: on the contrary, it only becomes more manifest that the unknown quantity can never be found. We feel ever more and more certain that fearless inquiry tends continually to give a firmer basis to all true Religion. The timid sectarian, alarmed at the progress of knowledge, obliged to abandon one by one the superstitions of his ancestors, and daily finding sundry of his cherished beliefs more and more shaken, secretly fears that all things may some day be explained; and has a corresponding dread of Science: thus evincing the profoundest of all infidelity—the fear lest the truth be bad. On the other hand, the sincere man of science, content fearlessly to follow wherever the evidence leads him, becomes by each new inquiry more profoundly convinced that the Universe is an insoluble problem. Alike in the external and the internal worlds, he sees himself in the midst of perpetual changes, of which he can discover neither the beginning nor the end. If, tracing back the genesis of things, he allows himself to entertain the still unproved hypothesis that all matter once existed in a diffused form, he finds it utterly impossible to conceive how this came to be so; and equally, if he speculates on the future, he can assign no limit to the grand succession of phenomena ever evolving themselves before him. On the other hand, if he looks inward, he perceives that both terminations of the thread of consciousness are beyond his grasp: he cannot remember when or how consciousness commenced, and he cannot examine the consciousness that at any moment exists; for only a state of consciousness that is already past can become the object of thought, and never one which is passing. When, again, he turns from the succession of phenomena, external or internal, to their essential nature, he is equally at fault. Though he may succeed in resolving all properties of objects into manifestations of force, he is not thereby enabled to realize what force is; but finds, on the contrary, that the more he thinks about it, the more he is baffled. Similarly, though analysis of mental actions may finally bring him down to sensations as the original materials out of which all thought is woven, he is none the forwarder; for he cannot in the least comprehend sensation—cannot even conceive how sensation is possible. Inward and outward things he thus discovers to be alike inscrutable in their ultimate genesis and nature. He sees that the Materialist and Spiritualist controversy is a mere war of words; the disputants being equally absurd—each believing he understands that which it is impossible for any human being to understand. In all directions his investigations eventually bring him face to face with the unknowable; and he ever more clearly perceives it to be the unknowable. He learns at once the greatness and the littleness of human intellect—its power in dealing with all that comes within the range of experience; its impotence in dealing with all that transcends experience. He feels, with a vividness which no others can, the utter incomprehensibleness of the simplest fact, considered in itself. He alone truly *sees* that absolute knowledge is impossible. He alone *knows* that under all things there lies an impenetrable mystery.

# Florence Nightingale

1820: Born 12 May in Florence, Italy

1851: Trained at the Institute for Protestant Deaconesses, Kaiserswerth, Germany

1853: Became Superintendent of the Institution for the Care of Sick Gentlewomen, London

1854: Superintendent of Nurses of the English Hospitals in the Crimea

1858: *Notes on Matters Affecting the Health, Efficiency, and Hospital Administration of the British Army*

1860: Established the Nightingale Training School for Nurses; *Notes on Nursing: What It Is and What It Is Not*, *Suggestions for Thought to the Searchers After Truth Among the Artizans of England*

1861: Established the Training School for Midwives at King's College Hospital, London

1910: Died 13 August in London

---

## CASSANDRA

---

The saintly "Lady of the Lamp" to her contemporaries, Florence Nightingale nursed the soldiers of the Crimean War and founded the modern nursing profession. After returning to England, Nightingale capitalized on her reputation and her ability to conduct careful statistical research in order to improve the sanitary conditions of the British Army in England and India, to influence Poor Law and Contagious Diseases legislation, and to provide advice on nursing and hospital architecture.

Until she was in her thirties, Nightingale had been prevented by her family from pursuing a vocation. She expressed her frustration and unhappiness in Suggestions for Thought, *written between 1850 and 1852. Originally intended for working-class readers,* Suggestions for Thought *is a philosophical and theological consideration of oppressive social customs and institutions; the second volume includes an essay on women's lives,* "Cassandra." *An earlier novelistic version of the manuscript contains a character called Cassandra, but in 1859 Nightingale revised her three-volume text, removing all indications that "Cassandra" had been drafted as a novel. She had the manuscript privately printed as a "review edition" and sent six copies to family and friends, including John Stuart* Mill *and Benjamin Jowett. Mill advised publication, but Jowett disliked Nightingale's anger and recommended major revisions. Jettisoning the project without making the suggested changes, she had only a few additional copies printed. Although* Suggestions for Thought *was never read by the Victorian public, "Cassandra" did have an impact on Victorian thinking: some of Mill's arguments in* The Subjection of Women *echo Nightingale's, and he alludes to her work indirectly. "Cassandra" records the voice of a woman who sees the injustice and hypocrisy of Victorian social customs in denying women meaningful work, but Nightingale herself did not subscribe to the Victorian feminist movement. She preferred individual initiative to theorizing. Refusing Mill's request that she serve on the board of the National Society for Women's Suffrage (although she later agreed to join), she argued that, while women should be able to vote, agitation for the franchise would hinder the progress of more important practical reforms.*                                                    LMF

## II

"Yet I would spare no pang,
   Would wish no torture less,
The more that anguish racks,
   The earlier it will bless."[1]

GIVE US BACK OUR SUFFERING, we cry to Heaven in our hearts—suffering rather than indifferentism; for out of nothing comes nothing. But out of suffering may come the cure. Better have pain than paralysis! A hundred struggle and drown in the breakers. One discovers the new world. But rather, ten times rather, die in the surf, heralding the way to that new world, than stand idly on the shore!

Passion, intellect, moral activity—these three have never been satisfied in woman. In this cold and oppressive conventional atmosphere, they cannot be satisfied. To say more on this subject would be to enter into the whole history of society, of the present state of civilization.

Look at that lizard—"It is not hot," he says, "I like it. The atmosphere which enervates you is life to me." The state of society which some complain of makes others happy. Why should these complain to those? *They* do not suffer. *They* would not understand it, any more than that lizard would comprehend the sufferings of a Shetland sheep.

The progressive world is necessarily divided into two classes—those who take the best of what there is and enjoy it—those who wish for something better and try to create it. Without these two classes, the world would be badly off. They are the very conditions of progress, both the one and the other. Were there none who were discontented with what they have, the world would never reach anything better. And, through the other class, which is constantly taking the best of what the first is creating for them, a bal-

1. Quoted partially and inexactly from Emily Brontë's "The Prisoner," published in *Poems by Currer, Ellis, and Acton Bell* (1846).

ance is secured, and that which is conquered is held fast. But with neither class must we quarrel for not possessing the privileges of the other. The laws of the nature of each make it impossible.

Is discontent a privilege?

Yes, it is a privilege to suffer for your race—a privilege not reserved to the Redeemer and the martyrs alone, but one enjoyed by numbers in every age.

The common-place life of thousands; and in that is its only interest—its only merit as a history: viz., that it *is* the type of common sufferings—the story of one who has not the courage to resist nor to submit to the civilization of her time—is this.

Poetry and imagination begin life. A child will fall on its knees on the gravel walk at the sight of a pink hawthorn in full flower, when it is by itself, to praise God for it.

Then comes intellect. It wishes to satisfy the wants which intellect creates for it. But there is a physical, not moral, impossibility of supplying the wants of the intellect in the state of civilization at which we have arrived. The stimulus, the training, the time, are all three wanting to us; or, in other words, the means and inducements are not there.

Look at the poor lives which we lead. It is a wonder that we are so good as we are, not that we are so bad. In looking round we are struck with the power of the organizations we see, not with their want of power. Now and then, it is true, we are conscious that *there* is an inferior organization, but, in general, just the contrary. Mrs. A. has the imagination, the poetry of a Murillo,[2] and has sufficient power of execution to show that she might have had a great deal more. Why is she not a Murillo? From a material difficulty, not a mental one. If she has a knife and fork in her hands during three hours of the day, she cannot have a pencil or brush. Dinner is the great sacred ceremony of this day, the great sacrament. To be absent from dinner is equivalent to being ill. Nothing else will excuse us from it. Bodily incapacity is the only apology valid. If she has a pen and ink in her hands during other three hours, writing answers for the penny post; again, she cannot have her pencil, and so *ad infinitum* through life. People have no type before them in their lives, neither fathers and mothers, nor the children themselves. They look at things in detail. They say, "It is very desirable that A., my daughter, should go to such a party, should know such a lady, should sit by such a person." It is true. But what standard have they before them? of the nature and destination of man? The very words are rejected as pedantic. But might they not, at least, have a type in their minds that such an one might be a discoverer through her intellect, such another through her art, a third through her moral power?

Women often try one branch of intellect after another in their youth, *e.g.*, mathematics. But that, least of all, is compatible with the life of "society." It is impossible to follow up anything systematically. Women often long to enter some man's profession where they would find direction, competition (or rather opportunity of measuring the intellect with others), and, above all, time.

In those wise institutions, mixed as they are with many follies, which will last as long as the human race lasts, because they are adapted to the wants of the human race; those institutions which we call monasteries, and which, embracing much that is contrary to

2. Bartolomé Esteban Murillo (1617–82), Spanish painter.

the laws of nature, are yet better adapted to the union of the life of action and that of thought than any other mode of life with which we are acquainted; in many such, four and a half hours, at least, are daily set aside for thought, rules are given for thought, training and opportunity afforded. Among us, there is *no* time appointed for this purpose, and the difficulty is that, in our social life, we must be always doubtful whether we ought not to be with somebody else or be doing something else.

Are men better off than women in this?

If one calls upon a friend in London and sees her son in the drawing-room, it strikes one as odd to find a young man sitting idling in his mother's drawing-room in the morning. For men, who are seen much in those haunts, there is no end of the epithets we have; "knights of the carpet," "drawing-room heroes," "ladies' men." But suppose we were to see a number of men in the morning sitting round a table in the drawing-room, looking at prints, doing worsted work, and reading little books, how we should laugh! A member of the House of Commons was once known to do worsted work. Of another man was said, "His only fault is that he is too good; he drives out with his mother every day in the carriage, and if he is asked anywhere he answers that he must dine with his mother, but, if she can spare him, he will come in to tea, and he does not come."

Now, why is it more ridiculous for a man than for a woman to do worsted work and drive out every day in the carriage? Why should we laugh if we were to see a parcel of men sitting round a drawing-room table in the morning, and think it all right if they were women?

Is man's time more valuable than woman's? or is the difference between man and woman this, that woman has confessedly nothing to do?

Women are never supposed to have any occupation of sufficient importance *not* to be interrupted, except "suckling their fools;" and women themselves have accepted this, have written books to support it, and have trained themselves so as to consider whatever they do as *not* of such value to the world or to others, but that they can throw it up at the first "claim of social life." They have accustomed themselves to consider intellectual occupation as a merely selfish amusement, which it is their "duty" to give up for every trifler more selfish than themselves.

A young man (who was afterwards useful and known in his day and generation) when busy reading and sent for by his proud mother to shine in some morning visit, came; but, after it was over, he said, "Now, remember, this is not to happen again. I came that you might not think me sulky, but I shall not come again." But for a young woman to send such a message to her mother and sisters, how impertinent it would be! A woman of great administrative powers said that she never undertook anything which she "could not throw by at once, if necessary."

How do we explain then the many cases of women who have distinguished themselves in classics, mathematics, even in politics?

Widowhood, ill-health, or want of bread, these three explanations or excuses are supposed to justify a woman in taking up an occupation. In some cases, no doubt, an indomitable force of character will suffice without any of these three, but such are rare.

But see how society fritters away the intellects of those committed to her charge! It is said that society is necessary to sharpen the intellect. But what do we seek society for? It does sharpen the intellect, because it is a kind of *tour-de-force* to say something at a pinch,—unprepared and uninterested with any subject, to improvise something under difficulties. But what "go we out for to seek?" To take the chance of some one having something to say which we want to hear? or of our finding something to say which *they* want to hear? You have a little to say, but not much. You often make a stipulation with some one else, "Come in ten minutes, for I shall not be able to find enough to spin out longer than that." You are not to talk of anything very interesting, for the essence of society is to prevent any long conversations and all *tête-à-têtes*. "Glissez, n'appuyez pas"[3] is its very motto. The praise of a good "*maîtresse de maison*"[4] consists in this, that she allows no one person to be too much absorbed in, or too long about, a conversation. She always recalls them to their "duty." People do not go into the company of their fellow-creatures for what would seem a very sufficient reason, namely, that they have something to say to them, or something that they want to hear from them; but in the vague hope that they may find something to say.

Then as to solitary opportunities. Women never have half an hour in all their lives (excepting before or after anybody is up in the house) that they can call their own, without fear of offending or of hurting some one. Why do people sit up so late, or, more rarely, get up so early? Not because the day is not long enough, but because they have "no time in the day to themselves."

If we do attempt to do anything in company, what is the system of literary exercise which we pursue? Everybody reads aloud out of their own book or newspaper—or, every five minutes, something is said. And what is it to be "read aloud to?" The most miserable exercise of the human intellect. Or rather, is it any exercise at all? It is like lying on one's back, with one's hands tied and having liquid poured down one's throat. Worse than that, because suffocation would immediately ensue and put a stop to this operation. But no suffocation would stop the other.

So much for the satisfaction of the intellect. Yet for a married woman in society, it is even worse. A married woman was heard to wish that she could break a limb that she might have a little time to herself. Many take advantage of the fear of "infection" to do the same.

It is a thing *so* accepted among women that they have nothing to do, that one woman has not the least scruple in saying to another, "I will come and spend the morning with you." And you would be thought quite surly and absurd, if you were to refuse it on the plea of occupation. Nay, it is thought a mark of amiability and affection, if you are "on such terms" that you can "come in" "any morning you please."

In a country house, if there is a large party of young people, "You will spend the morning with us," they say to the neighbours, "we will drive together in the afternoon," "tomorrow we will make an expedition, and we will spend the evening together." And this is thought friendly, and spending time in a pleasant manner. So women play through life. Yet time is the most valuable of all things. If they had come every morning and afternoon

3. "Touch lightly; don't dwell."
4. Mistress of the house.

and robbed us of half-a-crown we should have had redress from the police. But it is laid down, that our time is of no value. If you offer a morning visit to a professional man, and say, "I will just stay an hour with you, if you will allow me, till so and so comes back to fetch me;" it costs him the earnings of an hour, and therefore he has a right to complain. But women have no right, because it is "*only* their time."

Women have no means given them, whereby they *can* resist the "claims of social life." They are taught from their infancy upwards that it is wrong, ill-tempered, and a misunderstanding of "woman's mission" (with a great M.) if they do not allow themselves *willingly* to be interrupted at all hours. If a woman has once put in a claim to be treated as a man by some work of science or art or literature, which she can *show* as the "fruit of her leisure," then she will be considered justified in *having* leisure (hardly, perhaps, even then). But if not, not. If she has nothing to show, she must resign herself to her fate.

## III

"I like riding about this beautiful place, why don't you? I like walking about the garden, why don't you?" is the common expostulation—as if we were children, whose spirits rise during a fortnight's holidays, who think that they will last for ever—and look neither backwards nor forwards.

Society triumphs over many. They wish to regenerate the world with their institutions, with their moral philosophy, with their love. Then they sink to living from breakfast till dinner, from dinner till tea, with a little worsted work, and to looking forward to nothing but bed.

When shall we see a life full of steady enthusiasm, walking straight to its aim, flying home, as that bird is now, against the wind—with the calmness and the confidence of one who knows the laws of God and can apply them?

What *do* we see? We see great and fine organizations deteriorating. We see girls and boys of seventeen, before whose noble ambitions, heroic dreams, and rich endowments we bow our heads, as before *God incarnate in the flesh*. But, ere they are thirty, they are withered, paralysed, extinguished. "We have forgotten our visions," they say themselves.

The "dreams of youth" have become a proverb. That organizations, early rich, fall far short of their promise has been repeated to satiety. But is it extraordinary that it should be so? For do we ever *utilize* this heroism? Look how it lives upon itself and perishes for lack of food. We do not know what to do with it. We had rather that it should not be there. Often we laugh at it. Always we find it troublesome. Look at the poverty of our life! Can we expect anything else but poor creatures to come out of it? Did Michael Angelo's genius fail, did Pascal's die in its bud, did Sir Isaac Newton become a commonplace sort of man? In two of these cases the knife wore out the sheath. But the knife itself did not become rusty, till the body was dead or infirm.

Why cannot we *make use* of the noble rising heroisms of our own day, instead of leaving them to rust?

They have nothing to do.

Are they to be employed in sitting in the drawing-room, saying words which may as well not be said, which could be said as well if *they* were not there?

Women often strive to live by intellect. The clear, brilliant, sharp radiance of intellect's moonlight rising upon such an expanse of snow is dreary, it is true, but some love its solemn desolation, its silence, its solitude—if they are but *allowed* to live in it; if they are not perpetually baulked and disappointed. But a woman cannot live in the light of intellect. Society forbids it. Those conventional frivolities, which are called her "duties," forbid it. Her "domestic duties," high-sounding words, which, for the most part, are but bad habits (which she has not the courage to enfranchise herself from, the strength to break through) forbid it. What are these duties (or bad habits)?—Answering a multitude of letters which lead to nothing, from her so-called friends—keeping herself up to the level of the world that she may furnish her quota of amusement at the breakfast-table; driving out her company in the carriage. And all these things are exacted from her by her family which, if she is good and affectionate, will have more influence with her than the world.

What wonder if, wearied out, sick at heart with hope deferred, the springs of will broken, not seeing clearly *where* her duty lies, she abandons intellect as a vocation and takes it only, as we use the moon, by glimpses through her tight-closed window-shutters?

The family? It is too narrow a field for the development of an immortal spirit, be that spirit male or female. The chances are a thousand to one that, in that small sphere, the task for which that immortal spirit is destined by the qualities and the gifts which its Creator has placed within it, will not be found.

The family uses people, *not* for what they are, nor for what they are intended to be, but for what it wants them for—for its own uses. It thinks of them not as what God has made them, but as the something which *it* has arranged that they shall be. If it wants some one to sit in the drawing-room, *that* some one is to be supplied by the family, though that member may be destined for science, or for education, or for active superintendence by God, *i.e.*, by the gifts within.

This system dooms some minds to incurable infancy, others to silent misery.

And family boasts that it has performed its mission well, in as far as it has enabled the individual to say, "I have *no* peculiar work, nothing but what the moment brings me, nothing that I cannot throw up at once at anybody's claim;" in as far, that is, as it has *destroyed* the individual life. And the individual thinks that a great victory has been accomplished, when, at last, she is able to say that she has "no personal desires or plans." What is this but throwing the gifts of God aside as worthless, and substituting for them those of the world?

Marriage is the only chance (and it is but a chance) offered to women for escape from this death; and how eagerly and how ignorantly it is embraced!

At present we live to impede each other's satisfactions; competition, domestic life, society, what is it all but this? We go somewhere where we are not wanted and where we don't want to go. What else is conventional life? *Passivity* when we want to be active. So many hours spent every day in passively doing what conventional life tells us, when we would so gladly be at work.

And is it a wonder that all individual life is extinguished?

Women dream of a great sphere of steady, not sketchy benevolence, of moral activity, for which they would fain be trained and fitted, instead of working in the dark, neither knowing nor registering whither their steps lead, whether farther from or nearer to the aim.

For how do people exercise their moral activity now? We visit, we teach, we talk, among "the poor;" we are told, "don't look for the fruits, cast thy bread upon the waters: for thou shalt find it after many days." Certainly "don't look," for you won't see. You will *not* "find it," and then you would "strike work."

How different would be the heart for the work, and how different would be the success, if we learnt our work as a serious study, and followed it out steadily as a profession!

Were the physician to set to work at *his* trade, as the philanthropist does at his, how many bodies would he not spoil before he cured one!

We set the treatment of bodies so high above the treatment of souls, that the physician occupies a higher place in society than the schoolmaster. The governess is to have every one of God's gifts; she is to do that which the mother herself is incapable of doing; but our son must not degrade himself by marrying the governess, nor our daughter the tutor, though she might marry the medical man.

But my medical man does do something for me, it is said, my tutor has done nothing.

This is true, this is the real reason. And what a condemnation of the state of mental science it is! Low as is physical science, that of the mind is still lower.

Women long for an education to teach them *to teach*, to teach them the laws of the human mind and how to apply them—and knowing how imperfect, in the present state of the world, such an education must be, they long for experience, not patch-work experience, but experience followed up and systematized, to enable them to know what they are about and *where* they are "casting their bread" and whether it *is* "*bread*" or a stone.

How should we learn a language if we were to give to it an hour a week? A fortnight's steady application would make more way in it than a year of such patch-work. A "lady" can hardly go to "her school" two days running. She cannot leave the breakfast-table—or she must be fulfilling some little frivolous "duty," which others ought not to exact, or which might just as well be done some other time.

Dreaming always—never accomplishing; thus women live—too much ashamed of their dreams, which they think "romantic," to tell them where they will be laughed at, even if not considered wrong.

With greater strength of purpose they might accomplish something. But if they were strong, all of them, they would not need to have their story told, for all the world would read it in the mission they have fulfilled. . . .

# Richard Francis Burton

## A DAY AMONGST THE FANS

*In an era of travelers and explorers, Richard Burton stands out as one of the most prolific and controversial. He spoke approximately thirty languages and many dialects. He explored portions of Asia, Africa, the Middle East, South America, and North America, and he published his findings in dozens of books, translations, and over a hundred articles. Despite his fame and his broad knowledge of geography, linguistics, archaeology, anthropology, literature, and non-Western religions, Burton was neglected and often criticized by official organizations, in great part because of his tendency to make enemies. While he received support from the Royal Geographical Society to search for the source of the Nile, the credit for the "discovery" went to John Hanning Speke, who traveled with Burton, explored Lake Tanganyika with him, and went without him to the shores of the lake he named Victoria. Speke returned to England ahead of Burton and claimed—correctly, as it turned out— that he had found the major source of the Nile. Burton's detailed scientific information from the expedition was overlooked.*

*Burton took pains to study and to immerse himself in the cultures he encountered, even donning disguises. His tolerance of non-European customs was unusual for his time, but his ideas about racial difference were extreme. He embraced contemporary myths and evolutionary theories of Africans as savages and children, subject to the corruption of Western influence. "A Day Amongst the Fans" is representative of Burton's observations and attitudes: it*

*was Burton's report of an expedition he made to the Gabon territory in 1862, while he was*
*Consul at Fernando Po, an island off the west African coast. Read on March 24, 1863,*
*before the Anthropological Society of London, which Burton helped to found, it was pub-*
*lished that year in the society's* Anthropological Review.                    LMF

. . . IN THE COOL OF THE MORNING Fitevanga, king of Máyyáⁿ, lectured me upon the short and simple annals of the Fans.[1] They are but lately known to fame, having, within the memory of man, crossed the Sierra del Crystal,[2] or West African Ghauts, and dislodged the less warlike Bakele and Mpongwe. In 1842 few were seen upon the head waters of the Gaboon, now they are known to visit the factories at the mouth of the river. They were accompanied in their westward migration by a kindred tribe, the Osheba, and both were, doubtless, driven seawards by the pressure of the inner tribes. These are successively, beginning from the west or seaward, the Báti, the Okáná, the Yefá, and the Sensoba, the latter being the easternmost known to my negro informants. You will vainly look for these names in the best of our modern charts. All the lands lying eastward of the Gaboon river-head are purely white. All these races are described as brave, warlike, and hospitable to strangers. I would here draw your attention to a fundamental error in African ethnology, made by Dr. Livingstone, who, deriving all his knowledge from the southern corner of the vast continent, asserts that "*no African tribe ever became extinct.*" The contrary is emphatically the case; nowhere does the selection of species, so to speak, fight more fiercely the battle of life, than in maritime Africa. The tenants of the coast are rarely ancient peoples. Demoralized by the contact of European and Asiatic civilization, and having, like the Turks, less inducement to bar the coast to their inner neighbours, than the latter have to secure free transit for their merchandise to the ocean, the world's highway of commerce, they degenerate and gradually die out. I will instance in the present day the Mpongwe and the Efik, or old Calabar races.[3] During the last half century both notably have declined, and they are in a fair way to become extinct, or to be merged into other tribes, before the year of grace 1900.

The name of this Fan nation deserves correction. The Mpongwe of the Gaboon river know them as Mpángwe, the Europeans as Pauouin, or Paouen—corruptions both. They call themselves Pánwe, Fánwe, and Fáⁿ, with a highly nasalized N. The plural is Bá-Fáⁿ.[4] The word Fan pronounced after the English fashion would be unintelligible to them. Their tongue, which belongs to the northern or equatorial branch of the great south African family of language, is soft and sweet, a contrast to their harsh voices and *criard*[5] utterance. They are intelligent as regards speech. During my short stay I collected, assisted by Mr. Tippet,[6] a short vocabulary from the chief's son and others. It was subsequently

---

1. The Fan participated in a great migration southward in the eighteenth and nineteenth centuries from the southern part of present-day Cameroon into Gabon, and then toward the west coast.
2. A mountain range extending inland north of the Gaboon River.
3. Calabar was a trading town in the Cross River estuary on the Nigerian coast near the modern Cameroon border. The Efik lived further upstream along the lower Cross River.
4. Fán in their tongue means a man. [Burton's note]
5. Shrill.
6. A trader in ebony and ivory who was from the United States and employed by Burton's host in Gabon.

corrected by a comparison with an unpublished MS., the work of the Rev. Mr. Preston, of the A.B.C.F. Mission, an able linguist, who has resided for some time, and seen some queer adventures among the Fans. If you desire it, it is freely offered to you.

After a bath in the muddy Mbokwe I returned to the village, and found it in a state of ferment; the sister of a young warrior had lately been killed and "chopped" by the king of a neighbouring Osheba hamlet, "Sán-Kwí," and the brother was urging his friends to up and arm. All the youths seized their weapons, the huge war-drum, the hollowed base of a tree, was set up in the middle of the street; preparations for the week's singing and dancing, which inaugurate a campaign, were already in hand, and one man gave earnest of bloodshed by spearing a goat, the property of Mr. Tippet. It being my interest that the peace should be kept till our return from the sources of the Gaboon river, I repaired to the palava house,[7] and lent weight to the advice of my host, who urged these heroes to collect ivory, ebony, and rubber, and not to fight till his stores were full. He concluded by carrying off the goat. After great excitement the warriors subsided into a calm, which, however, was broken two days afterwards by the murder of a villager, the suspected lover of a woman higher up the Mbokwe river; he went to visit her and was at once speared by the "injured husband."

The Fans, like most African tribes, with whom fighting is our fox-hunting, live in a chronic state of ten days war; such is the case even where the slave trade has never been known. Battles, however, are not bloody; after the fall of two or three warriors they are dragged off to be devoured, and their friends disperse. If the whole body cannot be removed, the victors content themselves with a "*gigot*"[8] or two, to make soup. The cannibalism of the Fans is by no means remarkable, limited, as it is, to the consumption of slain enemies; the practice extends sporadically from the Nun to the Kongo,[9] and how much further south I cannot at present say. In the Niger and the Brass the people do not conceal it; in Bonny I have seen all but the act of eating; it is execrated by the old Kalabarese, whilst practised by their Ibo neighbours to the north-west; the Duallas of Camaroons number it among their "country fashions;" and though the Mpongwe eschew even the chimpanzie, the Fans invariably eat their foes.[10]

Still no trace of the practice was seen at Máyyán; this, however, is not caused by its civilization. The Rev. W. M. Walker, and other excellent authorities, agree that it is a rare incident even in the wildest parts, but it is rendered unusual only by want of opportunity. The corpse when brought in is carried to a hut in the outskirts, and is secretly eaten by the men only, the cooking pots being finally broken. No joint of man is ever seen in the settlements. The people shouted with laughter when a certain question was asked. The sick are not devoured, the dead are decently interred, except slaves, who, as usual, are thrown into the forest. The chiefs, stretched at full length and wrapped in a mat, are secretly buried, the object being to prevent some strong fetish or medicine being made

7. Space set aside for negotiations, or "palaver," between residents and explorers.
8. Leg of meat, usually mutton.
9. Rivers of west-central Africa; the Nyong River is in southern Cameroon.
10. Niger, Brass, and Bonny are all locations along the Nigerian coast; the Niger River Delta includes at its eastern end two island ports, Brass and Bonny. The Ibo were the largest ethnic group in the eastern Niger River Delta. The modern town of Douala, Cameroon, is named after the Duallas.

by enemies from various parts of the body; in some tribes those of the same family are interred near one another; the commonalty are put singly under ground. During my peregrinations I never saw even a skull. Mr. Tippet, who had lived three years with this people, only knew three cases of anthropophagy; yet the Fan character has its ferocious side. Prisoners are tortured with horrible ferocity, and children may be seen licking the blood from the ground. It is a curious ethnological consideration, this peculiar development of destructiveness in the African brain; cruelty seems to be with him a necessary of life. All his highest enjoyments are connected with causing pain and inflicting death. His religious rites—how different from the Hindu's!—are ever causelessly bloody. As an instance, take the Efik, or old Calabarese. For two hundred years they have had intercourse with Europeans, who certainly would not encourage these profitless horrors, yet no savages could show such an extent of ferocity as the six thousand wretched remnants of the race. I cannot believe this abnormal cruelty to be the mere result of uncivilization. It appears to me rather the work of an arrested development, which leaves to the man all the bloodthirstiness of the carnivor.

After the palaver had been temporarily settled, I wandered through the settlement and sketched the huts. Our village contains about four hundred souls, and throughout the country the maximum would be four thousand, the minimum a hundred or so. The Fan homes are most like those of the Mpongwe, in fact, after the fashion that begins at Camaroons river; they are not, however, so neat and clean as those of the seaboard. A thatching, whose long eaves form deep verandahs facing towards the one street, surmounts neat walls of split bamboo (*Pirnifera*), planted upon raised platforms of earth. The usual two doors make the hut a thoroughfare, through which no one hesitates to pass; and windows being absent the ceiling is painted like coal tar by soot. The walls are garnished with weapons and nets; in making these they are equally expert; and the furniture consists of mats, cooking utensils, logs of wood for pillows and seats, and dwarf stools cut out of a solid block. The only illumination is by a torch, such as the Mpongwe use, a yard of acacia gum mixed with and bound up in dried plantation leaves. The sexes are not separated; but the men, as in Unyamwezi,[11] to quote no other place, are fond of their clubs, whilst the women are rarely allowed to be idle in the house. The latter must fetch water, nurse the baby, and cook, while the former talk, smoke, and doze. The number of the children makes the hut contrast favourably with the dreary home of the debauched Mpongwe, who puts no question provided his wife presents him with a child.

The dietary of these barbarians would astonish the half-starved sons of civilization. When shall we realize the fact, that the great thing needful to the prosperity of England is, not alm-houses, and hospitals, and private charities, but the establishment, advocated by Mr. Carlyle,[12] of a regular and efficient emigration! The crassest ignorance only prevents the listless pauper, the frozen out mechanic, and the wretched agricultural labourer from quitting a scene of misery, and from finding scattered over Earth's surface spots where the memory of privations endured in the hole which he calls his home would make

11. The Nyamwezi inhabited the region in East Africa south of Lake Victoria and east of Lake Tanganyika.
12. In *Past and Present* (1843), Thomas CARLYLE advocates the establishment of an emigration service that would take members of the English working class to new areas of the world (4.3).

his exile a paradise. We expect from a national system of emigration, our present great want, not the pilgrimage of a few solitary hands who—Nostalgia is a more common disease than men suppose—are ever pining for the past, but the exodus of little villages, which, like those of the Hebrides in the last century, bore with them to the New World their lares and penates, their wives, families, and friends. . . .

The rest of my day and the week following were devoted to the study of this quaint people, and these are the results. Those who have dealings with the Fans, universally prefer them for honesty and manliness to the Mpongwe, and the other coast races. They have not had time to be thoroughly corrupted; to lose all the lesser, without acquiring any of the greater virtues. Chastity is still known amongst them. The marriage tie has some significance, and they will fight about women. It is an insult to call a Fan liar or coward, and he waxes wroth if his mother be abused. Like all tribes in West Africa, they are but moderately brave. They are fond of intoxication, but not yet broken to ardent spirits. I have seen a man rolling upon the ground and licking the yellow clayey earth, like one in the convulsions of death-thirst; this was the effect of a *glass* of trade rum. They would willingly traffic for salt and beads. *The wretched custom of the coast—the White coast   is to supply vile alcohols, arms, and ammunition. How men who read their bibles and attend their chapels regularly, can reconcile this abomination to their consciences, I cannot say.* [13] *May the day come, when unanimity will enable the West African merchants to abstain from living upon the lives of those who pour wealth into their coffers!!* . . .

13. Burton here alludes to his frequently expressed dislike of missionaries, such as David LIVINGSTONE. He considered Livingstone's plans for Christianizing Africa to be "rot."

# Lucie Duff Gordon

## LETTERS FROM EGYPT AND THE CAPE

*Although Lucie Duff Gordon began her publishing career as a translator of German tales,
she is best known as the author of two collections of letters written in South Africa and
Egypt, where she spent the last years of her life in hopes of recovery from tuberculosis. Both
collections illustrate Duff Gordon's sympathy with and attempts to understand the native
peoples she sketches.* Letters from the Cape *began as private correspondence to her husband and family; soon, her husband and her mother, Sarah Austin, encouraged her to publish her letters to finance her travel for her health. Austin, an author herself, prepared the
letters for publication. Mother and daughter together edited Duff Gordon's Egyptian letters
for a public readership. Unlike many European travelers in the century, Duff Gordon saw
Egypt, its customs and personalities, with an appreciative rather than a critical eye.
Commenting upon Harriet* MARTINEAU's Eastern Life, Present and Past, *she regretted
Martineau's "bigotry" and her belief that "the differences of manners are a sort of impassable
gulf;—the truth being that their feelings and passions are just like our own." Duff
Gordon's analysis of her surroundings, significant both for its acknowledgement of cultural
differences between European and Arab and for its contempt for the effects of colonialism,
was popular with the Victorian reading public and quickly reprinted.* LMF

## LETTERS FROM THE CAPE

*Caledon, Jan. 28th. 1862*

WELL, I HAVE BEEN TO Gnadenthal, and seen the "blooming parish," and a lovely spot it is. A large village nestled in a deep valley, surrounded by high mountains on three sides, and a lower range in front. We started early on Saturday, and drove over a mighty queer road, and through a river. Oh, ye gods! what a shaking and pounding! We were rattled up like dice in a box. Nothing but a Cape cart, Cape horses, and a Hottentot driver, above all, could have accomplished it. Captain D— rode, and had the best of it. On the road we passed three or four farms, at all which horses were *galloping out* the grain, or men were winnowing it by tossing it up with wooden shovels to let the wind blow away the chaff. We did the twenty-four miles up and down the mountain roads in two hours and a half, with our valiant little pair of horses; it is incredible how they go. We stopped at a nice cottage on the hillside belonging to a *ci-devant*[1] slave, one Christian Rietz, a *white* man, with brown woolly hair, sharp features, grey eyes, and *not* woolly moustaches. He said he was a "Scotch bastaard," and "le bon sang parlait—très-haut même,"[2] for a more thriving, shrewd, sensible fellow I never saw. His *father* and master had had to let him go when all slaves were emancipated, and he had come to Gnadenthal. He keeps a little inn in the village, and a shop and a fine garden. The cottage we lodged in was on the mountain side, and had been built for his son, who was dead; and his adopted daughter, a pretty coloured girl, exactly like a southern Frenchwoman, waited on us, assisted by about six or seven other women, who came chiefly to stare. Vrouw Rietz was as black as a coal, but *so* pretty!—a dear, soft, sleek, old lady, with beautiful eyes, and the kind pleasant ways which belong to nice blacks; and, though old and fat, still graceful and lovely in face, hands, and arms. . . .

But first I must tell what struck me most. I asked one of the Herrenhut brethren whether there were any *real* Hottentots,[3] and he said, "Yes, one;" and next morning, as I sat waiting for early prayers under the big oak-trees in the Plaats (square), he came up, followed by a tiny old man hobbling along with a long stick to support him. "Here," said he, "is the *last* Hottentot; he is a hundred and seven years old, and lives all alone." I looked on the little, wizened, yellow face, and was shocked that he should be dragged up like a wild beast to be stared at. A feeling of pity which felt like remorse fell upon me, and my eyes filled as I rose and stood before him, so tall and like a tyrant and oppressor, while he uncovered his poor little old snow-white head, and peered up in my face. I led him to the seat, and helped him to sit down, and said in Dutch, "Father, I hope you are not tired; you are old." He saw and heard as well as ever, and spoke *good* Dutch in a firm voice. "Yes, I am above a hundred years old, and alone—quite alone." I sat beside him, and he put his head on one side, and looked curiously up at me with his faded, but still piercing little wild eyes. Perhaps he had a perception of what I felt—yet I hardly think so; perhaps he thought I was in trouble, for he crept close up to me, and put one tiny brown paw into my hand, which he stroked with the other, and asked (like most coloured people) if I had

1. Former.
2. "Good blood was speaking—very high indeed."
3. White person's term for South African people who once occupied the region near the Cape of Good Hope.

children. I said, "Yes, at home in England;" and he patted my hand again, and said, "God bless them!" It was a relief to feel that he was pleased, for I should have felt like a murderer if my curiosity had added a moment's pain to so tragic a fate.

This may sound like sentimentalism; but you cannot conceive the effect of looking on the last of a race once the owners of all this land, and now utterly gone. His look was not quite human, physically speaking;—a good head, small wild-beast eyes, piercing and restless; cheek-bones strangely high and prominent, nose *quite* flat, mouth rather wide; thin shapeless lips, and an indescribably small, long, pointed chin, with just a very little soft white woolly beard; his head covered with extremely short close white wool, which ended round the poll in little ringlets. Hands and feet like an English child of seven or eight, and person about the size of a child of eleven. He had all his teeth, and though shrunk to nothing, was very little wrinkled in the face, and not at all in the hands, which were dark brown, while his face was yellow. His manner, and way of speaking were like those of an old peasant in England, only his voice was clearer and stronger, and his perceptions not blunted by age. He had travelled with one of the missionaries in the year 1790, or thereabouts, and remained with them ever since.

I went into the church—a large, clean, rather handsome building, consecrated in 1800—and heard a very good sort of Litany, mixed with such singing as only black voices can produce. The organ was beautifully played by a Bastaard lad. The Herrenhuters use very fine chants, and the perfect ear and heavenly voices of a large congregation, about six hundred, all coloured people, made music more beautiful than any chorus-singing I ever heard.

Prayers lasted half an hour; then the congregation turned out of doors, and the windows were opened. Some of the people went away, and others waited for the "allgemeine Predigt."[4] In a quarter of an hour a much larger congregation than the first assembled, the girls all with net-handkerchiefs tied round their heads so as to look exactly like the ancient Greek headdress with a double fillet    the very prettiest and neatest coiffure I ever saw. The gowns were made like those of English girls of the same class, but far smarter, cleaner, and gayer in colour    pink, and green, and yellow, and bright blue; several were all in white, with white gloves. The men and women sit separate, and the women's side was a bed of tulips. The young fellows were very smart indeed, with muslin or gauze, either white, pink, or blue, rolled round their hats (that is universal here, on account of the sun). The Hottentots, as they are called—that is, those of mixed Dutch and Hottentot origin (correctly, "bastaards")—have a sort of blackguard elegance in their gait and figure which is peculiar to them; a mixture of negro or Mozambique blood alters it altogether. The girls have the elegance without the blackguard look; *all* are slender, most are tall; all graceful, all have good hands and feet; some few are handsome in the face and many very interesting-looking. The complexion is a pale olive-yellow, and the hair more or less woolly, face flat, and cheekbones high, eyes small and bright. These are by far the most intelligent—equal, indeed, to whites. A mixture of black blood often gives real beauty, but takes off from the "air," and generally from the talent; but then the

4. General sermon.

blacks are so pleasant, and the Hottentots are taciturn and reserved. The old women of this breed are the grandest hags I ever saw; they are clean and well dressed, and tie up their old faces in white handkerchiefs like corpses,—faces like those of Andrea del Sarto's old women; they are splendid. Also, they are very clean people, addicted to tubbing more than any others. The maid-of-all-work, who lounges about your breakfast table in rags and dishevelled hair, has been in the river before you were awake, or, if that was too far off, in a tub. They are also far cleaner in their huts than any but the *very best* English poor. . . .

## LETTERS FROM EGYPT

*Sunday, Feb. 7, 1864.*

We have had our winter pretty sharp for three weeks, and everybody has had violent colds and coughs,—the Arabs I mean. I have been a good deal ailing, but have escaped any violent cold altogether, and now the thermometer is up to 64°, and it feels very pleasant. In the sun it is always very hot, but that does not prevent the air from being keen, and chapping lips and noses, and even hands. It is curious how a temperature which would be summer in England makes one shiver at Thebes; El-hamdu-lilláh,[5] it is over now!

My poor Sheykh Yoosuf[6] is in great distress about his brother, also a young sheykh (*i.e.* one learned in theology, and competent to preach in the mosque). Sheykh Mohammad is come home from studying in El-Azhar at Cairo,—I fear, to die. I went with Sheykh Yoosuf, at his desire, to see if I could help him, and found him gasping for breath, and very, very ill; I gave him a little soothing medicine, and put mustard plasters on him, and as they relieved him, I went again and repeated them. All the family and a number of neighbours crowded in to look on. There he lay in a dark little den with bare mudwalls, worse off, to our ideas, than any pauper in England; but these people do not feel the want of comforts, and one learns to think it quite natural to sit with perfect gentlemen in places inferior to our cattle-sheds. I pulled some blankets up against the wall, and put my arm behind Sheykh Mohammad's back, to make him rest while the poultices were on him; whereupon he laid his green turbaned head on my shoulder, and presently held up his delicate brown face for a kiss, like an affectionate child. As I kissed him, a very pious old moollah said "Bismilláh!" (In the name of God!) with an approving nod, and Sheykh Mohammad's old father (a splendid old man in a green turban) thanked me with "effusion," and prayed that my children might always find help and kindness. I suppose if I confessed to kissing a "dirty Arab" in a hovel, civilized people would execrate me; but it shows how much there is in "Muslim bigotry," "unconquerable hatred of Christians," etc.; for this family are Seyyids (descendants of the Prophet), and very pious. Sheykh Yoosuf does not even smoke, and he preaches on Fridays.

I rode over to a village a few days ago, to see a farmer named Omar; of course I had to eat, and the people were enchanted at my going alone, as they are used to see the English armed and guarded. Seedee Omar, however, insisted on accompanying me home,

5. "Praise be to God."
6. An Islamic scholar who gave Duff Gordon lessons in Arabic.

which is the civil thing here. He piled a whole stack of green fodder on his little nimble donkey, and hoisted himself atop of it without saddle or bridle, (the fodder was for Mustafa Agha,[7]) and we trotted home across the beautiful green barley-fields, to the amazement of some European young men who were out shooting. We did look a curious pair certainly, with my English saddle and bridle, habit, and hat and feather, on horseback, and Seedee Omar's brown shirt, bare legs, and white turban, guiding his donkey with his chibouque; we were laughing very merrily, too, over my blundering Arabic.

To-morrow or next day, Ramadán[8] begins, at the first sight of the new moon; it is a great nuisance, because everybody is cross. Omar[9] did not keep it last year, but this year he will; and if he spoils my dinners, who can blame him?

There was a wedding close by my house last night, and about ten o'clock all the women passed under my window, with cries of joy—"El Zaghareet,"—down to the river. I find on inquiry, that in Upper Egypt, as soon as the bridegroom has "taken the face" of his bride and left her, the women take her down to "see the Nile;" they have not yet forgotten that the old god is the giver of increase, it seems.

I have been reading Miss Martineau's book;[10] the descriptions are excellent, and it is true as far as it goes; but there is the usual defect;—to her, as to most Europeans, the people are not real people, only part of the scenery. She evidently knew and cared nothing about them, and had the feeling of most English travellers, that the differences of manners are a sort of impassable gulf;—the truth being that their feelings and passions are just like our own. It is curious that all the old books of travels that I have read mention the natives of strange countries in a far more natural tone, and with far more attempt to discriminate character, than modern ones,—e.g. Carsten Niebuhr's Travels here and in Arabia, Cook's Voyages, and many others. Have we grown so very civilized since a hundred years, that outlandish people seem to us like mere puppets, and not like real human beings? Miss Martineau's bigotry against Copts and Greeks is droll enough, compared to her very proper reverence for "Him who sleeps in Philæ," and her attack upon the hareems is outrageous. She implies that they are scenes of debauchery. I must admit that I have not seen a Turkish hareem, and she apparently saw no other, and yet she fancies the morals of Turkey to be superior to those of Egypt. Very often a man marries a second wife, out of a sense of duty, to provide for a brother's widow and children, or the like. Of course licentious men act loosely here as elsewhere. "We are all sons of Adam," as Sheykh Yoosuf says constantly, "bad-bad and good-good;" and modern travellers show strange ignorance in talking of foreign nations *in the lump*, as they nearly all do.

7. An Egyptian merchant who offered Duff Gordon a home in Luxor (Thebes).
8. Annual period of fasting in the Muslim tradition.
9. This Omar, Omar Abu Halaweh ("Father of the Sweets") was Duff Gordon's interpreter, servant, guide, and cook.
10. Harriet MARTINEAU's *Eastern Life, Present and Past* (1848).

# Frances Power Cobbe

1822: Born 4 December at Newbridge, Dublin County, Ireland

1855: *Essay on the Theory of Intuitive Morals*

1863: *Essays on the Pursuits of Women*

1864: *Religious Duty*

1872: *Darwinism in Morals and Other Essays*

1875: *The Moral Aspects of Vivisection*

1881: *The Duties of Women. A Course of Lectures*

1894: *Life of Frances Power Cobbe*

1904: Died 5 April at Hengwrt, Wales

## WOMAN AS A CITIZEN OF THE STATE

*Journalist Frances Power Cobbe was a well-known activist for women's rights and, later in her life, a campaigner against animal vivisection. Publicly endorsing women's entitlement to university examinations, Cobbe also addressed women's medical, legal, and economic concerns. Her study of wife-abuse, published as "Wife-Torture in England" in 1878, influenced the revision of the Matrimonial Causes Act. Cobbe's feminism combined an insistence on women's rights with a belief in their moral superiority—a belief also held by John* Ruskin. *In 1880 and 1881 she delivered a set of lectures to an audience of women in London and Clifton; these lectures discussing philosophical and ethical questions in the context of feminism were published as* The Duties of Women, *one of Cobbe's most popular works. As she explains in Lecture 6, printed here, women must attain political emancipation and representation in order to fulfill their "Social Duty of contributing to the virtue and happiness of mankind." Cobbe believed, as did John Stuart* Mill, *that only when women were accorded legal personhood would they be able to influence legislation and so change the social conditions under which they lived. While Cobbe's beliefs about women's capacity for public service were progressive, she acknowledged that women were not "to neglect any private duties already incurred for the sake of new public duties subsequently adopted."* LMF

. . . WE NOW TURN DIRECTLY TO consider how stands the Duty of Women in England as regards entrance into public life and development of public spirit.[1] What ought we to do at present, as concerns all public work wherein it is possible for us to obtain a share?

The question seems to answer itself in its mere statement. We are bound to do *all* we can to promote the virtue and happiness of our fellow men and women, and *therefore* we must accept and seize every instrument of power, every vote, every influence which we can obtain to enable us to promote virtue and happiness. To return to the thought which to me seems so beautiful and fertile,—we must, if we desire to spread the "Kingdom of God," necessarily desire and seek the *means* by which we can extend it far and wide through the whole world. I am unable to imagine such a paradoxical person as one who should earnestly wish that Justice and Truth and Love should prevail, and yet should decline to accept the direct and natural means of influencing the affairs of his country in the direction of Justice, Truth, and Love.

All true Enthusiasm of Humanity, all genuine love of Justice, it seems to me, must spur those who feel it, to do what in them lies, not merely to exert the small powers they may find in their hands, but also to strive to obtain *more extended* powers of beneficence.

When one of us, women, sees a wrong needing to be righted, or a good to be achieved, or a truth to be taught, or a misery to be relieved, we wish for wealth, for influence, for the tongue of an orator, or the pen of a poet to achieve our object. These are holy wishes, sacred longings of our heart, which come to us in life's best hours and in the presence of God. And why are not we also to wish and strive to be allowed to place our hands on that vast machinery whereby, in a constitutional realm, the great work of the world is carried on, and which achieves by its enormous power tenfold either the good or the harm which any individual can reach, which may be turned to good or turned to harm, according to the hands which touch it? In almost every case it is only by legislation (as you all know) that the *roots* of great evils can be touched at all, and that the social diseases of pauperism and vice and crime can be brought within hope of cure. Women, with the tenderest hearts and best intentions, go on labouring all their life-times often in merely pruning the offshoots of these evil roots,—in striving to allay and abate the symptoms of the disease. But the nobler and much more truly philanthropic work of plucking up the roots, or curing the disease, they have been forced to leave to men.

You will judge from these remarks the ground on which, as a matter of *Duty*, I place the demand for woman's political emancipation. I think we are bound to seek it in the first place, as a *means*, a very great means, *of doing good*, fulfilling our Social Duty of contributing to the virtue and happiness of mankind; advancing the kingdom of God. There are many other reasons, viewed from the point of expediency; but this is the view from that of Duty. We know too well that men who possess political rights do not always, or often, regard them in this fashion; but this is no reason why we should not do so. We also know that the individual power of one vote at any election seems rarely to affect any appreciable difference; but this also need not trouble us, for, little or great, if we can

---

1. In the first section of her lecture, omitted here, Cobbe provides examples of historical and contemporary women who proved themselves adept at governing nations, performing acts of heroism, engaging in philanthropic reforms, holding local public office, and educating themselves and other women.

obtain any influence at all, we ought to seek for it; and the multiplication of the votes of women bent on securing conscientious candidates would soon make them not only appreciable, but weighty. Nay, further, the *direct* influence of a vote is but a small part of the power which the possession of the political franchise confers: its indirect influence is far more important. In a government like ours, where the basis of representation is so immensely extensive, the whole business of legislation is carried on *by pressure*—the pressure of each represented class and party to get its grievances redressed, to make its interests prevail. The non-represented classes necessarily go to the wall, not by mere wilful neglect on the part of either ministers or members of Parliament, but because they must attend to their constituents first and to their pressure (they would lose their places and seats if they did not)—and the time for attending to the non-represented people, amid the hurry and bustle of the Session, never arrives. To be *one of a represented class* is a very much greater thing in England than merely to drop a paper into a ballot-box. It means to be able to *insist* upon attention to the wants of that class; and to all other matters of public importance which may be deemed deserving of attention. It is one of the sore grievances of women in particular that, not possessing representation, the measures which concern them are forever postponed to the bills promoted by the represented classes (*e.g.*, the Married Woman's Property Bill[2] was, if I mistake not, six times set down for reading in one Session in vain, the House being counted out on every occasion).

Thus in asking for the Parliamentary franchise we are asking, as I understand it, for the power to influence legislation generally; and in every other kind of franchise, municipal, parochial, or otherwise, for similar power to bring our sense of justice and righteousness to bear on Public affairs. To achieve so great an end we ought all to be willing to incur trouble, and labour, and the loss of that privacy we some of us so highly value; with the ridicule and obloquy of silly men and sillier women.

What is this, after all, my friends, but *Public Spirit*—in one shape called Patriotism, in another, Philanthropy—the extension of our sympathies beyond the narrow bounds of our homes; the disinterested enthusiasm for every good and sacred cause? As I said at first, all the world has recognized from the earliest times how good and noble and wholesome a thing it is for *men* to have their breasts filled with such Public Spirit; and we look upon them when they exhibit it as glorified thereby. Do you think it is not just as ennobling a thing for a *woman's* soul to be likewise filled with these large and generous and unselfish emotions? Do you think *she* does not rise, even as man does, by stretching beyond the petty interests of personal vanity or family ambition, and feeling her heart throb with pride for the glory of her country, with indignation against wrongs and injustices and perfidies and with the ardent longing to bring about some great step of progress, some sorely needed reform? . . .

But there is a special reason why we, women of the upper classes in England, should at this time stir ourselves to obtain influence in public affairs. That reason is, the miserable oppressions, the bitter griefs, the cruel wrongs our sister women are doomed to suffer, and which might be relieved and righted by better legislation. I have explained just

2. The Married Women's Property Acts (1870 and 1882) gave married women the right to their own property; prior to the passage of these laws, a woman's legal existence was subsumed by her husband's upon marriage.

now how every unrepresented class in a constitutional country *must* be neglected by ministers and members of Parliament,—and in the case of women there are such enormous arrears of bad laws regarding them lying over from far off times of barbarism and needing now to be revised, that this difficulty of obtaining attention to our concerns is a double cruelty. Instead of needing no legislation, because their interests are so well cared for (as some senators have audaciously asserted)—I boldly affirm that there is no class of men in England who could not better, and with less consequent injustice, forego the franchise, than women.

There are thousands of poor women who suffer the worst of these wrongs; some who are placed legally at the mercy of savage husbands, or who are driven by misery and ill-paid, hopeless labour into the Dead Sea of vice; and some, of a little higher class whose children are torn from their arms, perhaps to satisfy a dead or a living husband's religious fanaticism. These most piteously wronged of all God's creatures, are breaking their hearts day by day and year by year all around us; no *man* much understanding their woes; no *man* having leisure to seek their remedy. And can *we* sit patiently by, and know all these things, and long to relieve all this agony and stop all these wrongs, and yet accept contentedly as a beautiful dispensation—not of God but of man,—the law which leaves us tongue-tied and hand-bound, unable to throw the weight of one poor vote into the scale of justice and mercy? Can we think our wretched drawing-room dignities and courtesies, and the smiles and approval of a swarm of fops and fools worth preserving at the cost of the knowledge that we *might* do something to lift up this load, and do it *not*? . . .

Practically, I think that every woman who has any margin of time or money to spare should adopt some one public interest, some philanthropic undertaking, or some social agitation of reform, and give to that cause whatever time and work she may be able to afford; thus completing her life by adding to her private duties the noble effort to advance God's Kingdom beyond the bounds of her home. Remember, pray,—that I say emphatically "*adding* to her private duties,"—not *subtracting* from them. I should think it a most grievous and deplorable error to neglect any private duties already incurred for the sake of new public duties subsequently adopted. But in truth though we read of "Mrs. Jellybys" in novels,[3] I have failed yet to find, in a pretty large experience of real life, a single case in which a woman who exercised Public Spirit, even to the extent of self-devotion, was not *also* an admirable and conscientious daughter, wife, mother, or mistress of a household. This spectre of the Female Politician, who abandons her family to neglect, for the sake of passing bills in Parliament, is just as complete an illusion of the masculine brain as the older spectre whom Sydney Smith[4] laid by a joke; the woman who would "forsake an infant for a quadratic equation." . . .

We are, many of us, in these days wandering far and wide in despairing search for some bread of life whereby we may sustain our souls, some *Holy Grail* wherein we may drink salvation from doubt and sin. It may be a long, long quest ere we find it; but one thing is ready to our hands. It is DUTY! Let us turn to that, in simple fidelity, and labour

3. Mrs. Jellyby is a character in Dickens's *Bleak House* who neglects her family while devoting her energies to foreign philanthropy in Borrioboola-Gha.
4. Sydney Smith (1771–1845), English clergyman and founder of the *Edinburgh Review*.

to act up to our own highest ideal, to *be* the very best and purest and truest we know how, and to *do* around us every work of love which our hands and hearts may reach. When we have lived and laboured like this, then, I believe, that the light will come to us, as to many another doubting soul; and it will prove true once more that "they who do God's will shall know of his doctrine;" and they who strive to advance his kingdom here will gain faith in another Divine realm beyond the dark River, where Virtue shall ascend into Holiness, and Duty be transfigured into Joy.

## LIFE OF FRANCES POWER COBBE

*Cobbe intended her autobiography to elucidate the history of her commitment to women's rights. Contained within the narrative of her family life, her education, her humanitarian pursuits, and her work for women's causes is a chapter entitled "Religion," in which she describes the process by which she rejected traditional Christianity and ultimately embraced a version of Theism, a belief in a God at work in the world but neither a part of it nor apart from it. Cobbe's loss of orthodox religious faith, initiated by her doubts about the literal truth of the Bible, resembles the crisis of belief experienced by many Victorian intellectuals, including George ELIOT, whom Cobbe mentions. An agnostic for a time during her twenties, Cobbe was distressed by the thought that, without religious faith, she could imagine no reunion with her dead mother. She came to adopt a belief in an intuited morality that pointed to the existence of a God who was compassionate, rational, and just. In addition to writing about religious issues, Cobbe put her moral philosophy into practice throughout her life, particularly in her campaigns against vivisection, on the one hand, and, on the other, against the abuse and denigration of women in marriage.*                LMF

I DO NOT THINK THAT any one not being a fanatic, can regret having been brought up as an Evangelical Christian. I do not include Calvinistic Christianity in this remark; for it must surely cloud all the years of mortal life to have received the first impressions of Time and Eternity through that dreadful, discoloured glass whereby the "Sun is turned into darkness and the moon into blood." I speak of the mild, devout, philanthropic Arminianism of the Clapham School, which prevailed amongst pious people in England and Ireland from the beginning of the century till the rise of the Oxford movement, and of which William Wilberforce and Lord Shaftesbury were successively representatives. [1] To this school my parents belonged. The conversion of my father's grandmother by Lady

---

1. Arminianism is the anti-Calvinist school of theology named after Jacobus Arminius (1560–1609), a Dutch theologian. The "Clapham sect," composed of upper-middle-class Evangelicals, members of the Low Church wing of the Anglican church, campaigned for abolition and the moral improvement of the lower classes. William Wilberforce (1759–1833) was a member of Parliament who led the campaign against the slave trade; Lord Ashley, seventh earl of Shaftesbury (1801–85), fought for factory reform and the improvement of conditions for the poor. The Oxford Movement of the 1830s and 1840s, led by John Keble, John Henry NEWMAN, Richard H. Froude, and Edward Pusey, responded to attempted governmental interference with church authority with a reassertion of High Church doctrine and a return to ritualism and theology.

Huntingdon, of which I have spoken, had, no doubt, directed his attention in early life to religion, but he was himself no Methodist, or Quietist, but a typical Churchman as Churchmen were in the first half of the century. All our relatives far and near, so far as I have ever heard, were the same. We had five archbishops and a bishop among our near kindred,—Cobbe, Beresfords, and Trenchs, great-grandfather, uncle, and cousins,—and (as I have narrated) my father's ablest brother, my god-father, was a clergyman. I was the first heretic ever known amongst us.

My earliest recollections include the lessons of both my father and mother in religion. I can almost feel myself now kneeling at my dear mother's knees repeating the Lord's Prayer after her clear sweet voice. Then came learning the magnificent Collects, to be repeated to my father on Sunday mornings in his study; and later the church catechism and a great many hymns. Sunday was kept exceedingly strictly at Newbridge in those days; and no books were allowed except religious ones, nor any amusement, save a walk after church. Thus there was abundant time for reading the Bible and looking over the pictures in various large editions, and in Calmet's great folio *Dictionary*,[2] beside listening to the sermon in church, and to another sermon which my father read in the evening to the assembled household. Of course, every day of the week there were Morning Prayers in the library,—and a "Short Discourse" from good, prosy old Jay, of Bath's "Exercises."[3] In this way, altogether I received a good deal of direct religious instruction, beside very frequent reference to God and Duty and Heaven, in the ordinary talk of my parents with their children.

What was the result of this training? I can only suppose that my nature was a favourable soil for such seed, for it took root early and grew apace. I cannot recall any time when I could not have been described by any one who knew my little heart (I was very shy about it, and few, if any, did know it)—as a very religious child. Religious ideas were from the first intensely interesting and exciting to me. In great measure I fancy it was the element of the sublime in them which moved me first, just as I was moved by the thunder, and the storm and was wont to go out alone into the woods or into the long, solitary corridors to enjoy them more fully. I recollect being stirred to rapture by a little poem which I can repeat to this day, beginning:

> Where is Thy dwelling place?
> Is it in the realms of space,
> By angels and just spirits only trod?
> Or is it in the bright
> And ever-burning light
> Of the sun's flaming disk that Thou art throned, O God?

One of the stanzas suggested that the Divine seat might be in some region of the starry universe:

2. Probably *Dictionnaire historique, géographique, critique, chronologique, et littéral de la Bible* (1720), an exegetical work by Antoine Augustin Calmet (1672—1757), French Benedictine theologian.

3. William Jay (1769—1853), English Nonconformist minister of the Argyle Independent chapel in Bath. He published a number of religious works, including *Morning and Evening Exercises*.

> Far in the unmeasured, unimagined Heaven,
>
> So distant that its light
>
> Could never reach our sight
>
> Though with the speed of thought for endless ages driven.

Ideas like these used to make my cheek turn pale and lift me as if on wings; and natural-ly Religion was the great storehouse of them. But I think, even in childhood, there was in me a good deal beside of the *moral*, if not yet the *spiritual* element of real Religion. Of course the great beauty and glory of Evangelical Christianity, its thorough amalgamation of the ideas of Duty and Devotion (elsewhere often so lamentably distinct), was very prominent in my parents' lessons. God was always to me the All-seeing Judge. His eye looking into my heart and beholding all its naughtiness and little duplicities (which of course I was taught to consider serious sins) was so familiar a conception that I might be said to live and move in the sense of it. Thus my life in childhood morally, was much the same as it is physically to live in a room full of sunlight. Later on, the evils which belong to this Evangelical training, the excessive self-introspection and self-consciousness, made themselves painfully felt, but in early years there was nothing that was not perfectly wholesome in the religion which I had so readily assimilated. . . .

Up to my eleventh year, my little life inward and outward had flown in a bright and even current. Looking back at it and comparing my childhood with that of others I seem to have been—probably from the effects of solitude—*devout* beyond what was normal at my age. I used to spend a great deal of time secretly reading the Bible and that dullest of dull books *The Whole Duty of Man*[4] (the latter a curious foretaste of my subsequent life-long interest in the study of ethics)—not exactly enjoying them but happy in the feeling that I was somehow approaching God. I used to keep awake at night to repeat various prayers and (wonderful to remember!) the Creed and Commandments! I made all sorts of severe rules for myself, and if I broke them, manfully mulcted myself of any little plea-sures or endured some small self-imposed penance. Of none of these things had any one, even my dear mother, the remotest idea, except once when I felt driven like a veritable Cain, by my agonised conscience to go and confess to her that I had said in a recent rage (to myself) "*Curse them all!*" referring to my family in general and to my governess in par-ticular! The tempest of my tears and sobs on this occasion evidently astonished her, and I remember lying exhausted on the floor in a recess in her bedroom, for a long time before I was able to move.

But the hour of doubt and difficulty was approaching. The first question which ever arose in my mind was concerning the miracle of the Loaves and Fishes. I can recall the scene vividly. It was a winter's night, my father was reading the Sunday evening Sermon in the dining-room. The servants, whose attendance was *de rigueur*, were seated in a row down the room. My father faced them, and my mother and I and my governess sat round the fire near him. I was opposite the beautiful classic black marble mantelpiece, sur-mounted with an antique head of Jupiter Serapis[5] (all photographed on my brain even

---

4. A highly popular devotional work, published in 1658 by Richard Allestree (1619–81).
5. A god combining the qualities of the Roman Jupiter and the Egyptian god Serapis.

now), and listening with all my might, as in duty bound, to the sermon which described the miracle of the Loaves and Fishes. "How did it happen exactly?" I began cheerfully to think, quite imagining I was doing the right thing to try to understand it all. "Well! first there were the fishes and the loaves. But what was done to them? Did the fish grow and grow as they were eaten and broken? And the bread the same? No! That is nonsense. And then the twelve basketsful taken up at the end, when there was not nearly so much at the beginning. It is not possible!" "O! Heavens! (was the next thought) *I am doubting the Bible!* God forgive me! I must never think of it again."

But the little rift had begun, and as time went on other difficulties arose. . . . I have always considered that in [the] summer in my seventeenth year I went through what Evangelical Christians call "conversion." Religion became the supreme interest of life; and the sense that I was pardoned its greatest joy. I was, of course, a Christian of the usual Protestant type, finding infinite pleasure in the simple old "Communion" of those pre-ritualistic days, and in endless Bible readings to myself. Sometimes I rose in the early summer dawn and read a whole Gospel before I dressed. I think I never ran up into my room in the daytime for any change of attire without glancing into the book and carrying away some echo of what I believed to be "God's Word." Nobody knew anything about all this, of course; but as time went on there were great and terrible perturbations in my inner life, and these perhaps I did not always succeed in concealing from the watchful eyes of my dear mother.

So far as I can recall, the ideas of Christ and of God the Father, were for all practical religious purposes identified in my young mind. It was as God upon earth,—the Redeemer God, that I worshipped Jesus. To be pardoned through his "atonement" and at death to enter Heaven, were the religious objects of life. But a new and most disturbing element here entered my thoughts. How did anybody know all that story of Galilee to be true? How could we believe the miracles? I have read very carefully Gibbon's XV. and XVI. chapters,[6] and other books enough to teach me that everything in historical Christianity had been questioned; and my own awakening critical, and reasoning, and above all, ethical,—faculties supplied fresh crops of doubts of the truth of the story and of the morality of much of the Old Testament history, and of the scheme of Atonement itself.

Then ensued four years on which I look back as pitiful in the extreme. In complete mental solitude and great ignorance, I found myself facing all the dread problems of human existence. For a long time my intense desire to remain a Christian predominated, and brought me back from each return to scepticism in a passion of repentance and prayer to Christ to take my life or my reason sooner than allow me to stray from his fold. In those days no such thing was heard of as "Broad" interpretations of Scripture doctrines. We were fifty years before *Lux Mundi* and thirty before even *Essays and Reviews.*[7] To be a "Christian," then, was to believe implicitly in the verbal inspiration of every word of the

---

6. The controversial fifteenth and sixteenth chapters of Edward Gibbon's *History of the Decline and Fall of the Roman Empire* (1776) describe the growth of Christianity.
7. The so-called Broad Church within the Church of England called for ecumenism and tolerance for religious difference and religious doubt. *Essays and Reviews* (1860) contained seven essays on the relevance of scientific, historical, and linguistic inquiry to the study of scripture and Christianity as a religion. *Lux Mundi* (1889), a volume of essays by a group of High Church theologians at Oxford, argued for the compatibility of faith in Christ with historical and Biblical criticism.

Bible, and to adore Christ as "very God of very God." With such implicit belief it was permitted to hope we might, by a good life and through Christ's Atonement, attain after death to Heaven. Without the faith or the good life, it was certain we should go to hell. It was taught us all that to be good only from fear of Hell was not the highest motive; the *highest* motive was the hope of Heaven! Had anything like modern rationalising theories of the Atonement, or modern expositions of the Bible stories, or finally modern loftier doctrines of disinterested morality and religion, been known to me at this crisis of my life, it is possible that the whole course of my spiritual history would have been different. But of all such "raising up the astral spirits of dead creeds," as Carlyle called it, or as Broad churchmen say, "Liberating the kernel of Christianity from the husk," I knew, and could know nothing. Evangelical Christianity in 1840 presented itself as a thing to be taken whole, or rejected wholly; and for years the alternations went on in my poor young heart and brain, one week or month of rational and moral disbelief, and the next of vehement, remorseful return to the faith which I supposed could alone give me the joy of religion. As time went on, and my reading supplied me with a little more knowledge and my doubts deepened and accumulated, the returns to Christian faith grew fewer and shorter, and, as I had no idea of the possibility of reaching any other vital religion, I saw all that had made to me the supreme joy and glory of life fade out of it, while that motive which had been presented to me as the mainspring of duty and curb of passion, namely, the Hope of Heaven, vanished as a dream. . . . In short my poor young soul was in a fearful dilemma. On the one hand I had the choice to accept a whole mass of dogmas against which my reason and conscience rebelled; on the other, to abandon those dogmas and strive no more to believe the incredible, or to revere what I instinctively condemned; and then, as a necessary sequel, to cast aside the laws of Duty which I had hither to cherished, to cease to pray or take the sacrament; and to relinquish the hope of a life beyond the grave.

It was not very wonderful if, as I think I can recall, my disposition underwent a considerable change for the worse while all these tremendous questions were being debated in my solitary walks in the woods and by the seashore, and in my room at night over my Gibbon or my Bible. I know I was often bitter and morose and selfish; and then came the alternate spell of paroxysms of self-reproach and fanciful self-tormentings.

The life of a young woman in such a home as mine is so guarded round on every side and the instincts of a girl are so healthy, that the dangers incurred even in such a spiritual landslip as I have described are very limited compared to what they must inevitably be in the case of young men or of women less happily circumstanced. It has been my profound sense of the awful perils of such a downfall of faith as I experienced, the peril of moral shipwreck without compass or anchorage amid the tempests of youth, which has spurred me ever since to strive to forestall for others the hour of danger.

At last my efforts to believe in orthodox Christianity ceased altogether. In the summer after my twentieth birthday I had reached the end of the long struggle. The complete downfall of Evangelicalism,—which seems to have been effected in George Eliot's strong brain in a single fortnight of intercourse with Mr. and Mrs. Bray,[8]—had taken in my case

---

8. Charles and Caroline Bray, friends of George ELIOT, introduced her to Charles Hennell's *An Inquiry Concerning the Origin of Christianity* (1838), which played a part in her rejection of her Evangelical beliefs.

four long years of miserable mental conflict and unspeakable pain. It left me with something as nearly like a *Tabula rasa* of faith as can well be imagined. I definitely disbelieved in human immortality and in a supernatural revelation. The existence of God I neither denied nor affirmed. I felt I had no means of coming to any knowledge of Him. I was, in fact (long before the word was invented), precisely—an Agnostic.

One day, while thus literally creedless, I wandered out alone as was my wont into a part of our park a little more wild than the rest, where deer were formerly kept and sat down among the rocks and the gorse which was then in its summer glory of odorous blossoms, ever since rich to me with memories of that hour. It was a sunny day in May, and after reading a little of my favorite Shelley, I fell, as often happened, into mournful thought. I was profoundly miserable; profoundly conscious of the deterioration and sliding down of all my feelings and conduct from the high ambitions of righteousness and holiness which had been mine in the days of my Christian faith and prayer; and at the same time I knew that the whole scaffolding of that higher life had fallen to pieces and could never be built up again. While I was thus musing despairingly, something stirred within me, and I asked myself, "Can I not rise once more, conquer my faults, and live up to my own idea of what is right and good? Even though there be no life after death, I may yet deserve my own respect here and now, and, if there be a God, He must approve me."

The resolution was made very seriously. I came home to begin a new course and to cultivate a different spirit. Was it strange that in a few days I began instinctively, and almost without reflection, to pray again? No longer did I make any kind of effort to believe this thing or the other about God. I simply addressed Him as the Lord of conscience, whom I implored to strengthen my good resolutions, to forgive my faults, "to lift me out of the mire and clay and set my feet upon a rock and order my goings." Of course, there was Christian sentiment and the results of Christian training in all I felt and did. I could no more have cast them off than I could have leaped off my shadow. But of dogmatical Christianity there was never any more. I have never from that time, now more than fifty years ago, attached, or wished I could attach, credence to any part of what Dr. Martineau[9] has called the *Apocalyptic side of Christianity*, nor (I may add with thankfulness) have I ever lost faith in God.

The storms of my youth were over. Henceforth through many years there was a progressive advance to Theism as I have attempted to describe it in my books; and there were many, many hard moral fights with various Apollyons[10] all along the road; but no more spiritual revolutions. . . .

. . . [T]he perfect clearness and straightforwardness of my position was, and has ever since been, a source of strength and satisfaction to me, for which I have thanked God a thousand times. My inner life was made happy by my simple faith in God's infinite and perfect love; and I never had any doubt whether I had erred in abandoning the creed of my youth. On the contrary, as the whole tendency of modern science and criticism

9. James Martineau (1805–1900), Unitarian minister, philosopher, and professor of mental and moral philosophy and political economy at Manchester New College.

10. A reference to John Bunyan's allegory *Pilgrim's Progress*, a favorite book of Cobbe's youth. On his route to the Celestial City, the pilgrim Christian is beset by the fiend Apollyon and Giant Despair.

showed itself stronger and stronger against the old orthodoxy, my hopes were unduly raised of a not distant New Reformation which I might even live to see. These sanguine hopes have faded. As Dean Stanley[11] seems to have felt, there was, somewhere between the years '74 and '78, a turn in the tide of men's thoughts (due, I think, to the paramount influence and insolence which physical science then assumed), which has postponed any decisive "broad" movement for years beyond my possible span of life. But though nothing appears quite so bright to my old eyes as all things did to me in youth, though familiarity with human wickedness and misery, and still more with the horrors of scientific cruelty to animals, have strained my faith in God's justice sometimes even to agony,—I know that no form of religious creed could have helped me any more than my own or as much as it has done to bear the brunt of such trial; and I remain to the present unshaken both in respect to the denials and the affirmations of Theism. There are great difficulties, soul-torturing difficulties besetting it; but the same or worse, beset every other form of faith in God; and infinitely more, and to my mind insurmountable ones, beset Atheism.

For fifty years Theism has been my staff of life. I must soon try how it will support me down the last few steps of my earthly way. I believe it will do so well.

11. Arthur Penrhyn Stanley (1815–81), dean of Westminster and a leading liberal theologian.

# Matthew Arnold

1822: Born 24 December at Laleham, Surrey

1845: Elected Fellow at Oriel College, Oxford

1849: *The Strayed Reveller and Other Poems*

1851: Appointed Inspector of Schools, a post he held until 1886

1852: *Empedocles on Etna, and Other Poems*

1853: *Poems, a New Edition*

1857: Elected Professor of Poetry at Oxford

1865: *Essays in Criticism*, first series

1869: *Culture and Anarchy*

1873: *Literature and Dogma. An Essay Towards a Better Apprehension of the Bible*

1885: *Discourses in America*

1888: Died 15 April in Liverpool; *Essays in Criticism*, second series

## CULTURE AND ANARCHY

*By the late 1860s when Matthew Arnold began publishing the essays that would become* Culture and Anarchy, *he was already a respected literary figure. His poems of the 1840s and 1850s had spoken to the spiritual crises of many of his contemporaries, although Arnold himself was dissatisfied that his poetry, often characterized by melancholy and frustration, did not attain his classical ideals of cheerfulness and serenity. His lectures as Professor of Poetry at Oxford and his periodical essays, most notably "The Function of Criticism at the Present Time," had established him as a significant literary critic and the foremost advocate of criticism, loftily defined by him as "the disinterested endeavour to learn and propagate the best that is known and thought in the world." In the 1860s Arnold turned more directly to an examination of social problems.* Culture and Anarchy *is a product of and a response to specific political issues of that decade, particularly the agitation and debates leading to the passage of the 1867 Reform Bill (increasing the electorate), which for Arnold exemplified a tendency toward spiritual and intellectual anarchy. But* Culture and Anarchy *is also an expression of Arnold's more general diagnosis of the excesses and failings of modern England—its materialism, parochialism, self-satisfaction, divisiveness, over-valuing of personal liberty, and reliance on stock notions or "machin-ery"—and his faith in the expanded notion of "Culture," the pursuit of "harmonious perfec-tion," as a social and moral agent.*

*The volume* Culture and Anarchy *grew out of Arnold's Oxford lecture "Culture and Its Enemies" (June 1867) and a series of essays published in the* Cornhill Magazine *(July 1867 to August 1868). In 1869 Arnold gathered the essays together and added a preface for the first edition in book form. In the second edition in 1875, from which the selections below are taken, he eliminated many topical references and added the now famous chapter titles.*                                                                                    RM

## SWEETNESS AND LIGHT

THE DISPARAGERS OF CULTURE MAKE its motive curiosity; sometimes, indeed, they make its motive mere exclusiveness and vanity. The culture which is supposed to plume itself on a smattering of Greek and Latin is a culture which is begotten by nothing so intellec-tual as curiosity; it is valued either out of sheer vanity and ignorance, or else as an engine of social and class distinction, separating its holder, like a badge or title, from other peo-ple who have not got it. No serious man would call this *culture*, or attach any value to it, as culture, at all. To find the real ground for the very differing estimate which serious peo-ple will set upon culture, we must find some motive for culture in the terms of which may lie a real ambiguity; and such a motive the word *curiosity* gives us.

I have before now pointed out that we English do not, like the foreigners, use this word in a good sense as well as in a bad sense. With us the word is always used in a some-what disapproving sense. A liberal and intelligent eagerness about the things of the mind may be meant by a foreigner when he speaks of curiosity, but with us the word always conveys a certain notion of frivolous and unedifying activity. In the *Quarterly Review*, some little time ago, was an estimate of the celebrated French critic, M. Sainte-Beuve, and a very inadequate estimate it in my judgment was.[1] And its inadequacy consisted chiefly in this: that in our English way it left out of sight the double sense really involved in the word *curiosity*, thinking enough was said to stamp M. Sainte-Beuve with blame if it was said that he was impelled in his operations as a critic by curiosity, and omitting either to perceive that M. Sainte-Beuve himself, and many other people with him, would consid-er that this was praiseworthy and not blameworthy, or to point out why it ought really to be accounted worthy of blame and not of praise. For as there is a curiosity about intel-lectual matters which is futile, and merely a disease, so there is certainly a curiosity,—a desire after the things of the mind simply for their own sakes and for the pleasure of see-ing them as they are,—which is, in an intelligent being, natural and laudable. Nay, and the very desire to see things as they are, implies a balance and regulation of mind which is not often attained without fruitful effort, and which is the very opposite of the blind and diseased impulse of mind which is what we mean to blame when we blame curiosi-

1. [F. T. Marzials], "M. Sainte-Beuve," *Quarterly Review* (January 1866). Charles Augustin Sainte-Beuve (1804–69), French literary critic.

ty. Montesquieu says:—'The first motive which ought to impel us to study is the desire to augment the excellence of our nature, and to render an intelligent being yet more intelligent.'[2] This is the true ground to assign for the genuine scientific passion, however manifested, and for culture, viewed simply as a fruit of this passion; and it is a worthy ground, even though we let the term *curiosity* stand to describe it.

But there is of culture another view, in which not solely the scientific passion, the sheer desire to see things as they are, natural and proper in an intelligent being, appears as the ground of it. There is a view in which all the love of our neighbour, the impulses towards action, help, and beneficence, the desire for removing human error, clearing human confusion, and diminishing human misery, the noble aspiration to leave the world better and happier than we found it,—motives eminently such as are called social,—come in as part of the grounds of culture, and the main and pre-eminent part. Culture is then properly described not as having its origin in curiosity, but as having its origin in the love of perfection; it is *a study of perfection*. It moves by the force, not merely or primarily of the scientific passion for pure knowledge, but also of the moral and social passion for doing good. As, in the first view of it, we took for its worthy motto Montesquieu's words: 'To render an intelligent being yet more intelligent!' so, in the second view of it, there is no better motto which it can have than these words of Bishop Wilson: 'To make reason and the will of God prevail!'[3]

Only, whereas the passion for doing good is apt to be overhasty in determining what reason and the will of God say, because its turn is for acting rather than thinking and it wants to be beginning to act; and whereas it is apt to take its own conceptions, which proceed from its own state of development and share in all the imperfections and immaturities of this, for a basis of action; what distinguishes culture is, that it is possessed by the scientific passion, as well as by the passion of doing good; that it demands worthy notions of reason and the will of God, and does not readily suffer its own crude conceptions to substitute themselves for them. And knowing that no action or institution can be salutary and stable which is not based on reason and the will of God, it is not so bent on acting and instituting, even with the great aim of diminishing human error and misery ever before its thoughts, but that it can remember that acting and instituting are of little use, unless we know how and what we ought to act and to institute.[4]

This culture is more interesting and more far-reaching than that other, which is founded solely on the scientific passion for knowing. But it needs times of faith and ardour, times when the intellectual horizon is opening and widening all round us, to flourish in. And is not the close and bounded intellectual horizon within which we have long lived and moved now lifting up, and are not new lights finding free passage to shine in upon us?

2. Charles de Secondat, Baron de Montesquieu (1689–1755), French philosopher.
3. Bishop Thomas Wilson (1663–1755), in *Sacra Privata*.
4. Elsewhere in *Culture and Anarchy*, Arnold uses the terms "Hellenism" and "Hebraism" to distinguish between the passion for knowing and truth and the passion for doing, described here. "Hellenism" is his term for spontaneity of consciousness, disinterestedness, the pursuit of beauty and knowledge, and the full development of the "whole man," while "Hebraism" is his catchword for that instinct directed toward conduct, moral action, and strictness of conscience. Arnold conceives of the two as dialectical forces operating throughout history, vacillating in dominance, but ideally in balance. Modern England, according to Arnold, is unbalanced; its excessive Hebraism has led to narrow dogmatism and intellectual, spiritual anarchy.

For a long time there was no passage for them to make their way in upon us, and then it was of no use to think of adapting the world's action to them. Where was the hope of making reason and the will of God prevail among people who had a routine which they had christened reason and the will of God, in which they were inextricably bound, and beyond which they had no power of looking? But now the iron force of adhesion to the old routine,—social, political, religious,—has wonderfully yielded; the iron force of exclusion of all which is new has wonderfully yielded. The danger now is, not that people should obstinately refuse to allow anything but their old routine to pass for reason and the will of God, but either that they should allow some novelty or other to pass for these too easily, or else that they should underrate the importance of them altogether, and think it enough to follow action for its own sake, without troubling themselves to make reason and the will of God prevail therein. Now, then, is the moment for culture to be of service, culture which believes in making reason and the will of God prevail, believes in perfection, is the study and pursuit of perfection, and is no longer debarred, by a rigid invincible exclusion of whatever is new, from getting acceptance for its ideas, simply because they are new. . . .

If culture, then, is a study of perfection, and of harmonious perfection, general perfection, and perfection which consists in becoming something rather than in having something, in an inward condition of the mind and spirit, not in an outward set of circumstances,—it is clear that culture, instead of being the frivolous and useless thing which Mr. Bright, and Mr. Frederic Harrison,[5] and many other Liberals are apt to call it, has a very important function to fulfil for mankind. And this function is particularly important in our modern world, of which the whole civilisation is, to a much greater degree than the civilisation of Greece and Rome, mechanical and external, and tends constantly to become more so. But above all in our own country has culture a weighty part to perform, because here that mechanical character, which civilisation tends to take everywhere, is shown in the most eminent degree. Indeed nearly all the characters of perfection, as culture teaches us to fix them, meet in this country with some powerful tendency which thwarts them and sets them at defiance. The idea of perfection as an *inward* condition of the mind and spirit is at variance with the mechanical and material civilisation in esteem with us, and nowhere, as I have said, so much in esteem as with us. The idea of perfection as a *general* expansion of the human family is at variance with our strong individualism, our hatred of all limits to the unrestrained swing of the individual's personality, our maxim of 'every man for himself.' Above all, the idea of perfection as a *harmonious* expansion of human nature is at variance with our want of flexibility, with our inaptitude for seeing more than one side of a thing, with our intense energetic absorption in the particular pursuit we happen to be following. So culture has a rough task to achieve in this country. Its preachers have, and are likely long to have, a hard time of it, and they will much oftener be regarded, for a great while to come, as elegant or spurious Jeremiahs, than as friends and benefactors. That, however, will not prevent their doing in the end good service if they persevere. And meanwhile, the mode of action they have to pursue,

5. Both John Bright (1811–89), liberal member of Parliament and campaigner for the extension of the franchise, and Frederic Harrison (1831–1923), Positivist and critic, had attacked Arnold's notion of "culture."

and the sort of habits they must fight against, ought to be made quite clear for every one to see, who may be willing to look at the matter attentively and dispassionately.

Faith in machinery is, I said, our besetting danger; often in machinery most absurdly disproportioned to the end which this machinery, if it is to do any good at all, is to serve; but always in machinery, as if it had a value in and for itself. What is freedom but machinery? what is population but machinery? what is coal but machinery? what are railroads but machinery? what is wealth but machinery? what are, even, religious organisations but machinery? Now almost every voice in England is accustomed to speak of these things as if they were precious ends in themselves, and therefore had some of the characters of perfection indisputably joined to them. I have before now noticed Mr. Roebuck's[6] stock argument for proving the greatness and happiness of England as she is, and for quite stopping the mouths of all gainsayers. Mr. Roebuck is never weary of reiterating this argument of his, so I do not know why I should be weary of noticing it. 'May not every man in England say what he likes?'——Mr. Roebuck perpetually asks; and that, he thinks, is quite sufficient, and when every man may say what he likes, our aspirations ought to be satisfied. But the aspirations of culture, which is the study of perfection, are not satisfied, unless what men say, when they may say what they like, is worth saying,——has good in it, and more good than bad. In the same way the *Times*, replying to some foreign strictures on the dress, looks, and behaviour of the English abroad, urges that the English ideal is that everyone should be free to do and to look just as he likes. But culture indefatigably tries, not to make what each raw person may like, the rule by which he fashions himself; but to draw ever nearer to a sense of what is indeed beautiful, graceful, and becoming, and to get the raw person to like that.

And in the same way with respect to railroads and coal. Every one must have observed the strange language current during the late discussions as to the possible failure of our supplies of coal. Our coal, thousands of people were saying, is the real basis of our national greatness; if our coal runs short, there is an end of the greatness of England. But what *is* greatness?——culture makes us ask. Greatness is a spiritual condition worthy to excite love, interest, and admiration; and the outward proof of possessing greatness is that we excite love, interest, and admiration. If England were swallowed up by the sea to-morrow, which of the two, a hundred years hence, would most excite the love, interest, and admiration of mankind,——would most, therefore, show the evidences of having possessed greatness,——the England of the last twenty years, or the England of Elizabeth, of a time of splendid spiritual effort, but when our coal, and our industrial operations depending on coal, were very little developed? Well, then, what an unsound habit of mind it must be which makes us talk of things like coal or iron as constituting the greatness of England, and how salutary a friend is culture, bent on seeing things as they are, and thus dissipating delusions of this kind and fixing standards of perfection that are real! . . .

. . . But the point of view of culture, keeping the mark of human perfection simply and broadly in view, and not assigning to this perfection, as religion or utilitarianism assign to it, a special and limited character,——this point of view, I say, of culture is best

6. John Arthur Roebuck (1801–79), Radical reformer and Benthamite.

given by these words of Epictetus:— 'It is a sign of ἀφυΐα,' says he,—that is, of a nature not finely tempered,— 'to give yourselves up to things which relate to the body; to make, for instance, a great fuss about exercise, a great fuss about eating, a great fuss about drinking, a great fuss about walking, a great fuss about riding. All these things ought to be done merely by the way: the formation of the spirit and character must be our real concern.'[7] This is admirable; and, indeed, the Greek word εὐφΐα, a finely tempered nature, gives exactly the notion of perfection as culture brings us to conceive it: a harmonious perfection, a perfection in which the characters of beauty and intelligence are both present, which unites 'the two noblest of things,'—as Swift, who of one of the two, at any rate, had himself all too little, most happily calls them in his *Battle of the Books*,— 'the two noblest of things, *sweetness and light.*' The εὐφυής is the man who tends towards sweetness and light; the ἀφυής, on the other hand, is our Philistine. The immense spiritual significance of the Greeks is due to their having been inspired with this central and happy idea of the essential character of human perfection; and Mr. Bright's misconception of culture, as a smattering of Greek and Latin, comes itself, after all, from this wonderful significance of the Greeks having affected the very machinery of our education, and is in itself a kind of homage to it.

In thus making sweetness and light to be characters of perfection, culture is of like spirit with poetry, follows one law with poetry. Far more than on our freedom, our population, and our industrialism, many amongst us rely upon our religious organisations to save us. I have called religion a yet more important manifestation of human nature than poetry, because it has worked on a broader scale for perfection, and with greater masses of men. But the idea of beauty and of a human nature perfect on all its sides, which is the dominant idea of poetry, is a true and invaluable idea, though it has not yet had the success that the idea of conquering the obvious faults of our animality, and of a human nature perfect on the moral side,—which is the dominant idea of religion,—has been enabled to have; and it is destined, adding to itself the religious idea of a devout energy, to transform and govern the other.

The best art and poetry of the Greeks, in which religion and poetry are one, in which the idea of beauty and of a human nature perfect on all sides adds to itself a religious and devout energy, and works in the strength of that, is on this account of such surpassing interest and instructiveness for us, though it was,—as, having regard to the human race in general, and, indeed, having regard to the Greeks themselves, we must own,—a premature attempt, an attempt which for success needed the moral and religious fibre in humanity to be more braced and developed than it had yet been. But Greece did not err in having the idea of beauty, harmony, and complete human perfection, so present and paramount. It is impossible to have this idea too present and paramount; only, the moral fibre must be braced too. And we, because we have braced the moral fibre, are not on that account in the right way, if at the same time the idea of beauty, harmony, and complete human perfection, is wanting or misapprehended amongst us; and evidently it *is* wanting or misapprehended at present. And when we rely as we do on our religious organisations,

7. Epictetus, first- and second-century Roman philosopher, in *Encheiridion*.

which in themselves do not and cannot give us this idea, and think we have done enough if we make them spread and prevail, then, I say, we fall into our common fault of over-valuing machinery.

Nothing is more common than for people to confound the inward peace and satisfaction which follows the subduing of the obvious faults of our animality with what I may call absolute inward peace and satisfaction,—the peace and satisfaction which are reached as we draw near to complete spiritual perfection, and not merely to moral perfection, or rather to relative moral perfection. No people in the world have done more and struggled more to attain this relative moral perfection than our English race has. For no people in the world has the command to *resist the devil*, to *overcome the wicked one*, in the nearest and most obvious sense of those words, had such a pressing force and reality. And we have had our reward, not only in the great worldly prosperity which our obedience to this command has brought us, but also, and far more, in great inward peace and satisfaction. But to me few things are more pathetic than to see people, on the strength of the inward peace and satisfaction which their rudimentary efforts towards perfection have brought them, employ, concerning their incomplete perfection and the religious organisations within which they have found it, language which properly applies only to complete perfection, and is a far-off echo of the human soul's prophecy of it. Religion itself, I need hardly say, supplies them in abundance with this grand language. And very freely do they use it; yet it is really the severest possible criticism of such an incomplete perfection as alone we have yet reached through our religious organisations.

The impulse of the English race towards moral development and self-conquest has nowhere so powerfully manifested itself as in Puritanism. Nowhere has Puritanism found so adequate an expression as in the religious organisation of the Independents. The modern Independents have a newspaper, the *Nonconformist*,[8] written with great sincerity and ability. The motto, the standard, the profession of faith which this organ of theirs carries aloft, is: 'The Dissidence of Dissent and the Protestantism of the Protestant religion.' There is sweetness and light, and an ideal of complete harmonious human perfection! One need not go to culture and poetry to find language to judge it. Religion, with its instinct for perfection, supplies language to judge it, language, too, which is in our mouths every day. 'Finally, be of one mind, united in feeling,' says St. Peter.[9] There is an ideal which judges the Puritan ideal: 'The Dissidence of Dissent and the Protestantism of the Protestant religion!' And religious organisations like this are what people believe in, rest in, would give their lives for! Such, I say, is the wonderful virtue of even the beginnings of perfection, of having conquered even the plain faults of our animality, that the religious organisation which has helped us to do it can seem to us something precious, salutary, and to be propagated, even when it wears such a brand of imperfection on its forehead as this. And men have got such a habit of giving to the language of religion a special application, of making it a mere jargon, that for the condemnation which religion itself passes on the shortcomings of their religious organisations they have no ear; they are sure to cheat themselves and to explain this condemnation away. They can only be

8. Weekly Congregational paper, founded in 1841.
9. 1 Peter 3: 8.

reached by the criticism which culture, like poetry, speaking a language not to be sophis-ticated, and resolutely testing these organisations by the ideal of a human perfection on all sides, applies to them. . . .

. . . And I say that the English reliance on our religious organisations and on their ideas of human perfection just as they stand, is like our reliance on freedom, on muscular Christianity, on population, on coal, on wealth,—mere belief in machinery, and unfruit-ful; and that it is wholesomely counteracted by culture, bent on seeing things as they are, and on drawing the human race onwards to a more complete, a harmonious perfection.

Culture, however, shows its single-minded love of perfection, its desire simply to make reason and the will of God prevail, its freedom from fanaticism, by its attitude towards all this machinery, even while it insists that it is machinery. Fanatics, seeing the mischief men do themselves by their blind belief in some machinery or other,—whether it is wealth and industrialism, or whether it is the cultivation of bodily strength and activ-ity, or whether it is a political organisation, or whether it is a religious organisation,—oppose with might and main the tendency to this or that political and religious organisa-tion, or to games and athletic exercises, or to wealth and industrialism, and try violently to stop it. But the flexibility which sweetness and light give, and which is one of the rewards of culture pursued in good faith, enables a man to see that a tendency may be necessary, and even, as a preparation for something in the future, salutary, and yet that the generations or individuals who obey this tendency are sacrificed to it, that they fall short of the hope of perfection by following it; and that its mischiefs are to be criticised, lest it should take too firm a hold and last after it has served its purpose. . . .

The pursuit of perfection, then, is the pursuit of sweetness and light. He who works for sweetness and light, works to make reason and the will of God prevail. He who works for machinery, he who works for hatred, works only for confusion. Culture looks beyond machinery, culture hates hatred; culture has one great passion, the passion for sweetness and light. It has one even yet greater!—the passion for making them *prevail*. It is not sat-isfied till we *all* come to a perfect man; it knows that the sweetness and light of the few must be imperfect until the raw and unkindled masses of humanity are touched with sweetness and light. If I have not shrunk from saying that we must work for sweetness and light, so neither have I shrunk from saying that we must have a broad basis, must have sweetness and light for as many as possible. Again and again I have insisted how those are the happy moments of humanity, how those are the marking epochs of a people's life, how those are the flowering times for literature and art and all the creative power of genius, when there is a *national* glow of life and thought, when the whole of society is in the fullest measure permeated by thought, sensible to beauty, intelligent and alive. Only it must be *real* thought and *real* beauty; *real* sweetness and *real* light. Plenty of people will try to give the masses, as they call them, an intellectual food prepared and adapted in the way they think proper for the actual condition of the masses. The ordinary popular liter-ature is an example of this way of working on the masses. Plenty of people will try to indoctrinate the masses with the set of ideas and judgments constituting the creed of their own profession or party. Our religious and political organisations give an example of this way of working on the masses. I condemn neither way; but culture works differently. It does not try to teach down to the level of inferior classes; it does not try to win them for this or that sect of its own, with ready-made judgments and watchwords. It seeks to do away with classes; to make the best that has been thought and known in the world current everywhere; to make all men live in an atmosphere of sweetness and light, where they may use ideas, as it uses them itself, freely,—nourished, and not bound by them.

This is the *social idea*; and the men of culture are the true apostles of equality. The great men of culture are those who have had a passion for diffusing, for making prevail, for carrying from one end of society to the other, the best knowledge, the best ideas of their time; who have laboured to divest knowledge of all that was harsh, uncouth, difficult, abstract, professional, exclusive; to humanise it, to make it efficient outside the clique of the cultivated and learned, yet still remaining the *best* knowledge and thought of the time, and a true source, therefore, of sweetness and light. Such a man was Abelard in the Middle Ages, in spite of all his imperfections; and thence the boundless emotion and enthusiasm which Abelard excited. Such were Lessing and Herder in Germany, at the end of the last century; and their services to Germany were in this way inestimably precious.[10] Generations will pass, and literary monuments will accumulate, and works far more perfect than the works of Lessing and Herder will be produced in Germany; and yet the names of these two men will fill a German with a reverence and enthusiasm such as the names of the most gifted masters will hardly awaken. And why? Because they *humanised* knowledge; because they broadened the basis of life and intelligence; because they worked powerfully to diffuse sweetness and light, to make reason and the will of God prevail. With Saint Augustine they said: 'Let us not leave Thee alone to make in the secret of thy knowledge, as thou didst before the creation of the firmament, the division of light from darkness; let the children of thy spirit, placed in their firmament, make their light shine upon the earth, mark the division of night and day, and announce the revolution of the times; for the old order is passed, and the new arises; the night is spent, the day is come forth; and thou shalt crown the year with thy blessing, when thou shalt send forth labourers into thy harvest sown by other hands than theirs; when thou shalt send forth new labourers to new seed-times, whereof the harvest shall be not yet.'[11]

## DOING AS ONE LIKES

. . .When I began to speak of culture, I insisted on our bondage to machinery, on our proneness to value machinery as an end in itself, without looking beyond it to the end for which alone, in truth, it is valuable. Freedom, I said, was one of those things which we thus worshipped in itself, without enough regarding the ends for which freedom is to be desired. In our common notions and talk about freedom, we eminently show our idolatry of machinery. Our prevalent notion is,—and I quoted a number of instances to prove it,—that it is a most happy and important thing for a man merely to be able to do as he likes. On what he is to do when he is thus free to do as he likes, we do not lay so much stress. Our familiar praise of the British Constitution under which we live, is that it is a

10. Peter Abelard (1079–1142), scholastic philosopher; Gotthold Ephraim Lessing (1729–81), German dramatist and critic; Johann Gottfried von Herder (1744–1803), Romantic philosopher.
11. St. Augustine, *Confessions*, 13.

system of checks,—a system which stops and paralyses any power in interfering with the free action of individuals. To this effect Mr. Bright, who loves to walk in the old ways of the Constitution, said forcibly in one of his great speeches, what many other people are every day saying less forcibly, that the central idea of English life and politics is *the assertion of personal liberty*. Evidently this is so; but evidently, also, as feudalism, which with its ideas and habits of subordination was for many centuries silently behind the British Constitution, dies out, and we are left with nothing but our system of checks, and our notion of its being the great right and happiness of an Englishman to do as far as possible what he likes, we are in danger of drifting towards anarchy. We have not the notion, so familiar on the Continent and to antiquity, of *the State*,—the nation in its collective and corporate character, entrusted with stringent powers for the general advantage, and controlling individual wills in the name of an interest wider than that of individuals. We say, what is very true, that this notion is often made instrumental to tyranny; we say that a State is in reality made up of the individuals who compose it, and that every individual is the best judge of his own interests. Our leading class is an aristocracy, and no aristocracy likes the notion of a State-authority greater than itself, with a stringent administrative machinery superseding the decorative inutilities of lord-lieutenancy, deputy-lieutenancy, and the *posse comitatûs*,[12] which are all in its own hands. Our middle class, the great representative of trade and Dissent, with its maxims of every man for himself in business, every man for himself in religion, dreads a powerful administration which might somehow interfere with it; and besides, it has its own decorative inutilities of vestrymanship and guardianship, which are to this class what lord-lieutenancy and the county magistracy are to the aristocratic class, and a stringent administration might either take these functions out of its hands, or prevent its exercising them in its own comfortable, independent manner, as at present.

Then as to our working class. This class, pressed constantly by the hard daily compulsion of material wants, is naturally the very centre and stronghold of our national idea, that it is man's ideal right and felicity to do as he likes. I think I have somewhere related how M. Michelet[13] said to me of the people of France, that it was 'a nation of barbarians civilised by the conscription.' He meant that through their military service the idea of public duty and of discipline was brought to the mind of these masses, in other respects so raw and uncultivated. Our masses are quite as raw and uncultivated as the French; and so far from their having the idea of public duty and of discipline, superior to the individual's self-will, brought to their mind by a universal obligation of military service, such as that of the conscription,—so far from their having this, the very idea of a conscription is so at variance with our English notion of the prime right and blessedness of doing as one likes, that I remember the manager of the Clay Cross works in Derbyshire told me during the Crimean war, when our want of soldiers was much felt and some people were talking of a conscription, that sooner than submit to a conscription the population of that district would flee to the mines, and lead a sort of Robin Hood life under ground.

12. "Power of the county": group of men assisting the sheriff in enforcing the law and quelling riots.
13. Jules Michelet (1798–1874), French historian.

For a long time, as I have said, the strong feudal habits of subordination and deference continued to tell upon the working class. The modern spirit has now almost entirely dissolved those habits, and the anarchical tendency of our worship of freedom in and for itself, of our superstitious faith, as I say, in machinery, is becoming very manifest. More and more, because of this our blind faith in machinery, because of our want of light to enable us to look beyond machinery to the end for which machinery is valuable, this and that man, and this and that body of men, all over the country, are beginning to assert and put in practice an Englishman's right to do what he likes; his right to march where he likes, meet where he likes, enter where he likes, hoot as he likes, threaten as he likes, smash as he likes. All this, I say, tends to anarchy; and though a number of excellent people, and particularly my friends of the Liberal or progressive party, as they call themselves, are kind enough to reassure us by saying that these are trifles, that a few transient outbreaks of rowdyism signify nothing, that our system of liberty is one which itself cures all the evils which it works, that the educated and intelligent classes stand in overwhelming strength and majestic repose, ready, like our military force in riots, to act at a moment's notice,—yet one finds that one's Liberal friends generally say this because they have such faith in themselves and their nostrums, when they shall return, as the public welfare requires, to place and power. But this faith of theirs one cannot exactly share, when one has so long had them and their nostrums at work, and sees that they have not prevented our coming to our present embarrassed condition. And one finds, also, that the outbreaks of rowdyism tend to become less and less of trifles, to become more frequent rather than less frequent; and that meanwhile our educated and intelligent classes remain in their majestic repose, and somehow or other, whatever happens, their overwhelming strength, like our military force in riots, never does act.

How, indeed, *should* their overwhelming strength act, when the man who gives an inflammatory lecture, or breaks down the Park railings, or invades a Secretary of State's office, is only following an Englishman's impulse to do as he likes; and our own conscience tells us that we ourselves have always regarded this impulse as something primary and sacred? Mr. Murphy[14] lectures at Birmingham, and showers on the Catholic population of that town 'words,' says the Home Secretary, 'only fit to be addressed to thieves or murderers.' What then? Mr. Murphy has his own reasons of several kinds. He suspects the Roman Catholic Church of designs upon Mrs. Murphy; and he says, if mayors and magistrates do not care for their wives and daughters, he does. But, above all, he is doing as he likes; or, in worthier language, asserting his personal liberty. 'I will carry out my lectures if they walk over my body as a dead corpse; and I say to the Mayor of Birmingham that he is my servant while I am in Birmingham, and as my servant he must do his duty and protect me.' Touching and beautiful words, which find a sympathetic chord in every British bosom! The moment it is plainly put before us that a man is asserting his personal liberty, we are half disarmed; because we are believers in freedom, and not in some dream of a right reason to which the assertion of our freedom is to be subordinated. Accordingly, the Secretary of State had to say that although the lecturer's language was

14. William Murphy, anti-Catholic agitator, who in 1867–8 gave inflammatory lectures against nunneries and the "dangers" of the confessional.

'only fit to be addressed to thieves or murderers,' yet, 'I do not think he is to be deprived, I do not think that anything I have said could justify the inference that he is to be deprived, of the right of protection in a place built by him for the purpose of these lectures; because the language was not language which afforded grounds for a criminal prosecution.' No, nor to be silenced by Mayor, or Home Secretary, or any administrative authority on earth, simply on their notion of what is discreet and reasonable! This is in perfect consonance with our public opinion, and with our national love for the assertion of personal liberty. . . .

But by our *best self* we are united, impersonal, at harmony. We are in no peril from giving authority to this, because it is the truest friend we all of us can have; and when anarchy is a danger to us, to this authority we may turn with sure trust. Well, and this is the very self which culture, or the study of perfection, seeks to develop in us; at the expense of our old untransformed self, taking pleasure only in doing what it likes or is used to do, and exposing us to the risk of clashing with every one else who is doing the same! So that our poor culture, which is flouted as so unpractical, leads us to the very ideas capable of meeting the great want of our present embarrassed times! We want an authority, and we find nothing but jealous classes, checks, and a deadlock; culture suggests the idea of *the State*. We find no basis for a firm State-power in our ordinary selves; culture suggests one to us in our *best self*.

It cannot but acutely try a tender conscience to be accused, in a practical country like ours, of keeping aloof from the work and hope of a multitude of earnest-hearted men, and of merely toying with poetry and æsthetics. So it is with no little sense of relief that I find myself thus in the position of one who makes a contribution in aid of the practical necessities of our times. The great thing, it will be observed, is to find our *best* self, and to seek to affirm nothing but that; not,—as we English with our over-value for merely being free and busy have been so accustomed to do,—resting satisfied with a self which comes uppermost long before our best self, and affirming that with blind energy. In short,—to go back yet once more to Bishop Wilson,—of these two excellent rules of Bishop Wilson's for a man's guidance: 'Firstly, never go against the best light you have; secondly, take care that your light be not darkness,' we English have followed with praiseworthy zeal the first rule, but we have not given so much heed to the second. We have gone manfully according to the best light we have; but we have not taken enough care that this should be really the best light possible for us, that it should not be darkness. And, our honesty being very great, conscience has whispered to us that the light we were following, our ordinary self, was, indeed, perhaps, only an inferior self, only darkness; and that it would not do to impose this seriously on all the world.

But our best self inspires faith, and is capable of affording a serious principle of authority. For example. We are on our way to what the late Duke of Wellington, with his strong sagacity, foresaw and admirably described as 'a revolution by due course of law.' This is undoubtedly,—if we are still to live and grow, and this famous nation is not to stagnate and dwindle away on the one hand, or, on the other, to perish miserably in mere anarchy and confusion,—what we are on the way to. Great changes there must be, for a revolution cannot accomplish itself without great changes; yet order there must be, for without order a revolution cannot accomplish itself by due course of law. So whatever brings risk of tumult and disorder, multitudinous processions in the streets of our crowded towns, multitudinous meetings in their public places and parks,—demonstrations perfectly unnecessary in the present course of our affairs,—our best self, or right reason, plainly enjoins us to set our faces against. It enjoins us to encourage and uphold the occupants of the executive power, whoever they may be, in firmly prohibiting them. But it does this clearly and resolutely, and is thus a real principle of authority, because it does it with a free conscience; because in thus provisionally strengthening the executive power, it knows that it is not doing this merely to enable our aristocratical baronet to affirm himself as against our working-men's tribune, or our middle-class Dissenter to affirm himself as against both. It knows that it is stablishing *the State*, or organ of our collective best self, of our national right reason. And it has the testimony of conscience that it is stablishing the State on behalf of whatever great changes are needed, just as much as on behalf of order; stablishing it to deal just as stringently, when the time comes, with our baronet's aristocratical prejudices, or with the fanaticism of our middle-class Dissenter, as it deals with Mr. Bradlaugh's street-processions.[15]

---

# LITERATURE AND SCIENCE

*Matthew Arnold's job as a school inspector gave him first-hand knowledge of the educational issues troubling his times. What kind of education best serves an individual living in a modern, industrialized, and democratized nation? What ought the educated person know in an age when new forms of knowledge, especially scientific knowledge, proliferate? To what ends should education aspire? Arnold tackles these questions in "Literature and Science," while simultaneously answering his friend Thomas Henry HUXLEY's attack on traditional, classical education in "Science and Culture." At the opening of Josiah Mason's Science College in Birmingham on October 1, 1880, Huxley had defended college benefactor Mason's injunction that "mere literary instruction and education" were to be excluded from the curriculum and had accused Arnold, "our chief apostle of culture," of elitism and of clinging to the past. Admittedly, Arnold's ideal education universalizes the education of the bourgeois intellectual, and his prescription of a common culture is that of "high culture." In this response to Huxley, Arnold quotes Huxley, as Huxley had quoted him, in the process redefining the terms of the debate and enlarging its scope. Education, he argues, should be more than the accumulation of pieces of knowledge; it should serve the aims of culture to know ourselves and our world; it should relate knowledge to "our sense for conduct" and "our sense for beauty."*

   *Arnold delivered an earlier version of this lecture at Cambridge University in June 1882 and published it in the August 1882 issue of* The Nineteenth Century. *During his*

---

15. Charles Bradlaugh (1833–91), an outspoken social activist and member of the Reform League, organized a reform meeting that led to riots in Hyde Park in July 1866.

tour of America in 1883–4, he delivered the revised "Literature and Science" to numerous
audiences. In 1885 he published the American version in Discourses in America, the
source of the following selection.                                              RM

PRACTICAL PEOPLE TALK WITH A smile of Plato and of his absolute ideas; and it is impossible to deny that Plato's ideas do often seem unpractical and impracticable, and especially when one views them in connexion with the life of a great work-a-day world like the United States. The necessary staple of the life of such a world Plato regards with disdain; handicraft and trade and the working professions he regards with disdain; but what becomes of the life of an industrial modern community if you take handicraft and trade and the working professions out of it? The base mechanic arts and handicrafts, says Plato, bring about a natural weakness in the principle of excellence in a man, so that he cannot govern the ignoble growths in him, but nurses them, and cannot understand fostering any other.[1] Those who exercise such arts and trades, as they have their bodies, he says, marred by their vulgar businesses, so they have their souls, too, bowed and broken by them. And if one of these uncomely people has a mind to seek self-culture and philosophy, Plato compares him to a bald little tinker, who has scraped together money, and has got his release from service, and has had a bath, and bought a new coat, and is rigged out like a bridegroom about to marry the daughter of his master who has fallen into poor and helpless estate.

Nor do the working professions fare any better than trade at the hands of Plato. He draws for us an inimitable picture of the working lawyer, and of his life of bondage; he shows how this bondage from his youth up has stunted and warped him, and made him small and crooked of soul, encompassing him with difficulties which he is not man enough to rely on justice and truth as means to encounter, but has recourse, for help out of them, to falsehood and wrong. And so, says Plato, this poor creature is bent and broken, and grows up from boy to man without a particle of soundness in him, although exceedingly smart and clever in his own esteem.

One cannot refuse to admire the artist who draws these pictures. But we say to ourselves that his ideas show the influence of a primitive and obsolete order of things, when the warrior caste and the priestly caste were alone in honour, and the humble work of the world was done by slaves. We have now changed all that; the modern majority consists in work, as Emerson declares;[2] and in work, we may add, principally of such plain and dusty kind as the work of cultivators of the ground, handicraftsmen, men of trade and business, men of the working professions. Above all is this true in a great industrious community such as that of the United States.

Now education, many people go on to say, is still mainly governed by the ideas of men like Plato, who lived when the warrior caste and the priestly or philosophical class were alone in honour, and the really useful part of the community were slaves. It is an education fitted for persons of leisure in such a community. This education passed from Greece and Rome to the feudal communities of Europe, where also the warrior caste and the

1. Plato, Republic 6:495.
2. Ralph Waldo Emerson, "Literary Ethics," Nature, Addresses, and Lectures (1849).

priestly caste were alone held in honour, and where the really useful and working part of the community, though not nominally slaves as in the pagan world, were practically not much better off than slaves, and not more seriously regarded. And how absurd it is, people end by saying, to inflict this education upon an industrious modern community, where very few indeed are persons of leisure, and the mass to be considered has not leisure, but is bound, for its own great good, and for the great good of the world at large, to plain labour and to industrial pursuits, and the education in question tends necessarily to make men dissatisfied with these pursuits and unfitted for them!

That is what is said. So far I must defend Plato, as to plead that his view of education and studies is in the general, as it seems to me, sound enough, and fitted for all sorts and conditions of men, whatever their pursuits may be. 'An intelligent man,' says Plato, 'will prize those studies which result in his soul getting soberness, righteousness, and wisdom, and will less value the others.'[3] I cannot consider *that* a bad description of the aim of education, and of the motives which should govern us in the choice of studies, whether we are preparing ourselves for a hereditary seat in the English House of Lords or for the pork trade in Chicago.

Still I admit that Plato's world was not ours, that his scorn of trade and handicraft is fantastic, that he had no conception of a great industrial community such as that of the United States, and that such a community must and will shape its education to suit its own needs. If the usual education handed down to it from the past does not suit it, it will certainly before long drop this and try another. The usual education in the past has been mainly literary. The question is whether the studies which were long supposed to be the best for all of us are practically the best now; whether others are not better. The tyranny of the past, many think, weighs on us injuriously in the predominance given to letters in education. The question is raised whether, to meet the needs of our modern life, the predominance ought not now to pass from letters to science; and naturally the question is nowhere raised with more energy than here in the United States. The design of abasing what is called 'mere literary instruction and education,' and of exalting what is called 'sound, extensive, and practical scientific knowledge,' is, in this intensely modern world of the United States, even more perhaps than in Europe, a very popular design, and makes great and rapid progress.

I am going to ask whether the present movement for ousting letters from their old predominance in education, and for transferring the predominance in education to the natural sciences, whether this brisk and flourishing movement ought to prevail, and whether it is likely that in the end it really will prevail. An objection may be raised which I will anticipate. My own studies have been almost wholly in letters, and my visits to the field of the natural sciences have been very slight and inadequate, although those sciences have always strongly moved my curiosity. A man of letters, it will perhaps be said, is not competent to discuss the comparative merits of letters and natural science as means of education. To this objection I reply, first of all, that his incompetence, if he attempts the discussion but is really incompetent for it, will be abundantly visible; nobody will be taken in; he will have plenty of sharp observers and critics to save mankind from that dan-

3. *Republic* 9:591.

ger. But the line I am going to follow is, as you will soon discover, so extremely simple, that perhaps it may be followed without failure even by one who for a more ambitious line of discussion would be quite incompetent.

Some of you may possibly remember a phrase of mine which has been the object of a good deal of comment; an observation to the effect that in our culture, the aim being *to know ourselves and the world*, we have, as the means to this end, *to know the best which has been thought and said in the world*.[4] A man of science, who is also an excellent writer and the very prince of debaters, Professor Huxley, in a discourse at the opening of Sir Josiah Mason's college at Birmingham, laying hold of this phrase, expanded it by quoting some more words of mine, which are these: 'The civilised world is to be regarded as now being, for intellectual and spiritual purposes, one great confederation, bound to a joint action and working to a common result; and whose members have for their proper outfit a knowledge of Greek, Roman, and Eastern antiquity, and of one another. Special local and temporary advantages being put out of account, that modern nation will in the intellectual and spiritual sphere make most progress, which most thoroughly carries out this programme.'

Now on my phrase, thus enlarged, Professor Huxley remarks that when I speak of the above-mentioned knowledge as enabling us to know ourselves and the world, I assert *literature* to contain the materials which suffice for thus making us know ourselves and the world. But it is not by any means clear, says he, that after having learnt all which ancient and modern literatures have to tell us, we have laid a sufficiently broad and deep foundation for that criticism of life, that knowledge of ourselves and the world, which constitutes culture. On the contrary, Professor Huxley declares that he finds himself 'wholly unable to admit that either nations or individuals will really advance, if their outfit draws nothing from the stores of physical science. An army without weapons of precision, and with no particular base of operations, might more hopefully enter upon a campaign on the Rhine, than a man, devoid of a knowledge of what physical science has done in the last century, upon a criticism of life.'

This shows how needful it is for those who are to discuss any matter together, to have a common understanding as to the sense of the terms they employ,—how needful, and how difficult. What Professor Huxley says, implies just the reproach which is so often brought against the study of *belles lettres*, as they are called: that the study is an elegant one, but slight and ineffectual; a smattering of Greek and Latin and other ornamental things, of little use for any one whose object is to get at truth, and to be a practical man. So, too, M. Renan talks of the 'superficial humanism' of a school-course which treats us as if we were all going to be poets, writers, preachers, orators, and he opposes this humanism to positive science, or the critical search after truth.[5] And there is always a tendency in those who are remonstrating against the predominance of letters in education, to understand by letters *belles lettres*, and by *belles lettres* a superficial humanism, the opposite of science or true knowledge.

---

4. Familiar Arnoldian phrases. See especially "The Function of Criticism at the Present Time," *Essays in Criticism* (1865).
5. Ernest Renan, *Souvenirs d'enfance et de jeunesse* (1883).

But when we talk of knowing Greek and Roman antiquity, for instance, which is the knowledge people have called the humanities, I for my part mean a knowledge which is something more than a superficial humanism, mainly decorative. 'I call all teaching *scientific*,' says Wolf, the critic of Homer, 'which is systematically laid out and followed up to its original sources. For example: a knowledge of classical antiquity is scientific when the remains of classical antiquity are correctly studied in the original languages.'[6] There can be no doubt that Wolf is perfectly right; that all learning is scientific which is systematically laid out and followed up to its original sources, and that a genuine humanism is scientific.

When I speak of knowing Greek and Roman antiquity, therefore, as a help to knowing ourselves and the world, I mean more than a knowledge of so much vocabulary, so much grammar, so many portions of authors in the Greek and Latin languages. I mean knowing the Greeks and Romans, and their life and genius, and what they were and did in the world; what we get from them, and what is its value. That, at least, is the ideal; and when we talk of endeavouring to know Greek and Roman antiquity, as a help to knowing ourselves and the world, we mean endeavouring so to know them as to satisfy this ideal, however much we may still fall short of it.

The same also as to knowing our own and other modern nations, with the like aim of getting to understand ourselves and the world. To know the best that has been thought and said by the modern nations, is to know, says Professor Huxley, 'only what modern *literatures* have to tell us; it is the criticism of life contained in modern literature.' And yet 'the distinctive character of our times,' he urges, 'lies in the vast and constantly increasing part which is played by natural knowledge.' And how, therefore, can a man, devoid of knowledge of what physical science has done in the last century, enter hopefully upon a criticism of modern life?

Let us, I say, be agreed about the meaning of the terms we are using. I talk of knowing the best which has been thought and uttered in the world; Professor Huxley says this means knowing *literature*. Literature is a large word; it may mean everything written with letters or printed in a book. Euclid's *Elements* and Newton's *Principia* are thus literature. All knowledge that reaches us through books is literature. But by literature Professor Huxley means *belles lettres*. He means to make me say, that knowing the best which has been thought and said by the modern nations is knowing their *belles lettres* and no more. And this is no sufficient equipment, he argues, for a criticism of modern life. But as I do not mean, by knowing ancient Rome, knowing merely more or less of Latin *belles lettres*, and taking no account of Rome's military, and political, and legal, and administrative work in the world; and as, by knowing ancient Greece, I understand knowing her as the giver of Greek art, and the guide to a free and right use of reason and to scientific method, and the founder of our mathematics and physics and astronomy and biology,— I understand knowing her as all this, and not merely knowing certain Greek poems, and histories, and treatises, and speeches,—so as to the knowledge of modern nations also. By knowing modern nations, I mean not merely knowing their *belles lettres*, but knowing

6. Friedrich August Wolf (1759–1824), classical scholar.

also what has been done by such men as Copernicus, Galileo, Newton, Darwin. 'Our ancestors learned,' says Professor Huxley, 'that the earth is the centre of the visible universe, and that man is the cynosure of things terrestrial; and more especially was it inculcated that the course of nature had no fixed order, but that it could be, and constantly was, altered.' But for us now, continues Professor Huxley, 'the notions of the beginning and the end of the world entertained by our forefathers are no longer credible. It is very certain that the earth is not the chief body in the material universe, and that the world is not subordinated to man's use. It is even more certain that nature is the expression of a definite order, with which nothing interferes.' 'And yet,' he cries, 'the purely classical education advocated by the representatives of the humanists in our day gives no inkling of all this!'

. . .The reproach of being a superficial humanism, a tincture of *belles lettres*, may attach rightly enough to some other disciplines; but to the particular discipline recommended when I proposed knowing the best that has been thought and said in the world, it does not apply. In that best I certainly include what in modern times has been thought and said by the great observers and knowers of nature.

There is, therefore, really no question between Professor Huxley and me as to whether knowing the great results of the modern scientific study of nature is not required as a part of our culture, as well as knowing the products of literature and art. But to follow the processes by which those results are reached, ought, say the friends of physical science, to be made the staple of education for the bulk of mankind. And here there does arise a question between those whom Professor Huxley calls with playful sarcasm 'the Levites of culture,' and those whom the poor humanist is sometimes apt to regard as its Nebuchadnezzars.[7]

The great results of the scientific investigation of nature we are agreed upon knowing, but how much of our study are we bound to give to the processes by which those results are reached? The results have their visible bearing on human life. But all the processes, too, all the items of fact, by which those results are reached and established, are interesting. All knowledge is interesting to a wise man, and the knowledge of nature is interesting to all men. It is very interesting to know, that, from the albuminous white of the egg, the chick in the egg gets the materials for its flesh, bones, blood, and feathers; while, from the fatty yolk of the egg, it gets the heat and energy which enable it at length to break its shell and begin the world. It is less interesting, perhaps, but still it is interesting, to know that when a taper burns, the wax is converted into carbonic acid and water. Moreover, it is quite true that the habit of dealing with facts, which is given by the study of nature, is, as the friends of physical science praise it for being, an excellent discipline. The appeal, in the study of nature, is constantly to observation and experiment; not only is it said that the thing is so, but we can be made to see that is it so. Not only does a man tell us that when a taper burns the wax is converted into carbonic acid and water, as a man may tell us, if he likes, that Charon is punting his ferry-boat on the river Styx, or that Victor Hugo is a sublime poet, or Mr. Gladstone the most admirable of statesmen;

7. Babylonian king (reigned *ca.* 605–562 B.C.) who captured and sacked Jerusalem.

but we are made to see that the conversion into carbonic acid and water does actually happen. This reality of natural knowledge it is, which makes the friends of physical science contrast it, as a knowledge of things, with the humanist's knowledge, which is, say they, a knowledge of words. And hence Professor Huxley is moved to lay it down that, 'for the purpose of attaining real culture, an exclusively scientific education is at least as effectual as an exclusively literary education.' And a certain President of the Section for Mechanical Science in the British Association is, in Scripture phrase, 'very bold,' and declares that if a man, in his mental training, 'has substituted literature and history for natural science, he has chosen the less useful alternative.'[8] But whether we go these lengths or not, we must all admit that in natural science the habit gained of dealing with facts is a most valuable discipline, and that every one should have some experience of it.

More than this, however, is demanded by the reformers. It is proposed to make the training in natural science the main part of education, for the great majority of mankind at any rate. And here, I confess, I part company with the friends of physical science, with whom up to this point I have been agreeing. In differing from them, however, I wish to proceed with the utmost caution and diffidence. The smallness of my own acquaintance with the disciplines of natural science is ever before my mind, and I am fearful of doing these disciplines an injustice. The ability and pugnacity of the partisans of natural science make them formidable persons to contradict. The tone of tentative inquiry, which befits a being of dim faculties and bounded knowledge, is the tone I would wish to take and not to depart from. At present it seems to me, that those who are for giving to natural knowledge, as they call it, the chief place in the education of the majority of mankind, leave one important thing out of their account: the constitution of human nature. But I put this forward on the strength of some facts not at all recondite, very far from it; facts capable of being stated in the simplest possible fashion, and to which, if I so state them, the man of science will, I am sure, be willing to allow their due weight.

Deny the facts altogether, I think, he hardly can. He can hardly deny, that when we set ourselves to enumerate the powers which go to the building up of human life, and say that they are the power of conduct, the power of intellect and knowledge, the power of beauty, and the power of social life and manners,—he can hardly deny that this scheme, though drawn in rough and plain lines enough, and not pretending to scientific exactness, does yet give a fairly true representation of the matter. Human nature is built up by these powers; we have the need for them all. When we have rightly met and adjusted the claims of them all, we shall then be in a fair way for getting soberness and righteousness, with wisdom. This is evident enough, and the friends of physical science would admit it.

But perhaps they may not have sufficiently observed another thing: namely, that the several powers just mentioned are not isolated, but there is, in the generality of mankind, a perpetual tendency to relate them one to another in divers ways. With one such way of relating them I am particularly concerned now. Following our instinct for intellect and knowledge, we acquire pieces of knowledge; and presently, in the generality of men, there arises the desire to relate these pieces of knowledge to our sense for conduct, to

8. Charles Watkins Merrifield, speaking in 1876 in Glasgow.

our sense for beauty,—and there is weariness and dissatisfaction if the desire is baulked. Now in this desire lies, I think, the strength of that hold which letters have upon us. . . .

And the more that men's minds are cleared, the more that the results of science are frankly accepted, the more that poetry and eloquence come to be received and studied as what in truth they really are,—the criticism of life by gifted men, alive and active with extraordinary power at an unusual number of points;—so much the more will the value of humane letters, and of art also, which is an utterance having a like kind of power with theirs, be felt and acknowledged, and their place in education be secured.

Let us therefore, all of us, avoid indeed as much as possible any invidious comparison between the merits of humane letters, as means of education, and the merits of the natural sciences. But when some President of a Section for Mechanical Science insists on making the comparison, and tells us that 'he who in his training has substituted literature and history for natural science has chosen the less useful alternative,' let us make answer to him that the student of humane letters only, will, at least, know also the great general conceptions brought in by modern physical science; for science, as Professor Huxley says, forces them upon us all. But the student of the natural sciences only, will, by our very hypothesis, know nothing of humane letters; not to mention that in setting himself to be perpetually accumulating natural knowledge, he sets himself to do what only specialists have in general the gift for doing genially. And so he will probably be unsatisfied, or at any rate incomplete, and even more incomplete than the student of humane letters only.

I once mentioned in a school-report, how a young man in one of our English training colleges having to paraphrase the passage in *Macbeth* beginning,

'Can'st thou not minister to a mind diseased?'[9]

turned this line into, 'Can you not wait upon the lunatic?' And I remarked what a curious state of things it would be, if every pupil of our national schools knew, let us say, that the moon is two thousand one hundred and sixty miles in diameter, and thought at the same time that a good paraphrase for

'Can'st thou not minister to a mind diseased?'

was, 'Can you not wait upon the lunatic?' If one is driven to choose, I think I would rather have a young person ignorant about the moon's diameter, but aware that 'Can you not wait upon the lunatic?' is bad, than a young person whose education has been such as to manage things the other way.

Or to go higher than the pupils of our national schools. I have in my mind's eye a member of our British Parliament[10] who comes to travel here in America, who afterwards relates his travels, and who shows a really masterly knowledge of the geology of this great country and of its mining capabilities, but who ends by gravely suggesting that the United States should borrow a prince from our Royal Family, and should make him their king,

9. William Shakespeare, *Macbeth*, 5.3.
10. H. Hussey Vivian, *Notes of a Tour in America* (1878).

and should create a House of Lords of great landed proprietors after the pattern of ours; and then America, he thinks, would have her future happily and perfectly secured. Surely, in this case, the President of the Section for Mechanical Science would himself hardly say that our member of Parliament, by concentrating himself upon geology and mineralogy, and so on, and not attending to literature and history, had 'chosen the more useful alternative.'

If then there is to be separation and option between humane letters on the one hand, and the natural sciences on the other, the great majority of mankind, all who have not exceptional and overpowering aptitudes for the study of nature, would do well, I cannot but think, to choose to be educated in humane letters rather than in the natural sciences. Letters will call out their being at more points, will make them live more. . . .

# Thomas Henry Huxley

1825: Born 4 May at Ealing

1842–5: Studied medicine at University of London and Charing Cross Hospital

1846–50: Employed as assistant-surgeon aboard H.M.S. *Rattlesnake*

1854: Appointed Lecturer of Natural History, Royal School of Mines

1860: Debated Bishop Samuel Wilberforce at Oxford

1863: *Evidence as to Man's Place in Nature*

1868: "On the Physical Basis of Life"

1880: "Science and Culture" delivered as lecture; published the following year in *Science and Culture, and Other Essays*

1895: Died 29 June at Eastbourne

## SCIENCE AND CULTURE

*Although Thomas Henry Huxley is probably best known today for his championing of Charles Darwin's theory of evolution, Huxley's own scientific work in comparative anatomy, his philosophical investigations of the relationship between ethics and science, his role as a popularizer of science, and his powerful advocacy of scientific education made him a formidable presence in major debates of the second half of the century. An impressive lecturer and teacher, Huxley could explain science plainly to a lay audience, using a piece of chalk or a lump of coal to elucidate a principle or discovery. An outspoken advocate of educational reform, Huxley campaigned for the inclusion of scientific studies in schools and universities.*

*His 1880 address at the opening of Josiah Mason's Science College in Birmingham focuses on the importance of scientific knowledge and methods to education and culture. Defending College benefactor Josiah Mason's dictum to exclude "mere literary instruction and education" from the college's curriculum, Huxley takes aim at the proponents of classical education, including the "chief apostle of culture," Matthew Arnold. Borrowing Arnold's language, Huxley argues that literature alone, especially the acquaintance with Latin and Greek that sometimes passes for classical education, does not provide an individual with the "criticism of life" that constitutes "culture."* RM

. . . FROM THE TIME THAT THE first suggestion to introduce physical science into ordinary education was timidly whispered, until now, the advocates of scientific education have met with opposition of two kinds. On the one hand, they have been pooh-poohed by the men of business who pride themselves on being the representatives of practicality; while, on the other hand, they have been excommunicated by the classical scholars, in their capacity of Levites in charge of the ark of culture and monopolists of liberal education.

The practical men believed that the idol whom they worship—rule of thumb—has been the source of the past prosperity, and will suffice for the future welfare of the arts and manufactures. They were of opinion that science is speculative rubbish; that theory and practice have nothing to do with one another; and that the scientific habit of mind is an impediment, rather than an aid, in the conduct of ordinary affairs.

I have used the past tense in speaking of the practical men—for although they were very formidable thirty years ago, I am not sure that the pure species has not been extirpated. In fact, so far as mere argument goes, they have been subjected to such a *feu d'enfer*[1] that it is a miracle if any have escaped. But I have remarked that your typical practical man has an unexpected resemblance to one of Milton's angels. His spiritual wounds, such as are inflicted by logical weapons, may be as deep as a well and as wide as a church door, but beyond shedding a few drops of ichor, celestial or otherwise, he is no whit the worse. So, if any of these opponents be left, I will not waste time in vain repetition of the demonstrative evidence of the practical value of science; but knowing that a parable will sometimes penetrate where syllogisms fail to effect an entrance, I will offer a story for their consideration.

Once upon a time, a boy, with nothing to depend upon but his own vigorous nature, was thrown into the thick of the struggle for existence in the midst of a great manufacturing population. He seems to have had a hard fight, inasmuch as, by the time he was thirty years of age, his total disposable funds amounted to twenty pounds. Nevertheless, middle life found him giving proof of his comprehension of the practical problems he had been roughly called upon to solve, by a career of remarkable prosperity.

Finally, having reached old age with its well-earned surroundings of "honour, troops of friends," the hero of my story bethought himself of those who were making a like start in life, and how he could stretch out a helping hand to them.

After long and anxious reflection this successful practical man of business could devise nothing better than to provide them with the means of obtaining "sound, extensive, and practical scientific knowledge." And he devoted a large part of his wealth and five years of incessant work to this end.

I need not point the moral of a tale which, as the solid and spacious fabric of the Scientific College assures us, is no fable, nor can anything which I could say intensify the force of this practical answer to practical objections.

We may take it for granted then, that, in the opinion of those best qualified to judge, the diffusion of thorough scientific education is an absolutely essential condition of industrial progress; and that the College which has been opened to-day will confer an inestimable boon upon those whose livelihood is to be gained by the practice of the arts and

---

1. Literally, "fire of hell."

manufactures of the district.

The only question worth discussion is, whether the conditions, under which the work of the College is to be carried out, are such as to give it the best possible chance of achieving permanent success.

Sir Josiah Mason, without doubt most wisely, has left very large freedom of action to the trustees, to whom he proposes ultimately to commit the administration of the College, so that they may be able to adjust its arrangements in accordance with the changing conditions of the future. But, with respect to three points, he has laid most explicit injunctions upon both administrators and teachers.

Party politics are forbidden to enter into the minds of either, so far as the work of the College is concerned; theology is as sternly banished from its precincts; and finally, it is especially declared that the College shall make no provision for "mere literary instruction and education."

It does not concern me at present to dwell upon the first two injunctions any longer than may be needful to express my full conviction of their wisdom. But the third prohibition brings us face to face with those other opponents of scientific education, who are by no means in the moribund condition of the practical man, but alive, alert, and formidable.

It is not impossible that we shall hear this express exclusion of "literary instruction and education" from a College which, nevertheless, professes to give a high and efficient education, sharply criticised. Certainly the time was that the Levites of culture would have sounded their trumpets against its walls as against an educational Jericho.

How often have we not been told that the study of physical science is incompetent to confer culture; that it touches none of the higher problems of life; and, what is worse, that the continual devotion to scientific studies tends to generate a narrow and bigoted belief in the applicability of scientific methods to the search after truth of all kinds. How frequently one has reason to observe that no reply to a troublesome argument tells so well as calling its author a "mere scientific specialist." And, as I am afraid it is not permissible to speak of this form of opposition to scientific education in the past tense; may we not expect to be told that this, not only omission, but prohibition, of "mere literary instruction and education" is a patent example of scientific narrow-mindedness?

I am not acquainted with Sir Josiah Mason's reasons for the action which he has taken; but if, as I apprehend is the case, he refers to the ordinary classical course of our schools and universities by the name of "mere literary instruction and education," I venture to offer sundry reasons of my own in support of that action.

For I hold very strongly by two convictions—The first is, that neither the discipline nor the subject-matter of classical education is of such direct value to the student of physical science as to justify the expenditure of valuable time upon either; and the second is, that for the purpose of attaining real culture, an exclusively scientific education is at least as effectual as an exclusively literary education.

I need hardly point out to you that these opinions, especially the latter, are diametrically opposed to those of the great majority of educated Englishmen, influenced as they are by school and university traditions. In their belief, culture is obtainable only by a liberal education; and a liberal education is synonymous, not merely with education and instruction in literature, but in one particular form of literature, namely, that of Greek and Roman antiquity. They hold that the man who has learned Latin and Greek, however little, is educated; while he who is versed in other branches of knowledge, however deeply, is a more or less respectable specialist, not admissible into the cultured caste. The stamp of the educated man, the University degree, is not for him.

I am too well acquainted with the generous catholicity of spirit, the true sympathy with scientific thought, which pervades the writings of our chief apostle of culture to identify him with these opinions; and yet one may cull from one and another of those epistles to the Philistines, which so much delight all who do not answer to that name, sentences which lend them some support.

Mr. Arnold tells us that the meaning of culture is "to know the best that has been thought and said in the world." It is the criticism of life contained in literature. That criticism regards "Europe as being, for intellectual and spiritual purposes, one great confederation, bound to a joint action and working to a common result; and whose members have, for their common outfit, a knowledge of Greek, Roman, and Eastern antiquity, and of one another. Special, local, and temporary advantages being put out of account, that modern nation will in the intellectual and spiritual sphere make most progress, which most thoroughly carries out this programme. And what is that but saying that we too, all of us, as individuals, the more thoroughly we carry it out, shall make the more progress?"[2]

We have here to deal with two distinct propositions. The first, that a criticism of life is the essence of culture; the second, that literature contains the materials which suffice for the construction of such a criticism.

I think that we must all assent to the first proposition. For culture certainly means something quite different from learning or technical skill. It implies the possession of an ideal, and the habit of critically estimating the value of things by comparison with a theoretic standard. Perfect culture should supply a complete theory of life, based upon a clear knowledge alike of its possibilities and of its limitations.

But we may agree to all this, and yet strongly dissent from the assumption that literature alone is competent to supply this knowledge. After having learnt all that Greek, Roman, and Eastern antiquity have thought and said, and all that modern literatures have to tell us, it is not self-evident that we have laid a sufficiently broad and deep foundation for that criticism of life which constitutes culture.

Indeed, to any one acquainted with the scope of physical science, it is not at all evident. Considering progress only in the "intellectual and spiritual sphere," I find myself wholly unable to admit that either nations or individuals will really advance, if their common outfit draws nothing from the stores of physical science. I should say that an army, without weapons of precision and with no particular base of operations, might more hopefully enter upon a campaign on the Rhine, than a man, devoid of a knowledge of what physical science has done in the last century, upon a criticism of life. . . .

2. *Essays in Criticism*, p. 37. [Huxley's note]

This distinctive character of our own times lies in the vast and constantly increasing part which is played by natural knowledge. Not only is our daily life shaped by it, not only does the prosperity of millions of men depend upon it, but our whole theory of life has long been influenced, consciously or unconsciously, by the general conceptions of the universe, which have been forced upon us by physical science.

In fact, the most elementary acquaintance with the results of scientific investigation shows us that they offer a broad and striking contradiction to the opinions so implicitly credited and taught in the middle ages.

The notions of the beginning and the end of the world entertained by our forefathers are no longer credible. It is very certain that the earth is not the chief body in the material universe, and that the world is not subordinated to man's use. It is even more certain that nature is the expression of a definite order with which nothing interferes, and that the chief business of mankind is to learn that order and govern themselves accordingly. Moreover this scientific "criticism of life" presents itself to us with different credentials from any other. It appeals not to authority, nor to what anybody may have thought or said, but to nature. It admits that all our interpretations of natural fact are more or less imperfect and symbolic, and bids the learner seek for truth not among words but among things. It warns us that the assertion which outstrips evidence is not only a blunder but a crime.

The purely classical education advocated by the representatives of the Humanists in our day, gives no inkling of all this. A man may be a better scholar than Erasmus,[3] and know no more of the chief causes of the present intellectual fermentation than Erasmus did. Scholarly and pious persons, worthy of all respect, favour us with allocutions upon the sadness of the antagonism of science to their mediæval way of thinking, which betray an ignorance of the first principles of scientific investigation, an incapacity for understanding what a man of science means by veracity, and an unconsciousness of the weight of established scientific truths, which is almost comical.

There is no great force in the *tu quoque* argument, or else the advocates of scientific education might fairly enough retort upon the modern Humanists that they may be learned specialists, but that they possess no such sound foundation for a criticism of life as deserves the name of culture. And, indeed, if we were disposed to be cruel, we might urge that the Humanists have brought this reproach upon themselves, not because they are too full of the spirit of the ancient Greek, but because they lack it. . . .

We cannot know all the best thoughts and sayings of the Greeks unless we know what they thought about natural phenomena. We cannot fully apprehend their criticism of life unless we understand the extent to which that criticism was affected by scientific conceptions. We falsely pretend to be the inheritors of their culture, unless we are penetrated, as the best minds among them were, with an unhesitating faith that the free employment of reason, in accordance with scientific method, is the sole method of reaching truth.

Thus I venture to think that the pretensions of our modern Humanists to the possession of the monopoly of culture and to the exclusive inheritance of the spirit of antiqui-

---

3. Erasmus (*ca.* 1466–1536), Christian humanist.

ty must be abated, if not abandoned. But I should be very sorry that anything I have said should be taken to imply a desire on my part to depreciate the value of classical education, as it might be and as it sometimes is. The native capacities of mankind vary no less than their opportunities; and while culture is one, the road by which one man may best reach it is widely different from that which is most advantageous to another. Again, while scientific education is yet inchoate and tentative, classical education is thoroughly well organised upon the practical experience of generations of teachers. So that, given ample time for learning and destination for ordinary life, or for a literary career, I do not think that a young Englishman in search of culture can do better than follow the course usually marked out for him, supplementing its deficiencies by his own efforts.

But for those who mean to make science their serious occupation; or who intend to follow the profession of medicine; or who have to enter early upon the business of life; for all these, in my opinion, classical education is a mistake; and it is for this reason that I am glad to see "mere literary education and instruction" shut out from the curriculum of Sir Josiah Mason's College, seeing that its inclusion would probably lead to the introduction of the ordinary smattering of Latin and Greek.

Nevertheless, I am the last person to question the importance of genuine literary education, or to suppose that intellectual culture can be complete without it. An exclusively scientific training will bring about a mental twist as surely as an exclusively literary training. The value of the cargo does not compensate for a ship's being out of trim; and I should be very sorry to think that the Scientific College would turn out none but lop-sided men.

There is no need, however, that such a catastrophe should happen. Instruction in English, French, and German is provided, and thus the three greatest literatures of the modern world are made accessible to the student.

French and German, and especially the latter language, are absolutely indispensable to those who desire full knowledge in any department of science. But even supposing that the knowledge of these languages acquired is not more than sufficient for purely scientific purposes, every Englishman has, in his native tongue, an almost perfect instrument of literary expression; and, in his own literature, models of every kind of literary excellence. If an Englishman cannot get literary culture out of his Bible, his Shakspeare, his Milton, neither, in my belief, will the profoundest study of Homer and Sophocles, Virgil and Horace, give it to him.

Thus, since the constitution of the College makes sufficient provision for literary as well as for scientific education, and since artistic instruction is also contemplated, it seems to me that a fairly complete culture is offered to all who are willing to take advantage of it. . . .

---

## AGNOSTICISM AND CHRISTIANITY

---

*Huxley's skeptical empiricism led him to reserve judgment about a deity whose existence could not be demonstrated by physical evidence. To believe in an assertion that "outstrips evidence," he maintained in "Science and Culture," is both a blunder and a crime. In 1869 he coined the word "agnostic" to describe his own attitude of "not-knowing." Two decades later, when Dr. Henry Wace, Principal of King's College, and Dr. W. C. Magee, Bishop of Peterborough, denounced agnosticism and accused agnostics, and particularly Huxley, of "evasion," of hiding behind the new term rather than using the more accurate word "infidel," the disagreement spilled over into the pages of* The Nineteenth Century. *The following essay, the fourth of Huxley's contributions on the subject, was published in the magazine's June 1889 issue.*                                                    RM

CONTROVERSY, LIKE MOST THINGS IN this world, has a good and a bad side. On the good side, it may be said that it stimulates the wits, tends to clear the mind, and often helps those engaged in it to get a better grasp of their subject than they had before; while, mankind being essentially fighting animals, a contest leads the public to interest themselves in questions to which, otherwise, they would give but a languid attention. On the bad side, controversy is rarely found to sweeten the temper, and generally tends to degenerate into an exchange of more or less effective sarcasms. Moreover, if it is long continued, the original and really important issues are apt to become obscured by disputes on the collateral and relatively insignificant questions which have cropped up in the course of the discussion. No doubt both of these aspects of controversy have manifested themselves in the course of the debate which has been in progress, for some months, in these pages. So far as I may have illustrated the second, I express repentance and desire absolution, and I shall endeavour to make amends for any foregone lapses by an endeavour to exhibit only the better phase in these concluding remarks.

The present discussion has arisen out of the use, which has become general in the last few years, of the terms 'Agnostic' and 'Agnosticism.'

The people who call themselves 'Agnostics' have been charged with doing so because they have not the courage to declare themselves 'Infidels.' It has been insinuated that they have adopted a new name in order to escape the unpleasantness which attaches to their proper denomination. To this wholly erroneous imputation, I have replied by showing that the term 'Agnostic' did, as a matter of fact, arise in a manner which negatives it; and my statement has not been, and cannot be, refuted. Moreover, speaking for myself, and without impugning the right of any other person to use the term in another sense, I further say that Agnosticism is not properly described as a 'negative' creed, nor indeed as a creed of any kind, except in so far as it expresses absolute faith in the validity of a principle which is as much ethical as intellectual. This principle may be stated in various ways, but they all amount to this: that it is wrong for a man to say that he is certain of the objective truth of any proposition unless he can produce evidence which logically justifies that certainty. This is what Agnosticism asserts; and, in my opinion, it is all that is essential to Agnosticism. That which Agnostics deny and repudiate, as immoral, is the contrary doctrine, that there are propositions which men ought to believe, without logically satisfactory evidence; and that reprobation ought to attach to the profession of disbelief in such inadequately supported propositions. The justification of the Agnostic principle lies in the success which follows upon its application, whether in the field of natural, or in that of civil, history; and in the fact that, so far as these topics are concerned, no sane man thinks of denying its validity.

Still speaking for myself, I add, that though Agnosticism is not, and cannot be, a creed, except in so far as its general principle is concerned; yet that the application of that principle results in the denial of, or the suspension of judgment concerning, a number of propositions respecting which our contemporary ecclesiastical 'gnostics' profess entire certainty. And in so far as these ecclesiastical persons can be justified in their old-established custom (which many nowadays think more honoured in the breach than the observance) of using opprobrious names to those who differ from them, I fully admit their right to call me and those who think with me 'Infidels:' all I have ventured to urge is that they must not expect us to speak of ourselves by that title.

The extent of the region of the uncertain, the number of the problems the investigation of which ends in a verdict of not proven, will vary according to the knowledge and the intellectual habits of the individual Agnostic. I do not very much care to speak of anything as unknowable. What I am sure about is that there are many topics about which I know nothing; and which, so far as I can see, are out of reach of my faculties. But whether these things are knowable by any one else is exactly one of those matters which is beyond my knowledge, though I may have a tolerably strong opinion as to the probabilities of the case. Relatively to myself, I am quite sure that the region of uncertainty—the nebulous country in which words play the part of realities—is far more extensive than I could wish. Materialism and Idealism; Theism and Atheism; the doctrine of the soul and its mortality or immortality—appear in the history of philosophy like the shades of Scandinavian heroes, eternally slaying one another and eternally coming to life again in a metaphysical 'Nifelheim.'[1] It is getting on for twenty-five centuries, at least, since mankind began seriously to give their minds to these topics. Generation after generation, philosophy has been doomed to roll the stone uphill; and, just as all the world swore it was at the top, down it has rolled to the bottom again. All this is written in innumerable books; and he who will toil through them will discover that the stone is just where it was when the work began. Hume saw this; Kant saw it;[2] since their time, more and more eyes have been cleansed of the films which prevented them from seeing it; until now the weight and number of those who refuse to be the prey of verbal mystifications has begun to tell in practical life.

It was inevitable that a conflict should arise between Agnosticism and Theology; or rather I ought to say between Agnosticism and Ecclesiasticism. For Theology, the science, is one thing; and Ecclesiasticism, the championship of a foregone conclusion[3] as to the truth of a particular form of Theology, is another. With scientific Theology, Agnosticism has no quarrel. On the contrary, the Agnostic, knowing too well the influence of prejudice and idiosyncrasy, even on those who desire most earnestly to be impartial, can wish for nothing more urgently than that the scientific theologian should not only be at perfect liberty to thresh out the matter in his own fashion, but that he should, if he can, find

---

1. In Norse mythology, "Misty Hel," a dark, northern region.
2. Immanuel Kant (1724–1804), German philosopher; David Hume (1711–76), Scottish empiricist philosopher.
3. 'Let us maintain, before we have proved. This seeming paradox is the secret of happiness' (Dr. Newman: Tract 85, p. 85). [Huxley's note]

flaws in the Agnostic position, and, even if demonstration is not to be had, that he should put, in their full force, the grounds of the conclusions he thinks probable. The scientific theologian admits the Agnostic principle, however widely his results may differ from those reached by the majority of Agnostics.

But, as between Agnosticism and Ecclesiasticism, or, as our neighbours across the Channel call it, Clericalism, there can be neither peace nor truce. The Cleric asserts that it is morally wrong not to believe certain propositions, whatever the results of a strict scientific investigation of the evidence of these propositions. He tells us 'that religious error is, in itself, of an immoral nature.'[4] He declares that he has prejudged certain conclusions, and looks upon those who show cause for arrest of judgment as emissaries of Satan. It necessarily follows that, for him, the attainment of faith, not the ascertainment of truth, is the highest aim of mental life. And, on careful analysis of the nature of this faith, it will too often be found to be, not the mystic process of unity with the Divine, understood by the religious enthusiast—but that which the candid simplicity of a Sunday scholar once defined it to be. 'Faith,' said this unconscious plagiarist of Tertullian, 'is the power of saying you believe things which are incredible.'

Now I, and many other Agnostics, believe that faith, in this sense, is an abomination; and though we do not indulge in the luxury of self-righteousness so far as to call those who are not of our way of thinking hard names, we do feel that the disagreement between ourselves and those who hold this doctrine is even more moral than intellectual. It is desirable there should be an end of any mistakes on this topic. If our clerical opponents were clearly aware of the real state of the case, there would be an end of the curious delusion, which often appears between the lines of their writings, that those whom they are so fond of calling 'Infidels' are people who not only ought to be, but in their hearts are, ashamed of themselves. It would be discourteous to do more than hint the antipodal opposition of this pleasant dream of theirs to facts.

The clerics and their lay allies commonly tell us, that if we refuse to admit that there is good ground for expressing definite convictions about certain topics, the bonds of human society will dissolve and mankind lapse into savagery. There are several answers to this assertion. One is that the bonds of human society were formed without the aid of their theology, and in the opinion of not a few competent judges have been weakened rather than strengthened by a good deal of it. Greek science, Greek art, the ethics of old Israel, the social organisation of old Rome, contrived to come into being without the help of any one who believed in a single distinctive article of the simplest of the Christian creeds. The science, the art, the jurisprudence, the chief political and social theories, of the modern world have grown out of those of Greece and Rome—not by favour of, but in the teeth of, the fundamental teachings of early Christianity, to which science, art, and any serious occupation with the things of this world, were alike despicable.

Again, all that is best in the ethics of the modern world, in so far as it has not grown out of Greek thought, or Barbarian manhood, is the direct development of the ethics of old Israel. There is no code of legislation, ancient or modern, at once so just and so mer-

4. Dr. Newman, *Essay on Development*, p. 357. [Huxley's note]

ciful, so tender to the weak and poor, as the Jewish law; and, if the Gospels are to be trusted, Jesus of Nazareth himself declared that he taught nothing but that which lay implicitly, or explicitly, in the religious and ethical system of his people.

> And the scribe said unto him, Of a truth, Teacher, thou hast well said that
> he is one; and there is none other but he: and to love him with all the
> heart, and with all the understanding, and with all the strength, and to love
> his neighbour as himself, is much more than all whole burnt offerings and
> sacrifices. (Mark xii. 32, 33.)

Here is the briefest of summaries of the teaching of the prophets of Israel of the eighth century; does the Teacher, whose doctrine is thus set forth in his presence, repudiate the exposition? Nay; we are told, on the contrary, that Jesus saw that he 'answered discreetly' and replied, 'Thou art not far from the Kingdom of God.'

So that I think that even if the creeds, from the so-called 'Apostles' ' to the so-called 'Athanasian,' were swept into oblivion; and even if the human race should arrive at the conclusion that, whether a bishop washes a cup or leaves it unwashed, is not a matter of the least consequence, it will get on very well. The causes which have led to the development of morality in mankind, which have guided or impelled us all the way from the savage to the civilised state, will not cease to operate because a number of ecclesiastical hypotheses turn out to be baseless. And, even if the absurd notion that morality is more the child of speculation than of practical necessity and inherited instinct, had any foundation; if all the world is going to thieve, murder, and otherwise misconduct itself as soon as it discovers that certain portions of ancient history are mythical; what is the relevance of such arguments to any one who holds by the Agnostic principle?

Surely, the attempt to cast out Beelzebub by the aid of Beelzebub is a hopeful procedure as compared to that of preserving morality by the aid of immorality. For I suppose it is admitted that an Agnostic may be perfectly sincere, may be competent, and may have studied the question at issue with as much care as his clerical opponents. But, if the Agnostic really believes what he says, the 'dreadful consequence' argufier (consistently I admit with his own principles) virtually asks him to abstain from telling the truth, or to say what he believes to be untrue, because of the supposed injurious consequences to morality. 'Beloved brethren, that we may be spotlessly moral, before all things let us lie,' is the sum total of many an exhortation addressed to the 'Infidel.' Now, as I have already pointed out, we cannot oblige our exhorters. We leave the practical application of the convenient doctrines of 'Reserve' and 'Non-natural interpretation' to those who invented them.

I trust that I have now made amends for any ambiguity, or want of fulness, in my previous exposition of that which I hold to be the essence of the Agnostic doctrine. Henceforward, I might hope to hear no more of the assertion that we are necessarily Materialists, Idealists, Atheists, Theists, or any other *ists*, if experience had led me to think that the proved falsity of a statement was any guarantee against its repetition. And those who appreciate the nature of our position will see, at once, that when Ecclesiasticism declares that we ought to believe this, that, and the other, and are very wicked if we don't, it is impossible for us to give any answer but this: We have not the slightest objection to believe anything you like, if you will give us good grounds for belief; but, if you cannot, we must respectfully refuse, even if that refusal should wreck morality and insure our own damnation several times over. We are quite content to leave that to the decision of the future. The course of the past has impressed us with the firm conviction that no good ever comes of falsehood, and we feel warranted in refusing even to experiment in that direction. . . .

# Dinah Maria Mulock Craik

1826: Born 20 April at Stoke-on-Trent, Staffordshire

1849: *The Ogilvies*

1850: *Olive*

1856: *John Halifax, Gentleman*

1857–8: *A Woman's Thoughts About Women*

1859: *A Life for a Life*

1875: *The Little Lame Prince and His Travelling Cloak*

1886: *King Arthur*

1887: Died 12 October at Shortlands, Kent

---

## A WOMAN'S THOUGHTS ABOUT WOMEN

---

*A widely read journalist and novelist, Dinah Maria Mulock Craik published over fifty volumes of fiction, children's literature, poetry, essays, travel accounts, and translations. A Woman's Thoughts About Women originally appeared in Chambers's Edinburgh Journal in 1857. In 1858 it was issued as a book, from which the following selection is taken. Written after her best-selling self-help novel,* John Halifax, Gentleman, A Woman's Thoughts About Women *similarly shapes and helps to reinforce middle-class values—as do the advice manuals of Samuel SMILES and Sarah Stickney ELLIS—even as it conveys Craik's understanding of the difficulties faced by independent single women. In addressing the problems of single women explicitly, Craik contributes to Victorian discourse about what were called "redundant" or "odd" women: the three-quarters of a million women (according to W. R. GREG's estimate) whom the 1851 census recorded as unmarried. Craik acknowledges the social, vocational, and emotional problems faced by single women, but she advises individual initiative, discipline, and "solid work—daily, regular, conscientious work," rather than organized feminist activism.*

LMF

## SOMETHING TO DO

I PREMISE THAT THESE THOUGHTS do not concern married women, for whom there are always plenty to think, and who have generally quite enough to think of for themselves and those belonging to them. They have cast their lot for good or ill, have realised in greater or less degree the natural destiny of our sex. They must find out its comforts, cares, and responsibilities, and make the best of all. It is the single women, belonging to those supernumerary ranks, which, political economists tell us, are yearly increasing, who most need thinking about.

First, in their early estate, when they have so much in their possession—youth, bloom, and health giving them that temporary influence over the other sex which may result, and is meant to result, in a permanent one. Secondly, when this sovereignty is passing away, the chance of marriage lessening, or wholly ended, or voluntarily set aside, and the individual making up her mind to that which, respect for Grandfather Adam and Grandmother Eve must compel us to admit, is an unnatural condition of being.

Why this undue proportion of single women should almost always result from over-civilisation, and whether, since society's advance is usually indicated by the advance, morally and intellectually, of its women—this progress, by raising women's ideal standard of the "holy estate," will not necessarily cause a decline in the very *un*holy estate which it is most frequently made—are questions too wide to be entered upon here. We have only to deal with facts—with a certain acknowledged state of things, perhaps incapable of remedy, but by no means incapable of amelioration.

But, granted these facts, and leaving to wiser heads the explanation of them—if indeed there be any—it seems advisable, or at least allowable, that any woman who has thought a good deal about the matter, should not fear to express in word—or deed, which is better,—any conclusions, which out of her own observation and experience she may have arrived at. And looking around upon the middle classes, which form the staple stock of the community, it appears to me that the chief canker at the root of women's lives is the want of something to do.

Herein I refer, as this chapter must be understood especially to refer, not to those whom ill or good fortune—*query*, is it not often the latter?—has forced to earn their bread; but "to young ladies," who have never been brought up to do anything. Tom, Dick, and Harry, their brothers, has each had it knocked into him from school-days that he is to do something, to be somebody. Counting-house, shop, or college, afford him a clear future on which to concentrate all his energies and aims. He has got the grand *pabulum* of the human soul—occupation. If any inherent want in his character, any unlucky combination of circumstances, nullifies this, what a poor creature the man becomes!—what a dawdling, moping, sitting-over-the-fire, thumb-twiddling, lazy, ill-tempered animal! And why? "Oh, poor fellow! 'tis because he has got nothing to do!"

Yet this is precisely the condition of women for a third, a half, often the whole of their existence.

That Providence ordained it so—made men to work, and women to be idle—is a doctrine that few will be bold enough to assert openly. Tacitly they do, when they preach up lovely uselessness, fascinating frivolity, delicious helplessness—all those polite impertinences and poetical degradations to which the foolish, lazy, or selfish of our sex are prone to incline an ear, but which any woman of common sense must repudiate as insulting not only her womanhood but her Creator.

Equally blasphemous, and perhaps even more harmful, is the outcry about "the equality of the sexes;" the frantic attempt to force women, many of whom are either ignorant of or unequal for their own duties—into the position and duties of men. A pretty state of matters would ensue! Who that ever listened for two hours to the verbose confused inanities of a ladies' committee, would immediately go and give his vote for a female House of Commons? or who, on the receipt of a lady's letter of business—I speak of the average—would henceforth desire to have our courts of justice stocked with matronly lawyers, and our colleges thronged by

Sweet girl-graduates with their golden hair?[1]

As for finance, in its various branches—if you pause to consider the extreme difficulty there always is in balancing Mrs. Smith's housekeeping-book, or Miss Smith's quarterly allowance, I think, my dear Paternal Smith, you need not be much afraid lest this loud acclaim for "women's rights" should ever end in pushing you from your stools, in counting-house, college, or elsewhere.

No; equality of the sexes is not in the nature of things. Man and woman were made for, and not like one another. One only "right" we have to assert in common with mankind—and that is as much in our own hands as theirs—the right of having something to do.

That both sexes were meant to labour, one "by the sweat of his brow," the other "in sorrow to bring forth"— and bring up— "children"—cannot, I fancy, be questioned. Nor, when the gradual changes of the civilised world, or some special destiny, chosen or compelled, have prevented that first, highest, and in earlier times almost universal lot, does this accidental fate in any way abrogate the necessity, moral, physical, and mental, for a woman to have occupation in other forms. . . .

The difference between man's vocation and woman's seems naturally to be this—one is abroad, the other at home: one external, the other internal: one active, the other passive. He has to go and seek out his path; hers usually lies close under her feet. Yet each is as distinct, as honourable, as difficult; and whatever custom may urge to the contrary— if the life is meant to be a worthy or a happy one—each must resolutely and unshrinkingly be trod. But—*how?*

A definite answer to this question is simply impossible. So diverse are characters, tastes, capabilities, and circumstances, that to lay down a distinct line of occupation for any six women of one's own acquaintance, would be the merest absurdity.

Herein, the patient must minister to herself.[2]

To few is the choice so easy, the field of duty so wide, that she need puzzle very long over what she ought to do. Generally—and this is the best and safest guide—she will find her work lying very near at hand: some desultory tastes to condense into regular studies,

---

1. Quoted inexactly from Alfred Tennyson's *The Princess* (1847), Prologue.
2. Paraphrased from William Shakespeare's *Macbeth*, 5.3.

some faulty household quietly to remodel, some child to teach, or parent to watch over. All these being needless or unattainable, she may extend her service out of the home into the world, which perhaps never at any time so much needed the help of us women. And hardly one of its charities and duties can be done so thoroughly as by a wise and tender woman's hand.

Here occurs another of those plain rules which are the only guidance possible in the matter—a Bible rule, too—"*Whatsoever thy hand findeth to do, do it with thy might.*" Question it not, philosophise not over it—do it!—only *do it!* Thoroughly and completely, never satisfied with less than perfectness. Be it ever so great or so small, from the founding of a village-school to the making of a collar—do it "with thy might;" and never lay it aside till it is done.

Each day's account ought to leave this balance—of something done. Something beyond mere pleasure, one's own or another's—though both are good and sweet in their way. Let the superstructure of life be enjoyment, but let its foundation be in solid work— daily, regular, conscientious work: in its essence and results as distinct as any "business" of men. What they expend for wealth and ambition, shall not we offer for duty and love— the love of our fellow-creatures, or, far higher, the love of God? "Labour is worship," says the proverb: also—nay, necessarily so—labour is happiness. Only let us turn from the dreary, colourless lives of the women, old and young, who have nothing to do, to those of their sisters who are always busy doing something; who, believing and accepting the universal law, that pleasure is the mere accident of our being, and work its natural and most holy necessity, have set themselves steadily to seek out and fulfil theirs.

These are they who are little spoken of in the world at large. I do not include among them those whose labour should spring from an irresistible impulse, and become an absolute vocation, or it is not worth following at all—namely, the professional women, writers, painters, musicians, and the like. I mean those women who lead active, intelligent, industrious lives: lives complete in themselves, and therefore not giving half the trouble to their friends that the idle and foolish virgins do—no, not even in love-affairs. If love comes to them accidentally, (or rather providentially,) and happily, so much the better!—they will not make the worse wives for having been busy maidens. But the "tender passion" is not to them the one grand necessity that it is to aimless lives; they are in no haste to wed: their time is duly filled up; and if never married, still the habitual faculty of usefulness gives them in themselves and with others that obvious value, that fixed standing in society, which will for ever prevent their being drifted away, like most old maids, down the current of the new generation, even as dead May-flies down a stream.

They have made for themselves a place in the world: the harsh, practical, yet not ill-meaning world, where all find their level soon or late, and where a frivolous young maid sunk into a helpless old one, can no more expect to keep her pristine position than a last year's leaf to flutter upon a spring bough. But an old maid who deserves well of this same world, by her ceaseless work therein, having won her position, keeps it to the end.

Not an ill position either, or unkindly; often higher and more honourable than that of many a mother of ten sons. In households, where "Auntie" is the universal referee, nurse, playmate, comforter, and counsellor: in society, where "that nice Miss So-and-so," though neither clever, handsome, nor young, is yet such a person as can neither be omitted nor overlooked: in charitable works, where she is "such a practical body—always knows exactly what to do, and how to do it:" or perhaps, in her own house, solitary indeed, as every single woman's home must be, yet neither dull nor unhappy in itself, and the nucleus of cheerfulness and happiness to many another home besides.

She has not married. Under Heaven, her home, her life, her lot, are all of her own making. Bitter or sweet they may have been—it is not ours to meddle with them, but we can any day see their results. Wide or narrow as her circle of influence appears, she has exercised her power to the uttermost, and for good. Whether great or small her talents, she has not let one of them rust for want of use. Whatever the current of her existence may have been, and in whatever circumstances it has placed her, she has voluntarily wasted no portion of it—not a year, not a month, not a day.

Published or unpublished, this woman's life is a goodly chronicle, the title-page of which you may read in her quiet countenance; her manner, settled, cheerful, and at ease; her unfailing interest in all things and all people. You will rarely find she thinks much about herself; she has never had time for it. And this her life-chronicle, which, out of its very fulness, has taught her that the more one does, the more one finds to do—she will never flourish in your face, or the face of Heaven, as something uncommonly virtuous and extraordinary. She knows that, after all, she has simply done what it was her duty to do.

But—and when her place is vacant on earth, this will be said of her assuredly, both here and Otherwhere—"*She hath done what she could.*"

# Barbara Leigh Smith Bodichon

## REASONS FOR THE ENFRANCHISEMENT OF WOMEN

*An activist as well as a noteworthy landscape painter and philanthropist, Barbara Bodichon was one of the chief organizers of the mid-century feminist movement in Britain. In the 1850s and 1860s, along with her friends Bessie Rayner Parkes and Emily Davies, she led the Langham Place circle, considered by many to be the most influential feminist network of the mid-Victorian period. This group campaigned for legal, economic, and educational reforms for women; established the* English Woman's Journal *to promote women's causes; and formed the women's suffrage committee in England that solicited signatures to accompany John Stuart* MILL's *first petition to Parliament in 1866.* Reasons for the Enfranchisement of Women *was one of Bodichon's pamphlets on the vote for women. Initially delivered at the Social Science Association meeting in Manchester in October 1866—the only paper on women's suffrage presented—*Reasons *had little immediate effect. The sentiments of the country, expressed most vocally in the major periodicals, were largely against women's suffrage. Bodichon's awareness of the difficulties of the cause led her to advocate a limited franchise for women, one that would grant the vote to female freeholders and householders. In time Bodichon and her fellow cautious committee members differed with those members who favored more radical change, and the committee disbanded. In 1867 Bodichon withdrew from her earlier active public advocacy to cofound Girton College, Cambridge with Emily Davies.* LMF

THAT A RESPECTABLE, ORDERLY, INDEPENDENT body in the State should have no voice, and no influence recognised by the law, in the election of the representatives of the people, while they are otherwise acknowledged as responsible citizens, are eligible for many public offices, and required to pay all taxes, is an anomaly which seems to require some explanation. Many people are unable to conceive that women can care about voting. That some women do care, has been proved by the Petitions presented to Parliament. I shall try to show why some care—and why those who do not, ought to be made to care.

There are now a very considerable number of open-minded, unprejudiced people, who see no particular reason why women should not have votes, if they want them; but, they ask, what would be the good of it? What is there that women want which male legislators are not willing to give? And here let me say at the outset, that the advocates of this measure are very far from accusing men of deliberate unfairness to women. It is not as a means of extorting justice from unwilling legislators that the franchise is claimed for women. In so far as the claim is made with any special reference to class interests at all, it is simply on the general ground that, under a representative government, any class which is not represented is likely to be neglected. Proverbially, what is out of sight is out of mind; and the theory that women, as such, are bound to keep out of sight, finds its most emphatic expression in the denial of the right to vote. The direct results are probably less injurious than those which are indirect; but that a want of due consideration for the interests of women is apparent in our legislation, could very easily be shown. To give evidence in detail would be a long and an invidious task. I will mention one instance only, that of the educational endowments all over the country. Very few people would now maintain that the education of boys is more important to the State than that of girls. But, as a matter of fact, girls have but a very small share in educational endowments. Many of the old foundations have been reformed by Parliament, but the desireableness of providing with equal care for girls and boys has very seldom been recognised. In the administration of charities generally, the same tendency prevails to postpone the claims of women to those of men.

Among instances of hardship traceable directly to exclusion from the franchise and to no other cause, may be mentioned the unwillingness of landlords to accept women as tenants. Two large farmers in Suffolk inform me that this is not an uncommon case. They mention one estate on which seven widows have been ejected, who, if they had had votes, would have been continued as tenants.

The case of women farmers is stronger, but not much stronger, than that of women who, as heads of a business or a household, fulfil the duties of a man in the same position. Their task is often a hard one, and everything which helps to sustain their self-respect and to give them consideration and importance in the eyes of others, is likely to lessen their difficulties, and make them happier and stronger for the battle of life. The very fact that, though householders and tax-payers, they have not equal privileges with male householders and tax-payers, is in itself a *deconsideration*, which seems to me invidious and useless. It casts a kind of slur on the value of their opinions; and I may remark in passing, that what is treated as of no value is apt to grow valueless. Citizenship is an honour, and not to have the full rights of a citizen is a want of honour. Obvious it may not be, but by a subtle and sure process, those who without their own consent, and without sufficient reason, are debarred from full participation in the rights and duties of a citizen, lose more or less of social consideration and esteem.

These arguments, founded on considerations of justice and mercy to a large and important and increasing class, might in a civilised country, and in the absence of strong reasons to the contrary, be deemed amply sufficient to justify the measure proposed. There remain to be considered those aspects of the question which affect the general community. And among all the reasons for giving women votes, the one which appears to me the strongest, is that of the influence it might be expected to have in increasing public spirit. Patriotism, a healthy, lively, intelligent interest in everything which concerns the nation to which we belong, and an unselfish devotedness to the public service,—these are the qualities which make a people great and happy; these are the virtues which ought to be most sedulously cultivated in all classes of the community. And I know no better means, at this present time, of counteracting the tendency to prefer narrow private ends to the public good, than this of giving to all women, duly qualified, a direct and conscious participation in political affairs. Give some women votes, and it will tend to make all women think seriously of the concerns of the nation at large, and their interest having once been fairly roused, they will take pains, by reading and by consultation with persons better informed than themselves, to form sound opinions. As it is, women of the middle class occupy themselves but little with anything beyond their own family circle. They do not consider it any concern of theirs, if poor men and women are ill-nursed in workhouse infirmaries, and poor children ill-taught in workhouse schools. If the roads are bad, the drains neglected, the water poisoned, they think it is all very wrong, but it does not occur to them that it is their duty to get it put right. These farmer-women and business-women have honest, sensible minds, and much practical experience, but they do not bring their good sense to bear upon public affairs, because they think it is men's business, not theirs, to look after such things. It is this belief—so narrowing and deadening in its influence—that the exercise of the franchise would tend to dissipate. The mere fact of being called upon to enforce an opinion by a vote, would have an immediate effect in awakening a healthy sense of responsibility. There is no reason why these women should not take an active interest in all the social questions—education, public health, prison discipline, the poor laws, and the rest—which occupy Parliament, and they would be much more likely to do so, if they felt that they had importance in the eyes of members of Parliament, and could claim a hearing for their opinions.

Besides these women of business, there are ladies of property, whose more active participation in public affairs would be beneficial both to themselves and the community generally. The want of stimulus to energetic action is much felt by women of the higher classes. It is agreed that they ought not to be idle, but what they ought to do is not so clear. Reading, music, and drawing, needlework, and charity, are their usual employments. Reading, without a purpose, does not come to much. Music and drawing, and needlework, are most commonly regarded as amusements intended to fill up time. We have left, as the serious duty of independent and unmarried women, the care of the poor in all its branches, including visiting the sick and the aged, and ministering to their wants, looking after the schools, and in every possible way giving help wherever help is needed. Now education, the relief of the destitute, and the health of the people, are among the most important and difficult matters which occupy the minds of statesmen, and if it is admitted that women of leisure and culture are bound to contribute their part towards the solution of these great questions, it is evident that every means of making their co-operation enlightened and vigorous should be sought for. They have special opportunities of observing the operation of many of the laws. They know, for example, for they see before their eyes, the practical working of the law of settlement—of the laws relating to the dwellings of the poor—and many others, and the experience which peculiarly qual-ifies them to form a judgment on these matters ought not to be thrown away. We all know that we have already a goodly body of rich, influential working-women, whose opinions on the social and political questions of the day are well worth listening to. In almost every parish there are, happily for England, such women. Now everything should be done to give these valuable members of the community a solid social standing. If they are want-ed—and there can be no doubt that they are—in all departments of social work, their position in the work should be as dignified and honourable as it is possible to make it. Rich unmarried women have many opportunities of benefiting the community, which are not within reach of a married woman, absorbed by the care of her husband and children. Everything, I say again, should be done to encourage this most important and increasing class to take their place in the army of workers for the common good, and all the forces we can bring to bear for this end are of incalculable value. For by bringing women into hearty co-operation with men, we gain the benefit not only of their work, but of their intelligent sympathy. Public spirit is like fire: a feeble spark of it may be fanned into a flame, or it may very easily be put out. And the result of teaching women that they have nothing to do with politics, is that their influence goes towards extinguishing the unselfish interest—never too strong—which men are disposed to take in public affairs.

Let each member of the House of Commons consider, in a spirit of true scientific enquiry, all the properly qualified women of his acquaintance, and he will see no reason why the single ladies and the widows among his own family and friends should not form as sensible opinions on the merits of candidates as the voters who returned him to Parliament. When we find among the disfranchised such names as those of Mrs. Somerville, Harriet Martineau, Miss Burdett Coutts, Florence Nightingale, Mary Carpenter, Louisa Twining, Miss Marsh,[1] and many others scarcely inferior to these in intellectual and moral worth, we cannot but desire, for the elevation and dignity of the parliamentary system, to add them to the number of electors.

It need scarcely be pointed out that the measure has nothing of a party character. We have precedents under two very different governments, those of Austria and Sweden, for something very similar to what is now proposed. Now, let us calmly consider all the argu-ments we have heard against giving the franchise to women.

---

1. Mary Somerville (1780–1872), scientist; Harriet MARTINEAU (1802–76), journalist and popularizer of Political Economy; Angela Burdett-Coutts (1814–1906), philanthropist; Florence NIGHTINGALE (1820–1910), nurse and sanitary reformer; Mary Carpenter (1807–77), educator; Louisa Twining (1820–1912), social reformer; Anne Marsh (1791–1874), novelist.

Among these, the first and commonest is—Women do not want votes. Certainly that is a capital reason why women should not have votes thrust upon them, and no one proposes compulsory registration. There are many men who do not care to use their votes, and there is no law compelling them either to register themselves or to vote. The statement, however, that women do not wish to vote, is a mere assertion, and may be met by a counter-assertion. Some women do want votes, which the petitions signed, and now in course of signature, go very largely to prove. Some women manifestly do; others, let it be admitted, do not. It is impossible to say positively which side has the majority, unless we could poll all the women in question; or, in other words, without resorting to the very measure which is under discussion. Make registration possible, and we shall see how many care to avail themselves of the privilege.

But, it is said, women have other duties. The function of women is different to that of men, and their function is not politics. It is very true that women have other duties— many and various. But so have men. No citizen lives for his citizen duties only. He is a professional man, a tradesman, a family man, a club man, a thousand things as well as a voter. Of course these occupations sometimes interfere with a man's duties as a citizen, and when he cannot vote, he cannot. So with women; when they cannot vote, they cannot.

The proposition we are discussing practically concerns only women who have the qualification. Among these there are surely a great number whose time is not fully occupied, not even so much as that of men. Their duties in sick-rooms and in caring for children, leave them a sufficient margin of leisure for reading newspapers, and studying the *pros* and *cons* of political and social questions. No one can mean seriously to affirm that widows and unmarried women would find the mere act of voting once in several years arduous. One day, say once in three years, might surely be spared from domestic duties. If it is urged that it is not the time spent in voting that is in question, but the thought and the attention which are necessary for forming political opinions, I reply that women of the class we are speaking of, have, as a rule, more time for thought than men, their duties being of a less engrossing character, and they ought to bestow a considerable amount of thought and attention on the questions which occupy the Legislature. Social matters occupy every day a larger space in the deliberations of Parliament, and on many of these questions women are led to think and to judge in the fulfilment of those duties which, as a matter of course, devolve upon them in the ordinary business of English life. And however important the duties of home may be, we must bear in mind that a woman's duties do not end there. She is a daughter, a sister, the mistress of a household; she ought to be, in the broadest sense of the word, a neighbour, both to her equals and to the poor. These are her obvious and undeniable duties, and within the limits of her admitted functions; I should think it desirable to add to them—duties to her parish and to the State. A woman who is valuable in all the relations of life, a woman of a large nature, will be more perfect in her domestic capacity, and not less.

If we contemplate women in the past, and in different countries, we find them acting, in addition to their domestic part, all sorts of different *rôles*. What was their *rôle* among the Jews and the Romans? What was it in the early Christian churches? What is it amongst the Quakers? What is it in the colliery districts,—at the court of Victoria, and the Tuileries?[2] We can conjure up thousands of pictures of women performing different functions under varying conditions. They have done and do, all sorts of work in all sorts of ways. Is there anything in the past history of the world which justifies the assertion that they must and will do certain things in the future, and will not and cannot do certain other things? I do not think there is.

But to return to my argument, and supposing that there were enough data in the past to enable us to predict that women will never take sufficient interest in politics to induce even women to wish to vote once in several years, should we be justified in realising our own prediction, and forbidding by law what we declare to be contrary to nature? If anyone believes, as the result of observation and experience, that it is not a womanly function to vote, I respect such belief, and answer—only the future can prove. But what I do not respect, is the strange want of toleration which says—"You shall not do this or that." We do not want to compel women to act; we only wish to see them free to exercise or not, according as they themselves desire, political and other functions.

The argument that "women are ignorant of politics," would have great force if it could be shown that the mass of the existing voters are throughly well informed on political subjects, or even much better informed than the persons to whom it is proposed to give votes. Granted that women are ignorant of politics, so are many male ten-pound householders. Their ideas are not always clear on political questions, and would probably be even more confused if they had not votes. No mass of human beings will or can undertake the task of forming opinions on matters over which they have no control, and on which they have no practical decision to make. It would by most persons be considered waste of time. When women have votes, they will read with closer attention than heretofore the daily histories of our times, and will converse with each other and with their fathers and brothers about social and political questions. They will become interested in a wider circle of ideas, and where they now think and feel somewhat vaguely, they will form definite and decided opinions.

Among the women who are disqualified for voting by the legal disability of sex, there is a large number of the educated class. We shall know the exact number of women possessing the household and property qualifications, when the return ordered by Parliament has been made. In the meantime, the following calculation is suggestive. In the "London Court Guide," which of course includes no houses below the value of £10 a year, the number of householders whose names begin with A is 1149. Of these, 205, that is more than one-sixth, are women, all of whom are either unmarried or widows.

The fear entertained by some persons that family dissension would result from encouraging women to form political opinions, might be urged with equal force against their having any opinions on any subject at all. Differences on religious subjects are still more apt to rouse the passions and create disunion than political differences. As for opinions causing disunion, let it be remembered that what is a possible cause of disunion is also a possible cause of deeply-founded union. The more rational women become, the

2. The Tuileries: a royal palace in Paris, which was burned in 1871.

more real union there will be in families, for nothing separates so much as unreasonableness and frivolity. It will be said, perhaps, that contrary opinions may be held by the different members of a family without bringing on quarrels, so long as they are kept to the region of theory, and no attempt is made to carry them out publicly in action. But religious differences must be shown publicly. A woman who determines upon changing her religion—say to go over from Protestantism to Romanism—proclaims her difference from her family in a public and often a very distressing manner. But no one has yet proposed to make it illegal for a woman to change her religion. After all—is it essential that brothers and sisters and cousins shall all vote on the same side?

An assertion often made, that women would lose the good influence which they now exert indirectly on public affairs if they had votes, seems to require proof. First of all, it is necessary to prove that women have this indirect influence,—then that it is good,—then that the indirect good influence would be lost if they had direct influence,—then that the indirect influence which they would lose is better than the direct influence they would gain. From my own observation, I should say that the women who have gained by their wisdom and earnestness a good indirect influence, would not lose that influence if they had votes. And I see no necessary connexion between goodness and indirectness. On the contrary, I believe that the great thing women want is to be more direct and straightforward in thought, word, and deed. I think the educational advantage of citizenship to women would be so great, that I feel inclined to run the risk of sacrificing the subtle [in]direct influence, to a wholesome feeling of responsibility, which would, I think, make women give their opinions less rashly and more conscientiously than at present on political subjects.

A gentleman who thinks much about details, affirms that "polling-booths are not fit places for women." If this is so, one can only say that the sooner they are made fit the better. That in a State which professes to be civilised, a solemn public duty can only be discharged in the midst of drunkenness and riot, is scandalous and not to be endured. It is no doubt true that in many places polling is now carried on in a turbulent and disorderly manner. Where that is unhappily the case, women clearly must stay away. English women can surely be trusted not to force their way to the polling-booth when it would be manifestly unfit. But it does not follow that, because in some disreputable places some women would be illegally, but with their own consent, prevented from recording their votes, therefore all women, in all places, should be, without their own consent, by law disqualified. Those who at the last election visited the polling places in London and Westminster, and many other places, will bear me out in asserting that a lady would have had no more difficulty or annoyance to encounter in giving her vote, than she has in going to the Botanical Gardens or to Westminster Abbey.

There are certain other difficulties sometimes vaguely brought forward by the unreflecting, which I shall not attempt to discuss. Such, for example, is the argument that as voters ought to be independent, and as married women are liable to be influenced by their husbands, therefore unmarried women and widows ought not to vote. Or again, that many ladies canvass, and canvassing by ladies is a very objectionable practice, therefore canvassing ought to be the only direct method by which women can bring their influence to bear upon an election. Into such objections it is not necessary here to enter.

Nor is it needful to discuss the extreme logical consequences which may be obtained by pressing to an undue length the arguments used in favour of permitting women to exercise the suffrage. The question under consideration is, not whether women ought logically to be Members of Parliament, but whether, under existing circumstances, it is for the good of the State that women, who perform most of the duties, and enjoy nearly all the rights of citizenship, should be by special enactment disabled from exercising the additional privilege of taking part in the election of the representatives of the people. It is a question of expediency, to be discussed calmly, without passion or prejudice.

In England, the extension proposed would interfere with no vested interests. It would involve no change in the principles on which our Government is based, but would rather make our Constitution more consistent with itself. Conservatives have a right to claim it as a Conservative measure. Liberals are bound to ask for it as a necessary part of Radical reform. There is no reason for identifying it with any class or party in the State, and it is, in fact, impossible to predict what influence it might have on party politics. The question is simply of a special legal disability, which must, sooner or later, be removed.

# Margaret Oliphant

1828: Born 4 April in Wallyford, Scotland

1849: *Passages in the Life of Mrs Margaret Maitland, of Sunnyside, Written by Herself*

1863: *Salem Chapel*

1865–6: *Miss Marjoribanks*

1879: *A Beleaguered City*, in the *New Quarterly Magazine*

1883: *Hester: A Story of a Contemporary Life*

1890: *Kirsteen: The Story of a Scotch Family Seventy Years Ago*

1897: Died 25 June at Wimbledon; *Annals of a Publishing House: William Blackwood and His Sons, Their Magazine and Friends*

1899: *The Autobiography and Letters of Mrs M. O.W. Oliphant*

---

## THE AUTOBIOGRAPHY OF MRS M. O. W. OLIPHANT

---

Margaret Oliphant is a formidable figure both in terms of publications—nearly a hundred novels, more than fifty short stories, numerous travel accounts and biographies, and hundreds of articles and reviews—and in terms of critical influence. As a regular reviewer for Blackwood's for almost forty-five years, she helped to shape the values of the literary marketplace for which she wrote her fiction. Appreciated by her contemporaries—including Thomas Carlyle, William Gladstone, Alfred Tennyson, and Queen Victoria—Oliphant was seen as a hack writer for much of the twentieth century, due in part to the posthumous publication of her autobiography by her niece, Janet Wilson Oliphant, and her cousin, Annie Coghill. In the Autobiography, Oliphant deemphasizes her profession and her professionalism, accenting instead her role as mother and nurturer. She repeatedly suggests that it was her need to support her family financially that drove her to write with an eye to quantity rather than quality.

Eschewing the chronological format of traditional male autobiographies, Oliphant wrote a series of retrospective fragments over a period of more than thirty years. The deaths of her children in 1864, 1890, and 1894 mark the main sections of her text; within these sections, Oliphant recalls moments from her past as they come to her, sometimes retelling the

*same event from a later perspective, thus engaging in a continual reflection on and reevalu-*
*ation of her self and her decisions. The edited version of the autobiography published in*
*1899 omits some of the more emotionally revelatory passages of Oliphant's text and impos-*
*es a loosely linear chronology. The Margaret Oliphant of this* Autobiography *emerges as*
*someone who, like Florence* NIGHTINGALE, *understood the social constraints that women*
*faced, but, like Sarah Stickney* ELLIS, *never relinquished a belief in women's domestic and*
*moral mission. While this version of Oliphant is representative, it is incomplete: Oliphant's*
*fiction and letters reveal a complex understanding of the possibilities for women's lives and*
*women's choices, which she modified over the course of her life.*                    LMF

. . . I HAVE BEEN TEMPTED TO begin writing by George Eliot's life[1]—with that curious
kind of self-compassion which one cannot get clear of. I wonder if I am a little envious of
her? I always avoid considering formally what my own mind is worth. I have never had
any theory on the subject. I have written because it gave me pleasure, because it came
natural to me, because it was like talking or breathing, besides the big fact that it was necessary for me to work for my children. That, however, was not the first motive, so that
when I laugh inquiries off and say that it is my trade, I do it only by way of eluding the
question which I have neither time nor wish to enter into. Anthony Trollope's talk about
the characters in his books astonished me beyond measure, and I am totally incapable of
talking about anything I have ever done in that way. As he was a thoroughly sensible genuine man, I suppose he was quite sincere in what he says of them,—or was it that he was
driven into a fashion of self-explanation which belongs to the time, and which I am following now though in another way? I feel that my carelessness of asserting my claim is
very much against me with everybody. It is so natural to think that if the workman himself is indifferent about his work, there can't be much in it that is worth thinking about.
I am not indifferent, yet I should rather like to forget it all, to wipe out all the books, to
silence those compliments about my industry, &c., which I always turn off with a laugh.
I suppose this is really pride, with a mixture of Scotch shyness, and a good deal of that
uncomprehended, unexplainable feeling which made Mrs Carlyle[2] reply with a jibe,
which meant only a whimsical impulse to take the side of opposition, and the strong
Scotch sense of the absurdity of a chorus of praise, but which looks so often like detrac-
tion and bitterness, and has now definitely been accepted as such by the public in general. I don't find words to express it adequately, but I feel it strenuously in my own case.
When people comment upon the number of books I have written, and I say that I am so
far from being proud of that fact that I should like at least half of them forgotten, they
stare—and yet it is quite true; and even here I could no more go solemnly into them, and
tell why I had done this or that, than I could fly. They are my work, which I like in the
doing, which is my natural way of occupying myself, though they are never so good as I
meant them to be. And when I have said that, I have said all that is in me to say.

I don't quite know why I should put this all down. I suppose because George Eliot's

---

1. Oliphant reviewed J. W. Cross's *George Eliot's Life as Related in Her Letters and Journals* (1885) in the *Edinburgh Review* (April 1885). She later refers to novelist Anthony Trollope's *Autobiography* (1883).
2. See Jane Welsh CARLYLE.

life has, as I said above, stirred me up to an involuntary confession. How I have been hand-icapped in life! Should I have done better if I had been kept, like her, in a mental green-house and taken care of? This is one of the things it is perfectly impossible to tell. In all likelihood our minds and our circumstances are so arranged that, after all, the possible way is the way that is best; yet it is a little hard sometimes not to feel with Browning's Andrea, that the men who have no wives, who have given themselves up to their art, have had an almost unfair advantage over us who have been given perhaps more than one Lucrezia to take care of.[3] And to feel with him that perhaps in the after-life four square walls in the New Jerusalem may be given for another trial! I used to be intensely impressed in the Laurence Oliphants[4] with that curious freedom from human ties which I have never known; and that they felt it possible to make up their minds to do what was best, without any sort of *arrière pensée*,[5] without having to consider whether they could or not. Curious freedom! I have never known what it was. I have always had to think of other people, and to plan everything—for my own pleasure, it is true, very often, but always in subjection to the necessity which bound me to them. On the whole, I have had a great deal of my own way, and have insisted upon getting what I wished, but only at the cost of infinite labour, and of carrying a whole little world with me whenever I moved. I have not been able to rest, to please myself, to take the pleasures that have come in my way, but have always been forced to go on without a pause. When my poor brother's fam-ily fell upon my hands, and especially when there was question of Frank's education,[6] I remember that I said to myself, having then perhaps a little stirring of ambition, that I must make up my mind to think no more of that, and that to bring up the boys for the service of God was better than to write a fine novel, supposing even that it was in me to do so. Alas! the work has been done; the education is over; my good Frank, my steady, good boy, is dead. It seemed rather a fine thing to make that resolution (though in reali-ty I had no choice); but now I think that if I had taken the other way, which seemed the less noble, it might have been better for all of us. I might have done better work. I should in all probability have earned nearly as much for half the production had I done less; and I might have had the satisfaction of knowing that there was something laid up for them and for my old age; while they might have learned habits of work which now seem beyond recall. Who can tell? I did with much labour what I thought the best, and there is only a *might have been* on the other side.

In this my resolution which I did make, I was, after all, only following my instincts, it being in reality easier to me to keep on with a flowing sail, to keep my household and make a number of people comfortable, at the cost of incessant work, and an occasional great crisis of anxiety, than to live the self-restrained life which the greater artist impos-es upon himself.

What casuists we are on our own behalf!—this is altogether self-defence. And I know

---

3. In Robert Browning's dramatic monologue "Andrea del Sarto" (1855), the speaker speculates that he has failed to become the great painter he might have been because of the influence of his wife, Lucrezia.
4. Laurence Oliphant (1829–88), British novelist and travel writer, amateur philosopher, and visionary. He resigned a career as a Member of Parliament to join Thomas Lake Harris's religious community in America. Margaret Oliphant wrote a biography of her distant relative in 1891.
5. Mental reservation.
6. Francis Wilson (1854–79), Oliphant's nephew.

I am giving myself the air of being *au fond*[7] a finer sort of character than the others. I may as well take the little satisfaction to myself, for nobody will give it to me. No one even will mention me in the same breath with George Eliot. And that is just. It is a little justification to myself to think how much better off she was,—no trouble in all her life as far as appears, but the natural one of her father's death—and perhaps coolnesses with her brothers and sisters, though that is not said. And though her marriage is not one that most of us would have ventured on, still it seems to have secured her a worshipper unrivalled. I think she must have been a dull woman with a great genius distinct from herself, something like the gift of the old prophets, which they sometimes exercised with only a dim sort of perception what it meant. But this is a thing to be said only with bated breath, and perhaps further thought on the subject may change even my mind. She took herself with tremendous seriousness, that is evident, and was always on duty, never relaxing, her letters ponderous beyond description—and those to the Bray party giving one the idea of a mutual improvement society for the exchange of essays.

Let me be done with this—I wonder if I will ever have time to put a few autobiographical bits down before I die. I am in very little danger of having my life written, and that is all the better in this point of view—for what could be said of me? George Eliot and George Sand make me half inclined to cry over my poor little unappreciated self— "Many love me (*i.e.*, in a sort of way), but by none am I enough beloved." These two bigger women did things which I have never felt the least temptation to do—but how very much more enjoyment they seem to have got out of their life, how much more praise and homage and honour! I would not buy their fame with these disadvantages, but I do feel very small, very obscure, beside them, rather a failure all round, never securing any strong affection, and throughout my life, though I have had all the usual experiences of woman, never impressing anybody,—what a droll little complaint!—why should I? I acknowledge frankly that there is nothing in me—a fat, little, commonplace woman, rather tongue-tied—to impress any one; and yet there is a sort of whimsical injury in it which makes me sorry for myself.

*Feb. 8th.[1885]*

Here, then, for a little try at the autobiography. . . .

. . . We lived in the most singularly secluded way. I never was at a dance till after my marriage, never went out, never saw anybody at home. Our pleasures were books of all and every kind, newspapers and magazines, which formed the staple of our conversation, as well as all our amusement. In the time of my depression and sadness my mother had a bad illness, and I was her nurse, or at least attendant. I had to sit for hours by her bedside and keep quiet. I had no liking then for needlework, a taste which developed afterwards, so I took to writing. There was no particular purpose in my beginning except this, to secure some amusement and occupation for myself while I sat by my mother's bedside. I wrote a little book in which the chief character was an angelic elder sister, unmarried, who had the charge of a family of motherless brothers and sisters, and who had a shrine of sorrow

---

7. Fundamentally, at bottom.

in her life in the shape of the portrait and memory of her lover who had died young. It was all very innocent and guileless, and my audience—to wit, my mother and brother Frank—were highly pleased with it. (It was published long after by W. on his own account,[8] and very silly I think it is, poor little thing.) I think I was then about sixteen. Afterwards I wrote another very much concerned with the Church business, in which the heroine, I recollect, was a girl, who in the beginning of the story was a sort of half-witted undeveloped creature, but who ended by being one of those lofty poetical beings whom girls love. She was called, I recollect, Ibby, but why, I cannot explain. I had the satisfaction afterwards, when I came to my full growth, of burning the manuscript, which was a three-volume business. I don't think any effort was ever made to get a publisher for it. . . .

I forget when it was that we moved to Birkenhead—not, I think, till after the extraordinary epoch of the publication of my first book. From the time above spoken of I went on writing, and somehow, I don't remember how, got into the history of Mrs Margaret Maitland. There had been some sketches from life in the story which, as I have said, I burned; but that was pure imagination. A slight reflection of my own childhood perhaps was in the child Grace, a broken bit of reflection here and there from my mother in the picture of Mrs Margaret. Willie, after many failures and after a long illness, which we were in hopes had purified him from all his defects, had gone to London to go through some studies at the London University and in the College called the English Presbyterian, to which in our warm Free Churchism we had attached ourselves. He took my MS. to Colburn, then one of the chief publishers of novels, and for some weeks nothing was heard of it, when one morning came a big blue envelope containing an agreement by which Mr Colburn pledged himself to publish my book on the half-profit system, accompanied by a letter from a Mr S. W. Fullom, full of compliments as to its originality, &c. I have forgotten the terms now, but then I knew them by heart. The delight, the astonishment, the amusement of this was not to be described. First and foremost, it was the most extraordinary joke that ever was. Maggie's story! My mother laughed and cried with pride and happiness and amazement unbounded. She thought Mr S. W. Fullom a great authority and a man of genius, and augured the greatest advantage to me from his acquaintance and that of all the great literary persons about him. This wonderful event must have come most fortunately to comfort the family under new trouble; for things had again gone wrong with poor Willie—he had fallen once more into his old vice and debt and misery. . . .

. . . And then Mr Colburn kindly—I thought most kindly, and thanked him *avec effusion*—gave me £150 for 'Margaret Maitland.' I remember walking along the street with delightful elation, thinking that, after all, I was worth something—and not to be hustled about. I remember, too, getting the first review of my book in the twilight of a wintry dark afternoon, and reading it by the firelight—always half-amused at the thought that it was *me* who was being thus discussed in the newspapers. It was the 'Athenæum,' and it was on the whole favourable. Of course this event preceded by a couple of months the

8. The novel referred to is *Christian Melville*, published in 1856 under William or "Willie" Wilson's name.

transaction with Mr Colburn. I think the book was in its third edition before he offered me that £150. I remember no reviews except that one of the 'Athenæum,' nor any particular effect which my success produced in me, except that sense of elation. I cannot think why the book succeeded so well. When I read it over some years after, I felt nothing but shame at its foolish little polemics and opinions. I suppose there must have been some breath of youth and sincerity in it which touched people, and there had been no Scotch stories for a long time. Lord Jeffrey, then an old man and very near his end, sent me a letter of sweet praise, which filled my mother with rapture and myself with an abashed gratitude. I was very young. Oddly enough, it has always remained a matter of doubt with me whether the book was published in 1849 or 1850. I thought the former; but Geraldine Macpherson,[9] whom I met in London for the first time a day or two before it was published, declared it to be 1850, from the fact that *that* was the year of her marriage. If a woman remembers any date, it must be the date of her marriage![10] so I don't doubt Geddie was right. Anyhow, if it was 1850, I was then only twenty-two, and in some things very young for my age, as in others perhaps older than my years. I was wonderfully little moved by the business altogether. I had a great pleasure in writing, but the success and the three editions had no particular effect upon my mind. For one thing, I saw very few people. We had no society. My father had a horror of strangers, and would never see any one who came to the house, which was a continual wet blanket to my mother's cordial, hospitable nature; but she had given up struggling long before my time, and I grew up without any idea of the pleasures and companions of youth. I did not know them, and therefore did not miss them; but I daresay this helped to make me—not indifferent, rather unconscious, of what might in other circumstances have "turned my head." My head was as steady as a rock. I had nobody to praise me except my mother and Frank, and their applause—well, it was delightful, it was everything in the world—it was life,—but it did not count. They were part of me, and I of them, and we were all in it. After a while it came to be the custom that I should every night "read what I had written" to them before I went to bed. They were very critical sometimes, and I felt while I was reading whether my little audience was with me or not, which put a good deal of excitement into the performance. But that was all the excitement I had.

I began another book called 'Caleb Field,'[11] about the Plague in London, the very night I had finished 'Margaret Maitland.' I had been reading Defoe, and got the subject into my head. It came to one volume only, and I took a great deal of trouble about a Nonconformist minister who spoke in antitheses very carefully constructed. I don't think it attracted much notice, but I don't remember. Other matters, events even of our uneventful life, took so much more importance in life than these books—nay, it must be a kind of affectation to say that, for the writing ran through everything. But then it was also subordinate to everything, to be pushed aside for any little necessity. I had no table even to myself, much less a room to work in, but sat at the corner of the family table with my writing-book, with everything going on as if I had been making a shirt instead of writ-

9. Geraldine Macpherson was one of Oliphant's best friends and wife of painter Robert Macpherson.
10. It *was* 1849. [Coghill's note]
11. Published in 1851.

ing a book. Our rooms in those days were sadly wanting in artistic arrangement. The table was in the middle of the room, the centre round which everybody sat with the candles or lamp upon it. My mother sat always at needle-work of some kind, and talked to whoever might be present, and I took my share in the conversation, going on all the same with my story, the little groups of imaginary persons, these other talks evolving themselves quite undisturbed. It would put me out now to have someone sitting at the same table talking while I worked—at least I would think it put me out, with the sort of conventionalism which grows upon one. But up to this date, 1888, I have never been shut up in a separate room, or hedged off with any observances. My study, all the study I have ever attained to, is the little second drawing-room where all the (feminine) life of the house goes on; and I don't think I have ever had two hours undisturbed (except at night, when everybody is in bed) during my whole literary life. Miss Austen, I believe, wrote in the same way, and very much for the same reason; but at her period the natural flow of life took another form. The family were half ashamed to have it known that she was not just a young lady like the others, doing her embroidery. Mine were quite pleased to magnify me, and to be proud of my work, but always with a hidden sense that it was an admirable joke, and no idea that any special facilities or retirement was necessary. My mother, I believe, would have felt her pride and rapture much checked, almost humiliated, if she had conceived that I stood in need of any artificial aids of that or any other description. That would at once have made the work unnatural to her eyes, and also to mine. I think the first time I ever secluded myself for my work was years after it had become my profession and sole dependence—when I was living after my widowhood in a relation's house, and withdrew with my book and my inkstand from the family drawing-room out of a little conscious ill-temper which made me feel guilty, notwithstanding that the retirement was so very justifiable! But I did not feel it to be so, neither did the companions from whom I withdrew. . . .

I was reading of Charlotte Brontë the other day, and could not help comparing myself with the picture more or less as I read. I don't suppose my powers are equal to hers—my work to myself looks perfectly pale and colourless beside hers—but yet I have had far more experience and, I think, a fuller conception of life. I have learned to take perhaps more a man's view of mortal affairs,—to feel that the love between men and women, the marrying and giving in marriage, occupy in fact so small a portion of either existence or thought. When I die I know what people will say of me: they will give me credit for courage (which I almost think is not courage but insensibility), and for honesty and honourable dealing; they will say I did my duty with a kind of steadiness, not knowing how I have rebelled and groaned under the rod. Scarcely anybody who cares to speculate further will know what to say of my working power and my own conception of it; for, except one or two, even my friends will scarcely believe how little possessed I am with any thought of it all,—how little credit I feel due to me, how accidental most things have been, and how entirely a matter of daily labour, congenial work, sometimes now and then the expression of my own heart, almost always the work most pleasant to me, this has been. I wonder if God were to try me with the loss of this gift, such as it is, whether I should feel it much? If I could live otherwise I do not think I should. If I could move about the house, and serve my children with my own hands, I know I should be happier. But this is vain talking; only I know very well that for years past neither praise nor blame has quickened my pulse ten beats that I am aware of. This insensibility saves me some pain, but it must also lose me a great deal of pleasure. . . .

# William Morris

## HOW WE LIVE AND HOW WE MIGHT LIVE

*William Morris's dissatisfaction with the conditions of nineteenth-century life ("how we live") and his attraction to a more vital, heroic world in the imagined past—classical Greece, the Middle Ages, and Icelandic myth—informed his poetry, painting, and prose romances, as well as the wallpapers, tapestries, and stained glass he designed and the orna- mented editions he printed at his Kelmscott Press. Morris's disdain for the ugliness of indus- trialized England and the dehumanizing effects of capitalism and mass production is most overt and controversial in his works of social reform and his commitment to socialism. He professed this commitment in an Oxford lecture in November 1883. Inspired early in his career by Thomas CARLYLE and John RUSKIN and later influenced by his observation of the effects of mass production, Morris had grown disillusioned with what he saw as the failure of both the Conservative and Liberal parties to effect social change. He read Marx and joined the Social Democratic Federation; subsequently, he and several of the Federation lead- ers formed a new organization, the Socialist League. As a member of the league, Morris helped to found a paper, Commonweal, which he edited and financially supported until*

*1890. He lectured and proselytized for the socialist cause at outdoor mass meetings and on street corners. One of his lectures, "How We Live and How We Might Live," appeared first in* the Commonweal *and was included in* Signs of Change *(1888), a collection of seven of Morris's socialist lectures, from which this selection is taken.*                    LMF

THE WORD REVOLUTION, WHICH WE Socialists are so often forced to use, has a terrible sound in most people's ears, even when we have explained to them that it does not necessarily mean a change accompanied by riot and all kinds of violence, and cannot mean a change made mechanically and in the teeth of opinion by a group of men who have somehow managed to seize on the executive power for the moment. Even when we explain that we use the word revolution in its etymological sense, and mean by it a change in the basis of society, people are scared at the idea of such a vast change, and beg that you will speak of reform and not revolution. As, however, we Socialists do not at all mean by our word revolution what these worthy people mean by their word reform, I can't help thinking that it would be a mistake to use it, whatever projects we might conceal beneath its harmless envelope. So we will stick to our word, which means a change of the basis of society; it may frighten people, but it will at least warn them that there is something to be frightened about, which will be no less dangerous for being ignored; and also it may encourage some people, and will mean to them at least not a fear, but a hope.

Fear and Hope—those are the names of the two great passions which rule the race of man, and with which revolutionists have to deal; to give hope to the many oppressed and fear to the few oppressors, that is our business; if we do the first and give hope to the many, the few *must* be frightened by their hope; otherwise we do not want to frighten them; it is not revenge we want for poor people, but happiness; indeed, what revenge can be taken for all the thousands of years of the sufferings of the poor?

However, many of the oppressors of the poor, most of them, we will say, are not conscious of their being oppressors (we shall see why presently); they live in an orderly, quiet way themselves, as far as possible removed from the feelings of a Roman slave-owner or a Legree;[1] they know that the poor exist, but their sufferings do not present themselves to them in a trenchant and dramatic way; they themselves have troubles to bear, and they think doubtless that to bear trouble is the lot of humanity, nor have they any means of comparing the troubles of their lives with those of people lower in the social scale; and if ever the thought of those heavier troubles obtrudes itself upon them, they console themselves with the maxim that people do get used to the troubles they have to bear, whatever they may be.

Indeed, as far as regards individuals at least, that is but too true, so that we have as supporters of the present state of things, however bad it may be, first those comfortable unconscious oppressors who think that they have everything to fear from any change which would involve more than the softest and most gradual of reforms, and secondly those poor people who, living hard and anxiously as they do, can hardly conceive of any change for the better happening to them, and dare not risk one tittle of their poor pos-

1. Simon Legree: a brutal planter in Harriet Beecher Stowe's novel *Uncle Tom's Cabin* (1852).

sessions in taking any action towards a possible bettering of their condition; so that while we can do little with the rich save inspire them with fear, it is hard indeed to give the poor any hope. It is, then, no less than reasonable that those whom we try to involve in the great struggle for a better form of life than that which we now lead should call on us to give them at least some idea of what that life may be like. . . .

How do we live, then, under our present system? Let us look at it a little.

And first, please to understand that our present system of Society is based on a state of perpetual war. Do any of you think that this is as it should be? I know that you have often been told that the competition, which is at present the rule of all production, is a good thing, and stimulates the progress of the race; but the people who tell you this should call competition by its shorter name of *war* if they wish to be honest, and you would then be free to consider whether or no war stimulates progress, otherwise than as a mad bull chasing you over your own garden may do. War or competition, whichever you please to call it, means at the best pursuing your own advantage at the cost of some one else's loss, and in the process of it you must not be sparing of destruction even of your own possessions, or you will certainly come by the worse in the struggle. You understand that perfectly as to the kind of war in which people go out to kill and be killed; that sort of war in which ships are commissioned, for instance, "to sink, burn, and destroy;" but it appears that you are not so conscious of this waste of goods when you are only carrying on that other war called *commerce*; observe, however, that the waste is there all the same.

Now let us look at this kind of war a little closer, run through some of the forms of it, that we may see how the "burn, sink, and destroy" is carried on in it.

First, you have that form of it called national rivalry, which in good truth is nowadays the cause of all gunpowder and bayonet wars which civilized nations wage. For years past we English have been rather shy of them, except on those happy occasions when we could carry them on at no sort of risk to ourselves, when the killing was all on one side, or at all events when we hoped it would be. We have been shy of gunpowder war with a respectable enemy for a long while, and I will tell you why: It is because we have had the lion's share of the world-market; we didn't want to fight for it as a nation, for we had got it; but now this is changing in a most significant, and, to a Socialist, a most cheering way; we are losing or have lost that lion's share; it is now a desperate "competition" between the great nations of civilization for the world-market, and to-morrow it may be a desperate war for that end. As a result, the furthering of war (if it be not on too large a scale) is no longer confined to the honour-and-glory kind of old Tories,[2] who if they meant anything at all by it meant that a Tory war would be a good occasion for damping down democracy; we have changed all that, and now it is quite another kind of politician that is wont to urge us on to "patriotism" as 'tis called. The leaders of the Progressive Liberals, as they would call themselves, long-headed persons who know well enough that social movements are going on, who are not blind to the fact that the world will move with

2. Tories: older name for the Conservative political party, which tended to act to preserve the existing order and, in the Victorian period, to stress duties over rights. The Whig or Liberal Party, on the other hand, was associated with political progressivism and laissez-faire policies.

their help or without it; these have been the Jingoes[3] of these later days. I don't mean to say they know what they are doing: politicians, as you well know, take good care to shut their eyes to everything that may happen six months ahead; but what is being done is this: that the present system, which always must include national rivalry, is pushing us into a desperate scramble for the markets on more or less equal terms with other nations, because, once more, we have lost that command of them which we once had. Desperate is not too strong a word. We shall let this impulse to snatch markets carry us whither it will, whither it must. To-day it is successful burglary and disgrace, to-morrow it may be mere defeat and disgrace.

Now this is not a digression, although in saying this I am nearer to what is generally called politics than I shall be again. I only want to show you what commercial war comes to when it has to do with foreign nations, and that even the dullest can see how mere waste must go with it. That is how we live now with foreign nations, prepared to ruin them without war if possible, with it if necessary, let alone meantime the disgraceful exploiting of savage tribes and barbarous peoples, on whom we force at once our shoddy wares and our hypocrisy at the cannon's mouth.

Well, surely Socialism can offer you something in the place of all that. It can; it can offer you peace and friendship instead of war. We might live utterly without national rivalries, acknowledging that while it is best for those who feel that they naturally form a community under one name to govern themselves, yet that no community in civilization should feel that it had interests opposed to any other, their economical condition being at any rate similar; so that any citizen of one community could fall to work and live without disturbance of his life when he was in a foreign country, and would fit into his place quite naturally; so that all civilized nations would form one great community, agreeing together as to the kind and amount of production and distribution needed; working at such and such production where it could be best produced; avoiding waste by all means. Please to think of the amount of waste which they would avoid, how much such a revolution would add to the wealth of the world! What creature on earth would be harmed by such a revolution? Nay, would not everybody be the better for it? And what hinders it? I will tell you presently.

Meantime let us pass from this "competition" between nations to that between "the organizers of labour," great firms, joint-stock companies; capitalists in short, and see how competition "stimulates production" among them: indeed it does do that; but what kind of production? Well, production of something to sell at a profit, or say production of profits: and note how war commercial stimulates that: a certain market is demanding goods; there are, say, a hundred manufacturers who make that kind of goods, and every one of them would if he could keep that market to himself, and struggles desperately to get as much of it as he can, with the obvious result that presently the thing is overdone, and the market is glutted, and all that fury of manufacture has to sink into cold ashes. Doesn't that seem something like war to you? Can't you see the waste of it—waste of labour, skill, cunning, waste of life in short? Well, you may say, but it cheapens the goods. In a sense it

---

3. Professors of patriotism and England's readiness for war.

does; and yet only apparently, as wages have a tendency to sink for the ordinary worker in proportion as prices sink; and at what a cost do we gain this appearance of cheapness! Plainly speaking, at the cost of cheating the consumer and starving the real producer for the benefit of the gambler, who uses both consumer and producer as his milch cows. I needn't go at length into the subject of adulteration, for every one knows what kind of a part it plays in this sort of commerce; but remember that it is an absolutely necessary incident to the production of profit out of wares, which is the business of the so-called manufacturer; and this you must understand, that, taking him in the lump, the consumer is perfectly helpless against the gambler; the goods are forced on him by their cheapness, and with them a certain kind of life which that energetic, that aggressive cheapness determines for him: for so far-reaching is this curse of commercial war that no country is safe from its ravages; the traditions of a thousand years fall before it in a month; it overruns a weak or semi-barbarous country, and whatever romance or pleasure or art existed there, is trodden down into a mire of sordidness and ugliness; the Indian or Javanese craftsman may no longer ply his craft leisurely, working a few hours a day, in producing a maze of strange beauty on a piece of cloth: a steam-engine is set a-going at Manchester, and that victory over nature and a thousand stubborn difficulties is used for the base work of producing a sort of plaster of china-clay and shoddy, and the Asiatic worker, if he is not starved to death outright, as plentifully happens, is driven himself into a factory to lower the wages of his Manchester brother worker, and nothing of character is left him except, most like, an accumulation of fear and hatred of that to him most unaccountable evil, his English master. The South Sea Islander must leave his canoe-carving, his sweet rest, and his graceful dances, and become the slave of a slave: trousers, shoddy, rum, missionary, and fatal disease—he must swallow all this civilization in the lump, and neither himself nor we can help him now till social order displaces the hideous tyranny of gambling that has ruined him. . . .

. . . We have spoken first of the war of rival nations; next of that of rival firms: we have now to speak of rival men. As nations under the present system are driven to compete with one another for the markets of the world, and as firms or the captains of industry have to scramble for their share of the profits of the markets, so also have the workers to compete with each other—for livelihood; and it is this constant competition or war amongst them which enables the profit-grinders to make their profits, and by means of the wealth so acquired to take all the executive power of the country into their hands. But here is the difference between the position of the workers and the profit-makers: to the latter, the profit-grinders, war is necessary; you cannot have profit-making without competition, individual, corporate, and national; but you may work for a livelihood without competing; you may combine instead of competing.

I have said war was the life-breath of the profit-makers; in like manner, combination is the life of the workers. The working-classes or proletariat cannot even exist as a class without combination of some sort. The necessity which forced the profit-grinders to collect their men first into workshops working by the division of labour, and next into great factories worked by machinery, and so gradually to draw them into the great towns and centres of civilization, gave birth to a distinct working-class or proletariat: and this it was which gave them their *mechanical* existence, so to say. But note, that they are indeed combined into social groups for the production of wares, but only as yet mechanically; they do not know what they are working at, nor whom they are working for, because they are combining to produce wares of which the profit of a master forms an essential part, instead of goods for their own use: as long as they do this, and compete with each other for leave to do it, they will be, and will feel themselves to be, simply a part of those competing firms I have been speaking of; they will be in fact just a part of the machinery for the production of profit; and so long as this lasts it will be the aim of the masters or profit-makers to decrease the market value of this human part of the machinery; that is to say, since they already hold in their hands the labour of dead men in the form of capital and machinery, it is their interest, or we will say their necessity, to pay as little as they can help for the labour of living men which they have to buy from day to day: and since the workmen they employ have nothing but their labour-power, they are compelled to underbid one another for employment and wages, and so enable the capitalist to play his game.

I have said that, as things go, the workers are a part of the competing firms, an adjunct of capital. Nevertheless, they are only so by compulsion; and, even without their being conscious of it, they struggle against that compulsion and its immediate results, the lowering of their wages, of their standard of life; and this they do, and must do, both as a class and individually: just as the slave of the great Roman lord, though he distinctly felt himself to be a part of the household, yet collectively was a force in reserve for its destruction, and individually stole from his lord whenever he could safely do so. So, here, you see, is another form of war necessary to the way we live now, the war of class against class, which, when it rises to its height, and it seems to be rising at present, will destroy those other forms of war we have been speaking of; will make the position of the profit-makers, of perpetual commercial war, untenable; will destroy the present system of competitive privilege, or commercial war.

Now observe, I said that to the existence of the workers it was combination, not competition, that was necessary, while to that of the profit-makers combination was impossible, and war necessary. The present position of the workers is that of the machinery of commerce, or in plainer words its slaves; when they change that position and become free, the class of profit-makers must cease to exist; and what will then be the position of the workers? Even as it is they are the one necessary part of society, the life-giving part; the other classes are but hangers-on who live on them. But what should they be, what will they be, when they, once for all, come to know their real power, and cease competing with one another for livelihood? I will tell you: they will be society, they will be the community. And being society—that is, there being no class outside them to contend with—they can then regulate their labour in accordance with their own real needs.

There is much talk about supply and demand, but the supply and demand usually meant is an artificial one; it is under the sway of the gambling market; the demand is forced, as I hinted above, before it is supplied; nor, as each producer is working against all the rest, can the producers hold their hands, till the market is glutted and the workers, thrown out on the streets, hear that there has been over-production, amidst which over-plus of unsaleable goods they go ill-supplied with even necessaries, because the wealth which they themselves have created is "ill-distributed," as we call it—that is, unjustly taken away from them.

When the workers are society they will regulate their labour, so that the supply and demand shall be genuine, not gambling; the two will then be commensurate, for it is the same society which demands that also supplies; there will be no more artificial famines then, no more poverty amidst over-production, amidst too great a stock of the very things which should supply poverty and turn it into well-being. In short, there will be no waste and therefore no tyranny. . . .

Well, I will now let my claims for decent life stand as I have made them. To sum them up in brief, they are: First, a healthy body; second, an active mind in sympathy with the past, the present, and the future; thirdly, occupation fit for a healthy body and an active mind; and fourthly, a beautiful world to live in.

These are the conditions of life which the refined man of all ages has set before him as the thing above all others to be attained. Too often he has been so foiled in their pursuit that he has turned longing eyes backward to the days before civilization, when man's sole business was getting himself food from day to day, and hope was dormant in him, or at least could not be expressed by him.

Indeed, if civilization (as many think) forbids the realization of the hope to attain such conditions of life, then civilization forbids mankind to be happy; and if that be the case, then let us stifle all aspirations towards progress—nay, all feelings of mutual good-will and affection between men—and snatch each one of us what we can from the heap of wealth that fools create for rogues to grow fat on; or better still, let us as speedily as possible find some means of dying like men, since we are forbidden to live like men.

Rather, however, take courage, and believe that we of this age, in spite of all its torment and disorder, have been born to a wonderful heritage fashioned of the work of those that have gone before us; and that the day of the organization of man is dawning. It is not we who can build up the new social order; the past ages have done the most of that work for us; but we can clear our eyes to the signs of the times, and we shall then see that the attainment of a good condition of life is being made possible for us, and that it is now our business to stretch out our hands to take it.

And how? Chiefly, I think, by educating people to a sense of their real capacities as men, so that they may be able to use to their own good the political power which is rapidly being thrust upon them; to get them to see that the old system of organizing labour *for individual profit* is becoming unmanageable, and that the whole people have now got to choose between the confusion resulting from the break up of that system and the determination to take in hand the labour now organized for profit, and use its organization for the livelihood of the community: to get people to see that individual profit-makers are not a necessity for labour but an obstruction to it, and that not only or chiefly because they are the perpetual pensioners of labour, as they are, but rather because of the waste which their existence as a class necessitates. All this we have to teach people, when we have taught ourselves; and I admit that the work is long and burdensome; as I began by saying, people have been made so timorous of change by the terror of starvation that even the unluckiest of them are stolid and hard to move. Hard as the work is, however, its reward is not doubtful. The mere fact that a body of men, however small, are banded together as Socialist missionaries shows that the change is going on. As the working-classes, the real organic part of society, take in these ideas, hope will arise in them, and they will claim changes in society, many of which doubtless will not tend directly towards their emancipation, because they will be claimed without due knowledge of the one thing necessary to claim, *equality of condition*; but which indirectly will help to break up our rotten sham society, while that claim for equality of condition will be made constantly and with growing loudness till it *must* be listened to, and then at last it will only be a step over the border and the civilized world will be socialized; and, looking back on what has been, we shall be astonished to think of how long we submitted to live as we live now.

# Walter Horatio Pater

1839: Born 4 August in London

1864: Elected fellow at Brasenose College, Oxford

1873: *Studies in the History of the Renaissance*

1885: *Marius the Epicurean*

1887: *Imaginary Portraits*

1889: *Appreciations*

1893: *Plato and Platonism*

1894: Died 30 July at Oxford

## STUDIES IN THE HISTORY OF THE RENAISSANCE

*A quiet classics tutor at Oxford, Walter Pater gained fame and notoriety upon the publication of his* Studies in the History of the Renaissance *in 1873. In this collection of essays, which had been published earlier as individual periodical articles, Pater developed an aesthetic philosophy that reflected the influences of the British empiricist tradition, German idealism, and the French thought of Gautier, Baudelaire, and Flaubert. Rejecting the idea that the value of art lay in its "message" in favor of the idea of "art for art's sake," Pater believed that art was to be evaluated not, as John RUSKIN argued, according to its morality, but rather on the basis of its ability to produce pleasurable impressions in the viewer. His "Conclusion," with its vision of the perpetual creation and decreation of the world—a vision derived, on the one hand, from the philosophies of Descartes, Hume, and Kant and, on the other, from the discoveries of natural science—and its consequent exhortation to the reader to seek a life of full, pleasurable experience, shocked many of Pater's contemporaries and inspired a generation of Oxford students, including Oscar WILDE, Arthur SYMONS, and William Butler Yeats. Pater himself was influenced by Jacob Burckhardt's* The Civilization of the Renaissance in Italy *(1860), which shaped Pater's and our modern understanding of the Renaissance as an age that promoted individualism, not merely as the age in which classical learning was reborn.*

*Although some reviewers of* Studies in the History of the Renaissance *recognized Pater's departure from traditional art criticism and praised his prose style, particularly his description of the Mona Lisa in his essay on Leonardo da Vinci, many condemned what they saw as his immorality—his pagan vision and, as recent critics argue, his homosexual sensibilities. Pater, in the second edition of 1877, deleted numerous passages, omitted the "Conclusion," and changed the title to* The Renaissance: Studies in Art and Poetry. *He restored the "Conclusion" and made additional revisions to the third and fourth editions, published in 1888 and 1893. The following are selections from the 1873 text, the version that first startled Pater's contemporaries.* LMF

## PREFACE

MANY ATTEMPTS HAVE BEEN MADE by writers on art and poetry to define beauty in the abstract, to express it in the most general terms, to find a universal formula for it. The value of such attempts has most often been in the suggestive and penetrating things said by the way. Such discussions help us very little to enjoy what has been well done in art or poetry, to discriminate between what is more and what is less excellent in them, or to use words like beauty, excellence, art, poetry, with more meaning than they would otherwise have. Beauty, like all other qualities presented to human experience, is relative; and the definition of it becomes unmeaning and useless in proportion to its abstractness. To define beauty not in the most abstract, but in the most concrete terms possible, not to find a universal formula for it, but the formula which expresses most adequately this or that special manifestation of it, is the aim of the true student of æsthetics.

'To see the object as in itself it really is,'[1] has been justly said to be the aim of all true criticism whatever; and in æsthetic criticism the first step towards seeing one's object as it really is, is to know one's own impression as it really is, to discriminate it, to realise it distinctly. The objects with which æsthetic criticism deals, music, poetry, artistic and accomplished forms of human life, are indeed receptacles of so many powers or forces; they possess, like natural elements, so many virtues or qualities. What is this song or picture, this engaging personality presented in life or in a book, to *me*? What effect does it really produce on me? Does it give me pleasure? and if so, what sort or degree of pleasure? How is my nature modified by its presence and under its influence? The answers to these questions are the original facts with which the æsthetic critic has to do; and, as in the study of light, of morals, of number, one must realise such primary data for oneself or not at all. And he who experiences these impressions strongly, and drives directly at the analysis and discrimination of them, need not trouble himself with the abstract question what beauty is in itself, or its exact relation to truth or experience,—metaphysical questions, as unprofitable as metaphysical questions elsewhere. He may pass them all by as being, answerable or not, of no interest to him.

The æsthetic critic, then, regards all the objects with which he has to do, all works of art and the fairer forms of nature and human life, as powers or forces, producing pleasurable sensations, each of a more or less peculiar and unique kind. This influence he feels and wishes to explain, analysing it, and reducing it to its elements. To him, the picture,

---

1. Matthew ARNOLD's statement in "The Function of Criticism at the Present Time" (1864).

the landscape, the engaging personality in life or in a book, La Gioconda, the hills of Carrara, Pico of Mirandula,[2] are valuable for their virtues, as we say in speaking of a herb, a wine, a gem; for the property each has of affecting one with a special, unique impression of pleasure. Education grows in proportion as one's susceptibility to these impressions increases in depth and variety. And the function of the æsthetic critic is to distinguish, analyse, and separate from its adjuncts, the virtue by which a picture, a landscape, a fair personality in life or in a book, produces this special impression of beauty or pleasure, to indicate what the source of that impression is, and under what conditions it is experienced. His end is reached when he has disengaged that virtue, and noted it, as a chemist notes some natural element, for himself and others; and the rule for those who would reach this end is stated with great exactness in the words of a recent critic of Sainte-Beuve: 'De se borner à connaître de près les belles choses, et à s'en nourrir en exquis amateurs, en humanistes accomplis.'[3]

What is important, then, is not that the critic should possess a correct abstract definition of beauty for the intellect, but a certain kind of temperament, the power of being deeply moved by the presence of beautiful objects. He will remember always that beauty exists in many forms. To him all periods, types, schools of taste, are in themselves equal. In all ages there have been some excellent workmen and some excellent work done. The question he asks is always, In whom did the stir, the genius, the sentiment of the period find itself? who was the receptacle of its refinement, its elevation, its taste? 'The ages are all equal,' says William Blake, 'but genius is always above its age.'[4]

Often it will require great nicety to disengage this virtue from the commoner elements with which it may be found in combination. Few artists, not Goethe or Byron even, work quite cleanly, casting off all debris, and leaving us only what the heat of their imagination has wholly fused and transformed. Take for instance the writings of Wordsworth. The heat of his genius, entering into the substance of his work, has crystallised a part, but only a part, of it; and in that great mass of verse there is much which might well be forgotten. But scattered up and down it, sometimes fusing and transforming entire compositions, like the Stanzas on 'Resolution and Independence' and the Ode on the 'Recollections of Childhood,' sometimes, as if at random, turning a fine crystal here and there, in a matter it does not wholly search through and transform, we trace the action of his unique incommunicable faculty, that strange mystical sense of a life in natural things, and of man's life as a part of nature, drawing strength and colour and character from local influences, from the hills and streams and natural sights and sounds. Well! that is the *virtue*, the active principle in Wordsworth's poetry; and then the function of the critic of Wordsworth is to trace that active principle, to disengage it, to mark the degree in which it penetrates his verse.

2. Leonardo da Vinci's "La Gioconda" is also known as the *Mona Lisa*; "the hills of Carrara" in Italy contain white marble. Pico of Mirandula, or Pico della Mirandola (1463–94): an Italian philosopher whom Pater discusses in another essay included in *The Renaissance*.
3. "To confine themselves to knowing beautiful things intimately, and to sustain themselves by these, as sensitive amateurs and accomplished humanists do." This statement was in fact made by French critic Charles Augustin Sainte-Beuve himself.
4. From William Blake's annotations to *The Works of Sir Joshua Reynolds* (1798). Blake was responding to Reynolds' disparagement of the work of German painter and engraver Albrecht Dürer (1471–1528).

The subjects of the following studies are taken from the history of the Renaissance, and touch what I think the chief points in that complex, many-sided movement. I have explained in the first of them what I understand by the word, giving it a much wider scope than was intended by those who originally used it to denote only that revival of classical antiquity in the fifteenth century which was but one of many results of a general stimulus and enlightening of the human mind, and of which the great aim and achievements of what, as Christian art, is often falsely opposed to the Renaissance, were another result. This outbreak of the human spirit may be traced far into the middle age[5] itself, with its qualities already clearly pronounced, the care for physical beauty, the worship of the body, the breaking down of those limits which the religious system of the middle age imposed on the heart and the imagination. I have taken as an example of this movement, this earlier Renaissance within the middle age itself, and as an expression of its qualities, a little composition in early French; not because it is the best possible expression of them, but because it helps the unity of my series, inasmuch as the Renaissance ends also in France, in French poetry, in a phase of which the writings of Joachim du Bellay[6] are in many ways the most perfect illustration; the Renaissance thus putting forth in France an aftermath, a wonderful later growth, the products of which have to the full the subtle and delicate sweetness which belongs to a refined and comely decadence; just as its earliest phases have the freshness which belongs to all periods of growth in art, the charm of *ascesis*,[7] of the austere and serious girding of the loins in youth.

But it is in Italy, in the fifteenth century, that the interest of the Renaissance mainly lies, in that solemn fifteenth century which can hardly be studied too much, not merely for its positive results in the things of the intellect and the imagination, its concrete works of art, its special and prominent personalities, with their profound æsthetic charm, but for its general spirit and character, for the ethical qualities of which it is a consummate type.

The various forms of intellectual activity which together make up the culture of an age, move for the most part from different starting points and by unconnected roads. As products of the same generation they partake indeed of a common character and unconsciously illustrate each other; but of the producers themselves, each group is solitary, gaining what advantage or disadvantage there may be in intellectual isolation. Art and poetry, philosophy and the religious life, and that other life of refined pleasure and action in the open places of the world, are each of them confined to its own circle of ideas, and those who prosecute either of them are generally little curious of the thoughts of others. There come however from time to time eras of more favourable conditions, in which the thoughts of men draw nearer together than is their wont, and the many interests of the intellectual world combine in one complete type of general culture. The fifteenth century in Italy is one of these happier eras; and what is sometimes said of the age of Pericles is true of that of Lorenzo—it is an age productive in personalities, many-sided, centralised, complete. Here, artists and philosophers and those whom the action of the

---

5. Pater is referring to the Middle Ages.
6. Joachim du Bellay (1522–60), French poet and critic, discussed in an essay in *The Renaissance*.
7. Asceticism.

world has elevated and made keen, do not live in isolation, but breathe a common air and catch light and heat from each other's thoughts. There is a spirit of general elevation and enlightenment in which all alike communicate. It is the unity of this spirit which gives unity to all the various products of the Renaissance, and it is to this intimate alliance with mind, this participation in the best thoughts which that age produced, that the art of Italy in the fifteenth century owes much of its grave dignity and influence. . . .

## LIONARDO DA VINCI

. . . 'La Gioconda' is, in the truest sense, Lionardo's masterpiece, the revealing instance of his mode of thought and work. In suggestiveness, only the Melancholia of Dürer is comparable to it; and no crude symbolism disturbs the effect of its subdued and graceful mystery. We all know the face and hands of the figure, set in its marble chair, in that cirque of fantastic rocks, as in some faint light under sea. Perhaps of all ancient pictures time has chilled it least.[8] As often happens with works in which invention seems to reach its limit, there is an element in it given to, not invented by, the master. In that inestimable folio of drawings, once in the possession of Vasari, were certain designs by Verrocchio,[9] faces of such impressive beauty that Lionardo in his boyhood copied them many times. It is hard not to connect with these designs of the elder by-past master, as with its germinal prin-ciple, the unfathomable smile, always with a touch of something sinister in it, which plays over all Lionardo's work. Besides, the picture is a portrait. From childhood we see this image defining itself on the fabric of his dreams; and but for express historical testimony, we might fancy that this was but his ideal lady, embodied and beheld at last. What was the relationship of a living Florentine to this creature of his thought? By what strange affini-ties had she and the dream grown thus apart, yet so closely together? Present from the first, incorporeal in Lionardo's thought, dimly traced in the designs of Verrocchio, she is found present at last in Il Giocondo's[10] house. That there is much of mere portraiture in the picture is attested by the legend that by artificial means, the presence of mimes and flute-players, that subtle expression was protracted on the face. Again, was it in four years and by renewed labour never really completed, or in four months and as by stroke of magic, that the image was projected?

The presence that thus so strangely rose beside the waters is expressive of what in the ways of a thousand years man had come to desire. Hers is the head upon which all 'the ends of the world are come,' and the eyelids are a little weary. It is a beauty wrought out from within upon the flesh, the deposit, little cell by cell, of strange thoughts and fantas-tic reveries and exquisite passions. Set it for a moment beside one of those white Greek goddesses or beautiful women of antiquity, and how would they be troubled by this beau-ty, into which the soul with all its maladies has passed? All the thoughts and experience of the world have etched and moulded there in that which they have of power to refine and make expressive the outward form, the animalism of Greece, the lust of Rome, the

8. Yet for Vasari there was some further magic of crimson in the lips and cheeks, lost for us. [Pater's note] Giorgio Vasari was the author of *Lives of the Most Excellent Italian Painters* (1550).
9. Andrea del Verrocchio (1435–88), Florentine sculptor and painter.
10. Francesco del Giocondo, whose third wife Lisa may have been the subject of the *Mona Lisa*.

reverie of the middle age with its spiritual ambition and imaginative loves, the return of the Pagan world, the sins of the Borgias. She is older than the rocks among which she sits; like the vampire, she has been dead many times, and learned the secrets of the grave; and has been a diver in deep seas, and keeps their fallen day about her; and trafficked for strange webs with Eastern merchants; and, as Leda, was the mother of Helen of Troy, and, as Saint Anne, the mother of Mary; and all this has been to her but as the sound of lyres and flutes, and lives only in the delicacy with which it has moulded the changing lineaments and tinged the eyelids and the hands. The fancy of a perpetual life, sweeping together ten thousand experiences, is an old one; and modern thought has conceived the idea of humanity as wrought upon by, and summing up in itself, all modes of thought and life. Certainly Lady Lisa might stand as the embodiment of the old fancy, the symbol of the modern idea. . . .

## CONCLUSION

Λέγει που Ἡράκλειτος ὅτι πάντα χωρεῖ καὶ οὐδὲν μένει [11]

To regard all things and principles of things as inconstant modes or fashions has more and more become the tendency of modern thought. Let us begin with that which is without—our physical life. Fix upon it in one of its more exquisite intervals, the moment, for instance, of delicious recoil from the flood of water in summer heat. What is the whole physical life in that moment but a combination of natural elements to which science gives their names? But these elements, phosphorus and lime and delicate fibres, are present not in the human body alone: we detect them in places most remote from it. Our physical life is a perpetual motion of them—the passage of the blood, the wasting and repairing of the lenses of the eye, the modification of the tissues of the brain by every ray of light and sound—processes which science reduces to simpler and more elementary forces. Like the elements of which we are composed, the action of these forces extends beyond us; it rusts iron and ripens corn. Far out on every side of us these elements are broadcast, driven by many forces; and birth and gesture and death and the springing of violets from the grave are but a few out of ten thousand resulting combinations. That clear perpetual outline of face and limb is but an image of ours under which we group them—a design in a web, the actual threads of which pass out beyond it. This at least of flame-like our life has, that it is but the concurrence, renewed from moment to moment, of forces parting sooner or later on their ways.

Or if we begin with the inward world of thought and feeling, the whirlpool is still more rapid, the flame more eager and devouring. There it is no longer the gradual darkening of the eye and fading of colour from the wall,—the movement of the shore side, where the water flows down indeed, though in apparent rest,—but the race of the midstream, a drift of momentary acts of sight and passion and thought. At first sight experience seems to bury us under a flood of external objects, pressing upon us with a sharp importunate reality, calling us out of ourselves in a thousand forms of action. But when reflection begins to act upon those objects they are dissipated under its influence; the

---

11. "All things give way and nothing remains still," a saying of Heraclitus repeated by Socrates in Plato's *Cratylus*.

cohesive force is suspended like a trick of magic; each object is loosed into a group of impressions,—colour, odour, texture,—in the mind of the observer. And if we continue to dwell on this world, not of objects in the solidity with which language invests them, but of impressions unstable, flickering, inconsistent, which burn and are extinguished with our consciousness of them, it contracts still further; the whole scope of observation is dwarfed to the narrow chamber of the individual mind. Experience, already reduced to a swarm of impressions, is ringed round for each one of us by that thick wall of personality through which no real voice has ever pierced on its way to us, or from us to that which we can only conjecture to be without. Every one of those impressions is the impression of the individual in his isolation, each mind keeping as a solitary prisoner its own dream of a world.

Analysis goes a step further still, and tells us that those impressions of the individual to which, for each one of us, experience dwindles down, are in perpetual flight; that each of them is limited by time, and that as time is infinitely divisible, each of them is infinitely divisible also; all that is actual in it being a single moment, gone while we try to apprehend it, of which it may ever be more truly said that it has ceased to be than that it is. To such a tremulous wisp constantly reforming itself on the stream, to a single sharp impression, with a sense in it, a relic more or less fleeting, of such moments gone by, what is *real* in our life fines itself down. It is with the movement, the passage and dissolution of impressions, images, sensations, that analysis leaves off,—that continual vanishing away, that strange perpetual weaving and unweaving of ourselves.

*Philosophiren*, says Novalis, *ist dephlegmatisiren, vivificiren.*[12] The service of philosophy, and of religion and culture as well, to the human spirit, is to startle it into a sharp and eager observation. Every moment some form grows perfect in hand or face; some tone on the hills or sea is choicer than the rest; some mood of passion or insight or intellectual excitement is irresistibly real and attractive for us,—for that moment only. Not the fruit of experience, but experience itself is the end. A counted number of pulses only is given to us of a variegated, dramatic life. How may we see in them all that is to be seen in them by the finest senses? How can we pass most swiftly from point to point, and be present always at the focus where the greatest number of vital forces unite in their purest energy?

To burn always with this hard gem-like flame, to maintain this ecstasy, is success in life. Failure is to form habits; for habit is relative to a stereotyped world; meantime it is only the roughness of the eye that makes any two persons, things, situations, seem alike. While all melts under our feet, we may well catch at any exquisite passion, or any contribution to knowledge that seems, by a lifted horizon, to set the spirit free for a moment, or any stirring of the senses, strange dyes, strange flowers, and curious odours, or work of the artist's hands, or the face of one's friend. Not to discriminate every moment some passionate attitude in those about us, and in the brilliance of their gifts some tragic dividing of forces on their ways is, on this short day of frost and sun, to sleep before evening. With this sense of the splendour of our experience and of its awful brevity, gathering all we are

---

12. "To philosophise is to cast off inertia, to make oneself alive." Novalis: Friedrich von Hardenberg (1772–1801), German Romantic writer.

into one desperate effort to see and touch, we shall hardly have time to make theories about the things we see and touch. What we have to do is to be for ever curiously testing new opinions and courting new impressions, never acquiescing in a facile orthodoxy of Comte or of Hegel,[13] or of our own. Theories, religious or philosophical ideas, as points of view, instruments of criticism, may help us to gather up what might otherwise pass unregarded by us. *La philosophie, c'est la microscope de la pensée.*[14] The theory, or idea, or system, which requires of us the sacrifice of any part of this experience, in consideration of some interest into which we cannot enter, or some abstract morality we have not identified with ourselves, or what is only conventional, has no real claim upon us.

One of the most beautiful places in the writings of Rousseau is that in the sixth book of the 'Confessions,' where he describes the awakening in him of the literary sense. An undefinable taint of death had always clung about him, and now in early manhood he believed himself stricken by mortal disease. He asked himself how he might make as much as possible of the interval that remained; and he was not biassed by anything in his previous life when he decided that it must be by intellectual excitement, which he found in the clear, fresh writings of Voltaire. Well, we are all *condamnés*, as Victor Hugo says: *les hommes sont tous condamnés à mort avec des sursis indéfinis:*[15] we have an interval, and then our place knows us no more. Some spend this interval in listlessness, some in high passions, the wisest in art and song. For our one chance is in expanding that interval, in getting as many pulsations as possible into the given time. High passions give one this quickened sense of life, ecstasy and sorrow of love, political or religious enthusiasm, or the 'enthusiasm of humanity.' Only, be sure it is passion, that it does yield you this fruit of a quickened, multiplied consciousness. Of this wisdom, the poetic passion, the desire of beauty, the love of art for art's sake has most; for art comes to you professing frankly to give nothing but the highest quality to your moments as they pass, and simply for those moments' sake.

13. Auguste Comte (1798–1857), French founder of positivism (see George Henry Lewes); Georg W. F. Hegel (1770–1831), German philosopher.
14. "Philosophy is the microscope of thought."
15. "We are all under sentence of death but with a sort of indefinite reprieve." [Pater's translation in the 1893 edition] Victor Hugo (1802–85), French novelist and poet.

# Edmund William Gosse

## FATHER AND SON: A STUDY OF TWO TEMPERAMENTS

Despite his importance as a literary critic and biographer, Edmund Gosse's reputation rests upon his autobiography, Father and Son. This work, originally published anonymously but quickly attributed to Gosse, traces his gradual estrangement from his father's narrow Calvinism. A respected naturalist and zoological writer, Philip Henry Gosse (1810–88) had become the target of criticism and scorn in the scientific community with his publication of Omphalos (1857), in which he tried to resolve the contradiction between a literal interpretation of Genesis and recent geological discoveries. He suggested that fossils were merely evidence of his theory of "Prochronism," which argued that God at one moment created a world already bearing traces of organic development. Embittered by the response to his book and mourning the recent death of his wife, Philip Gosse became more severe and fanatical in his religious beliefs and practices. He raised his son according to the Puritan, evangelical precepts of the Plymouth Brethren. In its depiction of Edmund Gosse's gradual rebellion against his father's dogmatism and religion, as well as his assertion of independent selfhood, Father and Son reflects the impact of science and the questioning of authority upon one Victorian psyche, as some contemporary reviewers noted and a few condemned. While many early readers recognized their own spiritual journeys in Gosse's life, Father and Son combines moral fiction with authentic recollection. LMF

## CHAPTER 9

THE RESULT OF MY BEING ADMITTED into the communion of the "Saints"[1] was that, as soon as the nine days' wonder of the thing passed by, my position became, if anything, more harassing and pressed than ever. It is true that freedom was permitted to me in certain directions; I was allowed to act a little more on my own responsibility, and was not so incessantly informed what "the Lord's will" might be in this matter and in that, because it was now conceived that, in such dilemmas, I could command private intelligence of my own. But there was no relaxation of our rigid manner of life, and I think I now began, by comparing it with the habits of others, to perceive how very strict it was.

The main difference in my lot as a communicant from that of a mere dweller in the tents of righteousness was that I was expected to respond with instant fervour to every appeal of conscience. When I did not do this, my position was almost worse than it had been before, because of the livelier nature of the responsibility which weighed upon me. My little faults of conduct, too, assumed shapes of terrible importance, since they proceeded from one so signally enlightened. My Father was never tired of reminding me that, now that I was a professing Christian, I must remember, in everything I did, that I was an example to others. He used to draw dreadful pictures of supposititious little boys who were secretly watching me from afar, and whose whole career, in time and in eternity, might be disastrously affected if I did not keep my lamp burning. . . .

My attitude to other people's souls when I was out of my Father's sight was now a constant anxiety to me. In our tattling world of small things he had extraordinary opportunities of learning how I behaved when I was away from home; I did not realise this, and I used to think his acquaintance with my deeds and words savoured almost of wizardry. He was accustomed to urge upon me the necessity of "speaking for Jesus in season and out of season," and he so worked upon my feelings that I would start forth like St. Teresa, wild for the Moors and martyrdom. But any actual impact with persons marvellously cooled my zeal, and I should hardly ever have "spoken" at all if it had not been for that unfortunate phrase "out of season." It really seemed that one must talk of nothing else, since if an occasion was not in season it was out of season; there was no alternative, no close time for souls.

My Father was very generous. He used to magnify any little effort that I made, with stammering tongue, to sanctify a visit; and people, I now see, were accustomed to give me a friendly lead in this direction, so that they might please him by reporting that I had "testified" in the Lord's service. The whole thing, however, was artificial, and was part of my Father's restless inability to let well alone. It was not in harshness or in ill-nature that he worried me so much; on the contrary, it was all part of his too-anxious love. He was in a hurry to see me become a shining light, every thing that he had himself desired to be, yet with none of his shortcomings.

It was about this time that he harrowed my whole soul into painful agitation by a phrase that he let fall, without, I believe, attaching any particular importance to it at the

---

1. The Plymouth Brethren practiced adult baptism and extended the privilege of receiving communion only to adult believers who had undergone a conversion experience. Gosse's admission to full membership at the age of ten was considered extraordinary.

time. He was occupied, as he so often was, in polishing and burnishing my faith, and he was led to speak of the day when I should ascend the pulpit to preach my first sermon. "Oh! if I may be there, out of sight, and hear the gospel message proclaimed from your lips, then I shall say, 'My poor work is done. Oh! Lord Jesus, receive my spirit.' " I cannot express the dismay which this aspiration gave me, the horror with which I anticipated such a *nunc dimittis*.[2] I felt like a small and solitary bird, caught and hung out hopelessly and endlessly in a great glittering cage. The clearness of the personal image affected me as all the texts and prayers and predictions had failed to do. I saw myself imprisoned forever in the religious system which had caught me and would whirl my helpless spirit as in the concentric wheels of my nightly vision. I did not struggle against it, because I believed that it was inevitable, and that there was no other way of making peace with the terrible and ever-watchful "God who is a jealous God." But I looked forward to my fate without zeal and without exhilaration, and the fear of the Lord altogether swallowed up and cancelled any notion of the love of Him.

I should do myself an injustice, however, if I described my attitude to faith at this time as wanting in candour. I did very earnestly desire to follow where my Father led. That passion for imitation, which I have already discussed, was strongly developed at this time, and it induced me to repeat the language of pious books in godly ejaculations which greatly edified my grown-up companions, and were, so far as I can judge, perfectly sincere. I wished extremely to be good and holy, and I had no doubt in my mind of the absolute infallibility of my Father as a guide in heavenly things. But I am perfectly sure that there never was a moment in which my heart truly responded, with native ardour, to the words which flowed so readily, in such a stream of unction, from my anointed lips. I cannot recall anything but an intellectual surrender; there was never joy in the act of resignation, never the mystic's rapture at feeling his phantom self, his own threadbare soul, suffused, thrilled through, robed again in glory by a fire which burns up everything personal and individual about him.

Through thick and thin I clung to a hard nut of individuality, deep down in my childish nature. To the pressure from without, I resigned everything else, my thoughts, my words, my anticipations, my assurances, but there was something which I never resigned, my innate and persistent self. Meek as I seemed, and gently respondent, I was always conscious of that innermost quality which I had learned to recognise in my earlier days in Islington, that existence of two in the depths who could speak to one another in inviolable secrecy.[3]

"This a natural man may discourse of, and that very knowingly, and give a kind of natural credit to it, as to a history that may be true; but firmly to believe that there is divine truth in all these things, and to have a persuasion of it stronger than of the very thing we see with our eyes; such an assent as this is the peculiar work of the Spirit of God, and is certainly saving faith." This passage is not to be found in the writings of any extravagant

---

2. Permission to leave. An allusion to Simeon's words upon seeing the infant Jesus; see Luke 2:25–32.

3. Gosse alludes to an earlier incident in *Father and Son* when, at the age of six, he punched a hole in a water pipe and spoiled his father's fountain display. He kept his deed a secret from his parents and, in so doing, discovered that he had both an outer self by which others knew him and an inner, private self.

Plymouth Brother, but in one of the most solid classics of the Church, in Archbishop Leighton's "Commentary on the First Epistle of Peter."[4] I quote it because it defines, more exactly than words of my own could hope to do, the difference which already existed, and in secrecy began forthwith to be more and more acutely accentuated, between my Father and myself. He did indeed possess this saving faith, which could move mountains of evidence, and suffer no diminution under the action of failure or disappointment. I, on the other hand—as I began to feel dimly then, and see luminously now—had only acquired the habit of giving what the Archbishop means by "a kind of natural credit" to the doctrine so persistently impressed upon my conscience. From its very nature this could not but be molten in the dews and exhaled in the sunshine of life and thought and experience.

My Father, by an indulgent act for the caprice of which I cannot wholly account, presently let in a flood of imaginative light which was certainly hostile to my heavenly calling. My instinctive interest in geography has already been mentioned. This was the one branch of knowledge in which I needed no instruction, geographical information seeming to soak into the cells of my brain without an effort. At the age of eleven, I knew a great deal more of maps, and of the mutual relation of localities all over the globe, than most grown-up people do. It was almost a mechanical acquirement. I was now greatly taken with the geography of the West Indies, of every part of which I had made MS. maps. There was something powerfully attractive to my fancy in the great chain of the Antilles, lying on the sea like an open bracelet, with its big jewels and little jewels strung on an invisible thread. I liked to shut my eyes and see it all, in a mental panorama, stretched from Cape Sant' Antonio to the Serpent's Mouth. Several of these lovely islands, these emeralds and amethysts set on the Caribbean Sea, my Father had known well in his youth, and I was importunate in questioning him about them. One day, as I multiplied inquiries, he rose in his impetuous way, and climbing to the top of a bookcase, brought down a thick volume and presented it to me. "You'll find all about the Antilles there," he said, and left me with "Tom Cringle's Log"[5] in my possession.

The embargo laid upon every species of fiction by my Mother's powerful scruple had never been raised, although she had been dead four years. As I have said in an earlier chapter, this was a point on which I believe that my Father had never entirely agreed with her. He had, however, yielded to her prejudice, and no work of romance, no fictitious story, had ever come in my way. It is remarkable that among our books, which amounted to many hundreds, I had never discovered a single work of fiction until my Father himself revealed the existence of Michael Scott's wild masterpiece. So little did I understand what was allowable in the way of literary invention that I began the story without a doubt that it was true, and I think it was my Father himself who, in answer to an inquiry, explained to me that it was "all made up." He advised me to read the descriptions of the sea, and of the mountains of Jamaica, and "skip" the pages which gave imaginary adventures and conversations. But I did not take his counsel; these latter were the flower of the book to me. I had never read, never dreamed of anything like them, and they filled my whole horizon with glory and with joy.

4. Robert Leighton (1611–84), Archbishop of Glasgow and writer of popular sermons and commentaries.
5. By Michael Scott (1789–1835); published serially 1829–33 and in volume form in 1836.

I suppose that when my Father was a younger man, and less pietistic, he had read "Tom Cringle's Log" with pleasure, because it recalled familiar scenes to him. Much was explained by the fact that the frontispiece of this edition was a delicate line-engraving of Blewfields,[6] the great lonely house in a garden of Jamaican all-spice where for eighteen months he had worked as a naturalist. He could not look at this print without recalling exquisite memories and airs that blew from a terrestrial paradise. But Michael Scott's noisy amorous novel of adventure was an extraordinary book to put in the hands of a child who had never been allowed to glance at the mildest and most febrifugal story-book.

It was like giving a glass of brandy neat to some one who had never been weaned from a milk diet. I have not read "Tom Cringle's Log" from that day to this, and I think that I should be unwilling now to break the charm of memory, which may be largely illusion. But I remember a great deal of the plot and not a little of the language, and, while I am sure it is enchantingly spirited, I am quite as sure that the persons it describes were far from being unspotted by the world. The scenes at night in the streets of Spanish Town surpassed not merely my experience, but, thank goodness, my imagination. The nautical personages used, in their conversations, what is called "a class of language," and there ran, if I am not mistaken, a glow and gust of life through the romance from beginning to end which was nothing if it was not resolutely pagan.

There were certain scenes and images in "Tom Cringle's Log" which made not merely a lasting impression upon my mind, but tinged my outlook upon life. The long adventures, fightings and escapes, sudden storms without, and mutinies within, drawn forth as they were, surely with great skill, upon the fiery blue of the boundless tropical ocean, produced on my inner mind a sort of glimmering hope, very vaguely felt at first, slowly developing, long stationary and faint, but always tending towards a belief that I should escape at last from the narrowness of the life we led at home, from this bondage to the Law and the Prophets.

I must not define too clearly, or endeavour too formally to insist on the blind movements of a childish mind. But of this I am quite sure, that the reading and re-reading of "Tom Cringle's Log" did more than anything else, in this critical eleventh year of my life, to give fortitude to my individuality, which was in great danger—as I now see—of succumbing to the pressure my Father brought to bear upon it from all sides. My soul was shut up, like Fatima,[7] in a tower to which no external influences could come, and it might really have been starved to death, or have lost the power of recovery and rebound, if my captor, by some freak not yet perfectly accounted for, had not gratuitously opened a little window in it and added a powerful telescope. The daring chapters of Michael Scott's picaresque romance of the tropics were that telescope and that window. . . .

## CHAPTER 12

. . . There presently came over me a strong desire to know what doctrine indeed it was that the other Churches taught. I expressed a wish to be made aware of the practices of

---

6. A Moravian missionary house in Jamaica where Philip Gosse, sponsored by the British Museum, studied birds and produced two illustrated books about his studies.
7. Bluebeard's wife.

Rome, or at least of Canterbury, and I longed to attend the Anglican and the Roman services. But to do so was impossible. My Father did not, indeed, forbid me to enter the fine parish church of our village, or the stately Puginesque[8] cathedral which Rome had just erected at its side, but I knew that I could not be seen at either service without his immediately knowing it, or without his being deeply wounded. Although I was sixteen years of age, and although I was treated with indulgence and affection, I was still but a bird fluttering in the net-work of my Father's will, and incapable of the smallest independent action. I resigned all thought of attending any other services than those at our "Room," but I did no longer regard this exclusion as a final one. I bowed, but it was in the house of Rimmon,[9] from which I now knew that I must inevitably escape. All the liberation, however, which I desired or dreamed of was only just so much as would bring me into communion with the outer world of Christianity, without divesting me of the pure and simple principles of faith.

Of so much emancipation, indeed, I now became ardently desirous, and in the contemplation of it I rose to a more considerable degree of religious fervour than I had ever reached before or was ever to experience later. Our thoughts were at this time abundantly exercised with the expectation of the immediate coming of the Lord, who, as my Father and those who thought with him believed, would suddenly appear, without the least warning, and would catch up to be with Him in everlasting glory all whom acceptance of the Atonement had sealed for immortality. These were, on the whole, not numerous, and our belief was that the world, after a few days' amazement at the total disappearance of these persons, would revert to its customary habits of life, merely sinking more rapidly into a moral corruption due to the removal of these souls of salt. This event an examination of prophecy had led my Father to regard as absolutely imminent, and sometimes, when we parted for the night, he would say with a sparkling rapture in his eyes, "Who knows? We may meet next in the air, with all the cohorts of God's saints!"

This conviction I shared, without a doubt; and, indeed,—in perfect innocency, I hope, but perhaps with a touch of slyness too,—I proposed at the end of the summer holidays that I should stay at home. "What is the use of my going to school? Let me be with you when we rise to meet the Lord in the air!" To this my Father sharply and firmly replied that it was our duty to carry on our usual avocations to the last, for we knew not the moment of His coming, and we should be together in an instant on that day, how far soever we might be parted upon earth. I was ashamed, but his argument was logical, and, as it proved, judicious. My Father lived for nearly a quarter of a century more, never losing the hope of "not tasting death," and as the last moments of mortality approached, he was bitterly disappointed at what he held to be a scanty reward of his long faith and patience. But if my own life's work had been, as I proposed, shelved in expectation of the Lord's imminent advent, I should have cumbered the ground until this day.

To school, therefore, I returned with a brain full of strange discords, in a huddled mixture of "Endymion" and the Book of Revelation, John Wesley's hymns and *Midsummer Night's Dream*. Few boys of my age, I suppose, carried about with them such a confused

8. Design influenced by Augustus Welby Northmore Pugin (1812–52), architect of the Gothic revival.
9. See 2 Kings 5:18. Rimmon was an Assyrian divinity.

throng of immature impressions and contradictory hopes. I was at one moment devoutly pious, at the next haunted by visions of material beauty and longing for sensuous impressions. In my hot and silly brain, Jesus and Pan held sway together, as in a wayside chapel discordantly and impishly consecrated to Pagan and to Christian rites. But for the present, as in the great chorus which so marvellously portrays our double nature, "the folding-star of Bethlehem" was still dominant. I became more and more pietistic. Beginning now to versify, I wrote a tragedy in pale imitation of Shakespeare, but on a Biblical and evangelistic subject; and odes that were imitations of those in "Prometheus Unbound," but dealt with the approaching advent of our Lord and the rapture of His saints. My unwholesome excitement, bubbling up in this violent way, reached at last a climax and foamed over.

It was a summer afternoon, and, being now left very free in my movements, I had escaped from going out with the rest of my schoolfellows in their formal walk in charge of an usher. I had been reading a good deal of poetry, but my heart had translated Apollo and Bacchus into terms of exalted Christian faith. I was alone, and I lay on a sofa, drawn across a large open window at the top of the school-house, in a room which was used as a study by the boys who were "going up for examination." I gazed down on a labyrinth of gardens sloping to the sea, which twinkled faintly beyond the towers of the town. Each of these gardens held a villa in it, but all the near landscape below me was drowned in foliage. A wonderful warm light of approaching sunset modelled the shadows and set the broad summits of the trees in a rich glow. There was an absolute silence below and around me, a magic of suspense seemed to keep every topmost twig from waving.

Over my soul there swept an immense wave of emotion. Now, surely, now the great final change must be approaching. I gazed up into the faintly-coloured sky, and I broke irresistibly into speech. "Come now, Lord Jesus," I cried, "come now and take me to be for ever with Thee in Thy Paradise. I am ready to come. My heart is purged from sin, there is nothing that keeps me rooted to this wicked world. Oh, come now, now, and take me before I have known the temptations of life, before I have to go to London and all the dreadful things that happen there!" And I raised myself on the sofa, and leaned upon the window-sill, and waited for the glorious apparition.

This was the highest moment of my religious life, the apex of my striving after holiness. I waited awhile, watching; and then I had a little shame at the theatrical attitude I had adopted, although I was alone. Still I gazed and still I hoped. Then a little breeze sprang up, and the branches danced. Sounds began to rise from the road beneath me. Presently the colour deepened, the evening came on. From far below there rose to me the chatter of the boys returning home. The tea-bell rang,—last word of prose to shatter my mystical poetry. "The Lord has not come, the Lord will never come," I muttered, and in my heart the artificial edifice of extravagant faith began to totter and crumble. From that moment forth my Father and I, though the fact was long successfully concealed from him and even from myself, walked in opposite hemispheres of the soul, with "the thick o' the world between us."

# Mary Arnold (Mrs. Humphry) Ward

1851: Born 11 June at Hobart, Van Dieman's Land (Tasmania)

1856: Moved with family to England

1872: Married Thomas Humphry Ward, then tutor at Brasenose College, Oxford, and later art critic for the *Times*

1884: *Miss Bretherton*

1888: *Robert Elsmere*

1889: "An Appeal Against Female Suffrage"

1894: *Marcella*

1898: *Helbeck of Bannisdale*

1908: Founded Women's National Anti Suffrage League

1920: Died 24 March in London

## AN APPEAL AGAINST FEMALE SUFFRAGE

*Despite repeated calls for women's suffrage in the last four decades of the nineteenth century, women could not vote in national elections until the twentieth century. In 1918 the franchise was extended to women over thirty; in 1928 to women over twenty-one. "An Appeal Against Female Suffrage," appearing in the June 1889 issue of* The Nineteenth Century, *initiated a powerful protest by women, many of them privileged and titled, against female suffrage and probably helped to delay the extension of the vote to women. The "Appeal" was accompanied by a list of 104 female antisuffragists and a form that women readers who agreed with the appeal were requested to complete and return. The July issue contained a second request for signatures, next to a prosuffrage "Reply" by Millicent Fawcett and M. M. Dilke. In August* The Nineteenth Century *devoted twenty-nine pages to the names of approximately fifteen hundred antisuffrage respondents.*

*The author of the appeal, Mary Ward—granddaughter of Thomas Arnold of Rugby and niece of Matthew* Arnold—*had become by 1889 a famed novelist and woman of letters. The preceding year her controversial* Robert Elsmere *had shocked some and comforted others with its frank investigation of a clergyman's loss of religious faith. Mary Ward's vehe-*

*ment opposition to women's voting in parliamentary elections may seem somewhat odd,*
*given her own history as a prolific writer whose novels provided the major financial support*
*of her family's comfortable living; an active champion of women's education and one of the*
*forces behind the opening of Somerville Hall, Oxford; a campaigner for social causes, leader*
*in the settlement movement, and founder of children's play centers. Yet others, including*
*Florence NIGHTINGALE, also believed that the vote was less important than women's educa-*
*tion, although they might not share Ward's strong antipathy to suffrage. Ward's arguments*
*reveal deeply held cultural beliefs about sexual difference and the "sanctity" of the family. In*
*the "Appeal," reprinted here in its entirety, she uses the familiar argument from biology,*
*specifically nineteenth-century science's construction of woman as biologically inferior, and*
*voices the familiar refrain that a woman's moral influence—her sympathy and disinterest-*
*edness—requires no vote and indeed might be diminished by it.*                    RM

WE, THE UNDERSIGNED, WISH TO appeal to the common sense and the educated thought
of the men and women of England against the proposed extension of the Parliamentary
suffrage to women.

1. While desiring the fullest possible development of the powers, energies, and education of women, we believe that their work for the State, and their responsibilities
towards it, must always differ essentially from those of men, and that therefore their share
in the working of the State machinery should be different from that assigned to men.
Certain large departments of the national life are of necessity worked exclusively by men.
To men belong the struggle of debate and legislation in Parliament; the hard and exhausting labour implied in the administration of the national resources and powers; the conduct of England's relations towards the external world; the working of the army and
navy; all the heavy, laborious, fundamental industries of the State, such as those of mines,
metals, and railways; the lead and supervision of English commerce, the management of
our vast English finance, the service of that merchant fleet on which our food supply
depends. In all these spheres women's direct participation is made impossible either by
the disabilities of sex, or by strong formations of custom and habit resting ultimately
upon physical difference, against which it is useless to contend. They are affected indeed,
in some degree, by all these national activities; therefore they ought in some degree to
have an influence on them all. This influence they already have, and will have more and
more as the education of women advances. But their direct interest in these matters can
never equal that of men, whose whole energy of mind and body is daily and hourly risked
in them. Therefore it is not just to give to women direct power of deciding questions of
Parliamentary policy, of war, of foreign or colonial affairs, of commerce and finance equal
to that possessed by men. We hold that they already possess an influence on political matters fully proportioned to the possible share of women in the political activities of
England.

At the same time we are heartily in sympathy with all the recent efforts which have
been made to give women a more important part in those affairs of the community
where their interests and those of men are equally concerned; where it is possible for

them not only to decide but to help in carrying out, and where, therefore, judgment is weighted by a true responsibility, and can be guided by experience and the practical information which comes from it. As voters for or members of School Boards, Boards of Guardians, and other important public bodies, women have now opportunities for public usefulness which must promote the growth of character, and at the same time strengthen among them the social sense and habit. All these changes of recent years, together with the great improvements in women's education which have accompanied them, we cordially welcome. But we believe that the emancipating process has now reached the limits fixed by the physical constitution of women, and by the fundamental difference which must always exist between their main occupations and those of men. The care of the sick and the insane; the treatment of the poor; the education of children: in all these matters, and others besides, they have made good their claim to larger and more extended powers. We rejoice in it. But when it comes to questions of foreign or colonial policy, or of grave constitutional change, then we maintain that the necessary and normal experience of women—speaking generally and in the mass—does not and can never provide them with such materials for sound judgment as are open to men.

To sum up: we would give them their full share in the State of social effort and social mechanism; we look for their increasing activity in that higher State which rests on thought, conscience, and moral influence; but we protest against their admission to direct power in that State which *does* rest upon force—the State in its administrative, military and financial aspects—where the physical capacity, the accumulated experience and inherited training of men ought to prevail without the harassing interference of those who, though they may be partners with men in debate, can in these matters never be partners with them in action.

2. If we turn from the *right* of women to the suffrage—a right which on the grounds just given we deny—to the effect which the possession of the suffrage may be expected to have on their character and position and on family life, we find ourselves no less in doubt. It is urged that the influence of women in politics would tell upon the side of morality. We believe that it does so tell already, and will do so with greater force as women by improved education fit themselves to exert it more widely and efficiently. But it may be asked, On what does this moral influence depend? We believe that it depends largely on qualities which the natural position and functions of women as they are at present tend to develop, and which might be seriously impaired by their admission to the turmoil of active political life. These qualities are, above all, sympathy and disinterestedness. Any disposition of things which threatens to lessen the national reserve of such forces as these we hold to be a misfortune. It is notoriously difficult to maintain them in the presence of party necessities and in the heat of party struggle. Were women admitted to this struggle, their natural eagerness and quickness of temper would probably make them hotter partisans than men. As their political relations stand at present, they tend to check in them the disposition to partisanship, and to strengthen in them the qualities of sympathy and disinterestedness. We believe that their admission to the suffrage would precisely reverse this condition of things, and that the whole nation would suffer in consequence. For whatever may be the duty and privilege of the parliamentary vote for men,

we hold that citizenship is not dependent upon or identical with the possession of the suffrage. Citizenship lies in the participation of each individual in effort for the good of the community. And we believe that women will be more valuable citizens, will contribute more precious elements to the national life without the vote than with it. The quickness to feel, the willingness to lay aside prudential considerations in a right cause, which are amongst the peculiar excellencies of women, are in their right place when they are used to influence the more highly trained and developed judgment of men. But if this quickness of feeling could be immediately and directly translated into public action, in matters of vast and complicated political import, the risks of politics would be enormously increased, and what is now a national blessing might easily become a national calamity. On the one hand, then, we believe that to admit women to the ordinary machinery of political life would inflame the partisanship and increase the evils, already so conspicuous, of that life, would tend to blunt the special moral qualities of women, and so to lessen the national reserves of moral force; and, on the other hand, we dread the political and practical effects which, in our belief, would follow on such a transformation as is proposed, of an influence which is now beneficent largely because it is indirect and gradual.

3. Proposals for the extension of the suffrage to women are beset with grave practical difficulties. If votes be given to unmarried women on the same terms as they are given to men, large numbers of women leading immoral lives will be enfranchised on the one hand, while married women, who, as a rule, have passed through more of the practical experiences of life than the unmarried, will be excluded. To remedy part of this difficulty it is proposed by a large section of those who advocate the extension of the suffrage to women, to admit married women with the requisite property qualification. This proposal—an obviously just one if the suffrage is to be extended to women at all—introduces changes in family life, and in the English conception of the household, of enormous importance, which have never been adequately considered. We are practically invited to embark upon them because a few women of property possessing already all the influence which belongs to property, and a full share of that public protection and safety which is the fruit of taxation, feel themselves aggrieved by the denial of the parliamentary vote. The grievance put forward seems to us wholly disproportionate to the claim based upon it.

4. A survey of the manner in which this proposal has won its way into practical politics leads us to think that it is by no means ripe for legislative solution. A social change of momentous gravity has been proposed; the mass of those immediately concerned in it are notoriously indifferent; there has been no serious and general demand for it, as is always the case if a grievance is real and reform necessary; the amount of information collected is quite inadequate to the importance of the issue; and the public has gone through no sufficient discipline of discussion on the subject. Meanwhile pledges to support female suffrage have been hastily given in the hopes of strengthening existing political parties by the female vote. No doubt there are many conscientious supporters of female suffrage amongst members of Parliament; but it is hard to deny that the present prominence of the question is due to party considerations of a temporary nature. It is, we submit, alto-

gether unworthy of the intrinsic gravity of the question that it should be determined by reference to the passing needs of party organisation. Meanwhile we remember that great electoral changes have been carried out during recent years.[1] Masses of new electors have been added to the constituency. These new elements have still to be assimilated; these new electors have still to be trained to take their part in the national work; and while such changes are still fresh, and their issues uncertain, we protest against any further alteration in our main political machinery, especially when it is an alteration which involves a new principle of extraordinary range and significance, closely connected with the complicated problems of sex and family life.

5. It is often urged that certain injustices of the law towards women would be easily and quickly remedied were the political power of the vote conceded to them; and that there are many wants, especially among working women, which are now neglected, but which the suffrage would enable them to press on public attention. We reply that during the past half century all the principal injustices of the law towards women have been amended by means of the existing constitutional machinery; and with regard to those that remain, we see no signs of any unwillingness on the part of Parliament to deal with them. On the contrary, we remark a growing sensitiveness to the claims of women, and the rise of a new spirit of justice and sympathy among men, answering to those advances made by women in education, and the best kind of social influence, which we have already noticed and welcomed. With regard to the business or trade interests of women,—here, again, we think it safer and wiser to trust to organisation and self-help on their own part, and to the growth of a better public opinion among the men workers, than to the exercise of a political right which may easily bring women into direct and hasty conflict with men.

In conclusion: nothing can be further from our minds than to seek to depreciate the position or the importance of women. It is because we are keenly alive to the enormous value of their special contribution to the community, that we oppose what seems to us likely to endanger that contribution. We are convinced that the pursuit of a mere outward equality with men is for women not only vain but demoralising. It leads to a total misconception of woman's true dignity and special mission. It tends to personal struggle and rivalry, where the only effort of both the great divisions of the human family should be to contribute the characteristic labour and the best gifts of each to the common stock.

[Names of 104 female supporters of the appeal]
In furtherance of the foregoing Appeal —which has hitherto been only shown privately to a few persons—the accompanying proposed protest is laid before the readers of the *Nineteenth Century*, with the request that such ladies among them as agree with it will be kind enough to sign the opposite page and return it, *when detached*, to the EDITOR of this Review.

The difficulty of obtaining a public expression, even of disapproval, about such a question from those who entirely object to mixing themselves up in the coarsening struggles of party political life, may easily become a public danger. Their silence will be misinter-

---

1. The Third Reform Bill (1884) extended the male franchise further than the reform bills of 1832 and 1867. As Ward notes earlier, by 1889 women could vote in county and municipal elections and serve on local school boards and boards of Poor Law Guardians.

preted into indifference or consent to designs they most dislike, and may thus help to bring them about.

It is submitted that for once, and in order to save the quiet of Home life from total disappearance, they should do violence to their natural reticence, and signify publicly and unmistakably their condemnation of the scheme now threatened.

The deliberate opinion of the women readers of the *Nineteenth Century* might certainly be taken as a fair sample of the judgment of the educated women of the country, and would probably receive the sympathy and support of the overwhelming majority of their fellow countrywomen. EDITOR, *Nineteenth Century*

## FEMALE SUFFRAGE: A WOMEN'S PROTEST

The undersigned protest strongly against the proposed Extension of the Parliamentary Franchise to Women, which they believe would be a measure distasteful to the great majority of the women of the country—unnecessary—and mischievous both to themselves and to the State.

# Oscar Wilde

## THE SOUL OF MAN UNDER SOCIALISM

*1891 was a particularly good year for Oscar Wilde. During the previous decade, he had published poems and tales, lectured throughout North America, and above all, by the magnetic force of his personality and wit, become a popular sensation as the self-styled, self-parodying embodiment of both aestheticism and decadence. In 1891 Wilde wrote or published many of his most significant works:* The Picture of Dorian Gray *appeared in book form; he finished his first successful play,* Lady Windermere's Fan, *and completed* Salomé *in French; he produced a volume of prose entitled* Intentions *and published "The Soul of Man Under Socialism" in* The Fortnightly Review. *"The Soul of Man" challenges many conventional pieties and nineteenth-century values: altruism, the dignity of labor, the efficacy of suffering, capitalism, private property, the family, and artistic realism. Yet, despite its iconoclasm, the essay also evokes the familiar Victorian notion of individual and social organicism and a rather romanticized utopian future. Under Wilde's antiauthoritarian version of "Socialism, Communism, or whatever one chooses to call it," the individual will be freed to develop his "personality." The artist is the consummate individual, the dissident who disturbs the tyrannies of habit and authority, the agent of change. And Christ is the ideal individual and personality—not the suffering Christ of the Middle Ages, but a newly Hellenized Christ who preaches and embodies the liberation of personality.*

*In 1895 Oscar Wilde unsuccessfully sued the Marquess of Queensberry, the father of his lover Lord Alfred Douglas, for libel. Wilde was subsequently tried and convicted of "acts of gross indecency" with another male under the terms of the 1885 Criminal Law Amendment Act, and sentenced to two years in prison. However tempting it may be to read Wilde's life and works retrospectively in light of the events of 1895, Wilde still defies attempts to identify and totalize him. From his time into ours, Wilde has been labeled the apostle of beauty, a superficial dandy, a sodomite, a martyr of hypocritical sexual mores, a tragic victim of his own recklessness, a brilliant conversationalist, a bore, a social rebel, a social climber, a sentimentalist, an antisentimentalist, bourgeois, antibourgeois, modernist, and postmodernist. As complicated as our interpretation of Wilde's life is, so must our reading of his work, with its subversive irony and paradoxes, be.*                                              RM

THE CHIEF ADVANTAGE THAT WOULD result from the establishment of Socialism is, undoubtedly, the fact that Socialism would relieve us from that sordid necessity of living for others which, in the present condition of things, presses so hardly upon almost everybody. In fact, scarcely anyone at all escapes.

Now and then, in the course of the century, a great man of science, like Darwin; a great poet, like Keats; a fine critical spirit, like M. Renan[1]; a supreme artist, like Flaubert, has been able to isolate himself, to keep himself out of reach of the clamorous claims of others, to stand "under the shelter of the wall," as Plato puts it, and so to realise the perfection of what was in him, to his own incomparable gain, and to the incomparable and lasting gain of the whole world. These, however, are exceptions. The majority of people spoil their lives by an unhealthy and exaggerated altruism—are forced, indeed, so to spoil them. They find themselves surrounded by hideous poverty, by hideous ugliness, by hideous starvation. It is inevitable that they should be strongly moved by all this. The emotions of man are stirred more quickly than man's intelligence; and, as I pointed out some time ago in an article on the function of criticism, it is much more easy to have sympathy with suffering than it is to have sympathy with thought. Accordingly, with admirable though misdirected intentions, they very seriously and very sentimentally set themselves to the task of remedying the evils that they see. But their remedies do not cure the disease: they merely prolong it. Indeed, their remedies are part of the disease.

They try to solve the problem of poverty, for instance, by keeping the poor alive; or, in the case of a very advanced school, by amusing the poor.

But this is not a solution: it is an aggravation of the difficulty. *The proper aim is to try and reconstruct society on such a basis that poverty will be impossible.* And the altruistic virtues have really prevented the carrying out of this aim. Just as the worst slave-owners were those who were kind to their slaves, and so prevented the horror of the system being realised

---

1. Ernest Renan (1823–92), French critic, historian, and author of *Vie de Jésus.*

by those who suffered from it, and understood by those who contemplated it, so, in the present state of things in England, the people who do most harm are the people who try to do most good; and at last we have had the spectacle of men who have really studied the problem and know the life—educated men who live in the East-end—coming forward and imploring the community to restrain its altruistic impulses of charity, benevolence, and the like. They do so on the ground that such charity degrades and demoralizes. They are perfectly right. Charity creates a multitude of sins.

There is also this to be said. It is immoral to use private property in order to alleviate the horrible evils that result from the institution of private property. It is both immoral and unfair.

Under Socialism all this will, of course, be altered. There will be no people living in fetid dens and fetid rags, and bringing up unhealthy, hunger-pinched children in the midst of impossible and absolutely repulsive surroundings. The security of society will not depend, as it does now, on the state of the weather. If a frost comes we shall not have a hundred thousand men out of work, tramping about the streets in a state of disgusting misery, or whining to their neighbours for alms, or crowding round the doors of loath-some shelters to try and secure a hunch of bread and a night's unclean lodging. Each member of the society will share in the general prosperity and happiness of the society, and if a frost comes no one will practically be anything the worse.

Upon the other hand, *Socialism itself will be of value simply because it will lead to Individualism.*

Socialism, Communism, or whatever one chooses to call it, by converting private property into public wealth, and substituting cooperation for competition, will restore society to its proper condition of a thoroughly healthy organism, and insure the material well-being of each member of the community. It will, in fact, give Life its proper basis and its proper environment. But for the full development of Life to its highest mode of perfection, something more is needed. What is needed is Individualism. If the Socialism is Authoritarian; if there are Governments armed with economic power as they are now with political power; if, in a word, we are to have Industrial Tyrannies, then the last state of man will be worse than the first. At present, in consequence of the existence of pri-vate property, a great many people are enabled to develop a certain very limited amount of Individualism. They are either under no necessity to work for their living, or are enabled to choose the sphere of activity that is really congenial to them, and gives them pleasure. These are the poets, the philosophers, the men of science, the men of culture—in a word, the real men, the men who have realised themselves, and in whom all Humanity gains a partial realisation. Upon the other hand, there are a great many people who, having no private property of their own, and being always on the brink of sheer star-vation, are compelled to do the work of beasts of burden, to do work that is quite uncon-genial to them, and to which they are forced by the peremptory, unreasonable, degrad-ing Tyranny of want. These are the poor, and amongst them there is no grace of manner, or charm of speech, or civilization, or culture, or refinement in pleasures, or joy of life. From their collective force Humanity gains much in material prosperity. But it is only the material result that it gains, and the man who is poor is in himself absolutely of no importance. He is merely the infinitesimal atom of a force that, so far from regarding him, crushes him: indeed, prefers him crushed, as in that case he is far more obedient.

Of course, it might be said that the Individualism generated under conditions of private property is not always, or even as a rule, of a fine or wonderful type, and that the poor, if they have not culture and charm, have still many virtues. Both these statements would be quite true. The possession of private property is very often extremely demoralising, and that is, of course, one of the reasons why Socialism wants to get rid of the institution. In fact, property is really a nuisance. Some years ago people went about the country saying that property has duties. They said it so often and so tediously that, at last, the church has begun to say it. One hears it now from every pulpit. It is perfectly true. Property not merely has duties, but has so many duties that its possession to any large extent is a bore. It involves endless claims upon one, endless attention to business, endless bother. If property had simply pleasures, we could stand it; but its duties make it unbearable. In the interest of the rich we must get rid of it. The virtues of the poor may be readily admitted, and are much to be regretted. We are often told that the poor are grateful for charity. Some of them are, no doubt, *but the best amongst the poor are never grateful*. They are ungrateful, discontented, disobedient, and rebellious. They are quite right to be so. Charity they feel to be a ridiculously inadequate mode of partial restitution, or a sentimental dole, usually accompanied by some impertinent attempt on the part of the sentimentalist to tyrannize over their private lives. Why should they be grateful for the crumbs that fall from the rich man's table? They should be seated at the board, and are beginning to know it. As for being discontented, a man who would not be discontented with such surroundings and such a low mode of life would be a perfect brute. Disobedience, in the eyes of any one who has read history, is man's original virtue. It is through disobedience that progress has been made, through disobedience and through rebellion. Sometimes the poor are praised for being thrifty. But to recommend thrift to the poor is both grotesque and insulting. It is like advising a man who is starving to eat less. For a town or country labourer to practise thrift would be absolutely immoral. Man should not be ready to show that he can live like a badly-fed animal. He should decline to live like that, and should either steal or go on the rates, which is considered by many to be a form of stealing. As for begging, it is safer to beg than to take, but it is finer to take than to beg. No: a poor man who is ungrateful, unthrifty, discontented, and rebellious is probably a real personality, and has much in him. He is at any rate a healthy protest. As for the virtuous poor, one can pity them, of course, but one cannot possibly admire them. They have made private terms with the enemy, and sold their birthright for very bad pottage. They must also be extraordinarily stupid. I can quite understand a man accepting laws that protect private property, and admit of its accumulation, as long as he himself is able under those conditions to realise some form of beautiful and intellectual life. But it is almost incredible to me how a man whose life is marred and made hideous by such laws can possibly acquiesce in their continuance.

However, the explanation is not really difficult to find. It is simply this. Misery and poverty are so absolutely degrading, and exercise such a paralysing effect over the nature of men, that no class is ever really conscious of its own suffering. They have to be told of it by other people, and they often entirely disbelieve them. What is said by great employers of labour against agitators is unquestionably true. Agitators are a set of interfering, meddling people, who come down to some perfectly contented class of the community, and sow the seeds of discontent amongst them. That is the reason why agitators are so absolutely necessary. Without them, in our incomplete state, there would be no advance towards civilization. Slavery was put down in America, not in consequence of any action on the part of the slaves, or even any express desire on their part that they should be free. It was put down entirely through the grossly illegal conduct of certain agitators in Boston and elsewhere, who were not slaves themselves, nor owners of slaves, nor had anything to do with the question really. It was, undoubtedly, the Abolitionists who set the torch alight, who began the whole thing. And it is curious to note that from the slaves themselves they received, not merely very little assistance, but hardly any sympathy even; and when at the close of the war the slaves found themselves free, found themselves indeed so absolutely free that they were free to starve, many of them bitterly regretted the new state of things. To the thinker, the most tragic fact in the whole of the French Revolution is not that Marie Antoinette was killed for being a queen, but that the starved peasant of the Vendee voluntarily went out to die for the hideous cause of feudalism.[2]

It is clear, then, that no Authoritarian Socialism will do. For while under the present system a very large number of people can lead lives of a certain amount of freedom and expression and happiness, under an industrial-barrack system, or a system of economic tyranny, nobody would be able to have any such freedom at all. It is to be regretted that a portion of our community should be practically in slavery, but to propose to solve the problem by enslaving the entire community is childish. Every man must be left quite free to choose his own work. No form of compulsion must be exercised over him. If there is, his work will not be good for him, will not be good in itself, and will not be good for others. And by work I simply mean activity of any kind.

I hardly think that any Socialist, nowadays, would seriously propose that an inspector should call every morning at each house to see that each citizen rose up and did manual labour for eight hours. Humanity has got beyond that stage, and reserves such a form of life for the people whom, in a very arbitrary manner, it chooses to call criminals. But I confess that many of the socialistic views that I have come across seem to me to be tainted with ideas of authority, if not of actual compulsion. Of course authority and compulsion are out of the question. All association must be quite voluntary. *It is only in voluntary associations that man is fine.*

But it may be asked how Individualism, which is now more or less dependent on the existence of private property for its development, will benefit by the abolition of such private property. The answer is very simple. It is true that, under existing conditions, a few men who have had private means of their own, such as Byron, Shelley, Browning, Victor Hugo, Baudelaire, and others, have been able to realise their personality more or less completely. Not one of these men ever did a single day's work for hire. They were

2. Marie Antoinette (1755–93) was condemned to death by the Revolutionary Tribunal and executed in October 1793. From 1793 to 1796 some fifty thousand peasants of the Vendée in Western France opposed and fought against the Revolutionary forces.

relieved from poverty. They had an immense advantage. The question is whether it would be for the good of Individualism that such an advantage should be taken away. Let us suppose that it is taken away. What happens then to Individualism? How will it benefit?

It will benefit in this way. Under the new conditions Individualism will be far freer, far finer, and far more intensified than it is now. I am not talking of the great imaginatively-realised individualism of such poets as I have mentioned, but of the great actual Individualism latent and potential in mankind generally. For the recognition of private property has really harmed Individualism, and obscured it, by confusing a man with what he possesses. It has led Individualism entirely astray. It has made gain not growth its aim. So that man thought that the important thing was to have, and did not know that the important thing is to be. *The true perfection of man lies, not in what man has, but in what man is.* Private property has crushed true Individualism, and set up an Individualism that is false. It has debarred one part of the community from being individual by starving them. It has debarred the other part of the community from being individual by putting them on the wrong road, and encumbering them. Indeed, so completely has man's personality been absorbed by his possessions that the English law has always treated offences against a man's property with far more severity than offences against his person, and property is still the test of complete citizenship. The industry necessary for the making [of] money is also very demoralising. In a community like ours, where property confers immense distinction, social position, honour, respect, titles, and other pleasant things of the kind, man, being naturally ambitious, makes it his aim to accumulate this property, and goes on wearily and tediously accumulating it long after he has got far more than he wants, or can use, or enjoy, or perhaps even know of. Man will kill himself by over-work in order to secure property, and really, considering the enormous advantages that property brings, one is hardly surprised. One's regret is that society should be constructed on such a basis that man has been forced into a groove in which he cannot freely develop what is wonderful, and fascinating, and delightful in him—in which, in fact, he misses the true pleasure and joy of living. He is also, under existing conditions, very insecure. An enormously wealthy merchant may be—often is—at every moment of his life at the mercy of things that are not under his control. If the wind blows an extra point or so, or the weather suddenly changes, or some trivial thing happens, his ship may go down, his speculations may go wrong, and he finds himself a poor man, with his social position quite gone. Now, nothing should be able to harm a man except himself. Nothing should be able to rob a man at all. What a man really has, is what is in him. What is outside of him should be a matter of no importance. . . .

It will be a marvellous thing—the true personality of man—when we see it. It will grow naturally and simply, flower-like, or as a tree grows. It will not be at discord. It will never argue or dispute. It will not prove things. It will know everything. And yet it will not busy itself about knowledge. It will have wisdom. Its value will not be measured by material things. It will have nothing. And yet it will have everything, and whatever one takes from it, it will still have, so rich will it be. It will not be always meddling with others, or asking them to be like itself. It will love them because they will be different. And yet while it will not meddle with others it will help all, as a beautiful thing helps us, by being what it is. The personality of man will be very wonderful. It will be as wonderful as the personality of a child.

In its development it will be assisted by Christianity, if men desire that; but if men do not desire that, it will develop none the less surely. For it will not worry itself about the past, nor care whether things happened or did not happen. Nor will it admit any laws but its own laws; nor any authority but its own authority. Yet it will love those who sought to intensify it, and speak often of them. And of these Christ was one.

"Know Thyself" was written over the portal of the antique world. Over the portal of the new world, "Be thyself" shall be written. And the message of Christ to man was simply "Be thyself." That is the secret of Christ. . . .

Individualism, then, is what through Socialism we are to attain to. As a natural result the State must give up all idea of government. It must give it up because, as a wise man once said many centuries before Christ, there is such a thing as leaving mankind alone; there is no such thing as governing mankind. *All modes of government are failures.* Despotism is unjust to everybody, including the despot, who was probably made for better things. Oligarchies are unjust to the many, and ochlocracies are unjust to the few. High hopes were once formed of democracy; but democracy means simply the bludgeoning of the people by the people for the people. It has been found out. I must say that it was high time, for all authority is quite degrading. It degrades those who exercise it, and degrades those over whom it is exercised. When it is violently, grossly, and cruelly used, it produces a good effect, by creating, or at any rate bringing out, the spirit of revolt and individualism that is to kill it. When it is used with a certain amount of kindness, and accompanied by prizes and rewards, it is dreadfully demoralizing. People, in that case, are less conscious of the horrible pressure that is being put on them, and so go through their lives in a sort of coarse comfort, like petted animals, without ever realising that they are probably thinking other people's thoughts, living by other people's standards, wearing practically what one may call other people's second-hand clothes, and never being themselves for a single moment. "He who would be free," says a fine thinker, "must not conform." And authority, by bribing people to conform, produces a very gross kind of over-fed barbarism amongst us.

With authority, punishment will pass away. This will be a great gain—a gain, in fact, of incalculable value. As one reads history, not in the expurgated editions written for schoolboys and passmen, but in the original authorities of each time, one is absolutely sickened, not by the crimes that the wicked have committed, but by the punishments that the good have inflicted; *and a community is infinitely more brutalised by the habitual employment of punishment, than it is by the occasional occurrence of crime.* It obviously follows that the more punishment is inflicted the more crime is produced, and most modern legislation has clearly recognised this, and has made it its task to diminish punishment as far as it thinks it can. Wherever it has really diminished it, the results have always been extremely good. The less punishment, the less crime. When there is no punishment at all, crime will either cease to exist, or if it occurs, will be treated by physicians as a very distressing form of dementia, to be cured by care and kindness. For what are called criminals nowadays are not criminals at all. Starvation, and not sin, is the parent of modern crime.

That indeed is the reason why our criminals are, as a class, so absolutely uninteresting from any psychological point of view. They are not marvellous Macbeths and terrible Vautrins. They are merely what ordinary, respectable, commonplace people would be if they had not got enough to eat. When private property is abolished there will be no necessity for crime, no demand for it; it will cease to exist. Of course all crimes are not crimes against property, though such are the crimes that the English law, valuing what a man has more than what a man is, punishes with the harshest and most horrible severity, if we except the crime of murder, and regard death as worse than penal servitude, a point on which our criminals, I believe, disagree. But though a crime may not be against property, it may spring from the misery and rage and depression produced by our wrong system of property-holding, and so, when that system is abolished, will disappear. When each member of the community has sufficient for his wants, and is not interfered with by his neighbour, it will not be an object of any interest to him to interfere with anyone else. Jealousy, which is an extraordinary source of crime in modern life, is an emotion closely bound up with our conceptions of property, and under Socialism and Individualism will die out. It is remarkable that in communistic tribes jealousy is entirely unknown.

Now as the State is not to govern, it may be asked what the State is to do. The State is to be a voluntary association that will organize labour, and be the manufacturer and distributor of necessary commodities. *The State is to make what is useful. The individual is to make what is beautiful.* And as I have mentioned the word labour, I cannot help saying that a great deal of nonsense is being written and talked nowadays about the dignity of manual labour. There is nothing necessarily dignified about manual labour at all, and most of it is absolutely degrading. It is mentally and morally injurious to man to do anything in which he does not find pleasure, and many forms of labour are quite pleasureless activities, and should be regarded as such. To sweep a slushy crossing for eight hours on a day when the east wind is blowing is a disgusting occupation. To sweep it with mental, moral, or physical dignity seems to me to be impossible. To sweep it with joy would be appalling. Man is made for something better than disturbing dirt. All work of that kind should be done by a machine.

And I have no doubt that it will be so. Up to the present, man has been, to a certain extent, the slave of machinery, and there is something tragic in the fact that as soon as man had invented a machine to do his work he began to starve. This, however, is, of course, the result of our property system and our system of competition. One man owns a machine which does the work of five hundred men. Five hundred men are, in consequence, thrown out of employment, and having no work to do, become hungry and take to thieving. The one man secures the produce of the machine and keeps it, and has five hundred times as much as he should have, and probably, which is of much more importance, a great deal more than he really wants. Were that machine the property of all, every one would benefit by it. It would be an immense advantage to the community. All unintellectual labour, all monotonous, dull labour, all labour that deals with dreadful things, and involves unpleasant conditions, must be done by machinery. Machinery must work for us in coal mines, and do all sanitary services, and be the stoker of steamers, and clean the streets, and run messages on wet days, and do anything that is tedious or distressing.

*At present machinery competes against man. Under proper conditions machinery will serve man.* There is no doubt at all that this is the future of machinery, and just as trees grow while the country gentleman is asleep, so while Humanity will be amusing itself, or enjoying cultivated leisure—which, and not labour, is the aim of man—or making beautiful things, or reading beautiful things, or simply contemplating the world with admiration and delight, machinery will be doing all the necessary and unpleasant work. The fact is, that civilization requires slaves. The Greeks were quite right there. Unless there are slaves to do the ugly, horrible, uninteresting work, culture and contemplation become almost impossible. Human slavery is wrong, insecure, and demoralising. On mechanical slavery, on the slavery of the machine, the future of the world depends. And when scientific men are no longer called upon to go down to a depressing East-end and distribute bad cocoa and worse blankets to starving people, they will have delightful leisure in which to devise wonderful and marvellous things for their own joy and the joy of everyone else. There will be great storages of force for every city, and for every house if required, and this force man will convert into heat, light, or motion, according to his needs. Is this Utopian? A map of the world that does not include Utopia is not worth even glancing at, for it leaves out the one country at which Humanity is always landing. And when Humanity lands there, it looks out, and, seeing a better country, sets sail. Progress is the realisation of Utopias.

Now, I have said that the community by means of organization of machinery will supply the useful things, and that the beautiful things will be made by the individual. This is not merely necessary, but it is the only possible way by which we can get either the one or the other. An individual who has to make things for the use of others, and with reference to their wants and their wishes, does not work with interest, and consequently cannot put into his work what is best in him. Upon the other hand, whenever a community or a powerful section of a community, or a government of any kind, attempts to dictate to the artist what he is to do, Art either entirely vanishes, or becomes stereotyped, or degenerates into a low and ignoble form of craft. *A work of art is the unique result of a unique temperament. Its beauty comes from the fact that the author is what he is. It has nothing to do with the fact that other people want what they want.* Indeed, the moment that an artist takes notice of what other people want, and tries to supply the demand, he ceases to be an artist, and becomes a dull or an amusing craftsman, an honest or a dishonest tradesman. He has no further claim to be considered as an artist. *Art is the most intense mode of individualism that the world has known.* I am inclined to say that it is the only real mode of individualism that the world has known. Crime, which, under certain conditions, may seem to have created individualism, must take cognizance of other people and interfere with them. It belongs to the sphere of action. But alone, without any reference to his neighbours, without any interference, the artist can fashion a beautiful thing; and if he does not do it solely for his own pleasure, he is not an artist at all.

And it is to be noted that it is the fact that Art is this intense form of individualism that makes the public try to exercise over it an authority that is as immoral as it is ridiculous, and as corrupting as it is contemptible. It is not quite their fault. The public has always, and in every age, been badly brought up. They are continually asking Art to be popular, to please their want of taste, to flatter their absurd vanity, to tell them what they have been told before, to show them what they ought to be tired of seeing, to amuse them when they feel heavy after eating too much, and to distract their thoughts when they are wearied of their own stupidity. *Now Art should never try to be popular. The public should try to make itself artistic.* There is a very wide difference. If a man of science were told that the results of his experiments, and the conclusions that he arrived at, should be of such a character that they would not upset the received popular notions on the subject, or disturb popular prejudice, or hurt the sensibilities of people who knew nothing about science; if a philosopher were told that he had a perfect right to speculate in the highest spheres of thought, provided that he arrived at the same conclusions as were held by those who had never thought in any sphere at all—well, nowadays the man of science and the philosopher would be considerably amused. Yet it is really a very few years since both philosophy and science were subjected to brutal popular control, to authority in fact—the authority of either the general ignorance of the community, or the terror and greed for power of an ecclesiastical or governmental class. Of course, we have to a very great extent got rid of any attempt on the part of the community, or the Church, or the Government, to interfere with the individualism of speculative thought, but the attempt to interfere with the individualism of imaginative art still lingers. In fact, it does more than linger: it is aggressive, offensive, and brutalizing.

*In England, the arts that have escaped best are the arts in which the public take no interest.* Poetry is an instance of what I mean. We have been able to have fine poetry in England because the public do not read it, and consequently do not influence it. The public like to insult poets because they are individual, but once they have insulted them they leave them alone. In the case of the novel and the drama, arts in which the public does take an interest, the result of the exercise of popular authority has been absolutely ridiculous. No country produces such badly written fiction, such tedious, common work in the novel-form, such silly, vulgar plays as in England. It must necessarily be so. The popular standard is of such a character that no artist can get to it. It is at once too easy and too difficult to be a popular novelist. It is too easy, because the requirements of the public as far as plot, style, psychology, treatment of life, and treatment of literature are concerned are within the reach of the very meanest capacity and the most uncultivated mind. It is too difficult, because to meet such requirements the artist would have to do violence to his temperament, would have to write not for the artistic joy of writing, but for the amusement of half-educated people, and so would have to suppress his individualism, forget his culture, annihilate his style, and surrender everything that is valuable in him. In the case of the drama, things are a little better: the theatre-going public like the obvious, it is true, but they do not like the tedious; and burlesque and farcical comedy, the two most popular forms, are distinct forms of art. Delightful work may be produced under burlesque and farcical conditions, and in work of this kind the artist in England is allowed very great freedom. It is when one comes to the higher forms of the drama that the result of popular control is seen. The one thing that the public dislike is novelty. Any attempt to extend the subject-matter of art is extremely distasteful to the public; and yet the vitality and progress of art depend in a large measure on the continual extension of subject-matter.

The public dislike novelty because they are afraid of it. It represents to them a mode of Individualism, an assertion on the part of the artist that he selects his own subject, and treats it as he chooses. The public are quite right in their attitude. Art is Individualism, and Individualism is a disturbing and disintegrating force. Therein lies its immense value. For what it seeks to disturb is monotony of type, slavery of custom, tyranny of habit, and the reduction of man to the level of a machine. In Art, the public accept what has been, because they cannot alter it, not because they appreciate it. They swallow their classics whole, and never taste them. They endure them as the inevitable, and, as they cannot mar them, they mouth about them. Strangely enough, or not strangely, according to one's own views, this acceptance of the classics does a great deal of harm. The uncritical admiration of the Bible and Shakespeare in England is an instance of what I mean. With regard to the Bible, considerations of ecclesiastical authority enter into the matter, so that I need not dwell upon the point.

But in the case of Shakespeare it is quite obvious that the public really see neither the beauties nor the defects of his plays. If they saw the beauties, they would not object to the development of the drama; and if they saw the defects, they would not object to the development of the drama either. *The fact is, the public make use of the classics of a country as a means of checking the progress of Art.* They degrade the classics into authorities. They use them as bludgeons for preventing the free expression of Beauty in new forms. They are always asking a writer why he does not write like somebody else, or a painter why he does not paint like somebody else, quite oblivious of the fact that if either of them did anything of the kind he would cease to be an artist. A fresh mode of Beauty is absolutely distasteful to them, and whenever it appears they get so angry and bewildered that they always use two stupid expressions—one is that the work of art is grossly unintelligible; the other, that the work of art is grossly immoral. What they mean by these words seems to me to be this. When they say a work is grossly unintelligible, they mean that the artist has said or made a beautiful thing that is new; when they describe a work as grossly immoral, they mean that the artist has said or made a beautiful thing that is true. The former expression has reference to style; the latter to subject matter. But they probably use the words very vaguely, as an ordinary mob will use ready-made paving-stones. *There is not a single real poet or prose-writer of this century, for instance, on whom the British public have not solemnly conferred diplomas of immorality*, and these diplomas practically take the place, with us, of what in France is the formal recognition of an Academy of Letters, and fortunately make the establishment of such an institution quite unnecessary in England. Of course the public are very reckless in their use of the word. That they should have called Wordsworth an immoral poet, was only to be expected. Wordsworth was a poet. But that they should have called Charles Kingsley an immoral novelist is extraordinary.[3] Kingsley's prose was not of a very fine quality. Still, there is the word, and they use it as best they can. An artist is, of course, not disturbed by it. The true artist is a man who believes absolutely in himself, because he is absolutely himself. But I can fancy that if an artist produced a work of art in England that immediately on its appearance was recognised by the

3. Charles KINGSLEY (1819–75), author of *Alton Locke, Hypatia*, and other novels.

public, through their medium, which is the public press, as a work that was quite intelligible and highly moral, he would begin to seriously question whether in its creation he had really been himself at all, and consequently whether the work was not quite unworthy of him, and either of a thoroughly second-rate order, or of no artistic value whatsoever.

Perhaps, however, I have wronged the public in limiting them to such words as "immoral," "unintelligible," "exotic," and "unhealthy." There is one other word that they use. That word is "morbid." They do not use it often. The meaning of the word is so simple that they are afraid of using it. Still, they use it sometimes, and, now and then, one comes across it in popular newspapers. It is, of course, a ridiculous word to apply to a work of art. For what is morbidity but a mood of emotion or a mode of thought that one cannot express? The public are all morbid, because the public can never find expression for anything. *The artist is never morbid. He expresses everything.* He stands outside his subject, and through its medium produces incomparable and artistic effects. To call an artist morbid because he deals with morbidity as his subject matter is as silly as if one called Shakespeare mad because he wrote *King Lear*.

On the whole, an artist in England gains something by being attacked. His individuality is intensified. He becomes more completely himself. Of course the attacks are very gross, very impertinent, and very contemptible. But then no artist expects grace from the vulgar mind, or style from the suburban intellect. Vulgarity and stupidity are two very vivid facts in modern life. One regrets them, naturally. But there they are. They are subjects for study, like everything else. And it is only fair to state, with regard to modern journalists, that they always apologise to one in private for what they have written against one in public. . . .

. . . People sometimes inquire what form of government is most suitable for an artist to live under. To this question there is only one answer. *The form of government that is most suitable to the artist is no government at all.* Authority over him and his art is ridiculous. It has been stated that under despotisms artists have produced lovely work. This is not quite so. Artists have visited despots, not as subjects to be tyrannized over, but as wandering wonder-makers, as fascinating vagrant personalities, to be entertained and charmed and suffered to be at peace, and allowed to create. There is this to be said in favour of the despot, that he, being an individual, may have culture, while the mob, being a monster, has none. One who is an Emperor and King may stoop down to pick up a brush for a painter, but when the democracy stoops down it is merely to throw mud. And yet the democracy have not so far to stoop as the emperor. In fact, when they want to throw mud they have not to stoop at all. But there is no necessity to separate the monarch from the mob; all authority is equally bad.

There are three kinds of despots. There is the despot who tyrannizes over the body. There is the despot who tyrannizes over the soul. There is the despot who tyrannizes over soul and body alike. The first is called the Prince. The second is called the Pope. The third is called the People. The Prince may be cultivated. Many Princes have been. Yet in the Prince there is danger. One thinks of Dante at the bitter feast in Verona, of Tasso in

Ferrara's madman's cell.[4] It is better for the artist not to live with Princes. The Pope may be cultivated. Many Popes have been; the bad Popes have been. The bad Popes loved Beauty, almost as passionately, nay, with as much passion as the good Popes hated Thought. To the wickedness of the Papacy humanity owes much. The goodness of the Papacy owes a terrible debt to humanity. Yet, though the Vatican has kept the rhetoric of its thunders and lost the rod of its lightning, it is better for the artist not to live with Popes. It was a Pope who said of Cellini to a conclave of Cardinals that common laws and common authority were not made for men such as he; but it was a Pope who thrust Cellini into prison, and kept him there till he sickened with rage, and created unreal visions for himself, and saw the gilded sun enter his room, and grew so enamoured of it that he sought to escape, and crept out from tower to tower, and falling through dizzy air at dawn, maimed himself, and was by a vine-dresser covered with vine leaves, and carried in a cart to one who, loving beautiful things, had care of him.[5] There is danger in Popes. And as for the People, what of them and their authority? Perhaps of them and their authority one has spoken enough. Their authority is a thing blind, deaf, hideous, grotesque, tragic, amusing, serious and obscene. It is impossible for the artist to live with the People. All despots bribe. The people bribe and brutalize. Who told them to exercise authority? They were made to live, to listen, and to love. Someone has done them a great wrong. They have marred themselves by imitation of their inferiors. They have taken the sceptre of the Prince. How should they use it? They have taken the triple tiar of the Pope. How should they carry its burden? They are as a clown whose heart is broken. They are as a priest whose soul is not yet born. Let all who love Beauty pity them. Though they themselves love not Beauty, yet let them pity themselves. Who taught them the trick of tyranny? . . .

. . . It has been pointed out that one of the results of the extraordinary tyranny of authority is that words are absolutely distorted from their proper and simple meaning, and are used to express the obverse of their right signification. What is true about Art is true about Life. A man is called affected, now-a-days, if he dresses as he likes to dress. But in doing that he is acting in a perfectly natural manner. Affectation, in such matters, consists in dressing according to the views of one's neighbour, whose views, as they are the views of the majority, will probably be extremely stupid. Or a man is called selfish if he lives in the manner that seems to him most suitable for the full realisation of his own personality; if, in fact, the primary aim of his life is self-development. But this is the way in which everyone should live. *Selfishness is not living as one wishes to live, it is asking others to live as one wishes to live.* And unselfishness is letting other people's lives alone, not interfering with them. Selfishness always aims at creating around it an absolute uniformity of type. Unselfishness recognises infinite variety of type as a delightful thing, accepts it, acquiesces in it, enjoys it. It is not selfish to think for oneself. A man who does not think

---

4. Dante Alighieri (1265–1321), the great Italian poet; banished from his own city Florence, he lived for a time in Verona. In Canto 17 of *Paradiso*, Dante's ancestor Cacciaguida prophesies Dante's exile and says that he will know "the bitter taste of others' bread." Torquato Tasso (1544–95), Italian Renaissance poet, imprisoned by Duke Alfonso II for seven years as a madman, but actually for political and religious reasons.
5. Benvenuto Cellini (1500–71), goldsmith, sculptor, and autobiographer, was absolved of murder by Pope Paul III and later imprisoned for embezzling.

for himself does not think at all. It is grossly selfish to require of one's neighbour that he should think in the same way, and hold the same opinions. Why should he? If he can think, he will probably think differently. If he cannot think, it is monstrous to require thought of any kind from him. A red rose is not selfish because it wants to be a red rose. It would be horribly selfish if it wanted all the other flowers in the garden to be both red and roses. Under Individualism people will be quite natural and absolutely unselfish, and will know the meanings of the words, and realise them in their free, beautiful lives. Nor will men be egotistic as they are now. For the egotist is he who makes claims upon others, and the Individualist will not desire to do that. It will not give him pleasure. When man has realised Individualism, he will also realise sympathy and exercise it freely and spontaneously. Up to the present man has hardly cultivated sympathy at all. He has merely sympathy with pain, and sympathy with pain is not the highest form of sympathy. *All sympathy is fine, but sympathy with suffering is the least fine mode.* It is tainted with egotism. It is apt to become morbid. There is in it a certain element of terror for our own safety. We become afraid that we ourselves might be as the leper or as the blind, and that no man would have care of us. It is curiously limiting, too. One should sympathise with the entirety of life, not with life's sores and maladies merely, but with life's joy and beauty and energy and health and freedom. The wider sympathy is, of course, the more difficult. It requires more unselfishness. Anybody can sympathise with the sufferings of a friend, but it requires a very fine nature—it requires, in fact, the nature of a true Individualist— to sympathise with a friend's success. In the modern stress of competition and struggle for place, such sympathy is naturally rare, and is also very much stifled by the immoral ideal of uniformity of type and conformity to rule which is so prevalent everywhere, and is perhaps most obnoxious in England.

Sympathy with pain there will, of course, always be. It is one of the first instincts of man. The animals which are individual, the higher animals that is to say, share it with us. But it must be remembered that while sympathy with joy intensifies the sum of joy in the world, sympathy with pain does not really diminish the amount of pain. It may make man better able to endure evil, but the evil remains. Sympathy with consumption does not cure consumption; that is what Science does. And when Socialism has solved the problem of poverty, and Science solved the problem of disease, the area of the sentimentalists will be lessened, and the sympathy of man will be large, healthy, and spontaneous. Man will have joy in the contemplation of the joyous lives of others.

For it is through joy that the Individualism of the future will develop itself. *Christ made no attempt to reconstruct society, and consequently the Individualism that he preached to man could be realised only through pain or in solitude.* The ideals that we owe to Christ are the ideals of the man who abandons society entirely, or of the man who resists society absolutely. But man is naturally social. Even the Thebaid became peopled at last. And though the cenobite realises his personality, it is often an impoverished personality that he so realises. Upon the other hand, the terrible truth that pain is a mode through which man may realise himself exercised a wonderful fascination over the world. Shallow speakers and shallow thinkers in pulpits and on platforms often talk about the world's worship of pleasure, and whine against it. But it is rarely in the world's history that its ideal has been one of joy and beauty. The worship of pain has far more often dominated the world. Mediævalism, with its saints and martyrs, its love of self-torture, its wild passion for wounding itself, its gashing with knives, and its whipping with rods—Mediævalism is real Christianity, and the mediæval Christ is the real Christ. When the Renaissance dawned upon the world, and brought with it the new ideals of the beauty of life and the joy of living, men could not understand Christ. Even Art shows us that. The painters of the Renaissance drew Christ as a little boy playing with another boy in a palace or a garden, or lying back in his mother's arms, smiling at her, or at a flower, or at a bright bird; or as a noble stately figure moving nobly through the world; or as a wonderful figure rising in a sort of ecstasy from death to life. Even when they drew him crucified they drew him as a beautiful God on whom evil men had inflicted suffering. But he did not preoccupy them much. What delighted them was to paint the men and women whom they admired, and to show the loveliness of this lovely earth. They painted many religious pictures—in fact, they painted far too many, and the monotony of type and motive is wearisome, and was bad for art. It was the result of the authority of the public in art-matters, and is to be deplored. But their soul was not in the subject. Raphael was a great artist when he painted his portrait of the Pope. When he painted his Madonnas and infant Christs, he is not a great artist at all. Christ had no message for the Renaissance, which was wonderful because it brought an ideal at variance with his, and to find the presentation of the real Christ we must go to mediæval art. There he is one maimed and marred; one who is not comely to look on, because Beauty is a joy; one who is not in fair raiment, because that may be a joy also: he is a beggar who has a marvellous soul; he is a leper whose soul is divine; he needs neither property nor health; he is a God realising his perfection through pain.

The evolution of man is slow. The injustice of men is great. It was necessary that pain should be put forward as a mode of self-realisation. Even now, in some places in the world, the message of Christ is necessary. No one who lived in modern Russia could possibly realise his perfection except by pain. A few Russian artists have realised themselves in Art, in a fiction that is mediæval in character, because its dominant note is the realisation of men through suffering. But for those who are not artists, and to whom there is no mode of life but the actual life of fact, pain is the only door to perfection. A Russian who lives happily under the present system of government in Russia must either believe that man has no soul, or that, if he has, it is not worth developing. A Nihilist who rejects all authority, because he knows authority to be evil, and who welcomes all pain, because through that he realises his personality, is a real Christian. To him the Christian ideal is a true thing.

And yet, Christ did not revolt against authority. He accepted the imperial authority of the Roman Empire and paid tribute. He endured the ecclesiastical authority of the Jewish Church, and would not repel its violence by any violence of his own. He had, as I said before, no scheme for the reconstruction of society. But the modern world has schemes. It proposes to do away with poverty and the suffering that it entails. It desires to get rid of pain, and the suffering that pain entails. It trusts to Socialism and to Science as its methods. What it aims at is an Individualism expressing itself through joy. This

Individualism will be larger, fuller, lovelier than any Individualism has ever been. Pain is not the ultimate mode of perfection. It is merely provisional and a protest. It has reference to wrong, unhealthy, unjust surroundings. When the wrong, and the disease, and the injustice are removed, it will have no further place. It will have done its work. It was a great work, but it is almost over. Its sphere lessens every day.

Nor will man miss it. *For what man has sought for is, indeed, neither pain nor pleasure, but simply Life.* Man has sought to live intensely, fully, perfectly. When he can do so without exercising restraint on others, or suffering it ever, and his activities are all pleasurable to him, he will be saner, healthier, more civilized, more himself. Pleasure is Nature's test, her sign of approval. When man is happy, he is in harmony with himself and his environment. The new Individualism, for whose service Socialism, whether it wills it or not, is working, will be perfect harmony. It will be what the Greeks sought for, but could not, except in Thought, realise completely, because they had slaves, and fed them; it will be what the Renaissance sought for, but could not realise completely except in Art, because they had slaves, and starved them. It will be complete, and through it each man will attain to his perfection. The new Individualism is the new Hellenism.

# Mary Kingsley

## TRAVELS IN WEST AFRICA

Mary Kingsley's Travels in West Africa *describes her adventures and observations in West Africa in the mid 1890s. In 1892, after the death of her parents, Kingsley found herself to be what W. R. GREG described as a "redundant woman": thirty years old, unmarried, unemployed, self-educated but with no formal education. Her decision to leave England to study fetish and to collect fish on the West African Coast and in the interior of the Congo Français would establish her as a best-selling author and lecturer, as well as a curiosity— the intrepid spinster, forging her way through forests, trading tobacco and cloth, canoeing the Ogooué River, and befriending the Fan.*

*With self-effacing humor, Kingsley chronicles her own blunders and triumphs as an explorer and observer of West African customs. She is unusually sensitive to the blinding assumptions and limitations of her Eurocentric vision, aware that the mere presence of an English visitor alters what she has come to observe. As a consequence, Kingsley opposes British Colonial policy on the grounds that it is based on ignorance of indigenous peoples, their laws, customs, and beliefs. She criticizes Christian missionaries in general for their foolish, if well-intentioned zeal for civilizing and converting the African—a project she believes contaminates and destroys native cultures. Yet, although she opposed colonization, Mary Kingsley was no anti-imperialist; she argued for a form of economic imperialism, with West Africa as an expanding market for British trade.* **RM**

## INTRODUCTION

It was in 1893 that, for the first time in my life, I found myself in possession of five or six months which were not heavily forestalled, and feeling like a boy with a new half-crown, I lay about in my mind, as Mr. Bunyan would say, as to what to do with them. "Go and learn your tropics," said Science. Where on earth am I to go, I wondered, for tropics are tropics wherever found, so I got down an atlas and saw that either South America or West Africa must be my destination, for the Malayan region was too far off and too expensive. Then I got Wallace's *Geographical Distribution*[1] and after reading that master's article on the Ethiopian region I hardened my heart and closed with West Africa. I did this the more readily because while I knew nothing of the practical condition of it, I knew a good deal both by tradition and report of South East America, and remembered that Yellow Jack was endemic, and that a certain naturalist, my superior physically and mentally, had come very near getting starved to death in the depressing society of an expedition slowly perishing of want and miscellaneous fevers up the Parana.

My ignorance regarding West Africa was soon removed. And although the vast cavity in my mind that it occupied is not even yet half filled up, there is a great deal of very curious information in its place. I use the word curious advisedly, for I think many seemed to translate my request for practical hints and advice into an advertisement that "Rubbish may be shot here." This same information is in a state of great confusion still, although I have made heroic efforts to codify it. I find, however, that it can almost all be got in under the following different headings, namely and to wit:—

The dangers of West Africa.

The disagreeables of West Africa.

The diseases of West Africa.

The things you must take to West Africa.

The things you find most handy in West Africa.

The worst possible things you can do in West Africa. . . .

It was the beginning of August '93 when I first left England for "the Coast." Preparations of quinine with postage partially paid arrived up to the last moment, and a friend hastily sent two newspaper clippings, one entitled "A Week in a Palm-oil Tub," which was supposed to describe the sort of accommodation, companions, and fauna likely to be met with on a steamer going to West Africa, and on which I was to spend seven to *The Graphic* contributor's one; the other from *The Daily Telegraph*, reviewing a French book of "Phrases in common use" in Dahomey. The opening sentence in the latter was, "Help, I am drowning." Then came the inquiry, "If a man is not a thief?" and then another cry, "The boat is upset." "Get up, you lazy scamps," is the next exclamation, followed almost immediately by the question, "Why has not this man been buried?" "It is fetish that has killed him, and he must lie here exposed with nothing on him until only the bones remain," is the cheerful answer. This sounded discouraging to a person whose occupation

1. Alfred Russel Wallace, *The Geographical Distribution of Animals* (1876).

would necessitate going about considerably in boats, and whose fixed desire was to study fetish. So with a feeling of foreboding gloom I left London for Liverpool—none the more cheerful for the matter-of-fact manner in which the steamboat agents had informed me that they did not issue return tickets by the West African lines of steamers.

I will not go into the details of that voyage here, much as I am given to discursiveness. They are more amusing than instructive, for on my first voyage out I did not know the Coast, and the Coast did not know me, and we mutually terrified each other. I fully expected to get killed by the local nobility and gentry; they thought I was connected with the World's Women's Temperance Association, and collecting shocking details for subsequent magic-lantern lectures on the liquor traffic; so fearful misunderstandings arose, but we gradually educated each other, and I had the best of the affair; for all I had got to teach them was that I was only a beetle and fetish hunter, and so forth, while they had to teach me a new world, and a very fascinating course of study I found it. And whatever the Coast may have to say against me—for my continual desire for hair-pins, and other pins, my intolerable habit of getting into water, the abominations full of ants, that I brought into their houses, or things emitting at unexpectedly short notice vivid and awful stenches— they cannot but say that I was a diligent pupil, who honestly tried to learn the lessons they taught me so kindly, though some of those lessons were hard to a person who had never previously been even in a tame bit of tropics, and whose life for many years had been an entirely domestic one in a University town.

One by one I took my old ideas derived from books and thoughts based on imperfect knowledge and weighed them against the real life around me, and found them either worthless or wanting. The greatest recantation I had to make I made humbly before I had been three months on the Coast in 1893. It was of my idea of the traders. What I had expected to find them was a very different thing to what I did find them; and of their kindness to me I can never sufficiently speak, for on that voyage I was utterly out of touch with the governmental circles, and utterly dependent on the traders, and the most useful lesson of all the lessons I learnt on the West Coast in 1893 was that I could trust them. Had I not learnt this very thoroughly I could never have gone out again and carried out the voyage I give you a sketch of in this book. . . .

## CHAPTER 19: FETISH

. . . I will make an attempt to give a rough sketch of the African form of thought and the difficulties of studying it, because the study of this thing is my chief motive for going to West Africa. Since 1893 I have been collecting information in its native state regarding Fetish, and I use the usual terms fetish and ju-ju because they have among us a certain fixed value—a conventional value, but a useful one. Neither "fetish" nor "ju-ju" are native words. Fetish comes from the word the old Portuguese explorers used to designate the objects they thought the natives worshipped, and in which they were wise enough to recognise a certain similarity to their own little images and relics of Saints, "*Feitiço*." Ju-ju, on the other hand, is French, and comes from the word for a toy or doll,[2] so it is not

2. It is held by some authorities to come from gru-gru, a Mandingo word for charm, but I respectfully question whether gru-gru has not come from ju-ju, the native approximation to the French joujou. [Kingsley's note]

so applicable as the Portuguese name, for the native image is not a doll or toy, and has far more affinity to the image of a saint, inasmuch as it is not venerated for itself, or treasured because of its prettiness, but only because it is the residence, or the occasional haunt, of a spirit.

Stalking the wild West African idea is one of the most charming pursuits in the world. Quite apart from the intellectual, it has a high sporting interest; for its pursuit is as beset with difficulty and danger as grizzly bear hunting, yet the climate in which you carry on this pursuit—vile as it is—is warm, which to me is almost an essential of existence. Personally I prefer it to elephant hunting; and I shall never forget the pleasure with which, in the forest among the Fans, I netted one reason for the advantage of possessing a white man's eye-ball, and as I wrote it down in my water-worn notebook, saw it joined up with the reason why it is advisable to cut off big men's heads in the Niger Delta. Above all, I beg you to understand that I make no pretension to a thorough knowledge of Fetish ideas; I am only on the threshold. "Ich weiss nicht all doch viel ist mir bekannt," as Faust said[3]—and, like him after he had said it, I have got a lot to learn.

I do not intend here to weary you with more than a small portion of even my present knowledge, for I have great collections of facts that I keep only to compare with those of other hunters of the wild idea, and which in their present state are valueless to the cabinet ethnologist. Some of these may be rank lies, some of them mere individual mind-freaks, others have underlying them some idea I am not at present in touch with.

The difficulty of gaining a true conception of the savage's real idea is great and varied.

In places on the Coast where there is, or has been, much missionary influence the trouble is greatest, for in the first case the natives carefully conceal things they fear will bring them into derision and contempt, although they still keep them in their innermost hearts; and in the second case, you have a set of traditions which are Christian in origin, though frequently altered almost beyond recognition by being kept for years in the atmosphere of the African mind. For example, there is this beautiful story now extant among the Cabindas. God made at first all men black—He always does in the African story—and then He went across a great river and called men to follow Him, and the wisest and the bravest and the best plunged into the great river and crossed it; and the water washed them white, so they are the ancestors of the white men. But the others were afraid too much, and said, "No, we are comfortable here; we have our dances, and our tom-toms, and plenty to eat—we won't risk it, we'll stay here"; and they remained in the old place, and from them come the black men. But to this day the white men come to the bank, on the other side of the river, and call to the black men, saying, "Come, it is better over here." I fear there is little doubt that this story is a modified version of some parable preached to the Cabindas at the time the Jesuit Fathers had such influence among them, before they were driven out of the lower Congo regions more than a hundred years ago, for political reasons, by the Portuguese. The Cabindas have quite forgotten its origin— "it is old story"—and they keep it on, in much the same way as a neighbouring tribe keeps on the ringing of the old bells, morning and evening, that were once bells in a Jesuit monastery long since forgotten. "Our Fathers did it"; so palaver done set.

3. Loosely translated from Goethe's *Faust*: "I do not know everything but much is familiar to me."

In the bush—where the people have been little, or not at all, in contact with European ideas—in some ways the investigation is easier; yet another set of difficulties confronts you. The difficulty that seems to occur most easily to people is the difficulty of the language. My brother the other day derided me, as is his wont, saying, "What a great advantage it was, that peculiar power African travellers all seemed to have of conversing on the most obscure metaphysical questions with the natives; whereas when *he* was in Singapore, things were otherwise—if you said carefully, 'Pergi ka Mercantile Bank,' the chances were your rick-shaw runner took you to the waterworks." But the truth is that the West African languages are not difficult to pick up; nevertheless, there are an awful quantity of them and they are at the best most imperfect mediums of communication. No one who has been on the Coast can fail to recognise how inferior the native language is to the native mind behind it—and the prolixity and repetition he has therefore to employ to make his thoughts understood.

The great comfort is the wide diffusion of that peculiar language, "trade English"; it is not only used as a means of intercommunication between whites and blacks, but between natives using two distinct languages. On the south-west Coast you find individuals in villages far from the sea, or a trading station, who know it, and this is because they have picked it up and employ it in their dealings with the coast tribes and travelling traders.
. . .

The difficulty of the language is, however, far less than the whole set of difficulties with your own mind. Unless you can make it pliant enough to follow the African idea step by step, however much care you may take, you will not bag your game. I heard an account the other day—I have forgotten where—of a representative of her Majesty in Africa who went out for a day's antelope shooting. There were plenty of antelope about, and he stalked them with great care; but always, just before he got within shot of the game, they saw something and bolted. Knowing he and the boy behind him had been making no sound and could not have been seen, he stalked on, but always with the same result, until happening to look round, he saw the boy behind him was supporting the dignity of the Empire at large, and this representative of it in particular, by steadfastly holding aloft the consular flag. Well, if you go hunting the African idea with the flag of your own religion or opinions floating ostentatiously over you, you will similarly get a very poor bag.

A few hints as to your mental outfit when starting on this sport may be useful. Before starting for West Africa, burn all your notions about sun-myths and worship of the elemental forces. My own opinion is you had better also burn the notion, although it is fashionable, that human beings got their first notion of the origin of the soul from dreams.

I went out with my mind full of the deductions of every book on Ethnology, German or English, that I had read during fifteen years—and being a good Cambridge person, I was particularly confident that from Mr. Frazer's book, *The Golden Bough*, I had got a semi-universal key to the underlying idea of native custom and belief. But I soon found this was very far from being the case. His idea is a true key to a certain quantity of facts, but in West Africa only to a limited quantity.

I do not say, do not read Ethnology—by all means do so; and above all things read, until you know it by heart, *Primitive Culture*, by Dr. E. B. Tylor,[4] regarding which book I may say that I have never found a fact that flew in the face of the carefully made, broad-minded deductions of this greatest of Ethnologists. In addition you must know your Westermarck on *Human Marriage*, and your Waitz *Anthropologie*, and your Topinard[5]—not that you need expect to go measuring people's skulls and chests as this last named authority expects you to do, for no self-respecting person black or white likes that sort of thing from the hands of an utter stranger, and if you attempt it you'll get yourself disliked in West Africa. Add to this the knowledge of all A. B. Ellis's works;[6] Burton's *Anatomy of Melancholy*; Pliny's *Natural History*; and as much of Aristotle as possible. If you have a good knowledge of the Greek and Latin classics, I think it would be an immense advantage; an advantage I do not possess, for my classical knowledge is scrappy, and in place of it I have a knowledge of Red Indian dogma: a dogma by the way that seems to me much nearer the African in type than Asiatic forms of dogma.

Armed with these instruments of observation, with a little industry and care you should in the mill of your mind be able to make the varied tangled rag-bag of facts that you will soon become possessed of into a paper. And then I advise you to lay the results of your collection before some great thinker and he will write upon it the opinion that his greater and clearer vision makes him more fit to form.

You may say, Why not bring these home their things in the raw state? And bring them home in a raw state you must, for purposes of reference; but in this state they are of little use to a person unacquainted with the conditions which surround them in their native homes. . . .

However good may be the outfit for your work that you take with you, you will have, at first, great difficulty in realising that it is possible for the people you are among really to believe things in the way they do. And you cannot associate with them long before you must recognise that these Africans have often a remarkable mental acuteness and a large share of common sense; that there is nothing really "child-like" in their form of mind at all. Observe them further and you will find they are not a flighty-minded, mystical set of people in the least. They are not dreamers, or poets, and you will observe, and I hope observe closely—for to my mind this is the most important difference between their make of mind and our own—that they are notably deficient in all mechanical arts: they have never made, unless under white direction and instruction, a single fourteenth-rate piece of cloth, pottery, a tool or machine, house, road, bridge, picture or statue; that a written language of their own construction they none of them possess. A careful study of the things a man, black or white, fails to do, whether for good or evil, usually gives you a truer knowledge of the man than the things he succeeds in doing. When you fully realise this acuteness on one hand and this mechanical incapacity on the other which exist in the people you are studying, you can go ahead. Only, I beseech you, go ahead carefully. When you have found the easy key that opens the reason underlying a series of facts, as for example, these: a Benga spits on your hand as a greeting; you see a man who has been

4. Edward B. Tylor, *Primitive Culture* (1871).

5. Edward Westermarck, *The History of Human Marriage* (1891); Theodor Waitz, *Anthropologie der Naturvölker* (1859–71); Paul Topinard, *L'Anthropologie* (1876) and *Éléments d'anthropologie générale* (1885).

6. Alfred B. Ellis, *The Tshi Speaking, Ewe Speaking, and Yoruba Speaking Peoples of the West Coast of Africa* (1887–94).

marching regardless through the broiling sun all the forenoon, with a heavy load, on entering a village and having put down his load, elaborately steal round in the shelter of the houses, instead of crossing the street; you come across a tribe that cuts its dead up into small pieces and scatters them broadcast, and another tribe that thinks a white man's eye-ball is a most desirable thing to be possessed of—do not, when you have found this key, drop your collecting work, and go home with a shriek of "I know all about Fetish," because you don't, for the key to the above facts will not open the reason why it is regarded advisable to kill a person who is making Ikung; or why you should avoid at night a cotton tree that has red earth at its roots; or why combings of hair and paring of nails should be taken care of; or why a speck of blood that may fall from your flesh should be cut out of wood—if it has fallen on that—and destroyed, and if it has fallen on the ground stamped and rubbed into the soil with great care. This set requires another key entirely.

I must warn you also that your own mind requires protection when you send it stalking the savage idea through the tangled forests, the dark caves, the swamps and the fogs of the Ethiopian intellect. The best protection lies in recognising the untrustworthiness of human evidence regarding the unseen, and also the seen, when it is viewed by a person who has in his mind an explanation of the phenomenon before it occurs. For example, take a person who, believing in ghosts, sees a white figure in a churchyard, bolts home, has fits, and on revival states he has seen a ghost, and gives details. He has seen a ghost and therefore he is telling the truth. Another person who does not believe in ghosts sees the thing, flies at it and finds its component parts are boy and bed-sheet.

Do not applaud this individual, for he is quite conceited enough to make him comfortable; yet when he says the phenomenon was a boy and a bed-sheet, he is also telling the truth, and not much more of the truth than observer number one, for, after all, inside the boy there is a real ghost that made him go and do the thing. I know many people have doubts as to the existence of souls in small boys of this class, holding that they contain only devils; but devils can become ghosts, according to a mass of testimony. Great as the protection to the mind is, to keep it, as Hans Breitmann says, "still skebdical," I warn you that, with all precaution, the study of African metaphysics is bad for the brain, when you go and carry it on among all the weird, often unaccountable surroundings, and depressing scenery of the Land of the Shadow of Death—a land that stretches from Goree to Loanda.

The fascination of the African point of view is as sure to linger in your mind as the malaria in your body. Never then will you be able to attain to the gay, happy cock-sureness regarding the Deity and the Universe of those people who stay at home, and whom the *Saturday* so aptly called "the suburban agnostics." You will always feel inclined to ask this class of people, "Yes; well, what is Force? What is Motion; and above all, tell me what is Matter that you talk so glibly of? and if so why?" And the suburban agnostic looks down on you, and says pityingly, "Read Schopenhauer and Clifford," as if he were ordering you pills; which revolts you, and you retort "Read Kant and Darwin," and the conversation disappears into a fog of words.

The truth is, the study of natural phenomena knocks the bottom out of any man's conceit if it is done honestly and not by selecting only those facts that fit in with his pre-conceived or ingrafted notions. And, to my mind, the wisest way is to get into the state of mind of an old marine engineer who oils and sees that every screw and bolt of his engines is clean and well watched, and who loves them as living things, caressing and scolding them himself, defending them, with stormy language, against the aspersions of the silly, uninformed outside world, which persists in regarding them as mere machines, a thing his superior intelligence and experience knows they are not. Even animistic-minded I got awfully sat upon the other day in Cameroon by a superior but kindred spirit, in the form of a First Engineer. I had thoughtlessly repeated some scandalous gossip against the character of a naphtha launch in the river. "Stuff!" said he furiously; "she's all right, and she'd go from June to January if those blithering fools would let her alone." Of course I apologised.

The religious ideas of the Negroes, *i.e.*, the West Africans in the district from the Gambia to the Cameroon region, say roughly to the Rio del Rey (for the Bakwiri appear to have more of the Bantu form of idea than the negro, although physically they seem nearer the latter), differ very considerably from the religious ideas of the Bantu South-West Coast tribes. The Bantu[7] is vague on religious subjects; he gives one accustomed to the negro the impression that he once had the same set of ideas, but has forgotten half of them, and those that he possesses have not got that hold on him that the corresponding or super-imposed Christian ideas have over the true Negro; although he is quite as keen on the subject of witchcraft, and his witchcraft differs far less from the witchcraft of the Negro than his religious ideas do.

Witchcraft is a wonderful thing in its way. In Africa I constantly come upon ideas and methods of procedure in it that are identical with those of Irish, Devonian, and Semitic witchcraft, but this subject is too large to enter upon here.

The god, in the sense we use the word, is in essence the same in all of the Bantu tribes I have met with on the Coast: a non-interfering and therefore a negligeable quantity. He varies his name: Anzambi, Anyambi, Nyambi, Nzambi, Anzam, Nyam, Ukuku, Suku, and Nzam, but a better investigation shows that Nzam of the Fans is practically identical with Suku south of the Congo in the Bihe country, and so on.

They regard their god as the creator of man, plants, animals, and the earth, and they hold that having made them, he takes no further interest in the affair. But not so the crowd of spirits with which the universe is peopled, they take only too much interest and the Bantu wishes they would not and is perpetually saying so in his prayers, a large percentage whereof amounts to "Go away, we don't want you." "Come not into this house, this village, or its plantations." He knows from experience that the spirits pay little heed to these objurgations, and as they are the people who must be attended to, he develops a cult whereby they may be managed, used, and understood. This cult is what we call witchcraft. . . .

. . . A Fan told me that a man in the village, who was so weak from some cause or other that he could hardly crawl about, had fallen into this state by seeing the blood of a woman who had been killed by a falling tree. The underlying idea regarding blood is of course the old one that the blood is the life.

7. "Bantu" technically, and originally, refers to the major linguistic network (of "Bantu-speakers") linking numerous languages and peoples in central and southern Africa. Kingsley uses Bantu as an ethnic and cultural designation.

The life in Africa means a spirit, hence the liberated blood is the liberated spirit, and liberated spirits are always whipping into people who do not want them. In the case of the young Fan, the opinion held was that the weak spirit of the woman had got into him. I could not help being reminded of the saying one often hears from a person in England who has seen some tragedy,—"I cannot get the horror of it out of my eyes." This "horror" would mean to an African a spirit coming from the thing itself.

Charms are made for every occupation and desire in life—loving, hating, buying, selling, fishing, planting, travelling, hunting, &c., and although they are usually in the form of things filled with a mixture in which the spirit nestles, yet there are other kinds; for example, a great love charm is made of the water the lover has washed in, and this, mingled with the drink of the loved one, is held to soften the hardest heart. Of a similar nature is the friendship-compelling charm I know of on the Ivory Coast, which I have been told is used also in the Batanga regions. This is obtained on the death of a person you know really cared for you—like your father or mother, for example—by cutting off the head and suspending it over a heap of chalk, as the white earth that you find in river beds is called here, then letting it drip as long as it will and using this saturated chalk to mix in among the food of any one you wish should think kindly of you and trust you. This charm, a Bassa man said to me, "was good too much for the white trader," and made him give you "good price too much" for palm oil, &c., and that statement revived my sympathy for a friend who once said to me that when he used first to come to the Coast he had "pretty well had the inside raked up out of him" from the sickness caused by the charms that his local cook administered to him in the interest of the cook's friends. That man keeps an Accra cook now, and I trust lives a life of healthy, icy, unemotional calm.

Some kinds of charms, such as those to prevent your getting drowned, shot, seen by elephants, &c., are worn on a bracelet or necklace. A new-born child starts with a health-knot tied round the wrist, neck, or loins, and throughout the rest of its life its collection of charms goes on increasing. This collection does not, however, attain inconvenient dimensions, owing to the failure of some of the charms to work.

That is the worst of charms and prayers. The thing you wish of them may, and frequently does, happen in a strikingly direct way, but other times it does not. In Africa this is held to arise from the bad character of the spirits; their gross ingratitude and fickleness. You may have taken every care of a spirit for years, given it food and other offerings that you wanted for yourself, wrapped it up in your cloth on chilly nights and gone cold, put it in the only dry spot in the canoe, and so on, and yet after all this, the wretched thing will be capable of being got at by your rival or enemy and lured away, leaving you only the case it once lived in.

Finding, we will say, that you have been upset and half-drowned, and your canoe-load of goods lost three times in a week, that your paddles are always breaking, and the amount of snags in the river and so on is abnormal, you judge that your canoe-charm has stopped. Then you go to the medicine man who supplied you with it and complain. He says it was a perfectly good charm when he sold it you and he never had any complaints before, but he will investigate the affair; when he has done so, he either says the spirit has been lured away from the home he prepared for it by incantations and presents from other people, or that he finds the spirit is dead; it has been killed by a more powerful spirit of its class, which is in the pay of some enemy of yours. In all cases the little thing you kept the spirit in is no use now, and only fit to sell to a white man as "a big curio!" and the sooner you let him have sufficient money to procure you a fresh and still more powerful spirit—necessarily more expensive—the safer it will be for you, particularly as your misfortunes distinctly point to some one being desirous of your death. You of course grumble, but seeing the thing in his light you pay up, and the medicine man goes busily to work with incantations, dances, looking into mirrors or basins of still water, and concoctions of messes to make you a new protecting charm. . . .

# Arthur William Symons

1865: BORN 28 FEBRUARY AT MILFORD HAVEN, WALES

1886: *INTRODUCTION TO THE STUDY OF BROWNING*

1889: *DAYS AND NIGHTS*, FIRST VOLUME OF VERSE

1893: "THE DECADENT MOVEMENT IN LITERATURE" PUBLISHED IN *HARPER'S NEW MONTHLY MAGAZINE*

1896: EDITED *THE SAVOY*, WITH AUBREY BEARDSLEY

1900: *THE SYMBOLIST MOVEMENT IN LITERATURE*

1945: DIED 22 JANUARY AT WITTERSHAM, KENT

---

## THE DECADENT MOVEMENT IN LITERATURE

*Poet and critic Arthur Symons was chiefly known to his contemporaries as the defender of Decadence as an artistic movement. This reputation was shaped primarily by his essay, "The Decadent Movement in Literature," but assisted by his translations of Verlaine and the subjects and style of his own verse. "The Decadent Movement in Literature," according to Symons's biographer Karl Beckson, seems to have been Symons's answer to Richard Le Gallienne's attack on Decadence as "merely limited thinking, often insane thinking," in a review of Churton Collins's* Illustrations of Tennyson—*an attitude shared by many British readers.[1] Symons, in explaining the French tendency toward "an intense self-consciousness, a restless curiosity in research, an over-subtilizing refinement upon refinement, a spiritual and moral perversity," became the Decadent movement's spokesperson. His ideas in this essay and later in* The Symbolist Movement in Literature *influenced W. B. Yeats, Ezra Pound, T. S. Eliot, and James Joyce, and earned Symons his reputation as both defender of Aestheticism and anticipator of Modernism.* LMF

THE LATEST MOVEMENT IN EUROPEAN literature has been called by many names, none of them quite exact or comprehensive—Decadence, Symbolism, Impressionism, for

---

1. Karl Beckson, *Arthur Symons: A Life* (Oxford: Clarendon Press, 1987), pp. 95–6.

instance. It is easy to dispute over words, and we shall find that Verlaine objects to being called a Decadent, Maeterlinck to being called a Symbolist, Huysmans to being called an Impressionist.[2] These terms, as it happens, have been adopted as the badge of little separate cliques, noisy, brainsick young people who haunt the brasseries of the Boulevard Saint-Michel, and exhaust their ingenuities in theorizing over the works they cannot write. But, taken frankly as epithets which express their own meaning, both Impressionism and Symbolism convey some notion of that new kind of literature which is perhaps more broadly characterized by the word Decadence. The most representative literature of the day—the writing which appeals to, which has done so much to form, the younger generation—is certainly not classic, nor has it any relation with that old antithesis of the Classic, the Romantic. After a fashion it is no doubt a decadence; it has all the qualities that mark the end of great periods, the qualities that we find in the Greek, the Latin, decadence: an intense self-consciousness, a restless curiosity in research, an over-subtilizing refinement upon refinement, a spiritual and moral perversity. If what we call the classic is indeed the supreme art—those qualities of perfect simplicity, perfect sanity, perfect proportion, the supreme qualities—then this representative literature of to-day, interesting, beautiful, novel as it is, is really a new and beautiful and interesting disease.

Healthy we cannot call it, and healthy it does not wish to be considered. The Goncourts, in their prefaces, in their *Journal*, are always insisting on their own pet malady, *la névrose*.[3] It is in their work, too, that Huysmans notes with delight "le style tacheté et faisandé"—high-flavored and spotted with corruption—which he himself possesses in the highest degree. "Having desire without light, curiosity without wisdom, seeking God by strange ways, by ways traced by the hands of men; offering rash incense upon the high places to an unknown God, who is the God of darkness"—that is how Ernest Hello,[4] in one of his apocalyptic moments, characterizes the nineteenth century. And this unreason of the soul—of which Hello himself is so curious a victim—this unstable equilibrium, which has overbalanced so many brilliant intelligences into one form or another of spiritual confusion, is but another form of the *maladie fin de siècle*.[5] For its very disease of form, this literature is certainly typical of a civilization grown over-luxurious, over-inquiring, too languid for the relief of action, too uncertain for any emphasis in opinion or in conduct. It reflects all the moods, all the manners, of a sophisticated society; its very artificiality is a way of being true to nature: simplicity, sanity, proportion—the classic qualities—how much do we possess them in our life, our surroundings, that we should look to find them in our literature—so evidently the literature of a decadence?

Taking the word Decadence, then, as most precisely expressing the general sense of the newest movement in literature, we find that the terms Impressionism and Symbolism define correctly enough the two main branches of that movement. Now Impressionist

---

2. Paul Marie Verlaine (1844–96), French poet. Maurice Maeterlinck (1862–1949), Belgian poet, dramatist, and essayist. Charles Marie Georges Huysmans (1848–1907), French novelist who published under the name Joris-Karl Huysmans.
3. Edmond (1822–96) and Jules (1830–70) de Goncourt, French novelists, historians, art critics, collaborators on their *Journal*, parts of which were published in 1887–8 and 1890–2. "La névrose": neurosis.
4. Ernest Hello (1828–85), French writer.
5. End-of-the-century sickness.

and Symbolist have more in common than either supposes; both are really working on the same hypothesis, applied in different directions. What both seek is not general truth merely, but *la vérité vraie*, the very essence of truth—the truth of appearances to the senses, of the visible world to the eyes that see it; and the truth of spiritual things to the spiritual vision. The Impressionist, in literature as in painting, would flash upon you in a new, sudden way so exact an image of what you have just seen, just as you have seen it, that you may say, as a young American sculptor, a pupil of Rodin, said to me on seeing for the first time a picture of Whistler's, "Whistler seems to think his picture upon canvas—and there it is!" Or you may find, with Sainte-Beuve, writing of Goncourt, the "soul of the landscape"—the soul of whatever corner of the visible world has to be realized. The Symbolist, in this new, sudden way, would flash upon you the "soul" of that which can be apprehended only by the soul—the finer sense of things unseen, the deeper meaning of things evident. And naturally, necessarily, this endeavor after a perfect truth to one's impression, to one's intuition—perhaps an impossible endeavor—has brought with it, in its revolt from ready-made impressions and conclusions, a revolt from the ready-made of language, from the bondage of traditional form, of a form become rigid. In France, where this movement began and has mainly flourished, it is Goncourt who was the first to invent a style in prose really new, impressionistic, a style which was itself almost sensation. It is Verlaine who has invented such another new style in verse. . . .

An opera-glass—a special, unique way of seeing things—that is what the Goncourts have brought to bear upon the common things about us; and it is here that they have done the "something new," here more than anywhere. They have never sought "to see life steadily, and see it whole":[6] their vision has always been somewhat feverish, with the diseased sharpness of over-excited nerves. "We do not hide from ourselves that we have been passionate, nervous creatures, unhealthily impressionable," confesses the *Journal*. But it is this morbid intensity in seeing and seizing things that has helped to form that marvellous style—"a style perhaps too ambitious of impossibilities," as they admit—a style which inherits some of its color from Gautier, some of its fine outline from Flaubert,[7] but which has brought light and shadow into the color, which has softened outline in the magic of atmosphere. With them words are not merely color and sound, they live. That search after "l'image peinte," "l'épithète rare,"[8] is not (as with Flaubert) a search after harmony of phrase for its own sake; it is a desperate endeavor to give sensation, to flash the impression of the moment, to preserve the very heat and motion of life. And so, in analysis as in description, they have found out a way of noting the fine shades; they have broken the outline of the conventional novel in chapters, with its continuous story, in order to indicate—sometimes in a chapter of half a page—this and that revealing moment, this or that significant attitude or accident or sensation. . . .

Joris Karl Huysmans demands a prominent place in any record of the Decadent movement. His work, like that of the Goncourts, is largely determined by the *maladie fin de siècle*—the diseased nerves that, in his case, have given a curious personal quality of pes-

---

6. An allusion to Matthew ARNOLD's famous praise of Sophocles as one "who saw life steadily and saw it whole." See "To a Friend" (1849) and "On the Modern Element in Literature" (1869).
7. Théophile Gautier (1811–72), French poet and man of letters. Gustave Flaubert (1821–80), French novelist.
8. "L'image peinte": the painted image; "l' épithète rare": the uncommon epithet.

simism to his outlook on the world, his view of life. Part of his work—*Marthe*, *Les Sœurs Vatard*, *En Ménage*, *À Vau-l'Eau*⁹—is a minute and searching study of the minor discomforts, the commonplace miseries of life, as seen by a peevishly disordered vision, delighting, for its own self-torture, in the insistent contemplation of human stupidity, of the sordid in existence. Yet these books do but lead up to the unique masterpiece, the astonishing caprice of *À Rebours*, in which he has concentrated all that is delicately depraved, all that is beautifully, curiously poisonous, in modern art. *À Rebours* is the history of a typical Decadent—a study, indeed, after a real man, but a study which seizes the type rather than the personality. In the sensations and ideas of Des Esseintes we see the sensations and ideas of the effeminate, over-civilized, deliberately abnormal creature who is the last product of our society: partly the father, partly the offspring, of the perverse art that he adores. Des Esseintes creates for his solace, in the wilderness of a barren and profoundly uncomfortable world, an artificial paradise. His Thébaïde raffinée¹⁰ is furnished elaborately for candle-light, equipped with the pictures, the books, that satisfy his sense of the exquisitely abnormal. He delights in the Latin of Apuleius and Petronius, in the French of Baudelaire, Goncourt, Verlaine, Mallarmé, Villiers; in the pictures of Gustave Moreau, the French Burne-Jones, of Odilon Redon, the French Blake. He delights in the beauty of strange, unnatural flowers, in the melodic combination of scents, in the imagined harmonies of the sense of taste. And at last, exhausted by these spiritual and sensory debauches in the delights of the artificial, he is left (as we close the book) with a brief, doubtful choice before him—madness or death, or else a return to nature, to the normal life.

Since *À Rebours*, M. Huysmans has written one other remarkable book, *Là-Bas*, a study in the hysteria and mystical corruption of contemporary Black Magic. But it is on that one exceptional achievement, *À Rebours*, that his fame will rest; it is there that he has expressed not merely himself, but an epoch. And he has done so in a style which carries the modern experiments upon language to their furthest development. Formed upon Goncourt and Flaubert, it has sought for novelty, *l'image peinte*, the exactitude of color, the forcible precision of epithet, wherever words, images, or epithets are to be found. Barbaric in its profusion, violent in its emphasis, wearying in its splendor, it is—especially in regard to things seen—extraordinarily expressive, with all the shades of a painter's palette. Elaborately and deliberately perverse, it is in its very perversity that Huysmans' work—so fascinating, so repellent, so instinctively artificial—comes to represent, as the work of no other writer can be said to do, the main tendencies, the chief results, of the Decadent movement in literature.

Such, then, is the typical literature of the Decadence—literature which, as we have considered it so far, is entirely French. But those qualities which we find in the work of Goncourt, Verlaine, Huysmans—qualities which have permeated literature much more completely in France than in any other country—are not wanting in the recent literature

9. *Marthe, Histoire d'une Fille* (1876), *Les Sœurs Vatard* (1879), *En Ménage* (1881), *À Vau-l'Eau* (1882). His most famous novel, *À Rebours*, translated into English as *Against the Grain*, was published in 1884. Symons also mentions *Là-Bas* (1891).

10. A refined place of solitude.

of other countries. In Holland there is a new school of Sensitivists, as they call themselves, who have done some remarkable work—Couperus,[11] in *Ecstasy*, for example—very much on the lines of the French art of Impressionism. In Italy, Luigi Capuana (in *Giacinta*, for instance) has done some wonderful studies of morbid sensation; Gabriele d'Annunzio, in that marvellous, malarious *Piacere*, has achieved a triumph of exquisite perversity. In Spain, one of the principal novelists, Señora Pardo-Bazan, has formed herself, with some deliberateness, after Goncourt, grafting his method, curiously enough, upon a typically Spanish Catholicism of her own. In Norway, Ibsen has lately developed a personal kind of Impressionism (in *Hedda Gabler*) and of Symbolism (in *The Master-Builder*)—"opening the door," in his own phrase, "to the younger generation." And in England, too, we find the same influences at work. The prose of Mr. Walter Pater, the verse of Mr. W. E. Henley—to take two prominent examples—are attempts to do with the English language something of what Goncourt and Verlaine have done with the French. Mr. Pater's prose is the most beautiful English prose which is now being written; and, unlike the prose of Goncourt, it has done no violence to language, it has sought after no vivid effects, it has found a large part of mastery in reticence, in knowing what to omit. But how far away from the classic ideals of style is this style in which words have their color, their music, their perfume, in which there is "some strangeness in the proportion" of every beauty! The *Studies in the Renaissance*[12] have made of criticism a new art—have raised criticism almost to the act of creation. And *Marius the Epicurean*, in its study of "sensations and ideas" (the conjunction was Goncourt's before it was Mr. Pater's), and the *Imaginary Portraits*, in their evocations of the Middle Ages, the age of Watteau[13]—have they not that morbid subtlety of analysis, that morbid curiosity of form, that we have found in the works of the French Decadents? A fastidiousness equal to that of Flaubert has limited Mr. Pater's work to six volumes, but in these six volumes there is not a page that is not perfectly finished, with a conscious art of perfection. In its minute elaboration it can be compared only with goldsmith's work—so fine, so delicate is the handling of so delicate, so precious a material.

Mr. Henley's work in verse has none of the characteristics of Mr. Pater's work in prose. Verlaine's definition of his own theory of poetical writing—"sincerity, and the impression of the moment followed to the letter"—might well be adopted as a definition of Mr. Henley's theory or practice. In *A Book of Verses* and *The Song of the Sword*[14] he has brought into the traditional conventionalities of modern English verse the note of a new personality, the touch of a new method. The poetry of Impressionism can go no further, in one direction, than that series of rhymes and rhythms named *In Hospital*. The ache and throb of the body in its long nights on a tumbled bed, and as it lies on the operating-table awaiting "the thick, sweet mystery of chloroform," are brought home to us as nothing else

11. Louis Couperus (1863–1923); Luigi Capuana (1839–1915); Gabriele d'Annunzio (1863–1938); Emilia Pardo Bazaan (1851–1921); Henrik Ibsen (1828–1906).

12. *Studies in the History of the Renaissance*, first published in 1873; see Walter PATER in this volume. *Marius the Epicurean* (1885); *Imaginary Portraits* (1887).

13. Antoine Watteau (1684–1721), French painter.

14. William Ernest Henley (1849–1903), English writer whose works include *A Book of Verses* (1888), *The Song of the Sword* (1892), *London Voluntaries* (1893), and *In Hospital* (1903).

that I know in poetry has ever brought the physical sensations. And for a sharper, closer truth of rendering, Mr. Henley has resorted (after the manner of Heine[15]) to a rhymeless form of lyric verse, which in his hands, certainly, is sensitive and expressive. Whether this kind of *vers libre* can fully compensate, in what it gains of freedom and elasticity, for what it loses of compact form and vocal appeal, is a difficult question. It is one that Mr. Henley's verse is far from solving in the affirmative, for, in his work, the finest things, to my mind, are rhymed. In the purely impressionistic way, do not the *London Voluntaries*, which are rhymed, surpass all the unrhymed vignettes and nocturnes which attempt the same quality of result? They flash before us certain aspects of the poetry of London as only Whistler had ever done, and in another art. Nor is it only the poetry of cities, as here, nor the poetry of the disagreeable, as in *In Hospital*, that Mr. Henley can evoke; he can evoke the magic of personal romance. He has written verse that is exquisitely frivolous, daintily capricious, wayward and fugitive as the winged remembrance of some momentary delight. And, in certain fragments, he has come nearer than any other English singer to what I have called the achievement of Verlaine and the ideal of the Decadence: to be a disembodied voice, and yet the voice of a human soul.

15. Heinrich Heine (1797–1856), German poet and journalist.

# SELECTED BIBLIOGRAPHY ❧

## WILLIAM ACTON

Humphreys, Anne. Biographical Note. *Prostitution, Considered in its Moral, Social, and Sanitary Aspects* (1972).

Marcus, Steven. *The Other Victorians: A Study of Sexuality and Pornography in Mid-Nineteenth Century England* (1966, 1977).

Peterson, M. Jeanne. "Dr. Acton's Enemy: Medicine, Sex, and Society in Victorian England." *Victorian Studies* 29 (1986): 569–90.

——. *The Medical Profession in Mid-Victorian London* (1978).

Renner, Stanley. "William Acton, the Truth about Prostitution, and Hardy's Not-So-Ruined Maid." *Victorian Poetry* 30 (Spring 1992): 19–28.

Walkowitz, Judith R. *Prostitution and Victorian Society: Women, Class, and the State* (1980).

## PRINCE ALBERT

Bennett, Daphne. *King Without a Crown* (1977).

Fulford, Roger. *The Prince Consort* (1949).

Hobhouse, Hermione. *Prince Albert, His Life and Work* (1983).

Martin, Theodore. *The Life of His Royal Highness, the Prince Consort.* 5 vols. (1875–80).

Weintraub, Stanley. *Uncrowned King: The Life of Prince Albert* (1997).

## MATTHEW ARNOLD

Allott, Kenneth. *Matthew Arnold* (1975).

Allott, Miriam, ed. *Matthew Arnold 1988: A Centennial Review* (1988).

Altick, Richard. "The Comedy of *Culture and Anarchy.*" *Victorian Perspectives.* Ed. John Clubbe and Jerome Meckier (1989).

apRoberts, Ruth. *Arnold and God* (1983).

Bush, Douglas. *Matthew Arnold: A Survey of His Poetry and Prose* (1971).

Buckler, William E. *Matthew Arnold's Prose: Three Essays in Literary Enlargement* (1983).

Carroll, Joseph. *The Cultural Theory of Matthew Arnold* (1982).

Collini, Stefan. *Arnold* (1988).

Coulling, Sidney. "The Gospel of Culture and Its Critics." *Arnoldian* 15 (Winter 1987–8): 27–35.

Gallagher, Catherine. "The Politics of Culture and the Debate over Representation." *Representations* 5 (1984): 115–47.

Harris, Wendell V. "Interpretive Historicism: 'Signs of the Times' and *Culture and Anarchy* in their Contexts." *Nineteenth-Century Literature* 44 (1990): 441–64.

Honan, Park. *Matthew Arnold: A Life* (1981).

Machann, Clinton and Forrest D. Burt, eds. *Matthew Arnold in His Time and Ours: Centenary Essays* (1988).

Marcus, Steven. "*Culture and Anarchy* Today." *Southern Review* 29 (Summer 1993): 433–52.

Trilling, Lionel. *Matthew Arnold* (1939, 1949).

Walcott, Fred G. *The Origins of "Culture and Anarchy": Matthew Arnold and Popular Education in England* (1970).


## BARBARA LEIGH SMITH BODICHON

Burton, Hester. *Barbara Bodichon, 1827–1891* (1949).

Herstein, Sheila R. *A Mid-Victorian Feminist, Barbara Leigh Smith Bodichon* (1985).

Lacey, Candida Ann, ed. *Barbara Leigh Smith Bodichon and the Langham Place Group* (1986).

Nestor, Pauline A. "A New Departure in Women's Publishing: *The English Woman's Journal* and *The Victoria Magazine*." *Victorian Periodicals Review* 15 (1982): 93–106.

Pell, Nancy. "George Eliot and Barbara Leigh Smith Bodichon: A Friendship." *Nineteenth-Century Women Writers of the English-Speaking World*. Ed. Rhoda B. Nathan (1986).


## CHARLOTTE BRONTË

Alexander, Christine. *The Art of the Brontës* (1995).

Allott, Miriam, ed. *The Brontës: The Critical Heritage* (1974).

Barker, Juliet. *The Brontës* (1994).

Boumelha, Penny. *Charlotte Brontë* (1990).

Eagleton, Terry. *Myths of Power: A Marxist Study of the Brontës* (1975, 1988).

Fraser, Rebecca. *Charlotte Brontë* (1988).

Gary, Franklin. "Charlotte Brontë and George Henry Lewes." *PMLA* 51 (1936): 518–42.

Gaskell, Elizabeth. *The Life of Charlotte Brontë* (1857).

Gerin, Winifred. *Charlotte Brontë: The Evolution of a Genius* (1967).

Gezari, Janet. *Charlotte Brontë and Defensive Conduct* (1992).

Gilbert, Sandra M. and Susan Gubar. *The Madwoman in the Attic: The Woman Writer and the Nineteenth-Century Literary Imagination* (1979).

Gordon, Lyndall. *Charlotte Brontë: A Passionate Life* (1994).

Moglen, Helene. *Charlotte Brontë: The Self Conceived* (1976).

Shorter, Clement. *Charlotte Brontë and Her Circle* (1896).

Showalter, Elaine. *A Literature of Their Own* (1977).

Shuttleworth, Sally. *Charlotte Brontë and Victorian Psychology* (1996).

Smith, Margaret, ed. *The Letters of Charlotte Brontë 1829–1845* (1995).

Tayler, Irene. *Holy Ghosts: The Male Muses of Emily and Charlotte Brontë* (1990).

Voskuil, Lynn M. "Acting Naturally: Brontë, Lewes, and the Problem of Gender Performance." *English Literary History* 62 (1995): 409–42.

Wise, Thomas J. and J. A. Symonton, eds. *The Brontës: Their Lives, Friendships and Correspondence.* 4 vols. (1932).

## RICHARD FRANCIS BURTON

Brodie, Fawn M. *The Devil Drives: A Life of Sir Richard Burton* (1967).

Burne, Glenn S. *Richard F. Burton* (1985).

Farwell, Byron. *Burton: A Biography of Sir Richard Francis Burton* (1963).

Jutzi, Alan H., ed. *In Search of Sir Richard Burton: Papers from a Huntington Library Symposium* (1993).

Rice, Edward. *Captain Sir Richard Francis Burton: The secret agent who made the pilgrimage to Mecca, discovered the Kama Sutra, and brought the Arabian nights to the West* (1990).


## JANE WELSH CARLYLE

Burdett, Osbert. *The Two Carlyles* (1930).

Carlyle, Jane Welsh. *Letters and Memorials of Jane Welsh Carlyle Prepared for Publication by Thomas Carlyle*. Ed. James Anthony Froude. 3 vols. (1883).

Carlyle, Jane Welsh and Thomas Carlyle. *The Collected Letters of Thomas and Jane Welsh Carlyle*. Ed. Charles Richard Sanders, Clyde de L. Ryals, Kenneth Fielding. 24 vols. (1970–95).

Clarke, Norma. *Ambitious Heights: Writing, Friendship, Love: The Jewsbury Sisters, Felicia Hemans, and Jane Welsh Carlyle* (1990).

Hanson, Elisabeth and Lawrence. *Necessary Evil: The Life of Jane Welsh Carlyle* (1952).

Hardwick, Elizabeth. *Seduction and Betrayal* (1974).

Holme, Thea. *The Carlyles at Home* (1965).

Skabarnicki, Anne. "Seeing Jane Plain: Recovering the Art of Welsh Carlyle." *Modern Language Studies* 27 (1997): 47–65.

Tennyson, G. B. "The Carlyles: Jane Welsh Carlyle." *Victorian Prose: A Guide to Research.* Ed. David J. DeLaura (1973).

Wasko, Jean. "The Angel in the Envelope: The Letters of Jane Welsh Carlyle." *Modern Language Studies* 27 (1997): 3–18.

Woolf, Virginia. "Geraldine and Jane." *The Common Reader: Second Series* (1932).


## THOMAS CARLYLE

apRoberts, Ruth. *The Ancient Dialect: Thomas Carlyle and Comparative Religion* (1988).

Ashton, Rosemary. *The German Idea: Four English Writers and the Reception of German Thought, 1800–1860* (1994).

Baker, Lee C. R. "The Open Secret of *Sartor Resartus*: Carlyle's Method of Converting His Reader." *Studies in Philology* 83 (1986): 218–35.

Brookes, Gerry H. *The Rhetorical Form of Carlyle's Sartor Resartus* (1972).

Cazamian, Louis. *Carlyle* (1932).

Eliot, George. "Thomas Carlyle." *Essays of George Eliot*. Ed. Thomas Pinney (1963).

Fielding, K. J. and Rodger L. Tarr, eds. *Carlyle Past and Present* (1976).

Holloway, John. *The Victorian Sage: Studies in Argument* (1953).

Kaplan, Fred. *Thomas Carlyle: A Biography* (1983).

LaValley, Albert J. *Carlyle and the Idea of the Modern* (1968).

Le Quesne, A. L. "Carlyle." *Victorian Thinkers*. Ed. Keith Thomas (1993).

Levine, George. *The Boundaries of Fiction: Carlyle, Macaulay, Newman* (1968).

Miller, J. Hillis. "Hieroglyphical Truth in *Sartor Resartus*." *Victorian Perspectives*. Ed. John Clubbe and Jerome Meckier (1989).

Peckham, Morse. *Victorian Revolutionaries* (1970).

Rosenberg, John D. *Carlyle and the Burden of History* (1985).

Rosenberg, Philip. *The Seventh Hero: Thomas Carlyle and the Theory of Radical Activism* (1974).

Rundle, Vivienne. " 'Devising New Means': *Sartor Resartus* and the Devoted Reader." *Victorian Newsletter* 82 (1992): 13–22.

Tennyson, Georg B. *Sartor Called Resartus* (1965).

Vanden Bossche, Chris R. *Carlyle and the Search for Authority* (1991).

Waring, Walter. *Thomas Carlyle* (1978).

## ROBERT CHAMBERS

Darwin, Charles. *On the Origin of Species*. 3rd edition (1861).

Millhauser, Milton. *Just Before Darwin: Robert Chambers and "Vestiges"* (1959).

Postlethwaite, Diana. *Making It Whole: A Victorian Circle and the Shape of Their World* (1984).

Ruse, Michael. *The Darwinian Revolution* (1979).

Yeo, Richard. "Science and Intellectual Authority in Mid-Nineteenth-Century Britain: Robert Chambers and 'Vestiges of the Natural History of Creation.' " *Victorian Studies* 28 (1984): 5–31.

## FRANCES POWER COBBE

Bauer, Carol and Laurence Ritt. " 'A Husband Is a Beating Animal': Frances Power Cobbe Confronts the Wife-Abuse Problem in Victorian England." *International Journal of Women's Studies* 6 (1983): 99–118.

Caine, Barbara. *Victorian Feminists* (1992).

Frawley, Maria H. "Desert Places/Gendered Spaces: Victorian Women in the Middle East." *Nineteenth-Century Contexts* 15 (1991): 49–64.

Hallock, John. "Frances Power Cobbe." *Prose by Victorian Women*. Ed. Andrea Broomfield and Sally Mitchell (1996).

Levine, Philippa. *Victorian Feminism: 1850–1900* (1987).

## DINAH MARIA MULOCK CRAIK

Mitchell, Sally. *Dinah Mulock Craik* (1983).

Showalter, Elaine. "Dinah Mulock Craik and the Tactics of Sentiment: A Case Study in Victorian Female Authorship." *Feminist Studies* 2 (1975): 5–23.

## CHARLES DARWIN

Appleman, Philip. *Darwin* (1970, 1979).

Barrish, Philip. "Accumulating Variation: Darwin's *On the Origin of Species* and
    Contemporary Literary and Cultural Theory." *Victorian Studies* 34 (1991): 431–53.
Becquemont, Daniel. *Darwin, darwinisme, évolutionnisme* (1992).
Bowler, Peter J. *Evolution: The History of the Idea* (1984).
———. *Charles Darwin: The Man and His Influence* (1996).
Brent, Peter. *Charles Darwin: "A Man of Enlarged Curiosity"* (1981).
Browne, Janet. *Charles Darwin: A Biography* (1995).
Cosslett, Tess, ed. *Science and Religion in the Nineteenth Century* (1984).
Dennett, Daniel C. *Darwin's Dangerous Idea: Evolution and the Meanings of Life* (1995).
Desmond, Adrian and James Moore. *Darwin: The Life of a Tormented Evolutionist* (1992).
De Beer, Gavin. *Charles Darwin: Evolution by Natural Selection* (1963).
Ghiselin, Michael T. *The Triumph of the Darwinian Method* (1969, 1984).
Himmelfarb, Gertrude. *Darwin and the Darwinian Revolution* (1959).
Hull, David L. *Darwin and His Critics: The Reception of Darwin's Theory of Evolution by the
    Scientific Community* (1973).
Kohn, David, ed. *The Darwinian Heritage* (1985).
Levine, George. "Charles Darwin's Reluctant Revolution." *South Atlantic Quarterly* 91
    (1992): 525–55.
Lewes, G. H. "Mr. Darwin's Hypothesis." *Fortnightly Review* 16 (April 1868): 353–73.
Mayr, Ernst. *One Long Argument: Charles Darwin and the Genesis of Modern Evolutionary
    Thought* (1991).
Ruse, Michael. *The Darwinian Revolution* (1979).
    . *The Darwinian Paradigm* (1989).
Sedgwick, Adam. "Objections to Mr. Darwin's Theory on the Origin of Species."
    *Spectator* 33 (March 24, 1860): 285–6.
Shaw, Ian. " 'Of Plain Signification': Darwin's World in the First Edition of *The Origin of
    Species*." *University of Toronto Quarterly* 62 (1993): 356–74.
Wilberforce, Samuel. Review of *On the Origin of Species*. *Quarterly Review* 108 (July
    1860): 225–64.

## BENJAMIN DISRAELI

Blake, Robert. *Disraeli* (1966).
———. *Disraeli and Gladstone* (1970).
Brantlinger, Patrick. *Rule of Darkness: British Literature and Imperialism, 1830–1914* (1988).
Davis, Richard W. *Disraeli* (1976).
Eldridge, C. C. *England's Mission* (1973).
Feuchtwanger, E. J. *Disraeli, Democracy and the Tory Party* (1968).
Jerman, B. R. *The Young Disraeli* (1960).
Levine, Richard. *Benjamin Disraeli* (1968).
Machin, Ian. *Disraeli* (1995).
Monypenny, William F. and G. E. Buckle. *The Life of Benjamin Disraeli, Earl of Beaconsfield*
    (1929).
Shannon, Richard. *The Age of Disraeli, 1868–1881: The Rise of Tory Democracy* (1992).

Smith, Paul. *Disraelian Conservatism and Social Reform* (1967).

Vincent, John R. *Disraeli* (1990).

Weintraub, Stanley. *Disraeli: A Biography* (1993).

## LUCIE DUFF GORDON

Frank, Katherine. *A Passage to Egypt: The Life of Lucie Duff Gordon* (1994).

Frawley, Maria H. "Desert Places/Gendered Spaces: Victorian Women in the Middle East." *Nineteenth-Century Contexts* 15 (1991): 49–64.

Gendron, Charisse. "Lucie Duff Gordon's 'Letters from Egypt.' " *Ariel: A Review of International English Literature* 17.2 (April 1986): 49–61.

## GEORGE ELIOT

Ashton, Rosemary. *George Eliot: A Life* (1996).

Ermarth, Elizabeth. *George Eliot* (1985).

Haight, Gordon S. *George Eliot: A Biography* (1968).

—, ed. *The George Eliot Letters*. 9 vols. (1954–78).

Karl, Frederick R. *George Eliot, Voice of a Century: A Biography* (1995).

McSweeney, Kerry. *George Eliot: A Literary Life* (1991).

Pangallo, Karen L. *The Critical Response to George Eliot* (1994).

Taylor, Ina. *A Woman of Contradictions: The Life of George Eliot* (1989).

Tush, Susan Rowland. *George Eliot and the Conventions of Popular Women's Fiction: A Serious Literary Response to the "Silly Novels by Lady Novelists"* (1993).

Uglow, Jennifer S. *George Eliot* (1987).

## SARAH STICKNEY ELLIS

Colby, Vineta. *Yesterday's Woman: Domestic Realism in the English Novel* (1974).

Davenport, Randi. "The Mother's Mistake: Sarah Stickney Ellis and Dreams of Empire." *Victorian Literature and Culture* 22 (1994): 173–85.

## EDWARD EWART GLADSTONE

Cowling, Maurice. *1867: Disraeli, Gladstone, and Revolution: The Passing of the Second Reform Bill* (1967).

Crosby, Travis. *The Two Mr. Gladstones* (1997).

Eldridge, C. C. *England's Mission* (1973).

Feuchtwanger, E. J. *Gladstone* (1975).

Hammond, J. L. *Gladstone and Liberalism* (1965).

Jenkins, Roy. *Gladstone, A Biography* (1995).

Jenkins, T. A. *Gladstone, Whiggery, and the Liberal Party* (1988).

Matthew, H. C. G. *Gladstone, 1809–1874* (1986).

———. *Gladstone, 1875–1898* (1995).

Parry, J. P. *Democracy and Religion: Gladstone and the Liberal Party, 1867–1875* (1986).

Rooke, Patrick J. *Gladstone and Disraeli* (1970).

Saab, Ann Pottinger. *Reluctant Icon: Gladstone, Bulgaria, and the Working Classes, 1856–1878* (1991).

Shannon, Richard T. *Gladstone* (1982).

Vincent, John R. *The Formation of the Liberal Party, 1857–1868* (1966).


## EDMUND GOSSE

Allen, Peter. "Sir Edmund Gosse and His Modern Readers: The Continued Appeal of *Father and Son*." *English Literary History* 55 (1988): 487–503.

Barcus, James E. "Biological Evolution as Self-Explanation in Gosse's *Father and Son*." *Greyfriar: Siena Studies in Literature* 23 (1982): 57–67.

Charteris, Evan E. *The Life and Letters of Sir Edmund Gosse* (1931).

Dodd, Philip. "The Nature of Edmund Gosse's *Father and Son*." *English Literature in Transition, 1880–1920* 22 (1979): 270–80.

Henderson, Heather. *The Victorian Self: Autobiography and Biblical Narrative* (1989).

Hepburn, James. Introduction. *Father and Son: A Study of Two Temperaments* (1974).

Hoberman, Ruth. "Narrative Duplicity and Women in Edmund Gosse's *Father and Son*." *Biography* 11 (1988): 303–15.

Malone, Cynthia Northcutt. "The Struggle of *Father and Son*: Edmund Gosse's Polemical Autobiography." *A/B: Auto/Biography Studies* 8 (1993): 16–32.

Manarin, Karen Heaton. "'Flower-Like Thought of Our Departed': The Mother in *Father and Son*." *English Studies in Canada* 22 (1996): 59–70.

Thwaite, Ann. *Edmund Gosse: A Literary Landscape, 1849–1928* (1984).

Woolf, James D. "The Benevolent Christ in Gosse's *Father and Son*." *Prose Studies* 3 (September 1980): 165–75.

———. *Sir Edmund Gosse* (1972).


## WILLIAM RATHBONE GREG

Walkowitz, Judith R. *Prostitution and Victorian Society: Women, Class, and the State* (1980).


## THOMAS HENRY HUXLEY

Ashforth, Albert. *Thomas Henry Huxley* (1969).

Bibby, Cyril. *Scientist Extraordinary* (1972).

Cockshut, A. O. J. *The Unbelievers: English Agnostic Thought 1840–1890* (1964).

Desmond, Adrian. *Huxley: The Devil's Disciple* (1994).

Di Gregorio, Mario. *T. H. Huxley's Place in Natural Science* (1984).

Himmelfarb, Gertrude. *Darwin and the Darwinian Revolution* (1959).

Huxley, Leonard. *Life and Letters of Thomas Henry Huxley* (1900).

Irvine, William. *Apes, Angels, and Victorians: The Story of Darwin, Huxley, and Evolution* (1955).

Jensen, J. Vernon. *Thomas Henry Huxley: Communicating for Science* (1991).

Paradis, James. *T. H. Huxley: Man's Place in Nature* (1978).

## JAMES PHILLIPS KAY-SHUTTLEWORTH

Levy, Anita. *Other Women: The Writing of Class, Race, and Gender, 1832–1898* (1991).
Poovey, Mary. *Making a Social Body: British Cultural Formation, 1830–1864* (1995).
Smith, Frank. *The Life and Work of Sir James Kay-Shuttleworth* (1923).

## CHARLES KINGSLEY

Chitty, Susan. *The Beast and the Monk: A Life of Charles Kingsley* (1974).
Martin, Robert B. *The Dust of Combat: A Life of Charles Kingsley* (1960).
Uffelman, Larry K. *Charles Kingsley* (1979).
Vance, Norman. *The Sinews of the Spirit: The Ideal of Christian Manliness in Victorian Literature and Religious Thought* (1985).

## MARY KINGSLEY

Blunt, Alison. *Travel, Gender, and Imperialism: Mary Kingsley and West Africa* (1994).
Birkett, Dea. *Mary Kingsley: Imperial Adventuress* (1992).
Campbell, Olwen. *Mary Kingsley: A Victorian in the Jungle* (1957).
Frank, Katherine. *A Voyager Out: The Life of Mary Kingsley* (1986).
Huxley, Elspeth. Introduction. *Travels in West Africa* (1992).
Stevenson, Catherine Barnes. *Victorian Women Travel Writers in Africa* (1982).
Thiesmeyer, Lynn. "Imperial Fictions and Non-Fictions: Subversion of Sources in Mary Kingsley and Joseph Conrad." *Transforming Genres: New Approaches to British Fiction in the 1890s.* Ed. Nikki Lee Manos and Meri-Jane Rochelson (1994).

## PERCIVAL LEIGH

Altick, Richard. *Punch: The Lively Youth of a British Institution, 1841–1851* (1997).
Spielmann, M. H. *The History of Punch* (1895).
Stone, Harry. Introduction. *The Uncollected Writings of Charles Dickens: Household Words 1850–1859* (1969).

## GEORGE HENRY LEWES

Ashton, Rosemary. *G. H. Lewes: A Life* (1991).
Dale, Peter Allan. "George Lewes' Scientific Aesthetic: Restructuring the Ideology of the Symbol." *One Culture: Essays in Science and Literature.* Ed. George Levine and Alan Rauch (1987).
Gary, Franklin. "Charlotte Brontë and George Henry Lewes." *PMLA* 51 (1936): 518–42.
Hirshberg, Edgar W. *George Henry Lewes* (1970).
Kaminsky, Alice. *George Henry Lewes as Literary Critic* (1968).
Orel, Harold. *Victorian Literary Critics* (1984).
Postlethwaite, Diana. *Making It Whole: A Victorian Circle and the Shape of Their World* (1984).
Tjoa, Hock Guan. *George Henry Lewes: A Victorian Mind* (1977).
Voskuil, Lynn M. "Acting Naturally: Brontë, Lewes, and the Problem of Gender Performance." *English Literary History* 62 (1995): 409–42.

## DAVID LIVINGSTONE

Blaikie, William G. *The Personal Life of David Livingstone* (1881, 1969).

Brantlinger, Patrick. *Rule of Darkness: British Literature and Imperialism, 1830–1914* (1988).

Campbell, Reginald J. *Livingstone* (1929).

Jacobson, Dan. "Dr. Livingstone, He Presumed." *The American Scholar* 63 (1994): 96–101.

Jeal, Tim. *Livingstone* (1973).


## THOMAS BABINGTON MACAULAY

Bryant, Arthur. *Macaulay* (1932).

Clive, John. *Macaulay: The Shaping of the Historian* (1973, 1987).

Cruikshank, Margaret. *Thomas Babington Macaulay* (1978).

Gay, Peter. *Style in History* (1974).

Goldberg, Michael. " 'Demigods and Philistines': Macaulay and Carlyle—A Study in Contrasts." *Studies in Scottish Literature* 24 (1989): 116–28.

Morison, James C. *Macaulay* (1882, 1909).

Young, Kenneth. *Macaulay* (1976).


## HARRIET MARTINEAU

David, Deirdre. *Intellectual Women and Victorian Patriarchy* (1987).

Frawley, Maria H. "Desert Places / Gendered Spaces. Victorian Women in the Middle East." *Nineteenth-Century Contexts* 15 (1991): 49–64.

Gallagher, Catherine. *The Industrial Reformation of English Fiction* (1985).

Hoecker-Drysdale, Susan. *Harriet Martineau: First Woman Sociologist* (1991).

Pichanick, Valerie. *Harriet Martineau: The Woman and Her Work, 1802–1876* (1980).

Postlethwaite, Diana. *Making It Whole: A Victorian Circle and the Shape of Their World* (1984).

Thomas, Gillian. *Harriet Martineau* (1985).

Webb, R. K. *Harriet Martineau: A Radical Victorian* (1960).

Yates, Gayle Graham, ed. *Harriet Martineau on Women* (1985).


## HENRY MAYHEW

Englander, David. *Retrieved Riches: Social Investigation in Britain, 1840–1914* (1995).

Humphreys, Anne. *Henry Mayhew* (1984).

Maxwell, Richard. "Henry Mayhew and the Life of the Streets." *Journal of British Studies* 17 (1978): 87–105.

Taithe, Bertrand, ed. *The Essential Mayhew: Representing and Communicating the Poor* (1996).

Thompson, E. P. and Eileen Yeo, eds. *The Unknown Mayhew: Selections from the Morning Chronicle* (1971).

Woodcock, George. "Henry Mayhew and the Undiscovered Country of the Poor." *Sewanee Review* 92 (1984): 556–73.

## JOHN STUART MILL

August, Eugene. *John Stuart Mill: A Mind at Large* (1975).

Berger, Fred R. *Happiness, Justice, and Freedom: The Moral and Political Philosophy of J. S. Mill* (1984).

Briggs, Asa. Foreward. *The Autobiography of John Stuart Mill* (1964).

Britton, Karl. *John Stuart Mill* (1969).

Carr, Wendell R. Introduction. *The Subjection of Women* (1970).

Danahay, Martin. *A Community of One: Masculine Autobiography and Autonomy in Nineteenth Century Britain* (1993).

Donner, Wendy. *The Liberal Self: John Stuart Mill's Moral and Political Philosophy* (1991).

Ellery, John B. *John Stuart Mill* (1964).

Hekman, Susan. "John Stuart Mill's *The Subjection of Women*: The Foundations of Liberal Feminism." *History of European Ideas* 15 (1992): 681–86.

Himmelfarb, Gertrude. *On Liberty and Liberalism: The Case of John Stuart Mill* (1974).

Kamm, Josephine. *John Stuart Mill in Love* (1977).

Laine, Michael, ed. *A Cultivated Mind: Essays on J. S. Mill Presented to John M. Robson* (1991).

Lonoff, Sue. "Cultivated Feminism: Mill and *The Subjection of Women*." *Philological Quarterly* 65 (1986): 79–102.

Okin, Susan M. Introduction. *The Subjection of Women* (1988).

——. *Women in Western Political Thought* (1979, 1992).

Packe, Michael St. John. *The Life of John Stuart Mill* (1954).

Pugh, Evelyn L. "Florence Nightingale and J. S. Mill Debate Women's Rights." *Journal of British Studies* 21 (Spring 1982): 118–38.

Rossi, Alice. *Essays on Sex Equality: John Stuart Mill and Harriet Taylor Mill* (1970).

Schneewind, Jerome B. *Mill: A Collection of Critical Essays* (1968).

Semmel, Bernard. *John Stuart Mill and the Pursuit of Virtue* (1984).

Skorupski, John. *John Stuart Mill* (1989).

Stillinger, Jack. *The Early Draft of John Stuart Mill's Autobiography* (1961).

Tatalovich, Anne. "John Stuart Mill, *The Subjection of Women*: An Analysis." *The Southern Quarterly* 12 (1973): 87–105.

## WILLIAM MORRIS

Baker, Larry. "The Socialism of William Morris." *William Morris and Kelmscott* (1981).

Boos, Florence S. and Carole G. Silver, eds. *Socialism and the Literary Artistry of William Morris* (1990).

Faulkner, Peter. *Against the Age: An Introduction to William Morris* (1980).

Henderson, Philip. *William Morris: His Life, Work, and Friends* (1967).

Kirchhoff, Frederick. *William Morris* (1979).

MacCarthy, Fiona. *William Morris: A Life for Our Time* (1994).

Silver, Carole. "Eden and Apocalypse: William Morris' Marxist Vision in the 1880's." *University of Hartford Studies in Literature: A Journal of Interdisciplinary Criticism* 13 (1981): 62–77.

Skoblow, Jeffrey. *Paradise Dislocated: Morris, Politics, Art* (1993).

Thompson, E. P. *William Morris: Romantic to Revolutionary* (1955).

Thompson, Paul R. *The Work of William Morris* (1967, 1993).


## JOHN HENRY NEWMAN

Buckton, Oliver S. " 'An Unnatural State': Gender, 'Perversion,' and Newman's *Apologia Pro Vita Sua*." *Victorian Studies* 35 (1992): 359–83.

Bouyer, Louis. *Newman: His Life and Spirituality* (1958).

DeLaura, David D., ed. *Apologia Pro Vita Sua* (1968).

Chadwick, Owen. *The Spirit of the Oxford Movement* (1990).

Church, Richard W. *The Oxford Movement: Twelve Years. 1833–1845* (1891).

Culler, Dwight A. *The Imperial Intellect* (1955).

Dessain, Charles Stephen. *John Henry Newman* (1966).

Gilley, Sheridan. *Newman and His Age* (1990).

Harrold, Charles F. *John Henry Newman* (1945).

Holloway, John. *The Victorian Sage: Studies in Argument* (1953).

Houghton, Walter. *The Art of Newman's Apologia* (1945).

Jost, Walter. *Rhetorical Thought in John Henry Newman* (1989).

Ker, Ian T. and Alan G. Hill, eds. *Newman after a Hundred Years* (1990).

Ker, Ian T. *John Henry Newman: A Biography* (1988).

Loesberg, Jonathan. *Fictions of Consciousness: Mill, Newman, and the Reading of Victorian Prose* (1986).

Pattison, Robert. *The Great Dissent: John Henry Newman and the Liberal Heresy* (1991).


## FLORENCE NIGHTINGALE

Boyd, Nancy. *Three Victorian Women Who Changed Their World: Josephine Butler, Octavia Hill, Florence Nightingale* (1982).

Calabria, Michael D. and Janet A. Macrae, eds. *Suggestions for Thought, by Florence Nightingale: Selections and Commentaries* (1994).

Cook, Edward T. *The Life of Florence Nightingale*. 2 vols. (1913).

Hebert, Raymond. *Florence Nightingale: Saint, Reformer or Rebel?* (1981).

Jenkins, Ruth Y. "Rewriting Female Subjectivity: Florence Nightingale's Revisionist Myth of 'Cassandra.' " *Weber Studies: An Interdisciplinary Humanities Journal* 11 (1994): 16–26.

Landow, George P. "Aggressive (Re)interpretations of the Female Sage: Florence Nightingale's 'Cassandra.' " *Victorian Sages and Cultural Discourse: Renegotiating Gender and Power*. Ed. Thais E. Morgan (1990).

Pugh, Evelyn L. "Florence Nightingale and J. S. Mill Debate Women's Rights." *Journal of British Studies* 21 (1982): 118–38.

Showalter, Elaine. "Miranda and Cassandra: The Discourse of the Feminist Intellectual." *Tradition and the Talents of Women*. Ed. Florence Howe (1991).

———. "Florence Nightingale's Feminist Complaint: Women, Religion, and *Suggestions for Thought*." *Signs* 6 (1981): 395–412.

Snyder, Katherine V. "From Novel to Essay: Gender and Revision in Florence Nightingale's 'Cassandra.' " *The Politics of the Essay: Feminist Perspectives*. Ed. Ruth-Ellen Boetcher Joeres and Elizabeth Mittman (1993).

Stark, Myra. Introduction. *Cassandra* (1979).

Vicinus, Martha and Bea Nergaard, eds. *Ever Yours, Florence Nightingale: Selected Letters* (1989).

Woodham-Smith, Cecil. *Florence Nightingale, 1820–1910* (1950).

## CAROLINE NORTON

Acland, Alice. *Caroline Norton* (1948).

Chedzoy, Alan. *A Scandalous Woman: The Story of Carolyn Norton* (1992).

Huddleston, Joan. Introduction. *Caroline Norton's Defense: English Laws for Women in the Nineteenth Century* (1982).

Perkins, J. *The Life of Mrs. Norton* (1909).

Poovey, Mary. *Uneven Developments: The Ideological Work of Gender in Mid-Victorian England* (1988).

## RICHARD OASTLER

Alfred [Kydd, Samuel H. G.]. *The History of the Factory Movement* (1857).

Cole, G. D. H. *Chartist Portraits* (1941).

Driver, Cecil. *Tory Radical: The Life of Richard Oastler* (1946).

Gallagher, Catherine. *The Industrial Reformation of English Fiction* (1985).

Ward, J. T. *The Factory Movement* (1962).

## MARGARET OLIPHANT

Colby, Vineta. *The Equivocal Virtue: Mrs. Oliphant and the Victorian Literary Marketplace* (1966, 1981).

Jay, Elisabeth, ed. Introduction. *The Autobiography of Margaret Oliphant: The Complete Text* (1990).

———. *Mrs. Oliphant, "A Fiction to Herself": A Literary Life* (1995).

———. "Mrs. Oliphant: The Hero as Woman of Letters, or Autobiography, a Gendered Genre." *Caliban* 31 (1994): 85–95.

Trela, D. J., ed. *Margaret Oliphant: Critical Essays on a Gentle Subversive* (1995).

Williams, Merryn. *Margaret Oliphant: A Critical Biography* (1986).

## WALTER HORATIO PATER

Barolsky, Paul. *Walter Pater's Renaissance* (1987).

Brake, Laurel and Ian Small, eds. *Pater in the 1990's* (1991).

DeLaura, David J. *Hebrew and Hellene in Victorian England: Newman, Arnold, and Pater* (1969).

Hill, Donald L. *The Renaissance: Studies in Art and Poetry* (1980).

Levey, Michael. *The Case of Walter Pater* (1978).

McGrath, F. C. *The Sensible Spirit:Walter Pater and the Modernist Paradigm* (1986).

Monsman, Gerald C. *Walter Pater* (1977).

———. *Walter Pater's Art of Autobiography* (1980).

Seiler, R. M. *Walter Pater:The Critical Heritage* (1980).

Uglow, Jennifer. Introduction. *Essays on Literature and Art* (1973, 1990).

Williams, Carolyn. *TransfiguredWorld:Walter Pater's Aesthetic Historicism* (1989).


## MARY PRINCE

Edwards, Paul and David Dabydeen, eds. *Black Writers in Britain, 1760–1890* (1991).

Ferguson, Moira. Introduction. *The History of Mary Prince: A West Indian Slave* (1987, 1997).

———. *Subject to Others: British Women Writers and Colonial Slavery, 1670–1834* (1992).

Gates, Henry Louis, Jr., ed. *The Classic Slave Narratives* (1987).

Pouchet-paquet, Sandra. "The Heartbeat of a West Indian Slave: *The History of Mary Prince*." *African-American Review* 26 (1992): 131–46.


## PUNCH

Altick, Richard. *Punch, The Lively Youth of a British Institution, 1841–1851* (1997).

Briggs, Susan and Asa. Introduction. *Cap and Bell: Punch's Chronicle of English History in the Making, 1841–1861* (1972).

Prager, Arthur. *The Mahogany Tree: An Informal History of Punch* (1979).

Price, R. G. G. *A History of Punch* (1957).

Spielmann, M. H. *The History of Punch* (1895).


## ELIZABETH RIGBY, LADY EASTLAKE

Eastlake, Elizabeth Rigby. *Journals and Correspondence of Lady Eastlake*. Ed. Charles Eastlake Smith. 2 vols. (1895).

Lochhead, Marion. *Elizabeth Rigby, Lady Eastlake* (1961).

Poovey, Mary. *Uneven Developments:The IdeologicalWork of Gender in Mid-Victorian England* (1988).

Robertson, David A. *Sir Charles Eastlake and theVictorian ArtWorld* (1978).


## JOHN RUSKIN

Birch, Dinah. "Ruskin's 'Womanly Mind.' " *Essays in Criticism* 38 (1988): 308–24.

Brooks, Michael W. *John Ruskin andVictorian Architecture* (1987).

Evans, Joan. *John Ruskin* (1954, 1970).

Garrigan, Kristine O. *Ruskin on Architecture: His Thought and Influence* (1973).

Hewison, Robert, ed. *New Approaches to Ruskin:Thirteen Essays* (1981).

Hunt, John Dixon. *TheWider Sea: A Life of John Ruskin* (1982).

Kirchhoff, Frederick. *John Ruskin* (1984).

Landow, George P. *Ruskin* (1985).

Nord, Deborah Epstein. "Mill and Ruskin on the Woman Question Revisited." *Teaching*

Literature: What Is Needed Now. Ed. James Engell and David Perkins (1988).

Rosenberg, John D. The Darkening Glass: A Portrait of Ruskin's Genius (1961).

Sherburne, James Clark. John Ruskin; or the Ambiguities of Abundance (1972).

Wheeler, Michael and Nigel Whiteley, eds. The Lamp of Memory: Ruskin, Tradition, and Architecture (1992).

## SAMUEL SMILES

Briggs, Asa. "Samuel Smiles and the Gospel of Work." Victorian People (1954).

——, ed. Introduction. Self-Help (1958).

Clausen, Christopher. "How to Join the Middle Classes with the Help of Dr. Smiles and Mrs. Beeton." The American Scholar 62 (1993): 403–18.

Fielden, Kenneth. "Samuel Smiles and Self-Help." Victorian Studies 12 (1968): 155–76.

Jarvis, Adrian. Samuel Smiles and the Construction of Victorian Values (1997).

Thornton, A. H. Samuel Smiles and Nineteenth Century Self-Help in Education (1983).

Travers, Tim. Samuel Smiles and the Victorian Work Ethic (1987).

## HERBERT SPENCER

Burrow, J. W. Evolution and Society: A Study in Victorian Social Theory (1966).

Duncan, David. Life and Letters of Herbert Spencer (1908).

Kennedy, James. Herbert Spencer (1978).

Paxton, Nancy. George Eliot and Herbert Spencer: Feminism, Evolutionism and the Reconstruction of Gender (1991).

Peel, J. D. Y. Herbert Spencer: The Evolution of a Sociologist (1971).

Taylor, M. W. Men Versus the State: Herbert Spencer and Late Victorian Individualism (1992).

Turner, Jonathan H. Herbert Spencer, A Renewed Appreciation (1985).

Wiltshire, David. The Social and Political Thought of Herbert Spencer (1978).

## ARTHUR WILLIAM SYMONS

Beckson, Karl. Arthur Symons: A Life (1987).

——. London in the 1890s: A Cultural History (1992).

——. "The Tumbler of Water and the Cup of Wine: Symons, Yeats, and the Symbolist Movement." Victorian Poetry 28 (1990): 125–33.

——, ed. Aesthetes and Decadents of the 1890's (1966, 1981).

—— and John M. Munro, eds. Arthur Symons: Selected Letters, 1880–1935 (1989).

Block, Haskell M. "Yeats, Symons and The Symbolist Movement in Literature." Yeats: An Annual of Critical and Textual Studies 8 (1990): 9–18.

Munro, John M. Arthur Symons (1969).

## CHARLOTTE ELIZABETH TONNA

Fryckstedt, Monica Correa. "Charlotte Elizabeth Tonna and The Christian Lady's Magazine." Victorian Periodicals Review 14 (1981): 42–50.

Kestner, Joseph. Protest and Reform: The British Social Narrative by Women 1827–1867 (1985).

Kovacevic, Ivanka. *Fact into Fiction* (1975).

Kovacevic, Ivanka and S. Barbara Kanner. "Blue Book into Novel: The Forgotten Industrial Fiction of Charlotte Elizabeth Tonna." *Nineteenth-Century Fiction* 25 (1970): 152–73.

Mitchell, Sally. *The Fallen Angel: Chastity, Class, and Women's Reading: 1835–1880* (1981).

## VICTORIA, QUEEN OF ENGLAND

Cooper, Lettice. *The Young Victoria* (1961).

Duff, David. *Albert and Victoria* (1972).

Fulford, Roger, ed. *Dearest Child: Letters between Queen Victoria and the Princess Royal, 1858–1861* (1964).

———, ed. *Darling Child: Private Correspondence of Queen Victoria and the Crown Princess of Prussia, 1871–1878* (1976).

Homans, Margaret. " 'To the Queen's Private Apartments': Royal Family Portraiture and the Construction of Victoria's Sovereign Obedience." *Victorian Studies* 37 (1993):1–41.

Longford, Elizabeth. *Queen Victoria* (1964).

Strachey, Lytton. *Queen Victoria* (1921).

Thompson, Dorothy. *Queen Victoria: Gender and Power* (1990).

Weintraub, Stanley. *Victoria: An Intimate Biography* (1987, 1996).

Woodham-Smith, Cecil. *Queen Victoria* (1972).

## MARY ARNOLD WARD

Jones, Enid H. *Mrs. Humphry Ward* (1973).

Peterson, William S. *Victorian Heretic* (1977).

Smith, Esther M. G. *Mrs. Humphry Ward* (1980).

Sutherland, John. *Mrs Humphry Ward* (1990).

Trevelyan, Janet P. *The Life of Mrs. Humphry Ward* (1923).

## OSCAR WILDE

Beckson, Karl, ed. *Oscar Wilde: The Critical Heritage* (1970).

Danson, Lawrence. *Wilde's Intentions: The Artist in his Criticism* (1997).

Dellamora, Richard. *Masculine Desire: The Sexual Politics of Victorian Aestheticism* (1990).

Dollimore, Jonathan. *Sexual Dissidence* (1991).

Ellmann, Richard. *Oscar Wilde* (1988).

Gagnier, Reginia. *Idylls of the Marketplace: Oscar Wilde and the Victorian Public* (1986).

Hyde, H. Montgomery. *Oscar Wilde* (1975).

Price, Jody. *"A Map with Utopia": Oscar Wilde's Theory for Social Transformation* (1996).

Raby, Peter, ed. *The Cambridge Companion to Oscar Wilde* (1997).

Sedgwick, Eve Kosofsky. *Epistemology of the Closet* (1990).

Weintraub, Stanley. Introduction. *Literary Criticism of Oscar Wilde* (1968).

Willoughby, Guy. *Art and Christhood: The Aesthetics of Oscar Wilde* (1993).